D1565932

THOMAS MANN'S
SHORT FICTION

5-10-94

To Mary Louise Sullivan MSC
With admiration for your
work, My very best wishes
Esther H. Josès TOC

THOMAS MANN'S SHORT FICTION

An Intellectual Biography

Esther H. Lesér

EDITED BY

Mitzi Brunsdale

Rutherford • Madison • Teaneck
Fairleigh Dickinson University Press
London and Toronto: Associated University Presses

 # 17549476

Associated University Presses
440 Forsgate Drive
Cranbury, NJ 08512

Associated University Presses
25 Sicilian Avenue
London WC1A 2QH, England

Associated University Presses
P. O. Box 488, Port Credit
Mississauga, Ontario
Canada L5G 4M2

The paper used in this publication meets the requirements
of the American National Standard for Permanence of Paper
for Printed Library Materials Z39.48-1984.

Library of Congress Cataloging-in-Publication Data

Lesér, Esther H.
  Thomas Mann's short fiction.

  Bibliography: p.
  Includes index.
  1. Mann, Thomas, 1875–1955. 2. Novelists, German—
20th century—Biography. I. Brunsdale, Mitzi.
II. Title.
PT2625.A44Z7357 1989   833'.912 [B]   87-45369
ISBN 0-8386-3319-6 (alk. paper)

PRINTED IN THE UNITED STATES OF AMERICA

To My Husband Bernhardt
who died shortly before this book was completed

CONTENTS

PREFACE

Thomas Mann's Short Fiction: An Intellectual Biography has two intended roles: as a reference work in which each story may be read individually with its comprehensive study materials, and as an organic study of Thomas Mann's intellectual development. In both cases, extremely popular short stories are balanced with others that are virtually unknown, yet essential to the work as a whole. I hope that this study will also fill gaps that still exist between the burgeoning studies of Thomas Mann's mammoth novels, and through its chronological treatment offer fruitful insights to the general reader, the student, and the scholar through references to both original and secondary material.

The intricacy of Thomas Mann's fictional theory and expression requires a consultation of his own nonfiction and of the secondary literature on his work, not all of which has been translated. Therefore the in-text and endnote references will first list the standard English translation, *Thomas Mann: Stories of Three Decades*, trans. H. T. Lowe-Porter (New York: Alfred A. Knopf, 1974), referred to as *STD*. "The Transposed Heads," "Thou Shalt Have No Other Gods before Me," and "The Black Swan" are not included in the *Stories of Three Decades* and will be listed separately. Quotations from material not yet translated into English will be signed with the initials EHL. The standard German edition, *Gesammelte Werke*, 13 vols. (Frankfurt am Main: S. Fischer, 1974), will be referred to as *GW*. Translations of German expressions into English commonly lose some of the special implications and resonance that are attached to certain of these terms in Mann's works. For this reason, the special meaning conveyed by Mann's use of a particular German word will be emphasized by placing the German term in parentheses after its English equivalent, which will thereafter appear in quotation marks to distinguish this special usage from the standard definitions of these same English words. The reader is also referred to the Glossary for full explications of these terms.

The short stories are grouped into six chapters illustrating Thomas Mann's intellectual and artistic development, observing dates of composition rather than publication. The title of each chapter indicates the stage of his development. For ease of access the stories belonging to each phase will be listed in the table of contents and in each chapter heading.

Thomas Mann, an author of supreme craftsmanship deserves both a systematic examination conducted with a high degree of sensitivity, and a greater

familiarity on the part of the reader with his intellectual and spiritual environment and personal taste. The ambitious undertaking of providing a critical
guide to Thomas Mann's short fiction must depend in part on the vast amount
of scholarly research conducted on his work. No criticism of Thomas Mann's
distinguished translators is intended by the discussion of the various renditions of important passages. Variations in translation are inevitable in living
languages and make such study irresistibly attractive. The treatment of the
stories themselves, however, rests upon the author's interpretations, which
are new and perhaps controversial. These interpretations grew out of an
affection for Thomas Mann's work that is handled with the objectivity he
himself would have preferred.

Neither this book nor indeed any book of criticism should replace the work
of art that it discusses. Thomas Mann's short fiction offers a challenging reading experience with considerable opportunity for discovery through reading
with curiosity, attention, and reverence.

ACKNOWLEDGMENTS

I would like to express my deepest gratitude to the following individuals and institutions who have generously provided me various kinds of assistance and encouragement during the years I have been working on this book: the Thomas Mann Archives, Zurich, who shared their unique holdings with promptitude, dedication, and genuine friendliness; the Philosophical Society of America, whose grant for travel initiated the entire project; the Research and Development Department of the University of North Dakota, whose clerical and travel grants supplied essential assistance, and special thanks to Dr. Earl Freise, who gave me valuable time and advice; the staff of the Chester Fritz Library, University of North Dakota, especially Randy Pederson, Betty Gard, Janice Bolstad, and Mary Klave, for their untiring efforts; the staffs of the Rare Books Collections of the libraries of Yale University and Princeton University, for their patience and helpfulness; Dr. Hans Wysling, Director of the Thomas Mann Archives, whose expertise and concern proved an unfailing source of professional and personal strength along the way; Professor Emeritus Bernhardt Ulmer of Princeton University, who shared his memories of Thomas and Katia Mann and their family with me so warmly and brought them all to life for me in an endearing manner I will always treasure; Professor Magdalena Kerényi, who extended me her cherished friendship and her recollections of her late husband and his intimate friend, Thomas Mann; Dr. Carlo Cabrini for his valuable contributions, Dr. Geraldo Vettorazzo who provided singular research material on Venice, and Baroness Amalia von Inkey for her generous advice and hospitality during my research work in Europe; Professor Roger Nicholls, my former teacher, whose scholarship on Thomas Mann awoke my interest in the field many years ago; Dr. Bernard O'Kelly, Dean of the College of Arts and Sciences, and Dr. Paul Schwartz, at the University of North Dakota, whose advice and scheduling helped me to carry on my research and writing as well as my teaching and my duties for two years as Coordinator of the German Graduate Program; Pat Twedell, my secretary, Roger Anderson, my computer consultant, and Al Linden of the University of North Dakota Computer Center, who gave me indispensable help in their individual areas; Ursula Hovet, who typed the first version of the manuscript; all of the research assistants and graduate students who served as clerical assistants on this long and strenuous project; and to the members of the Fairleigh Dickinson University Publishing Committee, especially Dr. Harry Keyishian and Dr. Cummins, whose genial professionalism has both reassured and impressed me.

11

Two persons in particular made it possible for me to write this book. Dr. Mitzi Brunsdale, who edited the text, was once my student and is now a friend for life, a distinguished scholar of English literature with fluency in several languages, a person of style and talent, and a worker of incredible energy. It was a pleasure to work with her and learn from the rapport we share. I feel fortunate that she polished away my alien nuances and gave the text its clarity and easy flow. Without her unconditional dedication and friendship I could not have conveyed my message in English.

My late husband Bernhardt Lesér, a professor of Romance languages, wholeheartedly shared my interest, and I owe much of the growth of my ideas to our inestimably valuable conversations. He accompanied me with devotion through each phase of the work, even enduring my typing during his last illness with his unquenchable good humor, indefatigable patience, and remarkable insight. Our partnership not only enriched me but enabled me to pursue this project, making it only fitting for me to dedicate this work to his memory.

THOMAS MANN'S
SHORT FICTION

INTRODUCTION

Thomas Mann's childhood and adolescence, from 1875 to 1890, saw great changes in Germany's sociocultural patterns, and two opposing cultural impulses indelibly marked his personality and art. One side of Thomas Mann's world has been called "decadent" and "dilettante," while the other has become known as "socialistic" and "deterministic," with each set of proponents unacceptable to the other. This cultural dichotomy during the formative years of Thomas Mann's career is vital to the understanding of his fiction.

After 1830, the abstract ideals of German romanticism had been channeled toward social and national liberation throughout Europe, but once attempts to establish those ideals failed, many *geistig** individuals found themselves estranged from their intellectual milieu, and their ensuing disillusion caused many to accept Schopenhauer's world-denying *Weltanschauung.** Meanwhile, proponents of materialism flaunted their cynicism in new journalism supported by a rapidly developing scientific and industrial society. Because materialism rejected the subjective and abstract values that had embodied the classic and romantic Golden Age, many individuals felt violently severed from their heritage. Some practiced radical escapism—aestheticism, symbolism, spiritualism, and even satanism—while others accepted the rational and materialistic values that led to determinism, socialism, and ultimately Marxism.

However, individuals who did accept materialism and rationalism still needed imaginative subjectivity, which they sought and often found in a utopian vision of a rationally determined universe, optimistically offered to the masses in the expectation that technology would produce total self-sufficiency. They felt empowered by reason to advance aggressively, forcing their more abstract-minded contemporaries into the self-imposed isolation of non pragmatic values.

The arrogant adherents of each trend instinctively adopted a characteristic social posture and spurned each other. One side prided itself on its refinement and culture, the other on its young and popular brute strength. All were blind to the seeds of their self-destruction, shutting themselves away from values

---

*Thomas Mann's special terminology is listed in the Glossary. *Geist* and its forms and *Weltanschauung*, an international literary term, will be used in German because of their multiple meanings.

that might have mediated and healed. Those who escaped the mob were the "decadents" and "dilettantes" of the exquisitely isolated *fin de siècle*, while materialistic humanists shunned spiritual, moral and abstract values. Both extremes undermined the healthy equilibrium of human nature.

Thomas Mann's childhood and adolescence were particularly affected by the direct cultural flow from France to Germany. Preponderantly French literary currents entered Germany through the works of the symbolist poet Stefan George and the naturalistic plays and novels of Gerhart Hauptmann at the time when Thomas Mann, Hugo von Hofamannsthal, Rainer Maria Rilke, and Hermann Hesse, all born around 1875, were publishing their first works.

Following Goethe's death in 1832, the German nineteenth century did not produce internationally significant literature. Although the philosophical works of Hegel, Schopenhauer, and Marx did not reach the European general public prior to the second half of the century, in Germany itself the writings of these three powerfully influenced the nineteenth-century *Zeitgeist*. Richard Wagner sensed the influence; Nietzsche reacted against it; the entire *fin de siècle* could not have existed without it; and the scientific and industrial world unconsciously functioned in its atmosphere.

As the son of an old merchant family, leading patricians of Lübeck, Thomas Mann's intellectual inclination was inevitably established when the family business firm was dissolved following his father's death. The disillusionment typical of the "decadents" and the aesthetic intellectualism of the upper-class "dilettantes" became young Mann's pride, recognizable even in the titles of his first short stories: "Gefallen," "Wille zum Glück," "Enttäuschung," and "Der Bajazzo." Most of his recorded reactions reflect a *fin de siècle* ennui, because he was reacting against such radical social movements as women's emancipation and reveling in aestheticism, though symbolism and naturalism also played roles in his development.

Thomas Mann, however, would not have been a true child of his century had he not held the names of Schiller, Novalis, and above all, Goethe, firmly in his heart. Goethe eventually taught him the concept of *Weltliteratur*, enabling him in his fiction to free himself from space and time and thereby to treat universal themes. Goethe's example, too, helped him to establish his own position between *Bürgertum* and *Künstlertum*. Like Goethe, Thomas Mann had grown up as a *Bürger*'s son, and like Goethe, too, he had to mature in order to grasp and define the wide spiritual concept of the *Bürger*.

Although Mann wrote a few lyrics as a youth, he found prose the only art form capable of expressing his literary messages, and he even believed that the novel ideally conveyed the ideas of modern man. He had studied the classical epics enthusiastically, but after he had read Cervantes' *Don Quixote* and Goethe's *Wilhelm Meisters Lehrjahre*, he ranked the modern prose novel above its poetic precursors. From his very first attempts at literature, he relied on epic fiction to express himself, calling the novel a symphony, a complex monument, that substantialized his abstract messages.

Each plateau of Thomas Mann's development has one central theme. His progress resembles a flight of stairs with several landings, each of which raises him to a new level. He seems to have conceived the components of each of his vast major novels gradually, producing a cluster of letters, essays, theoretical pieces, short stories, and novellas around each novel like gigantic planets surrounded by constellations of literary satellites, demanding biographical data, his personal and theoretical writings, and considerable reference to his major novels in the discussion of his short fiction.

A systematic chronological exploration yields an especially refined reading and living experience of Thomas Mann's *oeuvre*, in which he generously reveals his most sensitive thoughts, emotions, and observations, a majestic literary talent expressing ideas and feelings as personally vital as they are universal. His work reflects his profound hopes, wishes, beliefs, and anguish, granting here a far fuller insight into his heart than any friend can ordinarily permit another.

This book cannot serve as a complete guide to Thomas Mann's entire canon, an impossibility without a thorough treatment of his great novels. Like Mann's short fiction itself, however, it may well serve as the first step on the path to a deeper experience of his work and an inspiration to the devoted examination his larger fiction so richly deserves.

1
THE PATH TO SELF-IDENTIFICATION

"Vision," "Gefallen," "Der Wille zum Glück,"
"Der Tod," "Disillusionment" ("Enttäuschung")

Photographs taken during Thomas Mann's last school years in Lübeck reveal a slim, handsome, rather tall youth, with a strongly modeled nose and heavy dark eyebrows that foreshadow his mature features and a solemn, stiff pose that made him seem already grown up. Years later he wrote:

> School I loathed and to the end failed to satisfy its demands. I despised it as a milieu, I was critical of the manners of its masters, and I early espoused a sort of literary opposition to its spirit, its discipline, and its methods of training. My indolence, necessary perhaps to my particular growth; an actual heaviness of spirit—even today I suffer from it—made me hate being urged to study, and react with feelings of contempt and scorn. (*SML*, 5; "*Lebensabriß*," *GW*, 11: 99)

Paul Thomas Mann was born at home[1] in Lübeck on 6 June 1875, the second son of Consul Thomas Johann Heinrich Mann and Julia Mann, née da Silva-Bruhns. Thomas and his brother Heinrich, born in 1871, lost their father on 13 October 1891; his will ordered the liquidation of the family's generations-old "Firma Johann Siegmund Mann." Although Consul and Senator Thomas Johann Heinrich Mann died of bladder cancer, Thomas Mann noted in *Sketch of My Life* that his father died of "blood poisoning."

In the following year, Julia Mann moved to Munich with her younger children, while Thomas finished his secondary education in Lübeck's Katharineum Realgymnasium where he declared a truce with his teachers after repeating two classes he had failed.[2] He made several pleasant friendships;[3] Otto Grautoff had been one of his most faithful friends since grammar school.[4] The two were inseparable in their passion for literature and in mischievous rebellion against school authority, and because Grautoff even failed his courses exactly when Thomas did, they were always in the same classes. After Mann left Lübeck, the boys kept up a rich correspondence until they were reunited in Munich in 1901. Otto Grautoff's letters to Thomas Mann have not been preserved, but the exhaustive collection of Mann's letters to Grautoff was published in 1975, the centennial of Mann's birth.[5] These letters are vital to understanding his early life, since he burned all his personal writings in 1896. His pre-1900 correspondence with his brother Heinrich has also been lost.

Heinrich's small literary successes had motivated Thomas's schoolboy belles lettres,[6] dramatic efforts for his puppet theater, a toy he admittedly played with until he was fourteen.[7] Much later he wrote,

> . . . it must have been around the period of my enchantment with that Viennese literary style that I dared to send the feuilleton editor of the paper in my native town Lübeck a pseudonymous piece of hypersensitive and overheated prose, titled "Color Sketch." It was an adventure with a humiliating ending. . . . beneath the politely printed rejection slip [the editor] wrote: "If you often have such ideas, then you should really do something about it."[8] (EHL)

Nothing remains of this early piece but its title.

Just before he left Lübeck Thomas Mann and his friends organized a student publication called "Spring Storm" ("Frühlingssturm"): "A Spring storm! Yes, like the spring storm [blowing] into dust-covered nature, so shall we blow with words and thoughts into the multitude of dust-covered brains, the ignorance and narrow-mindedness and the inflated Philistinism, which confronts us."[9] Probably because of a lack of funds and the opposition of the lampooned Katharineum faculty only two issues appeared: May 1893 and a double issue, June/July 1893, containing two poems,[10] a critical essay,[11] and a short sketch, "Vision."

"Vision"

No one knows when Thomas Mann wrote "Vision," as yet untranslated, and he might even have submitted it to a newspaper editor earlier than "Color Sketch."[12] Significantly, he never included "Vision" in any of his short story collections.

Mann's juvenilia clashes with the solemnity of his early photograph, for in his smart school slang ("*gippern*") he displayed youthful arrogance in his letters to Grautoff and his brother Heinrich. Peter de Mendelssohn calls this "feigned cynicism, fresh, frivolous, an overbearing rubbish-talk, a vainly gambled away self-irony, and satirizing of the surrounding world, monkey business, buffoonery and 'clownishness'" '(Introduction to *Thomas Mann: Briefe an Otto Grautoff 1894–1901, und Ida Boy-Ed 1903–1928*, xii [Frankfurt am Main: S. Fischer Verlag, 1975]). His high spirits, temporarily checked by natural shyness, were ready to explode, as "Vision" clearly indicates. "Vision" is set in a twilit room with an open window and a lamp. A poet, continually smoking, begins to dream, and out of the drifting smoke a dream-vision emerges: crystal vase with flowers and leaves, and near this a girl's hand with a pulsating blue vein, evoking bittersweet memories from the past. For a moment the vision clashes with the poet's passion before vanishing, carried away by a rising air bubble in the vase.

The structure and message of the one and a half page plotless "Vision" classify it as a sketch, divided into twelve short paragraphs, each clearly conveying a character and a message. The only protagonists are the poet and his vision, and the lyricism is balanced by sober rational irony. The first paragraph establishes the dreamy setting while the teasing language of the second evokes a troubled tension; reason gives free rein to the imagination as the poltergeist emerges. The tepid atmosphere is cut by sharp, hard repeated CK sounds: "Hinter mir kna*ck*t heimlich ne*ck*end die Stuhllehne" ("Behind me the back of the chair cracks secretly, teasingly"—EHL). In the next paragraph the tension intensifies with a mention of the devil, replete with occult-sounding *s*, *sch*, and *st* sounds. Next, the mounting magic recalls Faust's battle with the supernatural as the otherwordly element approaches amid wild punctuation and exhortational language. The poet rationally depicts a nonsensical "art work of coincidence . . . not large: small. Also not a whole, actually, but still complete formally. But infinite, fading out in all directions in the dark. One totality. One World" (EHL) (*GW* 8: 9–10. When the girl's hand appears, the soundless, unreal crepuscular vision of exploding forms and colors contrasts sharply with the earlier powerful sound painting. Extravagant baroque associations, like a ruby "bleeding on a ring," suit this exaltation, and the pulsing blue vein of the pale female hand engages the poet in wordless dialogue. With the girl's plea and a "cruel lust" in the poet's eye the Faust magic is superseded by the *Heidenröslein* tragedy.

This imaginative nonsense is absorbed by the pearly air bubble fading in the "bloody red" realm of the ruby. The vision is gone; a pleasant self-pity replaces it, and after a deep sigh, the poet affirms: "I know now as certainly as I knew then: you loved me after all . . . and this is why I can cry now" (EHL) (*GW*, 8: 10).

"Vision," though an adolescent experiment, exhibits Mann's painstaking description and his ability to imitate the shadowy symbolistic Viennese School inspired by Hugo von Hofmannsthal. "Vision" has no dramatic and poetic theme; and its implied "plot" is actually an evanescent bittersweet emotionalism. Youthful longing emerges through cigarette smoke and the memory of past amours; for the student at the Lübeck Gymnasium both the cigarette and the amour ambitiously attempted a veneer of sophistication. Certainly the girl's image in "Vision" was no "reflection of the past," as the sketch maintains, but purely a young man's active fancy. This little piece made only a literary ripple, and not surprisingly, Mann avoided mentioning it. However, the historical significance of "Vision" lies in its early revelation of his unique personal and literary qualities.

"Gefallen"

After graduating in 1901, Thomas Mann moved into his mother's eight-room apartment at 2 Rambergstraße in Munich's Schwabing district, where each of her five children had a separate room. The apartment was furnished in dark majestic antiques brought from Lübeck. This home, however, affluent, could hardly compare with their spacious Lübeck house, now sold. Their new neighbors matched them in position and respectability, and the neighborhood had recently been annexed to the city of Munich, though not all the streets were paved and streetcars were introduced only in 1895. This building, like the Mann home in Lübeck, was destroyed in World War II.

Julia Mann was forty-three then, a cordial hostess living comfortably on an income of about 12,000 marks a year. Thomas Mann rarely referred to his mother's personal life, but he did list the colorful personalities he had met at her receptions. Thomas and Heinrich, who had returned from a trip to Italy, each received about 600 marks per quarter, from which they paid their mother room and board. According to Viktor, their younger brother, Thomas, whom he called "Onkel Ommo," was always ready to play and tell him stories.

In April 1894, scarcely a month after his graduation, Thomas Mann became an unpaid trainee at an insurance firm, Süddeutsche Feuer-Versicherungsbank A. G. at Salvatorstraße 18, whose director had been his father's business friend. Mann later commented that he followed the decision of his legal guardian, Krafft Tesdorpf, "with the word 'temporary' in my heart," but his light work load let him pursue his writing. "I sat at my sloping desk surrounded by snuff-taking clerks and copied accounts; but secretly I also wrote my first tale, a love story called "Gefallen" which earned me my first literary success" (*SML*, 9; *GW*, 11: 101).[13]

The simple yet complex title "*Gefallen*" as yet untranslated has multiple German meanings and connotations of moral turpitude.[14] "Gefallen" approaches this concept first through the feminist Laube, one of the narrator Selten's audience, and then from Selten's more conservative viewpoint. The conflict turns on whether a woman must be considered "fallen" ("*gefallen*") if she has a love affair, and whether her male partner ought to be judged by the same standard.

Such problems probably mattered intensely to the scarcely mature Mann, whose letters to Grautoff indicate a distinct difficulty in approaching women. For Thomas Mann, "women" were either real people he knew or shimmering images of "immorality." Bridging the gap between them was difficult but greatly intriguing for him, and he may well have identified with Dr. Selten rather than Laube. Though Mann had apparently not experienced any disappointment in love as yet, his unfulfilled desires simultaneously surrounded that subject in "Gefallen" with tension, irritability, and fascination.

In contrast to "Vision," "Gefallen" is a genuine short story with setting, protagonists, plot and message, consisting of twenty-four unequally divided pages in a frame construction. The "story within the story" illustrates and elaborates the topic introduced by the four friends' conversation; in Meysenberg's rooms it is finally rounded off with a clear definition. Mann gradually unfolds an exotic and playful *fin de siècle* setting that reflects the multitudinous interests of these dilettantes who are accustomed to middle-class comforts and sensually savor their luscious decor and delectable food and drink— Roquefort, Benedictine, bonbons, and oranges—while they talk, a setting and mood reflective of Mann's own experience. Their mannerisms, their frequent use of French, and their pseudo-scientific ambitions all also reflect then-contemporary cosmopolitanism.

Laube's and Dr. Selten's personalities are antithetic. Laube opens the story: " 'The pitiful social position of the female' (he never said 'woman' but always 'female' because that made it sound more like natural science) 'is rooted in the prejudices, the idiotic prejudices of society!' " (EHL) (*GW*, 8: 12). As Laube continues vociferously, Dr. Selten suddenly illustrates his own position with a story, told in the third person, giving all names except the very young North German hero's, now a medical student in a mid-German city. Mann was wishfully describing himself; even given their physical similarities, Selten's relaxation and girls' "loving glances" were surely not his own direct experiences just then.

The hero is "innocent, pure in body and soul" (EHL) (*GW*, 8: 14), an important factor in the story's psychology, and the cynical rationalism of his somewhat older friend Rölling rudely shatters the hero's romantic daydreams. Finally, the young student writes an admiring letter to Fräulein Weltner, and as the winter passes with no reply, he lapses into melancholy. When spring comes, the student enters the girl's house, passing a fragrant lilac,[15] and strikes up a pure romantic friendship, upon which Rölling later comments impatiently.

The second section of Dr. Selten's tale opens in full-blown spring, a setting recalling *Faust*'s "Wood and Cave" scene. The pleasant weather has become "cruel heat" and "oppressive sultriness," and the student is "ill again," haunted by desire. "Rölling, this Mephisto" (EHL) (*GW*, 8: 26), is again responsible for the next move; Mann quotes Mephistopheles' lines from Goethe's *Faust*, Part I: "and then the noble intuition—[with gesture!]—of— need I say of what emission," but though the student wanders alone through natural scenery, his experience is not Faust's uplifting spiritual event. It is a bitter battle against his own tormenting desires.

Dr. Selten ironically adds that Rölling was " . . . only somewhat more well-meaning and less witty" (EHL) (*GW*, 8: 26) than Mephisto, shrinking Rölling's figure to the proportions of the mischievous student he actually is. When Mann detected in his own writing a developing similarity to another work, or recognized its subconscious influence, he indicated his source by a quotation or a direct allusion. In the conclusion of "Gefallen," he emphasizes the hero's innocence to focus on the girl's morality, presenting the topic through the student's normal male instinct, catalyzed by Rölling, who is responsible for the seductive ploy that the girl's virtue should have averted.

Mann places the turning point in the sixth section of "Gefallen," where the student unexpectedly finds an older man breakfasting with his mistress. After insulting him, the student reacts desperately and even sadistically, covering her with "Cruel scourging kisses." Selten cynically adds, "perhaps he already learned from these kisses that for him love would exist from now on only in hatred, and lust in vengeance" (EHL) (*GW*, 8: 40).

Why Thomas Mann wrote this violent scene is unknown; possibly he drew the student's insistence and his sadistic impulse from his own overheated imagination. Only in "Gefallen" did he describe sexual fulfillment in any detail. The student changes from "a good fellow" to a bitter, cynical man; he blindly rushes out and, cursing, rips up the lilac bush. Selten repeats the violence at the end of his story. In his ensuing argument with Laube, Selten maintains, "If a woman falls today for love, she will fall tomorrow for money. This is what I wanted to relate. Nothing more" (EHL) (*GW*, 8: 42).

Mann's "Gefallen" also clearly relates to the first episode of Goethe's *Wilhelm Meisters Lehrjahre*. The motif of a middle-class young man falling in love with a young actress is the main theme of "Gefallen," while it forms only one episode in Goethe's novel. In "Gefallen" the theme is cut off by the student's violence while Goethe carries it to its conclusion. Society's censure of actors is a major factor in both treatments, and in both a friend of the hero (Rölling and Werner), stands between the lovers. Goethe's Wilhelm differs fundamentally, however, from Mann's "good fellow," who never even considered marrying his Irma. Wilhelm, flushed with youthful enthusiasm, had even been willing to abandon his social position to marry Marianne. When Wilhelm learned of Marianne's relationship with Norberg, a wealthy business-man, he collapsed, but on his recovery he gave no sign of cynicism. In fact, Wilhelm's story did not end the episode, but began it, for after Marianne's death her son Felix taught Wilhelm the mature responsibilities of fatherhood.

Goethe treated the entire position of an unprotected, independent woman, while Mann touched only one of its aspects without a solution. Wilhelm's growth began through the experience, while Mann's injured hero regressed into cynical isolation.[16] Irma is handled objectively; her rebellion lacks depth, and her figure unexpectedly fades into oblivion. Goethe, however, convincingly motivates Marianne's degradation. In making her Felix's mother and allowing her early death, Goethe grants her double redemption as a mother and as a penitent.

Prior to its 1894 publication .in *Gesellschaft*, "Gefallen" appealed to the popular writer Richard Dehmel. Others had also noticed this story; Hermann Bahr, said to have imitated it in his novel *Die Gute Schule* (1890), pointed out in *Kritik der Moderne* that "Gefallen" departed from Zola's deterministic naturalism and shifted toward Paul Bourget's view. Bourget, a French psycho-novelist, believed in the Catholic middle-class principles of the *ancien régime*. Mann had studied Bourget's *Essais de psychologie contemporaine* and his novel *Cosmopolis*, published in Paris in 1892 and translated into German in 1894. Bourget developed the "epicurean intellectual" in *Cosmopolis*[17] as well as defining and rejecting the *fin de siècle* "dilettante" and "decadent," drawn from the philosophical determinism that had flourished after France's 1871 defeat in the Franco-Prussian War. All of "Gefallen" smacks of literary decadence, a sharp contrast to Goethe's ideal of well-balanced life, shown in Wilhelm and Marianne. Thomas Mann undoubtedly had had "dilettante" leanings but his interest in Bourget, his own healthy instincts, and especially his inclination toward equilibrium overcame them. Before 1900, his overriding theme is the struggle for liberation from the *fin de siècle* mentality.

"Vision" and "Gefallen," Mann's first stories, reflect his emotional condition and both consciously and subconsciously reveal his immaturity. In both "Vision" and "Gefallen" melodramatic defensiveness is linked to the theme, an obvious subject for an adolescent author. "Vision" and "Gefallen" lack the vigor of experience, and even the mood and colorful settings cannot hide the weakness of the personalities and the logical deficiency of the story's events.

In "Gefallen" Mann was attempting a contemporary intellectual topic. He appears as passive toward the problem as its conversationalists are in expressing the frustrations and anger then in his own heart. Formally this elegant, rather old-fashioned little story reflects the narrative heritage of late eighteenth- and early nineteenth-century literature, spiced with the tension of the end of the century.

"Gefallen" appeared a month after Thomas Mann had asked Richard Dehmel to publish another short story, "Der Kleine Professor," in *Pan*. Whether it was lost or destroyed is uncertain, but Dehmel graciously refused it, which no doubt disappointed the self-confident young author. He restlessly alternated carnival parties with writing, working on "Der alte König," a fairy tale in verse, and a short story, "Walter Weiler." "Der alte König," is also lost, but he presented "Walter Weiler" to Dehmel in early 1895. Dehmel accepted this story, but because of internal problems which led to the demise of *Pan* that fall, it was not published. Mann had also been reviewing minor books for *Das Zwanzigste Jahrhundert* since the spring of 1895.

Flushed with his first literary success, the young Mann enlisted his guardian's help in convincing his mother to let him leave the fire insurance company and support him while he prepared for a journalistic career. Julia Mann, proud of her sons' artistic and literary talents, readily agreed, and in 1892 young Thomas enrolled for the fall semester at Munich's Technische Hochschule, where he studied economics, history, Germanic mythology, aesthetics, and Shakespeare. He was only a "special" student because he had not passed his baccalaureate in Lübeck and thus could not receive regular academic credit;[18] initially fairly regular in class attendance, he soon left most of the pages of his notebooks empty. The young Munich intellectuals eagerly received the author of "Gefallen." After joining the Academic-Dramatic Society he played the businessman Werle in Ibsen's *The Wild Duck* under the direction of Ernst von Wolzogen, his only acting experience, although he remained a member of this group until World War I. His interest in Ibsen remained constant.

Mann spent July to October 1895 in Italy, and again from the fall of 1896 to 1898. During his first Italian visit,[19] he began "Wille zum Glück," published in the August–September 1896 issue of *Simplicissimus*.

Mann's letters to Grautoff show the spring and summer of 1895 passed quickly. Between "Gefallen" and his next published short story his intellectual and technical development is astonishing.[20] At the end of May 1895, he hinted at his attitude toward his own work: "You read a poetic text which impresses you, and then when you sit down to write, you instinctively feel and write in its style. You might call this dilettantism, or at least this [the imitation] is a part of it" (EHL). Though he had earlier prided himself on good imitations, he now sought the utmost in originality. His highly personal motivation for "Der Wille zum Glück," "Der Tod" and "Disillusionment"[21] caused him to analyze his own reactions, and the three stories share as motivation the impassioned search for fulfillment. Young Thomas Mann was attempting to communicate three vital concepts: the power of happiness, the power of the "I" over death; death, a power of nature, overruling a human challenge; and finally the individual's desire for ultimate experience.

The young Mann's observation was so intense that a moment of insight would crystallize into living experience (*Erlebnis*).[22] The stories which follow "Vision" and "Gefallen" demonstrate his urgent need to express his emotions creatively. His focus on human reactions to happiness, life, death, and beauty both suited his intellectual needs and conveyed the self-revelatory message he felt essential at this time.

The literature Mann devoured during 1895 guided the development of his *Weltanschauung*. Beyond the works of Goethe, Schiller, Heine, and E. T. A. Hoffmann, whose influences date from Mann's earliest youth and matured with him, his readings of Bourget, Ibsen, and Nietzsche and his gradual discovery of Wagner's operas, dating from 1892 in Lübeck, increasingly occupied him in Munich, where fine Wagnerian performances were presented.[23] He interpreted the fashionable *fin de siècle* catch-phrases of the decadent, the dilettante, and the cosmopolitan as Bourget had,[24] and Mann defined them and overcame them in the first stage of his own development.

Thomas Mann's sympathy for the dilettante derived from his inclination toward *fin de siècle* intellectual epicurism. Not merely superficial snobbery, his innate love of beauty and graceful living stimulated his creativity, and without such amenities the world saddened and even disgusted him. He followed the chic activity of international decadence with amusement, but he never abandoned his self-imposed standards, which harmonized with

Bourget's; he enjoyed dilettantism insofar as it did not inhibit his own needs, his creativity, and his logical observation.

At this point, when his instincts told him a topic no longer offered new insights into his intellectual and spiritual needs, Thomas Mann immediately approved a broader dimension of creativity. Each successive topic reflected his weightiest problem, and each consequently furnished a theme central to one of his works of art. He thus escaped the fashionable platitudinous stagnation found in dilettantes of the time and achieved exactly the vitality which Bourget had sought in vain. Paolo Hofmann, Mann's first "autobiographical" hero, is set apart by his unusual sensitivity, a mask either of estrangement or prestige. Paolo's sensitivity allows him special zest for coping with life; but the wisdom it offers also creates isolation. When Mann recognized these reactions in himself, he made their challenge the core of his art. His fictional heroes become significant parts of himself; in "Der Wille zum Glück," "Der Tod," and "Disillusionment" he personalized his own theme in order to overcome a problem while modulating it into a new artistic dimension and creating an ascending continuum of thought ("Lebensabriß," *GW*, 11: 109; *SML*, 21).

Thomas Mann later described one of his most powerful early stimuli, "the experience of Schopenhauer and Nietzsche. Probably the earliest prose writings of mine that saw the light of print betray the intellectual and stylistic influence of Nietzsche clearly enough. . . . Certainly the contact with Nietzsche was decisive to a high degree for an intellect still in its formative stage." Mendelssohn and Schröter, Mann's biographers, disagree on when he first read Nietzsche.[25] Even though the date of Mann's first contact with Nietzsche's works is uncertain, but he quoted *Beyond Good and Evil* (*Jenseits von Gut und Böse*) in his first Notebook, possibly before or while he wrote "*Der Wille zum Glück*," which directly cites[26] *On the Genealogy of Morals* (*Zur Genealogie der Moral*). Nietzsche's "to overcome" connotes comprehensive intellectual and emotional dedication, and Zarathustra's message teaches that only unconditional will can overcome limitations: "I teach you the overman. Man is something that shall be overcome. What have you done to overcome him?"[27]

"Der Wille zum Glück"

Thomas Mann's "Der Wille zum Glück"[28] first appeared in *Simplicissimus*, August and September 1896, prior to "Der Tod," though possibly he conceived these stories simultaneously.[29] He spent the fall of 1895 in Italy[30] with Heinrich and either took the preliminary draft of "Der Wille zum Glück" there or wrote it completely in Italy. Upon returning to Munich on 17 January 1896, he asked Grautoff to read and return "Der Wille zum Glück" in December of 1895 so that it could be published soon, and he even offered to pay Grautoff's return postage.

From the outset, Mann presents his fiction formally, "Der Wille zum

Glück" has three distinct parts: the introduction, Paolo Hofmann's youth; the body of the story, Paolo and Ada; and the denouement. The story, filled with enriching motifs, covers one decade in the hero's life, atypical of short fiction, but a distinguishing characteristic of his foreshadowing his later great novels. "Der Wille zum Glück" is one-third shorter than "Gefallen," with no poetic passages. A friend of Paolo Hofmann's narrates it in the first person.

The title "Der Wille zum Glück" ("the will to happiness") is vital because it immediately conveys the theme; and it overtly resembles Nietzsche's Will to Power (Der Wille zur Macht), but conceals a contrast in meanings.[31] The concept of "Will" is essentially Schopenhauerian, known to young Thomas Mann solely through Nietzsche's writings.[32] Here "will" is limited to his youthful longing to overcome obstacles to "happiness" or life. Such restrictions then appeared in his fiction as illness, the power of other people, and individual weakness. The somewhat melodramatic Baroness Ada is preserved from ludicrousness by contrast with the ironic realism of Paolo's will, energy, and burning faith. The genuine and profound theme movingly expresses Mann's own dreams, and Ada's proud self-confidence survives as a powerful illustration of Nietzsche's "will to power," his fictionalization of Nietzsche's theory (possibly a reference to Nietzsche's feelings for Cosima Wagner).

In the introduction to this story Mann typically presents his hero's origin, milieu, and character as surprisingly like his own.[33] "Hofmann," a common German name,[34] is combined with "Paolo,"[35] the Latinate spelling of "Paul" then common in Germany, a striking juxtaposition illustrating the hero's dual ethnic and cultural heritage—not as yet the central theme, as the title, "Der Wille zum Glück," indicates.[36] Paolo Hofmann's distinguishing characteristics are his German/Latin origin, his appearance, his talent, and his unusual sensitivity, which is the essence of the theme.

Thomas Mann's habit of first indicating obvious details of his hero's appearance and behavior and then revealing his hero's personality appears for the first time in this story. Paolo is a thin, sallow lad with black hair, the very image of his mother, wearing a conventional sailor suit while his undisciplined hair curled around his rather alien face.[37]

The narrator, neither named nor described, might be Paolo's alter ego,[38] an intelligent but otherwise ordinary man. These boys, similar in taste and upbringing, feel estranged from the rest of the classroom, even calling the others—including the teacher—"slugs" (Larven). "Toward most of our classmates . . . [we felt] that 'pathos of distance' which everyone knows who secretly reads Heine at fifteen" (EHL). Mann's disdain for traditional learning shows here, though he later became one of the most widely educated intellectuals of his time. "Pathos of distance" (Pathos der Distanz) is from Nietzsche's On the Genealogy of Morals, proof of Mann's thorough knowledge of Nietzsche's text during the second half of 1895.

This quotation used by a rich man's son at a public school indicates Mann's keen reaction to Nietzsche's wit. The boys' snobbishness recalls Nietzsche's controversial high mimetic explanation of the origin of "good" and "bad" in the first treatise of *Genealogy of Morals*,[39] and their mockery of their prosaic teacher and classmates reinforces the self-importance their soaring spirits had caught from Heine. Their upper-class backgrounds and their comical intellectual pretensions kept them together during early adolescence like Paolo and the narrator. As Paolo's natural sensitivity matured, the narrator no longer could share his "distinction," and thereafter merely served as Paolo's biographer, an emergence of the first essential component of the artist's isolation, one of Thomas Mann's major themes.

Paolo's puny frame, indicative of poor health, and a tracery of delicate blue veins on his temples are important; throughout fifty years of his fiction Mann used such veins to convey sensitivity and physical debilitation, a physical symptom that must have impressed him strongly as a youth.

In the seventh paragraph, the story establishes that the boys are about sixteen and exposes the main objectives of the theme. The first is love, which blossoms at dancing school, when the object of Paolo's affections, a vivacious blonde teenager, ignores him. From the start Mann stresses the blonde motif even though, as he observes in *A Sketch of My Life*, the hair of the real-life girl was brown: "What became of the brown-braided dance lesson partner to whom more love poetry was addressed, I cannot say" (EHL).

Later, the principal theme surfaces with Paolo's heart attack, a passage that might be sentimental, since only Paolo's will to seize happiness miraculously sustained him: "Would you believe [me] if I told you that I could simply lie down and die if I wanted to?" (EHL) (*GW*, 8: 57).

At the turning point of the story, Paolo's decision to rejoin Ada, Mann emphasizes his message with natural phenomena, a device he had learned from Goethe's *Werther* and employed earlier in "Gefallen." As Paolo and the narrator stroll through Rome that night, "It was still almost unbearably sultry, and the sky pulsed each second in rapid phosphorescence" (EHL).[40] At the Trevi Fountain, the narrator traditionally toasts Paolo, so that he may see Rome again. As Paolo lifts his glass, lightning flashes, he drops the glass and it smashes on the edge of the basin, a foreshadowing of his approaching death.

The narrator relates the bittersweet closing events, commenting: "It had to be this way. Was it not sheer will, the will to happiness alone, by which he [Paolo] had overcome death for so long? He had to die without struggle or opposition, to die as soon as his will for happiness was satisfied, because then he no longer had an excuse to live" (EHL).[41] Human will thus overcomes both blind fate and man's law, a testimony to the mysterious relationship between the man's deepest passions and natural forces. The decadent-dilettante elements, the uncertain and playful aspects of this story, all pale before the hero's firm faith in the abstract power of man over death. Valuing happiness over life also lends "Der Wille zum Glück" the appearance of an *histoire philosophique*, although the minute realistic details create the atmosphere with unusual clarity. Love there is merely the goal of the will; the central issue is man's will, with its powerful impetus toward happiness. The closing lines indicate that once happiness is attained, death must be un-equivocally accepted, but man's will may vanquish illness and death, power-ful forces of nature.

The physical description of the von Steins shows that possibly the baron and certainly his wife are of Jewish extraction, a scrap of realistic description that has been mistakenly considered evidence of Thomas Mann's anti-Semitism: "The baron was an elegant heavy-set gentleman, bald with a gray goatee . . . his spouse, however, was simply an ugly little Jewess in a gray, tasteless dress. In her ears large diamonds twinkled" (EHL).[42] The von Steins' circumstances strongly resemble the stilted social setting of Paul Bourget's *Cosmopolis*;[43] such details in "Der Wille zum Glück" authenticate Mann's description of the upper classes and their social code.[44]

When young Baroness Ada's name is mentioned, Paolo's body is strained, his eyes glow, and he radiates "powerful, tense" calm when he is in her presence—"gewaltsame[n], gespannte[n] Ruhe" (*GW*, 8: 47–51). This is repeatedly compared to an animal's attention, later to that of a "beast of prey" (*Raubtier*), and finally to a panther's gaze upon his victim.

Ada is a Semitic beauty, with sensually supple white skin and soft hands accentuated by billowing sleeves (*bauschige Ärmel*),[45] details that Paolo, who has lately exhibited a nude, clearly apprehends. The vocabulary describing Ada's beauty, her white skin, and her dark hair is surprisingly similar to the one Mann uses in his letters to Katia while courting her, and in the "Weary Hour," the later Schiller Novella.

Though Mann expresses abstract topics realistically, he does not achieve the impressive unity of his later work. The imagery of "Der Wille zum Glück" is vivid, based on his memories and impressions, but he does not clearly associate the governing thoughts of the story with the individual components of his imagery, as for example his repeated description of Paolo's mimicry, which relates only vaguely to the theme. Paolo's tension is not consonant with his gravity, and his calm is not adequately integrated with his final triumph, although it is a superhuman victory over the power of Death. As Paolo de-parts, his face radiates the will to happiness, as do Ada's features at Paolo's funeral.[46]

Thomas Mann's attempt to express his faith in the human will testifies to his optimism. "Der Wille zum Glück" is his protest against the materialism of his times,[47] and at the same time his pursuit of potentialities beyond the rationa-listic and deterministic. In man's talents and will rather than in his reason Mann hoped to find a quality powerful enough to assure man an autonomous position in creation, and in the title of his next short story, "Der Tod," he proved that an individual can attract death, dominate it, and command it to strike or stay away.[48]

"Der Tod"

"Der Tod" (untranslated) has received very little attention; it was first published in *Simplicissimus* in January 1897, and consists of sixteen short dated diaristic entries.[49] While Thomas Mann did not rank it among his best fiction, he included it in his first short story collection, *Der kleine Herr Friedemann.*[50]

The skillfully constructed prose of "Der Tod" is poetic, even rhythmic, with musical and pictorial effects and multiplicities of connotation. The story encompasses the tenth of September to the twelfth of October in four rising stages of inner stress conveyed through adjectives describing the sea, the wind, and the rain. Although the story has very little action, the diaristic style cleverly and accurately displays the narrator's innermost thoughts and past, present, and future events. The bare noun of the title, "Death," makes this lofty abstract power a distinctly personal antagonist.[51]

This first diary entry, 10 September, is fragmentary: "Now it is autumn, and summer will not return; I will never see it again. . . " (EHL) (*GW*, 8: 69). The archetypal image evokes a mysterious nostalgia, interrupting the hope of cyclic return, an indirect intimation of death continued in the next paragraph, which rhythmically explores the thought in three stages. The sea is gray and calm, with a somber rain falling (*GW*, 8: 69), and the diarist reacts with reverence and anguish to the word "date" (*Datum*).

This brief paragraph contains only technically relevant factors: the seaside setting; the early autumn of the diarist's fortieth year; the diarist as narrator; and a combination of expectation, anguish, and nostalgia achieved by the repetition of "now," such statements as "bid farewell to summer," and the adjective "inexorable," repeatedly used to approach "the [enigmatic] day, whose date I sometimes recall softly to myself" (EHL) (*GW*, 8: 69). The poetic method conveys the inevitability of circumstances which the sight of the autumnal sea has awakened in the narrator. He has grasped the power inherent in his long-maintained obsession with death, whose development is the theme of the story.

Other elements of the theme occur in the second and third entries, 12 and 15 September. Asuncion[52] appears in the second, and the mood of the gray manor house is almost elegiac, with heightened symbolic significance: ". . . gray, it [the house] overlooks the gray sea from the hill. The sidewalk leads behind it and also behind are the fields. But I do not pay any attention to that, I only regard the sea" (EHL). In the 15 September entry, the diarist stresses his desire for silent seclusion in this, his last autumn. He is a count, an aristocrat isolated from his fellow men. ". . . I do not want triviality and boredom to infringe upon my last days. I am concerned that Death might have something of the bourgeois and the everyday in it. The exotic, the strange should surround me on that great, grave, and enigmatic day, the twelfth of October." (*GW*, 8: 70). In his passion for the mysterious, the unusual and the extraordinary, the count's love for Asuncion is paramount, and his obsession with death, the culminating experience of his life, is inexorable. On 21 September he wrote, "My little Asuncion! If you [only] knew that I will have to leave you!" (EHL) (*GW*, 8: 71).

The next three entries (21, 23, 27 September) cite 12 October[53] with increasing gloom; it is the "date" mentioned in the first paragraph, the fulfillment of the count's prediction of his early death. The comic figure of Dr. Gudehus introduces the motif of medicine on 27 September.[54] Dr. Gudehus prohibits action and thought; he prescribes a heavy bromide to ensure the count's drugged sleep, a lethargy-inducing regimen. Thomas Mann intimates that this country doctor is ludicrously groping in the dark, ignorant of the spiritual powers at work. The servant's admirable devotion to his master also clashes with the doctor's blind faith in science, which ironically proves impotent when confronted with actuality. Each secondary figure plays an intimate part in the drama without actually understanding it.

In the 30 September entry, the count's tension and hypersensitivity have grown; it is now three o'clock[55] in the afternoon, and childishly he is counting the minutes until October twelfth. The count "could not sleep this night because the wind came up and the sea and the rain were murmuring" (EHL) (*GW*, 8: 72).

The longer second entry for October finally explains the aforementioned "date," which refers to the count's victory over an abstract unknown force, also a triumph over the others' ignorance. "I am not insane!" ("Ich bin nicht wahnsinnig!") the count cries out. "You can attract him [Death] to you, so that he approaches you at that very hour in which you believe . . . " (EHL). On the following day, the count ponders, "What is suicide? Death by free will? But no one dies against his will. . . . One does not die before one agrees to die. . . . Do I agree? It must be this way, because I believe that I would go mad if I did not die on October twelfth . . . " (EHL) (*GW*, 8: 73).

The third portion of "Der Tod" contains the diary entries for 7, 8, 9, and 10 October. By now "the wind has increased, the sea is raging and the rain drums on the roof" (EHL) (*GW*, 8: 72). The count records his anticipation for a climactic joy at the moment of death, which he envisions as "great, beautiful, and of a wild majesty" (EHL) (*GW*, 8: 74). On the ninth of October, when he asks Asuncion how she would feel if he left, she weeps.

Death visits him on the tenth, saying simply, "It is best to get it over with," and the count feels he has "never felt a colder, more scornful disillusionment" (EHL).[56] Death appears as prosaic as a dentist,[57] and the count, disgusted, orders him away.

The count's last entry, 11:00 P.M. on 11 October, relates how his frightened servant called him to his daughter's deathbed, where Dr. Gudehus diagnoses a fatal heart attack. "The sea and the rain raged outside, and the winds howled in the chimney." The count wrote:

It became so clear to me in a second that I struck the table! For twenty years I have been drawing Death to myself for this one day which is to begin one hour from now; and deep within me there has nevertheless been something, something I knew subconsciously, that made me unable to leave this child. I would not have been able to die after midnight; it had to happen this way! (EHL) (*GW*, 8: 75).

Now that Asuncion has gone, the count follows Death, closing his eyes at Death's commonplace invitation.

"Der Tod" prominently displays Thomas Mann's early use of form and motifs. Nature is both his setting and his tool to mold narrative mood, each part of the story individualized by the rhythmic images of sea, rain, and wind. Their increasing strength gives the story an ascending structure, which culminates in ultimate sound and fury.

Mann intentionally restricted the palette of "Der Tod" to gray, black, and white. The count caresses the child's black hair, inherited, like Paolo Hofmann's, from her mother, as he recollects the past. As Latin as Paolo Hofmann, Asuncion's whole small form reflects emotion, love, and sensitivity.

The entry for 12 October also contrasts the raging sea before the count and the silent house behind him, where Asuncion is sleeping.[58] The love that governs her and which she represents in the count's heart is stronger than his wish to dominate death, a factor that weakens the autosuggestive potential of his mental predetermination of his fatal moment. His own death recalls Paolo's will, which in its longing for happiness (*"Glück"*) mastered death, but the themes of the stories are reversed. Paolo's unconscious will to happiness, his love for Ada, proved stronger than biological death, while in "Der Tod," the count's powerful wish for death was limited by his love for Asuncion. His inability to leave her caused disharmony in his autosuggestion, so he himself unknowingly destroyed her, his innocent sacrifice, allowing death to keep their appointment. The youthful Thomas Mann was experiencing an increasing will to overcome natural powers at the same time that he gradually overcame a suicidal tendency fairly common in adolescence. The unconscious conquest of death in "Der Wille zum Glück" contrasts dramatically with the count's consciously planned campaign, in which the count expects death to furnish a superior experience. In "Der Wille zum Glück," Death is mastered, restricted, and ultimately rejected when the struggle for happiness is won. In "Der Tod" death becomes both an opponent and a partner, a "majesty" of mythical power. The count experienced a merciless disillusionment: Death proved to be simple, even ordinary. Dying, the count cries out, "Oh, these are rude and wretched words for delicate and mysterious things" (EHL) (*GW*, 8: 75).

Disillusionment, bitter guilt, and the realization of loss are the tragic components of the count's victory over Death. Disillusionment, the final mood of "Der Tod," is also the central theme of the last story in this cycle of Thomas Mann's development, the first story included in *Stories of Three Decades*.

"Disillusionment" ("Enttäuschung")

"Der Tod" was the last story Mann wrote in Munich; on 10 October 1896 he arrived for his first visit to Venice, where he stayed for about three weeks before joining Heinrich in Rome. Venice gave him the setting for his next short story, "Disillusionment" ("Enttäuschung").[59] The topic that absorbed him was the conquest of the natural forces of love and death, matters closely related to his self-identification[60] and self-discipline, which continued until his death on 12 August 1955. The secret of Mann's immense intellectual growth lies in his lifelong effort to understand and define each concept and phenomenon he encountered and to measure himself against them. As he wrote to Grautoff 8 November 1896,

> I observe everything silently, a little tired of loneliness. My thoughts glide back and forth, like a light on the water that seems to search for something on its dark surface. I think about my suffering, about the problem of my suffering. What makes me suffer? Science . . . will it destroy me? What makes me suffer? Sexuality . . . will this destroy me? How I hate this science which even forces art into compliance! How I hate sexuality, which employs all the results and effects of beauty for its own sake! Oh, this is the poison that lures everything that is beautiful. How can I free myself from science? Through religion? How can I free myself from sexuality? Through a diet of rice? (EHL)

He does not seem to have been romantically attached at this time, but he did discipline himself rigorously with long walks, a moderate diet, and cold showers to preserve a sober and detached objectivity.

He wrote "Disillusionment," as he said, about two months after his stay in Venice, probably in Rome during November or early December, and it seems logically connected with his other fiction of that time.[61] The story reflects Venice in late October, with an azure sky, a soft breeze, and the stranger's summer suit.[62]

The word "Disillusionment" names the hollow concept in the stranger's tale, which has a static theme lacking development and chronology. In contrast to the narrator of "Disillusionment," the count of "Der Tod" lyrically presented his experiences with mystery and sensitivity. On the other hand, the role of the curious, somewhat puzzled outsider in "Disillusionment" appealed strongly to Thomas Mann.

The lovely Venetian landscape, its weather, the pigeons in the piazza, the people around him, and even the "exceptional man"[63] he notices one autumn forenoon all delight the narrator.[64] Mann does not clearly reveal whether the narrator is impressed by the stranger's ideas or converted to his way of thinking—or even whether the writer approves of them, as the introduction proceeds in Mann's earlier manner. The enigmatic restless stranger appears against the spectacular facade of St Mark's Cathedral as viewed from a sidewalk café. The strange man seems alienated, and his sudden urge to confide in someone unknown to him is surprising. The conversation takes place in late afternoon, approaching evening.

In the body of the story (paragraphs 8–29), the "exceptional man" suddenly asks, "You are in Venice for the first time, Sir?" (*STD*, 24; *GW*, 8: 63). The question seems conventional enough for a Venetian café, but Thomas Mann always used Venice, the city where Richard Wagner died, symbolically.[65] The narrator also admits that the bewilderingly open conversation with the stranger affects him intensely,[66] and at the midpoint of the story comes the startling question, "Do you know, my dear sir, what disillusionment is?"[67]

A jejune atmosphere redolent of pathetic optimism and pulpit rhetoric appears in the stranger's concepts of "good" and "bad" and "beautiful" and "ugly":[68] "From man I expected divine virtue or hair-raising wickedness: from life either ravishing loveliness or else consummate horror" (EHL) (*GW*, 8: 64). All the "exceptional man" had rationally asked was a full life and all the values poets had led him to believe it offered. He had learned, though, that pain is limited by unconsciousness; he rejected love with oblivion: "Our human need for communication has found itself a way to create sounds which lie beyond these limits" (EHL).[69]

Werther's last lines also come from the mouth of the "exceptional man," reinforcing the thematic element of death. "What is man? asks young Werther once—man, the glorious demigod? Do his powers not fail him just where he needs them most? Whether he soars upward in joy or sinks down in anguish, is he not always brought back to bald, cold consciousness precisely at the point where he seeks to lose himself in the fullness of the infinite?" (EHL).[70] Death enters again at the close of "Disillusionment," recalling the ultimate disappointment of the count in "Der Tod." As in "Der Tod," the sea and land elegantly dominate the concept of the Infinite, which suffers by being bounded by physical laws: "Often I have thought of the day when I gazed for the first time at the sea. The sea is vast, the sea is wide, my eyes roved far and wide and longed to be free. But there was the horizon. Why a horizon, when I wanted the infinite from life?" (EHL) (*GW*, 8: 67).

Novalis's concept of the Night[71] in all its starry silent solitude links man's limited earthly life and the infinite. Mann's irony and his stern objectivity, however, discipline the romantic tendency, preventing it from becoming a religion or way of life (*Lebensweise*). The "exceptional man" can never forget the bitterly learned lesson of his own limitation, nor can he believe in mankind's poets any longer. He will dream, however, about his unquenchable thirst for a liberated life and calmly await death—even though he believes death will be his final disillusionment.

The story ends abruptly when the "exceptional man" suddenly breaks off, leaving the narrator perplexed at the stranger's complex "disillusionment." Despite the "exceptional man"'s bitter loss of poetic illusions, he, like the

Count in "Der Tod," does not leave a wholly pessimistic message. "Disillusionment" is optimistic, since its gloomy mood and the lofty bitterness are counterpoised by his objective anonymous narrator, who listens, observes, and absorbs without comment, a portrait of Thomas Mann as a young artist.

Isolation graced him with a peculiar prestige that was neither popular nor even understood by those around him, who tended to regard it with embarrassment and hesitant respect. The isolated figures of Paolo, the count, and the "exceptional man" each fall short of classical heroism. Their stature is not admirable, but strange, enigmatic, even questionable. All three, though, are nevertheless existential heroes according to Sartre's definition. Their powerful wills make them incorruptible, although in a superficial view their determination may appear self-destructive.

The "exceptional man" displays the initial intimations of Mann's highly individual irony because for the first time the setting, plot and presentation of the story do not spring solely from Thomas Mann's own observations, as they had in "Der Wille zum Glück" and "Der Tod," giving abstract logic rationally tangible form. The less spectacular plot of "Disillusionment" frames a strong theme; Mann must have realized that he could refrain from identifying with the basic message of his central figure, the "exceptional man," and remain the realistic ironic observer. The creation of artistic distance through irony, enabling him to treat his personal problems objectively, became one of his unconditional intellectual and artistic requirements. Irony as well becomes his weapon against personal emotions, partiality, and prejudice, for his genuine love of humanity, his compassion and his humor preserve him from sarcasm. Based on irony, his logic has intense clarity; his wit has a crystalline freedom without any trace of rancor; and his work radiates good humor and empathy. Above all, his irony allows the literary work to develop an intellectual realism which becomes so well balanced and aesthetically proportioned that it attains a perfection only classical literature could previously claim. Thomas Mann's smile is invariably "at us" rather than "at them."

All Thomas Mann's early stories contain gravity, pathos, and ecstasy, a combination that produced a few pedestrian paragraphs. He also employed fantasy for his plots; in "Der Wille zum Glück," Death is restrained by the Will to Happiness, and in "Der Tod," Death is attracted by the Will to Power over Death. "Disillusionment" has no such fictional message; its theme is as plain and negative as the announcement that all the poets' promises have caused people only disillusionment. This is not fiction, it is a personal admission, so true and so grievous that in order to handle it at all, Thomas Mann has to isolate it objectively and hence ironically to realize its triviality,[72] and when he begins to distance himself through irony, melodrama fades from his work.

Even though Thomas Mann's isolation caused him suffering, it also filled him with pride and self-esteem,[73] and Nietzsche's projected pride of isolation had become a part of his life by the time he wrote these three short stories.

"Feelings of distance," Nietzsche says, are the "prerequisite of every elevation of man." Again, in discussing what he means by "nobility," Nietzsche finds it in the sense of separation caused through the capacity for suffering. "Profound suffering makes noble: it separates"; and he says: "It almost determines the order of rank how deeply men can suffer." Nietzsche thus gave emphatic support to Mann's youthful pride in standing apart, and provided a justification for his sufferings. It is significant that Mann later described this early pride of isolation in very Nietzschean terms. In the essay "Goethe as a Representative of the Bourgeois Age" Mann speaks of "my youthful notion of aristocracy which quite definitely amounted to a sublime incapacity and lack of vocation for ordinary life."[74]

Isolation and its suffering become the hallmark of the three heroes of "Der Wille zum Glück," "Der Tod," and "Disillusionment," first intellectually as self-identification in the universe, in the world of man, or in the knowledge of himself; and then in physical suffering, which entails self-discipline, hard work, and logical forethought. Paolo, one of the few who read Heine, is set apart from boyhood by his illness, his sensitivity, and his talent. Since he loves in physical isolation, weak Paolo was spiritually stronger than his fellows. The count and the "exceptional man" are outstandingly receptive, but their ideas cut them off from society, a condition that the count desires and which the peculiar stranger does not seem to mind. Thomas Mann and Paolo, the count, and the "exceptional man," all proudly long for the isolation that hurts them. In 1896, Mann's characters are still experimental, their features not yet shaped by an acknowledged artist. The deaths of Paolo and the count are both dignified, for Mann told their stories seriously, but the "exceptional man" is as unfinished in his literary vehicle as is his message.

Once "Disillusionment" was completed in Rome Mann set it aside temporarily;[75] two years later, he would present it to S. Fischer for his first short story collection, *Der kleine Herr Friedemann*, 1898.

2
QUEST: FIRST CREATIVE EXPRESSION OF THE SELF

"Little Herr Friedemann" ("Der kleine Herr Friedemann"), "The Dilettante" ("Der Bajazzo")

"Little Herr Friedemann"

"Little Herr Friedemann" ("Der kleine Herr Friedemann")[1] and "The Dilettante" ("Der Bajazzo"), both of which appeared in Thomas Mann's first short story collection, share one vital theme.[2] "Little Herr Friedemann" was ready for publication first; its date of conception is uncertain,[3] but on 23 May 1896 he mentioned to Grautoff that he was beginning "a psychopathic story," later realized as "Little Herr Friedemann." He was probably working on its final version just after "Der Tod" and just before "Disillusionment," and he probably completed it before leaving for Italy in October 1896. Mann badly needed money to augment his allowance of 600 marks per quarter; disappointingly, he had not won the *Simplicissimus* prize he competed for with "Der Tod." Oscar Bie, editor of S. Fischer's literary journal, the *Neue deutsche Rundschau*, accepted "Little Herr Friedemann" and asked for all of Mann's work; it was the real beginning of his literary life, and in April 1897 he sent Fischer "Little Herr Friedemann," "Der Tod," "Der Wille zum Glück," "Disillusionment," and "Der Bajazzo." "Tobias Mindernickel," printed in the *Rundschau* for January 1898, joined this set, which led in part to his first novel, *Buddenbrooks*. Two major influences also affected Thomas Mann's early intellectual development: the Wagnerian performances he had attended in Munich and Nietzsche's writings on Wagner. For the first time, in "Little Herr Friedemann," Wagner's work plays an important role in his short fiction.

For the first time, too, the title directly characterizes the protagonist. Linking "little" (*kleine*) with "Herr" involves a paradox; "*kleine*" connotes a range from "small in size" to "insufficient," while "*Herr*," a gentleman's title, originally denoted a feudal lord. This contrast is effectively varied with phrases like "comic self-importance"[4] and "looking tiny and important,"[5] describing either the protagonist's small crippled body or his frame of mind. Friedemann, itself a fairly common name, means "man of peace." The ironic title "Little Herr Friedemann" refers to the protagonist, who becomes both plot and theme, an unusual circumstance for a short story that characterizes

"Little Herr Friedemann" in a fifteen-section epic narration.[6] In the first half, Friedemann is traced from birth to his thirtieth birthday, while sections 6 through 15 cover only the next few weeks, the dramatic reaction to Friedemann's earlier life, and then the story closes with his death. "Little Herr Friedemann" is a miniature novel whose miniature chapters present a full-scale theme, foreshadowing the technique of *Buddenbrooks*.

Certain autobiographical elements in "Der Wille zum Glück," "Der Tod," and "Disillusionment" help establish mood and atmosphere, but none of the earlier three was so clearly modeled on Thomas Mann's youthful environment as "Little Herr Friedemann."[7] His home is a mixture of memories from the ancestrally furnished Mann homes on the Mengstraße and the Beckergrube. Friedemann's three sisters[8] receive names and characteristic mannerisms only in the fifth section, and "Friedemann himself, according to Ilse Martens, was modeled, at least outwardly, on a cousin from Lübeck who was a hunchback" (EHL).[9]

Thomas Mann, a young rebel, often fictionalized a memorable dancing-class infatuation.[10] When Friedemann glimpses his idol behind a jasmine bush kissing a boy he knows well, he comically and most unheroically overreacts: "His head was sunk deeper than ever between his shoulders, his hands trembled, and a sharp pain shot upwards from his chest to his throat." He spurns suffering and feverishly decides, "Never again" (*Nie wieder*"). He firmly intends to escape all future pain by drowning himself in life's aesthetic pleasures. Some critics believe that Friedemann's physical condition caused his isolation, a deterministic view. In the present existential approach, whether Friedemann is crippled or not, he is responsible for choosing his response to his first disappointment.

This moment decides his life. He willingly and consciously isolates himself from human instinct, the source of love and suffering. Unlike Paolo, Friedemann rejects genuine emotion and adopts a substitute, independently choosing to surrender his fears.

The early accident which inhibited Friedemann's physical development did not limit his potential for free will at all. His family had loved him deeply, and he lived a normal life except that "He could not take part in their [his classmates'] games, and they were always embarrassed in his company,[11] so there was no feeling of good fellowship" (*STD*, 4; *GW*, 8: 79). The German text indicates that little Friedemann felt their indifference and withdrew from them. When Johannes's classmates discussed their romantic inclination, he felt—with a certain relief—that his disability excluded him from them as well as from sports, a legitimate excuse for remaining aloof.

The position on love a crippled adolescent boy should take is extremely sensitive.[12] Love's joy and its pain, superficially opposites, mean the utmost in living, a truth little Herr Friedemann cannot grasp. He immediately turns the scene behind the jasmine shrubs[13] into an excuse for justifying his escape from potentially hurtful situations. In the late 1800s such aestheticism had become a fashionable intellectual snobbery, where the vacuum an individual created about himself by overemphasizing his own emotions gave him a prestige he might otherwise not have been able to enjoy.

Although Thomas Mann felt by nature closer to the dilettantes than to materialistic social revolutionists, he could not accept dilettantism completely because it rejected such natural values as suffering, and replaced creativity with physical gratification. In his fiction he clearsightedly condemned intelligent but overrefined dilettantes for substituting false values for genuine emotions. On 6 April 1897 Mann wrote to Grautoff:

> . . . for some time I have been feeling as if chains have fallen from me, as if I have gained the space to express myself artistically, because only now have the means been given to me to express myself, to share myself. Since "Little Herr Friedemann" I can suddenly find the discrete forms and masks under whose cover I can walk with my experiences among other people, while, previously, when I wanted to express myself even to myself alone, I needed a secret diary. . . . (EHL)

And in July 1897 he wrote:

> . . . and while once I needed a diary to relieve my feelings in my little room, now I find novelistic forms and masks which can be made public so that I may shake off my love, my hate, my sympathy, my disdain, my pride, my scorn, and my accusations. This began, I believe, with "Little Herr Friedemann. (EHL)

Young Friedemann's decision near the jasmine bush to smother his natural emotions and channel his sensitivity into aesthetic pleasures was dilettantism. He felt deceptively relieved: "The resolution did him good. He had renounced, renounced forever. He went home, took up a book, or else played on his violin, which despite his deformed chest he had learned to do" (STD, 5; GW, 8: 80).[14]

Johannes Friedemann subsequently joined a business firm rather like that of Thomas Mann's father. Friedemann held fast to his decision by the jasmine bush. At his mother's death when he was twenty-one, he exhibited a dilettante's unnatural hypersensitivity; "He cherished this grief, he gave himself up to it as one gives oneself to a great joy, he fed it with a thousand childhood memories; it was the first important event in his life and he made the most of it" (STD, 5; GW, 8: 81). Friedemann heightened everyday phenomena, like walks, the perfume of flowers, and the songs of birds, into aesthetic delights, thinking he had attained happiness. He had laboriously perfected his receptivity to music and literature, ". . . yes, one might almost call him a connoisseur."[15] The word epicurean is also emphasized in the next German paragraph.

Friedemann's self-made vulnerability clearly appears in section five: "He possessed a dramatic sense which was unusually strong; at a telling theatrical effect or the catastrophe of a tragedy his whole small frame would shake with emotion" (*STD*, 6; *GW*, 8: 82). Thomas Mann's own reactions to music, especially Wagner's,[16] are heightened only slightly in Friedemann's.

Friedemann's serenity seems too passive today, even boring, but it convinces because Mann demonstrates that aesthetic pleasures have become the center of Friedemann's life. Little Herr Friedemann looks ahead with relaxed self-confidence, assuming that his future will match his past and present, literally living up to his name, "Mr. Peace."

The second part of the story contains a turning point in section 6, the only passage in which little Herr Friedemann does not appear. One month after his birthday, the new District Commandant von Rinnlingen and his twenty-four-year-old wife, Gerda, have arrived in the small country town, causing local consternation. The town ladies do not like her, but Gerda seems well-bred, with only a hint of eccentricity.[17]

After he sees Gerda von Rinnlingen for the first time, a brilliant and warmly ironic portrait, Friedemann will never be the same. The *large* businessman Stephens and the comically contrasted *little* Herr Friedemann walk together, their canes tapping in time; their dress and politics are similar, but their actions and words illustrate their dissonant personalities. Stephens is loud, vulgar and boisterous; Friedemann is reserved and well-mannered.[18]

In the careful description of Gerda von Rinnlingen, her red-blond hair and her meticulously delineated eyes stand out. Her hair catches the eye and becomes her trademark. Thomas Mann associates light with Gerda from this point,[19] while Friedemann's environment remains dull and dark. Friedemann's obvious distraction when he fails to reply to Stephens's slightly ridiculous comments shows that his first sight of the commandant's wife has affected him deeply; he realizes that she is exactly the danger against which he has been guarding himself.

Friedemann's long self-analysis and hypersensitivity have dire consequences. His voluntary isolation from love has forced him toward an enjoyment of the arts, which requires maximum sensitivity. His self-discipline may not be able to halt the mounting emotional tide. The situation is tragic, for as in "Der Tod," a protagonist's miscalculation threatens to turn against him, but Friedemann's story and its setting purposely lack the stature of genuine tragedy. Friedemann's existential decision at the age of sixteen has governed his existence, but it did not arise from admirable reasoning.

Friedemann's rising tide of emotions resembles the onset of a fatal disease, its crisis being little Herr Friedemann's attendance at a performance of Richard Wagner's *Lohengrin*,[20] which exemplifies Friedemann's hypersensitivity toward art, soon to be overwhelmed by his feelings for Gerda von Rinnlingen, to whom he has not yet been formally introduced. His repressed love explodes during *Lohengrin*, because of his abnormally intellectualized sensual appoach to art. Thomas Mann himself reacted similarly to Wagner's opera, a response probably aggravated by early sexual frustration.

Thomas Mann parallels sensual passion under the influence of art with an unnaturally suppressed sexual impulse through Friedemann's recurrent tremors ("twitching"; "*zittern*"), a symptom of his existential tension. This represents a vital energy beyond human feelings—in water, grass, flowers. "*Zittern*" is related to Friedemann's subconscious forcefully conveying the theme through an important leitmotif. Other leitmotifs are the color red, which consistently pertains to Gerda von Rinnlingen; the garden and the river, which represent "the living state" and "life" itself. The infant Friedemann's first vital sign was "twitching" ("*zucken*"), and later, "trembling" and "shaking" demonstrate his existential essense. Between his sixteenth and thirtieth years Friedemann could face life only by substituting emotional imagination, through art, for true living. When, in section 9, Friedemann sits in loge 13, right next to the lady he both fears and desires, they do not speak, because they still have not been introduced.[21] Colors, shapes, and fragrances—and Gerda von Rinnlingen's revealing décolletage—assault Friedemann's epicurean sensitivity. The performance of *Lohengrin* is simply a shadowy backdrop for his surging emotions, and his whole little body quivers, hypnotized by the lady in loge 13.

Was Gerda von Rinnlingen a coquette?[22] In Thomas Mann's day, she should probably have dropped her eyes at Friedemann's glance. To today's eyes she merely seems curious and independent, thanking the sweaty, trembling little gentleman for his attention with an ironic smile. Friedemann can no longer function normally, and his precipitous exit is an escape, not a rational decision. This is the turning point of the story, where Friedemann himself becomes aware of the change in his life. His will had served his secret desires in compensation for "the great happiness" ("*das grosse Glück*") he relinquished fourteen years ago near the jasmine bush, but now it cannot resist his raging emotions.

Friedemann feels humiliated by Gerda von Rinnlingen's stare: "But was she not a woman and he a man?"(*STD*, 6; *GW*, 8: 90), he asks himself. In his own sphere, Friedemann had all the male prerogatives of the 1890s because since his father's death he has been the master of his house. He had never experienced anything like Gerda von Rinnlingen's direct return of his gaze, and it deeply wounded his male dignity: "And those strange brown eyes of hers—had they not positively glittered with unholy joy?" (*STD*, 12; *GW*, 8: 90). Whether her eyes had actually gleamed, Friedemann thought they did, and it electrified him. The barriers he had built for his own peace of mind began to fail, and exhausted, he pushes aside a gorgeous rose someone gave him: "No, no. That was all over. What was even that fragrance to him now? What any of all those things that up to now had been the well-springs of his joy?"[23]

From a heavy restless sleep Friedemann awakes to a lovely clear Sunday morning; he succumbs to the treacherous glory of this radiant morning, and to the magnetism of Gerda von Rinnlingen.[24] Then he walks from his home in the north end of the town to the von Rinnlingen's red house in the south. As he enters the foyer, a violent trembling overcomes him and he gives in to his internal sensations. Friedemann, who had once thought he could escape suffering by controlling his emotions, cannot muster even one argument to uphold his accustomed lifestyle. "The door suddenly opened and the maid came towards him across the vestibule; she took his card and hurried away up the red-carpeted stair,"[25] which leads to the room where Gerda von Rinnlingen will meet him. Friedemann is in a state of intense excitement: he "keeps on shaking" ("*zitterte unaufhaltsam*").

Gerda is wearing a simple red and black dress, and a sunbeam plays in her red-blond hair as she quizzically watches Friedemann. Their emphatic difference in size gives Friedemann's desperation a comic twist as he gazes up at her, thinking he sees "*zittern*"[26] in her eyes. She asks him to play some music with her, and again he believes he sees her eyes "*zittern*." He blushes[27] and stammers in embarrassment, and not even his education or his highly polished manners can help him when Gerda von Rinnlingen talks about the garden behind their house and leads down to the river. The garden and river images are connected with the recurrent motifs of the tremor and the color red; the river first occurred with Friedemann's initial employment, and again when he rushed from the theater.[28] The garden is an archetype of peace both during Friedemann's youth and at his end, and the vital current of his life is symbolized by water (*Wasser*) and river (*Fluß*)."

In the thirteenth section, the sensitive nature descriptions do not merely provide backdrop but convey the story's theme. Friedemann's instinct urges him to the ultimate escape, suicide, but the natural beauty that surrounds him touches him deeply:

> All his tender love of life thrilled through him in that moment, all his profound yearning for his vanished "happiness." But then he looked about him into the silent, endlessly indifferent peace of nature, saw how the river went its own way in the sun, how the grasses quivered and the flowers stood up where they blossomed, only to fade and be blown away; saw how all that was bent submissively to the will of life. (*STD*, 17–18; *GW*, 8: 98).

A complex autobiographical message connects Friedemann with nature. The jasmine fragrance of the final paragraph recalls his renuncilation of love's suffering fourteen years earlier; it is another summer day, but Friedemann is not the same, because he has surrendered to his future.

In the conclusion, little Herr Friedemann moves through the von Rinnlingens' party like a man trapped in a nightmare. Exhausted, Friedemann drinks a considerable amount of wine, and then Gerda von Rinnlingen asks him to take her into the garden. After they sit down on a bench overlooking the river, Gerda von Rinnlingen initiates a startlingly frank conversation, especially for Thomas Mann's time; she asks Friedemann how he came to be crippled and she hints at her own unhappiness, seeming to imply that she understands his feelings.[29] Abandoning his manners and his dignity, Friedemann melodramatically exposes his fuzzy emotions, scarcely knowing what he wants from this near stranger.[30] "He had touched her hand with his as it lay beside him on the bench, and clung to it now, seizing the other as he knelt before her, this little cripple, trembling and shuddering; he buried his face in her lap and stammered between his gasps in a voice which was scarcely human . . ." (*STD*, 22; *GW*, 8: 104). After a moment, this well-bred young woman of 1896 pushes him away and runs away without a backward glance. Friedemann's impression of the "laughter" he hears allows a variety of interpretations. His soiled clothes bring home to him the depth of his degradation, and quaking in self-disgust,[31] he forces his face into the mud until his life ebbs away.[32]

Like Goethe, young Thomas Mann clarified his problems in order to understand them, and sorted them out through his writing. Because he acknowledged his own dilettantism and rejected its forced intellectualism, Friedemann had to die in miserable self-disgust. Not only his body but also his spirit were crippled by the cowardly selfish hedonism that governed his existential decisions. To avoid pain, he had distorted his natural instincts for fourteen years and forced them to become weapons of self-destruction.[33] Thomas Mann clarified his own concept of life by permitting little Herr Friedemann to perish in self-disgust.

"The Dilettante" ("Der Bajazzo")

In the spring of 1895, Thomas Mann sent a new story to Richard Dehmel, then at the peak of his literary popularity. Dehmel earlier had refused "Der kleine Professor," but Thomas Mann now hoped he would help publish "Walter Weiler." Dehmel replied to Thomas Mann's shy, insecure letter of 15 May 1895: "Just to give it a try, I wanted to read only the first page, but I could not tear myself away. This will tell you enough. . . . Meanwhile, I will recommend 'Walter Weiler' to *Pan* [for publication]" (EHL).

Despite Dehmel's enthusiasm, *Pan* never published this story and probably returned it to Mann, who completely reworked the manuscript in Italy during the autumn of 1896. Its original text has been lost, but in a letter to Grautoff dated 5 April 1897 Mann announced that he had completed a new version under the title "Der Bajazzo." S. Fischer accepted "Der Bajazzo" for the *Der kleine Herr Friedemann* collection, 29 May 1897.[34]

"Der Bajazzo" is written in the first person, though its chronological narration is not diaristic. The story has three main divisions, with fourteen numbered sections and unnumbered opening and concluding paragraphs. The story's retrospective impression derives from the close dependence of the introduction on the end of the story, producing a form similar to a frame construction.

In "Der Bajazzo," the abstract setting assumes a leading role. The unnumbered introduction refers to "disgust" (*"Ekel"*)* and the suicidal notion; the second part presents Bajazzo's development at home, in the world, and alone; and part three shows Bajazzo's "disgust" in his self-evaluation. The story's basis is the concept of "disgust," and the significance of its various aspects to the protagonist. When Thomas Mann renamed "Walter Weiler" "Der Bajazzo," he changed from third person narration to first person, leaving the protagonist without a real name. Just as the "exceptional man" in "Disillusionment" became a personification of a frustrated disappointment, the Bajazzo figure stood for whatever "Bajazzo" signified.[35] Although Mann never explained his choice of title, he likely referred to the bitterly comic similarity between his story and the opera *Pagliacci*.

"Der Bajazzo" has numerous dilettante qualities;[36] Thomas Mann repeatedly referred to "Walter Weiler" as a dilettante,[37] but his opinion of the protagonist changed considerably, and "Der Bajazzo" became a confessional work. The *Bajazzo-Pagliaccio* figure hides his tragic secret, acting out the real tragedy of his life in the role he assumes.

Thomas Mann was happy to have found a form of expression for this character in the new title,[38] a figure not typical of the dilettante as Bourget and Thomas Mann understood it. The dilettante neither could nor would face his own problems; he would rather flee into death, as Friedemann and the young contessa in Bourget's *Cosmopolis* did. Bajazzo's severe self-judgment at the close of the story is vital: "To make an end—but would that not be almost too heroic for a 'Bajazzo'?" (EHL).[39] Thomas Mann chose Leoncavallo's *Pagliacci* for his personal and dramatized expression; Bajazzo parallels the tragic undertones of Leoncavallo's hero with the German connotations of the word *Bajazzo*.

The murder of the operatic lovers by Canio and the failure of Tonio, the two *Pagliacci* in the opera, is analogous to Bajazzo's action in burning the bridges connecting him to his environment. His actions condemn him to the deepest expression of hopelessness, a loneliness that cannot be assuaged by compassion or understanding.[40]

At the very end of "Little Herr Friedemann," Thomas Mann described: ". . . a disgust, perhaps of himself, which filled him with a thirst to destroy himself, to tear himself to pieces, to blot himself utterly out" (*STD*, 92; *GW*, 8: 105). Friedemann did indeed destroy himself in the connection of death to "disgust," a violent and intricate concept in itself. Such a linkage is the first and principal motif of "Der Bajazzo." This continuity in the development of

---

*The special message conveyed by Mann's use of a particular German word will be emphasized by placing it in parentheses after its English equivalent, which will thereafter appear in quotation marks to signal this special usage. The same English terms, when not enclosed in quotes, will carry their ordinary dictionary meanings. This will be applied at the beginning of each chapter. Also see glossary.

Mann's thought from one fictional work to the next makes the structural peculiarity of "Der Bajazzo" logical. The central thought of "disgust," the governing mood of "Little Herr Friedemann," immediately becomes the topic of "Der Bajazzo": "It can all be summed up, beginning, middle, and end—yes, and fitting valediction too, perhaps—in the one word: 'disgust.' The disgust which I now feel for everything and for life as a whole; the disgust that chokes me, that shatters me that hounds me out and pulls me down. . . (*STD*, 28; *GW*, 8: 106).

This narration is called "my story" ("*meine Geschichte*") and focuses Mann's concept through the elements of disgust presented in the introduction. The style of the first section is completely different from the introduction, whose peaceful tone opens the narration. Lübeck's centuries-old Nordic charm appears in the naïve images of white doors and red curtains, echoing with the soft elegance of Chopin's nocturnes. Mann also sketches the dreaming child-features of the mother and the gray whiskers and powerful brows of the dominant father. "Bajazzo" consciously chose his mother's spirit as his model.

The section describes Bajazzo's beloved puppet theater, a toy Mann also had as a boy.[41] He called this pastime "passionate" ("*leidenschaftlich*"), similar to his reaction to Wagner's music.

In "Der Bajazzo" Thomas Mann notes objectively: ". . . splendid bombastic verse with more rhyme than reason; in fact it seldom had any connected meaning, but rolled magnificently on. . ." (*STD*, 31; *GW*, 8: 110). This dispassionate judgment of his childhood games is the first of several statements which clearly show that the thirty-year-old writer of "my story" readily determined the roots of the superficiality and moodiness which governed his entire adult life. He referred as well to the intense sensual pleasure his early interaction with the arts gave him, without in any way motivating him to a thorough exploration of structure, technique, message, or even the meaning of such arts.

This section also sharply displays the obvious similarities and differences between Bajazzo and Friedemann, while steadily reflecting autobiographical material. The setting is the usual upper-middle-class Lübeck home, and the protagonist has two elder sisters.[42] In school his clever imitations of the instructors make him popular with his fellows.[43]

Bajazzo's inability to concentrate is by no means a physical incapability but a part of his "clown talent" ("*Bajazzobegabung*"), as the Father calls it. Seeking refuge in role playing with his "musical puppet theater" and in notions from his reading thus becomes "real" for him. The excellence of his parodies and his comic performance of Wagnerian music do reveal talent and the capacity for keen observation, without which others cannot see irony and be entertained by it. While Friedemann withdrew through fear of rejection, Bajazzo disdains the world, work, and personal involvement. His aesthetic pleasures, he thinks, give him independence and a sense of superiority over the contemptible masses. Bajazzo has musical talent, he sketches, and he loves reading, activities like young Thomas Mann's, who enjoyed his violin lessons even longer than Bajazzo did. Mann, however, never became a professional-level performer or composer,[44] and reproductions of his drawings appear only in his biographical works.

"Der Bajazzo" ' a relationship with his musical instrument is a masterpiece of self-exploration and child psychology. The benevolent irony with which young Mann chronicled his hero's musical exploits is a humorous admission at the same time that it pinpoints the story-hero's superficial immature approach to music. Bajazzo's self-taught style is caricatured in the story: "Being attracted by the black keys, I began with the F-sharp major chords. . . ."[45] Exploring the instrument by himself was the most attractive feature for him. "In the circle of my relatives and friends I was high-spirited and popular, being amiable out of sheer pleasure in playing the amiable part, though at the same time I began instinctively to look down on all these people, finding them arid and unimaginative" (*STD*, 32; *GW*, 8: 112). The conclusion of the third section indicates that the protagonist is starting to realize the two major factors in his life: first, that in living he was playing a role; and second, that his self-image was built upon disdaining others. His acting satisfied no inner needs; it was simply a shallow, worthless pastime.

The fourth section is the conclusion of the first division of "my story." Bajazzo overhears his parents discussing him. His father, who all along has expressed his disappointment at his son's scholastic failures, says he has a "*Bajazzobegabung*" (talent for clowning).[46] The father proceeds to cite his son's "*Clownerie und Blague*," a pejorative phrase that displays his contempt for his son's "artistic" performances. However, the father will listen to his son's wishes before taking him out of school. Typically, the son had none; his only reaction is relief at being free from irksome school discipline. The upshot is that Bajazzo will be sent out to learn a business, and in sections 5–7, Bajazzo appears in the world with people, using his "*Bajazzo*-talent."

The change from school to an apprenticeship with Herr Schlievogt[47] was practically nil for Bajazzo, who now mocks the whole world instead of his teachers. He spends carefree hours at the Schlievogt office with a young man named Schilling,[48] but while Schilling's goal is to become wealthy, Bajazzo dreams of concerts, operas, and books; ". . . my brain [is] filled with an unproductive chaos of half-thoughts and fanciful imaginings. . . ." For the second time, Bajazzo admits the superficial worthlessness of his artistic activity, and adds his inability to create. All this apparently did not bother him, and he told his mother he felt happy in his new way of life. The writer of "my story" skillfully maintains the distance of time between his early memories and the thirty-year-old man.

Bajazzo considers his situation at the Schlievogt business as "temporary." His wealth, his popularity, and his social position all made him say, ". . . why should I not be happy?" (*STD*, 34; *GW*, 8: 115). This attitude led to his isolation, since he was a stranger to others' problems; he felt superior to other people and rollicked joyously while mocking their limitations. Bajazzo's isolation stems from his very early youth, when he had acted without really living in the roles in which he wished to be observed. His unconscious alienation gave him an enjoyable feeling of false popularity and prestige that differentiates him from Friedemann, who instead withdrew entirely from people. While Friedemann was "different" because of his crippled body, Bajazzo was "different" because of his chosen lifestyle. Still, the result was the same: Bajazzo's mockery and Friedemann's shyness both ended in aesthetic addiction and fatal rejection of others.

In section 6, his father told Bajazzo he should have no false expectations, because the business had slipped and he himself was in poor health; Bajazzo must understand, the father said, ". . . that you will be flung upon your own resources" (*STD*, 35; *GW*, 8: 116). This statement does not reflect Thomas Mann's own circumstances as accurately as other descriptions do. Thomas Mann's father, Johann Heinrich Mann, was not bankrupt when, just before he died, he specified that the family firm be liquidated upon his death, in order to protect his survivors' interest.[49] First Heinrich and later Thomas disliked school and rejected the notion of following the family business, a bitter disappointment to their father, especially when his own health was failing, and his will, opened on 13 October 1981, clearly showed that he could not count on either of his sons as his successor. Mendelssohn has proved that the liquidation brought heavy losses to the family estate, but it precluded mismanagement by inept sons or employees. Neither Heinrich, also a school dropout, nor Thomas revealed guilt about the financial decline and termination of the family's firm. In fiction, both in "Der Bajazzo" and *Buddenbrooks*, the bankruptcy occurred well before the maturity of the two "artistic" sons, Bajazzo and Hanno Buddenbrook. In "Der Bajazzo" these events relieve "Bajazzo" from parental authority, work, and responsibility, just as the liquidation relieved the young Mann brothers, especially since they both soon received an allowance to live a meager, but independent, life. Bajazzo also took advantage of the situation, for his weak mother[50] died shortly, and Bajazzo cashed in his part of the inheritance, leaving on the sybaritic journeys he had always wanted to make. Bajazzo's joyous rejection of his family's business-centered life style closely resembles Friedemann's decision to renounce love; both were self-exiles from their society.[51] Bajazzo's travels may represent search or learning, or, simply a quest for new stimuli. Thomas Mann's trips to Italy enabled him, in fact, to round out his neglected education. At this time he enjoyed a close companionship with Heinrich. Later, though, Thomas Mann judged his own leisure years harshly.

In the seventh section, Bajazzo somewhat pedantically accounts for six years' spending of his money. Thomas Mann himself habitually kept minute financial accounts, and his own economic state was similar to Bajazzo's. Midway in this section, the young man entertains a group with an improvised Wagnerian parody, either to reveal his deepest feelings for the poet-composer, or merely to enjoy some applause. One old gentleman exclaims, "But you must, you certainly must become an actor or a musician!" (*STD*, 36; *GW*, 8: 118).

This performance resembled the genial prank of an artist who sketches a caricature on a tablecloth; immediately afterwards, Bajazzo became depressed, and went to a piano; for the first time, he realized his lack of identity and suddenly yearned to belong somewhere. His finances provided a good excuse to return to Germany, and at twenty-five, five years before he would narrate the story, he descended from a train at a station of a Bavarian city (Munich), eager to settle down and indulge his tastes.

In contrast to Friedemann, Bajazzo had prided himself on being an extremely fortunate person. He allowed life to slide by, taking none of it seriously. His first decision was not to care about the Schlievogt business; his second, to spend time and money traveling, which would have enriched his life if he had had the right attitude. His third was to settle into a life which excluded the "world" he mocked and to consecrate his existence to the exclusive enjoying of the arts. He had no need to live up to any standards; the puppet theater, music, and poetry were all simply pleasurable toys which he thought he could exploit without searching for deeper values.

When Bajazzo arrives in his chosen town, Mann details the carefully selected locale and decor of Bajazzo's new dwelling. "Boredom?" Bajazzo wonders; he has to admit that his pastimes may not always be satisfactory, and he confesses:

> I would. . . feel stealing over me a distaste of all the world, myself included. I would be possessed by fear, spring up and go out of doors, there to shrug my shoulders and watch with a superior smile the business men and labourers on the street, who lacked the spiritual and material gifts which would fit them for the enjoyment of leisure. (*STD*, 38–39; *GW*, 8: 122).

For the first time, he links himself and the "world" which he had mocked all of his life. Still, his feelings of superiority are strong enough to blur his rising anguish and to enable him to set himself above others on account of his capacity for leisure and enjoyment.

Bajazzo never examined the reasons for his failure to initiate himself fully into the arts he enjoyed, and Mann's ironic statements about this incapacity become increasingly emphatic. By the end of the eighth section, the only audience Bajazzo has left is himself, since he has shut out the world he had mocked. In the ninth section, Bajazzo states that the "temporary" aspect of his life has become immutable, but he is tiring of passivity and isolation. Bajazzo now feels the need of human companionship, but he senses the estrangement that his situation, his upbringing and needs, his tastes and his standards, all gradually forced him into; he neither can nor will surrender his values. "Bajazzo" accepts the full responsibility for his isolation, as he calls it "largely my own fault" (*STD*, 39; *GW*, 8: 123). In the turning point of the story, he recognizes his lack of self-identification:

> Besides, of course, I had given up society; I had broken with it when I took the liberty of going my own way regardless of its claims upon me. So if in order to be happy I needed "people," then I had to ask myself whether I should not have been by now busy and useful making money as a business man in a large way and becoming the object of respect and envy. (*STD*, 39; *GW*, 8:123)

He realizes the enormity of his guilt feelings even before the romantic episode, a large step in Mann's maturing conception of the protagonist. Bajazzo evaluates his emotions with some degree of objectivity, as his clear-headed and ironic definition of his own *Bajazzo*-talent shows. In the last difficult lines of section 9 his self-directed irony has all the symptoms displayed in "Disillusionment," a cry of heartfelt despair. Interestingly, this passage was written before Fischer had asked Thomas Mann to produce a sizable novel.

"Der Bajazzo"'s mood in section 10 is characteristic of the dilettante, nostalgia mixed with masochism. "Again a day come to an end, a day of which one cannot deny, thank God, it had a content" (EHL) (*GW*, 8: 124; see also *STD*, 40). The second paragraph of this section brilliantly presents a hypersensitive and cultivated man's sensuous and intellectual reaction to a work of art; it is emotional, passionate, overwhelming—very similar to little Herr Friedemann's to *Lohengrin*, referring to one of those works that "shatter, enrapture, torture, inspire, and overwhelm [the reader] with their foul splendor of wickedly ingenious dilettantism" (EHL) (*GW*, 8: 125; see also *STD*, 40).

Mann transfers his experience of art to the passionate urge for creation, and for becoming an artist (see glossary, *Künstler*) himself. The emerging of the artist motive is a powerful step toward his own development: "And with all that the compulsion, which forever urges them upwards and outwards, to display them, to share them, to 'make something of them.' . . . Suppose I were an artist in very truth, capable of giving utterance to my feelings in music, in verge, in sculpture—or best of all, to be honest, in all of them at once?" (*STD*, 40; *GW*, 8: 125). For the very first time in his short fiction, Mann confesses his longing for self-expression and artistry, the high point Bajazzo attains in his relationship to art. While Friedemann only used it for his egotistic ivory-tower happiness, Bajazzo's reaction is a sound desire to share, a quality which later allows him to realize the failure inherent in his voluntary isolation. Mann's elaboration on these paragraphs opens up another important insight, a panorama of Bajazzo's abstract existential concepts. There exist, he explains, both "outer" and "inner" happinesses, and the outward happiness had been given to the "children of light": "Perhaps the truth is that I resigned my claim to this 'outward happiness' when I withdrew myself from the demands of society and arranged my life to do without people"(*STD*, 41; *GW*, 8: 126).

Both Friedemann and Bajazzo wanted happiness. The motif of failing at achieving it and the consequent scorn for one's failing to belong to the "children of light" recur throughout the story and culminate in the "disgust" motif of the ending. Bajazzo is certain that he will escape through some narcotic, and his mood endlessly swings up and down.

In section 11 the archetypes of fatigue and approaching death are unexpectedly introduced with the imagery of autumn. The unnerved Bajazzo is suddenly electrified by a spring like day unnatural to this gloomy season. Just when the intellect dulls, nature unexpectedly moves in; as Bajazzo strolls in the splendid unseasonable weather, he encounters the elegant carriage of an older gentleman, driven by a young daughter. She never actually notices the protagonist, and when she is forced to confront him by selling him a glass of wine in the next section, she disdainfully rejects him. In "Gefallen" and to some extent in "Der Wille zum Glück," Mann passed through early fantasies and a trite love interest, while in "Der Bajazzo" the female character has a tendency to withdraw. Gerda von Rinnlingen's actions convulse Friedemann, but Fräulein Rainer's pure, detached charm incorporates the type of the "children of light" whose complete detachment makes Bajazzo recognize his incapacity for happiness: ". . . what I felt was pleasure and admiration, but at the same time a strange and poignant pain aroused a rough and crowding feeling—of envy? of love? I did not dare to think it through—[perhaps] of self-contempt?" (EHL).

As in "Little Herr Friedemann," Bajazzo's second encounter with the lady is accidental (section 12) and also takes place at a performance of an opera,[52] here Gounod's *Faust*.[53] The chaste vision of the young lady in her opera loge with her father is comparable to Faust's first view of Marguerite from a distance. Neither this young lady nor Gerda von Rinnlingen seemed at all flirtatious: "Gounod's spirited and tender music was, it seemed to me, not [a] bad accompaniment to this sight, and I harkened, completely enraptured, to a mild and passive mood, whose melancholy would perhaps have been even more painful without this music" (EHL) (*STD*, 44; *GW*, 8: 131). The musical mood modifies Bajazzo's experience: Thomas Mann directly indicates that Bajazzo did not follow the stage action, but only experienced Gounod's melodies, which neatly illustrated his emotions. Just as Wagner's *Lohengrin* had impassioned Friedemann and, together with Gerda's effect upon his senses, had even overwhelmed him, Gounod's light musical background focuses this charming and somewhat sentimental view of Bajazzo's young lady. For the second time Thomas Mann uses music for a dual purpose, to shape an emotion and to affect his protagonist; while music inflamed Friedemann, it only tempered Bajazzo's mood.

After a detailed description of the young lady, young Alfred Witznagel, obviously her suitor, is bitterly caricatured by Bajazzo. "For the rest, the gentleman was faultlessly built and moved with assurance" (*STD*, 45; *GW*, 8: 132). The young gentleman's clothing and mannerisms are described with rousing humor. Significantly the young gentleman is blond: and Bajazzo savagely skewers his vulgarity and obtuseness: "What wonderfully happy self-confidence such a young man must rejoice in!" "(*STD*, 45; *GW*, 8: 133). Self-confidence, a basic requirement for the "children of light" who live in "outward happiness," has become a major motif. Immaculately dressed, the blond athletic antagonist joins the blond dancing students of Thomas Mann's earlier fiction. His unconscious self-assurance, the obvious source of his success with the young lady, makes him enviable despite his lack of sensitivity, elegance and wit. The smiling faces in the loge above him drive Bajazzo to despair; he feels "shut out, unregarded, disqualified, unknown, *hors ligne—déclassé*, pariah, a pitiable object even to [himself]!"[54]

Bajazzo has changed since the first two stages of his life, home and travels, periods when he could still maintain his self-styled superiority through his buffoonery and could camouflage his isolation with his disdainful pose. In the third part, the isolated Bajazzo was able to apprehend his need for others and the ghastly vacuum his alienation had caused. With an anguished heart, Bajazzo followed the father, daughter and her suitor to their doorstep after the opera and learned that the old gentleman was "Justizrat Rainer."[55]

Bajazzo feels "sick to death of it all" (*STD*, 46; *GW*, 8: 134), a disgust that is the final motif of the story. He decides to meet the young lady on equal terms at a forthcoming charity bazaar. The climax occurs when Bajazzo asks the lady for a glass of wine she is selling for charity, but he completely fails to prove his point. As the moment approaches, his self-consciousness mounts. He sharply senses his gauche manners, his muddy trousers, and his ludicrous appearance, and he is so embarrassed that when he finally speaks to the lady, he is scarcely civil. Nothing really happens, heightening the scene's verisimilitude. Bajazzo alone realizes the humiliation he has suffered in the eyes of the lady, the gentlemen around the table, and the lady's suitor. "Since that moment it is all up with me" (*STD*, 48; *GW*, 8: 137), he says, and a few days later, when he reads of the engagement of Fräulein Rainer to the blond athlete, he feels nothing.

Bajazzo picks up the last motif of the previous section in the conclusion: "Since that moment it is all up with me. My last remaining shreds of happiness and self-confidence have been blown to the winds, I can do no more. Yes, I am unhappy; I freely admit it. I seem a lamentable and absurd figure even to myself" (*STD*, 48; *GW*, 8: 137). Again, he considers happiness a prestigious achievement. In contrast to "Little Herr Friedemann," the protagonist does not melodramatically succumb to the temptation of suicide;[56] he is not even sure whether this had been love at all. He concludes, "There is only one kind of unhappiness: to suffer the loss pleasure in oneself. No longer to be pleasant to oneself—that is the worst that can happen" (*STD*, 49; *GW*, 8: 138). As reinforcement, Thomas Mann improvises a little scene: Schilling, Bajazzo's happy companion from Schlievogt's, is now wealthy and successful and comes to spend a few days with him. All of Bajazzo's efforts to project an impression of contentment fail: "I had not the backbone, the courage or the countenance; I was languid and ill at ease, I betrayed my insecurity" (*STD*, 49; *GW*, 8: 139). Schilling is not taken in, and he disenchantedly leaves town before the appointed time.

Alfred Witznagel, with his stupid self-satisfaction, blond good looks, and starched shirt front, and Schilling as well, are "children of light" as Bajazzo sees and envies them.[57] The beautiful Anna Rainer is one of them, too, and Bajazzo's envy here is mixed with longing, self-pity and what he thinks is love for her.

The story closes with the disgust Bajazzo has come to feel for himself; he sees clearly enough that suicide does not suit his style; he must insure himself to being dull, wretched, and ridiculous. The ambiguous ending may be a melodramatic outcry, a statement that to be a Bajazzo is a crippling fatality. Perhaps his talents were not stimulated by a sufficient vocation; perhaps his talent was too much of a temptation and distraction in daily life; perhaps it was too attractive to please others, thus obviating any quest for deeper values.

Art is involved in each of Mann's short stories to this point. Paolo Hofmann was an artist, but beyond his talent and sensitivity, his art received no significant description and was unrelated to his emotional problems. The count, the "exceptional man," Friedemann, and Bajazzo all possess a more than normal capacity for enjoying art, and all snatch at sensual experience, like dilettantes. Bajazzo, however, is the first character to complain of his lack of identity and of his artistic sterility. In Thomas Mann's fiction at this point, too, literature and music had begun to prevail over the plastic arts. Both Heinrich and Thomas had shown talent in the visual arts as young men.

Young Thomas Mann was finding he had to define his place in society and select his priorities, and his realization that isolation caused pain and longing was not new. Bajazzo's chosen rejection of society in favor of "inward happiness" was unsatisfying because of its parasitic passivity and lack of creativity, and the depth of his despair shows Thomas Mann's genuine devotion to the quest for truth. The deeply felt sense of responsibility for his own actions and choices, also noted in "Little Herr Friedemann," is emphatically present in "Der Bajazzo." Bajazzo cannot repair, relearn, start over; he has made his own tragedy, which, as with Leoncavallo's *Pagliacci*, is complete; nothing can bring back Bajazzo's self-respect. The joyously oblivious superiority and self-assurance he had savored in the first two parts of the narration were irrevocably destroyed. But when Bajazzo lost his self-reliance, Mann unconsciously realized some of his own values. His new-found sensitivity showed him not only how to live an epicurean life, but also how to listen to himself so that his moods and emotions could lead him to self-discovery. Further, his trained intellect and limitless leisure for self-analysis made him logically pursue such emotional manifestations. When he experienced the vacuum his self-imposed isolation had caused, and when he painfully realized the sterility of his artistic talent, he suddenly discovered an urgent need for self-identification.

The imagery of "inward happiness" and "outward happiness" scrupulously presents the real problems in Thomas Mann's developing *Weltbild*. Newly gained values proved negative and even fatal for Friedemann and Bajazzo, who sank helplessly into despair when they gradually lost their comforting self-created illusions, but their downfalls simultaneously liberated Mann himself from personal misconceptions.[58] The abyss Bajazzo faced became his springboard to another dimension, leaving Bajazzo behind him, confronted, analyzed, and overcome, a fascinating development that can only be seen retrospectively in his lifework. Before he could advance, he had to overcome the vacuum that appeared to open before Bajazzo when he realized the nothingness of his pursuits; he had either to forsake his attempt to understand phenomena of universal stature or to continue the quest.

After "Der Bajazzo," Mann expressed a different aspect of this harrowing period of his development in "Tobias Mindernickel" and the short fiction that followed, which bridge the artistic gap between his early stories and his first *Künstlernovellen*, "Tristan" and "Tonio Kröger," short stories with inherent aesthetic messages. The "other side" for Thomas Mann became plain when he acknowledged his artistic vocation, thus opening up an entire new cycle of themes (*Themenkreis*) in his fiction.

3
FROM GROTESQUE DISHARMONY
TO THE VISION OF AN ABSTRACT
WELTBILD

**"Tobias Mindernickel," "Little Lizzy" ("Luischen"), "The
Wardrobe" ("Der Kleiderschrank"), "Gerächt," "The Way
to the Churchyard" ("Der Weg zum Friedhof"), "Gladius Dei,"
"Tristan"**

The strange short stories between "Der Bajazzo" (1897) and "Tristan" (1903),
are generally neglected, and even the origins and completion of "Tobias
Mindernickel," "Little Lizzy," "The Wardrobe," "Gerächt," "The Way to
the Churchyard," and "Gladius Dei" are hazy.[1]

"Tobias Mindernickel"

After "Der Bajazzo" in the summer of 1897, Mann wrote a startlingly brutal story, "Tobias Mindernickel."[2] This six-and-one-half-page account of a
peculiar old man who kills his dog seems to lack a theme, but it does feature
an isolated hero, a far more wretched creature than any Thomas Mann had
yet created. He spent part of his time that summer in Rome and part at the
Albergo Casa Bernardini in Palestrina,[3] gathering background for a larger
project from his mother and other relatives.[4] He also had literary infatua-
tions: "At the moment I am admiring Eckermann's Conversations with
Goethe—what a humbling delight it is to have this great, regal, self-assured
and lucid human being before you, to hear him talk, to see his actions! I
cannot get enough of [this delight] and I will [also] regret coming to the end
[with someone] spiritually more akin to us decadents, namely E. T. A. Hoffmann, that strange ill being with the fantas[ies] of a hysterical child, . . . I
read everything of his I could lay my hands on" (EHL) (letter to Grautoff, 24
July 1897).

The names of Thomas Mann's fictional figures, like his settings, always play
an important role in his work. Here he creates "a man named Mindernickel—
and Tobias to boot" (*STD*, 51; *GW*, 8: 141), a peculiar combination as typically middle-class German of the *fin de siècle* as Tobias's clothing, his Empire

55

chest of drawers, and certain traits of his behavior. Biblical names were often given then, and here, as in the Bible, "Tobias" indicates "the man with the dog."[5] "Mindernickel," an ordinary German name, again portrays the hero's personality.[6] "Tobias Mindernickel" also significantly shares Thomas Mann's initials. This story has three parts: the introduction, a second section equal in length, and the tragic denouement, slightly shorter.

"Tobias Mindernickel" opens on a gray indeterminate street in a desolate neighborhood. Tobias's low-life neighbors remain nameless, while Thomas Mann announces that Tobias Mindernickel's story is both "*rätselhaft*," and "*schändlich*,"[7] before he again meticulously describes the protagonist at his first appearance.

Tobias Mindernickel is outwardly "striking," "odd," and "ludicrous," with peculiar mannerisms that cause street urchins to taunt him while their parents look on laughing. Tobias appears shy and frightened, but he is used to such treatment. Thomas Mann deliberately chooses not to reveal Tobias's past life, although Tobias's furnishings, his clothes and his manner hint at a middle-class citizen brought down to an ungainly strange personage with nothing to do but sniff at the dirt-filled flowerpot in a window that opens onto a gray stone wall.

Then one of the urchins is hurt, and the usually shy Tobias suddenly becomes alert and purposeful. Tending the boy with his own handkerchief, Tobias speaks decisively and acts masterfully. His old-fashioned compassion harmonizes with his biblical first name,[8] and his language is polished and free of dialect. The episode displays Tobias Mindernickel's "riddle of character" as he fleetingly dominates the situation.

Tobias Mindernickel later buys a young hunting dog for ten marks and tugs it back to his gray home. "And I will call you Esau"[9] he tells the dog when they arrive, overfeeding and overprotecting him to the point of misbehavior, which frightens Tobias Mindernickel, himself suffering from repressed emotions. He beats Esau severely each time the dog's instincts assert themselves. Then he ineffectually tries to train him, provoking the dog's fatigue and inattention, and bringing on the very obstreperousness that calls for punishment. As he whips Esau, Tobias's frenzy produces role playing, and he treats the dog Esau as though he were human.

Finally, the dog accidentally injures himself on Tobias's bread knife. Tobias is filled with sympathy, as with the hurt child. The dog recovers and returns to his naturally rambunctious behavior; when Esau refuses to lie down to be petted:

> That which now happened was so shocking, so inconceivable, that I simply cannot tell it in any detail. Tobias Mindernickel stood leaning a little forward, his arms hanging down; his lips compressed, the balls of his eyes vibrated uncannily in their sockets. Suddenly with a sort of frantic leap, he seized the animal, a large bright object gleamed in his hand— and then he flung Esau to the ground with a cut which ran from the right

shoulder deeps into the chest. The dog made no sound, he simply fell on his side, bleeding and quivering. (*STD*, 75; *GW*, 8: 150)

When Esau died, Tobias wept and spoke no more.

"Tobias Mindernickel" seems almost a pathological study of an alienation that engenders a violent urge to dominate. Chance allowed Tobias to do so twice, first when he comforted the injured boy and later when he cared for the hurt dog; but in his blind desire to subdue the dog so that it will accept his perverse affection, he finally strikes out at Esau. Tobias deprived himself of the only creature that might have loved him, and he is left in desperate self-pity. If a "case study" reading applied, though, it would be the only such instance in all of Mann's voluminous writing, since he had no particular clinical interest in 1897. Whether Tobias killed the dog intentionally or accidentally, it reveals Tobias's perverse compulsion to dominate the animal. Esau's pitiable fate was to be saved from more suffering in life.[10]

"Tobias Mindernickel" might also seem to mask Mann's own psychological examination of his sexual frustration and his isolation from women at the time. The violent bitterness of the student's reaction in "Gefallen" and the masochism in "Little Herr Friedemann" and "Der Bajazzo" suggest a psychologically sound pattern, with Esau as a "beloved" that rejects Tobias, the "lover." The "lover's" violence is unpremeditated, a rape of the very being of the "beloved." Such a theory, however, involves a subconscious self-expression not in harmony with Mann's psychological development at that time.

Thomas Mann's messages are always deeply personal statements on his preoccupations at given times in his life. The message of "Tobias Mindernickel" appears through the title, the name of the hero and its initials, and his furnishings and surroundings, a private, personal existence essentially drawn from Mann's self. The powerful despair and bitter self-disgust he had exposed so glaringly in "Little Herr Friedemann" and "Der Bajazzo" spilled into "Tobias Mindernickel," continuing his exploration of self-disgust.[11] The gray town where Bajazzo lived is also the town of Tobias Mindernickel and the sunny Lerchenberg where the heroes find their "beloveds." The grotesque ridicule, the disgust, and shame from the initial paragraph, all suit the spirit of the closing passage of "Der Bajazzo," because Tobias's miserable crime is but Bajazzo's destructive self-rejection carried out upon the "beloved" dog.

In the end I shall go on living, eating, sleeping: I shall gradually get used to the idea that I am dull, that I cut a wretched and ridiculous figure. (*STD*, 50; *GW*, 8: 140)

Finally, like Bajazzo, Tobias Mindernickel lacks a backbone.[12]

Tobias Mindernickel's abasement is masterfully presented through the dog Esau, sadly cheated out of his inheritance of freedom. Tobias treated Esau[13] ("hairy one") as though he were human to assuage his own miserable self-pity, fear, loneliness, and guilt. By nursing Esau in his own bed, by telling the dog sobbingly he is "his only one," Tobias deceives the innocent animal, just as the name "Esau" implies. When the irate Tobias tries to force Esau into submitting to his perverse affection, the dog simply cannot understand, bringing on his destruction. Is it that Mann unveils his subconscious struggle for his art, his beloved, which he could express only with difficulty?[14] When Tobias, who had no interest in art, left his gray room in the gray house on a gray street for the happy sunny park, he bought the dog as a substitute for what the world failed to give him. Just as with Thomas Mann's earlier characters, Tobias too was acquiring a value he could substitute for the love that would make life meaningful.

But the will to seek happy companionship is as simple and dynamic as nature itself. In denying Esau a natural life, just as Friedemann and Bajazzo refused themselves the genuine values of life and art, Tobias shows himself as sadistic, violent, and bitter. His will to power in subjugating Esau becomes obsessive to the point of murder, leaving him alone with the self he hates. Like his fictional predecessors, Tobias is weakened by concentrated decadence and can no longer endure life. Tobias does not deal with art, but he deals directly with life, and for Thomas Mann life, like art, is an incorruptible absolute. Esau's life, simple, playful, loving, should have been accepted, not corrupted.[15] "Tobias Mindernickel" thus is not a case study but an impressive piece of art, confessing a lack of self-respect that goes hand in hand with the loss of self-control.[16]

While Thomas Mann, the man, can be equated even less with Tobias Mindernickel than with Bajazzo, these stories therapeutically uncover his subconscious concerns. When he condemned Tobias Mindernickel he was still far from overcoming his difficulties; he still had no path to follow as his powerful imagination shifted from the sordid picture of Tobias weeping over the body of his dead dog Esau, toward another, just as distasteful, setting.

"Little Lizzy"

In the same summer, Mann also wrote "Little Lizzy," similar to "Tobias Mindernickel" in form, message, and distasteful aggressive mood. Mann wrote to Grautoff from Rome[17] on 21 July 1897: "In the meantime I have, one might say, already begun a new volume with a brief novella by the name of "Little Lizzy" ['Luischen'] , which I, on invitation, have first sent to *Jugend*—[it is] a peculiar and ugly story, as suits my present view of the world and people" (EHL).

The previous May, S. Fischer had encouraged Mann to submit a longer work, perhaps even a novel. Thomas and his brother Heinrich had been contemplating a projected generational novel,[18] but this had nothing to do with the eventual evolution of *Buddenbrooks*, Thomas Mann's own first novel.[19]

"Little Lizzy,"[20] comprised of five unequal parts, shares a Munich-like setting[21] with "Der Bajazzo" and "Tobias Mindernickel." The title, " Luis-chen," from a then popular song, signifies something quite different to each person: for Jacobi, who wants to please his wife but is trapped in his repellent appearance, "Luischen" represents an amalgamation of his overwhelming emotions and his self-rejection; for Amra, "Luischen" expresses her humilia-tion at having chosen to wed this "monster."

The characters receive Mann's usual careful delineation. Amra's dark coloring does not convey sensitivity but rather sensuality, gorgeously stupid, something not seen previously in his stories. Her intellect is limited and she feels only momentary thrills as the involuntary target of a legal husband's passion; his emotion is tragically encased in a monstrous body made impotent by fathomless self-disgust.

Jacobi's unhappy reclusiveness leaves him no dignity whatsoever. His head is covered with "light coloured bristles" (*"hellblonde Borsten"*), emphasized by a "tall blond wig" (*"hohe, semmel-blonde Lockencoiffüre"*).[22] In denying his personality and surrendering his self-respect so that others will tolerate his repulsive cowardice and self-rejection, he sinks below those others, whom Mann describes as "light" (*hell*) and "flaxen" (*semmel*).[23]

Paolo Hofmann's "blond" dancing school partner had been healthy, strong, happy, and sociable, but Jacobi lacks all of these qualities; Amra's unthinking sensual revenge utterly defeats him. Depressed and disgusted with himself at this time, Mann allowed none of these characters to be admirable; actually *both* his own "blond" and "dark" qualities opposed his slowly de-veloping sexuality, as it seemed to threaten logic and creativity. For him, submitting to physical desire was weak, cheap, and vain.

He wrote to Grautoff on 21 July 1897:

> As I have already written to you, for some time, it feels as if I have gained elbow room, as if I have found ways and means of speaking out, of expressing myself, of living for myself artistically, and earlier, while I needed a diary just to relieve myself for my little space, I now find *novel-listic* forms and masks worthy of publishing to release my love, my hatred, my compassion, my disdain, my pride, my mocking sneer and my accusation. (EHL)

The relationship between Amra and Jacobi prior to the appearance of her lover, Läutner, appears in the second section. Jacobi's ponderous language and deliberately clumsy punctuation[24] make his emotion ludicrous as he kneels by Amra's bed: ". . . I love you beyond my strength. You do not understand that, I know; but you believe it, and you must say, just one single time, that you are a little grateful to me . . ." (*STD*, 60; *GW*, 8: 172). Amra holds an uncomprehending power over him: "Yes, yes, you good beast, you" (EHL).[25]

Läutner, Amra's lover, is blond, self-satisfied, healthy, and mediocre. He lightheartedly accepts Amra's favors, and she does not even recognize her adultery, which the entire city censures. She is too stupid even to have a bad conscience,[26] so her husband never suspects her.

In "Springtime," Amra decides to welcome the spring ale with a great party near the "Lerchenberg." Jacobi's first name, Christian, appears only in sections three and four, from the moment of the party's planning until the fatal episode. Section four ironically caricatures the program committee, all snobbish dilettantes. Witznagel ("joke-nail")[27] suggests that their program needs a *pièce de résistance*, an anticipation of Amra's shocking proposal that Jacobi perform the "Luischen" number. Everyone hysterically seizes upon it. Christian Jacobi alone firmly refuses, earning himself a scrap of respect that's shattered when his fear of offending Amra and her guests overcomes his reluctance.

Next, Amra is in Läutner's arms, reveling in the erotic pleasure she takes in humiliating Jacobi and completing the betrayal by proposing that she and Läutner accompany the gruesome dance.

In the party near the Lerchengberg[28] Mann changes the atmosphere through descriptions of secondary characters and in the words and actions of Läutner. He commented to Grautoff, 21 July 1897: "Lately it even happens that, at a viable occasion, I even interrupt the flow of action and start to express a general message, as for example in 'Luischen' where I hold a short serious speech against the foppish and mimic-like type of little modern 'artist.' "[29]

The evening's dilettantish program includes a minstrel number, the Anglicized lyrics of Mrs. Hildebrandt's song, and an amusing lecture. Finally when it is time for "Luischen," the audience reacts to Jacobi's ludicrous costume, Amra's frame of mind,[30] and the depth of degradation Jacobi has undertaken. "Luischen" is much more than Jacobi in disguise; "Luischen" incarnates the painful clash between Jacobi's burning emotions and the unresponsive outer world, the paradox of devotion and self-rejection, a bottomless expression of misery, suffering, and longing, all distorted and abased by ridicule, as Jacobi dances and sings and cries out desperately for mercy.

Mann achieves this crescendo of horrors through a musical analogy. The keys of F sharp and F major that accompany the cheap lyrics[31] illustrate the scene's multiple levels of meaning. The lyrics and the music are obviously Läutner's vulgar contribution, and lines 3 and 4 of the German text actually verbalize the entire tragedy. Jacobi's complicity in his own metamorphosis into "Luischen," is suggested by the word "*vollführt.*" Just before "*Ich bin,*" the song's central message, a dissonance propels attention toward the coming climax; the F sharp should resolve to F major, announcing "Luischen," but between the "Ich bin" F sharp and the "Luischen" F major the split-second drama occurs. Jacobi breaks off at the stressed *I*-sound, unable to voice the infamous self-identification because he has instantaneously recognized the scandal and the crowd's thirst for his blood, and he is overcome. Amra and Läutner sit complacently, back to back, Amra completely unaware of her role in Jacobi's collapse, as a young Jewish doctor with a small pointed beard pronounces Jacobi dead.

Thomas Mann defines Jacobi as "Luischen" in three concepts: Jacobi's grotesque shape itself, the intensity of his emotions, and his total lack of self-respect. Jacobi's monstrous body advances the concept of isolation Mann had been wrestling with since his earliest stories."Little Herr Friedemann" was not turned away from life because he was physically crippled; he was emotionally crippled because his fear of rejection had isolated him from life. Bajazzo had made more progress in self-analysis than Friedemann: "In the end I shall go on living, eating, sleeping; I shall gradually get used to the idea that I am dull, that I cut a wretched and ridiculous figure" (*STD*, 50; *GW*, 8: 140). Both stories somehow seem unfinished, because though both protagonists recognize their guilt in rejecting life, they have not thought the problem through to its conclusion. Both had enhanced their sensitivity without putting it to creative uses. Jacobi contrasts with Tobias in shape and docility, but their neurotic isolation and the linguistic expression Mann gives them are surprisingly similar. The scrawny Tobias and the fat Jacobi are uninteresting, ignorable people; they are ugly and therefore undesirable; being ridiculous, they are repulsively melodramatic, typical of Thomas Mann's mood at this time.[32]

The "Luischen" phenomenon also represents the dynamism of Jacobi's feeling. With Amra, Jacobi measures his devotion as a "value" on a metaphysical scale of logic. In Tobias's suffering, Mann showed for the first time "disgust" actually destroying the only sympathetic object it could reach, a situation he reversed in "Luischen," where Jacobi eagerly debases himself. He abandons everything—taste, beauty, his reputation and even his own desire for privacy—to please and thereby gain sympathy. Amra, for whom Jacobi held such exalted feelings, is just as primitive as Tobias's dog Esau, an embodiment of the parasitic fascinating female that the lonely, troubled young Mann may have occasionally considered. At this time he probably had no love interest but numerous letters to Grautoff and Heinrich refer to his difficulties in controlling his sexuality (*"Geschlechtlichkeit"*), which interfered with his concentration. In "Luischen" and the stories that follow, Thomas Mann fictionalized his bachelor restlessness.

The most important characteristic of "Luischen"-Jacobi is his repulsive humility, signaling his lack of self-esteem. Friedemann rejected himself with "disgust" when the emotional Gerda von Rinnlingen freed disintegrated his ivory tower. Bajazzo defined "disgust" as the only "kind of unhappiness: to suffer the loss of satisfaction in oneself" (*STD*, 49; *GW*, 8: 138). In agreeing to "Luischen," Jacobi exposes and prostitutes his purest emotions, himself betraying the love his limited wife cannot grasp. Similarly, Läutner prostitutes artistic creation, especially in terms of the earlier references to art in "Little Herr Friedemann" and "Der Bajazzo." Thomas Mann's insecurity about his art might possibly have matched his frustration toward women.

At this point Fischer had accepted Mann's first short story collection and

enthusiastically invited him to present a larger work.[33] However, Mann's belief in his own talent faltered at the immensity of *Buddenbrooks*, and it took a
heroic effort to force himself to work regularly on the gigantic novel.

In "Luischen" Mann fictionally accepts a hero for the first time as being
odd and antisocial without simultaneous feelings of guilt, for the first time
accepting the character's "difference" as a basic factor of the story. Early
hints at Thomas Mann's dilemma between the "artist" existence and the
"burgher" thus occurred subconsciously in "Little Herr Friedemann," and
barely half-defined in "Der Bajazzo." The theme developed in "Tristan" and
culminated at last in the duality of "Tonio Kröger," the most important
stories in Mann's self-evaluation as artist. The intervening stories demonstrate its increasing importance to him as a man and as an artist.

"The Wardrobe"

As *Buddenbrooks* demanded more and more of his time, he corresponded
with his family about their life in Lübeck. After a laborious winter in Rome,[34]
he returned to Munich in April 1898, where the first edition of his first short
story collection had just appeared, and he worked until January 1900 in the
editorial offices of *Simplicissimus*. On 25 October 1898 he also mentioned to
Grautoff that he had finished two stories of another collection. Possibly "The
Wardrobe" might have been one of these, because an entry in his third notebook indicates that this story was written from 23 November to 29 November
1898,[35] in a cheaper Schwabing apartment from which he bicycled to his
mother's flat for meals.[36]

The wardrobe[37] itself is supernatural and the hero, Albrecht van der
Qualen,[38] has an experience of questionable actuality. The other characters
remain nameless, and the story lacks a definite locale and purpose. The
subtitle, "A Story Full of Riddles" ("Eine Geschichte voller Rätsel"), recalls
E. T. A. Hoffmann, to whom Thomas Mann later refers directly. The dreamy
mood contains naturalistic features, which do not have much to do with the
appearance of the young girl, a longed-for vision rather than a rational problem. The wardrobe draws van der Qualen from sleep as his train moves
through the night.

This seven-page delicate fantasy is based on Mann's own experience; he
kept the original wardrobe, a model for the story's focus, in his apartment on
the Marktstraße.[39] Despite its brevity, "The Wardrobe" contains an introduction, a body, and a conclusion. Its realistic elements cut sharply into the
story's nucleus, making its imaginative aspect seem surrealistic. In the cool
humid dusk, van der Qualen's awakening in the train at the station and his
glances at his surroundings, like his glimpse of the old lady with her suitcase,[40]
are so realistic that the dreamlike quality of the later experiences is not
intimated.

Very early in his career Mann unconventionally creates relativity through the absence of measured time; van der Qualen has neither watch nor calendar, and lately he has not even bothered to keep track of months. He also missed the signpost where the train stopped, a pleasant sensation of freedom; he snatches his bright red luggage and leaves the train.[41] Coachmen offer him a ride to the "Hotel zum braven Mann" ("hotel for the good [or well-mannered] man"); the awkward name emphasizes van der Qualen's rejection of the mediocre once he has begun his enigmatic adventure. At the hidden faces of passersby he too turns up his collar.

Van der Qualen walks away from the station in limbo. The Dantesque "old gate," at St. Michele the "massive towers," the "long wooden boat" and the "river" suggest transcendence from life and reality to the occult, but Lübeck's impressive Holstentor and the Holsten bridge over the Untertrave are plainly present, though geographically confused, since Lübeck is north, not south, of Berlin.

Next Mann's personal impressions appear, connecting "The Wardrobe" with Friedemann, "Bajazzo" and Tobias.[42] However, van der Qualen comments positively about himself: "More remote, freer, more detached, no one can be, . . ." (*STD*, 73; *GW*, 8: 155). Like the hero of "Der Wille zum Glück," van der Qualen is terminally ill, a fact pertinent here only because he is disassociated from everything in his normal life; he enjoys dwelling between two worlds.[43] Like Mann's earlier dilettantes, he savors small sensual pleasures like tobacco, a bit of good cheese, and a mouthful of expensive cognac.

After walking through the misty town, van der Qualen finally knocks at the door of a strange dark house with a vacancy sign. Van der Qualen's direct reference to E. T. A. Hoffmann recalls many eccentric Hoffmannesque figures, as when an old lady steps before van der Qualen with archaic clothing, beautiful white hands, and a repulsive mole on her forehead.

The presence of the wardrobe dominates the body of the story. The candle and lamplight create dancing shadows over the room's painted chairs,[44] enormous bed, and the wardrobe. Van der Qualen unhesitatingly rents the apartment.

Once alone, van der Qualen examines the wardrobe, the rational backdrop to his fantastic vision of a nude. The wardrobe has no wooden back, only a gray cloth attached with a thumbtack. When van der Qualen leaves for dinner, he hears a metallic sound, perhaps the thumbtack dropping. His brief absence might have allowed the girl to enter the wardrobe from the back.

In the climax, van der Qualen returns after an exquisitely detailed dinner, enjoys a glass of cognac[45] and a cigar, and then opens the door of the wardrobe. All Mann reveals are the girl's beautiful deep dark eyes, eyes he consistently describes each time a sympathetic and sensitive character inhabits a piece of his fiction.

"The Wardrobe" marks the first time since "Gefallen" that he both treated sexual desire fictionally and abandoned his hostility toward women. "The

Wardrobe" also presupposes van der Qualen's aggression, not the girl's. "Gefallen"'s romance ended in bitter disappointment, but the entire experience of "The Wardrobe" leaves no such aftertaste. The phantasmagorical body of the story and the final paragraph resemble Strindberg's ambivalent dream plays; van der Qualen might not ever have awakened on the train.

Thomas Mann sketches several stages of awareness reflecting van der Qualen's inner reactions to the series of apparently unconnected scenes: the old lady with the suitcase: van der Qualen, in contrast to her, is not afraid; van der Qualen realizes his freedom from time and space; he picks up his luggage and leaves; he walks through the town (a step into a deeper sleep level); Dantesque associations; childhood Lübeck associations (a step into restlessness prior to the deep-sleep stage); the vision of the house with plate-glass windows; the appearance of the old lady with the mole on her forehead —at which point the dream passes into deep sleep, and the wardrobe becomes in dream logic part of the dream until the end, when it curves back to its beginning stage.

A sad single tale as indolently smooth as the girl herself appears in the story she tells to van der Qualen, sowing seeds of lust and sadism. Reminding the reader of "Vision," Mann gently removes the disciplined cover from his personal desires. The nudity of the girl in the wardrobe now acquires an active rather than passive significance. Van der Qualen is drinking alcohol excessively (as Anselm will do in "Gerächt"), thus displaying a trait that recurs in the short stories influenced by E. T. A. Hoffmann. The girl narrates an account of a past love—softly, sadly, tragically, and without clear factual details. But van der Qualen's reactions clearly point to awakening desire. Just as the rest of the story does, this phase remains nebulous, unreal, and without specifications. This melancholy passage is also governed by dream logic, with the same fatigued pallor as van der Qualen's confession of his own reactions. He mentions "forgetting himself," and Mann limns van der Qualen's approach to the lovely nude creature elusively; his protagonist "forgets himself" and the girl "did not resist him." Was this unsatisfied desire, a simple brush of the fingertips, complete sexual union, or merely a fleeting thought? For Thomas Mann the value of the artistic experience lay in his ability to conceive the beauty open to him and express his desire without rejection or rebellion. Whether the girl in the wardrobe represents beauty, sex, love, or art does not matter. The situation actually is very similar to the one in Mann's next story, "Gerächt," in which a girl relates the story of a past love and awakens the desire of the protagonist. While van der Qualen's experience is only a vague reference, Anselm will rudely express his sexual lust in rationalizing his desire, thus making the situation distasteful. This similarity in topic and contrast in mood and expression actually creates a clear picture of young Thomas Mann's intellectual and physical conflict regarding desire for women during this time of his maturation. It was indeed only to Grautoff he could write about these thoughts and experiences.[46]

Adding another riddle to the rest of "The Wardrobe," Thomas Mann closes with: "'Everything must be in the air . . .'" (*STD*, 77; *GW*, 8: 161), a recapitulation of van der Qualen's ideas: "Everything must be in the air—so he put it in his mind, and the phrase was comprehensive though rather vague" (ELH) (see also *STD*, 72; *GW*, 8: 153). This repetition of the earlier words emphasizes the unsettled and intangible character of the entire story. It is never even made clear whether the setting and the narrated action are real or a fantasy. The humorous connotations of the closing remove much of the absurd gravity of the pathos, explaining Mann's own reference to the mood.

Van der Qualen's spontaneous reaction to the old landlady with beautiful white hands and a repulsive mole points out Thomas Mann's inherently intellectual response to E. T. A. Hoffmann, all of whose works had compulsively read recently. Hoffmann's musical novella "Don Juan" has striking similarities to "The Wardrobe";[47] both stories have dream-atmospheres supported by realistic frameworks. Each hero awakens from deep sleep to an unexpected situation. For van der Qualen the station and the furnished room are the concrete setting from whence he discovers the alluring vision announced by a "sort of ringing in the other room: As though a gold ring were to fall into a silver basin, a soft, clear, metallic sound—but perhaps he was mistaken."[48] Hoffmann's traveler passed through a small wall-papered door into a world where the beauty of Donna Anna and the opera take his breath away.[49] The eyes of each woman are significantly expressive; both women recount their fatal loves to their perplexed male visitors. Both experiences fade away; the girl was seen by no one else and the opera was misunderstood. The stories' themes are also essentially similar. Don Juan constantly immerses himself in sensuality; "Is it a wonder that the devil throws his rope around his neck?" (EHL).[50] His partly abstract, partly sensual, longing for the unattainable arose from greedy licentiousness, thus producing guilt. No mere physical intoxication, even though alcohol appears in both stories, could explain these experiences; rather, intellectual and emotional needs produce these sensually imaginative visions. The lonely travelers' yearnings materialize in a woman's innocent beauty.[51] Hoffmann's technique carried the maturing Thomas Mann far beyond Bahr's emotional mysticism, which he had admired earlier.[52]

The power of Thomas Mann's longing for love and beauty, a longing that transcends the physical, blurs the rational limitations of time, place, and practicality into a relativity that allows the object of imagined desire to emerge incarnate, and only through this zone of boundlessness, a parallel to the zone of restlessness prior to deep sleep, is the image of the absolute made visible.

Mann himself might not have been able to define the motivation and the theme of "The Wardrobe." He later seldom commented on the story,[53] whose composition parallels an interest he had had in suspense stories since the "Bilderbuch für artige Kinder," as shown in the carefully selected "stage properties" and supernatural murder of the lovers in the story the girl tells van der Qualen. "The Wardrobe" was a relaxing change from *Buddenbrooks* between 23 and 29 November 1898, as he kept writing at his green desk beneath Tolstoy's severe stare, flanked by a few flowers.

"Gerächt"

While Thomas Mann continued to work both on "the long book" (*Buddenbrooks*) and several shorter projects, he wrote one of his few published poems, "Monolog," which appeared later in 1899[54] in *Gesellschaft*, and that July he finished "Gerächt," published in *Simplicissimus* the next month. He never thought highly of this story, and he neither cited it in his *Sketch of My Life* nor chose it for his next short story collection.[55]

Anselm, the hero of "Gerächt" corresponds to E. T. A. Hoffmann's Anselmus, an immature youth who is oblivious to the real character of the phenomena around him.[56]

"Little Lizzy" was the distorted reflection of "Tobias Mindernickel," where dominant violence opposes self-subjugation to such an extent that it leads to self-betrayal. Similarly, "Gerächt" opposes "The Wardrobe"; both sprang from the same need, but Mann shaped them differently. "Gerächt" is narrated in the first person by a twenty-year-old man who strongly resembles Thomas Mann.[57] In a family-run boarding house he encounters Dunja Stegemann, an unmarried intellectual born in Russia and raised there by her German parents; she now writes a literary-musical column for a second-rate newspaper. The two become friends and share vehement musical and psychological conversations. While Dunja, clearly devoid of feminine charm, seems perfectly at ease, the young narrator is torn between pleasure in a female intellectual friend whose mind functions like a man's, and an awkward tension when he is in her presence, mercilessly eyeing his own immaturity and weakness throughout. When they discuss Wagner's *Tristan und Isolde*, he is simultaneously impressed and disturbed by Dunja's detached manner, shown in her matter-of-fact use of such expressions as "nonmaterialized lust" (EHL) ("*entfleischte Brunst*").

The climax occurs after dinner at the narrator's flat; he is a shade giddy and feels his usual embarrassment in this intimate setting, although he also enjoys the appearance of defying convention.[58] Subconsciously, he is seething at his inability to shake off his fascination with her unattractive femininity. Anxious to clear the suffocating atmosphere, he cruelly asks, "Do you know what gives our relationship its most original and finest charm? It's the intimacy of our minds, which has become indispensable to me, in contrast to the pronounced revulsion I feel for you physically!" Silence follows, then she says, "Yes, yes, this is amusing!" (EHL).[59] She appears to pay no more attention to what he has said. Later, however, she suddenly says, "And then [there's] one thing [more] that must come up between us . . . in fact, you don't know I once had a love affair" (EHL) (*GW*, 8: 165). The young man is completely taken aback.

Dunja insists her affair was wholly unplatonic. The unease stemming from wine and suppressed desires makes the blood pulse in the young man's head and blurs his eyesight; he reveals himself through an interior monologue: "This woman has agreed to let someone make love to her. . . . Again I poured down—how many had there been?—another glass of red wine. There was silence" (EHL) (*GW*, 8: 165).

The young man asked Dunja for endless details of her affair. She answered him with icy calm, biding her time soberly. Then he cried, " 'How would it be with the two of us?' She answered, 'Oh, my dear, how can you imagine such a thing?—No, our relationship is exclusively spiritual. . .' " (EHL) (*GW*, 8: 165–6). When he absurdly, violently insisted, she prepared to leave, with a scornful smile twisting her unappealing lips. After she went, he pondered the events again and finally fell asleep.

One view of the title *"Gerächt"* ("Revenged") sees the protagonist reacting vengefully at his inability to accept a purely intellectual relationship with a woman. In his inexperience, he selfishly wounded a woman with whom he had spent many rewarding hours, and earned a humiliating lesson, the loss of her friendship.

"Revenge" can also be seen from Dunja's point of view. His tactless remark that she repelled him physically must have hurt her deeply. She possibly realized his problems and calculated her revenge ruthlessly, striking his most vulnerable spot and thus loosing his repressed demon of sexuality. She sees through him when she challenges his erotic fantasies and makes him desire her, just as she is—and then spurns him contemptuously. The psychological value of "Gerächt" lies in its chronological position; even though the narrator criticizes his own clumsiness, he is not "hopeless" in the sense Mann's earlier heroes are. Here he relentlessly exposes the male immaturity of the narrator of "Gerächt" and rationally analyzes the paradoxical contrast of logic with prejudice. This is the beginning of Thomas Mann's technique of "soul dissection" (*Seelengliederung*), his mature method of working through a problem; the master of it will be the satanic Dr. Krokovsky in *The Magic Mountain*. The quality of Thomas Mann's observance and impersonal analysis in "Gerächt" are new for him and permeate the works that follow.

The melodramatic yet tragic features with which Mann endowed Tobias Mindernickel appear consistently in each of these stories, which, though vastly varied, share the same themes: love and women, life and death, isolation and self-repudiation. The great adventure, love, in "Gefallen" and " Der Wille zum Glück," ended in disillusionment or ultimate illusion, each unreal to an inexperienced young man. In "Disillusionment," love was barely mentioned as a possible ingredient of happiness. In "Little Herr Friedemann" and "Der Bajazzo," the female character pertains to the hero's existential question; Gerda von Rinnlingen represents far more than the first love of an eccentric cripple, and in "Der Bajazzo," less detailed, the woman's character nevertheless catalytically impels Bajazzo toward dissolution. In his next

stories Mann drew upon his own psychology to express conscious and unconscious concepts of love, sex, women, and his personality.

The feminist movement of nineteenth-century Europe produced new views
of women, a cultural shift that troubled Thomas Mann, for the mother and
sister images once so comfortably established in his concept of the world,
now suddenly seemed impossibly idealistic. Driven by his strong late-
maturing sexuality and yet restrained by his bourgeois upbringing and natural
propriety, he visualized the "new woman" as a menacing traitress. The "new"
female characters in literature haunted him: Strindberg's neurotics with
their violent love-hatred, Ibsen's flesh and blood lovers, Zola's proletarian
wives, Huysmans's satanic visions, and the powerfully sensuous women
of Gogol, Tolstoy, and Dostoevsky. At the same time, he was desperately
trying to concentrate on his systematic research for *Buddenbrooks*. It is no
wonder that precisely while he was laying the groundwork for this novel in
1897–98, his short fiction was baring the turbulent other side of his inner life,
which urged him to break with rules, laws, and traditions of beauty and
ethics. This conflict vividly reflects Mann's anguished attitude toward women
at this time, an image at once erotically sadistic and capable of mystical adoration, radiating a peculiar mixture of hope, redemption from longing, and self-
rejection. Until he found Katia, Thomas Mann was yearning for a woman
who could be lover, mother, and intellectual partner. Before her, he had
dreaded the new woman's independence and departures from tradition; with
her, he gained a wife, the mother of his six children, a partner, and a friend.
Above all, Katia, with her independence and wit and training a man would
have had, was a true example of a woman who made decisions for herself.
This stage of Mann's maturation, the realization of fears and longing in a
rapidly changing era, is most dramatically expressed in the stories at hand;
and the destructively "liberated" woman never reappeared in his works.

These stories also give new artistic expression to Thomas Mann's concept
of life and death, his bittersweet feeling of isolation, and his cynical self-
rejection. He had based his previous short fiction on autobiographical experiences, but in these stories he began to create original and fascinatingly varied
settings and actions as vehicles for self-revelation.

At the end of August 1899, Thomas Mann took a vacation from his duties
at *Simplicissimus* and visited Aalsgaard, the Danish summer resort near Hels-
ingör at the Sund, facing Sweden. His recent work on *Buddenbrooks* had
awakened vivid boyhood memories of Lübeck, and so he stopped there before going to Denmark, a trip whose rich impressions eventually inspired
"Tonio Kröger." Even though he had already spent two fatiguing years on
Buddenbrooks, he typically resisted the temptation to attack his new theme
until after he had completed the novel.

However, after he returned to Munich in the late fall of 1899, Thomas
Mann had one of his most significant intellecual experiences, the encounter
with Arthur Schopenhauer's *The World as Will and Representation* which

came at a crucial point in his writing of *Buddenbrooks*. He was experiencing difficulty in achieving the turning point leading to the conclusion of the novel, at the fifth chapter of the novel's tenth section. His reading of Schopenhauer's work awakened long-dormant unconscious thoughts, allowing him to grasp concepts of life and death which both fascinated and satisfied him. These became so intimately a part of his own personality that he not only understood them, but modeled his further thinking on them and retained them as part of his mental makeup for the rest of his life. He painstakingly acknowledged Schopenhauer's profound effect upon him in *Sketch of My Life*.[60]

When he encountered *The World as Will and Representation* in 1899, Thomas Mann was discouraged with the seemingly endless *Buddenbrooks*, and he was especially receptive, emotionally and intuitively, to Schopenhauer's ideas because of his brief visit to Lübeck and his aesthetic experience of the North Sea at Aalsgaard. He had been preoccupied with the search for an acceptable concept of existence for a long time and at this moment he had accidentally discovered just what he needed: a book providing him a solidly constructed comprehensive metaphysical system and *Weltbild*. In all of his short fiction since "Der Wille zum Glück" problems defined in Schopenhauer's work had appeared as Mann's integral thematic concerns: the *Wille zum Leben*, the protest against human limitation, attraction to and doubts about death, the concept of the individual and his place in the world, the problem of isolation, self-rejection and the longing for community, the significance of values of Art, the aesthetic experiences, the emotional complex of love, the rational view of "sexuality" (*Geschlechtlichkeit*),[61] and the puzzling question of perception through reason, the objectivation of intangibilities versus intuitive, subjective, nonlogical perception.

Schopenhauer's style is startlingly clear and even colloquial, markedly free of jargon, and attractive even to twentieth-century readers. In fact, Schopenhauer's method of supporting abstract concepts with concrete illustrations is itself a splendid example of "objectivation," which provides tangible and logical form from metaphysical ideas. Mann first grasped Schopenhauer's message and then broke down the sensual imagery, in order to reach the essence of Schopenhauer's ideas. In this manner, when he represented Schopenhauer's message as a part of his personal system of thought, he ran no risk of the plagiarism he might have been accused of had he remained on the superficial level.

Thus Mann's reception of Schopenhauer's work achieved what Schopenhauer believed Music could accomplish, penetrating the essence of the "thing-in-itself," and not merely duplicating the "idea," which is also a part of the "representation." Schopenhauer's technique of expression must have appealed greatly to young Thomas Mann, encouraging him to adapt his own abstract vision into structured patterns of fiction. From his earliest literary attempts, his exquisite talent for minute observation and description had made his writing attractive, and now the depth of insight producing in him by his experience of Schopenhauer's work became naturally integrated into his own thoughts, invigorating each detail with vibrant meaning and organically unifying his fictional representations.[62] Now suddenly he gained the capacity to penetrate beyond surface representation and the instinctive drive of the *Wille zum Leben* into the significance of existence and origin, which is the Unity inherent in all.[63] The state of insight is a temporary achievement of the *Geist* which overcomes the limitations of individuality and thus achieves a vision of the Universal.[64] Because of human limitations, such an experience is only temporary, but it is attainable by and therefore relevant to all men. Such "insight" (*Erkenntnis*) enriched Mann's descriptive talent with the vivid vision of meaningful unity behind all representation, allowing it to be perceptible through the dynamic experience of the printing page.

Thomas Mann's ability to ignite the latent power of metaphysical, intellectual, and emotional experience in his fiction far surpasses mere fictional entertainment; it attains the perfection of Art.[65] Every detail emerges as alive and significant through such supranormal power, revealing metaphysical truth beneath realistic surface appearance. These are the first discernible symptoms of his later perception on two or more levels of understanding, which he called his "dual vision" (*doppelte Optik*). He referred to his reading of Schopenhauer's work as a "life-experience," because he recognized that his ideas had thus consciously become an organic part of his creative *Geist*, and the next stage of his development was marked indelibly with the central Schopenhauerian theme of the world comprised of will and representation, later to be present in everything he wrote.

Thomas Mann's permitting Thomas Buddenbrook, the fictional character, to experience reactions he himself had had through the reading of Schopenhauer's *The World as Will and Representation*[66] makes the fictional account overwhelmingly genuine, the fictional expression of his own conceptualization of the epiphany of "insight" (*Erkenntnis*), which momentarily frees him from the imprisonment of the "principle of individuation" or the *principium individuationis*, as Schopenhauer expresses it, the objectivated representation of the "will to live," "*Wille zum Leben*." During this blissful moment his tormenting limitations disappeared and the Schopenhauerian "worldvision" (*Weltbild*) suddenly became clear to him and seemed glorious compared to his representation of the world he had previously known. The autobiographical description of the experience blended directly into the fictional. Thomas Mann himself retained the *Geist*-related impact of this "insight" (*Erkenntnis*) so deeply that it influenced his entire worldvision for years to come. In fact, thirty-nine years later, in 1938, he wrote a powerful essay on Schopenhauer.[67]

Thomas Mann's intellectual equipment had included a knowledge of Wagnerian opera, particularly *Tristan*, revealed when he put a conversation about that work's metaphysical eroticism into the mouths of Dunja Stegemann and the young narrator of "Gerächt." Around 1899, this Wagner-

ian influence intensified for Mann, reaching a climax with his composition of
the short story "Tristan." Thomas Buddenbrook said, "Have I ever hated
life—this pure, strong, relentless life? Folly and misconception! I have only
hated myself, because I could not bear it" (EHL). This self-analysis pertains
not only to Mann's work of 1899, but to his earlier stories as well, and in
quoting them again in his "Schopenhauer" essay of 1938, he emphasized their
importance to him. They express the problem of inferiority in Friedemann,
Bajazzo, Tobias, and Jacobi, designating a complex which slowly begins to
lose its power over Thomas Mann after he finished *Buddenbrooks*. Their
original meaning for him faded through the stimulation of Schopenhauer's
work. There was, in fact, also a deep affinity between Mann's nature and
Schopenhauer's: ". . . for Schopenhauer victory lay in the ascetic denial of
the will—achieving of a condition where we are free from its power—[it is]
Nietzsche who sees precisely in the will the force of life that is creative and
affirmative."[68]

In his essay on Schopenhauer, Mann says that a saint overcomes his will by
actually doing what his will does not dictate him to do. The overcoming of the
power of instinct thus represents for Thomas Mann the victory of "insight,"
and Schopenhauer's ideas later became for him a "metaphysical magic potion" (*metaphysischer Zaubertrank*).[69] Thomas Mann's mind was filled with
such thoughts as he completed the final chapters of *Buddenbrooks*[70] and then
wrote "The Way to the Churchyard," "Gladius Dei," and "Tristan."

Mann's 1899 experience of Schopenhauer's work, integral to his own writing at that time, is a personal affinity between writer and philosopher that
sometimes occurs between two people of similar character, environment, and
experience whose modes of thought and patterns of mental "representation"
(*Vorstellung*) unconsciously parallel one another. Thomas Mann's comments
regarding his discovery of *The World as Will and Representation* (*Die Welt als
Wille und Vorstellung*) indicate he rediscovered Schopenhauer's ideas in himself, instead of encountering on altogether new philosophical system. He had
had many of these concepts earlier, and Schopenhauer's system, not its components, was the significant revelation. Schopenhauer's system bound Mann's
scattered thoughts into an organic unity appropriate to his personal inclination, with a clear mental structure for the representation that now affected the
meaning of everything in and around him. For him this was the utter truth.
His emotional and intellectual satisfaction stemmed from the appeal for
meaningful action based on his insight into the destructive self-knowledge to
overcome the "will to live" (*Wille zum Leben*), which metaphysically proved
a positive force in the service of truth. The "heroism from weakness" curbed
the negative decadent tendency of a mood displayed in Thomas Mann's short
fiction from "Little Herr Friedemann" onward, drawing him from self-pitying
stagnation toward an ecstatic "genial objectivation" of a universally relevant
metaphysical vision of the *Weltbild*. The "death experience" of Thomas Buddenbrook had already opened a new vista of truth through its supersession of

the limited self. In his next three stories, "The Way to the Churchyard," "Gladius Dei," and "Tristan," Mann gradually disentangled his message from restrictive self-centeredness and allowed it to become intellectually fertile.[71] His marriage to Katia Pringsheim eventually became his most significant normalizing factor, but in 1899, when he read Schopenhauer's work, young Mann, ironic and disdainful, saw a world quite similar to Schopenhauer's. Their most important parallelism is that both reached out for fundamental aesthetic values, accepting and promoting the concept of true aesthetic experience as one of the most valuable of human achievements.

Schopenhauer died forty years earlier, having achieved his lifework, and having gained recognition in his last years, and to young Thomas Mann, Schopenhauer was his master, the grand old man, a magician, who had given him insight into a *Weltbild* he could accept, one to which he gladly would attune his own thinking. To him, Schopenhauer's philosophy, generally thought extremely pessimistic, became a joyous gospel of liberation which he transmuted metaphysically through the colorful world of his fiction. This fictional imagery perfectly suited the *Weltbild* of representation which he had now accepted as his own, for he began the shaping of his Schopenhauerian vision, a representation of a fictional world, with Thomas Buddenbrook's ecstasty. But the grotesque, the ironic, and the paradoxical, which the objectivation of the "will to live" (*Wille zum Leben*) brought to the representation of the world, also strongly attracted him. E. T. A. Hoffmann had forever inspired in him a compelling colorful imagery, an integral part of his technique and imagination to be objectivated in the fictional figures of Lobgott in "The Way to the Churchyard" and Hieronymus in "Gladius Dei." Only somewhat later, in "Tristan," did Wagner's concept of art also infiltrate Mann's newly gained representation, and while Nietzsche always figured both consciously and subconsciously in the intellectual panorama of his *Geist*, Nietzsche's significance in Mann's complex developing world view would only still later gain importance. In the focus of his Schopenhauerian *Weltbild* at the end of 1899, Thomas Mann's short fiction as interpreted through his personal writings and through Schopenhauer's *The World as Will and Representation* uncovers the delicate horizon in his work where the metaphysical merges into fiction.

"The Way to the Churchyard"

"The Way to the Churchyard" was written during the summer of 1900. Long afterward, Thomas Mann observed that he had worked on this story to relax after completing his "long, long book" (*das lange lange Buch*), but since "The Way to the Churchyard" was published in *Simplicissimus* 20 September 1900, leaving little time for its composition after *Buddenbrooks*, he may have inadvertently erred.[72]

"The Way to the Churchyard" is an eight-page story[73] divided into three sections: the introduction; a description of the setting, the protagonist, Lobgott Piepsam, and his encounter with "Life"; and the close, Piepsam's downfall. The opening paragraph meticulously describes the path to the cemetery, and its extravagant description is virtually untranslatable. The "way" is more than a mere means of access; in the first sentence, the German text reads literally, "the way to the churchyard. . . ran. . . until it had reached its *goal*, the churchyard" (EHL; emphasis added) (see also *STD*, 78; *GW*, 8: 187). Thomas Mann next observes "human dwellings" (not "suburban houses"), which he contrasts with open fields.[74] The "way," which runs along the highway, is a pleasant footpath, recalling the biblical "path of life."[75] The story, doubtless allegorically, refers to the "way to the churchyard" as the "road of life" (*Lebensbahn*), which in German also connotes "career," the path each person takes through life, thus projecting an existential message.

When viewed in a universal focus, the theme of "The Way to the Churchyard" makes Lobgott Piepsam incorporate the comical and failing configuration that grotesquely exhibits the tragicomedy of his life. The scene in which this didactic *fabliau* is staged is the road from womb to productive life. "Then came the fields" and then a reference to old age, "gnarled beeches of considerable age," and finally the tomb, the ultimate destination or "goal" of life (*STD*, 78; *GW*, 8: 187). Everyone travels on this universally allegorical road of life; Mann is describing only one of the many who carry out their ritualistic journey to the grave. Piepsam is one of Mann's autobiographical figures with a natural position in the growth sequence his work reveals, and even though Piepsam represents "man" wandering on the path of "life," his character, his reaction, and his problems may be typical, but need not necessarily be so.

The second paragraph provides the story's setting, showing nature as uncommitted, insensitive, happy and healthy, full of bird song and a mild breeze. This face of nature is carefree and unchanging, unaffected by entrances and exits. This cheerfulness pervades "The Way to Churchyard," so that Piepsam's particular defeat is only a minor episode in no way disrupting the placid setting of the human tragicomedy. Piepsam is merely a puny pitiable fool, no more or less than the other ironically viewed figures of the story's paradoxical action.

Each of the passersby described in the following paragraph is ordinary, and all, even the small yellow dog,[76] go about their business seriously, humorously isolated from each other. Piepsam comes next, all alone on the cobblestones, in contrast to the groups moving on the more traveled road that parallels his. From his very first appearance he shares the isolation that marks all of Mann's previous heroes, and the italics in the German text draw attention to his isolation: "nur *ein* Mann," "only one man" or "only a man."

"The Way to the Churchyard" is narrated anonymously in a semi-ironic, lightly teasing tone. The narrator is aware of the meaning and message of the story and he manipulates both events and characters with an air of superiority,[77] calling attention to the protagonist's singular name. The name, like Tobias Mindernickel's, sounds typically German, with a "religious" given name and a common low German surname connoting inferiority and insufficiency. As with their names, so with their natures, on the one hand subdued and humiliated and on the other full of violent rage. Both characters are crude in language and action as well as in their sensitivity and emotionalism. "Lobgott" ("praise God") was a fairly common German given name from the seventeenth century.[78] This name, with solemn deep vowels and religious connotations, paradoxically contrasts with the character's oafishness and his loneliness, which erupt in his aggressive behavior. "Lobgott" also clashes with the low German "Piepsam," not particularly dignified in sound or in its birdlike connotations.[79]

In appearance, Lobgott Piepsam might have stepped out of E. T. A. Hoffmann's sketchbook. Though grotesquely common, Piepsam is carefully dressed, with a top hat and black kid gloves to emphasize the reverence of his visit to the graves of his wife and children. This *Kleinbürger*, with his biblical language, his patriarchal poise and obvious shortcomings, is a familiar part of the smiling German countryside.

This aspect, however, changes significantly when Piepsam inquiringly raises his head, and then "you got a glimpse of a strange face, a face, unquestionably, which you would not easily forget" (*STD*, 79; *GW*, 8: 188). Above all, it is the fantastic, improbable, artificial, and unhealthy nose that testifies to drastic alcoholism. His long-time love affair with the bottle became his abiding passion following the deaths of his wife[80] and children, robbing him of his self-respect; delirium tremens eventually will completely annihilate him. This overpowering vice has also caused him to lose his job, so his job obscenely ugly nose embodies his total failure.

Piepsam's nose in fact epitomizes Mann's abstract vision in "The Way to the Churchyard." Once upon a time, Piepsam had had his wife, his children, and his work to live for, but his children turned out incapable of living; then, when his wife could neither give him more children nor sustain her own life, his feeble resistance to alcohol collapsed and he filled the gap in his lonely life with the passion for drink. This man, incapable of serving the "will to live" (*Wille zum Leben*), began his own dissolution. "And self-contempt and bad conduct stand in the most frightful mutual relation: they feed each other, they play into each other's hands, in a way shocking to behold. Thus was it with Piepsam. He drank because he had no self-respect, and he had no self-respect because the continual breakdown of his good intentions ate it away." (*STD*, 80; *GW*, 8: 120)

Since the bottle Piepsam keeps in his wardrobe overmasters this self-hating man,[81] Thomas Mann draws a clear parallel between the situations of "The Wardrobe" and "The Way to the Churchyard," between van der Qualen's intense desire for the charming apparition in his wardrobe and Piepsam's repulsive longing for the bottle. Lobgott's coming incongruity stems from his failure to control his instinctual will through his intellect, which turns him into the tool of his growing barbaric desire. His fall is less tragic than burlesque, an example of life's capitulation in order to avoid loneliness. Poor miserable Piepsam is abandoned in the midst of amiable sunshine with the "gentle breeze [that] played about his nose too" (*STD*, 80; *GW*, 8: 190), the object of eager observation by both the author and his readers.

The nucleus of this story is a hostile encounter between Piepsam and the cyclist; Piepsam stubbornly orders Life out of the way, absurdly threatening to report him to the authorities. Life does not understand, since, he says, *every man* uses this path. When Piepsam angrily threatens him, Life wants to leave him, since this situation is too inconsequential to warrant wasting such a beautiful day. The enraged Piepsam rushes to seize the bicycle, but life does not tolerate this and roughly shoves Piepsam away, pedaling off for good into the laughing summer day. Helpless, Lobgott Piepsam at first tries to stop him and then calls out to the others to denounce him: "Foaming at the mouth, he uttered the most shameless objurgations, while his voice cracked in his throat and his writhings grew more fantastic" (*STD*, 83; *GW*, 8: 194).

Lobgott Piepsam's terrible grotesquely comic dance of death appears on the next page. All of his vengeful sentiments toward Life and the evil world, and especially himself, erupt, dimming his mind and tossing his whole body in frenzy. All the symptoms of approaching death assult him, and his whole life passes before him as he mixes ideas and memories in incoherent babble. Even a traditional symbol of death, a howling dog, is there. When the end suddenly comes, his fall is theatrical, inevitably ludicrous. His last word is "ignorant," a term he had emphatically used before when he insulted Life directly.

The final part of the story shows other people reacting to Lobgott's death, the usual social tidying-up. Mann's language, images, and the actors' precision performances are clean-cut, humorous, and ironic, altogether reminiscent of apish antics.[82] Piepsam's wretchedness contrasts sharply with the healthy strength of the young cyclist, who suits the early summer countryside so well. Thomas Mann simply refers to him as *Life*, an allegorical embodiment. Once the reader accepts the cyclist as *Life* on the way to the churchyard, the story becomes a small mystery play, a miniaturization of the world, with people moving from origin to destination, acting out their individual problems. Mann's repeated emphatic reference to the cyclist as "*Leben*," or Life, the cyclist's happy unawareness, his total lack of knowledge and disregard of rules and his sole concern of rushing into the sparkling sunshine, all can very well represent the Schopenhauerian concept of the "will to live" (*Wille zum Leben*). In sharp contrast to this pleasant image stands the forlorn, wretched figure of Lobgott Piepsam, who might play the allegoric role of rationalization as Schopenhauer conceived it. Paradoxical and dumb, this pseudological rationalization figure turns against its own *raison d'être*, life itself, becoming self-destructively unable to overcome the *Wille zum Leben*. In the final line of the story, Thomas Mann refers to the entire distorted life-act of the

Schopenhauerian *Weltbild* acted out by these allegorical figures as a "monkey theater" (*Affentheater*). Thomas Buddenbrook had defined his relationship to the world and acknowledged his weakness,[83] his death confirming the short-comings of his life. Piepsam's story was not restricted by the circumstances set down in Mann's "long, long book," *Buddenbrooks*, allowing him to trace absurdity with much more freedom than the character and circumstances of Thomas Buddenbrook permitted. Lobgott Piepsam failed miserably in a most unheroic manner.

"Gladius Dei"

Prior to writing "Gladius Dei" in the summer of 1901, Thomas Mann had several significant experiences, including his vacation at Aalsgaard, his reading of Schopenhauer in the fall of 1899, his meeting with Carl and Paul Ehrenberg in December 1899, and his introduction to Mary Smith when he was in Florence with Heinrich in late April of 1901.

Upon his return from Italy in the spring of 1898, Thomas Mann had not qualified for military service because of what doctors considered "insufficient lung capacity" and a nervous heart conditions. According to regulations, he re-applied for admission to service on 6 July 1900, just before he completed *Buddenbrooks*. Documents prove he was willing enough to do his duty, although both his physical and his intellectual makeup were nonmilitary, and he was pleased when he received his draft notice on 1 October of that year. He had first applied to the infantry, and when no openings occurred there, the artillery; finally he was admitted to the Leib-Artillerie-Regiment.[84] According to an enthusiastic description by his younger brother Viktor, Thomas Mann must have cut a dashing figure in his blue uniform with shiny buttons. His military experience, however, turned out to be a failure, because his fallen arches produced muscle inflammation on the marching drills, which repeatedly forced him to the military hospital. He was finally given a medical discharge just before the end of 1900. Not much happened with *Buddenbrooks* during this time, and Mann was feeling frustrated and depressed over it, particularly since the Fischer publishing house had made it clear that marketing such an immense manuscript would be extremely difficult. While in the hospital, he wrote desperately to S. Fischer, feeling he had nothing to lose and explaining why no cuts could be made in *Buddenbrooks* without ruining its structure. Fischer was moved to read the manuscript himself during the next few months.

In this gloomy mood, Mann studied secondary sources[85] for a project on Savonarola, probably conceived when he returned from his first trip to Italy. He repeatedly wrote to Heinrich during the fall and winter of 1900 that he would join him soon in Italy to pursue this project, but early in 1901 some hope arose that Fischer would publish *Buddenbrooks*. Finally on 23 March 1901, he received a contract proposal for the uncut novel to be published that fall.

Relief from many months of frustration, his enjoyment of Wagnerian performances, and his delight in new friends all combined to make it difficult for Mann to leave for Italy at once. At this time in his life his new relationship with Carl and Paul Ehrenberg was proving to be greatly significant, both intellectually and emotionally; Carl Ehrenberg was a gifted musician, and his brother Paul, one year Mann's junior, was noted for his wildlife paintings.[86] Mann spent many evenings with the Ehrenbergs and two distant relatives of his own, Lilli and Hilde Distel, playing music and enjoying heated conversations. They often met at Julia Mann's home, because the artists and intellectuals who frequented her social circle provided a stimulating atmosphere. Carl Ehrenberg often accompanied Mann's violin music and discussed serious topics with him, especially the art of Richard Wagner, since they attended all of Wagner's works. They especially singled out for comment the operas *Parsifal, Tristan und Isolde*, and *Götterdämmerung*.[87] Paul Ehrenberg played a special role in Mann's life, too, since his obvious physical resemblance to Mann's cherished school friend Armin Martens made them especially close.[88]

Blond, cheerful, witty Paul Ehrenberg whom Mann addressed in his letters as "my dear Paulus" (*mein lieber Paulus*), took his heart by storm; he was one of the very few whom Mann, generally shy and formal, addressed with the familiar "*du*" soon after their first meeting.[89] This new friendship developed at the time Mann's memorable reading of Schopenhauer was becoming integrated with his earlier experiences of Nietzsche's work and when, too, his profoundly emotional experiences of Wagner's music were deepening his concept of *Tristan und Isolde*'s mystical eroticism (*mystische Erotik*). Thomas Mann identified his emotional friendship with Paul Ehrenberg both with the feelings that Wagner's dynamic music aroused in him and also with his own growing consciousness of art, and such emotional experiences in the framework of Schopenhauerian *Weltbild* contributed greatly to his artistic developmemt.

Finally, however, at the end of April, he tore himself away from his comfortable situation in Munich and joined Heinrich in Florence. Thomas continually complained in letters about his lack of money,[90] and so Heinrich found them an inexpensive *cinque lire pensione*, a family-style boarding house, where they met two sisters from Great Britain, the younger of whom, Mary Smith, made a deep impression on Thomas. This was his first recorded emotional attachment to a woman, and it was serious enough for him to have suggested eventual marriage and to write profoundly about it to Paul Ehrenberg. After this time, Mann scarcely referred to this relation with Mary Smith—he seems to have conducted the affair with his usual reticence—but it left lasting traces on his heart and prepared him emotionally for the marital commitment he was soon to make to Katia Pringsheim. "Gladius Dei," his next short story, was dedicated in July 1901, "to M. S., in remembrance of our days in Florence."

Thomas Mann first called the projected Renaissance drama, for which he hoped to gather material in Florence,[91] "The King of Florence" ("Der König von Florenz") and later "the Savonarola drama." He completed it as *Fiorenza* in January 1905, shortly before his wedding to Katia Pringsheim.[92]

Possible written at Mitterbach, in a health spa Mann visited after his return from Florence that summer, "Gladius Dei" was published in July 1902, in *Die Zeit*, a Viennese paper edited by Hermann Bahr. The story is twelve pages long and divided into four unequal sections.[93]

The title *"Gladius Dei,"* a clear reference to Savonarola, cites the quotation at the end of the story: "Gladius Dei super terram . . . cito et velociter!" ("Sword of God over the earth . . . act and swiftly!"). Mann must have come across the line during his research on Savonarola, his purpose in staying in Florence that spring. Since Savonarola became one of the three main characters of *Fiorenza* and occupied the center of Thomas Mann's attention for a time, details of Savonarola's life illuminate "Gladius Dei."[94] Hieronymus represents his fictionalization of the fiery preacher, and his theme, paralleling Savonarola's character, is the story of the religious saint (or fanatic) denouncing the world's lustful abuse of the arts.[95]

The setting of "Gladius Dei" recalls the setting of "Disillusionment," exhibiting the influence E. T. A. Hoffmann's "Ritter Gluck" had had on Thomas Mann. The radiantly splendid city of Munich suggests Lorenzo de' Medici's Florence, a Renaissance Babylon in its sinfully hectic liveliness. He repeatedly called "Gladius Dei" a humorous and grotesque story, and an alluring double standard is obvious from the beginning. The mentions of the Notung Motif[96] evokes Wagner's sensual mysticism, and the palaces under the "blue silk" skies Mann describes resemble idealized luxurious stage settings, sharply contrasting with the reality of Blüthenzweig's art shop. Everything within the shop is expensive and attractive, but it is merely pseudo art, spurious reproduction. In the shop window is a photograph representing the Madonna whose model was the mistress of a well-known artist; the picture's sensuous nudity exemplifies superficial aestheticism. All of the offerings of the shop appear geared to epicurean sensuality and its pragmatic exploitation, with glossy illustrated manuals. The first section of *"Gladius Dei"* introduces the topic of the story, a discussion of artistic ethics and the *raison d'être* of art itself.[97] It closes upon the concept of art the setting proposes: "There was a downright cult of line, decoration, form, significance, beauty. Munich was radiant" (*STD*, 183; *GW*, 8: 200).

In the midst of a colorful, luxury-loving crowd with bicycles, Mann's protagonist Hieronymus[98] stands out awkwardly, wrapped in a monkish black gown and hood, his face modeled after the Renaissance portrait of Savonarola.[99] Distraught with the world around him, he flees into a church. Something is surprising about the mercilessly ironic fatal judgment hanging over this city, juxtaposed with the intimate sense of belonging with which Thomas Mann invests his descriptions of Munich and Hieronymus. He put something of himself into both: this is the same Munich he had found so hard to leave in the spring of 1901, with its merry cyclists, its jocular carefree upper-class attitude, and the Wagnerian melodies whistled on its streets. He loved this pulsating town and its splendid opportunities, but he was also attracted by the ascetic figure of Hieronymus, so like the historical Savonarola, the enemy of pagan art and sinfulness. Mann's Hieronymus is grotesquely dedicated to overcoming the ways of the world, a position dictated by his religious vocation and the stern incorruptibility of his moral sense. Poor, uncouth and ugly, he is altogether unimpressive, and both his noble intention of facing down a sinful world and his demand that the merchant destroy the sensuous Madonna are in part discredited by his overreaction to her physical appeal, which suggests an emotional personal problem as well as his overt concern for propriety. His fanaticism may be entirely spiritual or a flight from carnal temptation by a man who feels himself too unappealing to conquer the object of his desire.[100] The conflict allows the ridiculous to penetrate the dignity of the historical Hieronymus/Savonarola figure, suggesting the humorously ironical view the young author took of his own frailties.

Hieronymus had overheard a discussion between two young men which gave a perfectly clear view of the model's personal circumstances. They say that she herself is more "harmless" than her photograph. The statement qualifies the picture as a "work of art" of genuine Schopenhauerian character since it expresses the "idea" of sensual beauty of a level higher than nature provides: "We all recognize human beauty when we see it, but in the genuine artist this takes place with such clearness that he shows it as he has never seen it, and in his presentation he surpasses nature. Now this is possible only because *we ourselves* are the will, whose adequate objectification at its highest grade is here to be judged and discovered."[101] The second theme which emerges from the conversation the horrified Hieronymus overhears is the joking claim of the young men that the sexual appeal of the beautiful woman gives them doubts about the Immaculate Conception.

The third section of "Gladius Dei" is only a half page long, relating the depth of the shock to Hieronymus's piety. The Schopenhauerian idea that the picture expressed proved itself to be not only the allegorical representation of purity traditionally associated with the Madonna, but also the idea of the sensual appetite of the "will to live" (*Wille zum Leben*). Hieronymus finds this association blasphemous and turns to God in protracted prayer, receiving on the third night a heavenly command to "lift his voice against the frivolity, blasphemy, and arrogance of beauty." Whether Thomas Mann intended this as divine revelation or fanatical hallucination, or even as a grotesque means of expression, is unclear, but the *will*, said to be God's *will*, is stressed, and Hieronymus obeys with the fervor of a Desert Father, with not a single doubt about his vocation. Hieronymus might be a peculiar monkish replica of Savonarola trying to extinguish his fleshly desires, as Savonarola himself was said to have done in fleeing from his home to a monastery to escape the advances of a neighbor's daughter; or he might be making a powerful and hopelessly tragic effort to free himself from the rude domination of the "will to live". Determined to fight his battle out and bent on carrying out God's command, Hieronymus walks toward Blüthenzweig's shop, his hood pulled over his head.

The long final section of "Gladius Dei" provides the body, the action, the turning point, and the ending of the story, in which Hieronymus appears both a martyr and a prophet. The weather has turned hot (*schwül*), threatening a thunderstorm,[102] when he finally enters the shop and asks for Mr. Blüthenzweig, who is busy with a customer. Mann unleashes his biting irony on the customers, especially a gentleman with a black goatee and a jaundiced complexion who is looking at French drawings and emitting sporadic bleats of laughter. The other two customers are an old lady looking over fanciful floral embroideries and an Englishman, judiciously eyeing a nude statuette, on whom Blüthenzweig is waiting.

When Blüthenzweig finally attends to Hieronymus, their conversation is brief; as soon as the shopkeeper understands that Hieronymus is demanding the removal of the Madonna merely on his own authority, he goes about his business, ordering one of his employees to get rid of this embarrassing visitor. When the clerk approaches Hieronymus, Hieronymus expresses his opinion in five consecutive paragraphs whose fervor swells to an unequivocal message in paragraphs three and four, then into emotional exasperation, before finally lapsing into grotesque excess. The historical Savonarola took just such a position, much like Thomas Mann's personal and philosophical standpoint at this time,[103] torn between his aesthetic joys and his inclination to intellectualize art and love and seek out their genuine "insight" (*Erkenntnis*). However, Schopenhauer's message is clear to him, and he does not deny that will omnipresently exists in all artistic expression as well as in everything created, including man. Thomas Mann objects only to the commercial exploitation of man's natural magnetism to all manifestations of the "will to live" (*Wille zum Leben*). He shows Blüthenzweig and his kind financially profiting from it to the spiritual disaster of all. Hieronymus, on the other hand, wants to overcome the domination of the "will to live" and rejects the force of the *principium individuationis* with its material representation, turning to "pure and true" love.[104] Since an artistic work like "Gladius Dei" does not encompass an entire system of philosophy, merely subjective and objective expressions of some philosophical ideas, Mann's ending, which leaves the question open to speculation, is fully satisfying.

Blüthenzweig's surprised silence and that of his employees is interrupted only by the bleating laughter of the yellow-suited goateed man. Full of indignation, Hieronymus retorts:

". . . Beauty? What is beauty? What forces are they which use beauty as their tool today—and upon what does it work? . . . knowledge, I tell you, is the profoundest torture in the world; but it is the purgatory without whose purifying pangs no soul can reach salvation. It is not infantile, blasphemous shallowness that can save us, Herr Blüthenzweig; only knowledge can avail, knowledge in which the passions of our loathsome flesh die away and are quenched." (*STD*, 191; *GW*, 8: 211).

In this passage Thomas Mann displays his concern for clearly defining his criteria of art, as exemplified in literature, and love, not sexuality. The responsibility of the literary artist toward the layman, his dedication of self to lofty principles, and the urge to overcome the limitations of the flesh combine to cause him to reject corrupting mediocrity with genuine revulsion, the climax of his literary analysis of Hieronymus.

Duality runs throughout "Gladius Dei" since Mann maintained Hieronymus's ascetic principles in his deepest being, while at the same time life and creative vitality occupied his heart completely. His artistic view of Munich was the expression of his glorious inner life, harmonizing with the character of his Lorenzo and the city of Florence.

The man with the goatee bleats again, and the clerk asks Hieronymus to leave, but Hieronymus speaks out for the fourth time, now defining art metaphysically:

"... You tell me that I blaspheme art. I say to you that you lie. I do not blaspheme art. Art is no conscienceless delusion, lending itself to reinforce the allurements of the fleshly. Art is the holy torch which turns its light upon all the frightful depths, all the shameful and woeful abysses of life; art is the godly fire laid to the world that, being redeemed by pity, it may flame up and dissolve altogether with its shames and torments."

Hieronymus is finally carried away with his inspiration and bursts out in saintly ecstasy—or irrationality: "Take it out, Herr Blüthenzweig, take away the work of that famous painter out of your window—you would do well to burn it with a hot fire and strew its ashes to the four winds—yes, to all the four winds—" (*STD*, 191; *GW*, 8: 211). Hieronymus strikes a domineering pose while Blüthenzweig becomes the picture of righteous indignation, threatening him with a savagery that throws Hieronymus into a frenzy; he cries out: "Burn everything in your shop, Herr Blüthenzweig, for it is a filthiness in God's sight. Burn it, burn it!' " (*STD*, 192; *GW*, 8: 213). Blüthenzweig's immediately reacts arrogantly and decisively, and he puts an end to the incident, calling Krauthuber, his hired man.[105] This gigantic masterpiece of human musculature appears and following his master's orders with the gentleness frequently seen in the treatment of the the weak by the strong, lifts Hieronymus out of the shop and with a "final shove" pitches him onto the pavement.

Lying exposed to the ridicule of this radiant world of vanities, Hieronymus has a vision: "A yellow background of cloud had drawn over the Theatinerstraße, and from it issued wild rumblings; but what he saw was a burning fiery sword, towering in sulphurous light above the joyous city" (*STD*, 193; *GW*, 8: 214–15). In the "judgment" of the prophet society makes, the historical parallel Thomas Mann draws is clear; but the closing passage, *"Gladius Dei super terram. . . cito et velociter!"* may suggest either hope or a martyr's crown, or Thomas Mann may be ironically commenting on the whole grotesque scene.

During the summer of 1901, when Thomas Mann completed "Gladius Dei" while ruminating on *Fiorenza*, which continued to occupy his mind until 1905, he was simultaneously developing two other projects. He had conceived the initial setting and some of the motifs of "Tonio Kröger" while he was on vacation at Aalsgaard in the fall of 1899, and in 1901 he began what he called "a burlesque," the short story now known as "Tristan." All the themes of "Gladius Dei," "Tristan," and "Tonio Kröger" deal with the definition of art in the focus of the Schopenhauerian *Weltbild*.[106]

In his earliest stories, Thomas Mann showed heroes painfully yearning to join the very world from which their oddities excluded them. But in "Gladius Dei," unlike the preceding stories, the central issues is Thomas Mann's expression of a *Weltbild* focused on art.[107] In the stories that follow "Gladius Dei" Thomas Mann continues to develop his metaphysical approach to the relation of the protagonist to art. Both "Tristan," which expresses that approach, and "Tonio Kröger," which further develops the concept of the artist and his focus on the world, are rooted in topics Thomas Mann first presented in "Gladius Dei" and *Fiorenza*.

When the Fischer publishing firm announced its intention to publish *Buddenbrooks*, Thomas Mann experienced a breakthrough in his attitude toward the long novel. Even before it appeared in bookstores in October of 1901,[108] he knew he had succeeded in becoming a writer, an intoxicating feeling after his long frustrating fall and winter of 1900–1901. Even though he had always felt sure of his own ability, like most young artists, he had been harassed by doubts and by belittling critical opinions. But now that the publisher had accepted the uncut *"lange, lange Buch,"* Thomas Mann felt that his vocation was truly literary, and he discovered a new identity and a new purpose in life. His personal problems suddenly became newly pertinent to art, and he realized that something he had at first thought of as his shortcoming and then as his peculiarity, finally had a worthwhile position in his relationship with literary creation. He now realized that his defensive attempts at escapism had been futile; he had next to try to overcome his proclivity for the ordinary, the burgher mentality. "Gladius Dei" represents his first step toward this goal. He later achieved another step in "Tristan," and in "Tonio Kröger" he finally attained an understanding of himself as both a human being and as an artist.

Thomas Mann logically began his search for his basic concepts in historical examples, a method naturally suited to his intellect. When he found an adequate exemplar in the intellectual and spiritual components of the conflict between Savonarola and Lorenzo, he began to research that era, studying the finest works on the subject he could find, and finally breathing Florence's very air in the spring of 1901. Especially in the light of the underlying *Weltbild* of the Schopenhauer experience, his study was much too important and complex to be completed in a hurry and he did not finish *Fiorenza* until 1905.[109] Under such mental and emotional stress in the summer of 1901, Thomas Mann needed to pour out his heart's desire, his joy in the lovely sinful Munich to which he was so devoted, and at the same time express his artistic vocation. The absurd and grotesque "Gladius Dei" impulsively blends Mann's Savonarola studies with his personal message into a montage of dynamic scenes.

Thomas Mann's voice, linking the absurd and the deeply realistic, speaks through the clumsy, ugly Hieronymus. Because of Schopenhauer's invigorating influence, he for the first time made his aesthetic theory a part of his *Weltbild*, creating a new, inspiring theme that would eventually dominate his work. While "The Way to the Churchyard" identified the living components of the metaphysical structure Mann had glimpsed in Schopenhauer's *The World as Will and Representation*, the message of "Gladius Dei" far more significantly points toward Mann's personal attitude to life and his developing aesthetic ethics.

"Tristan"

"Tristan" stands with "Tonio Kröger" and "Death in Venice" as one of Thomas Mann's most popular pieces of short fiction. Although "Tristan" belongs to his youth production, it signals his breakthrough into a new thematic concern deeply connected to his desire for personal and artistic identity, an urge which led him away from the morass of self-pity into a more creative quest toward life. He now was absorbed thematically with the identification of the "artist" (*Künstler*) and the "Burgher" (*Bürger*) in his own "worldview" (*Weltbild*), which directed him toward an ever-flexible and expansive *Weltanschauung* which inspired his voluminous later *Questor* novels. Mann in fact laid the groundwork for all of his subsequent work with "Tristan," "Tonio Kröger," and "Death in Venice," stories of intense beauty and deep emotional and intellectual appeal. Remarkably, with the exception of *Royal Highness* (Königliche Hoheit), a short novel, he did not write a major novel between 1901, when he completed *Buddenbrooks* and conceived "Tristan," and 1924, when he finished *The Magic Mountain* (*Der Zauberberg*). From 1924, the production of his short fiction diminished while he worked almost ceaselessly on one mammoth novel after another until his death in 1955.

Mann's enormous development between "The Way to the Churchyard" and "Gladius Dei" and his achievement in "Tristan" and "Tonio Kröger" led from his first fictionalization of an abstraction in "Tristan" to a personalized *Weltanschauung* in "Tonio Kröger." His development owes much to the intellectual and spiritual experiences he had undergone while reading the works of Nietzsche and more recently Schopenhauer, and enjoying Wagnerian opera with the Ehrenberg brothers in the winter of 1901. Years later in his *Betrachtungen eines Unpolitischen*, Thomas Mann described Schopenhauer, Nietzsche, and Wagner as "a triple constellation of three eternally bound spirits" (EHL) (*GW*, 7: 79), whose impact he gradually absorbed around 1900.

As with "Gladius Dei," the exact date of composition of "Tristan" has not been determined. Oscar Bie asked Mann on 1 April 1901, for a short story to publish in *Neue deutsche Rundschau*, but he just then was about to leave for Florence and had nothing to offer. He also had to turn down a similar request from the Langen firm, who were considering the publication of a new collection of his short fiction, as then "Tristan," could not have been completed during the visit to Florence.

Whether Mann wrote "Tristan" before, during, or after his visit to a sanatorium called Mitterbad[110] is not clear, either; however, in "Tristan" he did describe both this spa and Riva, another sanatorium close to Lake Garda and also under the direction of Dr. Hartungen. Heinrich Mann had stayed in both institutions prior to July 1901, when the bothers spent a month together at Mitterbad; and both Mendelssohn and Bürgin indicate that "Tristan" was written between Thomas Mann's return to Munich from Italy in May of 1901 and his stay at Mitterbad, which may imply he based his descriptive passages on material from correspondence, now lost, with Heinrich.[111]

On 13 February 1901, in a letter to Heinrich, Thomas Mann first mentioned a new story: "I am now working on a burlesque which will probably be called 'Tristan.' (This is something! A burlesque called 'Tristan'!)" (EHL).[112] The title's paradox is all the more absurd because Thomas Mann had always deeply cherished Wagner's opera *Tristan und Isolde*,[113] and his frame of mind was just as serious as when he had dealt with the theme of Savonarola. Mann was still working under the profound influence of his 1899 experience of Schopenhauer, which had been integral to the closing chapters of *Buddenbrooks*. Here, he amalgamated Schopenhauerian concepts with Wagner's *geistig-erotic* mysticism in *Tristan und Isolde* and then combined them with his own ideas.[114] This intellectual integration, especially in the light of Mann's response to Nietzschean concepts he already knew, stands at the climax of "Tristan," expressing his newly achieved personal theme: the conflict between the "will to live" and its paradoxical rationalization and the metaphysical meaning of Art, both conceived on the abstract plane of the world representation fictionalized in the limited contrast between the artist and the "burgher," and here we speak about the "well-fed" burgher (*Spießbürger*). Mann typically called as elevated a theme as he treats in "Tristan" a "*Burleske*," because the story contains fictional characters who are incapable of metaphysical experience. These figures represent the components paradoxical to the harmony of the worldview Mann conceived, and hence their distortions make them the burlesque elements of the story. On the other hand, Mann sees music as the noblest of the arts[115] and uses it to convey the essence of his metaphysical message through Wagner's *Tristan und Isolde*, never ridiculing the opera. Mann invariably distinguishes the dignity of the universal theme from the ironically burlesque aspect of the story, in which Gabriele expresses the tragic element and the other characters, with their comic and scapegoat qualities, the burlesque.

In this *"Burleske"* Mann separates the genres of tragedy and comedy on two completely different levels of perception: tragic transcendence, which moves from the Wagnerian music through Gabriele's performance and death to the Schopenhauerian "insight" (*Erkenntnis*) of Art;[116] and the "will to live", shown through her husband Klöterjahn, who is incapable of understanding the role he plays in the metaphysically conceived world he inhabits.[117] Spinell, the third protagonist, is positioned between Gabriele and Klöterjahn. He rationally comprehends the intellectual relevance of the music, but his lack of creativity, his inability to experience "insight" through Art, which overcomes the "will to live" limits him. Between the high mimetic values Gabriele represents and the low mimetic expressed by Klöterjahn, Spinell might be called "tragicomic," belonging wholly to neither side; he is a caricature of the unsuccessful pedant, alienated from his realistic milieu, but unable to rise above it. Ironically, he is a writer who knows the limitations of his talent. Mann admires the self-sacrifice of the artist Gabriele because it provides insight into a higher dimension of being, and he belittles the earthy vigor of Klöterjahn; Spinell is traced with remorseless irony, but not completely without Mann's sympathy.

A similar pattern appears in the sturcture of the story. Gabriele's fatal performance of the piano transcription of Wagner's *Tristan und Isolde* marks her passage from the limited physical dimension *"Diesseits"* represented by the materialistic *"Erdgeist"* of the burgher to the metaphysical dimension *"Jenseits"*[118] to which her playing leads. Although Mann does not mention the opera *Tristan und Isolde* either before or after Gabriele's performance, both the plot and the theme of the story depend completely upon the opera. Gabriele's progress toward death hinges upon her decision to play, which her doctors had forbidden.

The plot of "Tristan" illustrates Mann's own intellectual and spiritual implementation of his Schopenhauerian and Wagnerian themes;[119] his infatuation with Schopenhauer's *Weltbild* and his rather Nietzschean personal attitude to Wagner's opera form the key to understanding his message as well as providing the formal and thematic core of "Tristan." Here, he defines his own insight into the concept of harmony using *Tristan und Isolde* as his focus, and clarifies the differences between his ideas and Schopenhauer's, while not diverging completely from Schopenhauer's philosophical system.

An examination of "Tristan's" setting provides the vital first impression of the story. "Einfried," its setting, is an invitingly-named sanatorium that promises tranquillity to its wealthy clientele.[120] It also resembles a gleaming mythical dwelling of Wagnerian gods: "behind the slate roofs, evergreen and massive, softly divided by ravines, the mountains reach heavenward" (EHL).[121] The strong suggestion of harmonious concepts in a superior sphere of existence whose "stillness" is repeatedly emphasized supports Thomas Mann's choice of title for this story.[122]

Of those who dwell at Einfried, its chief of medical staff, Dr. Leander, appears first, as a rather cynical and authoritarian secondary character. In his chilly fashion, he "holds the sufferers under his spell, all these individuals who are too weak to give themselves their own laws and then obey them, [who] deliver their fortunes to him, to be allowed to lean on his strength for support" (EHL).[123] At the outset, then, Dr. Leander is on the side of the "will to live." Another physician, Dr. Müller, is also mentioned in the last paragraph of the first section of the story, and both his position in the sanatorium and his ordinary name emphasize his insignificance. He tends the relatively well and the hopelessly ill patients, both groups reflecting his status by being considered relatively "unimportant" to the life of the institution.[124]

At this early point in the story, Mann also introduces an anonymous figure of major importance to its plot and theme, given some indication of the meaning of the man's name: "a man, with a name of some kind of mineral or precious stone, and who steals the Lord's days with his inactivity" (EHL).[125] Next, Mr. and Mrs. Klöterjahn arrive at Einfried, and the first words "heard" from him are: "Slowly, Gabriele, take care, my angel, and keep your mouth closed."[126] Klöterjahn[127] is bubbling over with well-meant admonitions to his wife, and Thomas Mann's good-natured irony permeates Klöterjahn's words and appearance. The description of the natural setting[128] now harmonizes with the feverish ebbing of young Mrs. Klöterjahn's life, in direct contrast to the uproarious health of her husband and child. Klöterjahn also repeatedly points out that their home physician, Dr. Hinzpeter,[129] diagnosed his wife's ailment as a tracheal catarrh, not as tuberculosis. Actually, the specific diagnosis is irrelevant, since Gabriele's life and death do not depend on ordinary norms.[130]

Mann plays down the physicians, the representatives of science, since both Dr. Leander and Dr. Müller treat Mrs. Klöterjahn exactly as her former doctor had done, giving her ice chips, morphine, and complete bed rest. All agree that to avoid harmful emotional stress she must be prevented from playing the piano.

Mrs. Klöterjahn appears an exceptional woman, and Mann does not apply either humor or irony in describing her frail beauty. She is a brunette, who, with her other charming features, bears a fine blue vein on her forehead, which annoyingly dominates her entire fine-featured face.[131] This little blue vein stands out as a leitmotif each time she registers an emotion, together with her glance, which is exhausted and fading. The pleasant description of the fragile young wife is abruptly cut off by Klöterjahn's simplistic chatter. He calls for coffee and sandwiches, his lusty energy and appetite an obvious contrast to his wife's frailty.

Young Mrs. Klöterjahn's refreshing impression on the residents of Einfried appears in the opening of the third section of the story, where Klöterjahn supplies her background: she came from Bremen and now lives on the northeast coast of Germany, where Mann's own Lübeck is located, and her health has been poor since the birth of her strapping son. She is suffering from a tracheal catarrh, he says, and needs a gentler climate; to Klöterjahn, who is in blomming health, with blond hair, blue eyes, and moist, hungry-looking lips, the reasons for her illness are elementary.

The writer, still nameless, is now heard from again, reacting favorably to Mrs. Klöterjahn's ethereal grace, but he is shocked and disgusted when he sees Klöterjahn making advances to a chambermaid in an out-of-the-way corner of the sanatorium. After a week, Klöterjahn leaves his wife "in good hands" and returns to his bloomish child and his flourishing business.

Mann pays good deal of attention to the extraordinarily healthy Klöterjahn baby, a reflection of his father's robust vitality and a striking contrast to his young mother's extreme frailty. Klöterjahn's departure from the sanatorium seems a little insensitive, although he cannot really be faulted for neglecting his wife, whose apparently genuine attachment to her rough, exuberant husband with his sensual appetites seems surprising and even paradoxical.[132] Mann's chronology is highly important, since he overlaps the time of events between parts four and six and narrates earlier events in the present tense. At the close of the third section, Klöterjahn has left for home and yet he is still described as present, perhaps in spirit, at Einfried.

Part four of "Tristan" deals with the writer mentioned earlier and only now called by his name, Detlev Spinell. As with earlier characters, notably Paolo Hofmann, Tobias Mindernickel, and Lobgott Piepsam, Mann stresses the foreign origin of a part of the character's name,[133] even though in this case the formulation is no longer foreign, not Italian, as Dr. Leander later emphasizes to Mrs. Klöterjahn.

Spinell is nicely built, with brown hair like Mrs. Klöterjahn's, in contrast to her husband's blondness. The writer's intellect is superior to the business-man's—Spinell can deal with metaphysical concepts—but his physique is nothing like Klöterjahn's. Spinell does not even show a beard growth, an indication of impotence causing the other residents to refer to him as "the overgrown baby," a pitiable, clownish figure. All of his mannerisms similarly reflect his lack of virility. Even though he is a writer, Spinell is not creative. His one book was a failure and he cannot even play the music he understands and loves. His failings bar him from heroism, and Mann's description of him stresses his inclination toward contemplative but sterile aestheticism.

The direct relationship between Spinell and certain Schopenhauerian concepts familiar to Mann is germane. Clearly, Spinell stands for objective thought, related to Schopenhauer's concept of "objectivation"[134] to which Mann will refer in his later Schopenhauer essay. "It puts in a nutshell the whole tendency and capacity of mankind to delude itself and imagine that its will receives its direction and content from its mind, whereas our philosopher asserts the direct opposite, and relegates the intellect . . . to a position as mere mouthpiece of the will: to justify it, to provide it will "moral" motivations, and, in short, to rationalize our instincts."[135]

The title of Schopenhauer's book is an excellent condensation of its main thought:

4	1	2	3
Welt als	*Wille*	*und*	*Vorstellung*
World as	Will	and (factor of intellec- tualizing)	Representation/ Mental Image

The "will to live" (1) is formless and senseless, a blind surging power that uses the intellect (2) to acquire substance in the form of the rationalized representation or mental image, (3), which ultimately represents the world (4). The intellectualization of one blind instinctive power by another power, itself limited, gives a comically pitiable effect.

The objectivation by the intellect (2) is paralleled by the perception of "genius," or "genial objectivation," as Thomas Mann says in his essay on Schopenhauer; Schopenhauer sees "genial objectivation" as able to reach the aesthetic level of knowledge or "insight" (*"Einsicht"* or Erkenntnis). This insight reveals the deception of the limiting and tormenting *principium individuationis*, the false vision of the division of things into the separated state of being in the representation or "mental image" (*Vorstellung*) of the world.[136] The "genius" in especially favorable moments can free itself from the will and experience a complete aesthetic work, conceiving Beauty. Art and Beauty cannot be simply learned; they are the pure gift of intuition.[137] Mann maintained that in such an experience "the intellect participate[d] to such an extent that it [was] that which made the world into a "mental image". . . . Thus one will recall that irony noted above and objectivity belong together and are *one"* (EHL) (*GW*, 9: 116). In terms of Mann's "Tristan," Schopenhauer's belief, like that of Nietzsche and of Wagner in his later years, that music had different qualities from the other arts, made music superior to them in its capacity of "insight."[138]

Mann brought Schopenhauer's abstract pattern to life in the chief characters of "Tristan." Klöterjahn and his baby represent the "will to live"; Gabriele stands for the intuitive portion of the objectivity of the genius; and Spinell represents the intellectual component of the objectivity. Spinell thus also assumes the comic or burlesque role in the story.

Spinell's fantasies of Beauty, like a dilettante's, possess a naïve candor. Many superficial details seem to make Detlev Spinell resemble Thomas Mann himself: Spinell's hair color, his liking for elegance, his shyness toward women, and of course, his one and only book, a novel,[139] as well as his thirst (*Durst*) for the music of Wagner. In these respects, Spinell is a grotesque shadow of young Thomas Mann, a means of treating himself ironically.

However, Mann had still another model for Spinell: Arthur Holitscher, whom he had met in the Café Luitpold in Munich in 1899. Holitscher came from a Hungarian-German-Jewish background in Budapest and was attracted to Thomas Mann, six years younger than himself, who traveled in the same circles as Holitscher. Holitscher was on good terms with Langen and S. Fischer, and Mann, as a reader for the periodical *Simplicissimus*, had participated in the publication of Holitscher's latest novel, an undeniably second-rate work. Arthur Holitscher had a difficult personality and was extremely defensive about his shortcomings. Mann modeled the physiological and psychological descriptions of Detlev Spinell on Holitscher, who had, as it happened, written more than one book. Although S. Fischer must have recognized Holitscher in the fictional Spinell, Fischer did not object to printing "Tristan" in Mann's second short story collection. Spinell at once caricatures both Arthur Holitscher and Thomas Mann himself, a burlesque figure who stands between two worlds of concepts and furnishes intellectual insight into both. Spinell, too, is anything but a heroic lover. His abstract insight clashes with Klöterjahn's well-fed burgherhood; although Spinell is naïve and world-shy (*weltfremd*), beauty attracts him, and his reaction to a beautiful woman is a perfect illustration of the Kantian definition, as Thomas Mann points out repeatedly by displaying Spinell's many physical signs of impotence.

The fifth section of "Tristan" returns to the time before Klöterjahn departs from Einfried, clarifying the point that Klöterjahn and Spinell had indeed been introduced and paving the way for Gabriele's subsequent letter to her husband about Spinell. This seemingly unimportant short scene provides the exact orientation of Gabriele, Klöterjahn, and Spinell with respect to one another, locating Spinell in the central position he will hold during the rest of the story. His viewpoint is introduced by his reaction to the name Klöterjahn, which his aesthete's tender ears find rude, vulgar, and ugly both in sound and connotation. Certain names not suiting their owners may even disfigure them, as Spinell feels about "Klöterjahn," which seems to mar Gabriele's gentle equanimity. Spinell instinctively rejects the paradoxical union of two so dissimilar people under one name—and *that* name. His aestehetic sense cannot accept this grotesque combination, and he sets out to do all he can to make the Klöterjahns just as aware of their mismatching.

In section six, matters are being settled; Klöterjahn has gone home to the North and the plot development begins at Einfried. Up to this point in the story, the young lady is consistently referred to as "Mr. Klöterjahn's wife," reflecting Mann's attitude toward names; here she claims no special attention for her own personality and speaks and acts merely as a shadow of her dynamic husband. Despite this, she still radiates and unconscious appeal to which others respond, Spinell in particular.

Spinell's behavior with the young lady is peculiar; he lowers his voice with extreme caution and stays at a proper distance from her. Mrs. Klöterjahn more and more readily grasps Spinell's train of conversation, although his notions strike her as novel. From a strictly pragmatic, materialistic viewpoint, Spinell's words do not make much sense, but on the abstract plane they are significant. It is the first time in "Tristan" that conversation between Spinell and Gabriele Klöterjahn reveals its future direction and the nature of their developing geistig relationship. Overcoming the "will to live"[140] amounts ultimately to doing what the individual does *not* want to do, which is a victory of the spirit (*Geist*) over the physical.[141] The restriction of Spinell's "overcoming" of the "will to live" to his getting out of bed early is naturally indicative of the ironic limitation of his personality.

The German text reveals that in this scene Gabriele Klöterjahn uses precisely the expression, "overcoming of self," that Nietzsche gave as a title to a chapter of his *Thus Spoke Zarathustra* (*Also sprach Zarathustra*), "of Self-overcoming."[142] Nietzsche's phrase suits the impression Thomas Mann has created of Spinell up to this point in "Tristan." This treatment of the theme of self-overcoming is somewhat ludicrous, since in Nietzschean terms its value consists of a "higher" goal. Mann could acceptably use ideas from both Schopenhauer's and Nietzsche's works in this conversation between Gabriele Klöterjahn and Spinell, since these ideas are relevant to this theme.[143] His own efforts at self-discipline began with a self-imposed schedule adopted first to write more efficiently, then to subdue his maturing sexual restlessness, and finally, to silence his feelings of guilt at his lack of literary success. The struggle to master his personal weaknesses became a part of his work habits for the rest of his life.[144]

Mrs. Klöterjahn's thoughts have been frequently occupied with Spinell's notions, while at the same time her health appears to be declining in symptoms that recur each time she experiences a heightening of her "insight"[145]— first during her conversations with Spinell, then during her moments of introspection, and finally in her piano performance. These experiences gradually lead her away from the powerful magnetism of the "will to live."

Mrs. Klöterjahn's conversations with Spinell aroused her new-found interest in her own personality. The contrast is developed between the earthbound service of the "will to live" and the capacity for the metaphysical (*geniale Objektivität*), introduced on the fictional level by Spinell's critical attitude toward the name Klöterjahn. The dominance of the "will to live" over abstract values is illustrated in Spinell's earlier images, which had expressed the paradox of the Klöterjahn's marriage: "Take some wonderful creature, a sylph, an airy wraith, a fairy dream of a thing, and what does she do? Goes and gives herself to a brawny Hercules at a country fair, or maybe to a butcher's apprentice. . . ." He brings the matter up again rudely in the seventh section: "You will in justice, madame, admit that anybody who calls you Klöterjahn ought to be thrashed . . . It is the abandonment of ugliness; it is grotesque to make you comply with the custom so far as to fasten your husband's name upon you; it is barbarous and vile" (*STD*, 144–45; *GW*, 8: 232).

Before her marriage, Mrs. Klöterjahn's name was Gabriele Eckhof, a name that reveals her early background, her home in Bremen with its "dreadfully wild and overgrown garden," and her father, and old businessman who played the violin well. Mrs. Klöterjahn, too, is devoted to music, but at Einfried she has been forbidden to touch the piano.[146]

Spinell and Gabriele Eckhof then discuss the garden of her girlhood home in Bremen, and he goes so far as to imagine "a little golden crown" in her hair.[147] Then, she tells Spinell, Klöterjahn came and saw her, "and three days later he proposed." When Spinell revealed his surprise at such a short engagement, Gabriele told him, "But I had set my heart on it" (literally, "But I had *wanted* it" (EHL).[148] This illuminates Thomas Mann's point: "Aber ich *wollte* es eben." The word "will" is crucial to this passage, since it refers to the Schopenhauerian "will to live", whose connotations vitally illumine the message of the story. The original text used the German word for "will" five times in the larger passage from which this sentence is taken:

1.	a. English translation (STD)	But I set my heart on it.
	b. Literal translation (EHL)	But I *had wanted* it.
	c. German original	Aber ich *wollte* es eben
2.	a.	Ah, so you set your heart on it.
	b.	Ah you *wanted* it.
	c.	Ah, Sie *wollten* es.
3.	a.	Yes, and I displayed great strength of purpose
	b.	Yes, and I have displayed a stable and considerable *will*.
	c.	Ja, und ich habe einen ganz festen und respektablen *Willen* gezeigt.
4.	a.	Yes, I forsook all that; nature has arranged things that way.
	b.	Yes, and I had left all this behind, because it is as nature *wants* it (or, because this is the *will* of nature)
	c.	Ja, ich verließ das alles, denn so *will* es ja die Natur.
5.	a.	Yes, I suppose that it is.
	b.	Yes, so [nature] *wants* it.
	c.	Ja, so *will* sie [die Natur] es wohl.

Thomas Mann's heavy emphasis on "will" in this passage, gradually ascending to the statement, "this is the will of nature," incontrovertibly proves that the passage contains the theme of *Die Welt als Wille und Vorstellung*,[149] the motivation of Gabriele's marriage to Klöterjahn, who on the metaphysical level represents the "will to live" and on the fictional level the burgher mentality. Like her father, Gabriele had an artistic vocation, but her call directed her to a happy, dreamy playfulness unenlightened by "insight." At home, she was dormant, but her blind instinctive "will to live" drew her toward Klöterjahn and a commonplace existence with him in order to perpetuate the species.[150] She had followed the "will to live" in marrying Klöterjahn, because he clearly embodied the physical life of the species. The lines that immediately follow those discussed above refer to her happiness at bearing the extraordinarily healthy scion of the Klöterjahns. To this, Spinell represents the voice of intellectual insight.[151]

At its conclusion, the seventh section of "Tristan" offers an evolution of insight, for Mrs. Klöterjahn then thinks often about her discussions with Spinell and compares her husband's earthly inclinations with her own artistic desires. When someone asks about her family, the balance in her mind seems to be shifting against the too-healthy Klöterjahns. Her declining health conveys Mann's implicit question of whether a relation exists between her physical debilitation and her increasing insight.[152]

In the centrally thematic eighth section, all of the residents of Einfried except those who are gravely ill go on an excursion one February day, but Mrs. Klöterjahn and *Rätin* Spatz choose to stay at the sanatorium. Spinell, who had declared he was going to stay home and "work," joins them in the drawing room, where, after some conversation, he persuades Mrs. Klöterjahn to defy her doctors' orders and play the piano. At first she agrees to play only one selection, but the magic of the music takes control of her, and she proceeds, deeply moved, to play several compositions, at last performing the strenuous piano transcription of Wagner's *Tristan und Isolde*. When she finishes, it is almost dark and the other patients are beginning to return from their outing.

Mann consistently referred to his heroine in the preceding pages as "Mrs. Klöterjahn," or "the wife of Mr. Klöterjahn," but at the moment she begins to act of her own volition, playing the piano and liberating herself from the "will to live," he abandons this unnatural terminology and calls her "Gabriele," a name which conveys her ethereal nature. Mann also matches his carefully described setting within Einfried with the physical conditions outside the sanatorium. ". . . The sun shines with the same penetrating clearness upon the lovely and the commonplace, and I for one am positively grateful to it for finally going under a cloud." "Don't you like the sun, Herr Spinell?" "Well, I am no painter . . . when there is no sun one becomes more profound. . . . It is a thick layer of grayish-white cloud" (*STD*, 150–51; *GW*, 8: 240–41). The seemingly superficial conversation about the weather introduces the main theme of this section of "Tristan," although at first, as before, Mrs. Klöterjahn does not answer Spinell's special message, couched in images of darkness and night that derive from German literary tradition.

Ever since Novalis's Romantic treatment of Night, it has held a special significance completely apart from its traditional archetypical imagery of death, sleep, evil, and so forth. For Novalis, Night was the time of dreams, which offered the possibility of union with the Ultimate. The stars, winking eyes of Eternity in the dark silent sky, invite the wanderer into a world completely free of pragmatic preoccupations (*Erdgeist*). Night, in Novalis's sense, can thus provide moments of ecstatic insight into life; through Night the German Romantic poet might transcend physical limitations and evolve upward into the sphere of the Infinite (*das Unendliche*).[153]

The cult of the Night is also integral to Wagner's *Tristan und Isolde*. The lovers' physical union is surpassed by their ardent desire for the eternal mystical units of their souls and inner beings (*Wesen*). The harsh realistic sunlight which strikes their faces represents the manifold obligations of man's normal world and cruelly emphasizes the human limitations of the lovers, who long for the privilege of living in a never-ending Night, free of the fear of approaching Day. The darkness of the Night is only a surrogate for the lovers' ultimate union in an everlasting unity beyond physical limitations.[154] Wagner took pains to demonstrate how the most profound movement of the soul is the substantialization of the work of art that brought it into being.[155]

In "Tristan," Mann makes Spinell point out the disappearance of the glaring sun, which allows a "more profound" activity of the *Geist*. Spinell then nostalgically notes the lack of music at Einfried, and asks Mrs. Klöterjahn to play. She tells him the doctors have forbidden her to touch the piano, but Spinell begs her to exercise her power of individual liberty to act, and play. Spinell does not appeal to her physically; he represents the logical intellect, his power over others resting in his close observation and his clever and persuasive use of words. He cannot convince her to play for *him*, but he can force her to it, mercilessly revealing her most intimate weaknesses: "If you are afraid it will do you harm, then we shall leave the beauty dead and dumb that might have come alive beneath your fingers. You were not always so sensible: at least not when it was the opposite question from what it is today, and you had to decide to take leave of beauty. Then you did not care about your bodily welfare; you showed a firm and unhesitating resolution when you left the fountain and laid aside the little crown" (*STD*, 151–52; *GW*, 8: 242). She plays Chopin first, one nocturne and then another, showing herself to be a consummate artist, playing not for him but for herself. At the corner of her eyes, the shadows begin to darken. The doctor's prohibition of her music and her own frailty at this moment matches the overwhelming physical and emotional stress she takes on by agreeing to play the piano,[156] a turning point in her life: on the surface level, her physical exhaustion will bring on her death; but metaphysically, in overcoming the *principium individuationis*, she will attain "insight" (*Erkenntnis*), the state of blissful stillness. When Spinell found the piano transcription of Wagner's *Tristan und Isolde* for Gabriele, she obviously knew it well, but she did not reveal an emotion comparable to his as she began to play and the note of " the *Sehnsuchtsmotiv*, roving lost and forlorn like a voice in the night lifted its trembling question. Then silence, a waiting."[157] After Wagner's lovers have drunk the magic potion they are constantly tormented by longing for one another, even when they are physically most close. The separation of their "essential being" (*Wesen*) tortures them because of their earthly limitations, and the incapacity to dissolve completely into one another is the ultimate torment of desire.[158]

Even though the following paragraphs of "Tristan" are easy to follow, tracing the libretto of Wagner's *Tristan und Isolde* is valuable, for Mann was thoroughly acquainted with the opera, and the popularity of Wagnerian music then in France and Germany ensured that his readers would have been nearly as familiar with his Wagnerian references.[159] Mann used the second and third acts of *Tristan und Isolde* to highlight the eighth section of his "Tristan." The second act shows the meeting of the lovers in the night, guarded by Brangäne, Isolde's maid, but despite her warning they are overcome by the king and his men in daylight. Fatally wounded in the encounter, Tristan falls into Kurwenal's arms. The Death motif appears in harmony with the motifs of Night and Love.[160]

The lovers' limitless 'melting" into one another represents the essence of the Wagnerian metaphysics of love as contrasted with Schopenhauer's *"Metaphysik der Geschlechtsliebe,"* and Thomas Mann's concept of love rests on this subtle contrast. Schopenhauer's thought relies heavily on logic, the natural sciences and both Platonic and Aristotelian philosophy. The *"Metaphysik der Geschlechtsliebe"* explains that any love, longing, and striving of the lovers originates from and serves the abstract concept of eternity, not the eternity of the lovers themselves, but the survival of the entire species. Schopenhauer's, *"Metaphysik der Geschlechtsliebe,"* therefore, only appears to be metaphysical. In reality, it wholly serves the blind "will to live" the instinctive drive to perpetuate the species in the world of representation. Wagner, on the other hand, maintained a transcendental metaphysical concept of love heavily influenced by Novalis's Neoplatonic *Weltbild*, which conceives of the ultimate unity of all concepts, emotions, feelings, and impulses as inherent in the *seelische Heimat*, the Infinite that precedes and follows earthly existence. In Novalis's poetry, the poet pursues his vision of the "blue flower" (*blaue Blume*), the symbol of this utter bliss, but in the Schopenhauerian universe, man's immortality consists of a perpetuated existence in the species that is dominated by the "will to live." Unless the counteraction of the "will" has freed the insight, such a concept does not pertain at all either to Novalis's Romantic theory or to Wagner's, where the captive life in the world, the rule of limitation, is "sunshine," and Night allows liberation from all boundaries, ensuring endless bliss. Wagner's Tristan and Isolde are certainly not ethereal characters. But their powerful sexual love is only one aspect of the magnetism which the magic potion ignited in them. Their frail human bodies were poisoned by a mutual attraction more powerful than their species can endure, and this magnetism unites the entire universe in the night of death.[161] The actual "togetherness" of their human forms becomes an agonized yearning for the nonmaterial *geistig* unity only possbible after death has given them the final bliss of peace.

The second act of *Tristan und Isolde*, then, reveals the lovers at first fearing only day, which would separate them by roughly delineating their physical features and forcing them into the ordinary human world. As Wagner subsequently penetrates the metaphysical aspect of love in this opera, Tristan and Isolde pass from fear to "longing" (*Sehnsucht*), at last attaining the "insight"

(*Einsicht*) that Death alone, endless Night, can unite them forever, freeing them from the fear of being separated. Wagner's conception of the ecstasy of their joyful union is only reached after the *Liebestod* (Love-death) marking the beginning of their endless bliss.[162]

Mann built the eighth section of his "Tristan" closely on Wagner's poetic libretto, and a comparison of literal translations reveals the strong resemblances between his and Wagner's treatments. At this point in "Tristan," Mann drops the clumsy locution "Mrs. Klöterjahn," and refers to his heroine as "Gabriele," thus removing all burlesque overtones from the passage. Gabriele's reaction to the experience is : "I don't understand all of it very well, Herr Spinell; I only suspect [the meaning] by feeling. But what does this mean: 'even then I am the world'?" (EHL).[163] She thus simply and soberly acknowledges the rational explanation of a mystery she has experienced for a long time but which she only now has learned to comprehend.

The turning point of "Tristan" is also the most delicate point of contact between the Schopenhauerian and Wagnerian insights that Mann maintains at this moment of epiphany for Gabriele Klöterjahn, whose death will have more relation to Wagner's "*Liebestod*" than to Schopenhauer's stillness which follows insight. That it is absurd to think of Spinell as the "lover of the story" is obvious both from his physical and from his *geistig* qualities; in fact, " the lover of the story" is not Spinell, not Klöterjahn, but "Tristan"—not Isolde's flamboyant knightly lover, but the concept of Art itself.

In his personal writings of 1901, Thomas Mann indicated that he never missed a performance of *Tristan und Isolde*, stressing the power of the music: ". . . the whole second act of Tristan! That is nearly too much!"[164] In "Über die Kunst Richard Wagners" (1911), he wrote: "It was a liaison—skeptical, pessimistic, enlightened, nearly hateful, at the same time absolutely passionate and of an indescribably vital attraction. Wonderful hours of deep lonely happiness amidst the theater crowds, full of shivering and short moments of bliss, full of the lust of the nerves and of the intellect, of insights into the moving and great meanings, as only this art, insurpassable, can offer" (EHL).

Previously, Gabriele had played music and loved it, but without the knowledge of the genius's insight Spinell had helped her to experience.[165] The recurrent motif of "stillness" in the setting of *Einfried*, also typical of Gabriele's personality, is a clear-cut Schopenhauerian reference. Her love for the music she has been forbidden to perform now would reach fulfillment, and as it had with Isolde, whose union with Tristan meant a world of bliss, so now Gabriele's initiation through music to the insight of Art would liberate her from the *principium individuationis*.

Gabriele's question, "But what does this mean: 'I am the world'" can only be fully understood by correlating Mann's fictional Wagnerian theme with pertinent Schopenhauerian and Wagnerian theories, since the height of Wagner's symbolist art is attained in *Tristan und Isolde*, especially the mysterious fusion of music with poetry in the "love-death" (*Liebestod*), movingly conveying the union for which the lovers have yearned so desperately.[166]

The answer Spinell makes to Gabriele's question is not known to the reader but it leads to the fictional embodiment of Thomas Mann's interpretation. When she asks for the meaning of the words: "'Even then—I am the world"'! (EHL) ("Selbst dann—bin ich die Welt!")[167] the only reply can be that if in their earthly lives the lovers mean the world—all of existence—to each other, then after death this will be even more so, since death liberates them and allows them to attain the principle of "oneness" (*Einheit*). The word "*Welt*" represents "universe" rather than being limited to the physical sense of "world" only.

In comparing Wagner's metaphysics of love with Schopenhauer's, the reciprocal magnetism between Wagner's lovers is seen as so intense that it far exceeds sexual attraction, and the words of the passage, individually pronounced but sung in duet, flow into one single melodic stream, symbolizing the lovers' wish to attain oneness of being, post-terrestrial eternal bliss. Life, representing the "world" (*die Welt*), is thus both an expression of the blind will and a state of insight into the total existential sphere.[168] Wagner's text includes both concepts, expressing the "disembodies lust" as the eternal union of the lovers' indestructible essences, in contrast to the "carnal lust" of the "will to live," necessarily attached to material things. In declaring, "Ich bin die Welt," the lovers proclaim that each is the other's sphere of existence and the "will to live" on the level of "genius's objectivation."

In the thematic focus of Thomas Mann's fiction, Gabriele's question makes it plain that her experience of Art is subjective and a priori, rather than intellectual. She consistently responds first with surface interest and then with an intuitive affirmation of concepts she encounters (usually from Spinell); finally, after mental and physical effort she grasps their entire meaning. Spinell, the representative of the objectivating intellect, awakens her "insight" with his explanations. At the moment of her overwhelming question, Gabriele is completely united subjectively with the living work of art she is performing, but she is still one with the "world," the material representation, she inhabits. Her subjective reaction to music is not sufficient for her to achieve "insight" unless she can reach into the genuine aesthetic experience with "genius's objectivation." In "Tristan," Mann substitutes music for Wagner's "magic potion"; music awakens "longing" (*Sehnsucht*) for unity and produces fulfillment in the "love-death" (*Liebestod*) the mystical union of the intuitive and the intellectual components of the living work of art. This actually substitutes for the presence of the two lovers. While in *Tristan und Isolde* the two lovers respond body and soul to one another in the same subjective and rational, physical and nonphysical manner, Gabriele responds to the physical and nonphysical values of the work of art. Since Mann's title "Tristan" represents the fictional hero of his work, the work of art, Gabriele responds to Wagner's opera *Tristan und Isolde*, becoming through her "insight" the loving bride of Art (Tristan) whose only path to bliss is the liberation from "Light," the symbol for material existence, the "will to live," and the *principium individuationis*, which plunges her into the magnetic maelstrom that swirls her toward physical death. Gabriele's experience initiates her into a higher mode of being, no longer restricted by the physical, and her death is a positive rather than a negative act, not a loss of life but the achievement of a liberated state of bliss, totally beyond longing (*Sehnsucht*) in the ultimate union with Art.

Gabriele follows her first question to Spinell with another: " 'Why can you understand it so well, and yet cannot play it?' " In his customary fashion, Mann emphasizes his more important passages with casual repetitions in his commentary. Here he makes Spinell display his embarrassment by blushing, wringing his hands, and finally producing an unsatisfactory answer, his obvious lack of virility thematically signifying his impotence for expression or creation. Spinell's deficiency is acknowledged in his final significant words to Gabriele; he looks clownish, with an overage baby face and oversized hands and feet, at the very moment he helps Gabriele unite the intellectual and the intuitive elements of her being to achieve oneness in the work of art. Spinell knew and understood the music Gabriele played; though he himself is not creative, he can comment intelligently on art, and he impressed her with his thinking. In her presence, he seemed interesting and somewhat tragic, quite unlike the unappealing and quasi-burlesque figure he cut with the other residents. In fact, Gabriele is the only person who takes him seriously.

As she continues to play Wagner's music, Mann paraphrases the lines of *Tristan und Isolde* to the end of the scene in which Kurwenal, Melot, and King Mark burst in upon the lovers. The line, "Oh, glad chromatic upward surge of metaphysical perception!"[169] prepares the audience for the *Liebestod* which closes the opera. The ecstasy evoked by the music Gabriele plays is abruptly interrupted by the entrance of *Pastorin* Höhlenrauch. This lady lost her reason after bearing nineteen children, and now her only purpose in life is "her pathetic, instinctive rounds of the house" (*STD*, 155; *GW*, 8: 186). Possibly Mann's purpose in his inclusion of the instinct-guided old slave to the "survival of the species" is to parallel the interruption of Wagner's lovers with the insensitive powers of the daylight world. The emphasis which Thomas Mann places on *Pastorin* Höhlenrauch's instinctive actions recalls, offkey, Schopenhauer's world of thoughts.

When *Pastorin* Höhlenrauch leaves and Gabriele is again alone with Spinell, she turns to the last pages of the opera transcription, the *Liebestod* (Love-death), and plays the passage of the fulfillment of the lovers' wish to unite in death, which in the opera is sung by Isolde alone over Tristan's body, leading to her own ecstatic death.[170] All of Gabriele's physical details—her pallor, her shadowy eyes, the tremulous little vein in her forehead—identify her with her art, her intuition, and her impending death.[171]

In the passage which follows, Mann again meticulously paraphrases Wagner's music and poetry. Isolde's powerful aria in praise of the illusion of love abruptly changes from contemplation to self expression and as suddenly ends in deep silence (*Stille*), dividing the world of "mental image" from the world of Art. Next, very quickly, sleigh bells and voices are heard from a distance, and Spinell, clumsy and pathetic, kneels sobbing before Gabriele in gratitude for an artistic experience he himself could not create.[172] Einfried returns to everyday reality.

Once the twilight spell of the eighth section has been broken, on the sunny pragmatic world introduces Mann's denouement.[173] He no longer calls Gabriele "Mr. Klöterjahn's wife," though the cumbersome title suits the storm of platitudes surrounding her better than her given name. Spinell and Klöterjahn quarrel, while Gabriele, freed from the murderous "will to live," fades into the background. In the burlesque altercation, Klöterjahn's point of view, the surface plot, opposes the figurative representation of the Schopenhauerian world as first Spinell and now Gabriele envision it. When Gabriele begins to decline, Dr. Müller, who oversees both insignificant and terminal cases, assumes her care, calling Klöterjahn and his flourishing child from his flourishing business to her deathbed.

Mann here satirizes egotistical medical naïveté as well as Klöterjahn junior, an infant who "in every way surrendered himself to his instincts" (*STD*, 157; *GW*, 8: 249). The boisterous child horrifies Spinell, who flees from the baby, defeated and humiliated by the overpowering physical will of the Klöterjahns, who he feels are inferior human beings. Spinell detests them, but he is helpless against their overweening physicality. Section 9 bridges the climax and the ending, for Gabriele's performance has brought on her inevitable collapse.

Detlev Spinell's voice dominates section 10. In his room[174] he struggles to write to Klöterjahn, in order to battle against the "will to live" with his own "mental image" (*Vorstellung*) of the world. Mann humorously criticized himself in Spinell, as Spinell's saying that "the words came in such a rush" that his pride made him relieve his feelings thus. While at work on *Buddenbrooks*, Thomas Mann often complained that writing comes harder to a writer than to anyone else, and he revealed both his introspection and humorous shyness in Spinell's letter: "It is my habit to yield to the impulse which urges me to put my own experience into flamingly right and unforgettable words and to give them to the world. And therefore hear me" (*STD*, 158; *GW*, 8: 251).

Thomas Mann successfully channeled his interest in the decadent, the pessimistic, the self-rejecting, and the self-denigrating from the desperation of "Little Herr Friedemann" and "Der Bajazzo" to the grotesque symbolic expression and contemplative ironic subjectivity of "Tobias Mindernickel." While in "Little Lizzy" and "Gladius Dei," aesthetic concerns occupied only a small part of Mann's whole message, in "Tristan" for the first time he could define his theoretical conception of art in the *Weltbild* animated by Schopenhauer's and Wagner's ideas, the real theme of the story.[175] The only way Thomas Mann could progress from the pessimistic self-scrutiny and stagnating self-pity that had plagued his earlier works, and evaluate himself, the art he served, and his tangible world, was to rationalize factual matters, preventing himself from backsliding discouragement by distancing irony. Now that the *"lange, lange Buch," Buddenbrooks*, was being printed, he was no longer hampered by its enormous form, and in "Tristan" he could erect the whole framework of his story according to the "mental images" of his idea.

In Thomas Mann's development, Spinell's letter to Klöterjahn is a crucial advance, since in a witty miniframe construction it allows Spinell to set his own opinions squarely on his side of the dual vision: that is, Spinell's vision of Gabriele's artistic vocation versus the pragmatic, realistic understanding Klöterjahn has. The clear stand Spinell takes was necessary to allow Klöterjahn, the other side of the dual vision, to express himself in section eleven, creating the story's vital equilibrium.[176]

Spinell maintains that Gabriele belongs to "death and beauty,"[177] and he bitterly accuses Klöterjahn of having profaned her ephemeral loveliness and of leading "her idle will astray." Bearing the boisterously healthy Klöterjahn infant, heir to all his father's physicality, had drained his frail mother's life force, and Spinell angrily accuses Klöterjahn and son of barbaric villainy, Spinell's artful close is a bitter testament to the worldly victory of the physically strong over the weak, containing the interpretations Thomas Mann at that stage of his growth held of the word "burgher" (*Bürger*): "Perhaps he [the Klöterjahn baby] will continue in the way of his father, become a well-fed, trading, tax-paying citizen; a capable, philistine pillar of society; in any case, tone-deaf, normally functioning individual, responsible, sturdy, and stupid, troubled by not a doubt" (*STD*, 161; *GW*, 8: 254).

Spinell's letter provokes Klöterjahn's wrath. In the boisterous eleventh section of "Tristan," rage, hatred, love, and despair all clash, Klöterjahn's response to the twin blows of Spinell's letter and his wife's physical decline. Klöterjahn here evinces both common sense and burlesque, turning the glare of pragmatism on Spinell's idealism. But Mann ensures sympathy for Spinell: "He stood there, crestfallen, like a big, unhappy, chidden, gray-haired schoolboy" (*STD*, 163; *GW*, 8: 256). Mann balances the comic catalogue of absurdities between the two as they trade insults, Klöterjahn ridiculing Spinell's obvious lack of virility and Spinell deriding Klöterjahn's malapropisms.

Their burlesque duel, however, is interrupted by a tearful apparition, *Rätin* Spatz, who calls Klöterjahn to his wife's deathbed: "She was sitting up quite quietly in bed and humming a little snatch of music . . . and there it came . . . my god."[178] Immediately the situation appears in a different light. Klöterjahn's insults cease in his consternation, and he is truly shaken: ". . . a burst of good, warm, honest human feeling came over him" (*STD*, 164; *GW*, 8: 260). He suffers simple, heartbreaking pain as he rushes away, dragging *Rätin* Spatz with him.

Spinell and Klöterjahn have different reasons for their deep attachment to the dying Gabriele. Neither can claim her completely, since in the end her personality bows to no limitations. The opponents Spinell and Klöterjahn seem pitiable examples of the *principium individuationis*: their quarrel in no way profanes her since she has attained inner harmony and needs neither of them any longer. She is the only character in "Tristan" that Mann keeps entirely free of burlesque.

In the final section, Spinell tries to regain his composure. He drinks some cognac,[179] stretches out on his bed, and hears a bird joyously announcing the onset of spring. Tormented, he mutters, "Unchanging calling" (*Unausbleiblicher Beruf*), the phrase Klöterjahn had mispronounced and taken out of context, instead of his own "unavoidable calling" (*Unausweichlicher Beruf*), the message of Spinell's own letter. Nonsense, Spinell thinks to himself; the vocation of the *Geist*, of beauty and death, Spinell's profession, has been ignored by the strong and articulate well-fed "burgher" (*gut speisender Bürger*). Spinell, the writer, a decadent *fin de siècle* aesthete, contrasts sharply with Klöterjahn the "burgher", they wholeheartedly despise each other.

When spring calls, the lonely and tormented Spinell is forced from his stylish Empire seclusion into a vernal orgy of sun and sound, where he must encounter the "will to live" in all the naked vigor of its reign.[180] The trees are still bare, but the old and wintry death has already yielded to the growing will of new reproductive life. Spinell "turned his head and lifted his eyes, slowly, scanning the house until he reached one of the windows, a curtained window on which his gaze rested awhile, fixed and somber" (*STD*, 165; *GW*, 8: 261). Behind this window Gabriele was achieving her final transcendence from life to death—from her limited sunlit life as Klöterjahn's wife to the eternal existence of the night. "Herr Spinell did not see the sun, the direction the path took hid it from his view. He walked with bent head 'humming a little snatch of music,'[181] a short phrase, a figure that mounted wailingly and complainingly upward—the *Sehnsuchtsmotiv*."[182] As Gabriele dies, Spinell's spirit communes with hers through their fellowship in Wagner's Opera. Spinell cannot see the sun, its absence stressing Wagner's Romantic concept of the night as the unifying and liberating power of metaphysical experience.

Suddenly the sun's glare smites him at a turn in the path, and he, a large, graying man, abruptly faces the object of his hatred, Klöterjahn junior, Gabriele Eckhof's rosy son. At once the baby laughs and jeers at him: ". . . an attack of sheer animal spirits gave rise to [his] wild outburst of merriment." Unable to face this sunny little apparition, Spinell tiptoes hastily away, with artifical poise concealing the fact that "inwardly, he is running away" (*STD*, 165; *GW*, 8: 262). In the end, Gabriele freed herself from the power of the "will to live" through her insight of Art, but the "will to live" had vanquished Spinell, the impotent aesthete, who ran away ". . . pursued by the youthful Klöterjahn's joyous screams" (*STD*, 166; *GW*, 8: 262).

Thomas Mann's "Tristan" marks his artistic transition from *Buddenbrooks* to "Tonio Kröger." The large scale of the novel had forced him to discipline his creativity, shaping his own Schopenhauer experience to the style and atmosphere of *Buddenbrooks*'s conclusion. Once the novel was accepted, his restored belief in his work invigorated him, and in the context of his Italian visit and his idyllic friendship with Mary Smith, his art became the focus of his life, and from this point onward he would identify, explore, and integrate his art through his personal experience. By 1901, he could simultaneously consider his objective reading of Schopenhauer with his deeply felt experience of Wagnerian opera, especially *Tristan und Isolde*. "Tristan" reflects Mann's individual creative response to the messages of Schopenhauer, Wagner, and Nietzsche, which gradually formulated his mature attitudes to life and art. Of Schopenhauer's philosophy, the "will to live," the overcoming of the "will to live" by the "counter-will" of the intellect, and the survival of the species through sexual propagation, are all fictionalized in "Tristan." Next, the Wagnerian metaphysics of love expressed through *Tristan und Isolde*[183] went far deeper than instinctive procreative attraction and relied heavily on Novalis's imagery of Night and transcendence from worldly existence to real eternal life through death. Finally, "Tristan" exhibits a Nietzschean concept of music and the "overcoming" of oneself through art.

The distillation of these philosophical concepts formed Thomas Mann's conviction that the metaphysical fusion of the subjective art experience and intellectual insight in the creative artist fulfills the work of art. During this process, the work of art rises above its purely aesthetic state and genuinely expresses a universal message, joining limited human experience to eternal unlimited absolute knowledge. Art, Mann says in "Tristan," catalyzes an experience beyond normal human capacities, having its normal dimension in an unrestricted universe only open to metaphysical perception. He himself was searching eagerly for a definition of art, and he achieved its first phase in "Tristan" by expressing his concept of the art experience in man's existence. In "Tristan," Gabriele Eckhof Klöterjahn, the performing artist, is the medium through which the fusion of the *geistig* individual and the aesthetic-subjective elements of the work of art takes place. Music in "Tristan" links the limited human world and the metaphysical realm, and Klöterjahn and his baby son represent the force of the earthbound *Erdgeist*, the embodiment of the "will to live". From these Mann produced his unique definition of art as the union of the intuitive (Gabriele) with the intellectual (Spinell), making art (music) a living experience. Schopenhauer's "will to live" and Novalis's *Erdgeist* (the Klöterjahns) remains blindly outside the vital experience.

Thomas Mann always had been concerned with the hero's relationship to art. At first he had seen the relation as secondary: Paolo Hofmann's "will to happiness" that surpassed his illness; Friedemann used art in vain to try to escape life's dangers; Bajazzo tried to mold aesthetic pleasures into narcotic, but he finally rejected himself completely; and "Little Lizzy" bitterly perverts art. In *Buddenbrooks*, art fundamentally uplifts a family caught in physical decline. As the robust "will to live" weakens, the artist acquires insights, but art in this novel is only represented vaguely as music and emotion, the reading of Schopenhauer and a toothache. Hieronymus of "Gladius

Dei" raises purely aesthetic questions: he is obsessed by corruption, sanctity, sensuality, and beauty, and Mann treats him both with irony and ultimate sympathy.

In all of his early work Mann connects art with illness and the concept of existence. The theme of "Tristan" anatomizes art in its physical, sensual and abstract essences, envisioning the art experience itself, neither discussing the wonder of the artist's creativity nor questioning the artist's identity per se or as a symptom of society. "Tristan" marks the first time that Thomas Mann gave art a central position in his fiction, overcoming the material aspect of life, a transition between the hyperintense self-analysis of his earlier fiction and the positive exploration of creativity , the essential concern of art, which he achieved in "Tonio Kröger."

Although aspects of Mann's own personality appear in Gabriele, in Spinell, and in the attitude toward music shown in "Tristan," he can in no way be identified with the earthbound "will to live" mentality of the Klöterjahns. In the years leading to *The Magic Mountain* (1924), Thomas Mann greatly modified his definition of the "burgher" and the anti-heroic Spinell is Mann's burlesque way of saying,"I have written only one book," or, as he wrote to his brother Heinrich in May, 1901, "Ich kann nicht mit" ("I cannot live up to it") (EHL). "Tristan," which involves Wagner's profound artistic work *Tristan und Isolde*, is a paradox, since with respect only to the spirit of *Tristan und Isolde*, Mann's "Tristan" is a tragedy, but with respect to Spinell's role, it is also a burlesque.[184] The Klöterjahns "will to live" element that fits neither scheme, have a place in the world, too. But who cares about them at this important moment?

Mann feels the disharmony in the plastic imagery he used in his fiction. He expresses this frustration with shocking paradoxes, and grotesque and bitter irony. The passionate love of Wagner's music, a new conception of the epic art, and a fascination with Schopenhauer's message lead him to the vision of a *Weltbild*. His experience of Schopenhauer and Wagner will stay part of him from now on, maturing but never fading. These new values grow in the short fiction before "Tristan," in which story they appear fully developed. From grotesque disharmony and bitter irony, this period of Mann's life leads to the first aesthetic statements.

Mann had no immediate luck publishing "Tristan." On 18 November 1901, he read "Tristan" during a lecture at the *Akademisch Dramatischer Verein*, and later he presented this story to Insel Verlag where it remained until it was finally printed in 1902.[185] Only in the spring of 1903 did S. Fischer agree to publish "Tristan" as the little story of a new collection of Thomas Mann's short fiction.

4
BÜRGER AND *KÜNSTLER*: THE CONTOUR OF A NEW BEGINNING

"The Hungry Ones" ("Die Hungernden"), "Tonio Kröger," "A Gleam" ("Ein Glück"), "The Infant Prodigy" ("Das Wunderkind"), "At the Prophet's" (Beim Propheten"), "A Weary Hour" ("Schwere Stunde"), "The Blood of the Walsungs" ("Wälsungenblut"), "Anekdote," "Railway Accident" ("Das Eisenbahnunglück"), "The Fight between Jappe and Do Escobar" ("Wie Jappen und Do Escobar sich prügelten")

In the summer of 1901 Thomas Mann finished both "Tristan" and "Gladius Dei," and *Buddenbrooks* appeared in October. He stayed at the Villa Cristoforo at Riva, a spa near Lake Garda, from 20 November to 19 December 1901, returning in January 1902 to Munich, where he took a new apartment at 24 Ungerstraße. On 2 June 1902 he observed to Kurt Martens, "I did not work this winter, but I had many humanistic experiences, and my conscience is appeased because I filled my notebook with observations" (EHL).

While Mann was writing "Tristan," his notebook entries for a "Savonarola project" were proliferating. He first titled this "The King of Florence," later changing it to *Fiorenza*. He gave more attention to it than to any other of his writings. He also defended it vehemently against hostile critics. With *Fiorenza* he was leaving his native world of *Buddenbrooks*, just as he gradually became estranged from his brother Heinrich after Fischer accepted *Buddenbrooks*. One of Mann's few close relationships was with his brother Heinrich, whom he had admired but did not always approve of, and it had led him to spend long periods of time in Italy, where Heinrich was far more at home than he was, especially since Thomas' heart had called him to Aalsgaard in late 1899. The closeness he had shared with Otto Grautoff since their youth was also fading by 1901, as their letters indicate.

Other profound emotional experiences intruded in 1901: the publication of *Buddenbrooks*, a deeper exposure to Wagner's music, and a close friendship with Carl and Paul Ehrenberg. Mann was especially disturbed by the stress of *Buddenbrooks* and by the ten-month hiatus before the book actually appeared.

This emotional complex underlies Mann's melancholy in 1901 as well as his growth through his tendencies toward analysis and positivism, which reinforced Nietzsche's admonition "to overcome." He was also instinctively seeking an object responsive to his developing sexuality when he encountered Wagnerian opera with his new friend Carl Ehrenberg, which, together with his emotional attachment to Carl's brother Paul, gave him a wholly new subjective outlook. About the latter complicated affair, he commented to Heinrich in a letter of 7 March 1907, "The whole thing is the metaphysics, the music, the eroticism of puberty: I never seem to emerge from puberty. . . . there is no question here of a love story, at least not in the common sense of the word, but of a friendship . . . my nervous constitution and philosophical direction has complicated the thing incredibly: it has a thousand aspects—the simplest and the intellectually most adventurous" (EHL). This attachment was in no sense homoerotic. He was then virtually a shy, mildly depressed ascetic, maintaining a disciplined routine of work and exercise. He also had an extraordinary capacity for sensing creativity, especially in music. The formal laws of beauty and the logical principles that guided his artistry left him devoid of sensuality. In short, Mann was segregating himself, almost like Friedemann, from the "good things of life" that other young people naturally enjoyed every day, and this restriction caused a conflict within his "worldview" (*Weltbild*).

This conflict had been reflected for a long time, subconsciously or consciously, in his short stories. These oppositions, though clear, are not a rigid pattern of "light and dark," "yes and no," but a flexible structure of vaguely defined components, shifting according to interpretations Mann gave them during the differing stages of his development. They varied from the libido, characterized by openness and the attraction of the subject toward the object, to his focus upon himself. In 1901 Mann was vulnerable, since he was recuperating from an urge toward excessive introversion. He had written "Tristan" under the direct influence of his reading of Schopenhauer in the fall of 1899, setting Schopenhauerian concepts into fictional form. Now for the first time he was contemplating a new object of attraction, "life" itself, and so his emotional needs and his unsolved intellected, spiritual, and intuitive problems attained an expression dependent upon his *geistig* impressions of the *Dreigestirn* (literally, a constellation of three heavenly bodies; meaning Schopenhauer, Wager, and Nietzsche acting as a sponsoring agent upon his fiction, providing their philosophical bases without causing the loss of independence of Mann's own worldview). The ideas, emotional responses, and concepts he developed from his experiences of the works of Schopenhauer, Wagner, and Nietzsche vacillated between two sides of his personality in the light of his changing conceptualization.[1] Just as Mann's reading of Schopenhauer in 1899 had profoundly affected his intellectual and emotional worlds, "Tristan" shows that it for a time had dominated his "worldview" and even gave a new, personal angle to his interpretation of Wagner, while his

Schopenhauerian vocabulary remained integral to his verbal expression. This overlapping of older and newer concepts, both expressed in the same vocabulary, now fostered enrichingly ambiguous ideas. However, besides his 1899 "Schopenhauer shock," Mann also responded significantly to Nietzsche, with considerable impact on his intellectual development. Several passages from Nietzsche's *Birth of Tragedy* relate dramatically to Mann's thought in "The Hungry Ones," "Tonio Kröger," and "Ein Glück." In addition, though ascertaining the development of Mann's response to Nietzsche is problematic because he seldom referred to it privately, his literary dependence upon Nietzsche became a leading influence in the years between "Tristan" and "Death in Venice," a period in which he discusses the achievement of identity and the definition of his life. Once he had accomplished this, his message encompassed the universal themes he later expressed in his epic novels.

Nietzsche himself in his early years had been infatuated with Schopenhauer's thought, but prior to the 1880s he openly repudiated it, even though certain of Schopenhauer's ideas remained pillars of Nietzsche's own philosophy. Nietzsche called Schopenhauer a "Christian moralistic metaphysician," whose ideas violent clashed with Nietzsche's own Dionysian-dithyrambic metaphysics. Such Nietzschean contrasts become even more confusing when Nietzsche uses the same vocabulary as Schopenhauer did but loads it with opposite meanings. Around 1871, when he wrote *The Birth of Tragedy*, Nietzsche himself was wrestling with his own liberation from both Schopenhauer and Wagner, whose work he also simultaneously loved and hated.[2] It seems only natural that Mann would have encountered Nietzsche's early works when he himself was experiencing a transition from his "Schopenhauer shock" to a Nietzschean self-liberation. Mann's intellectual quest often caused him to fuse ideational elements into totally new concepts, and when he expressed them in his fiction, they sometimes confusingly appeared under similar verbal labels, a mode highly attractive to his dilettante readers. Mann's stories, with moods ranging from self-pitying emotionalism to icy rationalism, allowed his warm human empathy to shine through reserved appearances. "Analytic" and "psychological" aspects so vital to the Freudian *Zeitgeist* made Mann's message even more accessible to his readers. Since the "troubled self" was his own, his personal experience possessed genuine power, but it needed space, rhythm, setting, and appropriate form for adequate expression. "Tonio Kröger," the longest and most highly sculpted story of this set, succeeds for this reason, while the significantly shorter "The Hungry Ones" and "Ein Glück" exhibits emotions overcrowded and overheated for their smaller scales.

The ideas of the *Dreigestirn* contributed materially to the *Zeitgeist* of the *fin de siècle* and the first decade of the 1900s, and they enormously enrich the atmosphere of Thomas Mann's world; so did the new, warm friendship with Carl and Paul Ehrenberg that grew during the winter of 1900–1. From the first, Mann had been especially attracted to Paul, the younger brother, a painter of undeniable talent, and in the following spring of 1901 they grew especially close. Paul Ehrenberg was not the first person to have touched Mann's heart; years ago as a high-school student in Lübeck, he had been innocently infatuated with his vigorous, blond and blue-eyed, rather shallow schoolmate Armin Martens.[3]

In 1901, Mann's friendship with Paul Ehrenberg seemed to prove "that something honest, warm and good, not only 'irony,' remained in me, that not everything had been devastated, had become artificial and gnawed in me by the damned literature" (to Heinrich Mann, 13 February, 1901). "The high tension of his [Thomas Mann's] emotion did not allow this to remain a simple friendships; his entire longing for life, intensified by Schopenhauer, Nietzsche, and Wagner, focused upon this one man, from whom he hoped to gain redemption, inner peace, and recovery" (EHL).

The friendship with Paul Ehrenberg was a strong factor in the development of one of Thomas Mann's most important sets of images, the duality of blond and brunette physical characteristics. By 1901, these had become an accepted pattern of expressing certain contrasting elements that parallel one another in his fiction, a pattern that appears in both his own life and in his fictional worlds. His mother Julia, his wife Katia, his early friend Otto Grautoff, were coincidentally all dark, like Thomas Mann himself, and shared his sensitivity to life and art. Other individuals, however, like Heinrich, to whom he was bittersweetly attracted, were quite different, healthy, handsome, and above all, blond and blue-eyed. Mann's excessive need for identity and belonging drew him to individuals who, he thought, shared in a unity from which he himself was excluded. His youthful admiration of Heinrich, then of Armin Martens, an early schoolmate, was the first of these; Marten's sister, Ilse, also blond and blue-eyed, a friend of his younger sister Carla, was also much admired by the young writer; he and Ilse spent many hours playing violin and piano duets in Mann's Munich apartment, but no romantic attachment existed between them, and the "blond type" seemed to hold no sexual fascination for him.

Mann's basic shyness caused him to express his deeper emotions only in letters, as his correspondence with both Grautoff and his brother Heinrich shows, not only regarding Mary Smith during his visit to Florence in the late spring of 1901, but also in connection with Paul Ehrenberg. Thomas Mann's intense but suppressed emotions appear in Hieronymus of "Gladius Dei," a tendency he developed in the Savonarola of *Fiorenza*, where the motivation for the prior's religious vocation is a "flight" from his rejection by the beautiful Fiore.

Mann shaped his Schopenhauerian concepts by incorporating them in the characters of *Fiorenza*; he embodied the "will to live" in Lorenzo de' Medici, in contrast to the "prophet" and "saint" (*Heilige*) Savonarola. Here Art is on the side of Life, clashing with *Geist* and the "overcoming of life," or death. *Fiorenza* and *Die Geliebten*, never completed or published, began by paralleling one another, but they contained basically opposing material, one topic an intellectual-spiritual concern and the other personal and emotional; the two intertwined, however, in Thomas Mann's 1902–3 short stories. The novella "The Hungry Ones" introduces "Tonio Kröger," itself following by "Ein Glück," stories which fictionalize emotions from Mann's notes for *Die Gelieb-ten*. At the same time, each story exhibits one facet of the intellectual com-plex springing from *Fiorenza* and involving Art, the "will to live" (*Wille zum Leben*), Power, Will and the Power to Overcome, and the concept of Great-ness. He developed these central ideas further in his unpublished essay "Geist und Kunst."

"The Hungry Ones"

Since Mann's vacation at Aalsgaard in the fall of 1899, he had been slowly formulating the setting and some motifs for "Tonio Kröger." His insight into the complicated topics he had introduced in "Tristan" had ripened gradually, and during the spring of 1902 he was reading widely and experiencing a great deal of music. During the following summer in Munich he was wrestling with "Tonio Kröger," tense, lonely, depressed, irritable, and having difficulty untangling his problems. In this stressful mood he produced "The Hungry Ones" ("Die Hungernden"), which he called "a psychological study."[5] "The Hungry Ones" is a plotless monologue which attempts to convey a young man's moods and thoughts; he feels rejected because his loved one prefers another and bitterly leaves a party, feeling isolated because of his "unalter-able calling" (EHL). (*STD*, 165; *GW*, 8: 260). Mann unhesitatingly classifies the autobiographical figure as an "artist" (*Künstler*), increasing the hero's torment by his pride in his artistry, tinged with somewhat artificial self-pity for the isolation that he feels adds to his prestige.

The title "The Hungry Ones" refers less to the missing plot than to Mann's basic concept, because both physically and on the abstract level, "hunger" represents an vital need. If "hunger" remains unsatisfied, it will lead to star-vation and finally destruction. The trivial ending of "The Hungry Ones," in which Detlef confronts a starving wastrel, would seem artificial if the "world-view" (*Weltbild*) Mann had derived from the *Dreigestirn* did not illumine "The Hungry Ones."[6] "Hunger," a distressing vacuum of the body or mind, is all the more frustrating because it can be satisfied by simple, natural means. Most terrifyingly, it recurs shortly after it has been satisfied, corresponding perfectly to Schopenhauer's concept of the unceasing striving for appease-ment of the "will to live" (*Wille zum Leben*), the most deceptive mirage of the *principium individuationis*, which by nature and purpose can never rest in peace. The *principium individuationis* is a kind of madness (*Wahn*), an eternal hunger, devouring the self (*Selbstkannibalismus*) in a never-ending senseless succession. Only the act of overcoming the *principium individua-tionis* allows the insight of stillness and unity behind the turmoil of the world of representation.

Mann dramatized his own uneasy mood in the summer of 1902 in the fictional setting of "The Hungry Ones" ("Die Hungernden"). The plural title alludes to lovers like Detlef who suffer from an unquenchable longing (*Sehnsucht*) equal to starvation, caused by the "will to live" in the world of "representation." The awkward, artificial ending of "The Hungry Ones" suggests that only love can overcome such torment.[7] The most significant contribution of "The Hungry Ones," a preparatory exercise for "Tonio Kröger," is the light it sheds on Mann's work and mood in the summer of 1902, for it represents a link in the gradual development of his thoughts from "Tristan" to "Tonio Kröger," and certain passages of "Tonio Kröger" seem more sophisticated versions of sections in "The Hungry Ones." Quite possibly he had already written the first section of "Tonio Kröger" that depressed summer, as he mentions that he had difficulty in proceeding after section four, Tonio's discussion with Lisabeta, but even though he hinted at a new short story in various letters, no evidence indicates that he had more than notes for "Tonio Kröger" prior to the summer of 1902.

The summer of 1902 found Mann in a vacuum; he had the will to write, but the "hunger for life," the awful emptiness between longing and achievement, immobilized him. "The Hungry Ones" is hard to read and harder to remember, because it is a patchwork of shredded thoughts and moods eager for life but without a defined goal. The closing statements are significant only in the Schopenhauerian context, and without it they might well seem one of the few touches of *Kitsch* from Mann's pen.

Detlef of "The Hungry Ones" is a writer, like Detlev Spinell in "Tristan," although Mann gives no clues to Detlef's writings. The setting of "The Hungry Ones" is colorful but artificial, rather like the party scenes in such earlier stories as "Little Herr Friedemann," but it lacks their zealous observation. Mann does refer to a grotesque clarinet rendition of the music of *Tristan und Isolde* in "The Hungry Ones," like Bajazzo's Wagnerian parody, a masochistic degradation of the message of "Tristan," which contains the experience of art. In "Tristan," Mann held Wagner's music in the highest esteem, satirizing only the impotent onlookers. In "The Hungry Ones," he reverses the situation, distorting the music itself to pander to the crowd's desire to exploit its inherent powers, but Detlef can sense this. "Four or five actors in peasant costume were parodying with clarinets and stringed instruments the chromatic wrestling of the *Tristan* music" (*STD*, 168; *GW*, 8: 264). Detlef's vacillation between his wish to seclude himself from the crowd and his longing to be accepted allows a new dimension to his conflict. *Einheitssehnsucht* (a word of Mann's coinage meaning the "longing for [universal] unity") emphasizes Schopenhauer's key concept. Its vision is an all-embracing version of the *Liebestod* ("Death by Love"), the ultimate message of *Tristan und Isolde*. A clarinet parody of the immortal music degrades the metaphysical concept[8] to a base desire to be at one with the eating, sweating, dancing, and loving mob.

The crux is Mann's admission of the love that attracts him to the common folk, the admission that had made his work on "Tonio Kröger" so painful, his desire to share the life of the "burgher" (*Bürger*) he had earlier rejected as the earthbound "will to live" seen in the elder and the younger Klöterjahns. His admission, however, does not simplify his concept, which at this point is complicated by the metaphysical and Schopenhauerian "longing for unity" ("*Einheitssehnsucht*), representing genuine "insight," a vision swept clear of the veil of Maya. In "The Hungry Ones," the first motif is the hero's withdrawal from the circle of the "others," dramatized by his passion for "one of them," the blond Lily; next "love" is intensified into the "longing for universal unity." Then the hero's tragic inability to reach this goal with his final attempt to reach another individual, one also suffering from "hunger" in the cold winter night is dramatized. "The Hungry Ones" reflect Mann's stern philosophical discipline, but his dramatic portrayal of emotions involves the melodramatic self-pity of his earlier stories. The hothouse fictional setting, structurally oversimplified, cannot express his condensed message, and so Mann fruitlessly tried to defend his profound ideas when this psychological study was unfavorably received.

Mann's admission of his attraction to the "ordinary" is completed by the statement that Detlef cannot be a part of the crowd because he is inherently different from them since he is an artist, an intrinsically different being with a special place in life. He wrote to Paul Ehrenberg on 28 January 1902; "I would have said 'come visit me one day' if I were justified in assuming that you do not belong to all the 'others' who find the talent most respectable and the man repulsive . . ." (EHL).

Mann's negative concept of the "burgher" changed radically after he wrote "Tristan," whereas he had represented them via the Klöterjahns, he now exemplified them in the "The Hungry Ones" with Lily possibly modeled after Lilli Teufel, a young painter from Munich who later married the artist Paul Ehrenberg. "The little painter" was possibly modeled on Paul Ehrenberg, notoriously casual in love affairs; but were blond[9] and blue-eyed, real children of the "will to live." Mann now cries out in "The Hungry Ones," "The realm of the pleasant, the normal, and the respectable, it is life in all its tempting, banal, everydayness that we want . . ." (*STD*, 169; *GW*, 8: 256–56). Even though some lines in "The Hungry Ones" correspond to certain new ideas Mann will present in "Tonio Kröger," "The Hungry Ones" retains certain basic images of "Tristan." The recurring darkness, for example, suggests introspective night, where enlightenment of the spirit can occur.[10]

In the closing of "The Hungry Ones" Mann attempts to juxtapose the physical and emotional concepts of hunger, but his ponderous Schopenhauerian arguments seem remote: "Ah, we are all brothers, we creatures of the *restlessly suffering will* [emphasis added], yet we do not recognize ourselves as such. Another love is needed, another love" (*STD*, 172; *GW*, 8: 270). The passage recalls Thomas Buddenbrook's speech after his "Schopenhauer trauma." Mann still hungered, however; "I am working, even if only painfully and more then usually, a line at a time, because what I am planning, a longer novella, again is something difficult, so that it absolutely will require some time . . ." (EHL) [letter to Kurt Martens, 10 October 1902). "The Hungry Ones" first appeared in *Zukunft* 11, no. 17 (24 January 1903), periodical published by Maximilian Harden.

"Tonio Kröger"

Thomas Mann's brief vacation at the Danish seaside resort of Aalsgaard[11] in the fall of 1899 saw the birth of "Tonio Kröger." His rigorous self-discipline and writing habits kept him from yielding to this tempting project, which might have given him welcome relief from the tension of the last chapters of *Buddenbrooks*. Aalsgaard provided him the inspiration for the setting and even part of the action of "Tonio Kröger," but the total theme, for which he needed growth, was far from clear in his mind in 1899. He eventually developed the theme through three crucial experiences: the reading of Schopenhauer he made a few weeks after the trip to Aalsgaard, a reading that inspired the closing chapters of *Buddenbrooks*; his construction of the theoretical and intellectual novella "Tristan"; and the warm critical reception of *Buddenbrooks*. Only after these could Thomas Mann approach the concept of "artisthood" (*Künstlertum*) that was growing in his consciousness, express it in aesthetic form, and at last live up to the stringent artistic standards he had set for himself.

Mann's notes also show that at times ideas in "Tristan" overlapped those for "Tonio Kröger." In fact, concepts discussed completely only in "Tonio Kröger" had begun to develop as he worked on *Buddenbrooks* and "Tristan" between 1899 and 1903. Even if Paolo Hofmann, Friedemann, and Bajazzo each appeared to be an artistic-fictional reflection of Thomas Mann himself at various stages, Tonio Kröger and the message his tale contains is a new theme that leads to a different perception of his personal situation. He could not substantialize and express his theme as a work of art until he had acknowledged and accepted his vocation as an artist or a "poet", as he liked to identify himself (*Künstler*) at the same time dissolving his earlier self-image of a misfit who escapes via art. This new estimate of the value of his own creativity began to take shape when S. Fischer accepted the unabridged manuscript of *Buddenbrooks* in the spring of 1901.

The genre of "Tonio Kröger" is entirely new for Mann. His "Tristan" presents a theoretical "worldview" framed from existential and paradoxical (*Burleske*) concepts, but "Tonio Kröger" is a delicate lyrical expression of the intellectual and emotional struggle of a soul for maturity. While "Tristan" can be considered the imaginative presentation of an intellectual vision, the rational structure of "Tonio Kröger" is carried on waves of intimate, passionate emotions, leading far deeper into the hero's heart than did "Tristan," as Thomas Mann himself observed: " 'Tonio Kröger' is a totally lyric little poetic work grown out of intimate experiences, which surely had unconscious deferences to the *geistig* situation of its time, but which in a strange manner continually touches young people of each new succeeding generation with its youthful lyricism" (EHL) (Thomas Mann's letter to Fritz Friedländer, 26 February 1953).

"Tristan"'s setting, action, and characters are all overwhelmingly symbolic, the fictional realization of Mann's concept of a Schopenhauerian universe. On the other hand, the same elements of "Tonio Kröger" belong to Mann's own sphere of existence, which enabled him to shape his personal experiences with meticulous sensitivity and verisimilitude.

In the decade preceding "Tonio Kröger," Mann had spent considerable time in Italy, chiefly because of Heinrich, who increasingly found the Italian Renaissance spirit more and more indispensable. Mann chose the North for his vacation in 1899 because he yearned for the environment of his childhood at the same time that he recognized his true feelings toward the Southern mentality.[12] In his address to the Nobel Prize Committee on 10 December 1929, Thomas Mann said:

> As a young person I wrote a story which still appeals well to young people, 'Tonio Kröger.' It is about the south and north and the mixture of both in one person, a mixture full of conflicts and productivity. The south is in this story the quintessence of all [that is] *geistig*, sensual adventures, of the cold passion of being an artist; the north, on the contrary, [is] the quintessence of cordiality and the burgher homeland, of all feelings residing in the depth of all intimate humanity. And now it [my homeland] embraces and welcomes me, this Nordic homeland of the heart, in a sparkling festival. . . . (EHL; *GW*, 11: 410)

The setting of "Tonio Kröger" faithfully reflects Mann's own experiences, but the journey from north to south *and back again* to the "point of origin" (*Ausgangspunkt*) is essential to the theme, allowing him to express a deeply Romantic search for fulfillment in the return to one's origins. Tonio's trip thus symbolizes the artist's journey toward mature insight.[13]

In a letter to Heinrich dated 29 December 1900. Mann mentioned that he was working on "a new novella of a bitter melancholy character. . . ." In the spring of 1901,[14] he suggested a new volume of short stories to contain, among others, "perhaps a long-planned novella with the unaesthetic but exciting title 'Litteratur' (*Illae* lacrimae!)," but this collection never materialized.[15] Mann's friendship with Paul Ehrenberg and his excitement at *Buddenbrooks*'s acceptance made it hard for him to join Heinrich in Florence in the spring of 1901. He might have already completed some pages of the new story—"Tonio Kröger"—when he finally did leave Munich, but clearly this was difficult, and subsequently he had to put it aside several times. "Tonio Kröger" was probably completed in Riva, from which he returned to Munich on 15 November 1902, taking a new apartment at 11 Konradstraße in

Swabing. Fischer must have received "Tonio Kröger" around the end of that
year, since the story appeared under that new and permanent title in the
February 1903 issue of the *Neue deutsche Rundschau*, where it was an immediate success. On 4 February 1903, Mann presented it in a public reading
for the Lessing Gesellschaft, with "The Way to the Churchyard," and again
the next day for the Verein der Berliner Presse. His 1903 short story collection was a sturdy book of 264 pages with an appealing little cover by Alfred
Kubin, selling well and achieving great popularity, especially among young
readers. To 1980 "Tonio Kröger" sold about 200,000 copies as Mann's most
popular piece of short fiction.

From the start "Tonio Kröger" was clearly the name of the story's hero,
but Mann settled on the title only while completing the story. His earlier title,
"Litteratur," pertains to the topic of its middle portion, section four, in
which Tonio Kröger discusses the art of writing with Lisabeta.[16] "Litteratur"
focuses on Thomas Mann's expression of his aesthetic theories, since art was
an intellectually "exciting" (*spannend*) topic to him. He initially wanted the
story to reveal the artistic insight of a hero whose name referred directly to
Mann's own intellectual conflict and dual nature. "Tonio," that Romantic
first name, possibly inspired by Leoncavallo's Tonio in *Pagliacci*, accompanies
Latin ethnic characteristics of dark hair and complexion, recalling Mann's
own artistic and musical South American mother; "Kröger," the name of the
paternal grandmother's family in *Buddenbrooks*, evokes the Nordic qualities
of dependability, a somewhat crass healthy vitality, and bourgeois virtue. The
dynamic stress in the name "Tonio Kröger" substantializes the story's theme,
simultaneously representing Mann's own structural and qualitative intellectual and emotional anatomy. Contrasting Apollinian[17] and Dionysian
concepts[18] appear in the conceptual stress represented by this name. In emphasizing the theme of "North" and South," "Tonio Kröger" also depends on
Goethe's similar "North-South" theme in *Faust*.[19] The name Tonio Kröger is
in itself the most important formal and thematic leitmotif of Mann's best-
loved story.

The originally purely theoretical subject of "Litteratur" is developed in
three stages, each reflecting a realization of Tonio Kröger's position and his
heartfelt conception of "artisthood" (*Künstlertum*), more meaningful, more
intimate, and yet more mature each time, becoming a profound confession of
a newly attained insight into the nature of art, the artist, and his place in the
world. Later he referred in his work to musical forms,[20] but it is not certain
that he had any conscious intentions to do so with "Tonio Kröger," though its
structure is often likened to sonate form. He did subsequently write in a letter
to Emil Preetorius 12 December 1947, "I am really not a man of the visual but
rather a musician transformed into literature . . ." (EHL). His expression of
"Tonio Kröger"'s theme encompasses harmony and rhythm that enhances its
lyric sensitivity.

"Tonio Kröger" is formally divided into nine unequal parts which differ in structure, thematic function and significance.[21] The opening paragraph immediately evokes the humid, windy atmosphere of the old Hanseatic town, and the second reveals the categories of prestige dominating the school's faculty and student body.[22] Mann suddenly abandons the descriptive mode when Tonio steps into the scene, asking, " 'Are you finally coming, Hans?' " (EHL) (*GW*, 8: 271; see also *STD*, 85). This simple question compresses all of Tonio's emotions—love, longing, and hope—which dominate the first section of the story and then change significantly as Tonio matures in *Geist*.[23] The sensitive Tonio is emotionally dependent on Hans, making their friendship one-sided.

Mann's Aalsgaard notes indicate that the very appropriate name of Tonio's friend Hans Hansen did not enter the story early. Mann had in fact collected Nordic names, and he had seriously considered the name Tage[24] before choosing the more German but still Northern-sounding "Hans Hansen." Hans Hansen, in his name as in his whole being, represents everything that Tonio Kröger is not, everything that had always attracted Thomas Mann. "Hans Hansen," with nearly identical first and last names marked by deep repeated 'ah' sounds, contrasts sharply with the deeply melodious "Tonio" and the high, finely-chiseled "Kröger." The straightforward sound pattern of "Hans Hansen" perfectly illustrates his character, in opposition to the restless combination of "Tonio" and "Kröger."

A recurrent motif in Mann's early short fiction is the opposition between the blond Nordic physical type and the brunette Latin characteristics of his protagonists.[25] Since "Der Wille zum Glück," dark features had represented Latin qualities he had inherited from his beloved, beautiful half-Portuguese mother Julia Mann, a sensitive and imaginative woman who played the piano well. Mann's propensity for hard work, efficiency, organization, discipline, and achievement came from his North German father, Johannes Heinrich Mann, the embodiment of all these virtues. Mann both strongly shared his parents' basic tendencies and loved them profoundly, and in him one side quite consciously observed the other. As a youngster, he felt the "uncommon" maternal qualities singled him out; he reached out longingly to the "other" side of his personality, his father's side, trying to understand, justify, and accept his own "difference," an exploration of self that formed a growing and highly personal theme in his work, the realization and ultimately the understanding of his own definition of *Künstlertum*. The concept of art and artistry, or being an artist—Künstlertum—has always been his major creative theme, but Mann's genuine self-expression of the artist's vocation appears to be an original creation.

One of Thomas Mann's individaul artistic qualities, his "dual optic" (*doppelte Optik*),[26] the substantialization of abstract concepts into obvious action in the plot , ties into an artistic message that appears to him as an intellectually sound structure. The surface action becomes the vehicle of the abstract concept of Mann's own experience of life, which then attains universal relevancy. Such recurrent "surface level" imagery is his parallel to Wagner's leitmotif.

The notion of becoming lonely and isolated (*Vereinsamung*) has now matured in Mann's work. His "difference" from his fellows weighed heavily on him, and in "Tonio Kröger," he confessed his problem of identification and confronted the choice between "burgerlyness" (*Bügertum*) and "artisthood" (*Künstlertum*). His focus on the theme represented the "surface" level of the "dual optic," and the fictionalized topic was at once heated by his deeply felt emotions and intellectualized by his inherent concepts of the Apollinian and the Dionysian concept as well as the contrast between the Socratic and the Barbaric images of the world in Nietzsche's *Birth of Tragedy*, parallels which illumine his repeated textual references.

The idealistic and emotional friendship Mann had developed with the young painter Paul Ehrenberg and his bride, the Munich artist Lilli Teufel, may have given him models for Hans Hansen and Ingeborg Holm in "Tonio Kröger." All of his early stories, including "Tonio Kröger," refer repeatedly to youthful crushes on blond and blue-eyed dancing classmates. Some of his fictional figures possess characteristics suited to both Armin Martens and Paul Ehrenberg—a cheery spirit, robust health, brash physicality, success with peers, and a superficial neglect of Mann's tender, dreamy, somewhat stuffy attachment. The dark, sensitive, artistically inclined Thomas Mann felt both dramatically different from and magnetically attracted to these beautiful, insensitive, healthy, and happy people, a problem that gradually became the major theme of his life, especially since he realized that certain qualities made him incapable of functioning among the "others," while those very qualities simultaneously represented his spark of *Künstlertum*. For Thomas Mann, *Künstlertum* mysteriously opposed health (*Buddenbrooks*) and even life ("The Way to the Churchyard"), and concurrently held the key to enduring superior metaphysical values. Such a person is "chosen," and so "being different" means to be "more" than the "others."[27]

Restricting Mann's contrast between blond and dark physical types to merely autobiographical expression would oversimplify a complex issue, for the motif of contrast had blossomed into the vehicle of his unsolved personal, intellectual, and emotional problems. Once he had overcome them, the motif of blond and dark as well as the thematic attraction to blond people disappears from his work, although names with contrasting characteristics continue to appear.

The upper-middle-class merchant background of Tonio Kröger and Hans Hansen is a natural setting for Mann's autobiographical theme. Out of this identical windy, chilly Hanseatic environment, the great dissimilarity of the boys' reactions became a near-ideal means of illustrating his theme. He established the contrast between the boys first through details of their expensive clothing, such as Hans's sailor cap and Tonio Kröger's fur hat, and then in their eyes and their different gaits. Once he has drawn attention to their extreme dissimilarity, he introduces their emotional and intellectual qualities; Hans seems pleasant, friendly, and completely decent; he is intelligent and has a sharp intellect, and he realizes quite well what Tonio's problem is. In his own way, he likes Tonio and now realizes he has hurt him. To make amends, he directly touches the sore spot, taking Tonio's arm and explaining that he had not forgotten their agreement to walk together. Compared to Hans's sensitivity, Tonio's is excessive.[28]

"The matter was, that Tonio loved Hans Hansen . . ." (*GW*, 8: 273). The paragraph that opens with these words probes Tonio's fourteen-year-old conception of love, a love whose intellecutal significance and psychological ramifications gradually convey the whole message. This development of Thomas Mann (*Entwicklung* and *Bildung*), the maturing consciousness of love, parallels Tonio's aesthetic growth and his deepening realization of his position in the "burgher" environment. In "Tonio Kröger," this process develops in three stages:

a. Tonio experiences the concepts of Love and Art through Schiller's *Don Carlos* and relates his ideas to his subjective feeling (sections 1–2);
b. Tonio objictifies and discusses the formal-objective and the emotional-subjective components of Art in his life (section 4);
c. Tonio grows to understand and to define his concept of Art and his place in the world, verbalizing his definitions (sections 5–9).

Mann conceptualizes the word "love" as a positive outgoing power without egocentric,[29] sensual, or sexual undertones, although the tension in these passages might be described as erotic.[30] The powerful complex of emotions known as "love" can cause both extreme happiness and pain, and Tonio Kröger knows and enjoys that pain as well as the bliss love causes him, since rather than trying to escape such experiences, he treasures them deeply.[31] Such experiences give his life a dimension beyond his classmates' ordinary growth. Tonio's violin, the fountain in the garden, the walnut tree, the North Sea, all evoke the dimension of his dreams; all are things he had loved since his childhood and which are connected with his writing. At this point Mann reveals that Tonio wrote verses, a questionable pastime in the eyes of his teachers. When Tonio Kröger's family background appears, he further emphasizes the contrast between his brunette Latin mother and the typically Nordic Consul Kröger.[32]

Tonio's love for his mother was quite different from his feeling for Hans. Tonio warmly admired her beauty and her music with a nonrational, pacific, and simple love that incorporated a touch of guilt. It strangely clashed with his heartfelt recognition of the orderliness, decency, and stability put into his life by his father, that blond, blue-eyed man with the wild flower in his buttonhold. This passage contains one of Mann's individual "pattern phrases," sometimes called leitmotifs, which he classified as "formal" and "thematic"; "Most of all, the oral 'leitmotif' in 'Tonio' was no longer merely naturalistic

[and] purely an exterior descriptive [term], as it had been in *Buddenbrooks*; now it had gained an ideal emotional transparency which freed it from its mechanical quality and lifted it into the musical" (EHL) (*GW*, 9: 247; *SML*, 32; *GW*, 8: 116). As an example, the boy Tonio, considering his own short-comings, weighs his father's stern principles against his mother's relaxed attitude, and adopts his father's viewpoint: "After all, we are not gypsies living in a green wagon; we are respectable people, the family of Consul Kröger."[33]

Tonio proceeds to wonder at his difference from his teachers and schoolmates, who represent the solid majority, and his casual youthful soliloquy, a childish recognition of his inherent difference from his fellows, presents the first stage of the theme of the entire story. Tonio's acceptance of both his rejection by the rest of humanity and his love and longing for them is embodied in Hans Hansen, whom he loved so much: ". . . because he was in every respect his own opposite and foil" (*STD*, 88; *GW*, 8: 275). Tonio even cries out in gentle envy: "If one could [only] have such blue eyes and could live in such perfect harmony with the whole world!" (EHL).[34] However, Tonio never wants to be just like Hans Hansen; Tonio values most the bliss of opposites that attract.

Tonio burns to share with Hans his secret treasure, the experience of Schiller's *Don Carlos*. The conversation is appropriate to the boys' age, with German repetitions of such words as "weeping" and "betray" lost in translation, as in Tonio's touching attempt to engage Hans by using "horsy" vocabulary to describe abstractions: " 'There are passages in it [*Don Carlos*], you will see, which are so beautiful they pull you up, so that it cracks [like a whip]. . .' " (EHL) (*GW*, 8: 277; see also *STD*, 89). Emotions do not ordinarily "pull you up," and the expression "*knallt*," generally used in connection with riding crops, would seem farfetched without Jimmerthal, the budding cavalryman. Hans himself does not immediately understand, and Tonio passionately seizes the chance to pour out his heart while describing King Philip's tragic loneliness, revealing himself so pointedly that Hans senses his emotions and takes his arm.

Their idyllic moment is interrupted by a schoolmate, Ervin Jimmerthal, one of "the others."[35] Hans Hansen turns to him and rattles on about favorite mounts and riding lessons. Hans now addresses Tonio as "Kröger," and even describes Tonio[36] as strange and slippery as he feeds Tonio's fruit toffees to Jimmerthal. After this Jimmerthal disappears from the story; he only serves to point up Tonio's discomfort and illustrate his distance from the "others' " world. Tonio recoils, feeling as though he could weep as bitterly as King Philip. The gusty wet wind embodies the boy's gray mood, but after Jimmerthal leaves, Hans says, " 'And I'll read *Don Carlos* pretty soon, too' "; after that, on their way home, the wind at Tonio's back, "he [Tonio] went off transfigured as though on wings" (*STD*, 91–92; *GW*, 8: 280–81).

The first section of "Tonio Kröger" thus introduces Mann's protagonists and his theme: Tonio's isolation. Supporting this theme are his love for Hans, the "other," and his poetry, which affords a striking glimpse into his hidden life. The closing lines of this section, however, introduce two new leitmotifs. The exceedingly happy moments marked by love, hope, enthusiastic rapture—"Damals lebte sein Herz"[37]—and a quivering pulsation of the heart recur several times for Tonio Kröger and these moments are marked in the story by this motif. The other motif is implicit in the assertion that "Sehnsucht war darin und schwermütiger Neid und ein klein wenig Verachtung und eine ganze keusche Seligkeit,"[38] a passage that differs only slightly from the last lines of the story. The earlier passage, cited above, employs the past narrative tense, since the author is narrating Tonio's feelings; and the present tense used at the end of the story empowers Tonio Kröger, the mature artist, consciously to express himself. The first section of "Tonio Kröger" thus introduces the protagonists and the theme: Tonio's isolation from the world. With Ingeborg Holm in section two, Tonio encounters another kind of love. Ingeborg's father, a physician, lived on the town plaza near an old Gothic fountain. The motifs of the fountain, the walnut tree, the violin, and the North Sea are "the things he, Tonio, loved." This love is not at all the same as that which Tonio had felt for Hans.[39] Tonio Kröger is now sixteen, and his first love for a woman brings him suffering and humiliation, at the same time that he cherishes the experience—just as he had with Hans Hansen.

In the deliciously humorous description of the peculiar dancing master, François Knaak, Tonio achieves a disillusioned definition of the "others."[40] The soaring contrast between Knaak's light elegance and Tonio's embarrassing mistake in the quadrille emphasizes Tonio's loneliness and humiliation. Magdalena Vermehren,[41] the shy, clumsy girl with the beautiful brown eyes who loved and understood Tonio, represents an important psychological element of Tonio's emotional and mental makeup, as the passage exhibits Tonio's indifference toward those who, like himself, long passionately for "the others" so different than themselves.

The last message of the second section closely resembles that of the first; even though love causes suffering, it still is essential to happiness. The motif *"Damals lebte sein Herz"* (see n. 37) recurs here as well, but this love also fades into oblivion. In the first two sections of the story, Tonio's love for Hans and Ingeborg kept his heart "alive"; he learned to suffer and thereby experienced great happiness.

The autobiographical material in the first part of section 3 forms a sketchy transition from Tonio's early youth to adulthood. His family's[42] decline in fortune and his father's death are followed by his travels to Italy, as he leaves behind his beloved home town, the cold damp wind off the North Sea, the fountain, and the walnut tree. Tonio Kröger then surrenders to pseudo-intellectual snobbery, which he defines as the power of the word upon the intellect; he "looked down on the lowly and vulgar life he had led so long" (*STD*, 98; *GW*, 8: 288). This makes him even more lonely;[43] now that he believes that he can analyze everything, his arrogant, fierce "rationalization"

(*Rationalisierung*) isolates him even more. At this point, the leitmotif "*Damals lebte sein Herz*" is reversed: now his heart is "dead and loveless" (*STD*, 99; *GW*, 8: 289–90; see n. 37). He helplessly snatches at carnal delights, which make him suffer even more, but such torment is his only "spiritual joy." He is torn between two extremes, driven from the rational to the physical. Tonio Kröger detests this tension between the two extremes of his life, and the gypsy motif occurs here for the third time in the story, this time more highly pitched.

As Tonio's health declines,[44] his aesthetic sensitivity and taste become keener.[45] The final passage of section three prepares for the high point at the center of the novella, the discussion between Tonio and Lisabeta, in which Mann fictionalizes his own basic problem through wit, form, and taste to avoid revealing himself completely to the hydra-headed public. When Walter Opitz complained to him of the distance between them, Thomas Mann replied (5 December 1903): "You complain that you have not arrived at a 'closer relationship' with me; but suppose that there were a reason to complain: would this not signify something like ingratitude? No one can come nearer to me than one who is, like you, a reader of 'Tonio Kröger';. . . Is this not making a confidence? Well, then, shame on you, and say nothing more about a 'relationship'!" (EHL). As he indicated in the recurrent phrase "his heart was alive," to live life to its fullest means to have emotions; but it also means to give of oneself untiringly. After his reading of Schopenhauer in 1899, Mann had suffered agonies of self-doubt along with Thomas Buddenbrook, finally dissecting this traumatic experience, regrouping it logically, and at last fictionalizing it in "Tristan."

The acceptance of *Buddenbrooks* had made the intellectual problem of "*Literatur*" or "Litteratur," as he refers to it at this time, a very personal issue for Mann. When he wrote about Tonio Kröger, he humbly probed his own preoccupations and brought himself to confirm them validly. The truth, the beauty, and the sensitivity of this confession make "Tonio Kröger" a work of art. The two aspects of the leitmotif—"his heart was alive" and "his heart was dead"—mark the thematic polarity of "Tonio Kröger." He had to unify them to achieve the theme of the novella, but at this point, Tonio Kröger cannot see any possibility of reconciling them. He rationalizes cynically when he says, ". . . one has to be dead in order to completely be someone who can create. . ." (EHL) (*STD*, 100; *GW*, 8: 292).

In "Tonio Kröger"'s triptych form the first three numbered sections form the first part; the fourth section, containing the exposition of Tonio's intellectual problem, the second part; and section five through nine the third part. In the first section Tonio is seen as a boy and in the second he is a sixteen-year-old; in the third, time has passed without any dialogue to simulate movement. The fourth section, the second part, has only one scene, entirely in dialogue; Tonio Kröger appears, hat in hand, at the studio door of his friend Lisabeta Ivanovna,[46] a painter, formally asking to be admitted. Lisabeta, an accomplished artist, jokes about Tonio's formality, which with his meticulous grooming and manners reveals his resemblance to his "burgher" father, Consul Kröger.

The detailed description of Lisabeta's work corresponds significantly to Tonio's mental panorama. The colored sketches around her easel are her intuitive notes for her initial inspirations. The enmeshed[47] schematic charcoal lines on the canvas, where the first colors are beginning to appear, depict the form, organization, and composition of her concept, and Lisabeta's artistic effort to correlate and balance the subjective and intuitively expressive color with formal perspective and composition demands her total concentration; she must ask Tonio to excuse her for a moment while she adjusts a detail.[48] The Slavic spirit had held a special magic for Mann ever since he had become acquainted with Russian literature, and, significantly, Lisabeta is Russian.[49]

His description of the setting is typically in focus; the large north window of the studio admits light and the song of birds, and the fragrances of spring and odors of oil and fixative blend together. The natural elements represent the joy of life, while the artistic aromas stand for the techniques of art (*Kunst*). The same light brightens both the severely bare walls of the work space and Lisabeta's little living room, contrasting artistic discipline "burgherly" (*bürgerlich*) comforts. The theme of polarities that attract each other climaxes in the conversation Tonio has with Lisabeta. The Dionysian element, represented by spring with all its vital intoxication, and the Apollinian, conveyed through the sensual and abstract symbols of art, clearly represent extremes. Lisabeta, who can reconcile the artist by overcoming the self, unites the Apollinian and the Dionysian and gives the instinctual Dionysian the realization of an Apollianian work of art. Tonio, who has not yet achieved his own concept of art, vacillates from one extreme to the other—from "dehumanized" technical structuralism to a reckless surrender to spring's intoxication.

Tonio Kröger's appearance is described in this section through contrast. Tonio's tastefully reserved grooming clashes with his upset, fatigued expression. He tells Lisabeta," '. . . inside my head it looks just the way it does on this canvas' "(*STD*, 96; *GW*, 8: 293), a statement that brings the internal conflict implicit, in his name into clear perspective. The characters Mann created for "Tristan" and those of "Tonio Kröger," are essentially dissimilar, since "Tristan" is his fictionalized *Weltanschauung* and "Tonio Kröger" his expression of self. In "Tristan," the characters are allegorical, while in "Tonio Kröger" they are the products of a distanced self-analysis.

All of Mann's earlier blond and blue-eyed characters were ancestors of Hans Hansen, but closest of all Hansen's fore-runners were the senior and junior Klöterjahns. Hans, whom Tonio loves but with whom he wants nothing in common, is not at all ridiculous, or repulsive, or even vulgar as were the Klöterjahns; Hans is an attractive, healthy, lovable representative of the "others," in the mainstream of human life. This contradiction is easy to understand: at the time Mann had just read Schopenhauer and had not yet begun "Tristan." He had theorized his topic with a somewhat supercilious disdain for its earthly element. Something of this pride[50] is discernible in Tonio's quasi-instinctive revulsion in the face of the spring, which, however, disappears completely by the end of the story. If the task of "Tonio Kröger" is to identify and define, it is section 4 of the story that identifies and sections 5 through 9 that define; in the center, section 4, Tonio's concept of art indeed resembles Lisabeta's unfinished canvas: it is a structural basis with as yet unidentifiable experiences.

While Hanno Buddenbrook's talent had not even allowed his sensitive personality to express a superior sort of music, and the impotent Spinell was a one-book caricature of an artist, Tonio's growth into *Künstlertum* gradually leads to fulfillment, because he is the first of Thomas Mann's characters capable of becoming a creative "artist." His problem was to identify himself as a person and understand the concepts of art. Discovering a balance of opposites he could accept and live with was Mann's first step toward the classical *Weltanschauung* and a significant understanding of Goethe, a serious, reverent, profoundly Romantic attraction, without the disdain, irony, or cynicism with which he had sometimes reacted to Nietzsche.[51] This explains Tonio's positive vitality, which appears in none of the other characters Mann connected with art. Since Tonio Kröger was attracted to the common human element (*das gewöhnlich Menschliche*), he had to learn to justify his art without rejecting the love of human beauty and the commonplace things of the world that represent life.[53] Tonio's love for the world was also rational because he loved it for its taste, its order, its proportions, and its existing harmonies. Finally, the sensitive Tonio loved life for its *walnut trees*, *violins*, *fountains*, and the *North Sea*. All of these represent the undercurrent of the Dionysian, but they also stand for the simply emotional and spontaneous commonplace; in using them in his art, Thomas Mann attained their union with the symbolic Apollinian expression of art as well as the substantialization which would be meaningful to receptive minds. Similarly, Tonio Kröger sought to bring these contrasting elements into a union within himself.

In both "Tristan" and "Tonio Kröger" a third protagonist mediates between two extremes; in "Tristan" it is Detlev Spinell, and in "Tonio Kröger" it is Lisabeta Ivanovna. Lisabeta has nothing of Spinell's ridiculous artificiality; she is all heart and insight and seems to be not only a creative artist but a warm human being, while Spinell was only a poor imitation of an artist. Only Lisabeta, the accomplished artist and the motivating factor for the hero's action, can comprehend both sides of Tonio Kröger. She maintains the balance of the story, since her personality represents static harmony and inspires dynamic action in helping the instinctive element in Tonio develop into the symbolic.

Even though the Schopenhauer experience had a primary significance for Mann at this time, the Nietzschean Apollinian and Dionysian elements he would later elaborate upon in "Death in Venice" were becoming increasingly important to him, with the clash between the formal, self-controlled, harmonious logic of the Apollinian and the instinctive subjective powers of Dionysian intoxication. Nietzsche believed that one of these forces could not exist without the other, and that the weight of emphasis constantly shifted between them. When perfect balance between the Apollinian and the Dionysian is reached, a Golden Age of cultural expression appears, fostering the perfect work of art. Tonio Kröger bitterly bursts out to Lisabeta about his conflicts, amidst the spring fragrances and the fixatives, the bewildering intoxication of the spring[53] and "sensible ideas," and "the detached and elevated sphere of the literary man."[54] At this moment he has no satisfactory personal concept of art: "The comic and misery—the comic and misery. There came with the torment and the arrogance of "insight," loneliness. . . ."[55] Lisabeta could understand his dilemma because she knew both sides of the problem. Moreover, she wanted to help Tonio overcome his obduracy. He had told her about his friend Adalbert, who had asked him to a café to escape the invigorating but unsettling influence of spring, and she both opposes Tonio's view of Adalbert's position and disapproves of Tonio's one-sided definition of the artist, to which he refers in section 4 as unchangeable fact. Another interesting term used in this passage is "adventurer" (*Abenteurer*); in this case the adventure is a spiritual experience, and the adventurer stands between a questor and a "swindler" (*Hochstapler*).[56] At this point in the story, Tonio feels that an "artist" (*Künstler*) is just that sort of individual. The "artist" as the servant of the all-powerful word can shape truth and manipulate reactions through his cynical rationalization.

Tonio does not understand his own disharmony: ". . . whether I should envy Adalbert or despise him for his ignorance . . ." (*STD*, 102; *GW*, 8: 295). This confession is the first step toward his development, and Lisabeta's sympathetic understanding and wise challenge guides him. Typically of Mann's analytic bent,[57] Tonio Kröger now dissects his problem into its components so that he can carry his thinking to its conclusion. Tonio tries to defend himself from the trap of the "feelings," where "feeling" represents the mixture of "feeling" (*Gefühl*) and "sensitivity" (*Empfindung*) without an insight into the delicate difference between the two, here buried in the text and omitted in the translation.[58] Tonio found it hard to admit a genuine feeling that contradicted his accepted value judgment of his environment.[59] He even goes so far as to call his literary vocation a curse. Indeed, he claims, " '. . . everyone knows you are not a human being, but something else: something queer, different, inimical" (*STD*, 104; *GW*, 8: 298). He feels the artist deserves admiration for enduring the suffering his isolation causes him, but the lack of trustworthiness which springs from the otherworldly element in his nature makes him unattractive. Tonio refers to artist with the expressions "dubious" (*fragwürdig*) and "suspicious" (*verdächtig*), terms which become key expressions for Thomas Mann in reference to the realms of the subconscious.

A reference to Wagner's *Tristan und Isolde* here not only clarifies Mann's concept of the "artist" (*Künstler*), but it also pertains to his statements regarding Wagner himself. The Schopenhauerian focus Mann had first had upon *Tristan und Isolde* now has changed into the point of view of a "burgher" (*Bürger*), who fears the questionable power this work of art could exert on him.[60]

Lisabeta appears to sympathize with Tonio's predicament. She urges him to have tea, assuring him it is not strong, and tells him to relax with a cigarette.[61] Just now, though, Tonio's spring-induced irritability makes him ignore her words, though nonetheless they are extremely important: "'I mean, Tonio Kröger, that one can consider them just exactly as well from another side. . . . of the purifying and healing influence of letters, the subduing of the passions by knowledge and eloquence; literature as the guide to understanding, forgiveness, and love, the redeeming power of the word, literary art as the noblest manifestation of the human mind, the poet as the most highly developed of human beings, the poet as saint. Is it to consider things not curiously enough, to consider them so?'"(*STD*, 106; *GW*, 8: 299–300).

Lisabeta's question has a variety of interpretations, she might be suggesting a definition of literature, part of the original goal Mann had had for this story, or she might have been teasing Tonio gently with an overstatement. Her character, too, suggests differing readings, for she might be so opposed to his position she can only patiently lead him to finding his own way. She may also represent either the "artist" (*Künstler*) par excellence,[62] or "sacred Russian literature." Possibly she provides a Schopenhauerian thought in her suggestion of the "most highly accomplished human being" (*vollkommener Mensch*) as something like *geniale Objektivität*, concurrently the "saint" (*Heiliger*), according to Thomas Mann's own definition.[63] She may even refer to the opposition of the Dionysian and the Apollinian, or the impulse toward the sensitive but sober equilibrium of Goethe. All of these concepts affected Mann's thinking, based on his intellectual affinity with the concepts of the *Dreigestirn* and Goethe and his *Zeitgeist*. In all of this, Tonio cannot yet understand Lisabeta completely, since he continues to refer to a psychological and analytic "insight" (*Erkenntnis*), a rationalizing process of enlightenment which brings on the "disgust at insight" (*Erkenntnisekel*).[64] Mann wrote about this word in "Freud und die Zukunft," April/May 1936: ". . . the word '*Erkenntnisekel*' is in 'Tonio Kröger.' It is of good Nietzschean coinage, and its youthful melancholy points toward the Hamlet-like [element] in Nietzsche's nature, in which his own [was] reflected, a nature with a vocation for knowledge without being born to it. They are youthful pains and sadnesses that I speak of here, and which have been led, by more mature years, toward the cheerful and more tranquil" (EHL). He also wrote in "On Myself" (p. 17): ". . . it [Tonio Kröger] is a typical work of youth, with its Hamlet-like melancholy, its "disgust at insight": filled with the same *geistig* and moral sensitivity against the common reality of the world with which the same theme is varied in the less personally colored 'Tristan,' written at the same time: the bashful love of the *geistig* for the flat, healthy life; a love, mixed from 'longing, melancholy envy and a little disdain' " (EHL). Hamlet's inability to act can be compared to Tonio's, for Tonio, despite his unusual gifts, has no self-determination. His raising the motif to a rational concept when he makes it ironic (*hamletische Redseligkeit*) ("Hamlet-like flow of oratory") (*STD*, 109; *GW*, 8: 305), shows, however, that he had an inner capacity for survival. At this point Tonio Kröger sees art as only cynical intellectualizing, but he has the strength not to take himself seriously.[65]

Tonio Kröger proceeds to analyze and deprecate the "artist" who is a "vain and frigid charlatan." The word *erledigt* is used with a touch of contempt: "That which is enunciated, so his creed went, is settled. If the world were enunciated, then it is settled, redeemed, dismissed . . ." (EHL).[66] Here Tonio attacks the cold analytic position of the "man of letters" (*Literat*) Lisabeta had previously mentioned. Tonio Kröger swings from one extreme to the other like a pendulum, and his acknowledgment of his love becomes a condemnation of the "artist's" (*Künstler's*) life. Life, he feels, the normal, the respectable and the "lovable" (EHL),[67] is the kingdom of our longing: " '. . . life, in all its seductive banality . . . the longing, Lisabeta, for the bliss of the commonplace!' " (EHL) (*STD*, 108; *GW*, 8: 302).

In the next paragraph, Tonio Kröger reaches the definition of his antithetic concepts. He sees that there are two types of people who do not understand him, the blue-eyed "others" who do not need the "*Geist*" and those with "fine souls in uncouth bodies, people who are always falling down in the dance" like Magdalena Vermehren. The concept of to "disdain" (*verachten*) reveals a clannish solidarity among those who sacrifice their lives to the arts by suffering and living as the "artist" must. Tonio's anecdote about the hapless poetry-writing lieutenant shows that a dilettente who dabbles in art is pitiable.

Lisabeta's final *ex cathedra* statements are in contrast with her earlier cautious counsel. She had only been helping Tonio proceed with his monologue, but her reaction seems to show that she had lived through the problem herself. She acts rather like a therapist who analyzes his patient through "talk," precisely what she does at the end of this section. Tonio's self-sacrificing acceptance of his artistry makes it seem harsh of her to call him simply a "burgher," an epithet that Tonio, in many ways the alter ego of Thomas Mann himself and hardly that of Klöterjahn, might justifiably protest, but Lisabeta does temper her assessment. "You are a "burgher" on a lost path, Tonio Kröger—a "burgher" gone astray" (EHL).[68] But Tonio Kröger cannot help but view the world and the problem of his own "artisthood" (*Künstlertum*) from the "burger's" standpoint: he swings from contemplation of his own "inhumanity" (*Unmenschlichkeit*) to his unconditional love of the commonplace.

Why should Lisabeta call Tonio "a "burgher" gone astray"? Though she classes him as a "burgher," she cannot dismiss him as a dilettante,[69] because of his intellectual insight won from deep suffering, which gives him certain of the *Künstler*'s rights. Lisabeta is meant to be enigmatic: should he abandon the notion of becoming an artist, or should she help him find himself? The closing of Tonio's letter to her at the end of the story suggests that she might not approve of his solution ("Do not chide this love, Lisabeta") (*STD*, 132; *GW*, 8: 338). His friendship with Lisabeta did not change, and barring some apprehension seen in his surprised and embarrassed departure, he seems to have accepted her message.

Tonio's statement at the end of section four, "Nun Kann ich getrost nach Hause gehen. Ich bin erledigt,"[70] can be read literally: " 'Well, then, I can go home [in confidence]. It's settled for me" (EHL). After such a confession, a person generally would not leave so abruptly; irony is always possible with Thomas Mann. "*Erledigt*" actually puts Lisabeta just where Tonio had earlier put the charlatan, as she now opens up his unconscious world for him. Tonio's hasty departure, either a contradiction of her or a reaction to her challenge, allows him to pursue the existential question: Will he be able to make his own decisions? In section five, he does so, and pleases both himself and Lisabeta by seeking out his roots.

Obviously more mature the next fall, Tonio tells Lisabeta Ivanovna his travel plans,[71] stressing his preference for the North over the South in his admiration for his father and Northern writers.[72] He particularly loves the music in the language, and he is filled with yearning for the land of Hamlet.[73] At Lisabeta's question, he admits, a little flustered, that he would like to see his home town again, his "point of departure" (*Ausgangspunkt*).[74]

The sixth section begins in a fairy tale–like mood interlaced with bittersweet irony, a combination appropriate to the modern German Romantic Käte Hamburger saw in Thomas Mann.[75] He allows the time long past to live again without slowing the story's action; his verisimilitude, as in the adult view of scenes from childhood now shrunken, portrays familiar phenomena to establish the dreamy moment Tonio returns home. Through the veil of the thirteen years since the death of his father, the living images of Hans Hansen and Ingeborg Holm wander with him on the narrow streets of the little old town. The damp salty wind summons him back to relative reality under the gaze of Lübeck's "sneezing lions,"[76] and he retains all his "burgherly" poise and grooming, though as always when he is frustrated, he whistles.

During his long sleep that night Tonio has peculiar dreams, a significant experience on the eve of an important change in his life. While emotional sensations are Dionysian, Apollinian dream perceptions reveal the initial stages of the substantialization of the subconscious; and Tonio's experience of a basically natural phenomenon begins the "life-rehabilitation" of his "dead heart." Before talking with Lisabeta in the spring, Tonio Kröger had been consciously resisting his emotions and his subjectivity. The many years he had spent aimlessly wrestling with his ideas and feelings were over, and he was now ready to let the stream of his inner feelings flow without battling them with rationalizations. His exhaustion came not only from his long journey but also from his powerful emotional and intellectual experiences. Mann mentions Tonio Kröger's dreaming sleep for the first time, for heretofore "dreaming" had only been mentioned among his waking actions. Later Tonio Kröger has another, more explicit sleeping dream, which marks a vital existential experience in his life, but at this time his dreams in his small hotel room are confused and yearning,[77] an exact reflection of his waking mood and a real stage on the path of his development.

Tonio took exceptional pains as he dressed,[78] listening "to the anxious beating of his heart" (*STD*, 113; *GW*, 8: 310). Earlier his love-torn heart had been described as "living," for his love for Hans and Ingeborg and the pain that came from that love had made it so, but in the long years while Tonio Kröger had served the demands of the Word, his heart had been "dead." Now after a night filled with anxious dreams, the meticulously groomed Kröger listened for what Tonio's heart might tell him.

Once out on the street, Tonio Kröger hoped that he would not be recognized, and since time had changed him, he was not. The motif of an actor's mask taking over a personality, first introduced in section four, now has a variation, the change in outward appearance stemming from deep intellectual and emotional torment appearing as the hallmark of *Künstlertum*. In the following three paragraphs, the wind[79] represents reality, as it strikes Tonio Kröger in the face, awakening his past. When Tonio Kröger enters his boyhood home, nearly identical to the Buddenbrooks house,[80] he finds a public library on the ground floor, a clever fictional detail to allow "strangers" to visit the house. The vapid anemic librarians, inconsequential figures, offer refreshing relief from Tonio Kröger's increasingly stuffy sleepwalking mood. As he lifts a book from the shelf, Tonio Kröger recalls his youth: his verses and his violin are gone, but the walnut tree with the north wind in its branches remains.[81]

After visiting these cherished spots, Tonio returns for his baggage to the hotel, where he has a peculiar and important experience before taking the ferry to Denmark. Because a criminal has escaped, Tonio, as a stranger, must identify himself to the hotel manager, Herr Seehaase,[82] but Tonio carries no identification. Herr Seehaase had been an acquaintance of his father's, and one word from Tonio would immediately allow him to continue his trip. Tonio does not speak that word and Herr Seehaase cannot see Consul Kröger's son in this "stranger," an encounter crucial to the theme of identity, since identification papers or a reference to his father would define his position but not Tonio's personal identity. Mann uses the word *Hochstapler* ("swindler" or "rogue") as Tonio faces the entirely legitimate and unprejudiced questions of the two men, all alone and unknown, and for the last time the pattern phrase enters, now grown into a leitmotif: ". . . no gypsy in a green wagon, but the son of the late Consul Kröger, a member of the Kröger family." Tonio Kröger's attitude toward his own identity has materially changed; his first shield against the "others" had been his father's respectability and prestige, which alone balanced the awkwardness of his strange name, his sensitivity, and his appearance, and attached him, though tenuously, to the "others." Just as he once had agreed with his father's scolding over his bad school grades, Tonio now agrees with the officials' precautions, but the difficulty comes to an embarrassing halt when the two inspectors accidentally discover some manuscript pages in his briefcase. In the hotel in his home town, alone, unrecognized and suspect, Tonio Kröger for the first time does not want his father's standard of respectability to apply to him, so he explains that these pages are a part of his new work, soon to be published, a passage whose "emphasis and effect" (*Pointe und Wirkung*)[83] rather please him. He answers the policeman's questions about his profession; but Mann does not provide his exact words: "Tonio Kröger gulped and gave the name of his trade in a firm voice" (*STD*, 117; *GW*, 8: 316). The lack of a name for Tonio's trade is especially important, because heretofore Thomas Mann had precisely worded anything touching *Künstlertum*, but here he does not reveal whether Tonio Kröger called himself a "poet" (*Dichter*), a "literary man" (*Literat*), a "writer" (*Schriftsteller*), or a "short story writer" (*Novellist*). At any rate, however, the men credit his trustworthiness once they have read from the manuscript, the first time Tonio Kröger has been identified and treated politely, despite his oddities, for his work alone. This event takes place at his very departure, his "point of departure" (*Ausgangspunkt*).

At last Tonio Kröger on the boat that will carry him to Denmark, the land of Hamlet. The wind is blowing, he is absorbed with memories of his father, his dreams, the walnut tree, and the seashore of his youthful vacations. The sea intoxicates him, a Dionysian reference as Mann's description of the wind and water swells in beauty and significance.

A fellow passenger joins him, a red-blond businessman speaking a naïvely spontaneous low German dialect. This prototypical mediocre "well-fed burgher" (*Spießbürger*), who eats crudely like Klöterjahn, is utterly devoid of vocabulary, manners, grooming, and any hint of Hans Hansen's attractiveness. Even though he is ridiculous, Tonio Kröger loves him for the simple and moving honesty with which he expresses the deepest "feelings" (*Gefühle*) of which he is capable.[84]

Overnight the weather turns vicious, the wind whipping up huge waves, and Tonio Kröger's "heart is restless with sweet anticipation" (EHL). Mann's description of the roaring sea is exquisitely formulated and deserves reading aloud; Tonio Kröger's expectant heart revels in dynamic forces of nature around him. As he rejoices with a love song to the sea resounding in him, "his heart was alive" (ELH) (*sein Herz lebte*)[85] in a marvelously reverberant leitmotif. A poem was taking shape in his heart, but the passionate experience (*Empfindung*) drowned everything else in joyous intoxication.

Tonio's experience of the stormy sea, connected to his earlier dream, swirls up familiar forces from unknown depths, with a mythical magnitude impossible in dilettante art.[86] The parallel basic themes of "Tonio Kröger," the long-ing and striving for fulfilled humanity, find an equilibrium of universal values in him at last, a position that can be greatly illuminated through Goethe's *Faust*.[87] Many motifs in Thomas Mann's sea-storm description closely refer to Goethe's *Walpurgisnacht* (Walpurgis night) in *Faust I*, and the country dance at Aalsgaard (in part eight of "Tonio Kröger") parallels the classical *Walpur-gisnacht* of *Faust II*. In *Faust I* the *moon* dimly lights up the scene (I, 3852), while at the end of the classical *Walpurgisnacht* the scene glows with dazzling fantastic light when Homunculus unites with water, the source of life (II, 8455–60, 8472–73). Also in "Tonio Kröger" the nocturnal orgy of the stormy waves is lit by a moon behind racing clouds, the wind's howls mixed with those of the animals in the bowels of the boat. The dancing sea (*STD*, 121; *GW*, 8: 321) recalls the wild orgiastic dancing of the witches' Sabbath. The stormy scene brings Tonio's heart to life again, but because he has not yet completed his search he cannot yet create poems as he had when he was a boy. He has overcome the slavery of the *Literat*'s imposed philistine mentality,[88] but he has not yet been consecrated as a poet. As he breathes the moist sea air, his longing draws him toward his goal.

The short paragraph that describes Tonio Kröger's stay in Copenhagen closes with the statement, "He could no longer endure the joyous city" (EHL).[89] His longing for the sea is so strong that Mann conveys it in a lover's vocabulary; the name "Aalsgaard," where he had stayed some years pre-viously, is actually used in "Tonio Kröger," and brilliant sunshine, omitted in translation, plays its glittering light upon the scene. But even on gray stormy days, Tonio finds himself intimately involved with the sea, the wind, and the beech grove. His heart's emotions have won, freeing him from the bounds of his former existence. This state of affairs develops until a very special weekend.

He awakens to a glorious sunrise that seems supernatural to his drowsy eyes. The sun and the beautiful sea promise him an extraordinary day; he swims, takes a long walk, and sees that tourists have come up to enjoy the seashore. As they enter the hotel, he suddenly discovers *Hans Hansen* and *Ingeborg Holm* (italics in original) among them. Time has not changed them at all, and they do not recognize him. The "Hans" and "Ingeborg" he now sees are types; their individuality does not really matter, for Tonio Kröger does not love them as individuals, he loves them as representatives of the blond and blue-eyed "others" world. The world of the "others" does not care about him even if he has become important,[90] but Tonio Kröger has at least identified himself, and he knows that his suffering will give his heart the very life which it has lacked for so long.

Tonio Kröger follows Hans and Ingeborg with his eyes: " 'To be like you! . . . to live free from the curse of "insight" and the sufferings of creativity, to love and praise in a blessed state of mediocrity,' he cried" (EHL) (*GW*, 8: 332; see also *STD*, 128). His past relives itself, and even the quadrille must be danced as it had been in the past when he had missed the *Moulinet des Dames* and, just as many years ago, comes the galop and a girl much like Magdalena Vermehren falls.[91] Tonio Kröger gallantly helps her up, advising," 'You should not dance any longer, Fräulein' " (*STD*, 130; *GW*, 8: 336). Tonio leaves the ballroom to fight out his own battle, his heart filled with torment and love—a heart that now lives again.[92] Once in his room he "sobbed with remorse and nostalgia for his home" (EHL).[93]

In the third section of the novella, Tonio confronts his beloved, the ideal of the human and the natural. The dance at the vacation hotel represents the reconciliation of extremes, a confirmation of life and the fulfillment of self. The cynical Nietzschean spirit has given way to a reverent, wholehearted, rather sad Romantic plea, and with Tonio, Mann responds positively to life in section eight, the final and highest stage in his fulfillment. In a letter of 18 September 1931, he wrote to Jean Schlumberger, "The little book ['Tonio Kröger'] also was the expression of the inner mood of an entire generation" (EHL), and when Tonio Kröger writes to Lisabeta in section nine, he reveals that he has found his true dimension.

The theme of Germanic longing for ultimate beauty[94] is not only Nietzsche's conception, it originally pertained to Goethe's Faustian striving for human fulfillment. In the German cultural sphere, the longing to overcome the inherent contrast in man's nature was expressed in the opposing poles of North and South in the classical *Walpurgisnacht* of *Faust II*, evoking the quintessence of the classic Greek *Geist*.[95]

The day of the dance described in section eight of "Tonio Kröger" is explicitly connected to the imagery of the sun, in contrast to the moon of the stormy sea scene. That morning, the sun rose like a magical vision, reminiscent of the fiery blast at the moment of Homunculus's union with the life-giving water. The glass door of Tonio's room facing the sea is mentioned twice in this paragraph, paralleling Homunculus's glass tube, the protection for his *geistig* personality. "In a joyous daze" Tonio hurries to submerge himself in the "crisply glittering sea." The dance at Aalsgaard mirrors Goethe's classical *Walpurgisnacht*, past and present blend together, events take on relative timeless meaning, and characters become representations of already conceived types.

Since Mann was young and at the beginning of his career when he wrote "Tonio Kröger," and the ideas in it were desperately urgent to him, readers generally relate more easily to Tonio as the sensitive emotional youth than to Tonio the argumentative theoretician. Tonio's experience of his "classical *Walpurgisnacht*" matures him and he now can face the duality of his life as "artist" (*Künstler*) and as "burgher" (*Bürger*); he has found the incubator of his true being. Just as Goethe overcame his own *Sturm und Drang* crisis by creating Werther, Mann freed himself for new dimensions of creativity when he achieved "Tonio Kröger," overcoming his youthful problems. He observed on 19 August 1931: "The standpoint of the conflict between the burgher and the artist ways of life, which had played a strong role in my youthful production, had, over the course of time, lost its central significance for me" (EHL).

The ninth section of "Tonio Kröger," a letter he writes to Lisabeta Ivanovna, is very short, but it answers all of the fourth section's unsolved questions, referring directly to Lisabeta's earlier pronouncement that he was "a "burgher" (*Bürger*) gone astray." Tonio declares, "I stand between two worlds. I am at home in neither and I suffer in consequence. You artists call me a *bourgeois*, and the *bourgeois* try to arrest me. . . . I don't know which makes me feel worse" (*STD*, 132; *GW*, 8: 337). He counters this rather negative statement with: "For if anything is capable of making a poet of a literary man, it is my *bourgeois* love of the human, the living and usual. It is the source of all warmth, goodness, and humour; I even almost think it is itself that love of which it stands written that one may speak with the tongues of men and of angels and yet having it not is as sounding brass and tinkling cymbals"[96] At last Thomas Mann's strong words sprang as much from a living heart as from his artistic vocation:[97] "Do not chide this love, Lisabeta; it is good and fruitful. There is longing in it, and a gentle envy; a touch of contempt[98] and no little innocent bliss" (*STD*, 132; *GW*, 8: 382). The leitmotif is complete; Tonio Kröger's two opposing worlds are united through his personal "insight." Now that he can value the two worlds meeting in him, he realizes that he could never have become "a poet" (*Dichter*) without both the love of life and the skill that must be won through suffering. He promises Lisabeta, "The work I have so far done is nothing or not much—as good as nothing. I will do better, Lisabeta—this is a promise. As I write, the sea whispers to me and I close my eyes. I am looking into a world unborn and formless, that needs to be ordered and shaped; I see into a whirl of shadows of human figures who beckon to me to weave spells to redeem them: tragic and laughable figures and some that are both together—and to these I am drawn. But my deepest and secretest love belongs to the blond and blue-eyed, the fair and living, the happy, lovely, and commonplace" (*STD*, 132; *GW*, 8: 338).

Thomas Mann's "Tonio Kröger" was truly his child of suffering, for its relatively few pages cost him more than any of his other short stories. In "Tonio Kröger," he made a giant step toward his own insight into art and toward a *Weltanschauung* based on both personal and cultural values. From this time Mann related in a new way to his *Dreigestirn*;[99] now the constellation illumined him as well as guided his steps. He also acknowledged as his master and spiritual companion the ultimate "burgher" (*Bürger*) and poet of the German Golden Age, Johann Wolfgang von Goethe.

"Tonio Kröger" was published in fifty-one translations prior to Mann's death in 1955.[100] Its popularity continues to increase and it is, as Thomas Mann himself said, especially loved by young people.

"A Gleam"

Mann never commented very favorably on this little story, which he called "a study."[101] He had finished "A Gleam" before "The Infant Prodigy," although "The Infant Prodigy" was published first.[102] The plot of "A Gleam" was inspired by Mann's visit to the home of his friend Kurt Martens at Tegernsee during the summer of 1903.[103] Martens, who had praised Mann's *Tristan* collection highly in the *Literarische Echo*, told him a tale from his cavalry days,[104] a story with a noisy social affair in a ballroom, much like the setting of "The Hungry Ones." "A Gleam" is far easier to enjoy because of its characters, plot, and milieu, and hence it had a better reception.

"A Gleam" also occupies an important position in Mann's development.[105] Previously in "Tristan" he expressed the concept of "Life" (*Leben*) in the "will to live" a Schopenhauerian term denoting the instinct for survival. As he moved from the Klöterjahns to Hans and Ingeborg of "Tonio Kröger," Mann had to convert this concept into something more desirable and personal. After "Tonio Kröger," a new theme gradually became apparent in "A Gleam," the superiority of the lonely ones, their right and even obligation to be exceptional, in the image of royalty and the "artist."

Literally translated, "Ein Glück" means "One [or "a"] Happiness" ("felicity" or "bliss"; also "luck"), a close approximation of the story's theme. Contrary to the experience of Detlef in "The Hungry Ones," Tonio Kröger did experience moment of utter bliss when "his heart was alive"—that is, when his love was close to heartbreak. Tonio's love and longing for the "others" at first included a feeling of rejection, but later he realized that it was his artist's insight that set him apart from them. Finally, the two sides of his nature were reconciled through the acknowledgment his letter conveyed to Lisabeta. "Ein Glück" carries this development one step further: "*Glück*" or "happiness" is a *geistig* experience which Mann articulated in a letter to his brother Heinrich a year later (23 December 1904): "Never have I believed that happiness was an easy and gay thing, but I always believed that it was something as serious, difficult and severe as life itself. . ." (EHL). This letter was written after his engagement to Katia Pringsheim on 3 October 1904. Such happiness is a profound state beyond the turmoil of the senses ("will to live"). Consciously or unconsciously, Mann was searching for insight into something naïve and pure, superior to the clumsy evil force represented by the *principium individuationis*, something both more "human" (*menschlich*) and more "ordinary" (*gewöhnlich*). Therefore, even the final line of "The Hungry Ones" sounds simplistic: "Little children, love one another" (*STD*, 172; *GW*, 8: 270), suggesting an innocence able to ignore convention. In "Ein Glück," this is precisely what the unsophisticated little singer, the "swallow" (*Schwalbe*), does when she reveals her love and respect for the Baroness, stepping "from one side" to "the other." The German title "*Ein Glück*" presents an existential value, the experience of harmony in a fictional life situation incompatible with fleeting sensation.

Mann called this little story describing a state of mind "a sketch," only nine pages long, with no subdivisions. "Anna, poor little Baroness Anna" (*STD*, 273; *GW*, 8: 349) is the protagonist. Aristocratic characters appear infrequently in Mann's writings, since his own experience made him far more comfortable with middle-class settings and people. In the time and the army-officer situation of "Ein Glück," such a mingling of classes was not done, but Mann explains in detail how this unusual social combination of female entertainers, cavalry officers, and aristocratic officers' ladies came about. Twentieth century readers may find it difficult to appreciate the humiliation foisted upon properly reared Victorian ladies forced to accept an indecorous situation their gentlemen have created, but such indeed was the case for Baroness Anna.

Only Mann's masterful compromise makes "Ein Glück" enjoyable for a twentieth century audience. He first presents the *Schwalben* as girls of limited education but natural charm, with good manners and irreproachable morality, treated punctiliously by the officers. Second, he indicates the ladies' naïveté by their unquestioning acceptance of the entertainment. Frau Rittmeister von Hühnemann[106] herself dances with a *Schwalbe* and is surprised that the girls are so well educated, for the girl can recite the geographical locations of all the cavalry companies in the entire *Reich*. Also, the conflict of the evening is not the social clash in the "soul study" of Baroness Anna, but the emotional torment her hypersensitivity causes her.

At the time Thomas Mann wrote "Ein Glück," a few months before he began *Royal Highness*, he created a genuinely warm human being in Baroness Anna, using her social position both because of Martens's tale and to emphasize the degrees of distance between Anna's silent, lonely, sensitive world and the lively world of song and dance the little singer (*Schwalbe*) represents. Baroness Anna's high mimetic dignity and her fairy-tale position mirror Thomas Mann's sensitivity, like the "poet"'s isolation. The symbolic gesture of respect, the *Schwalbe*'s kiss on the Baroness's hand is also a symbolic apology from "Life" for having ignored Love's eternal values and rights. The chronology of Thomas Mann's development of thought indicates the source of the ideas which enrich his fiction.

Baron Harry typifies the blond element in his role as the aristocratic cavalry officer of the *fin de siècle*. Baron Harry's carousing is deftly shown not to be a result of excessive sensuality, for even after he has drunk a great deal, "his mood was a free and hilarious one, unclounded by any passion" (*STD*, 280; *GW*, 8: 358). Another reason for his exuberance was his vanity, perfectly suiting his personality. Thomas Mann emphasizes this attitude, calling it "harmless jolly conviviality" (*STD*, 278; *GW*, 8: 357), because this is an even more tragic and hopeless state of affairs than guilt. Harry simply does not understand how his wife feels and how his actions torment her.

A little furrow between the Baroness's eyebrows immediately recalls the tiny blue vein on Gabriele Klöterjahn's forehead. Anna's overabundant ash blond hair[107] and her pale hands indicate that she loves the blind, surging, instinctive power in the man she married, just as Gabriele loved the healthy Klöterjahn, and similarly Baron Harry imposed his lack of sensitivity, his attractiveness, and his strength on Anna, who could not match him on his own grounds. Once Anna and Gabriele were removed from their peaceful home, the world caused their sensitive personalities intense suffering. In "Ein Glück," though, not Music but Love fatally dominates the heroine.

The other two protagonists of the story are the *Avantageur*[108] and the little swallow (Schwalbe). The young *Avantageur*'s appearance is uncertain but dreamy, rather like the Baroness, with her "dreamy soul." The *Avantageur* "floated and swayed" when he walked, like a sleepwalker, and since he preferred not to dance he sat at the Baroness's table to keep her company. Though they tried hard, their conversation was unsuccessful, and when he plays the piano, he loses the beat and is asked to stop. On the other hand, *Leutnant* von Gelbsattel[109] has only one characteristic: his waltzes are exuberant and full of life like Baron Harry himself. Such social events were the little swallow's natural environment but during them she retained her sensitivity to human emotions. She had met people like Baron Harry before, and having a strong moral sense, was not at all affected by his flirting. When she realized that his jokes hurt the Baroness's feelings, she spontaneously put a stop to his behavior and directly apologized to the Baroness.

The personalities of the characters in "Ein Glück" and the concepts they represent give the story a dual layer of meaning, another instance of Mann's *doppelte Optik*; the story does not refer to a conventional love affair but to a *geistig* relationship he called "love," similar to the one he developed in his "blond and dark" imagery and the combined name "Tonio Kröger." Baroness Anna loves "life" (*Leben*), but through Baron Harry she is abused and exploited by it, while her heart, like Detlef's and Tonio's, longs to give and receive affection. Life has many varied aspects, but for Thomas Mann all of them attract love: as Tonio Kröger put it, "But my deepest and secretest love belongs to the blond and blue-eyed, the fair and living, the happy, lovely, and commonplace" (*STD*, 132; *GW*, 8: 338). The Baroness did recognize the true charm of the young girl: "If Harry had been in love with her, if he had burned and suffered for her sake, his wife could have forgiven that, she could have understood and sympathized. And suddenly she became conscious that her own feeling for the little Swallow was warmer and deeper than Harry's own" (*STD*, 280; *GW*, 8: 338). From this moment, the little Swallow (*Schwalbe*), the symbol of Life (*Leben*), has a name, a personality, and a role to play: "And the little Swallow herself? Dear me, her name was Emmy and she was fundamentally commonplace" (*STD*, 280; *GW*, 8: 338). When this girl sees the baroness resolutely and desperately leave the ballroom amid the stunned silence of the guests, Emmy takes a position. This is the circumstance that gives meaning to the closing words of the story.

"Ein Glück" had a good plot, exquisite descriptive passages, and brilliant form, but Mann was dissatisfied with it, probably for two reasons; he was expressing a concept that he had not as yet experienced himself, and he was using a plot in a fictional frame uncomfortable for him. The solution of Life (the *Schwalbe*) apologizing to Anna's retreating figure was Mann's wishful thinking, not his experience, and so although the scene is faithfully described, the final words have a touch of artificial pathos. For the first time, the auto-biographical elements of his "longing lovers" fall into an unnatural happy ending. The Swallow's generous wisdom is only a mirage, making the weak figure of Detlef far more credible than the attractive one of the Baroness.

Mann's continuity of thought from "The Hungry Ones" through "Tonio Kröger" to "Ein Glück" appears in corresponding scenes, which sometimes contain identical passages. One example is the heroes' complaint that only individuals who are like them can understand them—and that those whom they most long for never need them; this complaint is reflected in the titles of "The Hungry Ones" and the contradictory elements of the name "Tonio Krö-ger." It is also expressed thematically in the last paragraph of "Ein Glück": "For happiness touches the heart . . . when those two worlds . . . find each other" (EHL) (See *STD*, 282; *GW*, 8: 361).

"The Hungry Ones" and "Tonio Kröger" share many ideas, but in "Tonio Kröger" Mann's expression of his thoughts, the meaning of the complete work of art, and its relation to his process of composition, as well as the psychological growth of the hero, are all clearer and more aesthetically appealing than in the earlier story. "The Hungry Ones" shows no thematic relevance except the melancholy mood of the lovesick writer who abandons a ball. On the other hand, the corresponding passage is integral to the development of Tonio Kröger. "The Hungry Ones," too, contains an "either-or" ulti-matum: "Ah, just once to live, to love and to give thanks, to feel and know that feeling is all! Just once to share your life, ye living ones, just once to drink in magic draughts the bliss of the commonplace!" The implied conse-quence of not knowing that "feeling is all" is spiritual desolation. In "Tonio Kröger," however, the corresponding passage shows Tonio challenging Lisa-beta and the entire world: "The *bourgeois* are stupid, but you adorers of the beautiful, who call me phlegmatic and without aspirations, you ought to realize that there is a way of being an artist that goes so deep and is so much a matter of origins and destinies that no longing seems to it sweeter and more worth knowing than longing after the bliss of the commonplace." For Baro-ness Anna, in "A Gleam," the commonplace is represented by the little "Swallow" herself (*STD*, 170; *GW*, 8: 267; *STD*, 132; *GW*, 8: 337; *STD*, 280; *GW*, 8: 359).

Mann also reveals in "The Hungry Ones" a negative longing on behalf of *Künstlertum*, while "Tonio Kröger" contains the secret of *Künstlertum* itself, a victorious, jubilant statement stemming from the wealth of love and power of an undivided world.[110]

The plot and setting of Thomas Mann's sketch "Ein Glück" are enjoyable, but the little story is best appreciated in the overall progress of Mann's imagery from "Tristan" toward *Royal Highness* and onward to "Death in Venice." As a postlude to "Tonio Kröger," "Ein Glück" displays a playful, elegant, and utopian union of extremes, a thing Tonio knew to be impossible. And so while "Tonio Kröger" became one of Thomas Mann's greatest successes, it also obviated the originality and the relevance of "The Hungry Ones" and "Ein Glück," reducing them to stylistic and intellectual exercises.

Mann's meeting with Katia Pringsheim during the winter after "Tonio Kröger" changed his whole existence.[111] About 1903–4 Katia recalled, "I really only learned to know Thomas Mann after the streetcar adventure" (EHL).[112] Like him, she was a cycling enthusiast, but they often also took the same streetcar. One day after Katia had discarded her ticket and was ready to step off the car, the conductor asked her for the ticket. After heated discussion, Katia, furious, jumped off the tram. Mann had watched the little scene with amusement and he decided to be introduced to the young lady. Long before, in fact, fate had brought their paths together, unbeknownst to either. In Lübeck Mann had bought a reproduction of August Kaulbach's "Kinderkarneval" ("Children's Carnival"), with four little Pierrots and one Pierrette, for his study. Decades later, he learned that the Pringsheim children had posed for Kaulbach in 1892, and that the original hung in Katia's family home. He had also seen her at concerts and operas as early as 1902, prior to asking their mutual friends, the Bernsteins, to introduce them.[113] From the outset, Mrs. Pringsheim approved of his attention to her daughter, and Katia's twin brother Klaus also urged his suit. Though Professor Alfred Pringsheim[114] enthusiastically shared Mann's interest in Wagner, he was not particularly interested in literature and would have preferred a young scholar rather than a writer as a future son-in-law. He was agreeable, though, when Katia accepted Thomas Mann's proposal. At the beginning of April 1904, Mann wrote to Katia, "Yesterday when I had dinner at your house after the theater . . . I had a sore throat which I cured with your father's help. You naturally don't understand this because you don't know how zealously your father is concerned with my well-being" (EHL). This incident suggests the physical ailments recorded in Mann's correspondence.[115]

On 27 February 1904, Mann rapturously observed to Heinrich, "I am [now] socially introduced at the Bernsteins' and at the Pringsheims'. The Pringsheim [family] . . . [is] the father, a university professor, with a gold cigarette case; the mother, a Lenbach beauty; the youngest son a musician; and his twin sister Katja (she [actually] is called Katja) is a wonder, something indescribably unique and precious, a being who by merely existing equals 15 writers or 30 painters . . ." (EHL).[116]

Mann's courtship, as reported in his letters, diaries, and *Sketch of My Life*, is confirmed in Katia's published memoirs, but none conveys the intimate significance for his *geistig* and creative self that his novel *Royal Highness* does.[117] From their first encounter to their first happy months of married life in the spring of 1905, Mann completed "The Infant Prodigy" (December 1903), "At the Prophet's" (May 1904), *Fiorenza* (January 1905), and "A Weary Hour" (March 1905). He had also been working on *Royal Highness* since "Tonio Kröger," but the novel was not completed until February 1909.

"The Infant Prodigy"

Mann rapidly wrote "The Infant Prodigy"[118] for the Christmas issue of the *Neue Freie Presse*, 25 December 1903, and it has become one of his most popular short stories.[119] The English "infant prodigy" and the German "*Wunderkind*" both describe a young child with an unusually early-developing artistic talent, but "*Wunderkind*" also offers a heightened resonance of "miracle child," here indicating both the titular hero and the protagonist.

In the introduction, Mann uses "*Leute*" ("people") repeatedly, a collective noun which in German has no singular form.[120] *Leute* is a Hydra. Each hydra-head of the *Leute* functions separately but is restricted by the common body in its individual development. *Leute* is one of Mann's leitmotifs throughout "Das Wunderkind"; finally the *Leute* becomes a collective character with a composite mind, even another protagonist.[121] The third active power presented in the introductory paragraph, the "publicity machine" (*Reklameapparat*), provides unity throughout the story.

When the infant prodigy appears, his behavior mirrors the setting, which seethes with decadent *fin de siècle* colors and ornamentation. The child's affected gestures are studied and effeminate, and his immaturity is exaggerated to attract the public, making him appear his mother's toy rather than a little boy with individual rights. Mann points out his clothing, his hair, his behavior, and especially his name: "He was called Bibi[122] Saccellaphylaccas" (*STD*, 172; *GW*, 8: 339), another name, like Tonio Kröger's, whose first element clashes significantly with the last. Mann himself indicates this conflict, the gap between the ordinary citizen and the artist, when he discusses the impresario's reaction to the name. Any young lad in Munich might be called "Bibi," but "Saccellaphylaccas" immediately evokes distant Greece, a conflict between the innocence of the heart and the intricate burden carried by a child with a premature insight. The *Wunderkind* is a little boy with a soft unformed but lined face, the characteristics of his trade. Later Thomas Mann describes his strong well-trained hands, the dark complexion he inherited from his Greek ancestors, ". . . already a little tired," and the extravagant clothing and hair style his impresario requires.

Thomas Mann ironically picks up the notion of the deception inherent in the "artist" 's presentation of his art, earlier introduced by Tonio Kröger in his conversation with Lisabeta: "A little lie, they think, belongs to beauty. Where, do they [the people] think, would edification and elevation from the everyday living come from, if one did not contribute a little effort and accept things as they are presented? And they are quite right in their '*Leutehir-nen*' " (EHL) (*STD*, 173; *GW*, 8: 339). The "publicity machine" builds its success on the predictable uniformity of its audience, so the impressive French titles of the *Wunderkind*'s modest creations, like "*Le hibou et les moineaux*" ("The Owl and the Sparrows") are bound to make an effect.

Mann then deliberately reveals the *Wunderkind*'s mind and emotions. "Bibi made his face for the audience, because he was aware that he had to entertain them a little" (*STD*, 174; *GW*, 8: 340–41). The performing artist's feeling of superiority toward his audience is perfectly clear; little Bibi knows all the tricks to ensure an audience's response, but he genuinely feels music deeply, because it is a beloved world where each performance promises him an intimate *geistig* experience.

Mann himself knew the musical world well. He had taken violin lessons since he was seven years old, and he played quite well by ear, first with his mother, and later with Ilse Martens and Carl Ehrenberg.[123] As a youngster, he loved to act out the role of the virtuoso, just as he had enjoyed his puppet theater. Later in his life, he described a band he had seen during his boyhood on a happy vacation at Travemünde, and its "little, long-haired gypsy-looking" conductor named Hess.[124] He had also heard a nine-year-old Greek pianist named Loris Margaritis at the Munich conservatory where the Greek boy had studied. Much later, Margaritis's wife sent Mann a photograph of Margaritis at nine years old, with a letter stating that the pianist had enjoyed "The Infant Prodigy" very much.

The *Leute* observe the performance, the bows, and the entrances and exits of the *Wunderkind* and record humorous caricatures of the mother, the impresario, and other characters. Each episode has clear contours and a well-enunciated message, highlighted from at least two opposing angles. As Bibi plays, mentally commenting on his selections, and the *Leute* focus on him, the story's rich multiple angles become clearer. Mann simultaneously shows Bibi's real personality, the *Leute*'s viewpoint, and the spiritual relations between the artist and his audience. (*STD*, 176; *GW*, 8: 344).

The *Wunderkind*, as artist and as ally of the impresario, and the *Reklameapparat* are followed by the third protagonist, the *Leute*, represented by ten different characters from the gray, chewy, plump mass of the *Leute*, ten "*Leutehirne*" or "people-brains," willingly subordinate to the impresario. Each is hopelessly self-centered, deliberately cultivating personal weaknesses that bar him from the *Wunderkind*'s world: "All those people sat there in their regular rows, looking at the prodigy and thinking all sorts of things in their regular brains [*Leutehirnen*]" (*STD*, 177; *GW*, 8: 344). First Thomas Mann describes the "grey old man," using an interior monologue which supports his physical characteristics. The seal ring on the old man's index finger, omitted in the translation, shows that the old man has had a less refined upbringing than might be expected from an aristocrat, a finely crafted bit of irony confirmed by his sketchy experience with music and his use of a common form of German. His reactions are good-natured but naïve; for the price of a ticket, he receives romantic thoughts and "elevation."

The next "*Leute*" are a businessman concerned with nothing but economics, a selfish small-town piano teacher, and a young girl, whose fantasies are extinguished by the mere thought of cod liver oil. Her awakening womanhood, joined with an ardent imagination, suggests abstract disembodied love, which for her is a sensitive intellectual topic. The witless officer recalls the hapless versifying lieutenant in "Tonio Kröger."

"Then there was a critic, an elderly man in shiny black coat and turned-up trousers splashed with mud. He sat in his free seat and thought: '. . . He has in himself all the artist's exaltation and his utter worthlessness, his charlatanry and his sacred fire, his burning contempt and his secret raptures. Of course I can't write all that, it is too good. . .'" (*STD*, 178; *GW*, 8: 345–46). The critic's sharp insight has isolated him; his intelligence prevents him from escaping into illusion, as other "people-brains" do. But not being an artist himself, he cannot share Bibi's world; he serves the *Leute* as the *Reklameapparat* requires him to do. The critic's definition of Bibi also shows the essence of Mann's concept of the artist.[125] The *Wunderkind* becomes the central figure between the *Leute* and the *Reklameapparat*, while the critic is sometimes thought to represent Mann.

As soon as he has left his piano, Bibi becomes only a sweaty little boy. The crowd's attention is divided between two curiosities, Bibi and the old princess who is seated in the first row. When the two confront each other, the old princess acts candidly and routinely and the professional artist, a little boy, now that he has left the stage, shrinks in importance. He does not care enough about disclosing his personal experiences to answer the princess's dispirited questions coherently. After the musical experience which had united them, the princess and the infant prodigy part without having built any bridge of comprehension between them. Finally, "Outside in the cloakroom there was a crowd" (*STD*, 179; *GW*, 8: 347), and some highlights of various characters, both previously noted and newly appearing, break through the stuffiness. Mann again highlights the piano teacher with her envious display of professionalism and then a sparkle of beauty: a young blond blue-eyed[126] aristocratic girl with her two lighthearted officer brothers, followed by an uncouth, ungroomed, puberty-stricken, pseudo-intellectual girl, an old gentleman, and a depressed young lad. As the crowd dissipates, the individuals lose appeal, and the *Wunderkind* fades totally; the *Wunder* is over. The German text abandons the word *Leute*.

Mann's unity of composition and the essence of his message appear in the basic elements of the story—the *Wunderkind*, the *Reklameapparat*, and the *Leute*; the presentation of Bibi Saccellaphylaccas as Bibi plus Saccellaphylaccas, "Child" plus "Artist"; Bibi's relation to the *Leute*; Bibi as seen by "others," the *Leute*; and the interaction of the *Wunderkind* and the *Leute* as governed by the *Reklameapparat*. The interaction, relation and definition of

these elements express Mann's conception of the artist, the commoner, and
the reigning business apparatus at this point in his life. Mann himself was
pleased with his "Infant Prodigy." On 14 December 1903 he wrote to Fischer:
"At the moment I am writing a sketch for the Christmas issue of the *Neue
Freie Presse*, 'The Infant Prodigy.' It will be better than 'A Gleam'" (EHL).

"The Infant Prodigy" was an immediate success. On 11 December 1903,
Thomas Mann presented it in a lecture at the newly founded *Neuer Verein* in
Munich, and soon after, the *Neue Freie Presse* asked for a similar story for the
considerable sum of 300 marks. He often read "The Infant Prodigy" in public, its immense popularity deriving from its omnipresent delectable humor
and subtly ironic portraits, which never descend to cynicism.

Some of Mann's impressions and moods were troubling during early 1904,
and he discussed them candidly in a long letter to Heinrich (27 February
1904), reacting to "Jagt nach Liebe," a novella Heinrich had sent him, clearly
though unconsciously revealing the essential cause of his later estrangement
from Heinrich and also the motivation for his *Betrachtungen eines Unpolitischen* (1918), where he logically expressed long-held ideas that he, while writing, was beginning to overcome. The letter also illustrates his frame of mind
in early 1904:

> Much more peculiar, strangely interesting, still rather inconceivable for
> me is the development of your *Weltanschauung* toward liberalism, which
> is also formulated in this work. Strange, as [I] said, and interesting! . . .
> First, I understand little about "Freedom." For me it is a purely *geistig-
> moralistic* concept, synonymous with "honesty." (Some critics call this in
> me "coldness of the heart.") But for political freedom I have no interest
> at all. Has not the powerful Russian literature emerged from beneath
> overwhelming pressure? This would at least prove that the struggle
> for freedom is better than freedom itself. What actually is "freedom"?
> Because so much blood has already flowed for this concept, it has for
> me something eerie, weird, unfree, something outright medieval. . . .
> (EHL)

This passage exquisitely characterizes young Mann's abstract thought, and his
eagerness to clarify his own feverishly evolving metaphysical system of representation. Although he emphasized his lack of interest in political and
pragmatic reality in a naïve estrangement from the world, he would subsequently shape and fictionalize the patterns of his reality according to the way
he conceived of it. At this moment, when his budding love for Katia Pringsheim had aroused his will and emotions and lured him toward the world of
light, money, wit, and elegance, such expression was difficult for him, since he
hoped to court her properly and then establish with her a sound family unit in
a world he really neither knew nor cared about. Heinrich's new-found self-
identification, his expression of exploding sensuality and heated sociopolitical
ideas, are secondary to the impact that Heinrich's style, ideas, imagery, and
Weltanschauung made upon his brother Thomas by triggering his intellectual

defense mechanisms. Heinrich's position forced to reevaluate his own concepts and define them coherently to harmonize with his intellectual and his personal world, a considerable strain in early 1904. *Buddenbrooks* had provided him with fame and money,[127] but his work on *Fiorenza* was slow. He wrote to Ida Boy-Ed, 22 February 1904: ". . . I am nervous and tired. Lately I have come to realize my fame in the form of social events and intrusion by people and I find myself now in the near feverish state of *geistig* digestion" (EHL).

Mann's vital decisions did not come to a head for a long time. Katia, the daughter of a wealthy university professor who loved Wagner, collected rare art, and opened his house to colorful Munich society, did not even think about marrying at the moment. As she put it, "I was twenty and I felt well and happy under my skin, and also, I was very content with studies, [my] brothers, the tennis club and everything, and I really did not know why I now should leave it so soon" (EHL).[128] Thomas Mann remained in anxiety and hope.

"At the Prophet's"

Mann modeled the invisible prophet Daniel[129] of this story on Ludwig Derleth, author of *Proklamationen*, published in 1908 by Insel Verlag.[130] Like the fictional Daniel, Derleth lived in a fifth-floor apartment, Destouchesstraße 1, Schwabing, and had a sister, Anna Maria, who resembled Daniel's sister Maria Josepha. Anna Maria was four years younger than Derleth and totally devoted to her brother's thinking.[131] Mann had met this strange young lady at his mother's literary receptions.

The Derleths actually issued invitations for Good Friday with the insignia of an eagle holding a sword, just as described, "Mrs. Hedwig Pringsheim and Thomas Mann attended the lecture on Good Friday evening" (EHL)[132] Even the background story in "At the Prophet's" of Sonja, the "rich lady's" daughter, was based on real-life events.[133] Mann wrote to Heinrich on 27 March 1904: "Presently Katja is ill at the surgical clinic where today I sent a few nice flowers, with the permission of the pretty Lenbach-Mama who always smiles encouragingly when I speak in her presence simply of 'Katja'" (EHL). Mann admittedly portrayed Mrs. Pringsheim and Katia in "At the Prophet's," and so he showed the story to Mrs. Pringsheim before he sent it to the Viennese *Neue Freie Presse* for publication where it appeared in his new 1914 short story collection.

"At the Prophet's" is seven pages long with no thematic or formal division, but it does fall into three parts: the introduction of the characters and the setting; the disciple's presentation of the prophet's proclamations; and a brief conclusion. The title refers to a character not present in person, but whose spirit dominates its entire atmosphere. The eagle refers to the prophet's facial features, revealed in his photograph, and he is consistently called a "prophet," and not a "writer," "poet," or "intellectual," all of which Ludwig Derleth was in reality. The visitor's churchly behavior offers a hint of spiritualism, highly fashionable at the turn of the century, reinforced by the real or staged ecstasies of most of the visitors and the disciple's mysterious arrival from Switzerland at the time foretold. The stage properties convey the same pseudo-religious quality. The solemn tone of references to the "prophet" clashes against Mann's satiric nonsensical setting and plot. He wrote "The Infant Prodigy," "A Gleam," and "At the Prophet's" for money and at the request of his publisher, but in all three stories, he treated very personal and ideological matters.[134]

Munich, an intellectually stimulating town, contained an eccentric subculture. Even seventy-five years after this story was written, Mann's types are hilariously recognizable. On the surface, "At the Prophet's" might seem an altered version of "The Infant Prodigy," because both stories treat a performance, with comments by and about the audience, but since Bibi the infant prodigy bridged the "publicity machine" of the worlds and the "artist," the *Wunderkind* and his *Künstlertum* became the real theme of the story. The concept of the prophet is the central issue in "At the Prophet's."

Mann enlivens the abstract "worldview" by treating his human beings humorously in a realistic setting. His "novelist," a man who has overcome Tonio Kröger's problems, is a witty well-balanced writer and "burgher." Thus Mann's "novelist," an artist, for the first time is not lonely and "different" but a natural part of the "others." The tripartite Schopenhauerian "worldview" here is comprised of the blind "will to live" (*Ich*), verbalized by the "Proclamations of Daniel"; the crowd, the *principium individuationis*, individualized by the "rationalization" (*Rationalisierung*) and made asocial, lonely, and mute; and those who ". . . had a special relationship with life" (EHL) (*STD*, 283, 287, 289; *GW*, 8: 363, 368, 370). These are the "novelist," the "rich lady," and the absent Sonja, all of whom are healthy, beautiful, robust "burghers" with a large capacity for love. The prophet himself is not present physically, but nevertheless he is dynamically active through his ideas, his absurd, illogical reasoning, and his aggressive power of suggestion, which fascinates persons who have strayed away (*verirrt*) from normal social settings. Not the novelist but the other guests hang desperately on the prophet's words, since he is able to attract "unacknowledged geniuses" with the rationalized nonsense of his Proclamations.

The prophet's ideas parallel the Schopenhauerian spirit of the "rationalization" of the "will to live," the illogical and idolatrous power that engenders the concept of the *principium individuationis*.[135] The entire setting is an absurd "mental image" (*Vorstellung*) of the world of formless energy that the Proclamations defined and verbalized. The Proclamations themselves are as formless, rude and aggressive as the Will itself. Love has no place whatsoever in the Schopenhauerian representation of the World, and Mann emphasizes the novelist's love of life through the only leitmotif in the story, the phrase

"He and life were certainly on good terms!" occurring in the novelist's introduction and again as the last line of the story. Clearly the "novelist" is a good-natured ironic self-portrait of Mann.

Rather than a Schopenhauerian concepts of life, this leitmotif furnishes a "Tonio Kröger" definition of "life", with a seemingly insignificant autobiographical reference, the novelist's "trim moustache," an indication of Mann's own meticulous grooming confirmed in a letter of 29 October 1903 to S. Fischer: "Perhaps I will also compensate you by means of the industriously smitten symbols of my life, which are less uninteresting than my mustachioed personality" (EHL). The word "world" (*die Welt*), referring to the love of the world, is the only word which Mann italicized in the story. According to the prophet's last words, the world was to be given over to his "soldiers" for "looting and plunder." To the novelist, love of life and love of the world are identical, and so he sees the prophet's proclamation as a paradox. The novelist's semantic distinction holds the key to the story's levels of meaning. Mann's description of the prophet's disciple and his paraphrase of "Daniel's Proclamation" are a monstrous version of Spinell's rationalized insight and impotence. The disciple's low forehead, his brutal features, and his simultaneous awkwardness and weakness all substantialize the rationalizing power of the "will to live": "The youth displayed an odd and unpleasant mixture of brutality and weakness and the matter of his reading was in remarkable consonance with its manner" (*STD*, 287–88; *GW*, 8: 368). His audience is made up of failures, derailed lives, uninspired misfits, and outgrowths of hostile and perverse clashing elements. Compared to these pitiful creatures, the novelist's curiosity and the rich lady's boredom which brought them here are refreshingly positive. The only figure bridging the prophet and his followers and the "burgher"-novelist is Maria Josepha, the prophet's sister, but being enraptured by the prophet's rationalization, she can love only him. This love is paradoxical, since Daniel is the high priest of self-destruction, the self-devouring force of the *principium individuationis*.

The story's first sentence presents its three consecutive levels: real places, mental states, and the regions of *Geist*; and Mann describes the third as "the end: ice, chastity, null."[136] As in "The Hungry Ones" and "Tonio Kröger," ice connotes the emotional sterility resulting from the intellectual power of "art."[137] This image does not pertain to the novelist and there is no special mention of "art," since Mann had overcome his own stage of rigidity in "Tonio Kröger."

The room also holds a violently clashing collection of portraits. A huge likeness of Napoleon matches the recurrent eagle;[138] Luther the religious reformer is absurdly juxtaposed with Nietzsche the anti-ecclesiastic; and Moltke and Alexander appear with Robespierre and Savonarola.[139] The combination produces an antipathetic mixture of dictatorial egomania, weapons, passions, and spirits. The paradox, too, of Christ as Imperator Maximus, with a cruel tyranny of enforced obedience and humility, illogically associated with Bud-

dha, Alexander, and Napoleon, creates an almost unbearable tension during
the incredibly illogical nonsense being unfolded. "Daniel's Proclamation" is a
nebulous and endless composition, an indecipherable gospel: "The solitary
ego sang, raved, commanded. It would lose itself in confused pictures, go
down in an eddy of logical error, to bob up again suddenly and startlingly in
an entirely unexpected place. Blasphemies and hosannas—a waft of incense
and a reek of blood. In thunderings and slaughterings the world was conquered and redeemed" (*STD*, 288; *GW*, 8: 369). The listeners colorful descriptions, realistic and humorous, and their names are all as incongruous as
the meaning of the disciple's *Verlesung*.[140] As at the close of "The Infant
Prodigy," the audience crowds in to the dressing room, but no one speaks
except the novelist and the rich lady, who do not belong to this peculiar company. They exchange friendly words and mention Sonja, whom they love, the
link between them.

Mann did not comment much on "At the Prophet's," but he always included it in his short story collections. Its setting is strongly autobiographical,
as is its sensitivity because of his love for Katia and its philosophical implication of his Schopenhauerian themes.

Mann suffered a bitter disappointment in the summer of 1904. Dr. Pringsheim was suddenly taken ill and his wife and Katia left Munich to join him at
Kissingen. Katia later spent some time with her brother Klaus on the Baltic;
Katia commented, "Thomas Mann wrote wonderfully beautiful letters—
because he could write—which naturally made [an] impression on me and
which I answered less beautifully" (EHL).[141] After these elegant lyrical expressions, Thomas Mann and Katia Pringsheim were engaged on 4 October
1904.

Since 1901 Mann had been working on his Savonarola project, and simultaneously writing painfully at *Fiorenza* since the summer of 1903.[142] He had
promised Fischer he would deliver the finished manuscript at the beginning of
November, but his engagement changed everything, and he canceled lecture
engagements to meet Katia's relatives in Berlin. He did not complete *Fiorenza* until just before his wedding to Katia on 11 February 1905, observing to
Heinrich a week later, ". . . It [*Fiorenza*] was a heavy letdown, but it should
be rich in experience" (EHL).

Sobered by more than thirty years' objectivity, Mann wrote in "On Myself"
(1930): "The artist problem, the dialectic contrast of *Geist* and art on one side
and *Leben* on the other, continues to play a leading role in this cycle of production, which lasted until 'Death in Venice' and it also appeared in my only
dramatic attempt, *Fiorenza*. . . . While in 'Tonio Kröger' the *Geist* and art
are on one side against *Leben*, in *Fiorenza* the *Geist*, growing into asceticism
and becoming absolute nothingness, turns against art, which is considered the
lust for life sublimated" (EHL) (*GW*, 13: 145–146). To Heinrich he wrote on
18 February 1905: "in this play I posed them [life and art] as opponents. It led
to this Solnäs-fall,[143] this fiasco, the attempt to fill a *geistig* construction with

Leben" (EHL). Mann was relieved by *Fiorenza* and excited by his wedding, while his new father-in-law happily supervised the decoration of the young couple's future home. Thomas Mann also wrote to Heinrich on 18 February 1905 from his honeymoon residence, Hotel Baur au Lac near Zurich, since Heinrich and Carla Mann had been absent from the wedding: ". . . a completely new chapter shall begin in the novel of my life, a chapter which had been conceived in beautiful intoxication and which now wishes to be built up with love, art and trustfulness . . ." (EHL).

"A Weary Hour"

Mann wrote "A Weary Hour," which he called "a study," for the 9 May 1905 issue of Simplicissimus, commemorating the one-hundredth anniversary of Schiller's death.[144] He based the story upon Schiller's 1796–98 correspondence with Goethe, dealing with Schiller's *Wallenstein* trilogy and his aesthetic essay *Über naive und sentimentalische Dichtung*. Mann's youthful adoration of Schiller appears in Tonio Krögers' loving references to *Don Carlos*. He often referred to his intellectual and emotional links with Schiller, as he did in a letter to Kurt Martens on 28 March 1906: "What I mean is briefly and approximately expressed in the words of my Lorenzo: 'The effortless will not become great. . . Inhibition is the best friend of will. . .' ([These are] the words of Lorenzo, the lord of pleasures, whom I have portrayed not without a little empathy. . .)" (EHL). This became the theme of "A Weary Hour."

The English title "A Weary Hour" is not a literal translation of Mann's German title, "Schwere Stunde." The theme of this story reveals a creative crisis described by the word "*schwer*"—a "difficult," "hard," "severe," "grave," or "serious" crisis of self-evaluation when a poet's vocation suddenly forces him to envision his motivations clearly.[145] If his will to suffer and create masters his momentary depression, the crisis becomes a victory, affirming the individual's self-determination and greatness.

Like the three preceding stories, "A Weary Hour" is a sketch rather than a short story, even though it offers an analytic depth unusual to this genre. It deals with one crucial hour that encompasses a wealth of subject matter. The unnamed hero's reactions suit both Friedrich Schiller and Thomas Mann, who share certain biographical features. On a cold stormy night, the hero wrestles alone with his moment of discouragement, which leads him to an enlightening revelation and a new creative impulse. The poet's struggle takes place at Schiller's ascetic home at Jena, the abode of a scholarly professor of history, at the very end of the eighteenth century, as Schiller's correspondence and aesthetic essays indicate.[146] Such a setting could hardly be farther from the elegantly redecorated apartment of the newlyweds Thomas and Katia Mann at Franz-Joseph Straße 2 and the corner of Leopoldstraße, with the beautiful view of the garden of the Prince Leopold Palace that his wealthy father-in-law had provided. In spite of this disparity, the hero's state of mind is inseparable from the personalities of both Schiller and Mann.

The action of "A Weary Hour" is vaguely suggested by historical indications, such as Schiller's geographic separation from Goethe,[147] who was living in Weimar, and the reference to Schiller's *Wallenstein*, then in progress. Jubilee writings generally are so laudatory as to be critically negligible, but in his *Sketch of My Life* Mann called "A Weary Hour" a "highly subjective Schiller study" ("*sehr subjektive Schiller-studie*"), and his literary portrait of Schiller glows with candid honesty and warmth.

The two writers shared several biographical circumstances; at the moments focused upon by this story, both Schiller and Mann had been recently married and soon were to have children.[148] Both learned toward philosophical thought, scholarly accuracy, and a painstaking method of work; both were highly sensitive and rather shy, with scruples about their artistic capabilities; both were in somewhat fragile health. The several versions of Schiller's *Wallenstein* exhibit his self-discipline and ability to force himself to continue a task once begun, just as Mann had worked on *Fiorenza*, his only drama. "A Weary Hour" 's "work of art" ("*das Werk*") in progress refers both to Schiller's *Wallenstein* and Mann's *Fiorenza*.

One early morning, the poet is seized by a moment of despair. He is completely alone; his stove is nearly cold and the wind is howling outside. This rather romantic setting contrasts with the naturalistic description of the poet's common cold ("*Schnupfen*"), his swollen eyelids and reddened nose. Schiller never recovered from the illness that began in 1791, and he was compelled to stay indoors during bad weather.

In "A Weary Hour" the poet debates the cause of his writer's block—his illness or the work of art itself.[149] He needed distance to envision the concept, the materials, and the dimension of *Wallenstein*, and he was beginning to doubt his own capability. Schiller dramatically faced his past in the phrase "The excess of his youth" ("*Die Ausschweifungen seines Jugendmutes*"), greatly resembling Tonio Kröger's comment on his youthful dissipation, dramatically repeating the pattern-word "*Ausschweifung*." In "A Weary Hour" the hero refers to the limitation his pulmonary disease places on his life, and he again and again compares his method of approaching the work of art with Goethe's. Mann adds symbolic significance to these characters by never mentioning their names. The hero (Schiller) represents passionate suffering; the "other" (Goethe) represents wisdom and peaceful contemplation.

Mann here uses the unusual word "naive," in the sense of the aesthetic essay Schiller wrote shortly before he began work on *Wallenstein*, "Über naive und sentimentalische Dichtung," reflecting his *Weltanschauung*. Schiller proceeded in an Aristotelian vein,[150] by defining the term "naive": "Nature is in this viewpoint nothing other than freely accepted existence, the being of things in themselves, an existence according to their own and unalterable laws" (EHL).[151] Schiller's "naive" means an unbiased and nonpragmatic originality in all matters, a search for the essence, not the reason, of things: "We ascribe a 'naive' mentality to a person if he looks beyond artificial and unnatural circumstances when he makes a judgment, and if he guides himself solely by simply nature" (EHL).[152] In "A Weary Hour" Mann wrote: "Not to ascribe one's sufferings to bad air and constipation; to be well enough to cherish emotions, to scorn and ignore the material. Just on this one point to be naïve, though in all else sophisticated. To believe, to have strength to believe, in suffering. . . . But he *did* [emphasis only in the translation] believe in it; so profoundly, so ardently, that nothing which came to pass with suffering could seem to him either useless or evil" (*STD*, 293; *GW*, 8: 375).

Mann includes two topics new to him in "A Weary Hour," greatness and egocentricity. Like the "naive," Schiller's concept of "greatness" appears in "Über naive und sentimentalische Dichtung": ". . . not too often it happens that [in] looking above the unlimited ideal he would overlook the limited issue, and filled with the maximum, would miss the minimum, from which, in reality, all greatness derives" (EHL).[153] In Schiller's essay, the "naive" and the "great" are closely related by naturalness and genuineness. While Mann was working on "A Weary Hour," he became deeply involved with Schiller's logic ; he even adopted the same exultant "swing" ("*Schwung*") of the tone of Schiller's essay. Such creative personalities are also impelled to serve the artistic vocation, being unselfishly dedicated to becoming great (*groß*) by so doing. "For deeper still than his egoism lay the knowledge that he was freely consuming and sacrificing himself in the service of a high ideal, not as a virtue, of course, but rather out of sheer necessity" (*STD*, 294; *GW*, 8: 375). It is suffering that makes him great, and the only way that he knows is the difficult (*schwer*) way the "will to the difficult" (*Der Wille zum Schweren*), a reversal of Schopenhauer's "the will to live" (*Wille zum Leben*) and Nietzsche's "Will to Power." To face and then to overcome the "*Schwere*" is to transcend mediocrity. In exquisitely sensitive language Mann expresses this manifesto of the mystique of creation and its *geistig* realms. His indirect reference to the "other" ["man," *STD*, 295][154] ("*anderen*") indicates both Goethe the man and the "*sentimentalische*" realm Goethe represents, making the concept valid not only for Schiller in "A Weary Hour" but for Mann himself.[155]

As he endures this "*schwere Stunde*," the poet concentrates on Freedom, for Schiller one of the most profoundly conceived human capacities, but one that Thomas Mann completely articulated only much later in his life. The text of "A Weary Hour," however, points toward the concept of Freedom through Schiller's own ideas. Schiller began his aesthetic essay with the following passage: " 'No man must be obliged,' says the Jew Nathan[156] to the Dervish, and this word is true in a wider sense than perhaps one would give it credit [for being]. The will is the genetic characteristic of man, and reason itself is only an external rule of the same. All of nature act reasonably; his prerogative is only that it acts reasonably with consciousness and of his own volition. All other things *must*; man is the creature that *wills*" (EHL; emphasis added.)[157] The lonely poet of "A Weary Hour" ponders Freedom in relation to his own life.

The concept of Happiness is also closely related to the "naïve" in Schiller's definition of proximity to the essence of nature. "As long as we were only children of nature, we were happy and accomplished; we became free and lost both. Out of this emerges a dual, very dissimilar, longing for nature, one longing for its happiness, one longing for its accomplishment" (EHL).[158]

The description of Schiller's childlike and beautiful wife represents Mann at his lyric best, an example, in fact, of the "naïve" expression of love. The image of a pale beauty with dark curls ("a ringlet of dark hair lay across her cheek, that radiated with the paleness of pearl") (*STD* 296; *GW*, 8: 378) recurs in both his fiction and his correspondence.[159] The poet's interior monologue in "A Weary Hour," a love song, also contains the line "Bei Gott, bei Gott, ich liebe dich sehr!"[160] and a part of it was used in "Tonio Kröger," not only conveying his love for Katia, but also his more general longing for love. Stern artistic self-discipline reverses the mood: "And I must not be too utterly thine, never utterly happy in thee, for the sake of my mission " (*STD* 296; *GW*, 8: 379).

The last two paragraphs of "A Weary Hour" exhibit the poet's new beginning. The "difficult hour," the moment of human weakness and hesitation, is over, and the poet takes up his pen again. Creativity springs from the sympathetic involvement of the uncommitted poet, who can elicit the invisible universe that artistry can call to the visible world.[161] The ill, tormented Schiller reaches to the conceptual universe to transcend the human condition (*Menschentum*) through aesthetic insight, fighting the poet's way to Art despite bodily weakness, illness, and a momentary lack of inspiration. The hope, zeal, energy, and joy of resurgent creation are apparent as he forces himself to his heroic tasks: "No brooding! Work! Define, eliminate, fashion, complete!" (*STD*, 296; *GW*, 8: 379).

Whether the work is Schiller's *Wallenstein* or Mann's *Fiorenza* does not matter; only its birth from human suffering matters, forces from the depths of the "poet"'s soul, from music and idea, which reflect the universal "homeland" (*Heimland*) of the "other side." The closing lines of "A Weary Hour" glorify the poet's secret heroic struggle for the artistic creation his vocation demands, and they formulate the worthiest and most personal homage Thomas Mann could offer in honor of Schiller's.

"The Blood of the Walsungs"

After "The Weary Hour," Mann was absorbed in several other projects. His new and closer reading of Schopenhauer affected "Die Geliebten" and "Maya,"[162] and he was planning a "Fürsten Novelle," as he called it, a projected short story which grew into the novel *Royal Highness* (Königliche Hoheit). He was also researching the life and times of Frederick the Great of Prussia.[163] But suddenly in midsummer, 1905, Mann laid all of these aside for another short story, initially the "Tiergarten Novelle," now known as "The

Blood of the Walsungs" ("Wälsungenblut").[164] It was to appear in *Die Neue Deutsche Rundschau* in January 1906, but it was recalled from publication in December of 1905, and appeared only much later in French translation.[165] The story first appeared in German in 1921 as a single volume in an illustrated bibliophilic edition of 530 copies.[166]

"The Blood of the Walsungs" was written during Katia Mann's first pregnancy. In August 1905, the young couple went on vacation, first to relatives of Katia's, the Rosenbergs, in Berlin, and then to Zoppot, a little summer resort on the Baltic Sea.

The title of the story, "The Blood of the Walsungs," is the closing statement of the first act of Wagner's *Die Walküre*.[167] Wagner's treatment differs from Mann's in mood and attitude. The union of the semidivine Wagnerian figures celebrates a heroic victory,[168] but Mann's characters are decadent products of Western society who view their incest as a backhanded revenge upon it. He thus reduced the mythical operatic setting to naturalistic fiction, a difference that is crucial to the interpretation of this story.

Several possible motivations underlie the development of "The Blood of the Walsungs." Mann's own intellectual life, particularly his concepts of "worldview" and Art, provides the first salient approach. His attitude toward Wagner's music seems to have changed, and he was beginning to mistrust the subjective power of Wagner's works. The close connection he saw between Schopenhauerian concepts and Wagnerian art also appears to have been slackening. Either his self-defense against the magical Wagnerian music, which had ruled his subjectivity, might have been growing or his subconscious need to gain artistic equilibrium between his rational and his subjective reactions might have caused his increasing distance from Wagner's works.[169]

Mann might also first have been trying to express a vague epic vision still too powerful for him at this time, or he might have been seeking release from the dissonances of his various projects and his renewed reading of Schopenhauer. However, "The Blood of the Walsungs" might also be considered yet another subjective expression involving hidden personal problems like antisocial tendencies and narcissism. The paradoxical contrast between self-directed "disgust" (*Ekel*) and narcissism neurotically manifests the magnetism of opposites typical of Mann's romanticism. When he needed a sobering distance, he normally reacted with satire. The incest in "The Blood of the Walsungs" might then have been either an assault on Wagner's *Liebstod* concept in *Tristan und Isolde* or a shocking literary arabesque. This tendency also appears in "The Hungry Ones," where it grew from the need to create this in a paradoxical contrast between the *Künstler-Bürger* and the Walsung-human (Hunding) mentality.

At the time Mann was writing "The Blood of the Walsungs," conversations about Jewishness were commonplace and socially acceptable, and he himself was both objective and articulate.[170] Heinrich Mann was more critical of Jews, especially in his younger days; instead of coming to Thomas and Katia's wedding, he joined their sister Carla in sending a gift.[171] Later Heinrich and Katia had a pleasant, though not close relationship, possibly due to the conflict between the brothers that gradually developed.

Mann's many happy years with Katia demonstrate his total disregard of the Pringsheims' financial condition, which occasionally is cited by others as his motivation for marrying.[172] The solid foundation of his marriage was not shaken even during his worldwide fame, which coincided with the Holocaust. Because of the genuine human and intellectual attachment between Mann and his wife, "The Blood of the Walsung" was read to Katia and the other members of the Pringsheim family before it was sent to the publisher. Mann had satisfying personal relationships with individual Jews, and he also theoretically and idealistically expressed this in his *Royal Highness*.[173] For Mann, the so-called *Judenfrage* moved on the plane of the *Geist*. The complexity of the Holocaust makes it difficult for the non-Jewish majority of the population of Western countries to discuss the *Judenfrage* today. At the turn of the century anti-Semitism existed only in small independent radical movements. In middle-class society popular jokes and conversational slurs revealed the Jewish characteristics like that of any cultural group, as clearly demonstrated in *Cosmopolis*. As a minority culture the Jews endured some setbacks, but they were not persecuted, and families like the Pringsheims and the Dohms prospered and socialized not only with businessmen but also with intellectuals and artists. An example is Dr. Pringsheim's refusal to become a Christian as the basis for impediments to his promotion to a professorship, indicating a quasi-official prejudice against elevating non-Christians to higher echelons of government.[174] The Jewish families were, however, barred from mixing socially with the land-owning nobility, who rejected anyone not a member of their class, thus also the (Christian) burghers. The prestige of von Beckerath's name in the "The Blood of the Walsungs" is as important as is the silk comforter and the other valuables in the Aarenhold house. Von Beckerath's name and personality obviously ridicule the nobility and represent it in a boring *Kleinbürger*-type whose only desirable asset is his bloodline. Thomas Mann, the son of a respected patrician family, never felt comfortable in aristocratic circles, not even when he had attained world fame. Thus the irony here is directed against the unsophisticated Aarenhold parents as well as toward the utterly insignificant von Beckerath. The protagonists are the outsiders, the twins: Siegmund and Sieglinde. The image of the Jewish twins in "The Blood of the Walsungs," with the name of the "divine offspring" is Mann's realistic-satiric means of pointing toward highly complex topic. There is no reference to indicate whether Mann knew Wagner's text-sketch of the *Saracen Women* (Paris 1841; lost, 1843, which was then published 1889 in the "Bayreuter Blätter"), which would then interestingly relate the topic to Disraeli's, Steward Chamberlain's and Arthur de Gobineau's ideas in the 1840s. Mann felt that the heritage of the Hebrew was the ideal vehicle for conveying a bitterly ironic statement on Western decadence. Since the Jews are the "others," the extraordinary chosen people of God, they are separated from the Gentiles, this not only giving them a privileged position, but also making them disliked and isolated (*vereinsamt*) due to their "difference." The ironic tragedy is, however, that the same sons of God's chosen people do not live up to their standard either. The shocking paradoxical parallel between the incestuous Jewish twins, representing both the Walsung and Israel, and their "revenge" on von Beckerath (standing for Hunding), as well as the setting and the theme of Wagners *Die Walküre* seemed ideal for expressing both Mann's own personal disenchantment with Wagner's suggestive dominance, as well as his world around him, in creating a slapstick of *Die Walküre*. This would prove his father-in-law, Professor Pringsheim, right in his disapproval of the satirical criticism of Wagner.

Thomas Mann found it hard to endure what he now considered Wagner's artistic deception, and he wanted the whole world to justify his feelings: "As a *Geist*, as character, he seemed suspect to me, as an artist irresistible, even if deeply questionable . . ." (EHL) (*GW*, 10: 840–41). This statement validly expresses the *fin de siècle* decadence, as well as Thomas Mann's personal situation, since he was undergoing a painful awakening and an unpleasant liberation from Wagner's influence. In *Die Walküre* Siegmund and Sieglinde are the proud and hated offspring of the god Wotan; and Hunding, the philistine, is just as flat and as boring as Thomas Mann portrays him in the persona of him in von Beckerath. Siegmund and Sieglinde Aarenhold, expressing the *Weltanschauung*-satire, are colorful and true images of their sensual and materialistic dependence, and thus are distorted, naturalistically dissonant renditions of both the Nordic and the Abrahamic ideals. Their similarity is extravagantly absurd narcissistic, and unique, and von Beckerath (Hunding) is patently ridiculous, representing the common mainstream. The tripartite relations initially bewilder but soon become plain, for the story ridicules Wagnerian scenic effects and stage props, cynically and satirically stripping the scenes of their heroic effect. The opera sexually excites the twins, especially Siegmund,[175] and Mann's ironic and pejorative description of the Aarenholds satirizes their *nouveau riche* pretensions and their unmotivated existence. Von Beckerath, the parasite, does not come off any better, and even worse, he lacks the twins' wit and detachment. Mann describes a wealthy upper-class household with numerous children, but he did not model it neither on the Mann's as he did in *Buddenbrooks* nor on the Pringsheim familes; this is a parodistic parallel to the opera with a contrasting-paralleling clash effect between the descendents of the north Divinities and the sons of Abraham. "The Blood of the Walsungs" was even mistakenly understood by some individuals who had access to the manuscript as an anti-Semitic parody of the Pringsheim family by Thomas Mann, with the twins caricaturing Katia and her twin brother Klaus. Such speculations produced a scandal that made Mann cancel its German publication.[176] Two different endings exist to the story: the original close was: "What will happen to him? We have deceived him, [and] him a Christian!" (EHL).[177] This drastic original ending was questioned by Oskar Bie at Frischer Verlag, and after a brief hesitation and consultation with Heinrich, who did not feel a change was needed, Mann wrote the ending familiar today: ". . . he ought to be grateful to us. His existence will be a little less trivial, from now on."[178]

In December of 1905 Thomas Mann left his young wife and his baby daughter Erika for a lecture tour that included Prague, Dresden, and Breslau. When he returned on 15 December, he was met at the railroad station by Klaus Pringsheim, Katia's twin, who told him about the scandal that had rocked Munich for the last few days; Fischer Verlag had used some pages of faultily printed copies of the as yet unpublished "Blood of the Walsungs" as wrapping paper; they had been accidentally discovered and read by a bookstore clerk, and immediately vicious rumors spread all over the city. No family repercussions ensued at all between Mann and the Pringsheims as the story was known to them, except for mild displeasure on Dr. Pringsheim's part. He was not particularly literary, but as an ardent Wagnerian he resented any irreverent handling of *Die Walküre*. Mrs. Pringsheim, Klaus, and of course Katia had all approved the story when Thomas Mann had showed it to them, as he had with "At the Prophet's," before he sent the material to Fischer. Rumors flared up again when "The Blood of the Walsungs" was published in French in 1931 under the title of "Sang réservé," with the original ending and accompanied by an article in *Nouvelle Littéraire* that resurrected the 1905–6 scandal.[179]

Thomas Mann's indignation at these insinuations was best expressed in his short polemic piece, "Bilse und ich":[180]

> Already [when I was] a child, the public's fad of scenting a personal lead when faced with an absolute achievement outraged me. I was drawing a bit, [and] I painted little men with [my] pencil on paper and they seemed beautiful to me. But if I showed them to people in hopes of harvesting praise for my artistry, they asked me, "Whom shall this represent?" I screamed and was close to crying, "It should't be anyone!" I screamed and nearly cried, "It is a man, as you see, a drawing which I did, made out of contours, darn it . . ." This has not changed [at all]. Still they search: "Who will this be?" (EHL) (*GW*, 10: 17)

The settings of "The Blood of the Walsungs" are the house of a vastly wealthy Jewish railroad magnate, Aarenhold, and a performance of Wagner's opera *Die Walküre*. The twenty-three–page story includes an introduction, a performance of *Die Walkü*re, and an act of incest, but it has no formal textual division. The protagonists are the Aarenhold twins Siegmund and Sieglinde, backed by an supporting cast of insignificant characters—Herr von Beckerath, Sieglinde's suitor, and other members of the Aarenhold family. Mrs. Aarenhold, an ugly *parvenue*, resembles Baron Stein's wife in "Der Wille zum Glück": a tiny graceless woman, festooned with enormous diamonds and incapable of witty reflection on her surroundings. Her uneducated Yiddish-sprinkled speech and her unbecoming hairdo and clothing exhibit her lack of taste. The four children are all brassy—the twins, Kunz the soldier, and Märit the liberated spinster. Herr von Beckerath, a minor government functionary, is a mediocrity who owes his place in the *nouveau riche* firmament, unattainable to the Aarenholds, to his name and his job in the ministry.

The story moves in three dimensions. Father Aarenhold gets his money in the outside world to support his house and its microcosm. Von Beckerath comes from outside each noon to feed at the Aarenhold table, and Kunz and Märit both find their interest outside as well. The house itself is a plush buffer between "outside" and "inside" worlds, the refuge of the Aarenholds where their cultural trappings make life comfortable. Mr. Aarenhold loves the house he built and revels in it like a child with a new toy; he is freshly surprised each day by his pure silk comforter and the exquisite menu served in his pompous dining room and he intends to savor such pleasures every day of his life. His primitive joy in material splurging does not corrupt him, like the early Buddenbrooks with their uncomplicated pleasure in life's physical joys. The twins' world is an entirely different dimension, housing two creatures born into this house without any commitment to the outside world, from which indeed they feel excluded. They have cherished each other since birth, clinging to each other's moist fingers. As with Tonio Kröger and François Knaak, the incongruous juxtaposition of their Wagnerian first names[181] with their Old Testament last name paradoxically blends the mythical Old Norse tradition with their biblical Hebrew heritage. The twins wallow in comfortably wealthy blasé seclusion, a luxuricously decadent life style. Sieglinde and Siegmund are nearly identical physically as well as psychically, typically Semitic in voice, complexion, facial features, and thought patterns; they are inseparable by habit and choice. They shun the world outside, which can neither stimulate them nor accept them, for each other's continual company.

Mann says more about Siegmund Aarenhold than about Sieglinde; even though she resembles her brother so closely, Mann seems more comfortable expressing subtleties through a male character. He depicted many colorful women, but with them he never attains the sensitive creative reality of little Herr Friedemann, Bajazzo, Thomas or Hanno Buddenbrook, or Tonio Kröger. He seems to prefer modeling women from outside as types. Siegmund was the character closest to Mann in "The Blood of the Walsungs," and Sieglinde's existence was merely a formal necessity to caricature *Die Walküre* and to help express the story's narcissistic motif.

The twins' dress, unlike their mother's, was tastefully selected, an enhancement of their self-assurance, as it was for other fictional characters and for Mann himself. The fifteenth-century Florentine gown weighing down Sieglinde's frail shoulders recalls the refinement of Western civilization he had portrayed in *Fiorenza*, and the Oriental pearl on her forehead, a gift from her twin brother, dimly evokes a harem jewel or an Eastern caste mark. Siegmund too wears many colors and jewels of great value, and Sieglinde's gift to him, a golden chain he wears on his wrist, is also significant. In German, the word "*Fessel*" connotes "shackles" instead of "bracelet," an indication of forced dependence on his sister. Their linked red, cold and moist fingers, form a distasteful motif, a jarring element in their punctilious grooming.

Von Beckerath is not yet permitted to address his fiancée Sieglinde with the informal "*Du.*" Her distaste for further intimacy typifies not only her personality but also the whole family's attitude toward von Beckerath, as flat, dull, and gray a personality as his name indicates.[182] The cynical twins mock von Beckerath while they corruptly accept his marriage proposal in order to enjoy the prestige of his name. Von Beckerath does not have the behavior and mental processes of an aristocrat but those of a middle-, not upper-class, "burgher" (*Bürger*); he is an unpleasant ironic parallel to Hunding of *Die Walküre*, who assures "respectability" to the kidnapped god-begotten Volsung girl through a forcibly imposed marriage. The difference between von Beckerath and Hunding is the difference between the quasi heroics of the Old Norse impostor's crime and the ignoble surreptitious corruption of the modern decadent, as is the downfall of Abraham into materialistic mediocrities.

Mann carefully describes the twins' private language, characterized by slangy terms he had never used in his earlier fiction. A touch of this smart, challenging, humor-filled speech appears when Mann cites Katia and even in the conversations published in her *Meine ungeschriebenen Memoiren*, and Mann repeatedly mentions her sharp tongue in their courtship correspondence. The twins' conversational style reveals their quick minds, their cynicism, their irritability, and their discontent.

The Aarenholds serve gourmet dinners that do not exactly suit Mr. Aarenhold's humble origin, and neither do this elegant antique furniture, the old organ, or the oft-mentioned heavy Oriental rugs, but the younger generation takes their fashionable life style for granted, their criteria for civilization.

Several recurrent motifs point up significant moods, although these do not qualify as thematic leitmotifs. One of these is Siegmund's eyebrows, which he drew together "till they formed two black folds at the base of his nose."[183] Sieglinde's characterizing trail occurs with variations: the ". . . expectant gaze of her sparkling black eyes—a gaze as vacant of thought as any animal's."[184] Each mannerism is related to the omnipresent sensuality of these spoiled darlings.

When Siegmund prepares for the evening, his heavy dark beard and the abundant hair on his arms and chest[185] display a stubborn contrast to the "blond," the "other side," mentioned here for the only time in the story: ". . . how much occasion for making up his mind lay in that moment, recurring two or three times daily, when he had to select his cravat! And it was worth the effort. It was important. The blond-haired citizenry of the land might go about in elastic-sided boots and turn-over collars, heedless of the effect. But he—and most explicitly he—must be unassailable and blameless of exterior from head to foot" (*STD*, 306; *GW*, 8: 393).

Mann narrates this passage analyzing Siegmund's relationship to Sieglinde and the world, and not allowing Siegmund an interior monologue. A delicate balance exists between Siegmund's escape from the inimical, evil-smelling real world and the narcissistic love for his twin sister he has nurtured. The mere thought of von Beckerath makes Siegmund's typifying mannerism, the two "black [facial] folds" (*zwei schwarze Falten*), reappear. He more then despises his future brother-in-law, he feels a strong racial antagonism toward him, demonstrated when he calls von Beckerath "the Germanic one" (*Den Germanen*).

Before leaving for the opera, the twins kiss and fondle each other, even for normally affectionate youngsters an unusual familiarity, shading gradually into perversity. Their exit through the red-lighted stone corridor to the waiting carriage strongly suggests a classical descent into hell fraught with orgiastic symbolism. The name of one of the horses, Baal, suggests the erotic rites repugnant to the Old Testament Children of Israel, while Zampa, the other horse's name, evokes the motif of betrayal of the betrothed Hunding (Beckerath).[186] In their closed carriage, the twins are as secluded from the outside world as they were in their mother's womb.

Mann's details of *Die Walküre* today satisfy an opera lover. As the twins duplicate the stage action of the first act, Siegmund Aarenhold is a suddenly seized by vague sensations, ideas, and emotions: "Creation? How did one create? . . . it came to him as in a yearning vision that creation was born of passion and was reshaped anew as passion. . . . He saw his own life, and knew its contradictions, its clear understanding and spoilt voluptuousness, its splendid security and idle spite, its weakness and wittiness, its languid contempt; his life, so full of words, so void of acts, . . ." (*STD*, 314–15; *GW*, 8: 404). As the operatic hatred and passion swell, Sieglinde responds harmoniously to her brother; the performance ends, the two go home, and the tension becomes so unbearable that Siegmund leaves the table without finishing his meal. In his room he gives himself over to the scents of perfume and tobacco.[187]

The operatic Volsung twins know exactly what they are doing; they choose each other's love in conscious rebellion, for vengenance. Inflamed by sensual emotions, however, accustomed to their own way in everything, mingling rationalization with suppressed guilt, the Aarenhold twins yield to perversity. After their incestuous act, they remain benumbed, searching vainly for justification. A kind of illogical rationalization appears in Mann's hate-filled final sentence. Whether they say the "Goy" or the "cow-legged "burgher" " does not matter; they have sacrificed themselves to destructive hatred. She, sitting on the bearskin like one of Wagner's Volsungs, he shamefacedly rocking to and fro; the twins of Mann's "Blood of the Walsungs" are incarnations of the pitiable decadence of the *fin de siècle*, unable to give life to a Siegfried.

On 25 October 1940, Thomas Mann wrote in English to Lulla Adler from Princeton:

The story The Blood of the Walsungs [sic] must not be thought of in terms of present day conditions. It was written thirty-five years ago, when anti-semitism was rare in Germany and when a Jewish setting for a story had no particular significance . . . If you happen to have read the preface to the Stories of Three Decades [sic] you may have noticed that in the preface to the book I mentioned that The Blood of the Walsungs [sic] was a study of the mores of Berlin and had as its theme the isolation-motif. Certainly the story contained in it no deliberate impugning of any race or people, and for anyone to arrive at such a conclusion is quite erroneous.

"The Blood of the Walsungs" did not mark an important stage in Mann's work; he wrote to Gottfried Bermann Fischer on 11 November 1931, ". . . I really have never valued this story greatly . . ." (EHL).

This comment also indicates that Mann did not consider "The Blood of the Walsungs" to be a travesty of Wagner's *Die Walküre*; he used the story instead to express the cultural and sociological phenomena he had experienced in Berlin and employed a rationalizing irony to create necessary artistic distance and approach the quintessence of a subjective concept of his own.

Between "The Blood of the Walsungs" (1905)[188] and "Death in Venice" (1911) Thomas Mann produced only "Anekdote" (late 1907 or spring 1908), "The Railway Accident" (Christmas 1908), and "The Fight between Jappe and Do Escobar" (late 1910). He wrote them partly for money, partly to satisfy Fischer, and partly for his own relaxation.

Shortly after his wedding, besides "*Geliebten*" and his projected novel on Frederick the Great, he began a "*Fürsten-Novelle*," which grew into *Royal Highness (Königliche Hoheit).*[189] In 1905 he also began work on the "Swindler" (Hochstapler) project later known as "Felix Krull," but he set it aside in 1911.[190]

He was working on theoretical and aesthetic essays as well, and these years of study contributed greatly to his interrupted education and allowed him to come to terms with problems vital to his personal and artistic growth. Much of this research, unpublished at that time, like his essay "Geist und Kunst," appeared in his later fiction.[191] Among Mann's published essays are "Versuch über das Theater," 1907; "Mitteilungen an die Literaturhistorische Gesellschaft in Bonn," 1907; "Der Alte Fontane," 1910; "Peter Schlemihls wundersame Geschichte," 1910; and "Über die Kunst Richard Wagners," 1911.

Since Mann fortunately could afford to spend time in reading and meditation, his reduced publication during 1905–11 did not inconvenience him financially. S. Fischer felt that Mann was one of his most valuable writers and was eager to secure the rights to all of his productions.[192]

Because Mann seldom mentioned the three 1905–11 stories in his correspondence, only external data can establish their possible sequence of composition. He may have written "Anekdote" (not translated into English) at the end of 1907 or in the spring of 1908; it was published in the June issue of

Mrz (vol. 2, no. 2, 1908) while he still was working on *Royal Highness*, lecturing widely, and meeting important people. He was also both fascinated and frustrated by topics he was researching but was not yet ready to develop systematically; as he wrote to Heinrich on 11 June 1906, "'Frederick,' and 'Maya,' the short stories which I would like to write, could possibly become masterpieces, but one tears oneself apart with the projects and [one] loses [the] courage to begin" (EHL).

The term "the veil of Maya" was Schopenhauer's name for the vicious mirage of the world's representation, and since the fall of 1899, when he first read *The World as Will and Representation*, this phrase had never ceased to be highly significant to Mann. Between 1905 and 1910 he undoubtedly read both Nietzsche and Schopenhauer closely again.

The passion with which Mann in his Schopenhauer essay (1938) comes to speak especially of this particular aspect of Schopenhauerian teaching allows us to gauge how deeply he himself must have been impressed in his youth by the experience that all longing relied only on the deception of the senses: "the longing and yearning, your desire of the World—all this comes from the deception of plurality" (9: 551) (EHL).[193] In this frame of mind, Thomas Mann wrote "Anekdote."

"Anekdote"

The setting of this story resembles that of "Gefallen," Mann's first novella, in which a group of friends enjoy a spirited after-dinner conversation. In "Anekdote,"[194] however, he offers no description of either the setting or the participants, identifying the narrator only vaguely as "somebody" (*jemand*). Instead he emphasizes the "speculative and somewhat emotional" (EHL) (*GW*, 8: 411) theme of their discussion, aiming at the Schopenhauerian "worldview." Such chic blasé intellectualism dominates this little story, blending naturalistic and descriptive images with ruthless sarcasm. Mann here abandons his usual benevolent irony for bitterness toward man's foolish gullibility, which brings about his downfall. "Shame (*Blamage*) of longing" was the "glittering deception" of the "veil of Maya" (EHL).[195] At this point, the title's meaning becomes clear,[196] since the definition of an "anecdote" illustrates the theme of this short story, the misconception built on false appearances and bitterness at the lack of foresight and sarcastic disdain for limited insight. The scandalous tale of poor Becker and his repulsive wife is not the story's real message, it is only the misleading "representation" of the plot. Even the story's phraseology used then-fashionable "Schopenhauer jargon," and it falls into a logical pattern.

The story opens with the physical description of "heavenly little Angela Becker" (EHL) (*GW*, 8: 411). The name "Angela" reinforces the adjective "heavenly," which acquires sarcastic overtones. The lovely blue-eyed blond Mrs. Becker represents what the "will to live" represented in the "Way to the

Churchyard" or "Tristan," but she has none of the healthy "ordinary' qualities of Hans Hansen and Ingeborg Holm. Nothing actually is ordinary in
Angela Becker except her conventional marriage to Ernst Becker. Her loveliness is extraordinary, and so are her hidden vices. She tragically entrances
those about her; everyone is taken in by the superficially delightful world of
will and representation (*Welt von Wille und Vorstellung*).

Ernst Becker, the unhappy victim, as his name illustrates, is an unimaginative, uninteresting Everyman, whose "serious" devotion to Angela is the
basis for his tragic fall.[197] Ultimately the "others," who fail to understand or
accept "insight" (*Erkenntnis*), defeat him. When he wants to share his "insight" with the crowd, his foolish, tragicomic flaw illustrates the gravity of the
lack of human "insight."

At the close of the second paragraph, Mann spells out the Schopenhauerian
pattern of the "will to live" not formally emphasizing this phrase here. Angela Becker was indeed the "ideal" of the people who inhabited the world
around her. She, the ideal, has such "vivifying power" (*belebende Macht*) that
the loss of it would likely mean the loss of the "will to live."

Becker's wife had come from elsewhere, the narrator observes, hinting at
the Oriental origin of the "veil of Maya." This allegorical couple's childless-
ness is Schopenhauerian; extreme suffering had brought Becker the "insight"
of Angela's (*Leben's*) deceitful appearance, and so, for someone with Becker's insight, biological survival is impossible in the world of representation.[198]
When pathetic Ernst Becker can no longer bear the burden of his "insight,"
he self-destructively unveils the truth about his union with Angela (*Leben*).

The ordinary Becker and his grotesque confession carry the seed of Mann's
later *Doctor Faustus*; the tragedy reaches its height of desperation when no
one he was trying to enlighten could or would listen to his message of insight
into the real nature of the deception.[199] Much as in the close of Doctor Faustus, Becker is helped out of the room and the company leaves. The powerful
"will to live" conquered Becker, pushing him aside and silencing his message.
His insight could not be allowed to tarnish the "glitter of deception" in the
"veil of Maya," and "Anekdote" ends upon the grotesque ridiculous exposition of a longing.

"The Railway Accident"

The date of "The Railway Accident" is debatable; Hans Wysling suggests
that Variant A was written in May 1905, and Variant B, quite similar, at the
latest in the spring of 1906. The story was finally published in *Nord und Süd*,
January–February 1908.[200] "The Railway Accident" begins in an atypical colloquial but stressed style Mann also used in any essay, "Versuch über das
Theater" (*GW*, 10: 23), and in his novel *Royal Highness*.[201] His restlessness
appears in his letter of 27 February 1906 to Ida Boy-Ed: "You cannot believe
what affliction about myself I have to wrestle with,—naturally not about 'me'

but my talent, my artistry; more and more I incline to fatigue, to disgust, a listlessness which consumes [me] because it is associated with raging impatience; because I *need* achievement in order to justify myself" (EHL). On 1 May 1906, he went to Dresden alone because Katia was not up to traveling; he lectured, briefly visited the Fischers in Berlin, and stayed three weeks at the Weißen Hirschen.[202] On the way to Dresden he experienced a minor railway accident, the basic for the short story. He may have at least sketched the story after his return to Munich in May 1906, or he wrote it from memory no earlier than December 1908 for the Christmas issue of the *Neue Freie Presse*, as he himself said. December 1908 is used here as the date of composition.

"The Railway Accident," an autobiographical tale, is a little less than eight pages long, with an introduction, the traveler's departure; the climax, the suggested loss of his work in the collision, and the concluding reestablishment of normality.

After the abrupt mock formalism of the introduction, the amused narrator settles down to search his memories. The story touches on the artist's natural exhibitionism and swindlery; the problem of the artist as comedian obsessed with the search for demagogic effects, as well as the concept of the Artist-Swindler, figures in contrast to the literary man, all issues serious to Mann. The trip in the sleeping car is a little like a vacation with a leisurely and luxurious atmosphere.

Mann's familiar ironic benevolent smile here tolerantly shines on human weakness. The moustachiod train conductor represents law and order, security and respect. At the moment of disaster, his human frailty shows, but when the adventure is over, he resumes his pomposity and reenfolds everyone in sweet secure lethargy. Both the gentleman with the little dog and the old lady who wanted the second class compartment become accustomed members of the little community united through the disaster of the "railway accident." The high point is not the moment of collision but the moment when the novelist faces the terrible news: "Demolished–the baggage car? Demolished. . . . Probably it [my manuscript] was destroyed, then, torn up, demolished. My honeycomb, my spider-web, my nest, my earth, my pride and pain, my all, the best of me—what should I do if it were gone? . . . What should I do? I inquired of my own soul and I knew that I should begin over again from the beginning. . . .—and perhaps this time it would come easier!" (*STD*, 325–26; *GW*, 8: 423–24). The novelist's confession reveals his innermost character: he has nothing left but his life and his talent, and his spontaneous self-confidence at this moment is new even to him. Out of the pleasant train ride emerges an existential human problem: the author suddenly realizes that his creative personality is infinitely stronger than he had believed, and not his manuscript but his own flexible talent means everything. When order is restored and he is back on the train again, he is a new person, hardly caring that his manuscript was not lost after all.

In 1908 the Manns had acquired a summer house at Tölz, where they entertained their family and close friends. In the fall of 1908, Mann also had an interesting time in Vienna. His letters, which mention writing "The Railway Accident" to buy Christmas presents, are accurate, the story perfectly suits his mood. At Christmas Katia was expecting her third child the next March,[203] and three-year-old Erika and two-year-old Klaus were both healthy and lively.

The publication of *Royal Highness* relieved Mann of a long-standing obligation.[204] He hardly mentioned the existence of the short stories between 1906 and 1911, since he was absorbed in the "Felix Krull" project, which he had begun in January 1910. He was profoundly shocked, too, when, on 10 July 1910, Carla Mann committed suicide, a tragedy that nearly wrecked the health of their mother Julia Mann. He later wrote of this event that ". . . for the first time since the passing of my father [death came to our family] and the loss shook me to my very depths. . ." (*Sketch of My Life*, 38; *GW*, 11: 119). Carla's death awakened guilt and revolt in Thomas, and he realized that the family stability he had always believed in so strongly suddenly had been shaken. On 4 August 1910, he wrote to Heinrich: ". . . My sense of brotherhood makes it seem that suddenly Carla's death [has made] our entire existence questionable and that our ties have been loosened" (EHL). His ever-controlled *Geist*, which had been guided by the self-created boundaries of the world he acknowledged, was flooded with the very "anxiety of existence" (*Existenzangst*) which matured and strengthened him for his coming works, especially "Death in Venice" and the *Betrachtungen eines Unpolitischen*. In his pain, he impulsively reached out to Heinrich to try to save what he could; he could not grasp what Carla's death had meant to Heinrich, who had been so close to Carla but kept his feeling to himself. The brothers aided each other at this time, Heinrich supporting Thomas's *Fiorenza* and Thomas helping Heinrich financially, but the first chinks[205] of a deep gulf between them were beginning to appear.[206] Thomas Mann viewed Heinrich's growing "liberalism" with alarm, a position that intensified with the years.[207] Nervous and depressed over Carla's death, Mann spent the fall of 1910 at Tölz and the winter in his Munich apartment.[208]

"The Fight Between Jappe and Do Escobar"

On 11 December 1910, near Christmas, Mann read "The Fight Between Jappe and Do Escobar" to his family circle.[209] This light-hearted twelve-page story recalls his cherished boyhood vacations by the North Sea. The first-person narration highlights only a few characters; "Jappe" possibly was among Mann's youthful memories,[210] while "Johnny Bishop" might be the alter ego of one of his Lübeck schoolmates, Johnny Eckhoff. The narrator's mother, a lonely widow quite different from the socially active and pretty Julia Mann, and his little sister appear vaguely in the background as he candidly confesses his experience. In the group of two combatants and two onlookers, those who watch reflect the qualities the fighters exhibit. Between them appears the dancing master François Knaak, who had played a part in Tonio Kröger's youthful dancing-class infatuation with Ingeborg Holm, and they are surrounded by a happy crowd of faceless vacationers.

This story brilliantly describes small colorful details of a North German resort. The early teenagers naïvely admire Jappe and Do Escobar. The formal battle becomes in Mann's lovingly ironic treatment a showcase for the fighters' instincts and the public's reactions. Jappe and Do Escobar together illustrate exactly the same contrast as do the name and nature of Tonio Kröger—Jappe the blond blue-eyed North German and Do Escobar, "an exotic stranger" of Latin origin (EHL) (*STD*, 330; *GW*, 8: 429). Like Tonio Kröger, the young sensitive narrator has an affinity to each side, deeply frightened as well as attracted by the fight.

Johnny Bishop is an example of the "English character" who though still a child is intrepid, stable, sturdy, and attractive. "Johnny rejoiced wholeheartedly in the fray,"[211] typical of his sense of security and his rational curiosity, which accepted the match as a nonthreatening adventure. The narrator, anticipating the drama in his heart, felt far differently: "I felt a certain sense of duty, along with other and conflicting emotions: a great shyness and shame, . . ." (*STD*, 331; *GW*, 8: 431).

Besides the hot summer day, the dunes, the site of the fight, and its preparation, Mann adds a touch of resentment and fear. François Knaak, the trivial dancing master, is to referee the fight.[212] The victory is not clear-cut, though Jappe could be the winner and Do Escobar obviously the loser. The crowd is disappointed because of the brevity; they call for more blood but when there was no response, the narrator's tension mounts: "What I had feared had come to pass: the challenge had become general . . . In an excess of self-consciousness mingled with vanity I was about to raise my hand and offer myself for combat when somewhere in the circle the shout arose: 'Herr Knaak ought to fight!' " (*STD*, 338–39; *GW*, 8: 442).

After the moment of action is over, attention focuses upon Knaak, who cleverly avoid any confrontation. When wrestling was suggested, the momentum of greatness and dedication fades from view, dignity and heroism vanish, and when Do Escobar insults the German fighting spirit, he loses his last vestige of glory. Johnny stands up, disappointed that a remarkable event is disappearing into the sand. It deteriorates into undignified turmoil instead of being elevated to a heroic encounter.

"By the way, this story is not worth much" (EHL), Thomas Mann commented in a letter to Hans von Hülsen (27 February 1911). Leading American critics, however, acknowledge its emotional and descriptive worth.[213] But what makes "The Fight between Jappe and Do Escobar" so successful, despite Mann's own low opinion of it, is that the brilliant autobiographical setting is as profound as the story's intellectual horizon: Tonio Kröger and

Hans Hansen confronting and reacting to the primitive features of their own personalities in the rich imaginative world of childhood, surrounded by the bleakly realistic world. For the first time in Mann's fiction, this unpretentious story touched upon the theme of the artists's fear and longing to be involved in a great and perilous "adventure" and the delicate balance between the worlds of reality and fantasy that would produce "Death in Venice," Mann's next story, so personally moving and so universally relevant to the aesthetic appreciation of *Künstlertum*.

Mann, after having reached an abstract concept of existence in "Tristan," had to define his place in the world among people and to find access to the abstractions in art and the call of an artist. "Tonio Kröger" stands centrally in this quest with the other stories supplementing its message. The concept of *Bürgertum* (being a conscientious citizen), and *Künstlertum* (being a creative artist), are clearly defined according to Mann's standards at that time. These concepts harmonize with, but are not derived from, the message of Goethe and Schiller. The abyss is overcome between "Tonio," with his solitary calling of a poet, and "Kröger," who feels heart-warming community with the middle-of-the-road crowd and its cheerful mediocrity. This is an essentially romantic approach, which reached new intellectual, personal, and aesthetic values as Mann reexamined his Nietzsche readings between 1901 and 1910, and started his married life with Katia. Thomas Mann now had to move on to examine the very essence of the concepts of this *Künstlertum*.

5
AN ARTIST'S CALL AND FATE:
THE NATURE OF BEAUTY

"Death in Venice" ("Der Tod in Venedig")

In her memoirs, Katia Mann describes a trip to Dalmatia in the spring of 1911. After Broni proved "not very pleasant," the Manns "traveled by steamer to Venice. My husband was very much attached to Venice and the Lido" (EHL).[1] For the first time, the Manns gained a new perspective by approaching Venice by boat. Many of the events recorded by Katia also appear in "Death in Venice," like the gondolier who left without his pay after taking them to the Lido and the bystander who told them that their gondolier was not licensed. The Hôtel des Bains, where the Manns always stayed in Venice, was the model for Aschenbach's hotel, and even the Polish lady with her nunlike daughters and her handsome young son were real. Katia Mann confirms that all of the major incidents of the novella arise from actual experience. "My husband transferred the delight which he took in this charming youngster to Aschenbach and stylized it [his delight] into an extreme passion."[2] Katia Mann also related that many years later her daughter Erika received a letter from a Polish aristocrat who had read a Polish translation of "Death in Venice," and recognized there a description of himself and his sisters. He was in no way displeased to have served as a model for Thomas Mann's story.[3]

Mann also commented in "On Myself," ". . . just as in the youthful 'Tonio Kröger,' so in 'Death in Venice'—not one feature was invented: the suspect gondolier, the boy Tadzio and those around him, the failure to depart because of mixed-up suitcases, the cholera, the honest clerk at the travel agency, the wretched ballad-monger—all were provided by reality and had only to be matched"[4] (EHL) ("On Myself," 19. March/April 1940; *GW*, 8: 148).

When Mann left on his vacation that spring, he was working on "Felix Krull" and did not plan to start another project. By the time he arrived at the Lido he was considering "Death in Venice" as a quick improvisation to insert into his work on the swindler novel ("On Myself," 19. March/April 1940; *GW*, 13: 147–48). The moving infatuation Goethe had in his old age with Ulrike von Levetzow was haunting him: ". . . I wanted to offer something like the tragedy of "masterhood" (*Meistertum*) . . . the story of Goethe's last love, the love of a seventy-year-old for a little girl whom he insisted he wanted to marry" (EHL).[5]

But Mann could not set the master's decline to paper.[6] Later, on 28 December 1937, he wrote to Alfred Neumann that he had had "an old dream: to let Goethe himself act in fiction. It [the dream] springs from the time of 'Death in Venice,' when I did not dare [to do] this as yet" (EHL). Aschenbach's enchantment with Tadzio provided Mann a good substitute project and allowed him to express symbolically the rational and emotional concepts inherent in the "problem of the artist" (*Künstlerproblem*). In Venice during May 1911, using the letterhead of the Hôtel des Bains, he also wrote a four-page essay on Richard Wagner, who wrote *Tristan und Isolde* in Venice and later died there,[7] to fulfill his commitment for the Bayreuth issue of *Der Merkur*,[8] but the essay comprises his personal statement on "dignity of the artist" (*Künstlerwürde*) and the questionable nature of *Künstlertum*.[9] Thomas Mann took his customary personal approach in this essay and portions of it significantly illumine the theme of "Death in Venice."

Mann considered Wagner's vocation and talent genuinely epic, but he felt that by achieving intoxicating "effects" (*Wirkung*) through technical means Wagner presented only the surface level of the "dual optic" (*doppelte Optik*), frittering away his greatness. This made Wagner in Mann's eyes one of the charlatans he had introduced in "The Infant Prodigy" and was developing in the Krull project. Perhaps either Nietzsche or his own struggle for emotional and intellectual independence had turned him against his youthful love and debt to Wagner, although he closed his Wagner essay with a bittersweet tribute: "But even now, when a sound [or] a significant phrase from Wagner's work unexpectedly strikes my ear, I quicken with you, a kind of nostalgia for home and the pain of youth comes to me, and again, as before, my *Geist* succumbs to the wise, sensual, yearning and refined magic" (EHL). Most likely, both love and rejection of Wagner blended in his mind in 1911.

In discussing Wagner, Mann defined his own ideal: "Wagner is the nineteenth century, through and through . . . when I think of the art work of the twentieth century something basically and I think favorably different appears to me, something extraordinarily logical, ultimate in form, clear, stern and serene, of no less will power than the other's [Wagner's] but cooler, more sophisticated, and healthier in spirit, . . . [searching] for its greatness not in the baroque and the colossal, and for its beauty not in intoxication. A new classicism, it seems to me, must come" (EHL). This was Mann's commitment to the epic concept crystallized for him by Goethe, whom he acknowledged as his teacher.[10]

"Death in Venice" marks a milestone in Mann's development, and its vision of *Künstlertum* broadened his perspective into mythic universality. When he first worked on this novella, he called it an "impossible conception" (EHL).[11]

"Death in Venice" has five uneven chapters with a coda. Mann italicized his chapter headings here, rather than using numbers, treating an eighty-one-page novella with the scope of an epic.

The title of this novella, often linked with Wagner, stresses the Queen City of the Lagoons long considered the decaying gem of the past, a combination of beauty, love, and death.[12] The title's thematic significance parallels the notions of decadence and the loss of *Künstlerwürde* of which Mann had accused Wagner, stripping both the "beloved" and the "lover" of dignity. The setting of Wagner's star paralleled the meaning of Mann's crises—Fiore-Savonarola, Goethe-Ulrike, and Aschenbach-Tadzio. In "On Myself," he described Goethe's Marienbad episode as

> ". . . the loss of dignity of a highly soaring *Geist* through the passion for a lovely innocent bit of life—that grave crisis of Goethe's . . . [that] nearly became his downfall, and in any case was a *death* before *death*. At that time [1911] I did not dare to invoke the figure of Goethe, I did not trust my strength, and [I] gave up. I created a modern hero, a hero of a fragile type, one I had already shaped with understanding, a brother to Thomas Buddenbrook and Girolamo Savonarola, a *hero out of weakness*, thus one who works on the edge of exhaustion and extends himself to the ultimate; in short: a hero of the kind that I have called an 'achievement ethic.'" ("On Myself," 19: *GW*, 13: 148)

The concept of death became the theme of "Death in Venice." The physical trespasses of Wagner or Aschenbach are only the visible facet of Mann's "dual optic"(*doppelte Optik*), while the loss of *Künstlerwürde* is his genuine focus. He observed later, ". . . my theme again was the revenging invasion of passion, the destruction of a modeled, seemingly mastered way of life, which would be stripped of dignity and pushed into the absurd by the 'foreign god,' by Eros-Dionysus. The "artist," captivated by the sensual, cannot really attain dignity" ("On Myself," 19–20); Aschenbach, the ethical achiever, became the debased prey of Eros-Dionysus.

"Death in Venice" possessed classic and epic qualities from its very inception. Before any action begins in the first chapter, Mann presents the hero, the setting and the theme. The hero, Gustav von Aschenbach,[13] who was awarded a patent of nobility at fifty,[14] is now somewhere past the prime of life. The century, but not the year, is indicated, and the novella begins in the archetypally significant spring. Gustav von Aschenbach lived on Munich's Prinzregentstraße, a specificity of address Mann had never before offered in a story. The tangibly real world is immediately paralleled in an unfathomable mythic vision.

Gustav von Aschenbach's strict daily schedule alternates work and healthy activities.[15] On this particular day, his will-generated creativity refuses to allow him his usual rest, inducing restlessness and stress. Mann refers to the power of the "*motus animi continuus*, ("continuous movement of the mind"), a rationally creative *geistig* power, as "*fortschwingen*," literally "swinging away," "swinging ahead," or "an onward sweep."[16] A thematic oscillation appears in all of his works, representing the urge to overcome and marking the dangerous extremes it attempts to level. Mann himself developed in periodic oscillation, advancing by swinging gradually between extreme contrasts. Aschenbach is hypersensitive and irritable because of "the difficult and risky work of the morning hours, demanding just now a highest degree of caution [and] circumspection, penetration and accuracy of the will. He could not stop the 'on-swing' of this productive mechanism in himself, the '*motus animi continuus*' in which, according to Cicero, the essence of eloquence consists" (EHL) (*STD*, 378). This power, suddenly aroused, seems to have overpowered his rational control,[17] creating a dissonance in his life and *Künstlertum*, since this spring he is having trouble mastering the "swinging-forth" (*fortschwingen*)[18] of his creative power, which had been his impetus to work. On this warm, hazy afternoon in early May he tries a commonsense remedy, leaving the noisy crowd for an increasingly "still" path.[19] At the North Cemetery while waiting for the streetcar home, he suddenly notices a man standing "above the two apocalyptic beasts that guarded the staircase" (*STD*, 379; *GW*, 8: 445), a repulsive vagrant with a large hat and shockingly assembled features that seem at first almost familiar. His coloring, his emaciation, his scrawny neck and snub-nosed face, his too-short lips and long, strong teeth, his grimace at the setting sun—all features that recall a predatory death's head—recur throughout "Death in Venice." Aschenbach stares, fascinated, until he realizes that the stranger is returning his gaze with hostility, and intense emotion also significant throughout the novella.[20]

Aschenbach suddenly has an intense vision of "a tropical marshland, beneath a reeking sky, steaming monstrous, rank—a kind of primeval wilderness-world of islands, morasses, and alluvial channels."[21] That matters greatly to him, "and he felt his heart throb with terror, yet with a longing inexplicable"(*STD*, 380; *GW*, 8: 446). Travel had always seemed a quasi-"hygienic measure" (EHL) to the intellectual Aschenbach, both in Munich and at his rough mountain retreat, his two perfect work places, but he is now beset by a temptation to roam at leisure, and his exotic vision clashes with the stark Alpine landscape where he should soon go. His decision to go south seems rational, but actually he is yielding to his heart's impulsive yearning.

The first chapter of "Death in Venice" presents much of Aschenbach's past and present personal life, his idiosyncrasies, and his strengths and weaknesses. Both an artistic expression and a personal confession, "Death in Venice" recalls a tragic dislocation of inherent creative powers that eventually causes Aschenbach's tragic Dionysian surrender to intoxication,[22] a *Walpurgisnacht* in the classical mode.

Aschenbach's strain is clear in the first chapter, although he still controls his life and work. The second chapter presents his intellectual achievements[23] as "The author of the lucid and vigorous prose epic on the life of Frederick the Great" (*STD* 382; *GW*, 8: 450). "Epic" is the key word by which Mann acknowledges the quality of Aschenbach's work as "the patient *Künstler* who had industriously woven a richly patterned carpet of a novel, uniting manifold human destinies beneath the shadow of one idea by the name 'Maya.' "[24] "Patiently" and "industriously" categorize this creativity as hard work, not inspired artistry. The catalogue of Aschenbach's other works ironically names Thomas Mann's own unfinished projects: the "strong narrative" (*GW*, 8: 450) "Ein Elender"[25] and the "passionate treatise" "Geist und Kunst,"[26] compared to Schiller's aesthetic treatise "Über naive und sentimentalische Dichtung." Mann then begins his hero's biography: "Gustav von Aschenbach was born at L——. . ." (*STD*, 382; *GW*, 8: 450).

Although overt parallels exist between Mann's career and Aschenbach's,[27] the two are not identical. Mann was only thirty-six when he visited the Lido with Katia and Heinrich, so Aschenbach's life and character as retrospectively described "at forty" and older must be purely fictional. The immense energy and self-discipline by which Aschenbach practiced his craft was, of course, central to Mann's art. Constant self-control and endurance[28] were the virtues that enabled Aschenbach to complete his epic projects. In detailing Aschenbach's development of self-discipline,[29] Mann may be ironically anticipating Aschenbach's coming fall or admiring achievements that he knows himself incapable of—or he might simply have been stating his view of the artist's fate.

The serene equilibrium of Aschenbach's art had attracted an admiring audience oblivious of his agony of self-denial and the drain of his own energy. Aschenbach saw the hero as sufferer,[30] an apparently passive attitude that is in actuality active: "Forbearance in the face of fate, *Anmut*[31] constant under torture, is not merely passive" (EHL).

In a letter to Wolfgang Born, 18 March 1921, Thomas Mann commented on the silently victorious figure of St. Sebastian, the personification of "grace" (*Anmut*): "Now in its imagery I experience, above all, the benefit that the novella moves completely out of the naturalistic perspective, that it purifies itself of the pathological and sensual [elements] in the topic and allows only the poetic to remain" (EHL). Mann referred in the same letter to the "seemingly transitory association of the emerging figure of the "graceful" (*anmutig*) martyr in the story" (EHL). The figure of St. Sebastian, in fact, remains pure, free of the fine intellectual irony which pervades "Death in Venice."[32] Immediately following, Mann unveils the secret intellectual force of Aschenbach's creativity; Aschenbach is a "born deceiver" (EHL), which associates him will Krull, while "the doubt of existence of any other kind of heroism than heroism born from weakness"[33] indicates Mann's inherently personal position.

The crucial pattern-word *auf[zu]schwingen*[34] also offers a paradox: the writer appears as a "moralizer of accomplishment,"[35] sacrificing the emotional component of his personality on the altar of Apollinian form and symbolic expression, driven to excess and cheating Dionysus of his due portion. Such self-exploitation results in a perfect and appealing textbook example of formal literature. In creating such literature, Aschenbach accepted poor substitutes for artistry, defrauding both Apollo and Dionysus.

Mann also discusses the meaning of "dignity" (*Würde*) (*STD*, 385; *GW*, 8: 454), which completes the reference to Schiller's "Über Anmut und Würde." Thomas Mann also "doubted the "artist" could gain "dignity"; I allowed my hero, who had tried it, to learn and admit it was not possible . . . But to make him perish, this 'new will'—and to give a skeptical pessimistic solution to this attempt—this seemed precisely moral as well as artistic to me" (EHL) (*emphasis added*) (*GW*, 8: 516).

Aschenbach's discussion of "dignity" precedes an exposition using the concept of "disgust" (*Ekel*) presented in "Tonio Kröger," part four, referring repeatedly to "Ein Elender." The morally conscious Aschenbach[36] frequently comments on "a psychology-ridden age,"[37] a rejection ironically questioned by the narrator of "Death in Venice," who ponders whether moral fiber is not actually a dangerous simplification. "Has form not two aspects? Is it not moral and immoral at once?" (*STD*, 386; *GW*, 8: 455). Aschenbach's disciplined shaping of his own feelings into the framework of his fiction had cost him dearly by depleting his psychic and physical strength, his creativity. By stressing the formalistic Apollinian element in his writing throughout his lifetime had had willfully subjugated his Dionysian powers, and at the moment of his greatest public success, Aschenbach finds himself exhausted, with works that now seem empty examples of perfect exterior form.

Thomas Mann modeled Aschenbach's physical appearance on Gustav Mahler. He wrote in a letter to Wolfgang Born, 18 March 1921, ". . . in the early summer of 1911 [I heard] the news of the death of Gustav Mahler, whose acquaintance I had the privilege of making earlier in Munich and whose intense, self-consuming personality had deeply impressed me" (EHL). Impressed by the dramatic newspaper accounts of Mahler's death, he continued: ". . . while later these agitations mixed with the impressions and ideas from which the short story ['Death in Venice'] emerged, I gave my hero, decaying in orgiastic decomposition, not only the first name of the great musician, but I also loaned him the mask of Mahler in the description of his appearance." Aschenbach's face bore the ravages of his work. Marks of the "artist" "adventure" which Tonio Kröger had mentioned had chiseled lines which not even the most "extravagant passions"[38] could have caused. The chapter closes on the thematic pattern phrase *ausschweifen*, having just shown the self-disciplined writer's inability to *auf[zu]schwingen*.

At this point Mann uses a chiaroscuro technique to delineate Aschenbach's life, his ideals, and his ideas, convincingly suggesting a point only to dismantle it the next moment with deft questions. Even though he was immensely successful, Aschenbach failed to achieve his ultimate artistic standard because of precisely that "self-discipline" (*Zucht*) which had brought him his success. When his inner drives force the exhausted and prematurely aged Aschenbach to follow his sudden passionate urge to wander, he cannot resist them.

The long third chapter forms the powerful heart of the novella, in itself containing a fully developed setting and both the turning point and the climax of "Death in Venice." After attending to some business in Munich, Aschenbach set out for Pola, but there he missed the "intimate relationship to the sea" (EHL)[39] (*GW*, 8: 457), sensing he had not yet reached his destination. Aschenbach unhesitatingly obeys the mysterious force drawing him toward his fate, and Mann describes the boat that took Aschenbach to Venice with a skillful blend of realistic humor and a capacity of the occult. This dark ghost ship was manned by an ugly gnomish crew, a ticket-selling goateed clerk, a hunchbacked sailor, and the nightmarish others.[40] Aschenbach's ticket transaction seems Mephistophelean, the change on the table may connote Judas's thirty pieces of silver, and the bony fingers of the agent call up thoughts of Death itself. The sensation of unreality is overwhelming; Aschenbach suddenly glimpses what seems a grotesque provocative youth leading a band of young men, he soon sees with horror that this is an old man, costumed and made up, prancing like a youngster. Under his wide-brimmed straw hat, the man wears a brown wig, his face is painted with dull carmine rouge, and his little moustache has wilted.[41]

Aschenbach "felt as if a dreamlike estrangement would begin a disfigurement of the world into the occult, which would extend and sprend about" (EHL) (see also *STD*, 390; *GW*, 8: 460). When they are at sea, its vastness and the wide sky make Aschenbach completely lose the concept of time, a foreshadowing of his passage into a dimension where a Dionysian feast or a *Walpurgisnacht* is possible.

Aschenbach, like Thomas and Katia Mann, now approached Venice for the first time by sea, a completely new perspective. Thinking of Dante,[42] he watches the bell towers of the city as the boat, like Charon's barque,[43] approaches the lagoon where it had to stop and await sanitary inspection, Venice's first contact. While they waited, the old clown, drunk, approached the travelers. He was drunk,[44] and his gestures were repulsively suggestive as he for a moment confronted Aschenbach.

Her intimacy with the water unites the beauty of Venice, a fairy-tale city, with the archetypes of the origin of life, and her fantastic architecture erases the barriers of time, blending reality and fantasy and making the concepts of life and death seem irrelevant. Aschenbach at this moment was enraptured by Venice.

Paralleling life and dream, the boat docks, leaving the pragmatic world behind, even as today Venice's heart is still untouched by technological despoliation. Today's visitors may admire myriad architectural ornaments, discover the empty, sunny piazzas with their ancient stone fountains, and countless bridges curving high over darkly glittering water. The gondolas[45] with their symbolic and elegantly curved prows share the secrets of lovers, conspirators, and mourners, people from all walks of life. The gondoliers inherit their ancient profession, and today, as members of trade unions, still execute their work with pride, art, and corruption.

Aschenbach is eager to leave the boat, but he is "still hindered in stepping down; his trunk[46] hampered him, which was just then pulled and dragged down the ladderlike stairs" (EHL) (see also *STD*, 392; *GW*, 8: 463). He is crowded by the repulsive old dandy, who wishes him a thick-tongued happy stay in Venice with his "sweetheart."

The foolish old drunk shares a few characteristics with the emaciated vagrant in Munich's North Cemetery. Although generally their garments are dissimilar, both wear wide-brimmed hats. Both the wanderer and the young-old drunk refer to death; the latter wears false hair and a painted complexion with strong teeth, all in a worn-out carcass and dominated by a corrupt mind, a macabre replica of the Seducer. Both seem almost to intoxicate Aschenbach, who resents the man's vulgar insinuations; but the stranger arouses something in Aschenbach he at first rationally rejects but later, drawn by instinct, ultimately finds attractive. The symbolic configuration of Death here refers not only to the end of Aschenbach's physical life, but also to the close of his exclusive service to Apollo, the rule of reason and self-discipline: "Death before Death" is the paradoxical loss of the artist's unattainable dignity (*"Künstlerwürde"*); Dionysus is opposed to Apollo. Aschenbach, who had yearned to live long enough to be able "to be fruitful in all stages characteristic of the human" (EHL) (*STD*, 383; *GW*, 8: 451), now must endure the contest of Apollinian and Dionysian powers in his *Geist*.

By serving Apollo alone and suppressing his own natural instincts, Aschenbach had betrayed Dionysus. The idea of fading boundaries between the Apollinian and Dionysian concepts grows throughout "Death in Venice," as the characters symbolically embody abstractions the senses cannot grasp, reflecting overlapping, shifting characteristics.

The scene of this metaphysical contest significantly is Venice, the city of beauty and "grace" (*Anmut*), the city of life (water), death, and decay, a city fraught with mythical meaning and actual corruption. In Venice Aschenbach could be consecrated into insight, either attaining the "artist's dignity" or succumbing to powers beyond his strength. As he slowly follows his coffinlike trunk down the boat's step, he can still hear the obscene jokes of the drunk behind him.

Aschenbach had to take a gondola to his hotel, and Mann's repetitions of "death" and "coffin" make the gondola a symbol of death itself.[47] It has soft dark-colored or black velvet cushions, as luxuriously comfortable as a coffin, and the "stillness of the water city" graciously surrounds Aschenbach, making him relax and wish "it could last forever" (EHL) (*STD*, 392–93; *GW*, 8: 464).

A breeze of a foreboding sirocco moves the air as Aschenbach rides in the gondola, and ". . . it grew stiller and stiller around him" (EHL); the gondolier mumbles to himself as he guides his vehicle to the open sea. The gondolier is blond, outlandish, brutal; he wears a large straw hat with rotting braid; his short snub nose and his narrow lips, baring his teeth to the gum, place him in the parade of mythical Death-Dionysus figures Aschenbach encounters.

Upon arriving at the Lido, Aschenbach goes to the nearby hotel to find change for the fare, but when he returns, the gondolier has left without his pay.

At last Aschenbach is installed in the Hôtel des Bains,[48] where his tall window looks out on the open sea, as Tonio Kröger's glass door had done at Aalsgaard. The setting resmebles a mortuary, with furniture made of precious wood, strongly scented flowers, and the trunk in the middle of his room.

At first, Aschenbach, like any tourist, walked, had tea, read the papers and watched the people around him. Pleasant and cultivated multinational guests representing many nations always attracted Mann.[49] A group of youngsters with their governess catches Aschenbach's eye, three strictly comported girls in gray ensembles that erase their charm and individuality. The boy with them, very different, immediately takes Aschenbach's fancy.

Aschenbach's first impression of the boy gave him a start; he saw a vision of perfect beauty, made infinitely attractive by an individually dignified "grace" (*Anmut*) in every gesture, a delightful combination of dignified "self-respect" (*Selbstachtung*) and "poise" (*Zucht*). Beauty, as compared to Goodness and Wisdom, is the only abstraction which by its nature can acquire from, substantializing itself so that it can be perceived by human senses. Because of the boy's "poise" (*Zucht*) and "grace" (*Anmut*), his physical beauty represents not only the abstraction of Beauty, but also an inner quality of his personality, as a part of human (*menschliche*) nature that Aschenbach immediately associates with images from classical mythology, especially of the god Apollo.[50] As the boy's magnetic image oscillates between reality and vision, it tends increasingly toward the mythic.

After a peaceful sleep and dream,[51] Aschenbach has been joyfully and purely admiring the boy, but the heat becomes oppressive, and "when Aschenbach opened his window he smelt the stagnant odour of the lagoons,"[52] a leitmotif combining concrete and abstract decay.

The smell that years before had driven him from Venice depresses Aschenbach[53] enough so that he does not unpack completely. Aschenbach's free will governs his actions and he is completely responsible for their consequences, even though powerful deathly and Dionysian forces seem to conspire with repressed instincts to weaken his objective judgment. The trunk-coffin housing his belongings is a dead weight when it is moved around, but it seems to adjust to the rhythm of events. Defying gravity, it had appeared to resist its descent from the boat upon Aschenbach's arrival at Venice. It was passive in the gondola, while in the hotel room with the windows facing seaward and surrounded by the heavy fragrance of the flowers, it again suggests a funeral parlor.

Aschenbach breakfasts and he misses the beautiful Polish boy; when the boy finally appears, the bare pronoun "he" emphatically points out Aschenbach's concentration on him alone, with abundant references to Greek mythology. "It was the head of Eros, with the yellowish bloom of Parian marble, with fine serious brows, and dusky clustering ringlets standing out in soft plenteousness over temples and ears" (*STD*, 399; *GW*, 8: 474).[54] Aschenbach also exclaims, "Aha, little Phaeax!" referring to an inhabitant of Phaeacia, the luxurious island in the *Odyssey* where Odysseus was driven by a storm. Aschenbach assumes the pampered Polish boy is allowed to sleep longer than his more regimented sisters.

But Aschenbach feels that even his vacation is a matter of duty, and so he organizes the details of his leisure on the beach. The beach attendant who helped him find his lounge chair wears a large straw hat, a leitmotif item again appearing on the head of someone who aids Aschenbach's spiritual Southern adventure. As Aschenbach watches the colorful movement around him, a rather unruly, somewhat out-of-place Russian family briefly attracts his attention. Aschenbach, who has still not unpacked his trunk, thinks, "So I will remain here" (EHL).[55] He seems to have found the intimate contact with the sea he had longed for and missed at Pola. "To rest at perfection is the yearning of one who strives for excellence; and is Nothingness not a form of perfection?" (EHL) (see also *STD*, 401; *GW*, 8: 475).

When the Polish boy suddenly appears, he casts some aspersions on the Russian family, and Aschenbach, observing, is delighted: "This childish exhibition of fanaticism directed against the good-naturedest simplicity in the world—it gave to the godlike and impressive the final human touch" (*STD*, 401; *GW*, 8: 476).

As someone called to the Polish boy, Aschenbach tried to catch the boy's first name, but he could not recognize it: "Adjiu, with a long-drawn-out *u* at the end. He liked the melodious sound, and found it fitting" (*STD*, 402; *GW*, 8: 476–77). Mann knew no Polish, but he set about finding a bona fide Polish name matching the sounds he and Aschenbach heard on the beach. He wrote to Olga Meerson,[56] who explained that the sounds he had heard as "Adgio" or more often "Adgiu" might have been "Tadzio," the nickname for "Tadeusz," or possibly "Wladzio," the nickname for "Wladyslaw." The boy's real name was Wladyslaw Moes, but Mann chose "Tadzio" as more appealing.

Aschenbach soon rejected the paper and pens he had brought along, soothing his thirst with some large ripe strawberries.[57] The first strawberry episode at the middle of the third chapter marks the first intellectual turning point of the story, in which Aschenbach, fascinated by the beauty and "grace" (*Anmut*) of the Polish boy, feels unusual desires. Aschenbach first felt with irrational delight that the boy's antipathy to the Russians brought Tadzio down from divine beauty to the "human" level.[58] The boy's melodic name was the next irrational attraction;[59] after capriciously tossing aside his writing equipment, "With closed lids Aschenbach listened to this in his inner-resounding song, and again he thought that it was good to be here and that he wanted to stay here" (EHL) (see also *STD*, 403; *GW*, 8: 478). Aschenbach has unknowingly been touched by Dionysus. In Aschenbach's *Geist*, emotions gradually dominate his rationally conceived ideas, undermining his principles and established concepts, even rationalizing irrational yearnings.[60] Once in his room, Aschenbach suddenly discovers a tired, graying old man in his mirror, and against beauty and youth, rationalizing on fame seems meaningless. His admiration of a beauty that is necessarily limited to others, robs him of narcissistic delight.

After dinner, Aschenbach meets Tadzio in the elevator and discovers that the boy's teeth are imperfect, rather jagged and bluish,[61] a flaw that only makes the frail Polish boy more attractive. The motif of physical weakness is closely related to the theme of decadence, and Beauty is not related to life, but to Death; for the Greeks, it never referred to fruitfulness and fertility. Being a concept of intellect conceivable in the flesh, Beauty guides intellect and emotion without raising the thought of paternity, either biologically or artistically. Aschenbach's possessive joy in the boy's frailty made Tadzio more understandable and more lovable to Aschenbach than a healthy red-cheeked boy would have been. Tadzio's fragility suited Aschenbach's mental concept of Beauty because he related the boy's beauty to the unearthly and the eternal.

That same day Aschenbach took the *vaporetto* to Venice. His daily walk helped him recover his judgment and govern his irrational moods, totally reversing[62] his train of thought. The sultriness, the sirocco, and his own febrility, all made him see the need to flee this city, which was devastating him. Exhausted, he sat on the edge of a stone fountain in the midst of a deserted piazza,[63] and later he seemed restored when he began to organize his departure, swiftly announcing his departure the next morning to the hotel staff and packing his trunk completely before he goes to bed.

The next morning the weather seems to cooperate with the adverse forces within him, and the fresh air makes his previous day's decision appear hasty. He does not cancel his departure, but he does not help the efficient staff to get him to his train on time. At the very last moment "Tadzio entered through the glass door" (EHL) (*STD*, 406; *GW*, 8: 482). Aschenbach's silent farewell is paternal, "Be blessed" (ibid.); his heart is filled with a lover's violent pain. Will and reason were interrupting the great adventure of his life, and involvement with metaphysical power in the apprehension of Beauty.

Aschenbach realizes that he is saying farewell forever to Venice, and his eyes well with tears as he leaves for the railway station by water.[64] The abstract relation of his stay in Venice seems incomparably more significant than his physical incapacity for the climate, which seems a humiliation.

At the railway station, though, he learns that his trunk has been sent to the wrong destination, forcing him to a decision for the second time that day. In the first, when Tadzio entered through the glass door, Aschenbach's reason had overcome his emotion, but now he cannot deny his emotion, as if his suffering and exhausted heart had been waiting for an excuse to throw itself into the "impossible and prohibited stay" (EHL),[65] as "an adventurous joy"

(*STD*, 406), ". . . an incredible gaiety" (EHL).[66] "Adventurous" and "adventure" (*Abenteuerlich* and *Abenteuer*) have special connotations in Thomas Mann's vocabulary; especially since "Tonio Kröger," they had formed a necessary characteristic for Thomas Mann's questor, the *Künstler*, also suggesting the dubious nature of the trickster. These terms also relate to Thomas Mann's concept of freedom in the context of reckless promiscuity, at a Dionysian feast or a *Walpurgisnacht*, a "strangely unbelievable, humiliating, comically dreamlike adventure" (EHL) (see also *STD*, 407; *GW*, 8: 484).

The gray of the sea changes to light green as Aschenbach watches from his new room at the Hôtel des Bains. As he "looked with himself" (*STD*, 409; *GW*, 8: 486), he executed a gesture of welcome and offering, ritualistically surrendering to the perilous adventure (*Abenteuer*) with all its bliss and suffering. The weather turns with the fourth chapter of "Death in Venice," the dominant sun now full of fertility, light, purity, and beauty—delightful days and fresh, lovely, fragrant nights that mirror the clear harmonic beauty appropriate to Apollo.[67] His misdirected trunk returns after a few days, and this time Aschenbach unpacks completely, signaling his intention to remain indefinitely in Venice. Mann actually avoids naming the trunk now, referring to it as Aschenbach's "cargo gone astray" (EHL).[68] The trunk has lost its function and remains a silent part of the symbolic funerary decor, to which the dying Aschenbach will be brought from the beach at the end of the tragedy.

Aschenbach who all his life has served the sober discipline of art, now spends his days "entirely dedicated to the sun and its feasts" (EHL).[69] No matter where he goes or what he does, he meets Tadzio constantly. Tadzio's honey-colored curls and his beautiful shape glow in the sun like a statue from antiquity, bringing Aschenbach infinite delight.[70]

Here in the first two chapters, the concept of art is presented through Aschenbach. Tadzio's beauty now becomes singularly abstract; Aschenbach had worked within the abstract rules of his own art, comparing his media, language, with the sculptor's marble in expressing mankind's *geistig* beauty.[71] He now glimpsed "form as divine thought, the only pure perfection which lives in the *Geist* and of which a human copy and likeness was here, lightly and chastely, presented for adoration. This was intoxication" (EHL) (*STD*, 412; *GW*, 8: 490).[72] Aschenbach's train of thought had begun with the union of intangible beauty with the tangible beautiful form; it then moved toward a ritualistic adoration of the symbolically expressed form, the Apollinian, but swung suddenly to its opposite, Dionysian intoxication. The sunshine has guided his attention from the intellectual to the sensual, and Aschenbach greedily welcomes such intoxication. "So, too, the god, in order to make visible the spirit, avails himself of the forms and colours of human youth, gilding it will all imaginable beauty that it may serve memory as a tool, the very sight of which then sets us afire with pain and longing (*STD*, 412; *GW*, 8: 491). And a charming vision wove itself for him out of the frenzy of the sea and out of the glaze of the sun . . ." (EHL).[73]

Aschenbach's fantasies culminate in an imaginary dialogue—actually a monologue of Socrates to Phaedrus in a classical setting, summing up Aschenbach's ideas at this point, a scene that Mann recapitulates at the end of chapter five.[74] Socrates' brilliant argument for beauty and art is modeled on Plato's *Phaedrus*, but Aschenbach's dream-vision is suggestively similar to Nietzsche's Socrates, not Plato's.

Mann's Socrates concludes, " 'So then Beauty is the emotion's pathway to the *Geist*, only the road is just a means, little Phaedrus.' And then he pronounced the most subtle thing of all, this cunning courtier, that the lover is more divine than the beloved because the god was in him but not in the other, perhaps the tenderest [and] most mocking thought ever conceived, from which [proceeds] all the roguishness and secret lustful bliss that springs from longing" (EHL) (*STD*, 413; *GW*, 8: 492). This mood is the opposite of the feeling that had led Aschenbach to try to escape from Venice.[75] His transformation from the sober paternal artist who is almost religiously reverent to the artist immolating himself to create through the passion of self, opens his path to ruin. Plato had observed, "He who is the victim of his passions and the slave of pleasure will of course desire to make his beloved as agreeable to himself as possible. Now to him who has a mind diseased anything is agreeable which is not opposed to him, but that which is equal or superior is hateful to him, and therefore the lover will not brook any superiority or equality on the part of his beloved; he is always employed in reducing him to inferiority" (Pl. *Ph.*, 277). In "Death in Venice," the Platonic Socrates and the Nietzschean Socrates ironically clash, and no longer can Aschenbach heroically dedicate his life to his craft.[76]

The desire to act, to embrace, to proceed, fills Aschenbach with a passionate urge to unite his overwhelming emotions with the *Geist*. His *geistig* adventure forces him to create from, or in spite of, the Apollinian and the Dionysian,[77] and becomes the climax of "Death in Venice" 's tragic denouement. Tempted, then seduced, by the imaginary Socratic discourse, "in this crisis the violence of our sufferer's [Aschenbach's] seizure was directed almost wholly towards production" (*STD*, 413; *GW*, 8: 492). Whether his rapture is Apollo's glorious fertility or the Dionysian drive toward generation or a mystery beyond human comprehension does not matter; Aschenbach has to verbalize his desire in Tadzio's presence, to transmute Tadzio's physical beauty, the music of his voice and the grace of his gestures, into the realm of the *Geist*, in the mysterious union of the opposing body and the *Geist*. Aschenbach's ecstasy born of experiencing two extremes made the words he set down seems Eros's native language. Upon completing this brief work of art, Aschenbach "felt exhausted, broken, and his conscience reproved him, as if after a debauch" (EHL).[78] This was the one genuine creation of his entire life, in which the passion (*Rausch* = intoxication) of his *geistig* infatuation with beauty substantialized in his medium, words, the Beauty born of the union of the physical inner grace (*Anmut*), a mystery modeled upon Nietzsche's concept of overcoming opposites into unity.

Aschenbach's self-sacrificing heroism hides a heart-breaking tragic irony in this single creative adventure.[79] The sweet sounds of Nietzsche's Socrates seduced his *Geist*, and the creation he produced incestuously mingled *Geist* and passion.[80]

Tragically because of this noble desire to know, and utterly without realizing it, Aschenbach at this moment loses the "dignity" (*Würde*) he believed he had attained. Since he had not reached the union of *Geist* and beauty in genuine "insight" (*Erkenntnis*) but by deceptive passion, its "grace" (*Anmut*) was blurred, and the empty shell of formal beauty[81] held no inner beauty but chaotic instinct.[82] He plunges toward his end exhausted by guilt, an initiation into the tragic irony of his human condition.[83]

In an abrupt shift from sobriety to infatuation, Aschenbach from this day on behaves like a lover[84] in Tadzio's presence, believing the boy had noticed him, too.[85] The key expressions[86] "discipline" (*Zucht*), "licentious folly" (*Zügellosigkeit*)[87] and "self-esteem" (*Selbstachtung*), abound in the German text. A wild oscillation from one extreme, *Zucht*, to the other, *Zügellosigkeit*, results from Aschenbach's rejection of self-criticism, self-esteem, and discipline, eradicating the conceptual contrast, producing the fading, then the mingling of the extremes.[88] *Selbstachtung*, Tadzio's dignity, which had attracted Aschenbach so deeply in the first place, and his *Anmut*, a part of his physical beauty, now aroused in Aschenbach a passion utterly lacking the chastity and simplicity of his earlier admiration. Beauty, the ultimate mystery of human nature, is mentally mingled with instinct, robbing Aschenbach of his capacity for lucid self-criticism. On the one hand, all Aschenbach has left is the fear of seeming ridiculous and a growing sense of guilt.[89] On the other, however, he does not think of returning to Germany, and he allows the unusual surfeit of sun, food, and leisure to lead him into frenetic fantasies. He sleeps only lightly, agitated, eagerly waiting for the next sun-filled day, the imagery of the mythological figures, glowing with love for the enchanting Eos,[90] parallels Aschenbach's desires.

The images of sun and water, wind and clouds, mythically significant on this exceptional day, recall Tonio's awakening at Aalsgaard. Such mythological imagery[91] conveys Aschenbach's emotions as they fluctuate among the love, sorrow, jealousy, fear, and longing brought on by the mystery of distance, a mystery soon to be shattered by Aschenbach's approach to the boy in person.

One night, the Polish family is late and Aschenbach waits feverishly, dressed in evening clothes and wearing a large straw hat, an unusual combination crucial through its collective impact: the Munich vagrant, the old drunk on the boat, the gondolier, and the caretaker at the beach. Together, they point Aschenbach toward his fateful appointment in Venice where he, the lifelong champion of Apollinian values, will succumb to the forces of Dionysus. When at last Tadzio approaches that evening, Aschenbach is so overcome that he can only praise the beauty confronting him with the words he thought he had dominated. This moment of insight erases the deceptive

Socratic vision's promise of divinity; Aschenbach realizes that his literary power can never match this beauty. As he gazes at the Polish youngster, Aschenbach suddenly sees that Tadzio's smile is Narcissus's dreamy passive smile,[92] seeking his own lovely reflection in the ravaged face of the old man with the straw hat.

That smile leaves Aschenbach shaken, and like Friedemann in the face of an overwhelming passion (*STD*, 12; *GW*, 90) toward which he is impotent, Aschenbach falls prey to his long suppressed emotions. The Socratic deception has loose a flood of unfamiliar experiences, from which Aschenbach rushes toward his own ruin, bereft of poise and dignity.[93]

By the opening of the fourth chapter, Aschenbach has spent four weeks at the Lido, and it is now the latter part of July, when wealthy Venetians generally escape the heat.[94] Aschenbach has spent his time on the beach and around the hotel, surrendering completely to inactivity in which everything looks unreal and forces the imagination to run free. Suddenly Aschenbach realizes that changes unconnected with his own "great adventure" are taking place in the "outer world."[95]

"Bad" (*Übel*)[96] symptoms in other guests; the transparently diversionary attitude of the barber; and the growing pervasiveness of the carbolic odor—these are three symptoms that unite and pursue Aschenbach to the end. Aschenbach's actions are closely related to his problem, and the "badness" of his psyche eventually merges into the "badness" of the physical; his symbolic "death before death" coincides with his physical death from Asiatic cholera.

Aschenbach reacts as a lover who must above all else remain near the object of his devotion: "Passion is like crime: it does not thrive on the established order and the common round; it welcomes every blow dealt the bourgeois structure, every weakening of the social fabric because therein it feels a sure hope of its own disadvantage" (*STD*, 419; *GW*, 8: 500). Aschenbach fears only that Tadzio may leave Venice, something Aschenbach realizes he cannot bear.[97] The whole infamous, precarious and passionate situation "made his heart fill with satisfaction at the adventure the outer world was to engage in" (EHL) (*STD*, 419; *GW*, 8: 500).[98] Aschenbach's home has faded away; he is no longer a tourist, because he "belongs" with Tadzio. Aschenbach's only reason for suppressing news of the outbreak is to keep Tadzio from departing.

The epidemic itself is "bad," its odor corrupting the air as death corrupts human bodies. Aschenbach first perceives the carbolic smell as "a peculiar aroma" (*eigentümliches Aroma*) (EHL) (*STD*, 419; *GW*, 8: 499) and a little later, Thomas Mann uses the term "odor" (Geruch),[99] a symbol for physical and moral decay, the whole gamut of everything "bad." To Aschenbach, the odor signifies cholera and temptation curiosity, ecstasy, chaos; ultimately, death.

One Sunday Aschenbach follows the Polish family to Mass at St. Mark's Cathedral; Tadzio turns his head searchingly toward Aschenbach, who lurks in the dusk, watching him.[100] After Mass, Aschenbach pursues Tadzio and his family on foot and by gondola. Even now, he frantically tries to maintain his *Würde*, the self-respect his craft has given him, but inevitably the "adventure of the outer world" merges "obscurely with that of his heart, feeding his passion with vague and lawless hopes" (EHL) (*STD*, 422; *GW*, 8: 503).[101]

Not long after, street singers entertain the hotel guests on the terrace, led by a baritone guitarist[102] with a vulgar provocative style. Aschenbach, sipping a glass of pomegranate juice, is peculiarly receptive to these cheap ditties, which earlier he would have disdained. Ostensibly watching the guitarist, he surreptitiously eyes Tadzio, who stiffly smiles at the singer. The aristocratic boy, like the other spectators, feels shock and fascination at this dubious performer,[103] the latest in the series of the vagrant, the old drunk, the gondolier, and the beach attendant. The guitarist's red hair protrudes from a snap-brim hat, his skinny neck has a naked-looking adam's apple, and his snub-nosed face is dominated by large strong teeth. The guitar with its Eastern origin and rich history evokes the inherent instinctual life and decay that the Asiatic brings to Venice. The guitar also represents orgiastic Dionysian cult practices, the tradition of the *nomos pythikos*. Mann places Aschenbach symbolically between Tadzio and the street singer, Apollo and Dionysus.

Aschenbach questions the guitarist about the "bad" (*Übel*) things, but the man, whose clothing reeks with carbolic acid, denies even the existence of anything of the sort. The guitarist's "laughing song" provokes the crowd to hypnotic hysterical laughter.[104]

Aschenbach is overcome;[105] after the singers have gone and the crowd breaking up, Aschenbach dares to look at Tadzio once more. The boy responds with a grave glance and a deep sigh,[106] which Aschenbach takes as innocent docility and a symptom of frailty; they ignite "the reckless exultation of his [Aschenbach's] heart."[107] Once alone, Aschenbach contemplates time's relativity in the image of an hourglass he had seen in his childhood, compulsively associating his growing passion with the endemic cholera in the "outer world," taking a peculiar pleasure in unveiling the epidemic, and feeling an irrational satisfaction at the embarrassment he causes.

An example is Aschenbach's inquiry at the English travel bureau, where the clerk colorfully explains the origin of the Asiatic mephitic vapor,[108] an elaborated version of Aschenbach's vision in the first chapter.[109] The Englishman's remarks are plausible; he notes that German tourists have already gone, being first to ascertain the facts, and he also observes that food supplies have likely been contaminated, the surface reason for Aschenbach's approaching illness and death. Venice's death rate and Venetian greed in wishing to save their tourist trade are both clear, a physical decay that is matched by moral degradation. The helpful Englishman suggests that Aschenbach leave immediately.

Aschenbach reaches another turning point, where he must choose whether to go or stay. He envisions himself paternally warning Tadzio's mother of the epidemic, realizing that for him his chaste *geistliche* delights have yielded to the lure of Dionysian chaos. That night in Aschenbach's dreams unknown Dionysian powers invade his soul and defeat his upbringing and his mind.[110] In this clash between lust and debauch ("*Wollust*"and "*Unzucht*"), lust wins, at last overpowering Aschenbach completely (*STD*, 431; *GW*, 8: 516–17). A multitude of sound images stress the *u* sound; a flute[111] trembles with the name of Tadzio; a "stranger god," implicitly Dionysus, inhabits a wooded hilly setting; amid swarming animals and mythological creatures, "Aschenbach was greatly repulsed and anguished, but his will steadfastly protected to the last what was his against this stranger, the enemy of the collected and dignified *Geist*" (EHL) (*STD*, 431; *GW*, 8: 517).[112]

After this shattering dream, Aschenbach even loses his cautious modesty and no longer hides his desire. Most panic-stricken tourists[113] are leaving Venice for their homes, but the Polish family remains, seemingly unaware of the danger, and "lost to shame,"[114] Aschenbach follows Tadzio constantly. Like any lover, Aschenbach desperately desires to please,[115] and since his old body disgusts him, he allows a mercenary barber to dye his graying hair and make up his face and lips. With a loud red tie and a large yellow straw hat Aschenbach now resembles the repulsive old *bon vivant* who had so disgusted him on the boat to Venice. The weather parallels Aschenbach's mood; a "lukewarm storm-wind had come up" (*STD*, 433; *GW*, 8: 591), and the steamy chaotic town lies at the mercy of the cholera.

Soon his passion drives Aschenbach to pursue Tadzio again, blindly following the Polish family. Exhausted, he loses them; and sweaty and thirsty, he buys strawberries from a street vendor. Aschenbach greedily eats the deadripe fruit which had lain exposed to flies and bacteria as he surreptitiously slouches toward a deserted piazza with a fountain he has seen before, now befouled by garbage and reeking with carbolic acid.

At this point, Mann refers ironically to Aschenbach as the "dignified author of the '*Elenden*'" (*STD*, 434; *GW*, 8: 521). Delirious, Aschenbach repeats words (*STD*, 412–13; *GW*, 8: 491–92) from Socrates' discourse to Phaedrus, but the words, slightly altered, lead to new excesses: ". . . for you must know that we poets cannot follow the road of beauty unless Eros joins us as a companion, forcing himself on us as [our] guide" (EHL) (*STD*, 434–35; *GW*, 8: 519–20). Aschenbach believes now in an *Erkenntnis*[116] new to him: "To us poets, I say insight and intoxication lead there [to the abyss], because we are unable to swing up, we are only able to swing out [debauch]."[117] The pattern words *aufschwingen* and *ausschweifen*, confirm the theme: the poet cannot attain "dignity" (*Würde*), by reconciling the *Geist* and emotion attributable to Apollo and the instinctual intoxication of Dionysus. Man cannot attain divinity, the divine realm cannot be reached and mastered by man, because a glimpse of beauty will destroy him, as Semele was destroyed. Human limitations allow him to achieve only "excess" (*ausschweifen*) and debauchery. As Aschenbach, still speaking as Socrates, finishes his feverish speech, he says, " 'And now, Phaedrus, I will go. You remain here; and only when you cannot see me any longer, then you, too, depart'" (EHL) (*STD*, 435; *GW*, 8: 522).

A few days later, feeling unwell, Aschenbach leaves his room a little later than usual and learns the Polish family will depart after lunch. His fear and depression spring from his just expressed insight, the clear view of his inner world after the Dionysian dream which had destroyed the "discipline" (*Zucht*) and "self-respect" (*Selbstachtung*) his will had maintained. His immolation granted the *Erkenntnis* he had always wanted, fearing "that the hourglass would run down before he had done his share and had given himself totally" (EHL) (*STD*, 380; *GW*, 8: 447–48). Now he sees that the hourglass is empty. The outward action in the Hôtel des Bains singularly parallels the events of his inner life, and since Tadzio's departure has been set his own secret pact with Phaedrus would be fulfilled. For the last time, he goes calmly, even indifferently, toward the sea, to the source of life with which he had been so intimate.

Thomas Mann's autumnal beach scene abounds in archetypes of decay and death.[118] The lonely camera stand is silhouetted in black, a fantastic clash of "modern" technology with the eternal mythic elements of sea and sand. Aschenbach watches Tadzio at play from his deck chair between the sea and the beach tents. Aschenbach sits between two worlds, the sea representing the unlimited and unknown dimension of life, and the beach tents suggesting the everyday world. Tadzio plays in the sand with his friend Jaschiu, until Jaschiu's rudeness stops their games.[119] After the fight, Tadzio shrugs off his companion, who tries in vain to mollify him, and walks alone toward the sea. Reality and dream coalesce as Tadzio, beauty incarnate, turns toward Aschenbach,[120] and it seems "as if he [Tadzio] smiled and vowed, as if lifting his hand from his hip he pointed ahead, floating into the promise-filled and prodigious. And as he had so often done before, he [Aschenbach] rose to follow him" (EHL) (*GW*, 8: 525).[121]

Unconscious, Aschenbach is taken back to his mortuary-like room at the Hôtel des Bains, and his death becomes an event for his worldwide audience who acclaim his fame and "dignity"(*Würde*), especially after his last brief masterpiece, the piece Aschenbach had written on the beach, under the glaring sun, watching Tadzio. No one grasps the artist's tragedy behind this famous man's death.

Thomas Mann calls "Death in Venice" a tragedy. The essence of the tragic lies in the very nature of beauty itself. Beauty is the only concept that can be perceived when appearing associated with the physical. This union carries the unrestrained of the *geistig* and the perishable of the matter-bound, also conceivable as the Apollinian and the Dionysian. The artist's fate, to be able to reach the utmost of his creativity only in the moment when he can balance these two, requires his unconditional dedication and heroism when exposing himself to the danger of decay. The artist while balancing the opposites in the moment of creativity is filled with the passionate addiction to both. This vital (erotic) power lends him the (divine) spark of creativity. The "artist" being only human, had thus betrayed the unconditional service to both Apollo and Dionysus and therefore will be destroyed, since the one who has viewed beauty is not permitted to attain and to retain "dignity" (*Würde*).[122] But the *oeuvre* of the "artist" will survive him.

After Venice the Manns stayed at Tölz until October 1911, when they returned to Munich. Katia Mann had been suffering from malaise and fever, and she became seriously ill with edema in January of 1912. After an unsatisfactory stay at the Ebenhauser Sanatorium near Munich, she left for Davos with her mother on 10 March. Thomas Mann's work on "Death in Venice" went slowly; he wrote to Heinrich on 4 February 1912, "My life is now somewhat difficult but disregarding a few days of illness, I never stopped work and I hope to finish 'Death in Venice' before I go to Davos at the beginning of May" (EHL). However, he did not complete "Death in Venice" until after the visit, sending the manuscript to the Neue Rundschau on 21 July 1912, where it appeared in November 1912. Fischer issued a limited luxury edition in February 1913.

"Death in Venice"'s theme involves the topic of intellectual artist bearing both a theoretical and a biographical character. Its concise form and precise language explores two levels of conception, a *doppelte Optik* that has contributed to an oversimplification of Aschenbach's tragic confrontation with "insight" (*Erkenntnis*) into abstract and physical beauty as merely an instance of homoeroticism. Mann wrote to Paul Amann on 10 September 1915: "But I know . . . that through [this] I have been most clumsily misunderstood" (EHL), a matter he elucidated several times. In August of 1925, he wrote in "Über die Ehe," "Plato said, 'Who sees Beauty with [his] eyes/is already given over to the realm of death.' But these two lines erect the original and basic definition of all aestheticism and legitimately and rightfully the homoerotic should be called the eroticism of aestheticism" (EHL) (*GW*, 10: 191). In "On Myself," 1940, Thomas Mann further commented, "Again, my theme was the devastating invasion of passion, the destruction of a formulated, seemingly definitely mastered existence, which is stripped of dignity and pushed into the absurd by the 'stranger god,' Eros-Dionysus. The artist who is chained to the sensual cannot really become truly dignified: this tendency toward a bitterly melancholy skepticism appears in the acknowledgment (formed on the pattern of Plato's dialogues) which I put into the mouth of the hero, already marked by death" (EHL). Finally, Thomas Mann wrote to Jürgen Ernestus on 17 June 1954:

In America it ["Death in Venice"] is considered a classic—a sign that it [the story] itself is not considered immoral in this puritanical sphere. And it is not immoral. It [the story] is an acknowledgment of a reasoning conscience and pessimistic love of truth. "Perverse"? The dissolution of Aschenbach by the boy Tadzio cannot be dismissed with this definitely bungling word, because this is no ordinary yearning but an intoxication with beauty, the annihilating invasion of the "stranger god" into a formally conceived life, which had become "dignified" (*würdig*) [by being] built upon the exemplary and the representative. (EHL)

"Death in Venice" ranks as one of Thomas Mann's great successes. He wrote to Ernst Bertram on 31 May 1924, "You should hear what the managing editor of *Dial* wrote to me:[123] 'May I add,' he writes, 'that every day fresh congratulations come to us over our good fortune in being able to publish your 'Death in Venice' which has made a real stir in the American literary world'" (EHL).

"Death in Venice" also marks the end of Mann's great productivity as a short story writer. While his long series of gigantic novels, beginning with *The Magic Mountain* (1924), would establish him as one of the most frequently read modern novelists, he produced only a few short stories after "Death in Venice," for his emerging epic talent eventually found its most appropriate expression in the panoramic novel. "Death in Venice" is a thematic turning point in his world as well, because he had exhausted the topic of identity, the process of defining the artist and his vocation; he was free now to assess Judeo-Christian culture in *The Magic Mountain* and then extend himself later into the universal and the mythical in his great *Joseph* novels, a realm strongly intimated in "Death in Venice."

His short visit with Katia at Davos in the spring of 1912 gave Thomas Mann the seeds of a new project, *The Magic Mountain*. He wrote to Bertram on 24 July 1913, ". . . I am preparing another novella in the nearest future, which seems to be becoming a kind of humorous counterpart to 'Death in Venice.'" This "novella" grew into an enormous novel exceeding the earlier "long book," *Buddenbrooks*. *The Magic Mountain* took Thomas Mann twelve more years to complete.

6
NEW HUMANISM: FADING OF FORMAL GENRE LIMITATIONS

"Disorder and Early Sorrow" ("Unordnung und frühes Leid"), "Mario and the Magician" ("Mario und der Zauberer"), "Transposed Heads" ("Die vertauschten Köpfe"), "Thou Shalt Have No Other Gods before Me" ("Das Gesetz"), "The Black Swan" ("Die Betrogene")

The Road to Maturity

In the summer of 1913, Thomas Mann was badly depressed. He wrote to Heinrich from Tölz on 13 August:

> How is it going with you and the "Untertan"?[1] I am suffering from a constitutional depression and [am] all tormented. There's too much worry: some of *bürgerlich*-human [concerns] and some of a *geistig* character, about myself and my work. Katia is coughing and really should [go] away again. . . . I am too much in debt: 10,000 marks advance, 70,000 marks on the mortgage and even more. . . . If only [my] strength and inclination for [my] work matched. But within: always a menacing exhaustion, so that each attack shakes me to the roots; to this [is added] the inability to orient myself in *geistig* and political [matters] as you have been able to do; a growing proclivity for death deeply inherent in me; my entire interest always favored decay, and that is probably what keeps me from . . . advancing. But what kind of chatter is this! It is bad when all the misery of the times and the Fatherland weighs upon one when one has no strength to affect it. But probably this is just a part of the misery of the times and the Fatherland. . . . I am looking forward more to your works than I am to my own. Spiritually, you are in better shape, and that is what makes the difference. I am used up, I think, and I should probably never have become a writer. *Buddenbrooks* was a *Bürger*-book and no longer for the twentieth century, "Tonio Kröger" was merely *larmoyant*, *Royal Highness* vain, "Death in Venice" half-formed and false. So these are the final insights and comfort for [my] little moment of death. That I write to you this way is naturally rude, because what could you reply? But now it's already written down. Best greetings and apologies. (EHL)

After the brilliant reception of "Death in Venice," Mann announced that he was going to write a "humorous" novella, but his euphoria did not last. The "affinity for death," from "Death in Venice," made him all too susceptible to the menace then looming on the European political horizon to contemplate a "humorous" work. He had always been overcareful about money, and when his finances declined, Katia's recurrent illness and repeated hospital stays left him helpless, sinking into a self-pity so intense that it produced grave psychosomatic symptoms.

Since the fall of 1912 the Manns had been thinking of building a home near the shore of the Isar, close enough to enjoy Munich's cultural life but still near the unspoiled countryside. On 25 February 1913, Thomas and Katia Mann purchased the lot at 1 Poschingerstraße, where their new home was ready around 5 January 1914. Thomas Mann and the children had to move alone, since Katia was ill again. On 6 January 1914, he wrote to Ernst Bertram:[2]

> I am very worried because my wife could not move with me. Since the day before yesterday she has been at Arosa; a stay in the high mountains was necessary again. It is hard. My work is very much behind again. Don't imagine that it is completed. By the way, it is called "The Magic Mountain" . . . and it could become something readable if my nerves will obey [me]. (EHL)

Spiritually depressed, physically ailing, beset by debts, and above all separated from Katia, Mann needed encouragement to overcome his melancholy and his artistic doubts. His correspondence with friends and fellow writers reveals a formal manner,[3] possibly defensive, and he was becoming less close to Heinrich.

In their relationship over the years, Thomas hardly over discussed philosophical problems, and he carefully avoided arguing with Heinrich's politics and social notions. Thomas seemed to have taken for granted that no substantial difference could separate them; pragmatic concerns came second to his strong sense of family. Heinrich had felt some natural stress when Thomas's "long, long book" had made a fortune, while his own books languished in limited editions, but nothing important had troubled the brothers' relations until Heinrich, as a matter of principle, became estranged from their sister Lula.[4] For the first time Thomas Mann became painfully aware of Heinrich's —and their sister Carla's—differing view of Thomas's "sense of brotherly solidarity."[5] He was deeply hurt and his grief over Carla's suicide was all the more painful, but it did not cut him off entirely from Heinrich, for when Heinrich had been courting Inez Schmied, Thomas had been ready to accept her even though he did not altogether approve of her.

On 7 January 1914, Thomas Mann wrote to Heinrich: "I have often been asked lately, '*Is* your brother actually married?' Then I reply, 'I do not believe so, since if he were, I would certainly know about it' " (EHL). This hint refers to Heinrich's new love, Maria Kanova (Mimi), a twenty-seven-year-old Czechoslovakian actress Heinrich had met in Berlin during February of 1913.

Thomas had accepted Heinrich's invitation to be his best man,[6] but things turned out differently, for World War I broke out in August 1914, and Thomas served instead as best man for Victor, who was married[7] just before leaving for the battlefield, and he attended the farewell to Katia's brother Heinz, then joining his cavalry regiment.

Mann had not expected war. He wrote to Heinrich on 30 July 1914: ". . . one must be ashamed not to have considered this [the war] possible, and not to have seen that the catastrophe had to come" (EHL). The war aggravated his financial problems: "Naturally I am earning nothing, my father-in-law's contributions have had to be cut in half, Fischer can only pay me a small fraction of the advance he had promised me, [and] the country house at Tölz is unsalable at the moment. . ." (EHL).[8] Mann had been rejected for military service, which also depressed him. Katia was still weak, but she was running her new household well, even though their sixth child arrived a year later.[9] Katia kept her husband's working hours undisturbed by shunting intrusions to the afternoon. Mann walked his dog twice a day for exercise and relaxation.[10] One of the other intellectuals who lived close by happened to be Bruno Frank, and a warm friendship developed between the two families.

Though he could not be a soldier, Mann's essay "Gedanken im Kriege"[11] ("Thoughts in War") "grew out of the need to put at least my humble head at the service of the German cause" (EHL).[12] He viewed the war as essentially an idealistic struggle between the concepts of *Kultur* and *Zivilisation*: "Yes, the *Geist* is civilian, is "burgher" (*Bürger*)-like: it is the sworn enemy of drives, of passions. . . it [the *Geist*] is antidemonic, anti-heroic" (EHL) (ibid., *GW*, 13: 529) and: "Art, however, like all culture, is the sublimation of the demonic" (EHL) (ibid., *GW*, 13: 531). "Because politics is a matter of the reason, of democracy and civilization, [while] morality is [a matter] of culture and the soul" (EHL) (ibid., *GW*, 13: 531) "what made the poets enthusiastic was war itself, as an affliction and an ethical compulsion" (EHL) (ibid., *GW*, 73: 533). Richard Dehmel wrote to Mann: "The day before yesterday, in the trenches, I read your thoughts about the war (*Neue Rundschau*). I must tell you that each word seemed as if spoken out of my soul" (EHL).[13] Thomas Mann's loyalty to his fatherland and all it stood for was emotional rather than intellectual. In "Gedanken im Kriege" he observed, "I identified myself with it [the fatherland]; this was the form and meaning of my wartime patriotism" (EHL).[14]

Mann's "Gedanken im Kriege" was written during August and September 1914, "Friedrich und die große Koalition" was written from September to December of that year, and in the spring of 1915 he produced the open letter "Brief an die Redaktion des 'Svenska Dagbladet' Stockholm."[15] These three war essays were later published together in book form.[16] Their moods are very similar, but they reveal a progression in Mann's handling of his subject.

"Gedanken im Kriege" displays the contrast between the Dionysian and the Apollinian—the demonic-heroic warlike spirit and the rational pragmatism of what Mann conceived of as "*Zivilisation*." This concept is strictly intellectual, far removed from political actuality and far above wartime journalism. Its real meaning appears more accurately in the light of the *Betrachtungen eines Unpolitischen*; both essays tend toward the lyrical expression of a vulnerable, nonpragmatic, nonpartisan, and apolitical artist.

"Friedrich und die große Koalition" grew from arduous research for Mann's projected biography of Frederick the Great. The essay is heavily historical, and it concludes, "Friedrich wrote the 'Antimachiavelli,' and this was not false, but he loved the humanist *Geist*, reason, rigid clarity. . . so he loved Voltaire, the son of the *Geist*, the father of enlightenment and of all anti-heroic *Zivilisation*. He kissed the hand which had written, 'I hate all heroes" (EHL) (*GW*, 10: 134). This essay also refers to contemporary events,[17] and the character of Frederick reflects certain qualities of Thomas Mann himself.

In his letter to Walter Opitz, 23 September 1915, Mann called "Brief an die Zeitung 'Svenska Dagbladet' Stockholm" "more a small relief expedition tailored for foreigners, than an intellectual achievement" (EHL). The Swedish title of this essay, "Thomas Mann on Tyskland och Världskriget" ("Thomas Mann on Germany and the World War") reinforces this estimate. The purifying role of war discussed in "Gedanken im Kriege" is treated as a didactic factor: "Education was always the favorite concept of the German *Geist*" (*GW*, 13: 552). He described "The intellectual conceptualization of what is a war of liberation, a war for freedom. . . suffocation and inner desolation" (EHL) (*GW*, 13: 552).

The idea of equilibrium between power and *Geist* is rooted in Mann's attempt to level the differences between Savonarola's qualities and Lorenzo's, a contrast he saw clearly around the time he began work on the Friedrich material. This lifted war for him from the pragmatic political level to a philosophical plane. Enormous public interest was taken in Thomas Mann's later *Betrachtungen* (1918) and in *The Magic Mountain*, published in 1924, which enjoyed overwhelming success as the synthesis of his intellectual and cultural reflections during World War I.

In his war essays, Mann wastes no feelings on either democracy or the *Politik* and *Zivilisation* of French rhetoricians. He links the "unheroic," civilization and politics, to the "French spirit,"[18] as exemplified in particular by Romain Rolland, who had bitterly attacked Germany's position in the war. To Paul Amann, who had studied Rolland's work, Mann wrote (25 February 1916): "I am so extremely grateful to you for all that your writing teaches me about young France. . . France of this war had repelled me and embittered me, so [much] I cannot [even] tell,—and then I had to hear my own brother talk like Mr. Deschanel or Mr. Hanotaux![19] What I despise is the Jacobin, the freedom theoretician, the rhetorician-bourgeois, whether he carries the imprint of French Revolutionary or Italian Freemasonry. But I always knew that there exists another kind of France, and when I read Claudel's *L'annonce faite à Marie*, first in German, then in the original, I was enchanted" (EHL). Mann repeatedly rejects "French fanatical hatred,"[20] and defends the German position of *Kultur* against the Western spirit of *Zivilisation*, since he believes it is right and since he attributes the inner meaning of the war to it.

In 1914, Mann was far from alone; even pacifists like Hesse greeted the war initially as a necessary evil and articles like Thomas Mann's appeared in the Fall 1914 *Neue Rundschau*, signed by Gerhart Hauptmann, Richard Dehmel, Alfred Kerr, and Robert Musil. When Thomas Mann read his brother's article, "Zola," however, he saw in one lightning flash the gulf between his *Weltanschauung* and Heinrich's.[21] On 15 January 1916, he wrote bitterly to Bertram: "I have read [the Zola article], and it hardly surprises me; it is more directed at me than [it is] against Germany" (EHL). The magnitude of his pain can be grasped only in his later work. Katia Mann remarked, "With Heinrich's Zola Essay came a rupture [between the brothers], and [it was] a rupture by which both suffered greatly. Who suffered more because of this brotherly discord is hard to tell. . . . Wounded beyond all understanding, he [Thomas] took the first part of the essay far more to heart than necessary."[22]

Heinrich Mann's seventy-page essay on Zola, a brilliantly wide-ranging achievement, deals with Zola's life, work, and intellectual and spiritual development. It includes a manifesto on the war and an apologia for his own convictions, which aggressively opposed Thomas Mann's. Heinrich drew parallels between his own life and Zola's, and made intense personal references to Thomas that outstripped their personal differences.

For the most part, Thomas Mann tried to maintain a scholarly stance. He wrote to Karl Streckel, 18 April 1919: "In me the Nordic-Protestant element has the upper hand and in my brother, the Romance-Catholic. Thus [there is] in me, more [of] the conscience, in him the activistic will. I am an ethical individualist, he a socialist— . . . the contrast . . . reveals itself in the *geistig*, the artistic, the political aspects, in short in all references" (EHL).

Passages in Thomas Mann's *Betrachtungen*[23] undeniably attack his brother. The term *"Zivilisationsliterat"* in particular portrays Heinrich savagely, as does the phrase "gegen Recht und Wahrheit," in chapter 6. He called the *Betrachtungen* "a huge *geistig* cleansing. . ." (EHL) (letter to Philipp Witkop, 16 December 1915). Thomas Mann had begun work on the *Betrachtungen* even before he had read Heinrich's Zola essay, but few direct references to the Manns' feud appear in Thomas's correspondence, and he rarely mentioned Heinrich's name in other private writings.[24]

This controversy was above all philosophical. The deep differences in their *Weltanschauung* did not surprise Thomas, and he could accept this rationally; but he was repulsed by his brother's exposure of extremely intimate details about his personality and talents to the general public, reducing intellectual issues to the subjective level, something that he considered unprofessional.[25] He also felt that Heinrich had betrayed family solidarity and their close brotherly relationship with such indiscretions. For Thomas Mann, the *Betrachtungen* was, ". . . a middle thing between an achievement and outpouring, composition and scribbling" (*GW*, 12: 10), ". . . the work of an artist and not a work of art; yes, because it grew from an artistry whose vital dignity was endangered and questioned" (EHL) (*GW*, 12: 12). From the autumn of 1915, he fought the battle out in the six hundred pages of his *Betrachtungen eines Unpolitischen*, and he stresses repeatedly that he would never have pursued this mammoth soul-searching without the emotional challenge of the Zola essay.

Thomas Mann chose who revealing epigraphs for the *Betrachtungen*: "Que diable allait-il faire dans cette galère?" and "Examine yourself! Discover what you are!"[26] This demanding work matured him, liberating him from dependence on his older brother so that he could face the new perspectives emerging in war-torn Europe. He demanded the right and the freedom to inquire, to search, to learn and to change his mind in superhuman intellectual effort: "I have suffered two years, struggled, [I have] neglected my dearest projects, I have convinced myself to silence my art, examined and compared myself" (EHL) (*GW*, 12: 9). He also felt it was a genuine service (*Dienst*) for the war effort, though the *Betrachtungen*, which he called a "monster," seemed unpublishable, a kind of purifying mental exercise, but not a book,[27] and its reception, though never indifferent, was mixed. The *Betrachtungen* finally allowed him, tender as his wounds still were, to awaken from his nightmare. His children recalled that their father had been silent and distant for some time, his nerves on edge, and he had spent little time with them, but *The Magic Mountain*, which he had also neglected to write the *Betrachtungen*, ultimately benefited from his intellectual crisis.

At this time Thomas Mann sold the family's summer residence in Tölz to buy war bonds,[28] joining material sacrifice to his intellectual war contribution.[29] It amounted to a total loss that he probably considered a part of his private warfare, a demonstration of his loyalty.

In the late summer of 1916 the Mann family acquired an odd-looking farm dog of mixed breed, to replace the aristocratic collie Motz, who had been portrayed in *Royal Highness*. Old Motz had to be put to sleep and was given a solemn funeral by the Mann children.[30] The new dog, Bauschan,[31] became Thomas Mann's faithful companion on at least one long walk a day, usually in the rural area near his home, walks that were high spots for him while he lived on Poschingerstraße. While working on the proofs for the *Betrachtungen* in March 1918, he began a tale he called an "idyll," with the title "A Man and His Dog" ("Herr und Hund"). That same spring, on 24 April, Katia gave birth to their last daughter, Elisabeth Veronika, whom Thomas Mann called "*Kindchen*" ("little child"). Although exhausted, he opened his warm heart to the small satisfactions of his life in the spring of 1918.

The Man and His Dog[32] has not been as popular in the United States as it has been in England. This "private" tale yields a wealth of pleasure in its minute descriptions; it is a bouquet of precious moments of decency and love grouped around the figure of Bauschan, the image of man's simple faithful companion. In this "idyll," Thomas Mann proved he could express himself through simple heart felt expressions of the self; the nature descriptions are unique in his work, providing a limpid stylization of his hidden meaning and his amazing visual gifts. He worked on *A Man and His Dog* until 15 October 1918.[33]

In his diary entries[34] notes about Bauschan and *"das Kindchen"* (baby Elisabeth) are gently mingled with everyday experience. On Saturday, 14 September, he noted his "feelings of love for the '*Kindchen*' and inner attempts at a hexameter poem.[35] But I also envisioned the thematic interdependence of my future works, with the sphere that surrounds me while reading: death-romanticism plus acceptance of life in the Magic Mountain . . ." (EHL) (Diary, Friday, 13 September 1918). As his thoughts on the hexameter poem developed, he was bringing himself to work again on *The Magic Mountain*.

Already the father of four, Mann felt quite differently toward the new baby Elisabeth. He felt he had become mature, even aged, over the last two years, enriched[36] with a lovely new insight: "The sweetness in this little face is due to Oriental derivation; it shows at times in the shape of the mouth, in the glance of the eye, which dominates this little face and, although blue, [the eyes] do darken often from the inside (Poem)" (EHL) (Diary, Tuesday, 26 November 1918).

When Thomas Mann began to write "Gesang vom Kindchen. Idyll" his home and family meant more to him than ever. He was reading Hamsun, Tolstoy, and above all *Hermann und Dorothea*.[37] As his creativity bloomed, he increasingly referred to Goethe, with whom he identified.[38]

Working on "A Man and His Dog" and "Gesang vom Kindchen" helped Thomas Mann overcome the stress of the war and his *Betrachtungen* in the genre of the lyric idyll, which he had never used before. "Gesang vom Kindchen" is not one of his most distinguished works, nor is it on Goethe's poetic level. But in his idyll Mann does communicate his experience of the "Kindchen"'s sacredness as one newly come into this world out of the mythical darkness of prelife, with the awakening of conceptions and the miracle of learning. Mann's themes of birth, time, and daily experience awoke here, through his emotional experience of the mystery of transcendence, and later emerged with grandeur in *The Magic Mountain* and *Joseph and His Brothers*. These creatively abundant ideas formed a decisive part of Thomas Mann's intellectual growth only after his identification of self, first accomplished between "Tristan" and "Death in Venice" and then in the intellectual liberation he had bought through the "slavery" of the *Betrachtungen*. By late 1918, his positive and generous simple humanistic values had overcome scrupulous rationalization.

This change in his personality is expressed in Thomas Mann's sensitive and modest gestures of love, the sacrifice of his family's summer home to the fading Fatherland, his spontaneous personal contact with nature, and his feeling for Bauschan, man's best friend. In this new manner he now experienced fatherhood, and when Heinrich was said to be gravely ill, Thomas rushed to his brother's bedside[39] in response to their bond of brotherhood and reached out for him. Heinrich accepted and claimed never to have read the *Betrachtungen*, and Thomas eventually modified passages referring to their dispute.[40] On 8 April 1919, he began to work again on *The Magic Mountain*; he had to gather the material[41] he had packed away long ago, reorganizing[42] and rewriting it. On 6 June 1919, he confidently told Josef Ponten: "I am writing again on the 'Magic Mountain' novel, whose basic theme (Romanticism and Enlightenment, Death and Virtue: the theme of Death in Venice [*sic*] once again and also the one of the *Betrachtungen*) has fascinated me once more. . . ."

Thomas Mann repeatedly emphasized in his correspondence that in this novel he was consciously trying to produce a new version of the Goethean *Bildungsroman*.[43] He was interrupted by several trips[44] and numerous writing assignments, and the novel became more and more voluminous:[45] "It is a big novel which I hope to finish in the next weeks, a monster of two large volumes, of which the Swedish and Hungarian translations are already worked on . . ." (EHL). Only on 27 October 1924, did he write to Hans von Hülsen: "The Magic Mountain is finished,—a triumph of stubbornness, even if nothing more" (EHL).

"Disorder and Early Sorrow"

Even before completing *The Magic Mountain*, Mann wrote "Disorder and Early Sorrow,"[46] which grew directly out of his two previous idylls, "The Man and His Dog" and "Gesang vom Kindchen."[47] Happy, but exhausted, he commented, "The novella will be my field again . . . I will not undertake a composition such as the Magic Mountain [*sic*] soon again" (EHL). The times were increasingly unsettled,[48] and Germany's financial crisis was growing.[49] Since November 1922 Mann had been writing for the *Dial*, an American publication; the last of his eight "German Letters" appeared on 4 July 1928. "Disorder and Early Sorrow" was an assignment for Fischer Verlag, as Thomas Mann observed in *On Myself*: "For the first time in my life I wrote something literary, one might say to order: the editorship of the Fischer *Neue Rundschau* published a *Festschrift* for my 50th birthday and they wanted it to contain a narrative contribution by the birthday child. So emerged 'Disorder and Early Sorrow,' a story which I like so much that I am tempted to count it among my very best" (EHL).

"Disorder and Early Sorrow" is a medium long "inflation story" (EHL)[50] without formal textual divisions. The setting contains postwar autobiographical references, such as the home, the atmosphere, the language and the characters themselves. The story opens during a family meal at home; inflation and the changing times clash with the vestiges of traditional prewar gracious living. The language is witty and a little arrogant, with set patterns and real or forced cheerfulness impossible to convey in translation.

The "big folk," the two eldest children, Ingrid and Bert, parallel Erika[51] and Klaus Mann. Xaver Kleinsgutl is a "servant" who has become almost a part of the family.[52] He and Bert, the same age, like costumes and acting. Neither has "social" consciousness and both are quite satisfied with their positions. Mann treats Xaver with heretofore unseen warmth, allowing the direct and spontaneous young man to solve the child's enormous problem, and to play an intimate role in the family's life.

Professor Cornelius,[53] the father and narrator, embodies the theme, as he responds to the disruption and to the warmth of his heart, shown principally with his small daughter Lorchen.[54] The "big folk's" party catalyzes the story in its three parts: the introduction; the party itself, where the younger generation contrasts the professor's feelings; and the representation of "disorder" as the source of little Lorchen's overwhelming experience. The characters' expressions are readily discernible in their dialogue. It reveals, for example, the obvious good nature with which the parents meet their disconcerting lack of means, the mother's worries, her fatigue and her inability to get away for a rest[55]—all are expressed with a light ironic fatalism.

The preparation for the party, in the slangy unconventional fashion of Ingrid and Bert, is a little suspect to the adults, but it seems to them attractive, even desirable. "The *bürgerlich* old ones have a harder time" (EHL) (*GW*, 8: 621; see also *STD*, 503). The "*Bürger*" concept here has nothing to do with the "*Künstler*" seen in earlier short stories, especially "Tonio Kröger." Also the concept of the *Bürger* has another meaning, and it is contrasted in a peculiar fashion with the young ones' ways, appearing nostalgic, old-fashioned, out of the main stream of things, but cultured and in a way respected. Nevertheless the young people show all the signs of respect to their hosts' parents; they are friendly and accept the presence of the "little ones" with good nature and without ceremony. The professor is almost shocked at these positive qualities.

The open-mindedness that helped Mann over the *Betrachtungen* also appears in this story's acknowledgment of the youngsters' basic decency. They are surmounting the paradoxes of a world gone mad, without the second thoughts or the regrets of the older generation. The evil "Disorder" of this world malignantly affects the people born into it, as Thomas Mann demonstrates through the distortions and paradoxical clashes of all these young people, culminating in Lorchen's outburst, a symptom of the disruption of the times.[56] Mann had already used the unusual expression "historical man" in the *Betrachtungen*, and he defined it clearly in this short story: ". . . professors of history do not love history when it happens, only when it already has happened; . . . they hate the upheaval of the present because they conceive it as lawless, lacking continuity, fresh, in one word, 'unhistorical' and . . .

their hearts belong to the historical part" (EHL) (see also *STD*, 506; *GW*, 8:
626–27). Mann's use of "historical" demonstrates the disengaged *Weltanschauung* of the "unpolitical." The professor Cornelius's goatee resembles
Heinrich Mann's, and his "long" nose and small mouth resemble those
of both father and his son.[57] Heinrich's pro-French, anti-German attitude
had changed, just as Thomas Mann had overcome his own emotional con-
servatism with the *Betrachtungen*, and both had been disillusioned by the
partisan profanity of postwar politics. Contributing wittily to the "disorder," Mann knowingly mingled their personal qualities, both physical and
geistig, in Professor Cornelius.

The "disorder" of the world has been forced upon the professor, and he is
caught between his own tendency to timeless historical "order" and the
shocking "disorder" all around him. He is no longer the respected master of
his house, but a questor, spurred by the thirst for discovery and gravely
anxious about the unknown. This semiautobiographical figure candidly expresses the *Künstler*-questor's simultaneous fear of and longing for the
world that Thomas Mann himself felt. This mood, an ironic antithesis of the
great questor heroes of cultural history, was for him a profound human experience. The solemn grandeur of the *nunc stans*, as the professor conceives
the historical past, illustrates all of man's existence.

The connotations of "disorder" as pertinent to the concepts of culture,
history, and the unpolitical illuminate Professor Cornelius's conceptual problems. In a "culture," a group of people accept a common *geistig* way as an
"order" they willingly accept; "order" is thus synonymous with "culture."
Within this formal and traditional frame the individual finds and gains self-
expression, which "order" keeps from infringing on others. In their golden
ages, nations possess this order or cultural unity, but after such periods
equilibrium loses appeal and becomes rigid, often phasing into hypocrisy and
corruption. In such an era, supposed claims for free expression are merely
fresh attempts to undermine the aging cultural order, eventually rusting out
the traditional mechanism that inertia keeps going. "Disorder" ranges from
"mutiny" to "vital new spirit"; it may cause a tragic collapse, or it may begin
new trends that could develop another golden age of "order." The cycles of
recurring cultural orders regulate general mores and styles of language, allowing the individual freedom of expression without limiting others. Achieving
such balance, however, is difficult without intellectual and spiritual excellence, free from pragmatic corruption and from the intellectualizing of *geistig*
values, which Professor Cornelius called "unhistory" and Thomas Mann considered the spirit of "Western civilization." "Order" or "disorder" is then a
geistig and artistic phenomenon rather than a symptom of civilization, which
tends toward rationalism and pragmatism. The professor's concept of the
"historical" parallels the "unpolitical," synonymous with "order," and he
therefore opposes the "disorder" of economic, behavioral, and cultural struc-
tures that allow blind impulse and instinct to rule.

At the professor's party, where the generations mix so strikingly, the guest's names and appearances are treated with sharp but good-natured humor, as for instance Mr. Hergesell's[58] painful shoes and Fräulein Plaichinger's[59] corpulence, a striking contrast with Lorchen's birdlike frailty. Hergesell is an ordinary young man who acts from decent instincts. His equivocal behavior also contributes to the general "disorder." Even though his inflation-period party shoes are "as hard as iron," he tries to meet the traditional standards of the conservative older generation. To please his host, he playfully dances with little Lorchen and promises to do so again. When he finally comes to the nursery to calm her, he recites scraps of literature to impress the professor, and comments on Lorchen's behavior without realizing that his tactlessness smites the professor in his most tender sport.

With a primitive logic, kind blue-faced Anna does the same, defining the embarrassing problem: "It is a matter of fact . . . that in the child feminine instincts come to the surface very actively" (EHL) (*STD*, 525; *GW*, 8: 653), a comment that irritates the professor.[60] The standard of his whole social order has exploded, and outlandish things are happening. The orderly little world Lorchen's parents maintain for her suddenly splits into surging disorder; her instincts are briefly awakened to impulses she is far from being able to grasp. Childishly she cries out, "Why isn't Max my brother?" (*STD*, 525; *GW*, 8: 653), entirely abandoning thought when Herr Hergesell arrives, and joyfully sinking into sleep, to awake the next morning completely free of the experience.

Thomas Mann incorporates "disorder" into his smallest detail, except for the mother, who embodies the mythical *nunc stans*. While writing "Disorder and Early Sorrow," his mood was fluctuating between the uplifting satisfaction he had gained through *The Magic Mountain* and a growing realization that his idealism was incompatible with the values of the postwar world. He felt, however, the past abandoned in the face of the "political" or "unhistorical" mentality of the present could not be denied. He ironically set the utter disorder amid stylish manners of his own household in the midst of soaring inflation with uprooted rules and nonexistent discipline. All of this turmoil victimized the most innocent member of the family, his cherished little girl.

The last lines of this story pay tribute to the healing power of sleep, revealing the deep optimism and faith in mankind that helped Mann overcome his uneasiness at surface "disorder," and follow his quest still further. Cornelius deeply recognized Lorchen's nameless fear and pain, which the warmth of his own heart could not overcome. While Thomas Mann, the questor, hints at profundity, his compassion and his faith survive in this heartwarming idyll of a father's devotion to his little daughter. The story was immediately popular upon publication.[61]

Mann felt that the writing of "Disorder and Early Sorrow" relaxed him after *The Magic Mountain*. The story's setting[62] already belonged to the past when he wrote it,[63] a no-man's-land where "disorder" ruled, where twilight and dawn were mingled beyond human reason. From the summer of 1921 to September 1929,[64] his letters and essays document his procedure of rationalization, including the essay *"Okkulte Erlebnisse,"*[65] the initial inspiration for the *Joseph and His Brothers* cycle;[66] the completion of *The Magic Mountain*;[67] essays on marriage,[68] on Lübeck,[69] and on Freud;[70] and his study on the theater.[71] During this time, Thomas Mann lost both his mother[72] and his sister, Julia Mann-Löhr;[73] but on 10 December 1929, from the hands of King Gustaf V of Sweden in the Konserthuset in Stockholm, he received the Nobel Prize for *Buddenbrooks*.

Mann had made some lecture tours during the writing of the *Betrachtungen*, but he had only infrequently accepted invitations during his final work on *The Magic Mountain*. He now traveled often with his family, then very close, and even undertook a cruise.[74] Since *The Magic Mountain* was doing exceedingly well, he bought a car, the first car the family owned, and in August 1929 he and Katia bought a lot in the dunes at Nidden in the Memelgebiet near the Baltic Sea, to replace their summer home at Tölz. The liberation that the *Betrachtungen* and *The Magic Mountain* had provided allowed him to approach new philosophical dimensions. He developed these slowly and cautiously, as the Joseph manuscript gradually grew in the context of his various activities.[75]

"Mario and the Magician"

An experience Mann had during a vacation at Forte dei Marmi from 31 August to 13 September 1926 provided the basis of "Mario and the Magician,"[76] which involved material from his earlier "Okkulte Erlebnisse" and his later essay on Freud.[77] His preoccupation with psychology, psychoanalysis, and the occult appears in *The Magic Mountain*,[78] and its fictional treatment in "Mario and the Magician" also involves his personal problems, like the power of the will, its ethical use, and the difficult matter of individual and universal humanism. These subjects are connected to his concepts of the "political" and "unpolitical," and they also found their way into his work on *Joseph and His Brothers*, then in progress.

The increasingly oppressive mood of "Mario and the Magician" appears in the worsening weather and the inexorable crescendo of gloomy motifs pointing toward the final tragedy. Here more than in his previous stories, Mann acknowledges biographical events: "It was not feasible to take the swollen bulk of my uncopied manuscript of Joseph upon this extended though easy trip . . . so I resolved to spend my mornings on the easy task of writing out an incident of a previous holiday in Forte dei Marmi, near Viareggio."[79] In a letter to Hoerth, 12 June 1930, he wrote: "the 'magician-artist' was there and behaved exactly as I describe it. Only the lethal conclusion was invented: In reality Mario ran away after the kiss in comical embarrassment and he was, when he served us tea the next day, highly cheerful and filled with factual

recognition of 'Cipolla's' work. In life it just went less passionately. . ."
(EHL).

The theme of "Mario and the Magician," the misuse of psychic powers, is
suggested by its subtitle: "A tragic travel experience" (EHL) ("Ein tragisches
Reiseerlebnis"). The fictional trip began badly, with more and more disrup-
tive experiences. The setting presents several thematic elements: the unpleasant recollection of the vacation at Torre di Venere; the clash between
political nationalism and the popular character; and the contrast between the
exasperating prudishness of one group and the narrator's common sense.
Next the magician enters and performs, mastering the audience, and finally,
Mario's tragedy climaxes the story.

In "On Myself" Mann describes the message of this story: ". . . a warning
against the rape [caused] by the dictatorial being who in the end was overcome and destroyed" (EHL) (*GW*, 13: 166). Thomas Mann's earlier preference for the Nordic over the Southern does not pertain here,[80] and his criticism of one segment of the Italian public is directed purely against their fascist
frenzy. He acutely contrasts Cipolla's fascism with simple, attractive, ordinary Italians uncontaminated by politics, like Mario and Signora Angiolieri.[81]
After the *Betrachtungen*, one of Mann's developments was his genuine openness toward neighboring nations, with whom he enthusiastically advocated
cooperation.[82] After *the Magic Mountain*, he addressed problems relevant to
all humanity in the panorama of Western culture.

The limited universe of the Italian summer resort holds two contrasting
worlds: the Grand Hotel, with the passionately maternal Italian princess and
the servile hotel manager, the horribly prudish beach crowd, and the frightful
Cipolla; and the Pensione Eleonora, with its hostess Signora Angiolieri, once
a friend of Duse,[83] the just doctor who serves enlightened science, and all the
children's friends, primarily Mario and the other young men of the beaches,
the fishermen, and the hotel employees. The "good" side is characterized by
common sense, also represented by the narrator, while the "bad" side's old
fashioned prudishness is combined with politically fashionable militaristic
aggression. By contrasting these mentalities, Mann prepares for the ultimate
encounter between Cipolla and Mario.

The sun is overwhelming, as in the middle section of "Death in Venice,"
but here it successfully paralyzes its exposed victims. The magician displays
Rome's fascist ruler, to whom the narrator refers as a spoil-sport advocating
the "greatness and dignity of Italy," as a contagious virulent influence (see
also *STD*, 535; *GW*, 8: 667). The narrator realizes that his own idleness and
his family's lead to conflict with the dominant status quo: that is, first the sun
cripples them, then general opinion and law enervates them, and at last
Cipolla's power disarms them.

Shortly thereafter, the removal of the little girl's wet and dirty bathing suit
is publicly denounced as a "*molto grave*" offense against the decency of the
great Italian nation. Suddenly the Italians depart, leaving the international

tourists in the majority in Torre de Venere. The narrator asks himself why he and his family stayed, not sure whether they are persevering or whether they are merely incapable of movement. He regretfully notes that if he had gone, he would have been spared the encounter with the fatal Cipolla. The sultry sirocco and the burning sun here, as in "Death in Venice," set the scene for the onset of an epidemic. The sirocco accompanies Cipolla's entrance, a figure whose idiosyncrasies force the stagnant atmosphere to active participation in the disaster.

Cipolla calls himself a *Forzatore*, *Illusionista*, and *Prestidigitatore*. His alluring advertisements here ignite contagious curiosity, and the narrator and his wife have allowed their young children to stay up beyond their bedtime just this once, much as little Lorchen and Beißer of "Disorder and Early Sorrow" had unhappily done. Like Lorchen, the children in "Mario and the Magician" are unfortunately exposed to a *geistig* intrusion whose significance, fortunately, they cannot as yet comprehend, and sleep removes them from the scene. The parents are ashamed and embarrassed at their submission to this moral contamination.

When Cipolla finally appears, he contradicts his advertised image. The professional pretense of the performing artist, on the realistic level, blends with the mysterious powers he represents. Since "Death in Venice," too, Mann had been treating the "*unanständige Psychologisieren*" in his fiction, dealing in "Mario and the Magician," with psychological matters[84] and hypnotic powers, and their use for good or ill,[85] questions dynamically relevant to the postwar preoccupations of both Thomas Mann and his readers.

Cipolla pretends eagerness to serve a public he actually disdains and manipulates. He will not entertain them as advertised, but will overpower, humiliate, and enslave them, recalling the suggestive street singer in "Death in Venice." Cipolla exerts a psychic power over the crowd, and he bears an invisible mask of Cain. Cheap cigarettes and drinks stimulate him as he performs, arrogantly attempting to dominate the audience and at last to penetrate Mario's mind. "You do what you want. Or have you ever not done what you wanted? Or even done what you did not want to do? [Done] what not you, [but someone], wanted to be done?" (EHL) (see also *STD*, 542; *GW*, 8: 676). Cipolla's entire technique is based on logic; first he fascinates the attention of all, then he cautiously involves single individuals to demonstrate his power, and then as he grows more intoxicated and the hour approaches midnight, Cipolla controls more and more people, battering down their resistance.

Chevalier Cipolla's trademark is a silver-handled riding crop with sinister and even demonic overtones, a symbol of power he uses to force his victims into submission. This little whip symbolizes debasement and captivity. It suits both Cipolla and his weak audience, lured into the hall under false pretenses and now allowing this charlatan to crack the whip over their heads.

Cipolla's speech is also an enslaving instrument. His quick tongue first fascinates the crowd, and by blurring their judgment, it allows him to exert his hypnotic power on them. The narrator explains to his children that Cipolla is a conjuror an "artist-magician" (*Zauberkünstler*),[86] who uses language to manipulate his audience, a combination of words Thomas Mann allowed only once here.[87] The notion that the magician-*Zauberer* overlapped the functions of the *Künstler* was becoming one of his major fictional themes, as in *The Magic Mountain*, as well as an autobiographical revelation.[88] The closest members of Mann's family—his children Erika, Klaus, Golo, and Monika as well as Katia—all called him "the Magician," because of his power to create mood while storytelling. To him, the "*Künstler*" and the "*Magician*" comprise the storyteller's gift; the *Künstler* captivates the imagination through illusion, alluring, magnetic, irresistible in its deception. The Magician initiates listeners to mythical reality through the medium of the story. This duality identifies the storyteller as both a wretched swindler and the bearer of a divine theme. Thomas Mann readily accepted this nickname, and Monika Mann recalls her father's choosing a magician's costume for a social event. Later in America and then Switzerland, when he was separated for long periods of time from his older children, he signed his letters to them with a capital *Z*, standing for "*Zauberer*."

As a young writer, Mann had expressed longing, anguish, and the unlimited ambition to master metaphysical powers. At that time he was unaware of the anatomy of his own conception of his *Künstlertum*, and he had to sort out the concepts and experiences thronging his mind. After *Buddenbrooks*, he modeled his ideas on the Schoperhauerian "worldview" (*Weltbild*) and shaped them into fiction. The tension between his deeply romantic longing and the unconditional determination of the questor allowed him momentarily to overcome the abyss between the opposing extremes of the "burgher" (*Bürger*) and the "artist" (*Künstler*) in "Tonio Kröger," and at last he dignified the topic of the *Künstler* with tragic expression in "Death in Venice."

Stunned by the enormity of the World War that raged in the interval between "Death in Venice" and *The Magic Mountain*, Thomas Mann exhaustively examined himself in the mirror of his *Betrachtungen eines Unpolitischen*; liberated from self-absorption and with broadened horizons, he became a new kind of storyteller. Everyday values suddenly took on mythical significance and from his original microconception of the *Bürger-Künstler*, he established a romantic balance between illusion and truth, roguishness and suffering, surface logic and the limitless world of the unconscious.

Beyond the strongly autobiographical presentation of the Magician in Cipolla, Mann also portrays a Mephistophelean character similar to the tempter of *The Magic Mountain*, Dr. Krokowski, whose trenchant humor, mastery of "soul dissection" (*Seelenzergliederung*), and ruthless goal of enslaving anyone who dares set foot on the "Magic Mountain" all illustrate a satanic nature. Cipolla the magician would do anything Dr. Krokowski can; their victims reveal Mann's criticism of those who blindly trust anything their limited minds cannot grasp. Krokowski robbed unsuspecting guests of their health and freedom, while Cipolla victimized unsophisticated members of his audience. Both have definite theories about the cause of prostration, illness, and defeat, attributing collapse to the individual's attempt to defy occult supreme powers.[89] Most of all, both Dr. Krokowski and Cipolla passionately debase love; Krokowski attempts to force Hans Castorp into betraying his love for his cousin Joachim Ziemssen,[90] and Cipolla tries to force Mario into believing that he, Cipolla, is his beloved Silvestra.

Hans Castorp succeeded in breaking Krokowski's spell, but Mario, like the hysterically dancing crowd, is totally oblivious, robbed of the powers of will and judgment. Obediently, even smiling happily, Mario exposes his innermost feelings to the audience and his rudely laughing antagonist. When Cipolla awakens him with a movement of his whip, Mario obviously realizes what has happened. He first recoils and tries to escape, then he reacts and destroys the magician.[92]

The hypnotic performances of Krokowski and Cipolla are analogous by first involving many individuals and then focusing on one. Both descriptions derive from a séance Mann described to Ernst Bertram on Christmas Day, 1922: "At Schrenck-Notzing's I participated in a séance with the medium Willi S., a 20 year old lad of unbelievable psychic powers. I cannot tell you today, but I have seen occult phantasms of organic life; (I have seen [them] uncorruptedly with my own eyes), [a topic that] fits more than easily into the frame of my novel" (EHL). In 1935, he again noted, ". . . what I do usually emerges from an unforeseen direct experience, and both the occult and the Mario novella are due to such personal experiences. . ." (EHL).[92] Thomas Mann candidly described this séance in "Okkulte Erlebnisse"; he had actively assisted the hypnotist as a test, and he was amazed that he had been able to detect no tricks; it was ". . . a seduction . . . to things which should not have anything to do with me, which, however, exercise upon my imagination as well as on my intellect a sharp and nervous fascination. . ." (EHL) (*GW*, 10: 136). His fascination with the occult evidences only a rational skepticism fictionalized in the repugnant Krokowski and Cipolla. Thomas Mann undertook the Schrenck-Notzing séance as a controlled, purposeful demonstration, with "reverence for the secret" (ibid., *GW*, 10: 141, 145).

Schrenck-Notzing's book title denotes the problem, *Materialization of Phenomena*,[93] and out of self-preservation Thomas Mann rejected such occult experiments.[94] "Okkulte Erlebnisse" records his fear of jeopardizing the balanced rationality upon which his peace of mind rested through Schrenck-Notzing's experimentation, where despite his frustration, he could not deny the fairness of the attempt. He strongly feared misuse of the occult by charlatans, since he genuinely revered the unknown power he sensed, and he shied away from further exploration. However, the threat of psychic manipulation could not disappear from the world. It was becoming ever more menacing, propagated by scientific and political demagogues. Thomas Mann's phrase "indecent toying with psychology" ("*unanständige Psychologisieren*") does not refer to Freud, whose integrity he acknowledged.[95] Claiming lack of expertise, Mann followed Nietzsche in professing his place in the conceptual world of light.

"Mario and the Magician" reveals this stage of Thomas Mann's thinking. Krokowski had abused Freud's theories,[96] and Cipolla succeeded him as a psychic demagogue and manipulator of the masses. Cipolla shows that when man's aggressive will pursues a specific goal, it proves invincible; "Freedom exists and also the will exists," he says, "but the freedom of the will does not exist, because a will which is focused upon its own freedom strikes a vacuum" (EHL).[97] Cipolla's demonic logic is paralyzing: "To command and to obey, build together only one principle, an unbreakable unity; the one who could obey, could also command, and the other way around" (EHL) (see also (*STD*, 553; *GW*, 8: 691). Fascinated and ashamed, as though frozen beneath the riding crop of this debauched hypnotist, the narrator cannot leave, even to take his sleeping children home.[98] Past midnight Cipolla controls not one, not two, but a horde of people, driving them like marionettes into a "dance orgy," a nightmarish *Walpurgisnacht* of military somnambulism.[99] Repeatedly his Fascist party jargon invokes the all-powerful State, whose leaders Cipolla claims to have entertained in Rome. Once Mario has been stripped of his illusions, he behaves primitively, his bullet destroying the magician but leaving uncontrolled hate-filled anarchy unleashed to enslave the world. Mann commented to Claire Goll, 21 September 1931: "It was peculiar to me to see how out of the personal and the private [experience] something symbolic and ethical grew" (EHL).

Many readers take the fascist element of "Mario and the Magician" to be its theme. Mann wrote to Hans Flesch, 26 June 1941, "I can only say that it is going much too far to see in the magician Cipolla simply a mask of Mussolini; on the other hand it is understood that the novella absolutely has a moralistic-political meaning. . . . After all, it [the story] should in its entirety be considered as a work of art, not an allegory of daily politics. . . . I am not pleased when this story is considered a work of political satire" (EHL). Later he wrote to Bedrick Fucik, 15 April 1932: "When I wrote it I did not believe that Cipolla could be possible in Germany. It was a patriotic overestimate of my nation. The irritation with which critics already received the story should have told me where the trend was leading, and that it all was possible. . in the most 'educated' of people" (EHL).[100]

His optimism became somewhat clouded after *The Magic Mountain*, for at last the veil of Maya had fallen; Thomas Mann could now discern the two opposing component of *Künstlertum*, the swindler and the sufferer. He eagerly began to shape his new vision, the story of Joseph, the mythical man free of historical boundaries: "Again and further are the right words, for the unresearchable plays a kind of mocking game with our researching ardor; it offers apparent holds and goals, behind which, when we have gained them, new stretches of the past still open out—as happens to the coastwise voyager, who finds no end to his journey, for behind each headland of clayey dune he conquers, fresh headland and new distances [that] lure him on" (EHL).[101]

The titles *The Magic Mountain* and "Mario and the Magician" include an abstract concept, the nature of the *Künstler*'s magic power, that lay dormant early in Thomas Mann's *geistig* development. In *The Magic Mountain*, he idealized that magic quality through growth, learning, and the ability to overcome temptation and then he had shown it corrupted in "Mario and the Magician." After the concept of "magic" had been revealed, he could identify it, define it, and isolate its contrasting qualities, preventing them from dimming his insight. The magnetism of the eternal paradoxical contrast remained in his heart, however, kindling his creative energies for still greater achievements.

"The Transposed Heads: A Legend of India"

More than a decade after Thomas Mann finished "Mario and the Magician,"[102] and despite his heavy commitments to the Joseph tetralogy, his activities related to the Goethe centennial, and his self-imposed exile, he wrote another novella, "The Transposed Heads: A Legend of India."[103] Since September 1938 the Mann family had been living in a spacious house in the middle of an attractive garden within walking distance of Princeton University, where Thomas Mann taught until the end of the 1940 academic year,[104] after which he concentrated on his literary work.[105] The family spent the summer of 1940 in Brentwood, near Los Angeles, in a comfortable rented house whose eucalyptus, cedar, and palm trees on the mountain slope reminded Mann of the Tuscan landscape. Later they bought California property, and after speeding the winter in Princeton, the family moved into a temporary California home in April 1941.[106] Thomas Mann wrote "The Transposed Heads" during the spring in Princeton and his vacation in California that summer.

After ten years of anxiety and exile, Thomas Mann produced a benevolently ironic work in the "The Transposed Heads."[107] After the Nobel Prize and "Mario and the Magician" Thomas Mann had been besieged with requests for public appearances, particularly readings of the Joseph novels and "Mario and the Magician." He always preferred to relax with travel, and the prestige of the Nobel Prize enabled him to do so to a greater extent than earlier.[108] In the spring of 1930, he made what he called "a significant voyage" (EHL).[109] In view of his work on the *Joseph* cycle, interrupted by his public and political appearances,[110] Mann's trip to Paris in May 1931 is especially interesting because of its warm intellectual bonds.[111] The year 1932 was highly important to his intellectual growth; this year of the German financial crisis also marked the centennial of Goethe's death, for which Mann was busy preparing a *Festschrift* on Goethe,[112] which set the stage for his own later work, *Lotte in Weimar*. The National Socialists also gained a substantial German majority[113] in July of that year, and in early 1933[114] Thomas Mann prepared an address for the fiftieth anniversary of Richard Wagner's death.[115] He left on 11 February for speeches in Amsterdam,[116] Brussels,[117] and Paris,[118] just when his brother Heinrich arrived in Paris as a penniless refugee.[119] Thomas and Katia decided to rest in Arosa, Switzerland, and await political developments; on 12 March their older children Erika and Klaus warned their parents of "the bad weather" in Germany, the beginning of Thomas Mann's long self-imposed exile.

Thomas and Katia Mann at first lived in Switzerland while their grown children traveled constantly. Erika rescued her father's manuscripts in April, including his handwritten copy of the *Joseph* material, and Golo helped to bring the youngest, Elisabeth and Michael, to freedom. Blanche Knopf, the representive of his American publisher, visited Mann for the first time at his residence at Sanary-sur-Mer, and on her second visit, in April 1934, at Küsnacht,[120] she invited him to the United States. Thomas Mann also began to correspond with the Hungarian-born Swiss classicist and mythologist Karl Kerényi on 27 January 1934, a significant intellectual contact for both men. During that year, his American publisher, Alfred A. Knopf, and his English translator, Helen T. Lowe-Porter, welcomed him to the United States for the first time. His exuberant triumphal procession was distinguished by a reception at the New York P. E. N. Club,[121] a lecture at Yale[122] and his honorary admission to the Authors Club before his return to Europe on 9 June. Before he finally decided to move to Princeton, Mann visited the United States three more times: June–July 1935, April 1937, and February 1938, each time enjoying many demonstrations of friendship and esteem.[123]

Mann could respond warmly to such profound experiences. His first two volumes of the *Joseph* novels[124] reveal a peaceful heart, a benevolent understanding and gentle humor, and a deep concern for temporal and eternal human values. The Mann household, with Katia at its heart,[125] had been scattered by world catastrophe, but parents and children were bound by close ties. Heinrich, too, survived the maelstrom. On 19 November 1936, Thomas Mann was stripped of his German citizenship and acquired Czechoslovakian citizenship at the Czech embassy in Zurich. Despite the frustrations of exile, illness, and his children's marital shifts, life went on as normally as possible. Mann preached the cause of a free Germany, which with *Joseph* was his strongest motivation. Although he had never been politically active, Thomas Mann's honor demanded that he examine, conceive and express Germany's *geistig* developments. He shared his idealistic involvement with other exiled German intellectuals like Werfel, Stefan Zweig, and Bruno Frank, and in Switzerland he developed a special bond with Hermann Hesse. Others, like Romain Rolland, whom he had earlier antagonized, also drew nearer, and he had to hire help, which Katia supervised, to deal with the burgeoning correspondence his sense of duty prompted him to carry on: "I am German culture; wherever I am, there is German culture, " he liked to say, expressing a profound Goethean sense of the *Bürger*, especially apt since he was then writing a novel on Goethe,[126] the greatest of all German *Bürgers*.

Thomas Mann was now able to balance the wartime world and the realm of universal values, something he could not do at the time of his *Betrachtungen eines Unpolitischen*. While he was delivering speeches,[127] he was also working on an essay on Schopenhauer,[128] to which his constant interest had drawn him. As was his usual practice, he waited until his other commitments were completed to begin the new essay. On 21 August 1924, he had written to Franz Mockrauer about a proposed lecture on Schopenhauer" "Also [there are] other commitments after . . . the novel [*The Magic Mountain*] which will hinder me from doing well by your wish this winter. For the future, however, I will not let the thought of it out of [my] sight" (EHL). He returned to a systematic reading of Schopenhauer in 1937, which provided the basis for a forty-page essay that brilliantly presents topics and Thomas Mann's interpretations of Schopenhauer's, *The World as Will and Representation* in thoughts markedly similar to those he had at the time of *Buddenbrooks*.

Thomas Mann was no longer emotionally dependent on but he was intellectually attracted to Schopenhauer's works all his life. "The pleasure we take in a metaphysical system, the gratification purveyed by the intellectual organization of the world into a closely reasoned, complete and balanced structure of thoughts, is always of a pre-eminently aesthetic kind. It flows from the same source as the satisfaction, the high and ever happy satisfaction we get from art, with its power to shape and order its material, to sort out life's manifold confusion so as to give us a clear and general view."[129] This joyful mood underlies "The Transposed Heads," written two years later, "a Maya grotesque . . . of the Great Mother's cult, in whose honor people cut off their heads—a game of separation into two . . . not too serious; it will at best be a curiosity and I don't even know whether I will make it to its end" (EHL).[130]

Mann called this story a "Maya grotesque," as he had called "Tristan" a "burlesque."[131] Thomas Mann viewed "Tristan" from conviction, the acceptance of the Schopenhauerian *Weltanschauung*, the representation of the world conceived through the absurdity of the rationalization of the "will to live" (*Wille zum Leben*), amid which Gabriele's existential experience with the music of *Tristan* acted as "insight" (*Erkenntnis*)."Tristan" thus parodied the world represented by the idea appearing in the reflection of Maya, an idea which reappeared in "Anekdote," without its original charm. Mann's later treatment of Maya, "The Transposed Heads," proceeds from deep admiration for the aesthetic creativity of Schopenhauer's philosophical system. He whimsically superimposed the extravagant Schopenhauerian system upon the tale of Sita of the beautiful hips and her two husbands. The Indian setting is entirely appropriate because Schopenhauer had owed his basic concepts to India's religious thought. The Schopenhauer vocabulary is again, as in "Tristan" used heavily. Mann succeeded in portraying Maya as grotesque without damaging his warm relation to the characters' human aspects, treating their faith and dedication with a warmth and humor hidden under the absurdities of the Maya representation of the world. The deceit of Maya, that richly detailed labyrinth of bizarre rationalization, however, never tarnishes the protagonists' attraction as they seek a path leading to a happiness worthy of their appealing human dignity. Their end—willing immolation—is acceptable because it employs an ancient Indian tradition, and it also parallels Schopenhauer's supreme "insight" (*Erkenntnis*), the road to freedom from the *principium individuationis*. The fate of the beautiful Sita after death is unclear; once she joins her dead husbands on the funeral pyre, her screams are muffled (if she screamed at all) by triumphal fanfares. The lovable Sita attains dignity, even an obelisk raised reverently in her memory. Mann's "Transposed Heads" does not express a special commitment to Schopenhauer's philosophy, but it celebrates the human values behind the deception of Maya, and thus has thematic significance.

Thomas Mann repeatedly called "The Transposed Heads" a "metaphysical jest."[132] He tended to play it down just after its publication, and it had very little success in the United States.[133] He did appreciate Käte Hamburger's sympathetic reaction;[134] he commented, ". . . as I needed a work to relax (after the Magic Mountain [*sic*] it was "Disorder and Early Sorrow"), . . . this Hindu mixture of sensuality and metaphysics, the confusion of identities, the murderous joking, the love- and personality-problem attracted me, so I allowed myself to be involved with the matter and I don't have to regret it, because I believe that something light and superior materialized" (EHL).[135] At first, Mann seemed insecure about this story; he later thought better of it and revised his opinion, but his overall reaction was quite hesitant, and he never defended it as vigorously as He had *Fiorenza*. This demonstrates his reverence for his youth experience of Schopenhauer, which he did not want tarnished by an unappreciative public.

Thomas Mann also told Käte Hamburger that he wrote "The Transposed Heads" to pursue his train of thought from a new angle and to express it in new imagery. He also said to Harry Slochower, ". . . 'Lotte' and [the] Indian jest [are], if not the continuation, then the offshoots of 'Joseph.' In 'Transposed Heads' I saw a little of the road back from Weimar into the mythical,— but indeed Weimar is a mythos too, Goethe is one [a myth himself], and here too it is a question of the realization of making a mythos clear with all the intimacy of the real and of the make-believe" (EHL).[136] The ideas in *Lotte in Weimar* were colored by Thomas Mann's lifelong commitment to Goethe and by personal associations. The theme of the sacrificial victim and the one to whom the sacrifice is offered, a theme that Cipolla had equivocally handled, had survived and matured. The aged Goethe tells Lotte, "You used an image nearer and dearer to me than any other, [one] by which my soul had ever been possessed: the moth and the fatal alluring flame. Before and after all, I am [the] sacrificial victim, as well as he who offers it [the sacrifice]. . . [addressing Lotte] Know [that] metamorphosis is most beloved and most intimate to your friend, his great hope and deepest longing, the play of eternal transformation . . . [the] unity, intermingling [all] things . . . Death, the final flight into the flame: in all-enveloping Unity, how should death be anything but a transformation?" (EHL).[137] The dullness of ordinary time is transfigured in these lines into a glowing existential act that Thomas Mann retained, clothing his thoughts in new light and radiant colors.

"The Transposed Heads" has twelve numbered sections of varying length.[138] Its language is light, soft, humorous, and descriptive, and the dialogue creates a fairy-tale mood blending fantastic and meditative logic, delicate humor, and philosophical satire directed against the absurdity of Maya. Since "The Transposed Heads" was not included in printings of *Stories of Three Decades*,[139] Mann and his American publisher evidently agreed that it would only disrupt the established short story collection. Mann referred to many typographical errors,[140] and he also felt it "presumably suffered through the translation."[141] The subtle verbal style Thomas Mann used in "The Transposed Heads" is indeed difficult to render in translation. Certain words, expressions, and word clusters shape mood and connotation by repetition, by syntactic placement, or by the use of eccentricity. Such artful shaping of the atmosphere calls forth subjective rather than rational conceptualization and creates much of the message. For example, the German *"lauschen"* ("watching," "listening," "eavesdropping," or "lurking") connotes an untranslatable reference to the mysterious, the intangible, to miraculous, an expression that occurs surprisingly often in Heinrich Zimmer's sound-sensitive language in his writings on Indian myth, with which Thomas Mann was familiar.[142] Thomas Mann even uses an unusual adjective, *lauschig*, from the verb *lauschen*. Shridaman and Nanda, conversing, define the concept: "'Listen, how *lauschig*! I use the word *"lauschig"* because it descends from the action of *lauschen*, which is only caused by silence. Because it makes us become alert to everything that is not completely still in it [silence] . . . Only Nirvana is completely still and filled with silence, that is why it cannot be called *lauschig*'" (EHL).[143] This passage demonstrates Thomas Mann's soft mediative argumentation and the sensitivity of his humor; such meticulous and charming exchanges, integral to the theme, abound in this story.

Mann also uses repeated qualitative phrases, as for instance, "Sita of the beautiful hips." The clumsiness of translation spoils the fluid musicality of the German phrase, *"schönhüftige* Sita," humorous and highly exotic, with a strong undercurrent of sensuality. This cluster of words characteristically accompanies Sita's name. It points to the source of the story's central mystery, the absurd concept of fertility, of which Sita's child is the tangible evidence, uniting all features in himself. Such repeated phrases individualize the tale, insistently highlighting the message. Such ideas are integral to each characterization, so that they stand out in the conceptual images of the subconscious and are ready when the plot reaches out for understanding, a formal feature which conveys the theme, the existential problem of individual identity versus the struggle for unity of beings caught up in sharply differentiated physical and psychic characteristics. Contrasts between the physical appearances and the castes of Schridaman and Nanda, as well as their intellectual upbringing, their personal qualities, and their modes of life exert a reciprocal attraction,[144] which opposes Schopenhauerian hate-filled reciprocal pursuit. But even this reciprocal attraction, like everything in the story, is a deception of Maya; their love brings the two men to a violent end, as their hate would have done in a Schopenhauerian world of bitter struggle. Schridaman and Nanda commit ritualistic self-sacrifice to satisfy dogma.[145] Existence in the world of representation, whether moved by love or hatred, must overcome individualizing boundaries in the act of overcoming the self. But even this supreme "insight" (*Erkenntnis*) seems questionable because of Neoplatonic magnetism;[146] striving toward ultimate union is as egotistical as sacrificial, and the heroes' faith is projected through the lens of the narrator's questioning humor. The difference between Schopenhauer's struggle of "all against all" and Mann's tale is reciprocal longing which affirms and strengthens each side's characteristics. Schridaman, whose intellect is reflected in his refined features and soft limbs, is admired by Nanda; Schridaman himself admires Nanda's powerful body; they share a closeness between castes unacceptable in their original culture. Each man's imperfection forms part of his individuality, which then seeks completion in the other. Schridaman's *geistlich* qualities stand out, and with Nanda, those of the senses.[147] A late reflection of the loving-hating shadows of Lorenzo and Savonarola united by their sinful love of Fiore, who represents beauty and sensuality, is nearly resurrected. In "The Transposed Heads," however, nothing remains of the bitter fortitude of the rulers of Florence, or of Tonio's heartbreaking longing.[148] Longing as a counterweight to centrifugal energy is conveyed through the qualities of the three friends; Sita, who represents beauty, is shown in images of love and sensuality. Her name means "furrow," and even though she has a lovely profile, she is just an average girl, wife, and mother of her caste. Even the impression of her beautiful hips is soon hidden beneath her floating sari, contrasting with the strong psychic and physical features of Schridaman and Nanda. Sita is a beautiful incomplete incarnation of the World Mother of the bloodthirsty womb, whose impersonal fecundity draws the *geistig* and the sensual potential that she, consciously or not, has thoughtlessly and greedily united. Sita may have disrupted the balance of power, first by mixing the distinguishing features of Schridaman and Nanda, and then by overturning the system that sustains attraction against centrifugal force. She also prevents the "weak" parts of each conceptual type from possessing her own beauty. The offspring of such candid beauty might have inherited qualities from each side, uniting them in an ultimate perfection that is unfit to live in the imperfect world of representation. Sita herself was terrified of bringing a "widow's child" pale and blind, into the world. But the World Mother's wisdom thunderously provided a solution: " 'Be good and let this be my worry! First of all, this is only a

stupid women's superstition, and secondly,' she thunders at Sita, 'in my re-
tinue there must also be pale and blind cripples' " (EHL) (see also *TH*, 99;
GW, 8: 758). She gave little Samadhi-Andhaka an attractive light complexion
and nearsighted star like eyes good enough for him to become the bard of the
king of Benares; he is weak and imperfect enough to be of this world, beautiful and skilled enough to conclude the tale happily.

"The Transposed Heads" has a frame construction, its initial paragraphs
introducing the theme, the trickery of Maya, and identifying the protagonists.
The friendship between Nanda and Schridaman "was based on the diversity
in their I- and my-feelings,[149] those of the one yearning towards those of the
other. Incorporation, that is, makes for isolation, isolation for difference; difference makes for comparisons, comparisons give rise to uneasiness, uneasiness to wonderment, wonderment tends to admiration; and finally admiration
turns to a yearning for mutual exchange and unity. *Etad vei tad*. This is that.
And the doctrine applies especially in youth, when the clay of life is still soft
and The I- and my-feelings not yet hardened into the division of the single
personality."[150] This passage offers illustrative approaches to the concept and
symptoms of the *principium individuationis*.

The action of the plot opens with the two young men visiting Kali's lustral
sanctuary near the little river called the "Gold Fly" (*TH*, 15; *GW*, 8: 716).
The prayer, ritual bath, and drink represent purification, and the submer-
gence symbolizes unification, religiously dramatizing the entire existential
problem of the story. Their holy duties done, Schridaman and Nanda enjoy a
calm "as beyond the six waves of hunger, thirst, old age, and death, pain, and
illusion" (EHL). (*TH*, 18; *GW*, 8: 719). They sink down into the sensual
delights of this paradise, fragrant with jasmine.[151] Their speech typifies their
contrasting personalities with a gentle humor that hints at peaceful life
together. Suddenly, a maiden steps unaware into the holiest spot and disrobes
for her prayers and ritual bath. "The loveliness of her body was dazzling. It
seemed made of Maya . . ." (EHL) (*TH*, 32; *GW*, 8: 725). Filled with admiration and suitably holy conversation, Nanda remembers that the name of the
girl is Sita and that he had known her before Schridaman. He pursues his
concept of the "insight" (*Erkenntnis*) he gains by the vision of the girl: " 'Because she is all, not only just one: Life and Death, Madness and Wisdom,
Magician and Liberator, don't you know that? Because this is what fascinates
and simultaneously liberates us, and it is exaltation[152] which blinds sensual
beauty and the *Geist*' " (EHL).[153] Indeed, the Brahmin Schridaman understands the problem of the plurality he is a part of and refers to the aesthetic
part Sita represents: " 'Because as Beauty and *Geist* flow into one another in
exaltation, so do Life and Death in Love' " (EHL).[154] Thus Schridaman enthusiastically summarizes the essence of this "metaphysical jest," and Nanda
appreciatively offers his friend some betel to chew.[155] Mann employs another
of his *ménages à trois*— Klöterjahn-Spinell and Gabriele; Tonio and Hans-
Ingeborg; Lorenzo-Savonarola and Fiore, all representing the overlapping
concepts of *Geist*, *Kunst*, and Beauty-*Schönheit* and/or Life-*Leben*.

This *ménage à trois* then goes to visit Sita's parents. The young wife, now pregnant, yearns passionately for her husband's athletic friend, and only her good upbringing and her self-respect keep her from revealing her feelings. Once their cart, drawn by an ox and a camel; is on its way, "The confusion of their own souls was favoured by the darkness, and unconsciously they projected their inward bewilderment into outward space—with the result that they lost their way,"[156] passing into a "deep forest," and finally stopping before the temple of the World Mother, where Schridaman briefly prays. The goddess, called variously Dewi, Durga, Kali, and other names, is heard but never seen, in this surrealistic realm that Mann calls a "subterranean slaughterhouse." His humor is built upon shocking naturalness, a mental state in which the most bizarre happenings seem credible and even common, "exalted" (*begeistert*) by the goddess, another aspect of Maya. So Schridaman felt when he was overwhelmed by "exaltation" (*Begeisterung*); he ". . . spoke these darkling words, seized up the sword from the floor, and severed his own head from his neck" (*TH*, 76; *GW*, 8: 748). Penetration into another level of existence, here illustrated first in the self-sacrifice and the mystery of the victim's blood returning and reentering the body of the World Mother, is thus a ritual of unification and purification of the three, a transcendence of self in a moment of highest "exaltation" (*Begeisterung*); it is comparable in nature to Schopenhauer's *geniale Erkenntnis*.

The World Mother's reversal of the young men's sacrifices is a truly paradoxical humorous way to clarify the new phase of life in the world of I and My, the confusion Sita's explanation creates. The World Mother's offended pride is delightfully feminine. She rejects Sita's theory about the two suicides: that the men killed themselves for the love of Sita. The World Mother of course took the deaths as offerings,[157] and now she releases them again. Such action is absurd, like her instructing Sita, in gobbledygook poured out like thunder, not to put the heads back to front.[158] Sita does her best but she either is confused or guided by suppressed desires, and she transposes the heads.

To decide who is now Sita's rightful husband, Schridaman's head or his body (considering that it had produced their offspring), the three visit the saintly hermit Kamadamana in the Dankaka Forest. Thomas Mann's family relished chapter 10 even before the story was completed: "I can tell you that I . . . read a new chapter of 'Transposed Heads' to my [family] and some friends, the one which plays at the ascetic in the Indian wood and that we all have laughed [unto] tears—not excluding the reader and author" (EHL) (Thomas Mann's letter to Agnes E. Meyer, 14 June 1940). At last the holy man designated Schridaman's head as Sita's rightful husband, and, overjoyed, the "wife," now the possessor of the fine-featured head and athletic body, bids farewell to Nanda's head, who, bitter at the deception, withdraws into the lonely jungle with his weak, rather chubby, body.

After fleeting joy, the head, with the lifestyle it dictates, begins a process of equalization. The refined head on the vigorous body becomes rough, while the body loses its athletic character, and the bliss of Sita of the beautiful hips is over. She sets off with her little son in search of Nanda. Mann wrote the account of her journey and reunion at Brentwood, and these passages reflect the charming climate and scenery he liked so much. Later, though, he had to struggle to finish the story.[159]

The tragic situation Sita created was actually not much worse than the original state the three had been in when the centrifugal and the attracting powers held matters in balance. However, that state of being had been natural; now it is emphatically substantialized, realized, and understood, another of Maya's deceptions.[160] At last, Sita says, decency and human dignity must win and reorder things peacefully after a final ritual self-sacrifice; [161] by these words, she earns the obelisk her compatriots raise to her memory. Joy pervades this story, and even the Schopenhauerian negatives are all wittily featured as deceptively positive, due, of course, to the influence of Maya.[162]

"The Transposed Heads" 's chief merit lies in the light humor and elegant irony with which Thomas Mann treated matters of great weight. He himself acknowledged this value: "It was only a scurrilous intermezzo, but in [my] younger days I would not have been able to write it, and what satisfies me [now] is the cheerfulness which I could pass on and maintain, which under today's circumstances is no small thing" (EHL).[163]

As he approached the end of "The Transposed Heads," Mann wrote, ". . . Now [I] hope to put down the Indic jest soon and I have my Joseph material with me . . ." (EHL).[164] A little later he announced, "Now I have the last volume of the Joseph in my head,"[165] and he reached toward a harmonization of his lifelong themes. Like "The Transposed Heads" in particular, the short story genre as a whole was the plateau on which he could sort and assimilate his thoughts, sometimes just satisfying his need to relax after an enormous effort or to assemble his ideas for another great novel. The epic of Wagner's operas that had impressed him in his youth had found a definition of his own in his mind. In his lecture "On the Novel" at Princeton in 1939, Thomas Mann had said,

> Allow me the personal and nonacademic confession that my love and interest belong, among the genres of art, especially to the genius of the Epic, and I do not excuse myself if a lecture on "The Art of the Novel" becomes without exception a thoroughgoing praise of the epic *Geist* of art. It is a powerful and majestic *Geist*, expansive, full of life, wide as the ocean in its rolling sameness, simultaneously magnanimous and minute, and wisely, contemplatively musical; it does not strive for the piecemeal, the episode, it desires the whole, the world with its countless episodes and particularities, at which it will rest forgetful of self . . . it has unlimited time; it is the *Geist* of patience, of true perseverance and slowness which becomes enjoyable through love, the *Geist* of enchanting ennui. It can hardly register otherwise than with the original beginning of

all things, and it might not at all want to reach an end. For from it the word of the poet is viable: "That you cannot end makes you great." But its greatness is mild, "calming," "cheerful," "wise,"—"objective." It stands at a distance from the things it is distanced from by nature; it [the greatness] floats above, and smiles down upon them so well that it involves the listener [*Lauschender*] or the reader in itself and waves them on. The art of the Epic is "Apollinian" art, as the aesthetic term sounds; because Apollo, the far-reaching, is the god of the far away, the god of distance, of objectivity, the god of irony. Objectivity is the *Geist* of Irony. (EHL) (*GW*, 10: 352–53)

In July 1940, Mann had finished polishing "The Transposed Heads," to be published in Stockholm[166] in October, and returned to his Joseph project. Shortly after, the Manns purchased a lot in Pacific Palisades, California, and moved there from Princeton in the spring of 1941, renting a house until their new home was ready in early 1942.[167] They stayed there until they left America in mid-1952 for Switzerland, where both Thomas and Katia Mann died. During the war, Thomas Mann made public anti-Nazi appearances[168] or gave readings from his work.[169] On 13–14 January 1941, Thomas and Katia Mann were the White House guests of President Roosevelt.

On 5 January 1943, Thomas Mann began a short story, "Das Gesetz," completed in record time on 13 March 1943, when he started to work on the notes for *Doctor Faustus*.

"Thou Shalt Have No Other Gods before Me"

The language and presentation of "Das Gesetz"[170] is shocking contrast to those of the Joseph novels. The epigrammatic language shows a blend of the narrative serenity of a fairy tale and factual objectivity, only the superficial aspects of the plot being taken from the Bible. The story, divided into twenty sections of slightly varying length is about fifty pages long, sharply interrupted by quotations and short, naturalistic dialogues.[171] "Das Gesetz," with a biblical plot and setting, has its own message. The text has passages of close paraphrase of the Luther Bible.[172]

Mann models his message here with scalpel sharpness[173] is an aggressive combination of biblical and fairy-tale qualities and absurd anachronisms, without losing the unity he achieved through the universality of his message. The harshly realistic text does not allow the comfort of a God-governed fate; Moses the man, enslaved by fleshly desires, still tenaciously craves the Ten Commandments. The law outlining ethics and civilization, as claimed here, is the first phonetically written text accessible to all men.[174]

"Das Gesetz" represents an interesting and obvious maturation of Thomas Mann's thought and expression, which is clearly based on meticulous research for his Joseph novels. It is a powerful sketch of his vision of the birth of Judeo-Christian culture.

"Das Gesetz," literally "The Law," was titled in the English translation "Thou Shalt Have No Other Gods before Me". This title lacks the laconic firmness and simple power of the original; it serves the Robinson project well, but in quoting the divine words it fails to reflect Thomas Mann's hero Moses, who stubbornly, passionately, and all alone serves the "invisible god." This deity remains absent in Thomas Mann's story and it is Moses' struggle against primal urges the "will to live" (*Wille zum Leben*): the flesh, superstition, ingratitude of man (shown in the short story through the Jewish tribe), that is the focus of Mann's message. This Moses is a roughly carved replica of Michelangelo, the artist himself. With his crushed and flattened nose, his unruly temper and his power to carve and shape his media, Thomas Mann's Moses is more impressive than any other artistic image of Moses. The originality of this Moses lies in the credibility of his shortcomings and his clumsy limited ability to serve his "invisible god." This Moses' speech was so unclear that his brother Aaron had to speak for him. Moses' own subjective powers were torn between his devotion to his "invisible god" and the wild cravings of his flesh, which debased him to the level of the mob he had to shape, educate, and discipline to the image of this "invisible God." Crippled by his limitations, Mann's Moses was a powerless tool of the "invisible god," shaking his huge fists in rage and stammering with a foaming mouth. This Moses mediates between the divine and the earthbound, a profoundly romantic concept of the poet (*Dichter*).

The fact that Mann's Moses was not simply a Hebrew foundling raised by Pharaoh's daughter, but a hybrid born of lust between the "divine" Egyptian princess and a Jewish slave who was later slaughtered, his body hidden under the all-covering desert sand, represents the fertile encounter of extremes, opening the topic to universality. Moses unites, in his flawed person, on the one hand, the divine blood of the pharaohs and that of the slaves; on the other hand, this stuttering mouthpiece of the "invisible god is a teacher unable to speak clearly and a ruler unable to control his own passions. Moses thus becomes a Faustian representation of man, in his virtue of unconditional striving. Thomas Mann's theme lauds the human element in his Moses.[175] The "invisible god" never speaks directly to the Hebrews, so, as an individual, Moses represents man himself.

Some critics, especially Jewish critics, have felt that Thomas Mann's narration was irreverent or even anti-Semitic;[176] however, the strength and credibility of this story is that Mann does not idealize the Hebrew nomads or put their qualities on levels which would not be realistically and normally credible. His Moses must deal with the imperfections and the curse of greatness of a man with the lucid perception of urgent needs for growth, with unconditional dedication—like a Frederick the Great, a Peter the Great, or a Cardinal Richelieu. Thomas Mann's Michelangelo-Moses must lead the people on a new path, playing an unappreciated and tragic role in history.

Moses, or the "invisible god" via Moses, does not only give the Hebrews an ethical code but also a means of self-expression by inventing writing. This is substantialized by the stone-carved Ten Commandments, products of Moses' *Geist* and his very "flesh and blood." This equilibrium of two opposing life powers represents the elements of all mankind.

Thomas Mann expresses this as the core of *Menschenbenehmen*, or human behavior, including ethics, decency, dignity, and respect of the self. The commandments and the gift of writing are not there for Israel only, but for all mankind. The universality of the message is clear; Moses and the Hebrews are merely its vehicle. The archetypal Word carved in stone with blood, the spirit, and flesh, belongs to all humanity.

The last paragraph of "Das Gesetz" features Moses' characteristic determination to enforce the Ten Commandments. His language is earthy, reflecting the mentality and phraseology of Eastern rulers. Moses threatens offenders against the new law, and he defines the concept of sin. This last paragraph, so important to the message of the entire story, does not single out any one commandment, as the English title does. The strength of Mann's story is in its emphasis upon the unity of the ten laws defining human dignity. To single one commandment out would weaken this concept and would cripple the equilibrium inherent in the concept of right and wrong. Similar is the idea of the gift of writing, a motif Mann strongly emphasizes. Writing represents universal communication, since all can read the phonetic system, and lifts the limitations of space and time.

It is uncertain how far Mann bows to divine intervention and how far he permits Moses to go in manipulating the superstitious; the chosen people of God are no different here from any undisciplined, selfish, pragmatic crowd. Mann noted, in a letter to Agnes E. Meyer, 13 March 1943: ". . . it [the story] treats naturally the human ethics and the whole ends, after a lot of ironic joking, with a real curse upon those who lead humans to shackle them [with the laws]."

The same concern with human ethics was central to "The Transposed Heads," where death by sword and fire leads the characters through purification of death into a peaceful ad decent existence. In a letter of 17 March 1943 to Helen T. Lowe-Porter, Thomas Mann significantly mentioned "Disorder and Early Sorrow," which, with his next and last short story, "Die Betrogene," embodied the same theme as "The Transposed Heads" and "Das Gesetz," namely the struggle for order and decency. He also wrote to Otto Basler on 1 September 1945, "Why is Michelangelo the model, [he] who . . . looks like the prophet Jeremiah in the Sistine—who has not much of the Jewish [character] either?" (EHL). Michelangelo's life and work are much closer to Mann's Moses figure than Michelangelo's patriarchal sculpture of Moses is. Mann's Moses is not necessarily a Hebrew; he could have been modeled on any person having the appropriate personality. It is a profound element of Thomas Mann's humanism that he, while believing in the corruptibility of human nature, also believed in stronger impulses or even spiritual interventions that could bring fate into the right path so that order prevailed after each irregularity. In "Disorder and Early Sorrow," Lorchen was cured by the blessed power of sleep; the three lovers were led by the angry goddess in "The Transposed Heads"; the Jews were scourged to the right path by Moses' words and threats, as well as Joshua's sword and the fear of the "invisible god." Rosalie, in the story to follow, Mann's last, was also led to the right path by the firm hand of Mother Nature herself.

"The Black Swan"

During the winter and spring of 1952, in Pacific Palisades, Thomas Mann worked on the *Felix Krull* manuscript which he had interrupted in May to start "Die Betrogene,"[177] which later received the English title "The Black Swan."[178] The next summer, the Manns left Pacific Palisades for Switzerland, first staying in Zurich and then St. Wolfgang and Gastein; they spent the fall of 1953 and the end of the year in Zurich, then moved to Erlenbach, and in early 1954 they settled in their last home in Kilchberg, near Zurich. "The Black Swan," which Mann had started in the United States, was completed in Switzerland.

"The subject of 'The Black Swan' was no less tabu than *The Holy Sinner*, a tragic insight into the deceit of life, which stemmed from a chance conversation with Katja."[179] Thomas Mann wrote,". . . . But there is life behind this story, a real anecdote, which I heard and which instantly had a productive reaction on me . . ." As soon as Mann became interested in the plot material he examined the medical facts with his medical advisor for *Doctor Faustus*, Dr. Frederick Rosenthal[180]. At an early stage, Mann had a grasp of the medical as well as the psychological issues implicit in his theme, as shown in his letters of 5 and 13 May 1952 to Rosenthal. He also painstakingly examined the geographical details around Düsseldorf; and he wrote to Dr. Oberloskamp,[181] and secured the correct Rhineland dialect from Grete Nikisch.[182]

"The Black Swan" involves sensitive, and for Mann, unusual, plot material. Hamilton comments, "It was a cruel story, and was to upset many of Thomas' staunchest admirers."[183] The reception of the story was mixed, and the secondary literature, especially in the United States, is comparable in neither depth, attitude, nor volume to that available for earlier stories. Some critics consider "The Black Swan" either a failure or a minor story.[184]

After the immense emotional and intellectual effort of writing *Doctor Faustus*, he was drained, and he now looked forward to working on "The Black Swan." He had been ailing and he referred to "unfavorable circumstances" (EHL) he experienced while writing it. On 6 January 1950, Mann wrote to Bruno Walter, "Hardly out of bed, which one ought not to do, I wrote the story to its end. . . ." Mann refers to "The Black Swan" as "a little myth about Mother Nature" (EHL).[185] The story was important to him; he was

hurt when it was belittled, but he did not defend it as he did *Fiorenza*.
In 1954 Mann wrote in *"Rückkehr"* (*GW*, 11: 529):

> There have been silly comparisons made between it [the story "The
> Black Swan"] and "Death in Venice", it ["The Black Swan"] has nothing
> to do with it ["Death in Venice"], neither considering its weight nor its
> theme. The only [thing] it ["The Black Swan"] has in common with it
> ["Death in Venice"] is that it is accidentally [written] by me and is actual-
> ly unmistakably from me. It could be from no one else and belongs with a
> certain necessary urgency to me and [the work of] mine. The event that I
> heard and which caught me due to the cruel demonic force of nature that
> is expressed in it, shocked me and immediately attracted me in a produc-
> tive manner." (EHL)

"The Black Swan" conveys Mann's characteristic thought, his way of expression, his imagery, his intellectual history, and especially the oscillating
pattern of reactions found throughout his work.

There is no doubt that similarities in minor details do exist between "Death
in Venice" and "The Black Swan" and might have called for the comments
that Mann rejected. "Death in Venice" is a *Künstlernovelle* the theme of
which suggests the ideal harmony of the Apollinian and Dionysian as the
key to the artist's fulfillment. "The Black Swan'" might be called "a nature
novella" since in a controversial manner, nature, repeatedly referred to as
"Mother Nature," seems to be on trial. However, she is mistress of Order and
Harmony and the source of beauty; she is totally in control of her realm.
Hidden behind the "veil of Maya," she is misunderstood and accused of betrayal when she energetically keeps her realm within the laws of the Nature
she rules. Rosalie might be considered either as villain or victim. When Mann
says that "The black Swan" is "another dimension" than "Death in Venice,"
this is accurate, since "Death in Venice" is a dramatic expression of his own
aesthetic growth, while "The Black Swan" was born from his need to express
a status quo.

Some motifs from "Death in Venice" are, however, recognizable in "The
Black Swan"; one example is the chance and the failure to avoid disaster and
the paradoxical pseudo-logical arguments (*Objektivierung des Wille zum
Leben*) to justify this: Aschenbach's inability to leave the sirocco plaguing
Venice, which was harmful to his health; Rosalie's refusal to send Kent
Keaton away or to leave town herself, as Anna suggests. Another example is
that in both stories the respected mature citizen uses cosmetics to please the
object of his/her infatuation. Also, the sense of smell is a powerful motif in
both stories, evoked through the odor of must in "The Black Swan" and of
carbolic acid and putrefaction in "Death in Venice." In both stories the infatuation occurs on the part of the older person and neither Tadzio nor Kent
realizes it at first; when they later do, they both manipulate the love-stricken
senior with playful flirtation. Thus, while Thomas Mann rejected the sugges-

tion of a direct reference to "Death in Venice," he did agree that "The Black Swan" is genuinely his own, which is an admission that similarities are naturally detectable. But this is also true in reference to stories other than "Death in Venice." A conversation between Rosalie and Anna, "Yes, you are clever and as an artist you are not on the best terms with nature . . ." (*TBS*, 30; *GW*, 8: 891), reminds us of Tonio Kröger's conversation with Lisabeta. Even the Baron Harry from "Gleam" reappears in the fading figure of the late von Tümmler and is reflected by the young Edward. The title of the short story "Disorder and Early Sorrow," could be slightly altered to "Disorder and *Later* Sorrow" for "The Black Swan." There is also the problem of the generation gap, which conveys Mann's own emotions in relation to Dr. Cornelius and Anna. Mann had not changed his attitude since "Disorder and Early Sorrow," and he never reached the bitterness the "sexual revolution" of the 1960s was to bring. The instinctual game deeply buried in the subconscious, which caused little Lorchen's sorrow, was objectivated with paradoxical logic by the older woman, Rosalie, when the same thing happens to her. While Lorchen was adversely touched by the postwar disorder, it is the mature Rosalie, driven by the power of her passion, who is willing to disrupt the order of man's value-based society and misinterprets Nature's order. Hence the doctor's diagnosis is crucial when he refers to "heaven knows what kind of stimulation" (*TBS*, 138–39; *GW*, 8: 949) as a cause of the sudden spreading of the cancer. The careful examination of the doctor's diagnosis shows "Mother Nature" in command. It is possible, even if not explicitly pointed out, that if Rosalie had acted according to Anna's advice and had broken off with Ken, the "stimulation" would not have caused the development of her tragic cancer. Significantly, Rosalie's newly youthful appearance occurred after her decision not to stop this relationship.

The presence of the *Liebestodmotiv* has been suggested without considering Thomas Mann's lifelong growth toward the concept. Rosalie's transitory bliss in death yields to nature without any trace of the Wagnerian theme of the union of the lovers in death.

Thomas Mann's attraction to this theme was owing to his need to follow the swing of the pendulum of his creative rhythm. As the Schopenhauerian "Worldview" (*Weltbild*) in "Tristan" was balanced by the self-definition in "Tonio Kröger" (the *Künstler-Bürger*), so now "The Black Swan" carries Thomas Mann's lifelong message. The concepts of the Apollinian are found in Anna's arguments, while the addiction to nature, freedom, permissiveness, and chaos are the Dionysian qualities, expressed by Rosalie. As Anna suggests, Rosalie turns her back on harmony, order, and self-discipline to reach for Dionysian infatuation.

Nature, a very important protagonist of the story, is referred to, usually with emphasis, in Thomas Mann's correspondence as "Mother Nature" ("*Mutter*" or "*Liebe Mutter Natur*"), accepted as an actual, active, independent character. This refers strongly to the mother figure in "The Transposed

Heads," where the Goddess Durga-Dewi, the "Mother" (*TH*, 79–80; *GW*, 8: 757–58), had an aggressively powerful role in the love entanglement, the dramatic turning point, and the conclusion of the story. There, as well as in "The Black Swan," the mother stands for order, harmony, and decency restored by death.[186] In neither story do the protagonists consider death to be a punishment. In "The Transposed Heads," as well as in "The Black Swan," death signifies a grace-filled transition from dishonoring life to a peaceful purification. The strong reference to Schopenhauer's "Worldview" (*Weltbild*) also appears in "The Transposed Heads" and in "The Black Swan."

While the setting and imagery of "The Black Swan" firmly rest on medical and scientific grounds, they stunningly, even naturalistically, portray the aging woman's physical and psychological earthbound problems, while the theme, the concept, and the reverence for order, are abstractions. Therefore, this story is an "idea novella" rather than a story built on social topics. "The Transposed Heads" had illustrated the three characters' power in choosing death to rise above the indecent instinctual passions inherent in the individual's paradoxical objectivation of the *principium individuationis*. At the swing of the pendulum, Rosalie, in spite of the cultivated responses she gives to Anna, chooses the paradoxical objectivation of her instinctive drives (*TBS*, 26–35; *GW*, 8: 889–93).

Thomas Mann's vocabulary in "The Black Swan" is closely related to the one used in his Schopenhauer essay (1938). The German text expresses this as "*gegen-sich-selbst-leben*,"[187] while Thomas Mann uses "*gegen Willenakt*" in his Schopenhauer article (*GW*, 9: 547).[188] The word and sound clusters are closely related one to the other in German. Also Anna uses the word "disrupted" "*zerrissen*" (*GW*, 8: 736; *TBS*, 10), which is identically used in The Schopenhauer article (*GW*, 9: 547). Death leads Rosalie to the blissful words, "Indeed, death is a great instrument of life . . . ," while we read in the Schopenhauer article, ". . . Death is but an upheaval of misunderstanding. . ." (EHL) (*GW*, 9: 551). The insight of Rosalie, the naïve lover of nature, has reached the Schopenhauerian "insight" (*Erkennung*). And then Rosalie's last line lifts the paradox of *principium individuationis*: "Nature—I have always loved her, and she has been loving to her child." Mann wrote Dr. Rosenthal 13 May 1952, "Death is a great means of natural life . . ." He answered Ludwig Marcuse from Kilchberg on 17 April 1954, when close to the end of his life, "Schopenhauer forgotten? Not by me! He was a powerful writer and his system remains an admirable work of art."

It might be asked why Thomas Mann in his private correspondence did not really "rehabilitate" Mother Nature when he gave his highest valuation to the concept of death. The death that Rosalie received from Mother Nature was charitable, dignified, sublime, and happy. One might step back from "The Black Swan" to relieve the characters Rosalie and Anna from their opposing roles. Though so closely related in the story they represent opposite poles: Rosalie, in spite of her poised manners and language, is an uncomplicated subjective soul whose love of nature is as unsophisticated and uncontrolled as her intellect; Anna, on the contrary, has been shaped by her physical handicap. She is fully in control of her existence after a painful past involvement which she has overcome with dignity. Her logic is clear and rational but she is capable of real compassion. Her self-discipline even controls her artistic expression as a painter, leaving no chance for subjective intoxications. The two women have defined in their conversations a varied scale of definition of the concepts of nature and of love. The multiple shades of these defined concepts appear in the elegant conversations of these poised women who have the ability to express the most intimate problems with sensitivity and taste.

Henry Hatfield's suggestion that the story is an allegory representing the values of Old Europe and those of the New World is certainly present in the story as a motive; but it is hardly meant to represent the central message. Also, typical comments from Thomas Mann the emigrant, noting some experiences with "typical" Americanisms, are to be found in his letters and diaries. Kent Keaton, the easy-going American, was a figure Mann had learned to like. The story's essential message, though, is modeled by the discussions of the two diametrically opposed views on nature and love: self-discipline and order versus the easy-going permissiveness of the two ladies. The denouement comes in Mother Nature's verdict to decree death to restore order, while allowing a blissful transition and fading individuation, restoring equilibrium. Consummation of this love would disturb the Order of Nature and is thus unthinkable.

This transition to the very essence of Nature, through death, is the road to unlimited bliss. Rosalie's naïve faith in and love of nature is presented here in a genuinely romantic fashion. At this moment of Rosalie's transition from life to death, she grasps the mystery in its simple totality, a concept inconceivable to plain ordinary rationalization.

At this point the imagery of "The Black Swan" displays its significance and it becomes clear why the English title was acceptable to Mann. The German title *"Die Betrogene"* (*"The Deceived One"*) has two meanings. First, and liternally, Rosalie is deceived when she mistakenly sees her first hemorrhage as a recurrence of her fertility. This would have been contrary to Nature's usual order, but Rosalie's blind passion and her paradoxical objectivation in the defense of her "will to live" (*Wille zum Leben*) allowed her no logical doubt. This reading deals with an insensitive concept of nature. Secondly, the title *"Die Betrogene"* might be conceived of as playful irony in which "Mother Nature," like the goddess in "The Transposed Heads," is personified, manipulating the fate of her naïve and passion-blinded "child," Rosalie. Mother Nature might even be considered generous to give Rosalie the chance to experience the magic of love without upsetting the order or nature she is ruling over. The episode ends when "Mother Nature" leads Rosalie peacefully through the transition to Death.

The medical diagnosis (". . . after the menopause, through heaven knows what process of stimulation, begin to develop malignantly. And then the organism, *post festum*, if you like, is shot through drenched, inundated, with estrogen, which leads to hormonal hyperplasia of the internal mucous membrane, with concomitant hemorrhages" [*TBS*, 139; *GW*, 949]) clearly maintains the double standard of the scientific and fictional messages of the story. "Mother Nature" must be seen as the supreme power that rules both the physical world of nature and the dimension of universal existence without limitations of the tangible; she is in charge and she furiously guards the natural order of both these dimensions. The beautiful black swan with "his blood-red bill, the black beating of his wings" (*TBS*, 140; *GW*, 8: 950) is her servant: the embodiment of tangible nature. In his dignified beauty, paradoxically confined within the moat of the rococo chateau, the black swan claims the food offering coming to him. Rosalie, in consuming some of the archetypal bread crumbs taken from home to feed the swans, actually commits blasphemy. Rosalie misguidedly believes she has the right to partake in this mystical offering to Nature, and the black swan reacts with violent anger. The beat of his powerful wings represents an image of a menacing death, the turning point of the story. After this, the events follow swiftly.

Rosalie in her misconception is blinded by the Veil of Maya and acts aggressively; her actions are trivial and unsophisticated, following her instincts to chaos. She pulls the young tutor through a secret door, separating them from the sightseers. In a dark, moldy, centuries-old love nest, Rosalie, without any self-restraint or her usual poise, confesses her passion to the young boy. The situation is embarrassing, the setting absurd. Ironically, Rosalie does not realize the paradox of her behavior; she insists on a rendezvous the following day. To the end of the story Thomas Mann significantly de-emphasizes the role of Kent Keaton. Kent does not speak in this scene, and after it his name is not even mentioned. The last phase of Rosalie's life reflects her relationship with (Mother) Nature—the theme of the story. Rosalie's death is not related to her passion for Kent. Thus there is no similarity to the Tristan/Isolde theme.

Their rendezvous the next day never materializes. At night Rosalie is found in a pool of blood; she is rushed to the hospital, where after surgery her terminal illness is diagnosed. The denouement is between Rosalie and "Mother Nature" as the "Veil of Maya" is lifted for the dying woman. The "dual vision" (*doppelte Optik*) of the story is focused through the surgeon's diagnosis (*TBS*, 140; *GW*, 8 : 949). During the weeks of Rosalie's semiconsciousness, the black swan did appear to her, expressing his outrage. But the climax is reached through her relationship to "Mother Nature." Rosalie expresses the message of Thomas Mann's last short fiction: "Anna, never say that Nature deceived me, that she is sardonic and cruel. . . . but, how could there be spring without death? Indeed, death is a great instrument of life, and if for me it borrowed the guise of resurrection, of the joy of love, that was not a lie, but a goodness and mercy" (*TBS* 140; *GW*, 8: 950). Rosalie reaches insight at her last moments "Nature—I have loved her, and she—has been loving to her child" (*TBS*, 141; *GW*, 8: 951). Rosalie's bliss at the moment of transition is thematically significant to the story.

Thomas Mann usually checked the English translation of his works painstakingly. He disliked changes and interpretative meanings in the text and argued the details tenaciously. This time he hardly commented upon Willard R. Trask's translation and his correspondence reflects his satisfaction. Thomas Mann's acceptance of the translator's significant change in title from "*Die Betrogene*" to "*The Black Swan*" illustrated this clearly and supports the reading above.

"The Black Swan" is a story very intimately personal to Thomas Mann. The use of the *doppelte Optik* is more dramatically powerful than ever, the "Veil of Maya" standing between the fictional setting and the thematic message. The plot and setting of the story reflect Thomas Mann's maturity. With humorous irony, he matches a trivial life-situation with his significant theme. The trivia of the fictional plot and setting is his vehicle for expressing his reverence for order and decency. The clash between the unimpressive fictional facade and the depth and simplicity of his message is Mann's mature achievement in "The Black Swan", which is a worthy exercise for *Felix Krull*, his last novel.

There were negative reactions to "The Black Swan,"[189] but even though Mann was depressed by them, he did not argue with them. He received the positive comments with pleasure[190]. It is difficult to pinpoint the reason that "The Black Swan" aroused so little interest. The striking success of *Felix Krull* proves clearly that, commercially speaking, Thomas Mann was not passé as a writer. It is possible that his vocabulary, reflecting his own Schopenhauerian imagery and his life long intellectual growth, which can only be familiar to his most faithful readers, has left the more superficial without a trail to follow. Thomas Mann's vocabulary, wording, and imagery became most personal, and as he himself said of "The Black Swan," it "was very much one of his own."

Conclusion

When Thomas Mann finished "The Black Swan," he immediately returned to his notes and reading for the "Luther Project." He was also considering themes involving Ulick von Hutten, Erasmus, Charles V, and Leo X. Typically self-disciplined, he then concentrated on completing his partially assembled Krull project.[191] He repeatedly said that he would not be able to finish all the projects his mind suggested, but he did finish the Krull project. Thomas Mann awaited the publication of *Felix Krull* with mixed feelings. He was pleasantly surprised when Bermann-Fischer's first issue sold swiftly, requiring several new printings.

The period between the completion in 1953 of "The Black Swan," his last short fiction, and 12 August 1955, the day of his death, was restless but very productive. Honorary doctorates, medals, and other recognitions, including the Legion of Honor, were showered upon him, imposing a hectic and exhausting schedule. Simultaneously, negative and hostile reaction also harassed him. The McCarthy committee and some voices of the West German press suspected him of being Stalinist, partly owing to his insistence on allowing his works, including speeches, articles, and recordings to appear in East Germany. Some of his candid definitions of socialism, communism and democracy were arbitrarily used by critics and the media, causing him to suffer from the misrepresentations. On 28 December 1945, Mann wrote to Klaus Pinkros, "I am an American citizen. Never, as such—even if there were no such thing as 'press'—would it occur to me abroad to speak unsympathetically or even depreciatingly of a country to which I belong now and in the future. . . . But of course, in our bloodily-divided world there is no end to misunderstanding, of spying, of insinuation, and denunciation; and so I suppose I shall not be left in peace to the end of my days." The result was that only after the walkout of half of the members of the *Bürgerschaft* was the town of Lübeck able to honor Mann with the freedom of the city for his eightieth birthday.[192]

These tensions weakened Thomas Mann physically and kept him from concentrating on his Luther project.[193] It was finally the preparation of the eulogy for Schiller's jubilee that recaptured his attention and once again gave him the zeal and pleasure of creativity.

His *Essay on Schiller*,[194] one of the finest of its genre, was too voluminous for the speeches and lectures Mann was invited to deliver and thus was trimmed by Erica to the desired length. The lectures were received with great enthusiasm in Stuttgart, Weimar (in East Germany where Schiller had died), Amsterdam, and Lübeck.

Exhausted after the Schiller lectures and the festivities of his eightieth birthday,[195] Thomas and Katia Mann took refuge at Noordwijk in Holland, in the month of July. Even though tired, Thomas Mann was at the peak of his mental activity, receptiveness, and creativity. He read and wrote regularly even during this vacation. A sudden pain in his left leg was recognized by physicians as thrombosis, and he was flown on 23 July to the Zurich Kantonhospital. He was heavily sedated most of the time. In accordance with Katia's wishes, the diagnosis was not passed on to him. During his last days he read Bernard Shaw's *Getting Married* as a background for his projected play, "Luther's Wedding." He joked with his physician in English and French late in the afternoon of 15 August, but after heavy sedation for pain, Thomas Mann fell asleep and died peacefully soon thereafter.

In writing the last lines of his Schiller eulogy Thomas Man had found the nucleus of the message he himself had sought: ". . . out of his gentle powerful will [some of] his drive to beauty, to truth, to the good, to the ethical, to inner freedom, to art, love, peace, and to salvaging men's self-respect should at this feast of his funeral and assumption transfer to us" (EHL) (*GW*, 9: 951). As earlier, Thomas Mann's love and understanding of Schiller was a joint recognition of Schiller and his own creative self-expression. The insight of the Schillerian bliss filled him with joyful fascination. He was writing furiously, enraptured by his Schiller essay. It was as if he now could overcome his own limiting individuality in touching ideas conceivable only beyond the boundaries of self. The "genius of Epic," at Thomas Mann calls his mode of expression, reaches beyond the definition of the genre of the novel, as he had defined it in his Princeton lecture of 1939. This definition had already borne the seeds of his later outreach toward the unlimited and timeless, the overcoming of individuality, and the apprehension of the secret of the "Veil of Maya."

Thomas Mann's short fictions are as satellites of the great novels and thus are an organic part of his *oeuvre*. The humorous self-criticism and heartwarming humanism that he had reached proves to be universally valid, not limited to place or time. Thomas Mann had developed the maturity to establish the ethical values of his concept of life. He had achieved this after discussing his ideas in terms of social, abstract, aesthetic, biblical, and nature-bound topics in his fiction. The expression of the inner message grows beyond the formal nature of the medium of art. The formal requirements of the genre fade, leaving fully realized, individually significant re-creations of the precious life-experience. This insight became the message the artist communicates to the world. For Thomas Mann it is the grasp of a glorious peaceful entity that he attempts to pass on within the concept of the "genius of Epic" expressed in the last words of the Schiller eulogy.

In critically viewing the reception of his *oeuvre* and his message, the life essence of Thomas Mann, it seems that some of its vital potential has been lost when evaluated and manipulated by the professional and commercial experts. The virginity of the *Dichter*'s message is damaged when catalogued under topics, titles, genres; dissected, studied, analyzed, criticized, and even forces into commercial or political interest patterns, with lack of reverence for the essential values. But still there are a few for whom the *Künstler*'s own life experience, his message is in reach. The deterioration of the basic skills of humanistic education in the last thirty years has created an abyss of understanding. Futhermore, the work of the *Künstler* on the one hand, owing to its nature of originality and its focus on the expression of the insight, is on the other hand handicapped by the pragmatic distribution of the "book" as merchandise, labeled and priced as a marketable commodity. The humanistic significance of Thomas Mann's *oeuvre* represents a unity, with a *raison d'être* of its own and of value to all. This message will either mature the stature of a work with the potential of becoming a classic, thus timeless, extending its significance free from limitations of time and circumstance, or it will be forgotten.

Thomas Mann's *oeuvre* therefore, like that of any creative artist, should not be carved into genre segments. The formal perfection of craftsmanship of any talented, dedicated author is a tool to express the abstract essence of his message, opening up his own microcosm when creating his work of art. This is an adventurous-*abenteuerlich* quest resulting in the work of art, the gift from the artist to the reader, and the nature of such a gift is a very personal legacy from the artist. Some are not granted the time to finish defining it.

At this point, the separation of Thomas Mann's work into "short fiction" and "novels" is no longer germane. This study was aimed at bridging the gap of the numerous and very uneven treatments of Mann's short fiction in secondary critical literature. Some works are hardly read or discussed and some remain untranslated, while others have a rich bibliography. This study has attempted to follow Thomas Mann's intellectual biography from his early beginning to his maturation and beyond, allowing the reader to trace the emotional, intellectual, and spiritual highlights that led to the development and unity of his *oeuvre*.

The existing rich secondary material on Thomas Mann is more meaningful in the light of his intellectual biography. His concept of the "genius of Epic" appears in his entire *oeuvre*, not only in his great novels. Therefore the message must be seen in the entire panorama of his life-work.

Thomas Mann's transition from life to death was a familiar homecoming rather than a departure. He worked to the last moments of his life. His ". . . objectivity was [is] the *Geist* of irony" permitting him to distance himself from personal emotion and thus allowing him to approach the essential. The ideas expressed in his work, which sometimes seem difficult and discouraging because of his amazing knowledge and his intensive intellectual association with imagery taken from different fields, are in actuality clear, simple, and true in the light of the last words of his Schiller eulogy and his concept of the "genius of Epic." They are as clear and as simple as great things always are.

GLOSSARY

ABENTEURER. Adventurer. Thomas Mann used singular connotations for this term, indicating the special *geistig* adventure of the *Dichter* who transcends the surface (double vision); he glimpses the secrets of human nature and being and expresses them. The divine spark and dubious quality of make-believe make Thomas Mann call the poet's extraordinary privilege and obligation an "adventure." Also used as an adjective: *abenteuerlich*.

ABWARTEN. To wait for; to await one's chance.

"ABWÄRTS." Lit. "downward," Thomas Mann first used this title for the project that later became *Buddenbrooks*, which he began in the summer of 1897 in Italy.

AFFENTHEATER. Lit. "monkey theater." Used by Mann as an ironic glimpse of a senselessly wasted life (see "The Way to the Churchyard").

ANMUT. This means grace, comeliness, attractiveness, charm, inner style, elegance. Thomas Mann used it in reference to *Über Anmut und Würde* by Friedrich von Schiller.

ANSTÄNDIGKEIT. Lit. "decency," this term conveys the virtue of the *Bürger* at the same time that it shows the *bürgerlich* limitations, that hinder the *Künstler* in his intellectual (*geistig*) adventure (*Abenteuer*).

APOLLINIAN. This is Walter Kaufmann's spelling. Nietzsche expressed the concept in *Die Geburt der Tragödie* (*The Birth of Tragedy*), 1871, as having the characteristics of the cult and alleged personality of the god Apollo, who inspired harmony, form, balance, logic, and organized dreams. The"Apollinian" concept opposes the "Dionysian."

AUFKLÄRUNG. This is the German term for the Age of Enlightenment. The German Aufklärung differs from similar eras in France and England because the German *Geist* was deeply influenced by Leibniz's acceptance of God as central to the *Weltbild*. The German *Aufklärung* is loosely dated from Johann Christoph Gottsched's ascendancy (ca. 1740) to the emotional reaction of the *Sturm und Drang*, ca. 1768.

AUFSCHWINGEN. An upward oscillation; surge. *See* AUSSCHWEIFEN; SCHWUNG.

AUSGANGSPUNKT. Lit. "point of departure." In "Tonio Kröger" this term refers to Tonio's home town, but it also means his point of departure as a *Künstler* (*Dichter*) (qqr.). German Romantics believed that a child's innocence could envision the subconscious image of, the identity (home) of the soul, *seelische Heimat*, more clearly than the man whose decentralized mind could not see through the turmoil in the world caused by the *Erdgeist*.

Außenwelt. Lit. "outer world." Its connotations in "Der Tod in Venedig" refer to the world beyond Aschenbach's fantasies.

AUSSCHWEIFEN. To be excessive, extravagant, debauched, licentious, dissolute, wild. *See* AUFSCHWINGEN.

"DER BAJAZZO." Thomas Mann's story was first drafted under the title "Walter Weiler," in 1897. S. Fischer accepted "Der Bajazzo" for the *Der kleine Herr Friedemann* collection published in 1898. *Bajazzo* is the Germanicized form of the Italian *Pagliaccio*, meaning "clown" or "joker."

BAJAZZOBEGABUNG. Lit. "clown's talent," the term is pejoratively used. It indicates someone who takes refuge in role playing.

BAJAZZOTUM. An expression Thomas Mann used in his letters to Grautoff to indicate "clownishness."

BEGEISTERUNG. Exaltation

BETRACHTUNGEN EINES UNPOLITISCHEN. Theoretical essay by Thomas Mann, written from fall 1915 to February 1918. First published by Fischer in Berlin, 1918 (*GW*, 12: 9–589).

BILDUNG. This is a formation, as in education; a shaping.

BILDUNGSROMAN. (German literary term) (*Bildung* f. = formation; *bilden* = "to build" or "to develop"). The *Bildungsroman* features the changes and growth in a protagonist's character. The genre was established by Goethe's *Wilhelm Meisters Lehrjahre*, 1795–97, and Novalis's *Heinrich von Ofterdingen*, 1799. *See also* ENTWICKLUNGSROMAN.

BLAUE BLUME. "Blue flower" of German Romanticism, a symbol introduced by Novalis (Friedrich Leopold Freiherr von Hardenberg) in his novel *Heinrich von Ofterdingen*, 1790, expressing the Neoplatonic longing of the poet for his "*seelische Heimat*," his soul's homeland.

BLONDE BESTIE. The "blond beast" was a Nietzschean image with no racial overtones, only a phrase that pertained to a mental attitude. See Nietzsche (Schlechta) 2: 786, 787, and 980.

BON VIVANT. (French) A person fond of good living.

BOURGEOIS. (French) Citizen, townsman, commoner, middle-class person. Here used to differentiate from "burgher," which is used for the German expression *Bürger* in the special sense indicated.

BÜRGER. Middle-of-the-road citizen, versus the lonely poet. The expression carries a variable signification in Thomas Mann's fiction. See especially "Tristan" and "Tonio Kröger." See also KLEINBÜRGER and SPIEßBÜRGER.

BÜRGERLICH. *Bürger*-like. *See* BÜRGER.

BÜRGERHIRN. Thomas Mann coined this word to indicate the *Bürger* mentality, a rather limited and deficient individuality, in terms of the capacity to grasp metaphysical matter. It becomes a motif in "Das Wunderkind" ("The Infant Prodigy").

BÜRGERSINN. Lit. "the mentality of the *Bürger*"; this term, in contrast to *Bürgerhirn*, has no ironic connotations.

CANNIBALISM OF THE SELF. This Schopenhauerian term (*Selbstkannibalismus*) indicates the senseless urge toward self-destruction triggered by the misconception of the *principium individuationis*.

CANTI CARNASCIALIESCHI. Worldly, sensual songs, typical of the festivities during the reign of Lorenzo de' Medici in Florence. Anathema to Savonarola.

CREDO. Creed, from the Latin *credere*, "to trust," or "to believe."

CYMBULA. Lit. (Greek) "shell"; the word "gondola" is sometimes suggested as a derivative. This is debatable.

DÉCLASSÉ. (French) One who has come down in the world. *See also* HORS DE LIGNE.

DICHTER. A poet; *see* DICHTUNG.

DICHTUNG. Poetry. This term is used for all imaginative literature with solely artistic inspiration, form, and purpose. Although Thomas Mann had written only a few poems in his youth, he took pride in being a *Dichter* (lit. "poet"), and referred to himself as a *Künstler* (lit. "artist"). He called his fiction his "*dichterisches Schreiben.*"

DIESSEITS. Lit. "on this side." Immanent or earthly life, in contrast to Jenseits, eternal life after death. *Diesseits* designates the earthbound *Weltanschauung* versus the transcendent one. The materialistic *Zeitgeist* concentrated on the *Diesseits*.

DIONYSUS. (Roman Bacchus), son of Zeus and Semele, a princess of Thebes; as the Greek god of vine, worshiped by bacchentes and maenades, he established viniculture. His attributes are the grape and the ivy.

DIONYSIAN. Nietzsche expressed the concept of the Dionysian in *The Birth of Tragedy*, 1871, as conveying the characteristics of the cult and alleged personality of Dionysus—intoxication, fertility, and sensuality, as opposed to the Apollinian, q.v.

DOPPELTE OPTIK. Lit. "dual vision," the term Thomas Mann probably borrowed from Nietzsche to describe his own ability to incorporate a metaphysical meaning (truth) vividly beneath realistic surface of fiction, thus creating two or more levels of understanding.

DREIGESTIRN. Thomas Mann called the triple influence of the philosophies of Schopenhauer, Nietzsche, and Wagner a *Dreigestirn* or "triple constellation," essential to his own intellectual development. See *Betrachtungen eines Unpolitischen*, *GW*, 8: 79ff.

DURST. Thirst. In the abstract sense, "longing for."

EINFRIED. Name of sanatorium in "Tristan." Lit. "one/peace," refers to Schoperian *Erkenntnis*, and reminds one of *Wahnfried*, the home of Wagner in Bayreuth.

EINHEIT. *Einheit*, as a Schopenhauerian term, indicates the unity of the world. The rationalization of the instinctual drive, *Wille zum Leben*, formulates the false concept of the *principium individuationis*.

EINHEITSDRANG. Lit. "urgency to be united"—a Schopenhauerian term meaning escape from the *principium individuationis* into the peaceful natural state of the Schopenhauerian world.

EINHEITSSEHNSUCHT. Lit. "longing for unity"; this Schopenhauerian term indicates the longing for the metaphysical dimension of the unity of the universe.

EINSICHT. Insight; as a Schopenhauerian term, is the same as "*Erkenntnis*," meaning "insight" or "knowledge" of the universe. *(See* EINHEIT.)

EKEL. Disgust, repulsion. Thomas Mann first developed the emotion in fiction in Johannes Friedemann's self-rejection when he could not control his emotions for Gerda. Utterly incapable of fitting into society, Bajazzo loses his self-esteem in his own brand of *Ekel*. See ERKENNTNISEKEL.

EMPFINDUNG. This is a perception via the senses; a realization, a sensation. *See* GEFÜHL.

"ENTFLEISCHTE BRUNST." This phrase (lit. "de- or nonmaterialized lust") refers to the concept of the *Liebestod* in Wagner's *Tristan und Isolde*: the passionate striving for complete and eternal unity after and beyond death. See Anselm's discussions with Dunja in "Gerächt."

ENTSTEHUNG. Birth, creation, formation, genesis, origin. *See* ENTSTEHUNGS-GESCHICHTE.

ENTSTEHUNGSGESCHICHTE. This is the history of the creation of a work of art.

ENTWICKLUNG. Development, evolution, unfolding.

ENTWICKLUNGSROMAN. A German novel form, a long prose narrative of epic dimension. It systematically and consciously develops the hero's character vis-à-vis the setting and his interplay with the *Zeitgeist*. *See also* BILDUNGSROMAN.

ENTWÜRDIGUNG. A degradation or derogation; it is the central theme of "Der Tod in Venedig."

ERDGEIST. Lit. "earth-spirit"; the materialistic and pragmatic spirit of the mob. The German Romantics introduced the concept.

ERKENNTNIS. Insight. *See* EINSICHT.

ERKENNTNISEKEL. Disgust of recognition or insight. The word was coined by Thomas Mann and explicitly discussed in "Tonio Kröger," part 4 (the discussion between Tonio and Lisabeta). It connotes the fear and repulsion of the formalist, who is technically motivated to shape his art and loses his "humanity" or contact with life's natural values. Tonio Kröger's *Erkenntnisekel* is a rejection of the code he mistakenly believes is artistry: analytic, dehumanizing insight (*Erkenntnis*). Tonio's ability to overcome his *Erkenntnisekel* makes him a genuine artist. His fear of a sterile artistic life contrasts with *Erkenntnis*, as shown in "Tristan."

ERLEBEN. Lit. "to live through it"; erleben means "to experience."

ERLEBNIS. Experience. Thomas Mann's fiction is based on his self-analysis of his significant life-experiences (*Erlebnisse*). The term has a special meaning in his writings in reference to *Erkenntnis* and *Einsicht* (qq. v.).

ERLEDIGEN. To adjust, arrange, settle, handle, attend to, deal with, dispose of, effect, execute, clear up, finish off. See the discussion in part 4 of "Tonio Kröger."

EXISTENZANGST. A German term used by existentialists, meaning the fear of existence, especially in the beginning of this century to express anguish due to the mechanized dehumanized world.

FABLIAU. A *fabliau* (French) is a popular medieval tale, often satiric in nature, instructing by giving humorous examples of society, the clergy, or human nature. It should not be confused with the fable.

"FAUST." *Faust* is Goethe's dramatic poem in 12,000 verses. The first part was finished in 1806 and the second in 1832. The basic motif of selling one's soul to the devil for superhuman powers, with ensuing damnation, originated in pre-Christian times in Jewish magic texts, with the evocation of satanism (*Höllenzwang*), and recurred in various forms during the Middle Ages. Goethe took the topic from the *Volksbuch*, a popularized and inexpensive version of medieval fiction in the 16th century, the *Historia von D. Joh. Fausten*, 1587. Christopher Marlowe (1564–93) used the same source for his *Tragical History of Doctor Faustus*. Goethe encountered the theme in puppet plays of English traveling companies in Frankfurt. Goethe's first version was the *Urfaust*, lost and again found after one hundred years.

Faust itself is considered Goethe's chief work. Its ideology, which allows Faust salvation through his striving and Gretchen's love instead of the traditional damnation, places *Faust* among the most intriguing artistic and spiritual works of all time. Its first part, containing the lyric sections of the love between Gretchen and Faust on earth, is called the "Gretchenepisode" or "Gretchentragödie," for she is seduced by Faust, yet her love survives after death and saves him. This section is often read alone, although this does not do justice to the entire work. Thomas Mann knew *Faust* well from his school years (see "Gefallen," his first published short story, where Rölling is comically modeled on Mephistopheles) and was fascinated with it during his whole life. Thomas Mann treated the Faust theme himself in the novel *Doctor Faustus*, 1947, the tragic fate of Adrian Leverkühn, the artist whose questionable ambitions come to naught.

FESTUNGSWALL. Thomas Mann repeatedly refers to the remnants of the medieval fortification or rampart which still surround the city of Lübeck.

FIN DE SIÈCLE. Lit. "end of the century" referring to the closing years of the 19th century, the period of Thomas Mann's adolescence and young manhood. In his time the term had progressive connotations, not commonly used today, but it now is an accepted literary term, standing for such terminology as "decadent" and "dilettante" qualities of that time. It is in this sense that the word is used here.

"FRÜHLINGSFEIER." A poem by Friedrich Gottlieb Klopstock.

FRÜHLINGSSTURM. Thomas Mann contributed to this student publication (Lübeck, summer of 1893) with his very first writings.

FÜHLEN. *See* EMPFINDUNG.

GEFÜHL. This is a sense of feeling, both physical and emotional. *See* EMPFINDUNG.

GEIST. One of the German words most heavily fraught with meaning, it covers a large range of concepts: spirit; mind; morale; mentality; intelligence; spiritual depth; intellectual capacity; mental power; wit; brilliance (of mind); esprit; character; genius; theologically, God; ghost; devil. If linked with concepts, it carries even more significance. The text above does not translate the term, since any attempt at equivalence would sadly restrict the wealth of the German term. See discussion on *Geist* in Thomas Mann's letter to Josef Hofmiller, Munich, 23 Nov. 1919.

GEISTIG. *See* GEIST.

"GELIEBTEN-MAJA." This refers to Thomas Mann's unpublished material, particularly in Notebook 7, for an unfinished novel, also called the "*Maja-Projekt*," held in the Zurich Thomas Mann Archives. See "Zu Thomas Manns 'Maja' Project," Hans Wysling, in Scherer und Wysling, *Quellenkritische Studien zum Werk Thomas Manns* (Bern and Munich: Francke Verlag, 1967). Referred to in the text as Wysling, "Maja."

"GENIALE EINSICHT." A geniuslike insight or knowledge. *See* "GENIALE ERKENNTNIS."

"GENIALE ERKENNTNIS." *See* GENIALE EINSICHT." This Schopenhauerian term means the metaphysical perception of an intuitive and a priori nature, reaching beyond the false concept of the *principium individuationis* toward genuine truth, the unity in peace.

GENIALE OBJEKTIVITÄT. Refers to the terminology Mann uses discussing Schopenhauer. This type of objectivity does not pertain to *"rationalizieren,"* as it refers to abstract "insight," the power of which leads to *"Erkenntnis."*

GERUCH. Lit. "smell," "odor." *"Fauliger Geruch"* is a stagnant or rotting odor. In "Der Tod in Venedig" the *mephitischer Odem* (mephitic vapor) represents Death; it repulses and intoxicates as the Dionysian powers become ascendant.

GESAMTKUNSTWERK. A work of art that unites the different art media. Wagner's operas are often referred to as such, since they united music, poetry, and dance.

GESANG. Lit. "song"; Thomas Mann uses the word for the purest form of artistic expression, poetry. It also stands for the musical element of the Dionysian temptation, as in the flute call of the *u* sound in "Der Tod in Venedig."

GESCHLECHTLICHKEIT. A Schopenhauerian term for sexuality.

GESELLSCHAFTSROMAN. Literally, a novel about society; this German term describes a novel that concentrates on a particular society of a particular time, upon which its plot is built.

GEWÖHNLICH. Commonplace. In Thomas Mann's novella "Tonio Kröger" the term refers to ordinary people, the "blond" and the "blue-eyed," belonging to the *Erdgeist. See* BLONDE BESTIE. See also the final section of "Tonio Kröger," Tonio's letter to Lisabeta.

GEWÖHNLICHKEIT. The "commonplace" refers to the crowd and its needs, in contrast to the isolated chosen poet.

GIOVANOTTO. This Italian terms means "young man." It is used in "Mario und der Zauberer."

GIPPERN. Young Thomas Mann coined this expression to indicate "feigned cynicism, or fresh, frivolous, overbearing cheapish chatter." He used the expression in letters to Grautoff and to his brother Heinrich.

GLÜCK. Joy, luck, happiness. (No reference to the meaning of "A Gleam.")

GONDOLA. Possibly from the Greek *cymbula*, "shell." A gondola is a long narrow canal boat with a cabin in the middle, a high pointed prow and stern. It is traditionally used in Venice, propelled by a gondolier. Gondoliers inherit their ancient profession and it is nearly impossible for applicants to get a license. Gondoliers are now unionized and ply their trade with pride, art, tradition, and corruption. The gondolier who took Aschenbach to the Hôtel des Bains for the first time foreshadows Death through his hat and features, playing the role of Charon.

GRETCHENEPISODE OR GRETCHENTRAGÖDIE. *See* FAUST.

GRUNDMOTIV. See LEITMOTIV.

GRÜNE WAGEN. The "green wagon" (associated with gypies) is one of the pattern phrases used as a leitmotiv in Thomas Mann's novella "Tonio Kröger." The gypsies were popularly linked with sloppy, unpredictable capriciousness and mysterious adventure.

HEIMAT. The German term for "homeland" is also a German Romantic term indicating Neoplatonic longing and mystical union with the original vital power.

HERZ. Heart. The expressions "sein Herz lebte" ("his heart was alive") and "sein Herz war tot" ("his heart was dead") form a pattern and a thematic leitmotiv in the novella "Tonio Kröger."

"HISTORICAL MAN." In contrast to the "unhistorical," this concept is developed in "Unordnung und frühes Leid." Thomas Mann uses "historical" to characterize the *Weltanschauung* of the "unpolitical" man, developed in his *Betrachtungen eines Unpolitischen* (q.v.)—a theoretical worldview detached from pragmatic interests.

HOCHSTAPLER. Swindler, rogue, charlatan, confidence man. With Thomas Mann, its special connotations include the make-believe qualities of the *Künstler*. See *Die Bekenntnisse des Hochstaplers Felix Krull*.

HORS DE LIGNE. (French) Out of line. *See* DÉCLASSÉ.

HÔTEL DES BAINS. The Manns and Gustav von Aschenbach of "Der Tod in Venedig" all vacationed here. Except for a new swimming pool and beach cabañas, the modernized hotel has not had a change of exterior since Thomas Mann stayed there in the summer of 1911.

"HOTEL ZUM BRAVEN MANN." ("Hotel for the good or well-behaved man"). This title appears in "Der Kleiderschrank," 1899.

ICH. This is the German pronoun for "I"; it is the basic concept of the *principium individuationis*, representing conscious emphasis on the Ego in reference to the frame of the surrounding world.

INSIGHT. *See* ERKENNTNIS.

INSTINKTVERSCHMELZUNG. Thomas Mann coined this expression (lit. "mingling of instincts") for the mixture of high and low mimetic components; it is an important thematic element in his novella "Der Tod in Venedig."

JENSEITS. Lit. on the other side. It indicates the eternal life after death in the religious sense, in contrast to *diesseits*. *Jenseits* connotes a *Weltanschauung* where earthly life is only a preparation for real eternal existence after the transcendence through death. Medieval Christianity focused on *jenseits*.

KLEINBÜRGER. Lesser burgher, of simple means. *See* BÜRGER; SPIESSBÜRGER.

KULTUR. Culture.

KUNST. Art.

KÜNSTLER. Artist. Thomas Mann's most essential existential value lies in the *Künstler*, the creative artist. The conflict between *Bürger* and *Künstler* was overcome in "Tonio Kröger." Talent both curses and blesses.

KÜNSTLERIDENTITÄT. Literally, the "identity of the artist."

KÜNSTLERNOVELLE. (German literary term.) A short story (novella) featuring a thematic problem involving the *Künstler*, his development, his personal difficulties related to his vocation, or aesthetic problems. See "Tonio Kröger" and "Der Tod in Venedig."

KÜNSTLERPROBLEM. A problem related to the existence of an artist.

KÜNSTLERROMAN. "Artist novel"; treats the theme of the development of the artist, with his problems, needs, observations, aesthetic ideas, expectations, and *Weltanschauung*.

KÜNSTLERTUM. This term expresses the intellectual and spiritual atmosphere created by the attitude of the artist.

KÜNSTLERWÜRDE. Lit. "dignity of the artist." The highest calling, the poet's, with its service and sacrifice to art, lifts him above the crowd, but the "make believe" element of art jeopardizes his purity and dignity (the *Künstlerwürde*).

LÄCHERLICH. To be laughed at. *See* SCHÄNDLICH.

LARMOYANT. (French) Tearful, lachrymose.

L'ART POUR L'ART. "Art for art's sake," a term introduced by Théophile Gautier (1811–72) in *Emaux et Camées*, 1852.

LEBEN. Life.

LEBENSBAHN. Career; one's way of living.

LEBENSBEJAHUNG. Lit. "saying yes to life."

LEBENSWEISE. Lit. the "way of life."

LEIDENSCHAFT. Passion.

"LEISTUNGS-ETHIKER." Lit. "achievement-moralist." Ethical value, according to a *"Leistungs-Ethiker"* in "Der Tod in Venedig," is measured by the attained achievement and the level of restraint applied. Such a person, like Gustav von Aschenbach, is a virtuoso of the form, with a firm grip on his emotions.

LEITMOTIF. This device come originally from Wagner's *Grundidee* (basic idea) motif, recurring in the narration and intentionally used for unity through repetition (formal leitmotif) or to express the central message (thematic leitmotif). Wagner's conscious technique of constructing his gigantic operas based on the leitmotif was admired and then adopted by Thomas Mann in his fiction. The formal leitmotif is identifiable from "Der kleine Herr Friedemann" onward. "Tonio kröger" introduces the genuine use of the thematic leitmotif.

LEUTEHIRNE. Lit. "people brains." Thomas Mann coined this expression for the collective and limited herd mentality. He used it systematically as a motif in "Das Wunderkind."

"LIEBESTOD." "Love-death," a concept from Wagner's *Tristan und Isolde*, whose protagonists, bewitched by a magic potion, reach total and eternal union.

LITERAT. This is a German term indicating a man of literature, scholar, or a writer. Thomas Mann used it perjoratively, in opposition to the term *Dichter*, meaning the romantic, inspirational (German) poet. Chapter 2, "Der Zivilisationsliterat" of *Die Betrachtungen eines Unpolitischen* (1918), discusses French rational humanism, which Thomas Mann considered a "dehumanization" of the German spirit (*GW*, 12: 68), as he hinted to his brother Heinrich in these discussions. See also "Der Künstler und der Literat," 1913 (*GW*, 10: 62).

LUSTSPIEL. This 18th-century German literary form replaced the previous term *Komödie* (comedy). *Lustspiel* exhibits the characteristics of Lessing's age, rationality, wit, typical German setting, and humor, unlike classical Greek comedy, which represents the low mimetic mode opposing the high mimetic tragedy. The early Greek comedy, universal in its appeal, poked fun at a scapegoat protagonist, but the *Lustspiel* reflects German settings and characteristics of its time. Thomas Mann's humor, irony, and personal wit, as well as his strongly "German" humanism, brings his art closer to the *Lustspiel* than to classical comedy.

MAGNETISMUS DER GEGENPOLE. Lit. "the magnetism of opposing poles." Terminology of German romanticism, emphasizing the attraction of contrasts.

MÄRCHEN. A fairy tale. The *Märchen* is a short narrative, with a simple story and naïve ethical concepts, beyond natural law. It appeals by its miraculous, fantastic, wishful, dreamy quality and is mostly anonymous, an example of popular expression.

MENSCHENBENEHMEN. Lit. "human behavior," used with ironic undertone.

MENSCHLICH. This adjective indicates *human* in nature, or decent, tolerable humane, in contrast to *unmenschlich*.

METAPHYSISCHER ZAUBERTRANK. A magic potion with not physical, but metaphysical powers.

MOULINET DES DAMES. (French) A dance expression for special dance figures.

NOVELLE. This German term is equivalent to the English "novella," not to be confused with the English "novel" (German *Roman*). A *novelist* in the German sense is thus a novella or short story writer.

NUNC STANS. Lit. "standing present." This is a concept of insight, of relativity of time, space, the relief from worldly boundaries (*see also* PRINCIPIUM

INDIVIDUATIONIS). Thomas Mann derived the concept of the present as undefined existence without limit melting into the endless organic continuity of history ("Unordnung und frühes Leid") and the qualities of nature (his novels) from his experience of Schopenhauer's works, and it developed during his writing of the *Betrachtungen eines Unpolitischen* and his post–World War I humanism.

PAGLIACCIO. Italian for clown. *See* "DER-BAJAZZO."

PIAGNONI. The *Piagnoni* (It. "those who weep") were followers of Savonarola.

PRESTIDIGITATORE. This Italian term means "juggler."

PRINCIPIUM INDIVIDUATIONIS. Lit. "the principle of the individual," this Schopenhauerian term indicates the false concept that each person is a separate unit driven to satisfy his own *Wille zum Leben*. It expresses the essence of all worldly evil—egotism, aggression, the urge to dominate, etc. It contrasts with Truth—the unity of the Universe, invisible to those who have not attained geniuslike insight (*Erkenntnis*).

QUESTOR. This hero is driven by the urge to discover and is beset by anxiety toward the unknown. A poet, the adventurer of the spiritual world, is a "*Künstler*," a questor, who strives on the dangerous and rewarding path of the unknown.

REKLAMAPPARAT. Publicity machine (see "The Infant Prodigy").

SCHÄNDLICH. Lit. "shameful," "disgraceful," "infamous."

SCHNUPFEN. This is the term for the common cold.

"SCHÖNE SEELE." Literally translated, "beautiful soul," this is a concept from the Pietistic tendency of the second part of the 18th century; it indicates the power of the individual to develop the positive qualities of his spiritual being (soul), as contrasted to someone oriented to fate.

SCHRIFTSTELLER. This German term, sometimes translated as "writer," in Thomas Mann's fiction is slightly derogatory, indicating a career writer rather than a servant of the arts. *See*, for contrast, KÜNSTLER and DICHTER.

SCHWALBEN. Swallows. Also a group of young girl singers in "A Gleam."

SCHWEIFEN. float.

SCHWER. Difficult, hard, grave, serious, burdensome, heavy (in weight), grievous, bad.

SCHWINDLER. *See* HOCHSTAPLER.

SCHWINGEN. Swing.

SCHWUNG. This German term means "swing" with a dynamic connotation. *See* AUFSCHWINGEN; AUSSCHWEIFEN; SCHWINGEN.

SEELE. The soul.

SEELENGLIEDERUNG. Dissection of the soul.

SEELISCHE HEIMAT. Terminology of German Romantics, lit. "the homeland of the soul"; the origin, the target of Neoplatonic longing.

SEHNSUCHTSMOTIV. Wagnerian term: the leitmotif of longing.

SPIESSBÜRGER. Well-fed burgher. Ordinary BÜRGER(s), with a derogatory connotation. *See also* BÜRGER; KLEINBÜRGER.

STOFF. This German literary term means the thematic or fictional material used to develop the work of art.

STREBEN. This German verb means "to strive," to live up to the God-given capacities of the Faustian hero. See Goethe's *Faust*.

STURM UND DRANG. The "Storm and Stress" period was a product of a literary and emotional trend dated from Herder's *Fragmente*, 1767, to the following classic period dominated by Schiller and Goethe.

THEMENKREIS. These are cycles of themes on a topic related to a centrally relevant problem of Thomas Mann's short fiction.

TODESROMANTIK. This is the poetic expression of the attraction to death that was articulated in "Der Tod in Venedig."

TON. In the Schopenhauerian sense, this is the purest element of music, without the rationalized technique of composed melody and rhythm, the only direct contact between the geniuslike insight (*geniale Erkenntnis*) and the unity of the universe; that is, between the represented world and real existence.

TOTO GENERE. In its colloquial use in the German text, this phrase means, "all," the "whole"—kind(s), clan(s), people(s).

TRAUMBANN. Lit. "dream spell."

ÜBEL. Lit. bad, or evil Thomas Mann uses it with ominous connotations in "Der Tod Venedig."

ÜBERMENSCH. This Nietzschean term literally means "over-man," a being that has evolved from a lower to a higher species through individual determination. *See* ÜBERWINDUNG. Walter Kaufmann uses the literal translation of *Übermensch* to avoid the misleading popular connotations of the word "superman" in his translations of Nietzsche's works.

ÜBERWINDUNG. This Nietzschean term literally means "overcoming" or "conquest of selfish instincts." It indicates self-restraint and self-control.

UMSCHWUNG. Rotation, revolution, swing around.

"UNANSTÄNDIGES PSYCHOLOGISIEREN." A phrase used by Thomas Mann meaning "indecent tampering with psychology."

UNAUSBLEIBLICHER BERUF. (See "Tristan.") A humorous play of words to demonstrate Klöterjahn's boorishness; lit. "the profession that cannot stay away."

UNAUSWEICHLICHER BERUF. (See "Tristan.") The genuine expression: a profession that cannot be denied (lit. avoided).

UNENDLICH(KEIT). A term from German Romantic diction, the *unendlich* describes the Infinite from whence man is "imprisoned" in the physical world and to which his longing drives him in dreams.

UNIO MYSTICA. The "mystical union" is an Augustinian term, referring to man's longing for reunion with God, his creator.

UNMENSCHLICHKEIT. In contrast to *Menschlichkeit*, this term indicates inhumanity, brutality, or cruelty.

UNORDNUNG. Disorder. See the discussion of "Unordnung und frühes Leid" (chap. 6).

UNWÜRDIG. Unworthy, disreputable, unseemly, undignified, beneath one's notice. *See* WÜRDE.

UNZUCHT. This means lewdness; indecency; lack of chastity; bestiality; sodomy and professional prostitution.

VAPORETTO. Canal motorboat providing public transportation in Venice and the Lido.

VERACHTEN. To disdain, to despise, to look down upon.

VERACHTUNG. Disdain, contempt, scorn, an attitude of looking down upon.

VEREINSAMUNG. This term from German Romantic diction represents the gradual isolation of the poet from his fellow man, i.e., the *Erdgeist* (world spirit). The *Vereinsamung* causes his suffering and purification, which ennobles his works and confers upon him dignity. The German Romantics believed this suffering was a part of the fate of the genuine poet.

VERIRRT. Puzzled, disconcerted, confused, dazed, entangled, lost. Used in part of "Tonio Kröger," his discussion with Lisabeta.

VERISMO. A naturalistic movement of Italian opera introduced by Pietro Mascagni in *Cavalleria Rusticana*, premiering 17 May 1890. Leoncavallo, Giordano, Puccini, and Zandonai all display *verismo*. With emphasis on the message of the libretto, *verismo* reflects common characters and circumstances, thus freeing the opera from traditional topics and settings. Its basic premise is expressed in the Prologue to Leoncavallo's *I Pagliacci*, sung by the clown Tonio.

VERLANGEN. Literally, "to ask"; "demand"; "command"; "compel"; "desire"; "want"; "crave." This expression represents more a demanding than a longing feeling, but Thomas Mann often used it interchangeably with "longing" or "yearning."

VERLESUNG. A play with words: misreading.

VERNUNFT. Reason.

VOLKSBUCH. This term indicates 16th-century retelling of medieval epic subjects, folktales, and other stories of mostly anonymous origin. *Volksbücher* were printed in book form in the 16th century and were very popular.

VOLLFÜHREN. To execute.

VORSTELLUNG. Vorstellung means "idea" plus "representation." A Schopenhauerian term, it represents the contrast with the geniuslike *Erkenntnis* (insight); it is the limited vision (Idea or Representation) of the world in which we live.

WELT. The world. The connotation of this term in Wagner's *Tristan und Isolde* and Thomas Mann's "Tristan" is not "world," but "universe."

WELTANSCHAUUNG. A living understanding of the world, open to impressions (lit. "world-viewing"). It is often incorrectly used for "philosophy of the world." A *Weltanschauung* is a mixture of objective, subjective, rational, and emotional perceptions, forming the open and living idea of the world, not preconceived or doctrinaire.

WELTBILD. A vision of the universe, of existence, of the physical and spiritual composition of the world man inhabits. In contrast to the *Weltanschauung*, the view or opinion of the world, the *Weltbild* is a stable glance, a vision of the whole conceived by factors that are intellectual and rational as well as subjective and emotional. A change of the *Weltanschauung* involving new rational insight can alter the vision of the *Weltbild* as well. It is thus less argumentative and more a visionary conception of the world.

WELTFREMD. Literally, this German Romantic term means "estranged from the world." When the poet follows his calling (the "blue flower") he gradually isolates himself from the world, rejecting the concerns of the *Erdgeist*. See BLAUE BLUME.

WELTHUNGER. World hunger. A Schopenhauerian term for the concept of the *principium individuationis*. *See also* CANNIBALISM OF THE SELF.

WELTLITERATUR. World literature. Goethe initiated the term, which has the special connotation of a wish for the future, not simply indicating the totality of already created literary works but including the implication of new literature emerging from the mutual respect of peoples and above all their knowledge of one another's heritages and cultural characteristics. Thus it suggests a growth that empowers such meaningful literary expression. Goethe did not imply suppression of national values but rather reciprocal understanding, and so *Weltliteratur* involves the intellectual and cultural heritage of all peoples. See: "Goethes wichtigste Äußerungen über Weltliteratur," *Goethes Werke*, 1963. Thomas Mann also had absorbed Goethe's concept and expressed its very essence in "Lübeck als geistige Lebensform," 1926 (*GW*, 11: 376–98).

WELTSCHMERZ. This is a pessimistic attitude particularly found among romantic poets, seeing man hurled on the mercy of the *Erdgeist* and functioning there as a penalized being. The word was coined by Jean Paul (Friedrich Richter) (1763–1825).

"WILLE ZUM LEBEN." Lit. "the will to life." This is one of the basic concepts of Schopenhauer's *Die Welt als Wille und Vorstellung*, 1818; it is the blind natural instinct to live and reproduce. It parallels the *Erdgeist*, because of its incapacity and unwillingness to attain to intellectual and spiritual transcendence. The *Wille zum Leben* is assisted by *Rationalisierung* (rationalization), a paradoxical logic rationally sustaining the blind drive to satisfy needs. The egotism of the *Wille zum Leben* creates the *principium individuationis*.

"WILLE ZUM SCHWEREN." Literally "the will to overcome the difficult." Thomas Mann used this expression in "Schwere Stunde" to transcend the threshold of mediocrity.

WIRKUNG. Lit. "an affect"; to Tonio Kröger, it rationally seems a betrayal of human nature (*Menschlichkeit*).

WOLLEN. To want, to wish, to will. The noun *der Wille* literally means "the will."

WOLLUST. Voluptuousness, lust, sensual pleasure, lasciviousness, orgasm, *See also* UNZUCHT.

WOLLUST DES UNTERGANGES. Literally "the lust of (for) destruction"; it indicates also a death wish.

WONNE DER WEHMUT. Lit. "the delight of sorrow," a mood typical of the German Storm and Stress (Sturm und Drang) period's mentality.

WUNDER. This is a wonder, a marvel, or something miraculous; not to be confused with something magical (*Zauber*).

WÜRDE. Literally "dignity"; this term comes from Schiller's "Über Anmut und Würde," as a reflection of the inner power of the individual. Thomas Mann emphasized it in "Der Tod in Venedig" in reference to St. Sebastian (*GW*, 8: 453; *TA*, 345), a characterization of chaste manliness, self-discipline, and the graceful triumph of the spirit. The poet's *Würde* is the theme of "Der Tod in Venedig"; the fate of the artist leads toward the overcoming of the opposition between the Apollinian and the Dionysian. The "spiritual" poet has to be initiated through the senses, sacrificing his purity to reach the height of artistry. The price of that creativity is his loss of *Würde*. See "Über Anmut und Würde" (*GW*, 13: 532).

ZAUBERER. Lit. "magician," this term held a special meaning throughout Thomas Mann's life, expressing the power to reach beyond the tangible and the power to create the appearance of reality. He liked to call himself the *Zauberer*, and appeared once at a masquerade ball as a magician. Such titles as "Mario und der Zauberer," 1930, and *The magic Mountain* (*Der Zauberberg*), 1924, hence are full of significance.

ZAUBERKÜNSTLER. Literally, this means "magical artist." *See* ZAUBERER.

ZEITGEIST. This term indicates the spirit or typical trend of an era's cultural expression.

ZITTERN. This verb means to tremble, quake, quiver (with fear or excitement), flutter, shake. The expression is noted in a special way in "Der kleine Herr Friedemann." *Zittern* connotes a less violent motion than *zucken*.

ZIVILISATION. The German term for "civilization"; Thomas Mann said, ". . . politics is a matter of reason, of democracy and civilization [while] morality, is [a matter] of culture and the soul. . . " (*GW*, 13: 528–29, 535, 361–68).

ZIVILISATIONSLITERAT. Thomas Mann coined this expression, obviously expressing disdain of the concept. Discussed in *Betrachtungen eines Unpolitischen*.

ZUCHT. Lit. "discipline" or "breeding." *See* WÜRDE, in contrast to ZÜGELLOSIGKEIT.

ZUCKEN. To twitch, jerk, palpitate, convulse, quiver.

ZÜGELLOSIGKEIT. Licentiousness, dissoluteness, or moral laxity; disorderly activity; extravagance. In "Der Tod in Venedig," this contrasts with *Würde*, dignity, self-esteem, or self-respect. *See also* ZUCHT.

NOTES

Chapter 1. The Path to Self-Identification

1. Thomas Mann, *A Sketch of My Life*, translated by H. T. Lowe-Porter (New York: Alfred A Knopf, 1960), 5. Hereafter identified as *SML*.

2. Dr. Carlo Cabrini, an Italian physician, has pointed out that as an adolescent Thomas Mann might have suffered from a hormone deficiency, possibly due to adenoidal infection. The adenoids are related to the function of the hypophysis and control of the pituitary (the chief endocrine gland) development, regulating among other functions metabolic processes, growth, and sexual development. Dr Cabrini refers in particular to the anterior pituitary's function in growth, development and activity of the adrenal cortex, sex glands, thyroid, and pancreas. At puberty, the pituitary gland stimulates the sex glands to mature; up to that time it controls development.

Dr. Cabrini's suggestion sheds new light upon Thomas Mann's youthful behavior, which included inattentiveness, irritability, and apparent dullness. At nineteen and later, he repeatedly mentioned sore throats to Grautoff, possibly due to infected adenoids, along with headaches and gastric upsets. His late sexual development, which he himself complained of and which Mendelssohn repeatedly indicates, appears in the symptoms Thomas Mann gave his fictional characters. His extreme shyness, his reluctance to approach women he liked, his need to idealize his natural proclivities, and his overreaction at being "betrayed" by women he did approach, all display a behavioral pattern supporting Dr Cabrini's suggestion of a physical cause for his symptoms.

3. Armin Martens (see also note 4), one of Thomas Mann's closest high school attachments, was no longer among the students.

4. Otto Grautoff, one year younger than Thomas Mann, was the son of the bookstore owner Ferdinand Hermann Grautoff, from a numerous Lübeck middle-class family. In 1879 this business went bankrupt, the family lived in reduced circumstances, and the father committed suicide in 1891. Since both Thomas Mann and Otto Grautoff lost their fathers the same year, their friendship was probably even more significant. Otto was outwardly unattractive, small, with uneven features and very nearsighted "pop eyes." He was socially and physically much inferior to his friend and had an inferiority complex. In a letter to Grautoff 28 March 1895 Thomas Mann expressed the secret of their friendship:

> Well, simply: in fact I need him a little. Only now, when I am among only strangers, who don't know me, do I realize that he meant a great deal to me. We were really intimate. With each other we were without embarrassment intellectually, which was so good and convenient. We pretended at most for the sake of fun. We understood each other down to the smallest points. (Translations by the present author are indicated by the initials EHL.)

As his letters to young Grautoff disclose, Thomas Mann's sexual maturity came late. He repeatedly mentioned a "brown-braided" girl from his dancing class, whose image recurs in his later short stories, usually as a "blond"-braided little girl. Thomas Mann possibly elaborated upon his "puppy love" in the personal writings he destroyed in 1896. Ilse Martens, sister of his former schoolmate and idol Armin, might have been the object of each romantic childhood dreams. Ilse, a close friend of Julia Mann, Thomas's sister, did move to Munich in later years and Thomas Mann played the violin with her. They seem never to have had any attachment.

5. Thomas Mann, *Briefe an Otto Grautoff 1894–1901, und Ida Boy-Ed 1903–1928*, ed. Peter de Mendelssohn (Frankfurt am Main: S. Fischer, 1975).

6. In 1891 and 1892, Heinrich turned away from poetic experiments and published a few critical essays in *Gesellschaft*. Then he fell severely ill and finished his first fiction in August 1892 while convalescing in the Black Forest. Heinrich, like Thomas, had refused to become a merchant; he left school before graduation and was apprenticed to a Dresden bookseller. Heinrich's first publication was a short story, "Beppo als Trauzeuge," in the *Lübecker Zeitung*, 23 May 1889.

7. Thomas Mann refers to "Aischa," his first dramatic writing, in the first letter he kept, addressed to Fried, 14 October 1889, Lübeck. He signed himself "Thomas Mann, lyric-dramatic poet" (*"Lyrisch-dramatischer Dichter"*).

8. Thomas Mann, "On Myself," in *Dokumente und Untersuchungen, Beitrage zur Thomas-Mann-Forschung*, by Hans Wysling; 74 (Bern and Munich: Francke Verlag, 1974). Thomas Mann used the pseudonym "Paul Thomas." "On Myself" is quoted from *GW*, 8: 27.

9. Hans Bürgin and Hans-Otto Mayer, *Thomas Mann: Eine Chronik seines Lebens* (Frankfurt am Main: Fischer Taschenbuch Verlag, 1974), 13.

10. "Nacht" (*GW*, 8: 1103–4) and "Dichters Tod" (*GW*, 8: 1104). Thomas Mann is known for short stories, novels, and theoretical essays. He wrote poetry only in his early youth.

11. In "Heinrich Heine, der 'Gute,'" *Der Frühlingssturm*, (Lübeck, June/July 1893), 3–4, Thomas Mann aggressively attacked an essay by Dr. Conrad Scipion in the *Berliner Tageblatt*.

12. Thomas Mann habitually carried a notebook throughout his life, now chronologically numbered by scholars. He jotted observations there as well as on many little pieces of paper, arranging them as he needed them in his fiction. An amazing quantity of this material eventually appeared in his final texts.

13. *Summary*: Four young people leisurely listen to Dr. Selten's after-dinner story; an anonymous young medical student from a northern town falls head over heels in love with Irma, an actress in the local Goethe theater of a mid-German university town. His older schoolmate Rölling cynically rationalizes the situation, urging him first to write the girl, then to visit her, and finally to become her lover. Time passes unnoticed for the youth, overwhelmed with his newfound joy, until he visits Irma unexpectedly one morning, discovering an older patron breakfasting with his beloved. He forces the man out, berates the girl, and finally storms away forever. The story closes with Selten's admission that he himself had been the student who loved the girl.

14. The German verb *gefallen* (*gef.allen*) = to please, the noun *Gefallen* (*Gef.allen*) = delight, and the adjective *gefallen* (*ge-fallen*) = fallen are all spelled the same way. *Gefallen* is also the past participle form of the verb to fall: *fallen, fiel, [ist] gefallen* (infinitive, preterite, past participle).

15. Lilacs grew in the backyard of Julia Mann's Rambergstraße home.

16. Richard Dehmel added a postscript to his letter of 4 November 1894, to Thomas Mann.

That the girl had fallen, is here not the immediate issue; the main thing is, and this gives the poetic depth to your tale that here a law of nature is expressed, a law of emotions. Basically the man had fallen too, through the girl, only in another sense; he had permitted her to break a strong something in him. I would give the story the title "The Cynic." (EHL)

Dehmel's suggestion for changing the title was logical; not surprising in the light of Thomas Mann's frame of mind, he did not take Dehmel's advice.

17. "It is much less a doctrine than a disposition of the mind. Very intelligent at the same time that it is very sensuous, it inclines us again and again toward the diverse forms of life, and leads us to lend ourselves to all these aspects without giving ourselves to any of them" (EHL). Paul Bourget, *Cosmopolis* (Paris: Librairie Plon, 1892), 55.

18. When Thomas Mann graduated from the Katharineum Realgymnasium, he had received an *Abgangszeugnis*, a document proving that he had completed the required courses, but it was not a *Reifezeugnis*, comparable to a U.S. bachelor's degree.

19. Confusion exists regarding Thomas and Heinrich Mann's dating of the early Munich period and the Italian years, for which Thomas Mann seems to have left rather incomplete references. In his personal notes and in *Sketch of My Life* Thomas treated his two Italian trips as a single visit, confusing dates, events, and even specific addresses and names. Possibly the brothers might have alluded indirectly to their life during this period to repudiate in part their involvement with *Das zwanzigste Jahrhundert*, a journal of dubious merit for which both briefly worked at this time. Peter de Mendelssohn warns that this confusion cannot be simply considered the result of failing memory, suggesting that Thomas Mann's autobiographical references of 1894–97 may be inconclusive (*Der Zauberer das Leben des deutchen Schriftstellers Thomas Mann 1875–1918* [Frankfurt am Main: S. Fischer, 1975], 214–21; hereafter referred to as *Zauberer*).

20. "I am utterly happy that you also liked my 'Gefallen'—well! I really had a smashing success with that one! . . . I am very busy, I have a great deal to read, very much to *learn*, and besides [all] this I am working on my fairy-tale play, 'Der alte König', ['The Old King'] the first act of which is finished" (EHL) (Letter to Grautoff, Munich, 8 January 1895).

21. "Der Wille zum Glück" and "Der Tod" have not as yet been translated into English. Stories that have been published in English translation are referred to by English titles with the exception of "Der Bajazzo." "Disillusionment" ("Enttäuschung") is the earliest short story by Thomas Mann translated into English.

22. Many years later, in 1913, after having written "Death in Venice," Thomas Mann pertinently commented in "Der Künstler und Literat": "The writer expresses while he experiences, he experiences in expressing, and he experiences in order to express" (EHL) (*GW*, 10: 66).

23. Beginning in the fall of 1894, Thomas Mann enrolled in lectures on Germanic mythology given by Dr. Wilhelm Hertz at the Technische Hochschule in Munich. In Notebook I, Thomas Mann referred to Wolfram von Eschenbach's *Parzival*, which Hertz had translated in 1882 as *Die Sage von Parzival und dem Gral*. Possibly Thomas Mann knew of a translation of Gottfried von Strassburg's *Tristan und Isolde* published by Hertz in 1877.

24. Bourget's *Essais de psychologie contemporaine* (Paris, 1886) and his novel *Cosmopolis* (Paris, 1892), which appeared in German translation in 1894, were familiar to Thomas Mann, who did not emphasize his dependence on Bourget, but repeatedly quoted from his works. In a letter to Grautoff from Munich dated 17 January 1896, he wrote, "Also, Bourget in the original is something incomparably different! And then a whole new literature opens up before one, the 1830 school, [such as] Balzac, Mérimée, Stendhal, and the big critics, who until now one only knew through Brandes!" (EHL). Thomas Mann indicated his familiarity with Bourget's *Cosmopolis* by references in a June 1896 review. At the time Thomas Mann wrote "Der Wille zum Glück," "Der Tod," and "Disillusionment," Paul Bourget, who rejected dilettantism in any form, would not have approved of him.

25. Notebook 1, pp. 51–56. According to Mendelssohn, *Zauberer*, 200, Thomas

Mann, the Wagner fan, probably knew Nietzsche's *Der Fall Wagner*, published in
1888, possibly alerted to it by his brother Heinrich, who knew at least *Also sprach
Zarathustra* (*Thus Spoke Zarathustra*) since 1891, and who referred to Nietzsche as his
"most essential reading" in 1892. Klaus Schröter, *Thomas Mann in Selbstzeugnissen
und Bilddokumenten* (hereafter referred to as *Thomas Mann*) (Reinbeck bei Hamburg: Rowohlt, 1964), 42, declares: "Thomas Mann began to read Nietzsche only in
October 1896. . . ." (EHL). Such a categorical statement is debatable; other facts indicate the possibility of Thomas Mann's earlier acquaintance with Nietzsche's works (see
also note 65).

26. "Pathos der Distanz," *GW*, 8: 44.

27. Friedrich Nietzsche, *Thus Spoke Zarathustra*, trans. Walter Kaufmann, in *The
Portable Nietzsche* (New York: Viking Press, 1954), Zarathustra's Prologue, part 3,
p. 124. "Lebensabriß," *GW*, 11: 109. "*Selbstüberwinder*" is literally translated as "the
self-overcomer." Thomas Mann discussed his lifelong fascination with Nietzsche in
detail much later in his *Die Betrachtungen eines Unpolitischen* (*Confessions of an Unpolitical Man*). However, only the direct references noted above exist regarding his
knowledge of Nietzsche's works during 1895–96, when "Der Wille zum Glück" was
conceived and written. While he repeatedly mentioned Bourget, Wagner, and other
French, Scandinavian, and Russian authors in his correspondence with Grautoff,
Thomas Mann did not include the name of Nietzsche.

28. *Summary*: Two youths, Paolo Hofmann and the narrator, are introduced in
their North German home town. An important episode recalls a sudden fainting spell
Paolo suffered at dancing school when a little blond girl he was infatuated with asked
another boy repeatedly to dance with her, revealing Paolo's extreme sensitivity and his
serious heart condition, both integral to the story.

After a five-year separation, the narrator meets Paolo in Munich, far to the south.
Paolo is now a promising artist, though he is gravely ill; he introduces his friend to the
von Steins, a nouveau riche baronial family: the baron, a retired businessman, his
Jewish wife, and their beautiful daughter Ada, whom Paolo loves. Paolo asks for
Ada's hand, but the baron refuses because of Paolo's ill health. Paolo then vanishes,
and Ada asks the narrator to tell him that she will marry no one else.

Five years pass without news of Paolo, who is supposedly drifting around the world;
by chance the narrator meets him in a Rome café. Paolo declares that he too had
sworn never to marry anyone but Ada, but he is so ill that only his will to happiness has
miraculously preserved him. A note from the baron tells them that Ada has refused a
proposal and the baron now consents to her marriage to Paolo. Paolo triumphantly
leaves for Munich but dies the day after the wedding. At his funeral the narrator
catches the same triumphant gleam of will in the eyes of Ada, Paolo's young widow.

29. In the current German S. Fischer edition (1975), which does not follow a strict
chronological order, "Disillusionment" ("Enttäuschung") is printed after "Der Wille
zum Glück," and before "Der Tod." In *Stories of Three Decades* (New York: Alfred
A. Knopf, 1974), "Disillusionment" follows "Little Herr Friedemann." This arrangement was probably made because although "Disillusionment" was written earlier, it
first appeared in this collection. Hans Bürgin and Hans-Otto Mayer, in *Thomas Mann,
Eine Chronik seines Lebens* (Frankfurt am Main: Fischer Taschen Verlag, 1974), 16,
refer to the summer of 1896 as the date of composition of this story.

30. Thomas Mann's autobiographical writings do not clearly date his travels to Italy
before completion of *Buddenbrooks* (See note 19).

31. See *Wille zum Leben* in glossary.

32. It is hard to tell whether at this time Thomas Mann had read Nietzsche's *Will to
Power*. Very possibly, however, he had read *On the Genealogy of Morals*, which also
discusses related topics and which he quotes in the story.

33. Thomas Mann's maternal grandfather, Johann Ludwig Hermann Bruhns (b. 1821), emigrated to Brazil and founded an export business in São Paulo. He later acquired a coffee and sugar plantation in Parati, near Rio de Janeiro, and owned rice fields in Boa Vista and Angra dos Reis. He married Maria da Silva, daughter of Dom Manoel Gaetano da Silva, a plantation owner at Ilha de São Sebastião, near Santos, Brazil. Maria died at an early age, and Bruhns did not return to Germany then, though their daughters, Julia and Maria, were raised by relatives in Lübeck. Julia grew up without a mother and corresponded in German with her father, who lived in South America with her brothers. Thomas Mann's grandfather Bruhns finally returned to Germany at the end of his life and died in Bavaria in 1893. Maria, five years younger than her sister Julia, married Heinrich Nicolaus Stolterfoht. Julia was engaged to Johann Heinrich Mann, Thomas Mann's father, on 4 February 1889.

34. "Hofmann" also suggests E. T. A. Hoffmann, whose name recurs in Thomas Mann's fiction and to whom, with Heine, Goethe, and Schiller, he refers frequently in his early years. E. T. A. Hoffmann's artistic abilities, as well as his talents for music and caricature, make him a prototype of the "artist" per se. Both Thomas and Heinrich Mann drew well, and for decades Heinrich found it difficult to decide whether his forte was writing or painting. Many of Thomas Mann's early sketches exist, too, indicating, like Goethe's, a youthful interest in art. The spelling "Hofmann" connotes the "man of the court," or a "courting man," a logical comment on the theme of this story.

35. Thomas Mann may have chosen the Latinate spelling of the name "Paolo" to commemorate his grandfather's residence in Brazil; also, Thomas Mann's first Christian name was Paul, and he signed some writings "Paul Thomas."

36. Later, of course, the clash expressed in the combination of names became increasingly important to him and developed into the powerful Leitmotiv of "Tonio Kröger."

37. Thomas Mann himself was slender, of medium height, and dark-haired, but he was not a sallow, sickly child, nor did he display either the physical or the emotional Latin characteristics. He had, however, felt attracted from his youth to the charm of the Latins and their Romance languages, even though when he stayed in Italy he repeatedly expressed his longing for the North. This combination of attractions later developed into Thomas Mann's theme of isolation, paralleling the theme of the tension between the artist and the *Bürger* which for him reached its peak in "Tonio Kröger."

38. Paolo inherited all of his physical characteristics from his Latin mother, and his *geistig* qualities differ from those of people around him. Although the circumstances of Paolo and the narrator are very similar, the narrator clearly belongs to the "majority," while Paolo, as far as *geistig* matters are concerned, is isolated. Without a name or physical description, the narrator still can observe and understand both Paolo and the people who surround him. Thomas Mann has thus labeled one side of a personality, the sensitive "Latin" artist and lover, with "Paolo," his own pseudonym, while substantializing the rational and objective side in the narrator of the story. The values of Paolo's industrious North German father also enter the story through the anonymous narrator.

39. *The Genealogy of Morals*, in *The Philosophy of Nietzsche*, trans. Horace B. Samuel, 634–35 (New York: Modern Library, n.d. [ca. 1927, 1954]: "Now the first argument that comes ready to my hand is that the real homestead of the concept 'good' is sought and located in the wrong place: the judgement 'good' did *not* originate among those to whom goodness was shown. Much rather has it been the good themselves, that is, the aristocratic, the powerful, the high-stationed, the high-minded, who have felt that they themselves were good, and that their actions were good, that is to say of the first order, in contradistinction to all the low, the low-minded, the vulgar,

and the plebeian. It was out of this *pathos of distance* [emphasis added] that they first arrogated the right to create values for their own profit, and to coin the names of such values; what had they to do with utility?"

40. "Es war noch jetzt fast unerträglich schwül, und der Himmel zuckte jede Sekunde in dem Phosphorlichte auf" (*GW*, 8: 59–60). "*Zucken*" and "*zittern*," meaning "to convulse, palpitate, tremble, and quiver," were words Thomas Mann used to express emotions, life, and passion, often in connection with the eyes.

41. *GW*, 8: 61. This again emphasizes Thomas Mann's idea, recurring in all three stories, that the individual must consent to death before he is ready to die.

42. Such passages of "Der Wille zum Glück" reflect Mann's unprejudiced view of the social atmosphere of his time. No evidence exists that he was anti-Semitic and in fact not long after he wrote this story, he married Katia Pringsheim, daughter of an intellectual middle-class Jewish family with artistic taste and good social connections. The von Stein family astonishingly resembles the Pringsheim family, although at this early time Thomas Mann certainly did not know either Katia Pringsheim or her parents.

43. Thomas Mann, who had read both Bourget's French original and the German translation of *Cosmopolis*, might have considered some parallels to Bourget's work. Bourget aimed to show how passions bring ethnic differentiations to the fore. Medieval Venice is represented in the modern Italian setting of *Cosmopolis* by the descendant of the doges, Countess Steno, the widow and her young daughter Alba, and the corrupt and bankrupt prince Ardea; the Slavic type is represented by the countess Steno's first lover, the Polish count Boleslas Gorka; America is typified by the widow's second lover, the painter Maitland, his mulatto wife Lyda, and her brother Florent Chapront; the countess Gorka represents the highly idealized English woman, a puritanical fanatic. The dehumanized Jewish-German businessman Hafner and his almost saintly daughter Fanny represent extremes. The two Frenchmen in the novel are the Marquis of Montfanon, a traditional Royalist Catholic, and Dorsenne the writer, the prototype of the cosmopolitan and the central figure of the book.

44. The title of baron was held by the von Steins in spite of their nonaristocratic origin and their lack of blood ties with the centuries-old German landowning or military nobility; their education and money had opened doors for them in the middle-class society of the intelligentsia. Thomas Mann himself was not at home in aristocratic circles, and he seldom described or even referred to such figures. The phenomenon of newly wealthy and recently ennobled families was common in the second part of the nineteenth century and was often a result of financial conditions which had arisen from the new industrialism and the bankruptcy of the older nobility, a situation also treated in Paul Bourget's *Cosmopolis*.

45. Other feminine characters of Thomas Mann's have an erotic appeal greatly relevant to his themes. His reason for choosing this cut of garment as a motif is uncertain; the style was common for well-dressed ladies of the time, but he must have deeply associated the image with his theme, for he used it throughout his works. The best known photograph of Katia Pringsheim as a young girl also shows her wearing puffed sleeves.

46. Paolo's death cannot be compared to the concept of the *Liebestod*, since it does not represent Wagner's idea of the fulfillment of love through the union of the lovers in Death.

47. Part of Thomas Mann's reaction was his rejection of a church-ruled faith. One reason for his turning away from Bourget's thinking at the end of the 1890s was Bourget's acceptance of orthodox Catholic morality.

48. There are striking similarities between Thomas Mann's thoughts in "Der Tod" and Nietzsche's in "Of Voluntary Death" ("Vom freien Tode"), in *Thus Spoke Zarathustra* (*Also sprach Zarathustra*), part one. There is no evidence, however, that

Thomas Mann took these ideas from Nietzsche directly, even though it is very possible that, along with his brother Heinrich, young Thomas had read *Zarathustra* in his youth. Some lines, like the following, seem especially pertinent to "Der Tod": "Meinen Tod lobe ich euch, den freien Tod, der mir kommt weil *ich* will" (*Zarathustra* in Nietzsche, ed. Schlechta, 2: 334). "Der Tod" in its fictionalized final form, however, presents a message quite different from Nietzsche's.

49. *Summary*: The first-person narrator, a count, relates in his diary that many years ago he conceived and accepted the notion that he would die on 12 October of his fortieth year, since he had attracted Death with his will power. During his last weeks, he reveals his most intimate reactions to his own death. He is filled with love for his daughter Asuncion, and when she dies hours before his own predicted date of death, he realizes that she does so because he would not have been able to accept Death wholeheartedly had he had to leave his child. At the end, he readily faces Death.

50. (Berlin: S. Fischer, 1898), containing: "Der kleine Herr Friedemann," "Der Tod," "Der Bajazzo," "Tobias Mindernickel," and "Luischen."

51. In this discussion, Death is capitalized when personified. In "Der Wille zum Glück" death was "just" a natural phenomenon, since Paolo himself did not even realize his position vis-à-vis death.

52. The Spanish word *asunción* means "assumption," an elevation to higher dignity, and the ascent of the Holy Virgin to heaven; commonly an assumption is the thing supposed, a postulate. The word is often used as a female name in Spanish-speaking countries. Thomas Mann's Asuncion intriguingly resembles Goethe's Mignon. Mignon, a major character in *Wilhelm Meister's Apprenticeship*, is an Italian girl filled with longing for her homeland and unconditionally devoted to Wilhelm, her master and her savior. Her feelings are absolute, pure, and without any materalistic motivation. Her ethereal love is symbolic and mystical rather than sensual. Her character lends a deep significance to Goethe's theme, and her death parallels the disappearance of art from the life of Wilhelm Meister.

53. Other influences possibly pertain: nineteenth-century *Schicksalsdrama*, especially Zacharias Werner's *Der vierundzwanzigste Februar*, Platen's *Verhängnisvolle Gabel* and Grillparzer's *Die Ahnfrau*.

54. To point up the Nordic setting, his name signifies the "house of God" in the Scandinavian languages.

55. Possibly this is an allusion to Christ's hour of death.

56. *GW*, 8: 75. "Enttäuschung" ("Disillusionment") is the title of Thomas Mann's next short story, whose theme is hopeless, humiliating disillusionment.

57. Dentisry and the condition of teeth becomes an increasingly typical motif in Thomas Mann's work representing a physical and psychical state of being.

58. See note 52.

59. Thomas Mann, *Stories of Three Decades*, trans. H. T. Lowe-Porter (New York: Knopf, 1974). The English translations used here are taken from this standard text, *STD*, unless otherwise stated.

60. Thomas Mann gradually developed the association of a Latin type with these qualities into the figure of the artist.

61. *Summary*: This framed story has a sketch as its body: one early autumn a stranger in the Piazza San Marco relates his disappointment with life to the narrator. The stranger accuses poets and scholars of raising false hopes; he feels life is mediocre, man is limited, and even death will not satisfy his excessive expectations.

62. That the setting and presentation of this story resemble those of E. T. A. Hoffmann's "Der Ritter Gluck" and that "Disillusionment" directly refers to Goethe's *Die Leiden des jungen Werther* prove Mann's continuing dependence on his reading. He also repeatedly referred to E. T. A. Hoffmann in his early works. Even though Thomas Mann did not directly refer in "Disillusionment" to Hoffmann's "Der Ritter

Gluck," in which the narrator meets a stranger, they converse in a public setting, and finally the stranger (Ritter Gluck himself), invites the narrator to listen to his piano playing and song, and shares with him the story of his condemnation as an artist, the setting, the mood, and even some motives remind the reader of Hoffmann's work. Hoffmann's late fall setting, even the vocabulary (*Spätherbst*), the plaza with the colorful crowd (*buntgemischt*) and the stranger's careful description, his anonymity, his nervous monologues, his disappointed pessimism, and the abrupt ending, strongly resemble those in Mann's "Disillusionment."

63. In the German text, the stranger is the *"sonderbare Herr."* The standard English translation renders the phrase "extraordinary man," but "extraordinary" does not convey the enigmatic quality of the German adjective. Here the term "exceptional" will be used.

64. The English translation incorrectly uses the term "afternoon" for "forenoon."

65. The edition of Nietzsche's *Der Fall Wagner* which Thomas Mann owned and annotated is marked with his name and the date 1895.

66. The German phrase is *"befremdliche Offenheit,"* "alienating openness." The English translation of "candour and friendliness" seems questionable.

67. *STD*, 24 (*GW*, 8: 64). "Disillusionment" is difficult to read, because in contrast to the earlier stories, it resembles a philosophical text; the fictional element and minimal action do not hold the reader's attention. Mann skillfully interwove his message into each word, making a translation extremely difficult.

68. These ideas and images strongly resemble those projected in Hermann Hesse's *Demian* (1914). Hesse knew all of Thomas Mann's early works. The setting the "exceptional man" describes as his own youthful environment, too, is not similar to Mann's, but to Hesse's. The similarity between "Disillusionment" and *Demian* possibly does not reflect a direct influence by Mann on Hesse, but manifests the *Zeitgeist* affecting both young authors.

69. *GW*, 8: 66; see also *STD*, 25. The stranger's bitter accusations do not mention Goethe by name, an author who also experienced a period of revolt and described it in his *Werther*, an early work of the *Sturm und Drang* period. (Goethe, *Die Leiden des jungen Werther*, in *Goethes Werke* [Hamburg: Christian Wegner Verlag, 1965], vol. 1.)

70. *GW*, 8: 67; *STD*, 36. These are the last lines Werther wrote in his diary; from here on, his friend, the editor of his legacy, finishes the tragic story (*Werther*, 92).

71. Novalis, *Hymnen an die Nacht* (Munich: Athenäum—Fassung Goldmans Gelbe Taschenbuch, 1964), 38. The problem of limitation is a central concept of German Romanticism. The Neoplatonic element of the German Romantic School longed for a reunion of the ego with the unlimited (*das Unendliche*); longing was an existential urge to attain a state beyond physical boundaries, which appears as the theme of "Der Tod." The count had overstepped the limits of human existence through autosuggestion, but he had been disillusioned by the ordinariness of Death itself. The tone, setting, mood, style, and reasoning of "Disillusionment" are all decidedly more suitable to Thomas Mann's own earthly personality than the phantasmagorical speculations of the count in "Der Tod." It is no wonder that "Disillusionment" has appeared in all German and English editions of Mann's short fiction, for its hero does not try to overstep his human status through some mystical manipulation of supernatural powers, and it harmonizes well with any collection of his subsequent works.

72. The romantic irony of Ludwig Tieck and E. T. A. Hoffmann.

73. Since the characters of these three stories belong to the social and intellectual upper class, they are naturally isolated from the crowd.

74. R. A. Nicholls, "Nietzsche in the Early Work of Thomas Mann," *University of California Publications in Modern Philology* 45 (1955): 9.

75. Whether coincidentally or as a result of brotherly conversations, Heinrich Mann was working on a piece of short fiction also bearing the title "Enttäuschung" at the same time.

Chapter 2. Quest: First Creative Expression of the Self

1. *Summary*: Little Herr Friedemann was accidentally crippled as an infant, and grew up a hunchback. During his adolescence, a girl rejects his loving friendship, and in order to escape the torment of rejection, he decides to renounce the love of women forever. Until he is thirty, he nurtures immense aesthetic sensitivity; then Gerda von Rinnlingen ignites his dormant passions. He cannot resist; he humiliates himself, and his self-disgust eventually leads to his suicide.

2. S. Fischer published these stories in 1898 in the volume *Der kleine Herr Friedemann*.

3. A manuscript, now lost, with the title "The Little Professor" ("Der kleine Professor"), might have been an early sketch for "Little Herr Friedemann." In November of 1894 Thomas Mann sent "The Little Professor" to Richard Dehmel, who had earlier shown an interest in "Gefallen," and asked Dehmel to help him have it published in the periodical *Pan*. Dehmel replied that this story was unsuitable, amicably citing a "too narrow" theme that gave no clue to the plot of the story. Later, Thomas Mann sent "The Little Professor" to *Gesellschaft*, where it was refused. Except for a few brief remarks in correspondence, Thomas Mann never mentioned "Der kleine Professor" again. *Gesellschaft* published a poem by Thomas Mann, "Siehst du Kind, ich liebe Dich," in January 1895.

4. *"Putzigen Wichtigkeit"* (*GW* 8: 82). The English translation "strutting comically" (*STD*, 6) does not provide this connotation at all.

5. *STD*, 8. *"winzig und wichtig"* (*GW* 8: 85).

6. The English version does not use the numbers Thomas Mann gave his sections, a system customary in German works in the last half of the nineteenth century.

7. The name Johannes became the traditional one in the Buddenbrook family; Thomas Mann's great-grandfather was Johann Heinrich Marty; his grandfather, Johann Siegmund Mann; his father, Senator Thomas Johann Heinrich Mann.

8. *Buddenbrooks*'s sources show that the sisters were patterned after Thomas Mann's cousins, the unmarried daughters Emmi, Auguste, and Luise of Johann Siegmund Mann.

9. Mendelssohn, *Zauberer*, 237.

10. This event, already noted in "Der Wille zum Glück," occurs repeatedly in Thomas Mann's stories, perhaps most notably in "Tonio Kröger."

11. A more accurate translation of the clause "und da sie ihm gegenüber eine befangene Zurückhaltung immer bewahrten" is "and since they always kept a self-conscious reserve toward him."

12. In any consideration of this problem, the enormous difference between the Victorian concept of love and current "liberated" adolescent sexual behavior is paramount.

13. "Love" is repeatedly connected to "spring." In "Gefallen," Thomas Mann pointed out the lilac and its strong fragrance, and here the higher fragrant jasmine hides the lovers from young Friedemann. Jasmine will reoccur in association with sensual love in this and other Thomas Mann fiction—even without the association with spring.

14. The phrase *"verwachsene Brust,"* translated as "deformed chest," has connotations the word *chest* is not able to convey. *"Brust"* (breast) is often used in German, especially by eighteenth-century poets, to indicate the seat of the emotions. The German phrase thus indicates not only Friedemann's physical deformity, but also his distorted emotions. Thomas Mann, a student of Nietzsche, believed that music transmitted emotional messages most sensitively and genuinely.

15. *STD*, 6. ". . .oh! man könnte beinahe sagen, daß er ein Epikureer war" (*GW* 8: 81). R. A. Nicholls's observation is indispensable:

In the original the term used is "Epikureer," and it is interesting that this Epicurean ideal to which Friedemann subscribes is an important symbol in Nietzsche's
work and a symbol used in very much the same way as Mann uses it here. Epicureanism had as its ideal the avoidance of pain and suffering. In Nietzsche's
interpretation: "To seek happiness would be nonsense, that would mean seeking
something negative! But to avoid suffering, that is the aim." Such an ideal, he
says, is essentially decadent.

Nicholls, 11. See the English translation "connoisseur" (*STD*, 6); a better translation
would have been "epicurean."

16. In *Die Betrachtungen eines Unpolitischen*, nearly twenty years after "Little Herr
Friedemann," Thomas Mann noted that his knees were weak "from enthusiasm at the
romantic message of the Lohengrin Overture" (EHL) (*GW* 12: 80).

17. Thomas Mann describes her as "*burschikos*" (hearty, unaffected, boyish), and
she is no coquette, but she lacks warmth for her husband. The news of her sensational
arrival must have reached Friedemann. Later she claims she has known unhappiness.

18. Thomas Mann's ability to provide the most important revelations of character
through dialogue became a typically brilliant feature of his fiction, especially in his
novels.

19. Several critics have pointed out physical similarities between Gerda von Rinnlingen and Gerda Buddenbrook, Thomas's wife: their hair color is similar; both are
musical and somehow not liked by average persons; both are cold to their respective
husbands and appear to enjoy manipulating men they have attracted. The dark
shadows near Gerda von Rinnlingen's eyes are repeatedly pointed out.

20. At this time Thomas Mann's close *geistig* dependence on Wagner's music was
just beginning. See Schröter, *Thomas Mann* 19: "The first <<Lohengrin>> performance [in Lübeck] especially blessed him with romantic tremors" (EHL). In Munich he
attended Wagnerian operas whenever possible. In "Little Herr Friedemann" Wagner's symbolistic music and poetry have not yet become centrally relevant to Thomas
Mann's theme. Acquaintance with the *Ring* cycle and *Tristan und Isolde* greatly
deepens an appreciation of Thomas Mann's work. According to Mendelssohn,
Zauberer 184, "Thomas Mann later candidly acknowledged that what in Wagner had
so fascinated and enraptured him in his youth was the extraordinary unleashed erotic
intensity of his music, which had had a liberating effect on his late-beginning sexual
development . . ." (EHL).

21. "The overture to Lohengrin gave the first too embarrassing, and too well turned
out example of how one can hypnotize with music" (EHL) (". . . das Lohengrin-
Vorspiel gab das erste, nur zu verfängliche, nur zu gut geratene Beispiel dafür, wie
man auch mit Musik hypnotisiert." Nietzsche, "Der Fall Wagner," in *Friedrich Nietzsche*, ed. Karl Schlechta, 3 vols. (Munich: Carl Hanser Verlag, 1955) 2: 918.

22. Mendelssohn, *Zauberer*, 235, cites Thomas Mann's letter to a female reader in
1909: "Frau von Rinnlingen is not a coquette; she is a sufferer, a character filled with
problems, who recognizes a fellow sufferer in the crippled man, but she is too proud at
the last moment to accept the acknowledgment of this fellow sufferer. This is briefly
her relationship to little Herr Friedemann" (EHL). Thomas Mann's own struggle
against his late-developing powerful sexuality did not permit emotional indulgences
that would have distracted him. In a letter to Grautoff, 5 March 1895, he observed:

I am saying you do *not need* to belittle the lower body. But you *may* very well do
so; in fact, I do it myself, too. I have recently developed a quasi-asceticism in
myself. I go on in my better times about pure aesthetic sensuality, the sensuality
of the spirit, the soul, the disposition in general. I tell you, let us separate the
lower part of the body from love! and so forth. Volumes could be written about

this. But this is a purely personal point of view which should not be generalized into a philosophy. (EHL)

23. *STD*, 12 (*GW* 8: 91). The original punctuation of "Glück" is important. The passage literally rendered is, "What were any of all those things that up to now had comprised his 'happiness'?"

24. Mendelssohn, *Zauberer*, 235, quotes Thomas Mann:

> This melancholy story of the little hunchback also represents a cornerstone in my personal history, insofar as it for the first time sounds the basic motif that plays the same role in the total work as the 'leitmotifs' do in the individual words. The main figure is a person badly treated by nature, who finds a way to come to terms with his fate in a mild, peaceful, philosophical manner, and who had based his life on restful contemplation and peace. The appearance of a remarkably beautiful woman who is also cold and cruel represents the intrusion of passion into this sheltered life, which overthrows the entire fabrication of it and destroys the quiescent hero himself. (EHL)

25. Besides Gerda's red leitmotif the traditional significance of "red carpet" is also ironic.

26. The English translation calls it an "uncannily flickering gaze."

27. This is the only instance in this story of the attribution of the color red to anyone or anything other than Gerda von Rinnlingen or objects that refer directly to her. The redness of Friedemann's face of course indicates the extent of the emotions she has aroused.

28. In Lübeck, the street from the theater actually leads toward the river, where many business firms are situated.

29. Critics have previously considered her manner provocative. Informal college surveys indicate that about half of young men find her words abrasive to Friedemann's dignity and 18 percent directly insulting, while 95 percent of the young women consider her approach as logical and compassionate; today's women feel that Friedemann should have been relieved by the conversation.

30. Thomas Mann's objectivity shows no hint that Gerda von Rinnlingen pushed Friedemann into his declaration. In the last crucial pages, Thomas Mann did not in the least abandon his veil of irony.

31. In the German text, *zittern* indicates all of Friedemann's tremors except those in his first and last appearances, where *zucken* is used. This is impossible to convey in English (*STD*, 57, 78).

32. An identical train of thought occurred in Thomas Mann's later work, *Königliche Hoheit* (*Royal Majesty*), in the sensitive romance between the Prince and the American millionaire's daughter, Imma. Both are sufferers, but when the young Prince loses his poise and like Friedemann falls to his knees before the woman, she does not reject him; however, at their next meeting she is cold and sarcastic, and replies:

> "For heaven's sake, Prince, allow this past event to be forgotten. To what are you returning! What do you remind yourself and me of! I thought that you had good reasons to cover these things with deepest silence. *To allow yourself to let go to such an extent! To lose your poise!*"—"If you knew, Imma, how indescribably good it felt *to lose my poise!*"—"I decline! This is *offensive*, do you know that? I insist that you keep your poise in my presence, the same [poise] which you maintain in the face of the whole world. I am not here so that you may recuperate from your princely existence, in my company." (EHL; emphasis added)

Imma and Gerda von Rinnlingen share the same pride, the typical reaction of a sensitive virginal heart that has previously been hurt. The difference is that the Prince, despite his deformity, does not give up and will go on fighting for his happiness. *Königliche Hoheit* was conceived and written during the time that Thomas Mann was courting Katia Pringsheim and displays many sensitive autobiographical details.

33. Letter to Grautoff, 17 February 1896:

> The destruction of a wicked impulse does not happen suddenly with a moral uprooting; that signifies nothing, and [afterward] one unavoidably slips backward, only more desperately. There is a need for a slow, careful, permitting of the drive to weaken and dry up, in which all possible intellectual artful tactics which suggest the instinct of self-preservation are helpful. Finally, one is too much of an *homme de lettres* and psychologist not to take a superior pleasure in such self-treatment. Any kind of despair would be senseless at your age. You have the time, and the urge toward serenity and self-satisfaction will force the dogs of the subterranean depths into chains. (EHL)

34. *Summary*: An unnamed child, son of a respectable businessman and a melancholy musical mother, grows up spending most of his energy on clowning to entertain people he secretly looks down upon. Because he largely neglects his studies for what his father calls his clownishness (*"Bajazzotum"*) , he is apprenticed to a businessman, a position the *"Bajazzo"* considers "temporary" and unattractive. After his father dies, he uses part of his inheritance to see the world and invests the rest to live in a mid-German town. He spends his time savoring the arts, but this secluded leisurely existence soon palls. One lovely day he sees a young lady in a carriage with her father and not long after sees her again at the opera. Aware of his rapturous feeling about her, he attends a charity bazzar where she is a hostess and is humiliated there, thus realizing that he has lost touch with "the world," whose members are "the children of light." As he becomes more and more aware of his isolation, the *"Bajazzo"* rationalizes his relationship with the rest of the world. Having lost his self-respect and self-assurance and finding even his childhood companion turning away from him, he, the outsider, remains desperately lonely.

35. The word *Bajazzo* is derived from Leoncavallo's *Pagliacci*, which belongs to the operatic verismo style. The opera had its premiere in May 1892, and the expression "der Bajazzo" became used in Germany. *"Pagliacci"* means "clowns,' referring to the two clown characters in the opera, Canio and Tonio. The Italian word "Pagliaccio" has become familiar both as noun and adjective in Germany (according to the *Grosse Duden* encyclopedia, *"Bajazzo"* means *"Possenreisser"* or "joker"), though its meaning today is fading. Due to the message in Thomas Mann's title, "Bajazzo" will be used instead of the "dilettante" of the English translation.

36. The thin prevalent connotations of "dilettante" came from Paul Bourget, the French *fin de siècle* thinker, novelist, and moralist, who defined the term as the decadent and cosmopolitan spirit in his *Essais de psychologie contemporaine* and his novel *Cosmopolis*, which Thomas Mann frequently quoted. The concept includes the spirit of *Laisser faire, laisser aller*, a hedonistic way of enjoying egotistically aesthetic and sensual values of life. Bourget believed this trend had caused the decay in French society.

37. Letter to Grautoff, 16 May 1895:

> But such a mood, which belongs only to fools and which had nothing to do with the reason or the will, passes as soon as it arrives, and the no-good decadent swiftly gives up [the attempt] to amount to something in the world [and] he satisfies himself with [the fact that] the world is something for him. . . ." (EHL)

38. Undated letter fragment to Grautoff, about January 1897: "The novella 'Walter Weiler' under another title and a changed organization (probably in the form of a diary) has received a painstaking *reworking* . . ." (EHL).

39. "I will make an end of it—alas, that is an attitude too heroic for a dilettante" (*STD*, 50; *GW*, 8: 140). A literal translation is given above.

40. After "Der Bajazzo," Thomas Mann repeatedly featured the concept of gradual isolation (*"Vereinsamung"*) in his "questor heroes," most movingly in the fate of the unfortunate Adrian Leverkühn of *Doctor Faustus*.

41. The motif of the puppet theater occurs in *Buddenbrooks*, where it characterizes the eccentric Christian Buddenbrook. Such theaters were a popular toy for youths in the eighteenth and nineteenth centuries; Goethe was introduced to the Faust theme by a puppet theater, and the young Ibsen played extensively with marionettes. "From their grandmother, old Frau Consul Elisabeth Mann, Heinrich [Mann] received a puppet theater as a gift . . . when Heinrich tired of the puppet theater, he passed it to his younger brother. He [Thomas] made something quite different of it" (EHL). Typically, he wrote "real" plays and charged "real" admissions for his performances.

42. Thomas Mann's two sisters, Julia and Carla, were younger than he, but Friedemann had three older sisters, modeled on Mann's three cousins.

43. Mendelssohn, *Zauberer*, 66. Thomas Mann gave reading sessions and lectures throughout his long life. He also told jokes well and mimicked: "Erika Mann inherited this talent from her father; she once said: 'Well, I am a monkey,' and then added, 'My father was also a monkey.' In an autobiographical sketch, Thomas Mann termed 'the original instinct to copy and to imitate' the primitive origin of all art" (EHL).

44. This must have happened at the latest in the fall of 1882, in the year of the move to the Beckergrube house, because Thomas Mann told his children that he had taken violin lessons from the age of seven or eight. He came home from school around 1:00 P.M., he was served a plate of sandwiches, and then he left for his violin lesson with Herr Winkelmann. He was home for the main meal of the day, which according to the upper-middle-class custom was taken about four o'clock.

45. *STD*, 32; *GW*, 8: 111. A literal rendering indicates Thomas Mann's point: "I learned a kind of special way of playing the piano on my own. I began by sounding the F-sharp major chords because I found the black keys to be especially attractive . . ." (EHL).

46. "Dilettante variety" ignores Thomas Mann's stress on the clown attitude rather than on the dilettante's. "Clownery" and "nonsense" cover the German message.

47. This name, also used in "Little Herr Friedemann," means "sly bird" in Low German dialect; the business is in a locale similar to that of Friedemann's first job.

48. "Schilling" is a piece of Austrian currency, here possibly used to emphasize this character's materialistic interests in contrast to Bajazzo's.

49. Viktor, the youngest Mann child, was born 12 April 1892, when his mother, Julia Mann, was thirty-nine.

50. Bajazzo's mother is unlike the passionate Southern mothers Thomas Mann gave to Paolo Hofmann and Tonio Kröger. "Bajazzo"'s mother is gentle, charming, and lonely, a faded blond who plays Chopin and tells stories. One of the boy's most cherished memories is her touch on his head. Though she appears only briefly, she is consistently mentioned until she vanishes after the father dies. She is the only one who takes the boy's talent seriously and hopes he will develop into an artist, a balance for the father's pragmatic efficiency. This charming figure remained in Thomas Mann's mind, to reappear as Gabriele Klöterjahn, one of the protagonists of "Tristan." Thomas Mann writes tenderly of these women, so delicate and so unable to function in the material world. Bajazzo's mother might have served as his inspiration, but Bajazzo was too superficial to pay attention to her.

51. The dilettante's travels from his original environment cannot be identified with

the symbolic wandering of the German Romantic heroes, nor should the Romantic search for the Blue Flower be confused with the intellectual and sensual pursuit of epicureanism. Bourget defined in *Cosmopolis* the dilettante's attitude of self-exile.

52. The opera in "Little Herr Friedemann" was performed in the town theater, which refers to Lübeck; in "Der Bajazzo" the performance takes place in a Munich opera house.

53. Thomas Mann refers to Gounod's protagonist, Marguerite, who is emphasized rather than the titular hero Faust. Here Marguerite's purity and innocence are stressed as they are in Goethe's *Faust*, even though the outcome favors Marlowe's Elizabethan version of the legend and emphasizes Faust's base method of seduction. This opera was quite popular for its lovely light melodies, but it never really won the hearts of the German public, probably because its libretto, which claimed to be based on Goethe's masterpiece, is actually poor in poetic and philosophic quality; a German audience would feel it a travesty of Goethe's work.

54. The use of *hors ligne* indicates that "Bajazzo" is a member of the upper class, even though his shortcomings make him feel estranged from it.

55. "The name 'Rainer' comes from '*Rain*' (boundary between fields), but it suggests 'rein' = 'pure'" (W. L. Robinson, "Name-Characterization in the Works of Thomas Mann," [diss., Univ. of Texas, 1959], 20).

56. The *monologue intérieur* attains extreme vivacity, and the argument between sentimental self-pity and cold rationality is brilliantly shaped: "I cannot stand this! I will not be ruined! I will shoot myself dead; shall it be today or tomorrow?" and then: "One does not perish from unhappy love. An unhappy love is an attitude. In an unhappy love one pleases oneself" (EHL) (*STD*, 48; *GW*, 8: 137–38). The *Werther* theme is briefly entertained and then briskly rejected, as is the attitude of "Der kleine Herr Friedemann."

57. Bajazzo foreshadows Gabriele in "Tristan." The Schilling character also conveys qualities typical of Klöterjahn in "Tristan," and Spinell possibly originates as well in Bajazzo's sterile aestheticism. "The children of light," as well as the mixed emotions Bajazzo displays toward them, mark the first expression of a growing motif which reached fruition in Hans and Ingeborg, the representatives of the "blond and blue-eyed" that Tonio Kröger came to love.

58. Such writing as "Der Bajazzo" was therapeutic for Thomas Mann.

Chapter 3. From Grotesque Disharmony to the Vision of an Abstract *Weltbild*

1. Except for "Gerächt," which is not translated yet, the stories of this chapter appear in *Stories of Three Decades*, and hence are referred to here by their English titles. "Tobias Mindernickel" and "Gladius Dei" are the same in both German and English versions.

2. *Summary*: Tobias Mindernickel is a lonely, aging eccentric, constantly mocked by street urchins. He is usually timid, but one day when a child is hurt and Tobias comforts him, Tobias's personality suddenly asserts itself. He then buys himself a young dog, and when the dog, alert and energetic, does not conform to Tobias' wishes, Tobias angrily chastises him, his emotions swinging wildly between fury and tenderness. After the dog is accidentally injured, Tobias devotedly nurses him back to health, but when the dog is able to romp again, Tobias stabs him to death in a sudden rage and then weeps bitterly over him.

3. More than forty years later, in *Dr Faustus*, the devil appeared to Adrian Leverkühn at the Albergo Casa Bernardini.

4. Thomas Mann first referred to this project as "Abwärts" ("Downward"). It evolved into *Buddenbrooks*.

5. Whether the Old Testament connections of Tobias with Abraham's wife Sarah, the Archangel Raphael, and his father's blindness pertain to Thomas Mann's choice of name for this protagonist is debatable. In Christian art, however, "Tobias" is consistently the name of a young man presented with his dog.

6. "The name Tobias Mindernickel is the most widely recognized example of Mann's use of '*redende Namen*'" (W. L. Robinson, "Name-Characterization in the Works of Thomas Mann," [hereafter referred to as "Names"], diss., Univ. of Texas, 1959, 20). "*Nickel*" can have two connotations: one, "Nikolaus," giving a composite meaning of "younger Nikolaus" or "son of Nikolaus"; and secondly, a coin of low value (*Nickel* = 10–50 *Pfennig*) and/or a metal of lesser value, hence insignificant; these emphasize the inferiority suggested in "*Minder*," (lesser) which also connotes a northern German locale. Further, in certain parts of German-speaking Europe, it is a popular custom to scold little boys who have temper tantrums by calling them "*wütender Tobias*" (raging Tobias).

7. The translation (*STD*, 51) uses the terms "puzzling" and "sinister," but these do not cover the concept at hand. "*Rätselhaft*" has connotations of "riddlesome," and "*schändlich*" indicates "shamefulness" (*GW*, 8: 141).

8. In the introduction the hero's first name is not mentioned without the family name, except in the urchins' taunts. The last name is emphatically singled out when Thomas Mann wishes to stress the negative aspects of the hero's personality. In the second section, when the hero has the dog, the first name, "Tobias," dominates, suiting the biblical image of the "man with the dog."

9. "Esau," from the Hebrew word for "hairy," was the name of the Old Testament figure cheated out of his inheritance by his brother Jacob.

10. Nicholls, *Nietzsche*, 13: "The suspect origin of gentleness and pity is an essential feature of Nietzsche's 'unmasking psychology.' One passage in *Human. All-too Human* expresses the theme of this story precisely. 'Pity . . . is in so far a consolation for the weak and suffering in that the latter recognize therein they possess still one power, in spite of their weakness, the *power of giving pain*. The unfortunate derives a sort of pleasure from this feeling of superiority of which the exhibition of pain makes him conscious; his imagination is exalted; he is still powerful enough to give the world pain.'"

11. In the stories that follow "Tobias Mindernickel," Thomas Mann repeatedly uses important motifs from previous works to construct subsequent ones. The state of mind and affairs expressed in Bajazzo's last words, added to the possibility that Bajazzo might have spent some time actually living that way, makes a strong case for a figure resulting in Tobias Mindernickel. The continuing use of the Lerchenberg image in the three stories "Der Bajazzo," "Tobias Mindernickel," and "Little Lizzy" supports this view, especially since the self-degradation, self-rejection, and even masochism intensify, the plots and imageries becoming increasingly grotesque.

12. (*STD*, 49). "I had not the backbone, the courage, or the countenance." "Mir fehlte jedes Rückrat. . . ." (*GW*, 8: 140).

13. Thomas Mann's "Herr und Hund" ("A Man and His Dog") is an idyllic autobiographical narrative about the close friendship between a man and his dog, Bauschan, whose honest and simple fidelity is a thoroughly uncomplicated emotion. The entire narrative is refreshing and cleansing, a portrait of a "real" relationship Thomas Mann took pride in. The love of dogs had long been a part of his personality; he later wrote, "in the course of my childhood, I made people give me gifts of china, papier-mâché and bisque dogs, little pugs and hunting dogs . . ." Mendelssohn, *Zauberer*, 66 (EHL). Thomas Mann himself loved dogs dearly, understanding their canine nature and never endowing them with unnatural human qualities.

14. In "Gefallen," the young actress, through her profession, represents arts; but her values prove corruptible, and Selten can never overcome his disappointment in

her, turning bitter and cynical. Friedemann and Bajazzo prostituted art to their unnatural epicurean pleasures and thus were destroyed.

15. The dichotomous love-hate attitude toward life can be traced through Thomas Mann's works in the contrast of the blond and blue-eyed, strong, healthy and playful figures, much like the dog Esau, opposed to the isolated, sensitive, artistic Latin types exemplified in Paolo Hofmann. Thomas Mann gave life its most complete expression in "Tonio Kröger"'s Hans Hansen and Ingeborg.

16. Within a short time, Thomas Mann reversed these roles in the story "Little Lizzy," where cold controlled disgust and unreasoning drives (Amra) destroyed a submissive wretch totally lacking the self-respect (Jacobi).

17. Via del Pantheon 57.

18. Although such close collaboration indicates the excellent relationship between Heinrich and Thomas, they did not share an apartment, as they had previously done in Rome. While Heinrich remained in the apartment at Via Argentina 34, Thomas lived at Via del Pantheon 57 during the winter of 1896–97. In the late fall of 1897 correspondence indicates that Thomas Mann had moved back to Via Torre Argentina 34 (postcard to Grautoff 11 December 1897).

19. Thomas Mann has pointed out that at this time he was reading the works of Scandinavian and Russian authors intensively. He must have been deeply impressed by their realism, their penetration of psychological problems and their vivid, powerful imagery (Bürgin, *Chronicle*, 17). He mentions Ibsen, Strindberg, and Kielland as well as Tolstoy and Dostoevsky in *Sketch of My Life*.

20. *Summary*: The three protagonists in "Luischen" form a romantic triangle: Jacobi, the husband, a lawyer, is immensely obese and smitten by an inferiority complex; Amra, his wife, is a beautiful, wealthy, hypersensuous, and vapid woman; Alfred Läutner, her young lover, is an unknown composer. This awkward pattern of life has become routine when Amra suddenly decides that she is going to host an unusual party. As entertainment she suggests that her huge husband perform "Luischen," a hit song; Läutner has composed new music for it, which Amra and he will play as an accompaniment for Jacobi's dancing and singing. After the initial shock, Amra's guests are infected by her hectic enthusiasm, and to please her, Jacobi reluctantly accepts the role. As he dances, Jacobi suddenly realizes the true import of the situation and is felled by a cerebral hemorrhage, to the consternation of onlookers.

21. Here the Lerchenberg is also mentioned.

22. Thomas Mann's theme of the blond Nordic and the dark Latin physiognomies gradually developed during his early short stories.

23. This is a degree of descriptive detail impossible to convey in an English translation.

24. The words and punctuation here resemble similar passages spoken by Tobias Mindernickel.

25. *STD*, 60. The translation "Yes, yes, good doggy, good doggy!" does not seem to render the German text adequately: "Ja!—Ja!—Du gutes Tier—!" (*GW*, 8: 172). The imagery of the dog is repeatedly used to illustrate both Jacobi's character and his obesity.

26. "Amra was not sensitive enough to . . ." (*STD*, 61); "Amra war auch dumm, um an bösem Gewissen. . ." (*GW*, 8: 173). The English phrase does not convey Thomas Mann's stress on Amra's limited intellect.

27. This flexible Beau Brummell with his dueling scars has the same name as the successful suitor of Anna Rainer in "Der Bajazzo." The name "joke-nail" characterizes him as well as the blond athlete, Dr Witznagel.

28. This word is a catalytic agent in all Thomas Mann's stories of the period, for Bajazzo first saw Anna Rainer, the future wife of Dr. Alfred Witznagel, on the Lerchenberg, the same place where Tobias bought his dog Esau.

29. This theme swells to major importance in "Gladius Dei." The passage Thomas Mann refers to is from *STD*, 61; *GW*, 8: 172–73.

30. "Oh, your wife is an artist, only an artist could have hit upon the idea!" (*STD*, 134). ("Ah, Ihre Frau Gemahlin ist eine Künstlerin, eine Künstlerin sage ich!" (*GW*, 8: 178).

31. Unfortunately the finesse of the high or low point is lost in the translation of the refrain, mainly due to the effort of rendering it in verse form. "*Ich bin Luischen*" (emphasis added), "is a statement of importance both to the speaker and to the addressee. When Jacobi pronounces these words, the realization of his situation becomes a real life-experience, causing his physical collapse, a public scandal, and the end to the pitiful Amra, Jacobi, Läutner triangle. Thomas Mann dramatized this statement in his Joseph novels: *Ich bins* (*GW*, 5: 1308) = "I am the one" becomes a Leitmotiv, starting when Joseph enters the prison after having overcome the temptation of Pohphar's wife, so expressing: "I am the one who trusts god." At the moment of his incarceration his miraculous ascent to the top of Pharao's empire starts and he is "the chosen one." He will be "the one" to help Israel to survive. "*Ich bins*" is recurs, from this "high-point" on, at each important scene when Joseph identifies himself. The way Thomas Mann turned the pitifully negative expression, this high/low-point of this early, hardly known short story into a powerfully affirmative humanistic self-appraisal in *Joseph*, more than thirty-five years later, is an essential detail illuminating Thomas Mann's intellectual growth. A literal translation is given here:

Original German:

Den Walzertanz und auch die Polke
Hat keine noch wie ich vollführt;
Ich bin Luischen aus dem Volke,
Die manches Mannerherz gerührt . . .

H. T. Lowe-Porter's translation:

I can polka until I am dizzy,
I can waltz with the best and beyond,
I'm the popular pet, little Lizzy,
Who makes all the menfolks so fond—

Literal translation (EHL):

To dance the waltz and also the polka
No one has yet executed as I do;
I am Luischen of the people
Who has moved the hearts of quite a few men—

The meaning of "*vollführt*," is reinforced by its position at the end of line two. No other word can be justified between "ich bin" and "Luischen," since this actually is the most basic statement of Thomas Mann's message. The dissonance of verse two builds up to the change of key in the word L U I S C H E N 's *I* sound; therefore the additional syllables and the additional *I* sounds erase the musical effect of the high point constructed by the author. See Glossary, s.v. "Vollführen."

32. Thomas Mann wrote to Grautoff 13 January 1897: "Happy? Ah, no, I am not happy, either; however, to the contrary, I am sufficiently irritated, gloomy and tired; . . ."

33. Letter to Grautoff 20 August 1897: "I myself had actually not believed that I ever could find the courage for such [an] undertaking" (EHL).

34. "When I started to write *Buddenbrooks* I was sitting in Rome, Via Torre Argentina trenta quattro 34, three flats high" (EHL) (*GW*, 10: 5).

35. "Der Kleiderschrank geschr. vom 23–29 Nov" (Third Notebook, 1898–99, p. 31). Torn pages were found in this notebook, obviously from another lost or destroyed notebook, with notes pertinent to the material of these stories. A list of possible story topics also is included here, of which only two themes were developed much later: "Gladius Dei" and "Wie Jappe und Do Escobar sich prügelten."

36. Bürgin-Meyer: 18–19: "1. Mai 1898 Erste Junggesellenwohnung: Theresien-straße 82. . . , bald umgezogen in die Barerstraße 69. . . November 1898 Neue Wohnung in der Marktstraße 5111 in Schwabing: Schilderung dieser Wohnung in der Novelle 'Der Kleiderschrank.'" Thomas Mann's one-and-a-half-year-old hunting dog left his household later this year. ("Titino" had moved to the mother's apartment in the Herzogstraße and belonged after this to Thomas younger brother Victor.) Mann commented, "I am glad to have my library all together once more and I feel as well as a poor neurasthenic can feel, within my four walls [with] my dog, my pictures, my grand piano and my violin" (EHL). Letter to Grautoff, 9 May 1898, from the There-sienstraße no. 82 apartment in Munich. On 14 May he refers to having read Knut Hamsun's *Mysterier*.

37. *Summary*: Van der Qualen wakes up at night on a train traveling from north to south. He leaves the train without knowing where he is. He arrives at a strange house where he rents a room, and during his stay a naked girl appears in the wardrobe of the room and they talk. The duration of this situation is as uncertain as the setting, and it is even uncertain whether it happened at all; van der Qualen might just have been dreaming as his train rushed south toward Rome. "All must remain [up] in the air . . ." are the last words of the story.

38. "*Qualen*" means "pain" and "suffering" in German.

39. Victor Mann has described his older brother's apartment as cheerful, with white walls partially covered with avocado green burlap and strawberry red chairs. The work table was also green; it held a flower-bedecked picture of Tolstoy and a heavy lamp, next to which lay the manuscript of *Buddenbrooks*. The apartment also held a rented piano with Thomas's violin case on it. Thomas had shown Victor and their mother the apartment, even the bedroom, on their first visit: "Thomas opened a quite ordinary wardrobe which belonged to the landlady and laughing, displayed the burlap which substituted for the missing back [of the cabinet]" (EHL) Mendelssohn, *Zauberer* 340.

40. This passage has, however, an unexpected turn which refers to van der Qualen's personal life rather than to the description: ". . . But each for himself, so things are arranged in life; and I stand here at this moment perfectly carefree, looking at you as might at a beetle that has fallen on its back" (*STD*, 71). ("Aber jeder für sich, so ist's eingerichtet, und ich, der ich in diesem Augenblicke ganz ohne Angst bin, stehe hier und sehe dir zu, wie einem Käfer, der auf den Rücken gefallen ist" *GW*, 8: 153). A more expressive translation would be: "and perfectly without fear," since *Angst* is a much stronger expression than "carefree."

41. The bright red of the luggage sharply cuts into the haze; similarly, the color of the painted chairs contrasts vividly with the shiny whipped-cream white of the room later in the story.

42. "'And I move with them,' he thought, 'and am as alone [and] as strange as probably no man has ever been before'" (*STD*, 73; *GW*, 8: 155). There is an obvious similarity to these lines from "Tobias Mindernickel": "What was the matter with this man, who was always alone and unhappy even beyond the common lot?" (*STD*, 52; *GW* 8: 142). They also recall Bajazzo's words: "The fact remained that my philosophic isolation disturbed me far too much" (*STD*, 39; *GW*, 8: 123).

43. This state of mind is not the same as the death wish of the count in "Der Tod."

44. ". . . I spent entire days squatting before the wicker chairs I had bought 'in the white' and painting them with red enamel" (SML, 15; *GW*, 11: 105). In *Story of My Life*, Thomas Mann points out the similarity between his own furniture at the Marktstraße in Schwabing and the pieces he carefully describes in "The Wardrobe."

45. "It is totally against my habit to drink before or during work. However, once during the long time while I was working principally in the forenoons, I wrote a novella in the evening, with the aid of cognac. One can recognize that in it [the novella]. . . . In general I do not think anything of 'inspiration' through alcohol. I do not believe in it, [and] that several great poets were drinkers does not prove anything" (EHL) (Thomas Mann, "Über den Alkohol," 1906, *GW*, 11: 718).

46. Thomas Mann uses "above the belt" (*"oberhalb des Gürtels"*) when writing to Grautoff in reference to the pain of the heart; in discussing sexual matters (*Geschlechtlichkeit*), he talks about "below the belt" (*"unter dem Gürtel"*).

47. Don Juan, the hero, a hotel guest, upon awakening to music is told that Mozart's opera *Don Juan* (usually known as *Don Giovanni*) will be presented near by. Delighted, he attends what he recognizes as an excellent performance. While the opera is still going on, Donna Anna, its female protagonist, visits the spectator in his loge, telling him the tragic secret of Don Juan's life. When he visits a restaurant after this experience, the guest realizes the public's lack of understanding of the "opera of all operas." In the second part of the story the protagonist sits alone with his writing equipment and a drink in the empty loge, pondering Donna Anna's words about herself and Don Juan. His Romantic search for the ultimate is corrupted by the intervention of the devil, and his striving becomes a reckless grasp at the sensual, endlessly unsatisfied. His disdain for common *Bürger* customs causes Don Juan's total isolation. Contaminated by his passion, the pure Donna Anna cannot save his soul. After his descent to Hell she refuses to marry her well-behaved but insignificant fiancé Ottavio; she asks for one year, but she will not live so long. Intoxicated by his drink and thoughts, the spectator believes he hears the voice of Donna Anna at 2:00 A.M. in the desolate locale. In the third part of the story the traveler learns the next day that the Italian singer who had played Donna Anna had died at 2:00 A.M. that morning.

48. *STD*, 75; *GW*, 8: 158. In E. T. A. Hoffmann's "Der goldene Topf" the presence of the beloved little snake Serpentina is repeatedly announced by a crystalline bell-like sound.

49. In E. T. A. Hoffman's "Der goldene Topf" the door of the Archivarius Lindhorst, for whom Anselm is to write fairy tales, is well guarded; it is the route to the world of imagination.

50. "Don Juan," in *E. T. A. Hoffmanns sämtliche Werke*, ed. Hannsludwig Geiger, 3 vols. (Berlin and Darmstadt: Tempel-Verlag, 1963), 1: 77.

51. ". . . charm to which the only answer is a sob" (*STD*, 76; *GW*, 8: 159).

52. E. T. A. Hoffmann's hotel guest is enriched by grasping the tragic secret of Don Juan and Donna Anna; his guiltless insight is his own aesthetic-sensual fulfillment, through sounds, colors and the beauty of the opera and Donna Anna. Only with the tragic Faustian figure of the brilliant reprobate Don Juan can van der Qualen be partially identified through his greedy desire for his lovely vision. Hoffmann follows Mozart's *Don Giovanni* closely, describing scenes, paraphrasing and evoking musical effects fictionally. Thomas Mann used this technique for the first time in explaining the effects in the "Little Lizzy" ("Luischen") song. He used it often again especially in "Tristan" and "Blood of the Walsungs" ("Wälsungenblut").

53. On 2 May 1943 Thomas Mann wrote to Alfred H. Unger about a planned English edition: "By the way, I could as well have recommended the story 'Der Kleiderschrank' ('The Wardrobe') for your anthology; yes, this little novella stands even literally higher than the other [he is talking about 'Das Wunderkind']." And

later, 22 January 1947, to Warner Angell: "I would suggest replacing these two short stories ['The Hungry,' 'Gladius Dei'] with 'The Wardrobe' and either 'At the Prophet's' or the Schiller study 'A Weary Hour.'. . . . This would be my choice if I had to decide."

54. This date is taken from Notebook 3, written in July 1899. First publication, *Die Gesellschaft* (Leipzig) 2, no. 15 (1899): 183.

55. In a letter to Kurt Martens, 4 August 1889, Thomas Mann wrote, "Don't think badly of me for what is to appear next in *Simplicissimus*. It is of little value, but until the novel is finished I must in one way or another keep myself in the public eye" (EHL).

56. "Der goldene Topf," a romantic story by E. T. A. Hoffmann, concerns Anselmus, who fell in love with the lovely little "snake" Serpentina. While copying stories for the Archivarius Lindhorst, Anselmus learns to recognize his real poetic vocation, and the fairy tale phenomena surrounding him gradually make sense, building a beautiful world at the end. Then Anselmus recognizes his dedication and marries Serpentina. The final message is: "Is Anselmus's happiness actually something other than life in poetry, where the sacred harmony of all beings is expressed as the deepest secret of nature?" (EHL) ("Der goldene Topf," in *E. T. A. Hoffmanns sämtliche Werke*, ed. Hannsludwig Geiger, 255).

57. *Summary*: A young humanist encounters Dunja Stegemann, an intellectual career woman several years his senior, and an unusual friendship develops between them. They enjoy an intimacy of the *Geist* the young man had believed impossible between opposite sexes. One night, after numerous glasses of wine, he suddenly tells her that he finds her physically repulsive. Under the cover of liberal intellectualism Dunja first does not react, then relates her past love affair. Shocked and confused, the young man loses control and propositions her. Cold and superior, Dunja refuses and leaves.

58. Late Victorian mores imposed very strict rules of social relations between the sexes. For a self-respecting woman to spend time in the dwelling of a man without a chaperon seriously compromised her reputation. If the visit was late in the evening and involved drinking and smoking, it obviously indicated the woman's moral laxity, men enjoying far more latitude in this respect. A man's usual means of proposing an immoral liaison was to invite the woman to his bachelor dwelling, and her acceptance of the invitation indicated capitulation. This form of socializing, even if held under the guise of "intellectual emancipation," ran counter to the era's general customs and the the young man's upbringing, and subconsciously pressured as well as stimulated him. Even though Mann makes no reference to this in the story, it is obvious that Dunja is at least emotionally a suffragette, an early advocate of woman's liberation.

59. The change from the formal to informal German address illustrates the shift in attitude from the admiring and respectful to the familiar, derogatory, and offensive. (*GW*, 8: 140).

60. See *SML*, 24–25; *GW*, 11: 111.

61. When Thomas Mann discussed the intimate problem in his letters to Grautoff, he used "Geschlechtlichkeit," the word in Schopenhauer's title of chapter 44, book 4, volume 2 of *The World as Will and Representation*, "The Metaphysics of Sexual Love" ("Metaphysik der Geschlechtlichkeit"), which he had read thoroughly at the time,

62. Thomas Mann's metaphysical vision, the *Weltbild* inspired by Schopenhauer's work, was later enriched by his growing experience of the art of Richard Wagner and the philosophical message of Nietzsche. Even though he had been acquainted with the works of both Wagner and Nietzsche prior to 1899, the reading of Schopenhauer's work in that year opened his mind markedly to the inspiration of philosophical thought. Mann had indeed mentioned Nietzsche's works and Wagner's music directly, as observed in the discussion of pre-1899 short fiction above. But these references

were autobiographical, not the expressions of deeply felt personal and *geistig* changes in him, as was his reading of Schopenhauer's *Weltbild*. He later commented, "Tonio Kröger says there is such a thing as being 'sick of knowledge.' The phrase quite accurately describes that sickness of my youth. If I remembered correctly, it played a large part in making me receptive to the philosophy of Schopenhauer, to which I came only after some acquaintance with Nietzsche. *That* was a spiritual experience of the absolutely first order and an unforgettable sort—whereas the Nietzsche experience was more intellectual and artistic" (*SML*, 24).

63. Surface "representation" (= *Vorstellung*) is a "rational objectivation" (*rationelle Objectiwierung*) of the "will to live" (*Wille zum Leben*). It appears as a mad world divided into countless individual apparitions: the *principium individuationis*, paradoxically the blind *Wille zum Leben*, is raging in each of them, making them devour each other (actually themselves, a self-cannibalism). The *Wille zum Leben* is the unintelligent instinctive power; the "thing-in-itself" (*das Ding an sich*). Universal "unity" is the metaphysical state of being of the "thing-in-itself," without objectivation in its natural form.

64. "Insight" is also "knowledge" (*Erkenntnis*), the geniuslike knowledge (*geniale Erkenntnis*), as opposed to rational objectivation. It frees the *Geist* from the imprisonment of the *Wille zum Leben* and permits the *Geist* to "know" the oneness of the universe.

65. "Art" (*aesthetische Erkenntis*) is aesthetic knowledge, a disinterested aesthetic reflection of beauty the "knowledge" of which can free the *Geist* from the rule of the *principium individuationis*. The arts reproduce beauty in the idea (representation); the highest of the arts is music, which actually can reach beyond the representation and reproduce the essence of the serene undivided universality.

66. The name of the author and the title of the book are not mentioned in *Buddenbrooks*, nor is Lübeck mentioned by name. Thomas Mann, however, accurately cited Schopenhauer's chapter 44 of book 4 in volume 2 of *Buddenbrooks*. Readers familiar with Novalis's German Romanticism might be tempted to relate the projected imagery in *Buddenbrooks* to those concepts, but Thomas Mann's concept and text are so close to Schopenhauer's chapter "On Death and Its Relation to the Indestructibility of Our Inner Nature" that the representations must be focused on Schopenhauer's ideological pattern. (Schopenhauer, *Die Welt als Wille und Vorstellung*, vol. 2, Supplement to bk. 4, chap. 41: "Über den Tod und sein Verhalten zur Unzerstörbarkeit unseres Wesens an sich.")

67. Such questions as whether an artist follows one or another system of philosophy—or even whether he has correctly understood or applied a particular philosophical system—are not particularly relevant as "classification" or "evaluation" of a writer. The study of the inspiration and influence of a philosophical system, or indeed of any cultural influence, however, is of the greatest interest in understanding serious literature.

> In this way artists often become "betrayers" of a philosophy, and thus was Schopenhauer "understood" by Wagner, when he put his erotic mystery play [*Tristan und Isolde*, left out in the translation] as it were under the protection of Schopenhauer's metaphysics. (*ETD*, 396; *GW*, 9: 561–62)

68. Nicholls, *Nietzsche*, 19.

69. This term reflects the influence of the metaphysical magic potion in Wagner's *Tristan*.

70. He wrote, "18 July 1900. the last line of *Buddenbrooks* written. The first chapters were reworked in the middle of August" (EHL). The MS was mailed 13 August 1900 to Fischer, who acknowledged its receipt on 15 August.

71. These aspects of Thomas Mann's Schopenhauer experience have not been discussed extensively, and thus "Schopenhauerian" characterics of his earlier work have been questioned. These are symptomatic phenomenological expressions of his conscious, but also and more certainly of his unconscious, reaction to a Schopenhauerian "destructive self-denial" which without the positive force of a unifying system endangered his motivation and his capacity for meaningful action. Close examination proves, however, that Thomas Mann's message had indeed changed considerably and that his thematic concern had moved from self-absorption to the observation of a universal self with objective, rather than subjective, reality.

72. Mendelssohn, *Zauberer*, 387, suggests an earlier date of composition for "The Way to the Churchyard," but he does not provide supporting references: "Other references indicate May, not August or September 1900; in September it [the story] was already printed" (EHL).

73. *Summary*: The plot is both simple and bizarre. The projected mood delivers the message, and each of the many details is vital. Lobgott Piepsam has become an alcoholic after losing his wife and children, and he has recently also lost his job as a copyist. Lonely and miserable, he now is going to visit the graves of his family. Suddenly a cyclist, referred to as "Life," passes him. Piepsam is annoyed and orders the cyclist off the road, but when he refuses to obey, Piepsam works himself into a fatal irate hysteria. The cyclist disappears and Piepsam's body is carried away.

74. The setting strongly resembles that of "Der Tod," in which behind the dwelling were cultivated fields, roads, and even a noisy delivery service, representing society. In front of the house was the moist green grass and the living, moving, powerful sea, which represented the unknown real powers of existence.

75. The German text personifies the two parallel roads, showing them acting out their purposes. This detail is highly significant, since other elements of the story, like the cyclist, are allegorically significant. Thomas Mann calls attention to his integral message through the subtle images which conceal a necessary inner significance. The entire panorama is vital—the roads, the houses, and the cemetery.

76. The little yellow dog, possibly a hunting dog, like Esau and Pepino, Thomas Mann's own dog, reminds us of Tobias Mindernickel and even Thomas Mann himself.

77. This arrogance is partially lost in the English text, which detracts from Thomas Mann's original intention, though not from the readability of the text.

78. Like Dr. Gudehus in "Der Tod," the man called Lobgott is neither a special servant of God nor particularly reverent. Both characters foolishly fail to understand the situations in which they are involved. Schopenhauer's calling religion "nonphilosophical" and Thomas Mann's placing the count's metaphysical fantasy in "Der Tod" "above" the doctor's scientifically limited views might suggest a denigrating use of God-related names.

79. Piepsam's frantic conduct is enhanced by the connotation of the name, which Henry Hatfield aptly describes as evocative of the futile chirping of a bird. Cited in Walter Langridge Robinson, "Name Characterization in the Works of Thomas Mann" (diss., Univ. of Texas, 1959), 52.

80. The only other personal name in this story is Mrs. Piepsam's maiden name, Lebzelt, literally "tent of life." Though she is never seen and is referred to only because of her death, Thomas Mann gave her a name reflecting life-giving power. Lebzelt is not a common German name, but its awkwardness is not disturbing.

81. Thomas Mann's emphasis on the word *wardrobe* (*Kleiderschrank*) in the German text refers to the earlier story. Thomas Mann "refrains from mentioning" the venomous liquor by name (presumably absinthe) in "The Wardrobe," "out of precaution" ("*aus Vorsicht*"), leaving the reader free to speculate on its nature. Such powerful liquor might represent uncontrollable sexuality as well as alcoholism, and its autobiographical significance suits the intellectual component of this period of Thomas

Mann's life. "But mine was essentially a metaphysical intoxication, closely related to a late and violent outbreak of sexuality (I am speaking of my twentieth year) and in its nature less philosophical than passionate and mystical" (*SML*, 25).

This story was written around the time of Thomas Mann's extensive reading of Schopenhauer's *Die Welt als Wille und Vorstellung*. The metaphysical "intoxication" that he mentions in the *Sketch of My Life* was genuinely significant to him then, and also the instinct or will, a Schopenhauerian concept of the propulsive force of the *Wille zum Leben*, emerges here. Once Piepsam's opportunity to procreate (and thus create his biological immortality) is gone with the death of Mrs. Piepsam (née Lebzelt), the *Wille zum Leben* turns its blind power toward self-destruction, here represented by Piepsam's alcoholism. Also, van der Qualen's "will to sexuality" estranges and even drives away the innocent beauty represented by the girl in the wardrobe. Both van der Qualen's girl and Piepsam's bottle are potentially highly explosive, but in the stories they are shown as perfectly static. It is the inner drive, the will, of the protagonists that impels them to action.

82. The English translation reflects neither the sound and rhythmic effect of the last lines nor the connotation of *Affentheater*—monkey theater.

83. Thomas Buddenbrook read Schopenhauer's work only once and tasted happiness, but by becoming frightened and confused he judged his *"Bürgerhirn"* to be too limited. *"Bürgerhirn"* was Thomas Mann's neologism, indicating a *Bürger*'s brain, thus rather limited. Because Thomas Buddenbrook felt his brain too weak to endure the power of the abstract message, he never faced the metaphysical experience again. The natural, instinctive power over him did not allow his intellect to overcome it, and an abscessed tooth struck him down, causing him to die ignobly, his face in a dirty mud puddle. (The dental images in "Der Tod" are relevant here.) But Thomas Buddenbrook had not been debased by a powerful drive; his only shortcoming was the lack of drive (Faustian *Streben*) to endure the superhuman experience.

84. Letter of 1 September to Grautoff: "I have nothing against riding and shooting. I hope that they still have openings" (EHL).

85. These were *Savonarola und seine Zeit*, by Pasquale Villari; *Kultur der Renaissance in Italien*, by Jacob Burckhardt; and Giorgio Vasari's *Lives of the most Eminent Painters and Architects*.

86. Mendelssohn, *Zauberer* 383: "Paul Ehrenberg's painting *Hetzjagd* hung for a longer time in Thomas Mann's workroom. . . . Thomas Mann's not too dominating sensitivity toward the visual arts remained surprisingly undeveloped and hence closed to [what was] new, and remained stagnant in the academically conventional. . . . During his lifetime he bought only a few pictures and they were not much more worth than a few nickels; but he thought since they pleased him they could not be all bad" (EHL).

87. Mendelssohn (ibid., 381) quotes from Carl Ehrenberg's diary: "Thomas Mann had probably inherited his love and talent for music from his mother, a good pianist. He played the violin quite nicely and proved to have a refined sensitivity, especially for the music of Richard Wagner, which I often had to play for him. This was probably what brought us especially close together" (EHL).

88. Earlier notes dating from Thomas Mann's schooldays repeatedly include the name of Armin Martens, whose tall, athletic, blond and blue-eyed good looks had been extremely attractive to him. Even after Martens left Lübeck to travel with an itinerant acting company, and was later reported to have died from alcoholism in Africa, Mann kept up his friendship with Martens's sister Ilse, who also moved from Lübeck to Munich and was a close friend of his sisters.

89. Mendelssohn, *Zauberer*, 385, sees Thomas Mann's interest in Paul Ehrenberg and Armin Martens as an indication of the lifelong attraction he felt toward the "blond and blue-eyed" physical type. Paul Ehrenberg's picture showed ". . . an unmistakable, even 'speaking' likeness to the picture of the youthful Armin Martens which was

[the picture] kept by his sister Ilse—no doubt: it was the same 'type'" (EHL). [German text omitted] The powerful magnetism of Hans Hansen on Tonio Kröger and of Pribislav Hippe upon Hans Castorp in *The Magic Mountain* reflects Mann's youthful experiences.

90. One much complaint was registered in the letter closest to this date, written to Heinrich 1 April 1901.

91. Some of the sources of inspiration Mann found there were the portrait of Savonarola in the Museo di San Marco, a clay bust of "Il Magnifico," and the portrait of Giovanna Tornabuoni by Domenico Ghirlandaio as the model for Fiore.

92. Since *Fiorenza* is not a short story but Thomas Mann's only drama, no detailed discussion of it is included here, but it rewards some attention because its topic and theme are closely related to Thomas Mann's experience of Schopenhauer's works, and also because until 1905 it reflects his prevailing emotional state.

93. *Summary*: Young Hieronymus lives in Munich, a city paradoxically and grotesquely reflecting the decadent Renaissance outlook of the Italian Golden Age, and there in an art shop he discovers a photograph which represents the Madonna and Child. He recognizes the model for the Madonna as the mistress of well-known artist, and he is shocked by the exposure the picture makes of her physical charms. He conceives of it as sacrilege, and a conversation he overhears between two bystanders impels him to believe he has heard a call from heaven to protest against this corruption by demanding that the shopkeeper remove the picture from the window and burn it. The brilliant satire and humor with which Thomas Mann describes the scene in the shop culminates in Hieronymus's exposition of his thesis on Art, Beauty, and Purity, given in four monologues of increasing emotional intensity. When the shop keeper tires of the harangue, he orders his handyman to "help" the young idealist out into the street, where he finds himself sitting in the dust envisioning God's sword of justice in the sky.

94. In the summer of 1492, the death of Pope Innocent VIII fulfilled Savonarola's prediction, and his spiritual message was at its height. The election of Cardinal Borgia to the papacy intensified popular devotion to Savonarola and popular fear of God's wrathful retribution for their sins, and as he preached, Savonarola became increasingly inflamed with mystic passion. During one such sermon, Savonarola had a vision of a hand bearing a sword in the heavens, with the words "*Gladius Domini supra terram cito et velociter*," accompanied by voices proclaiming God's wrath on the sinful and mercy to the faithful. In his vision, the sword bent down toward the earth, while the sky darkened and lightning flashed, destroying the earth. His contemporaries engraved Savonarola's vision and Latin words into medals, coins, and pieces of art, and it became the symbol of his message. Following the vision, his enemies exiled Savonarola because they feared his power, causing him to go to Prato and then Bologna, where he delivered sermons to fervent crowds. He was nearly put to death in Bologna, when he chided the wife of Bentivoglio, a leading official, for disturbing his sermon. Men were hired to assassinate him, but according to popular belief they fled when he addressed them.

95. During his whole life, Savonarola had denounced religious abuses and the Medici family, and he had predicted God's wrathful destruction of sinful humanity. For a short time his preaching succeeded in changing pleasure-loving Florence, causing the citizens to abjure worldly vanities and follow the path of asceticism. In 1496 Savonarola arranged a "carnival" to praise God through song and dance, and the next year this festival culminated in the burning of allegedly indecent books, pictures, and art objects in the Piazza della Signoria.

96. Savonarola was enchanted by Florence's beauty when he was transferred by his order to San Marco in 1482. But he soon realized with holy horror that religion had died in the hearts of the polished and cultured citizens of Lorenzo di Medici's city. The

streets rang with Lorenzo's bawdy songs, the sensual *canti carnascialieschi*. Thomas Mann, increasingly aware of the emotional and sensual effect of Wagner's music on himself, seems to be drawing a strong parallel between his own experience and Savonarola's.

97. Arthur Schopenhauer, *The World as Will and Representation*, trans. E. F. J. Payne (New York: Dover, 1889), 3: 45, 51. Schopenhauer's concept of art represents the metaphysics of "insight" (*Erkenntnis*) of the representation of the will. Music, not treated here, is the only one of the arts directly reflecting the "insight" (*Erkenntnis*) without its rationalized representation. The corruption of the visual arts by rationalization serving the list of will and pragmatic ends is the subject of this story.

98. The name "Hieronymus" belonged to two noted theologians whose lives resembled Savonarola's, and hence the strange name suits Mann's protagonist perfectly.

99. In *Bild und Text bei Thomas Mann: Eine Dokumentation*, ed. Hans Wysling (Bern/Munich: Francke Verlag, 1975), material is published on the pictures, documents, and art work Thomas Mann had studied or owned, providing a visual idea of the impressions he had as he wrote. The description of Hieronymus the hero corresponds with a reproduction he owned, now part of the collection of the Thomas Mann Archives in Zurich. The original of the picture is known as *Ritratto di Fra Girolamo Savonarola* by Fra Bartolommeo, now in Florence in the Museo di San Marco.

100. This double standard is not suggested in the description of Hieronymus but is clearly present in *Fiorenza*, where a fictional input into the Prior's past suggests that he had fled to the monastery of the Dominicans to overcome the torment of his rejected love for the girl who is later Fiore, Il Magnifico's mistress (and the symbol of the town of Florence). It also might suggest Thomas Mann's own relations to women—even his last involvement. Even though Mary Smith seemed to return his attention, his 7 May 1901 letters to Heinrich reveal a shy feeling of inferiority: ". . . but now I think I am getting too melancholy. She is so very clever, and I am so stupid to love always the ones who are clever, even though I cannot be with them in the long run" Mendelssohn suggest that the following note in Thomas Mann's notebook refers to his relationship to Paul Ehrenberg: "You came so full of life; this made me shy, this turned me suddenly desperate and made me mute for a full hour, unlikable and hopeless. I cannot be a part of it" (EHL) (422).

101. *The World as Will and Representation*, vol. 3, part 45, pp. 222, 225. Schopenhauer also refers to beauty and nudity in a manner that it employs in to the story: "Because beauty with grace is the principal subject of sculpture it likes the nude, and tolerates clothing only in so far as this does not conceal the form. This method of presentation greatly engrosses the understanding, since the understanding reaches the perception of the cause, namely the form of the body, only through the one directly given effect, that is to say, the arrangement of the drapery" (Schopenhauer/Schlechta, vol. 3, part 47, p. 229).

102. In both "Gefallen" and "Der Wille zum Glück" Thomas Mann used thunder and lightning, as well as references to Goethe's *Sorrows of Young Werther* to highlight critical moods. Also, Savonarola's history has a pertinent detail: it is believed that when he was about to be executed by hanging and then burning, a sudden thunderstorm unexpectedly forced a stay of execution, which his followers, the *Piagnori*, thought to be a miracle. Since the fall of 1900 Thomas Mann had been studying Villari's biography of Savonarola, which contains an account of a sudden strong wind blowing smoke away from the bodies of the three friars, briefly halting their immolation. The recurrent motif of the thunderstorm and sudden wind might also suggest God's wrath at the immorality of the city and/or the innocence of the executed man.

103. The following quotations from Schopenhauer supply an idea that motivated Thomas Mann's argumentation: "Whereas in the first book we were reluctantly forced to declare our own body to be mere representation of the knowing subject, like all the

other objects of this world of perception, it has now become clear to us that something in the consciousness of everyone distinguishes the representation of his own body from all the others that are in other respects quite like it. This is that the body occurs in consciousness in quite another way, *toto genere* different, that is denoted by the word *will*. It is just this double knowledge of our own body which gives us information about that body itself, about its action and movement following on motives, as well as about its suffering through outside impressions, in a word, about what it is, not as representation, but as something over and above this, and hence what it is *in itself*. We do not have such immediate information about the nature, action, and suffering of any other real objects" (vol, 1, bk. 2/19, p. 103). "Thus, although every particular action, under the presupposition of the definite character, necessarily ensues with the presented motive, and although growth, the process of nourishment, and all the changes in the animal body take place according to necessarily acting causes (stimuli), the whole series of actions, and consequently every individual act and likewise its condition, namely the whole body itself which performs it, and therefore also the process through which and in which the body exists, are nothing but the phenomenal appearance of the will, its becoming visible, the *objectivity of the will*." "Phenomenon means representation and nothing more. All representation, be it of whatever kind it may, all *object*, is *phenomenon*. But only the *will* is *thing-in-itself*; as such it is not representation at all, but *toto genere* different therefrom. It is that of which all representation, all object, is the phenomenon, the visibility, the *objectivity*. It is the innermost essence, the kernel, of every particular thing and also of the whole. It appears in every blindly acting force of nature, and also in the deliberate conduct of man, and the great difference between the two concerns only the degree of the manifestation, not the inner nature of what is manifested" (vol. 1, bk 2/21, pp. 108–10).

104. "It follows from all that has been said, that the denial of the *Wille zum Leben*, which is the same as what is called complete resignation or holiness, always proceeds from that quieter of the will; and this is the knowledge of its inner conflict and its essential vanity, expressing themselves in the suffering of all that lives. The difference, that we have described as two paths, is whether that knowledge is called forth by suffering which is merely and simply *known* and freely appropriated by our seeing through the *principium individuationis*, or by suffering immediately felt by ourselves. True salvation, deliverance from life and suffering, cannot even be imagined without complete denial of the will" (vol. 1, bk. 4/68, pp. 397–98). "On the other hand, all true and pure affection, and even all free justice, result from seeing through the *principium individuationis*; when this penetration occurs in all its force, it produces perfect sanctification and salvation, the phenomena of which are the state of resignation previously described, the unshakable peace accompanying this, and the highest joy and delight in death." (There is no reason not to render the German Liebe as the English *love*, rather than *affection*. EHL.) (vol. 1, bk. 4/68, pp. 438–39).

105. Robinson, "Names," 68. "The name Krauthuber is a South German equivalent to the Lübeck names Carl Smolt or Krischan Smut. It conveys the idea of brutality and stupidity, *huber* suggesting a heaver or lifter of heavy weights." One could reconstruct the name in translation as "the lifter of cabbage."

106. Thomas Mann's play *Fiorenza* shares this definition of art.

107. The roles of the two protagonists of *Fiorenza*, Savonarola and Lorenzo de' Medici, are similar: each relates to art in his own way.

108. The date Thomas Mann gave in the *Sketch of My Life* is considered incorrect.

109. Even then the play did not incorporate the spark of life essential to a work of art; its chief value is its revelation of Thomas Mann's thoughts at that time. *Fiorenza* stabilized Thomas Mann's research, and even though its long dialogues often make for feeble drama, they still validly pave the way for later, more meaningful, artistic expressions, like "Tonio Kröger."

110. Mitterbad is located in the Ulten Valley near Meran.
111. Mendelssohn, *Zauberer*, 444–45. Mendelssohn suggests the possibility that Thomas Mann relied on Heinrich's letters. Bürgin (24) states that Thomas Mann was back in Munich in June of 1901, and that the short story "Tristan" was finished then.
112. *Summary*: The setting is "Einfried," a sanatorium in the mountains, where patients come to recuperate from various illnesses. It is supervised by Dr. Leander and his assistant Dr. Muller. The protagonists are Mr. and Mrs. Klöterjahn and the writer Detlev Spinell. Mr Klöterjahn is a wealthy businessman who has brought his wife Gabriele to Einfried because of an undefined illness, and she has been forbidden to exert herself, especially by playing the piano, since emotional effort might prove fatal. Spinell and Mrs. Klöterjahn become friends, and one day when most of the other patients have gone on an excursion, Spinell persuades her to play the piano, climaxing in an impromptu performance of Wagner's *Tristan und Isolde* in piano transcription. A few days later, her husband and child are called to her deathbed. Spinell accepts an esoteric reason for her decline and writes an overwrought letter to Klöterjahn, who misses its point completely and is infuriated at Spinell's trespassing. While Gabriele is dying, Spinell comes upon the Klöterjahn infant, preternaturally full of health, and recognizing the infant's overwhelming "will to live" (*Wille zum Leben*), Spinell flees from the scene.
113. In 1854, around the time Wagner sent Schopenhauer the libretto of the first two operas of The Ring of the Nibelung, *Rheingold* and *Walküre*, in acknowledgment of his influence, Wagner met Otto and Mathilde Wesendonck. They became close friends, and in 1857 Otto Wesendonck invited the Wagners to a house close to his villa, the *Asyl*, on the outskirts of Zurich. The Wagner residence, *Grüne Hügel* (Green Hill), was not far from Kilchberg where, among other distinguished Germans, Thomas Mann also would one day stay. Wagner developed a romantic attachment to the beautiful Mathilde Wesendonck, which was ended by the good-natured reaction of Otto Wesendonck and the emotional protest of Minna Wagner, and the Wagners departed from Green Hill. The memory of Wagner's love, however, was immortalized in the "Wesendonck Lieder" and his opera *Tristan und Isolde*.
114. In the fall of 1854, Wagner wrote to Franz Liszt: "It is Arthur Schopenhauer, the greatest philosopher since Kant, whose thoughts—this is the way he expresses himself—he had thought out to the very end. . . . His main idea, the final denial of the *Wille zum Leben*, is frighteningly severe, but wholly redeeming. . . . When I think back to the storms in my heart, the horrible spasm in which it [my heart] clenched to the hope of life, yes, when it even now swells into a hurricane, then I have found only one calmative which helps me to sleep at last in my wakeful nights; it is the hearty and deep longing for death: the complete lack of sensation, total nonexistence, the disappearance of all dreams—the only final redemption!" (EHL).
Later, the Schopenhauerian concept Wagner expressed developed in the ten years he worked on *Tristan und Isolde* into a transcendental concept, influenced by German Romanticism, in which a limitless bliss of flawless and absolute union of the lovers is achieved in the "Love-Death" (*Liebestod*). A comparison with Thomas Buddenbrook's "Death Vision" and its powerfully positive attitude displays the conceptual differences. This illustrates Thomas Mann's own representation of Death, *overcoming* petty limitations and independent love, but represented as a metaphysical vision, in itself a vigorous means of affirming (*bejahen*) all phases of a transcendentally balanced *Weltbild*.
115. This is in accordance with Schopenhauer's, Nietzsche's, and Wagner's views, and was readily acknowledged by Thomas Mann.
116. *Erkenntnis* has a a special connotation in Schopenhauer. The expression is most frequently translated into English as "knowledge" or "insight." The German expression used above emphasizes the implied significance. Here "insight" will be used.

117. Interpretations that stress the *"Burleske"* by focusing on "Tristan" as a traves-ty of Wagner's *Tristan und Isolde* are perfectly acceptable, because they represent the perspective of those who are incapable of the experience of Art; instead of contradict-ing the philosophical interpretation, they rather refer to Thomas Mann's presentation of "Tristan." Northcote-Bade's interpretation is a notable example of this line of thought.

118. This discussion follows the structural division of the original text, which the English translation does not observe, a twelve-part division with section eight con-siderably longer than the rest and situated roughly in the middle of the story. Seven shorter sections serve as the introduction and four somewhat longer ones form the conclusion. Both the climax and the turning point of the plot appear in the eighth section, the only one that contains reference to Wagner's *Tristan und Isolde*, the key to both the story's action and its theme. In his essay "Schopenhauer" (*GW*, 9: 536–37), Mann refers to Plato and Kant, paralleling the *Diesseits* with the "immanent" and the *Jenseits* with the "transcendent," the "immanent" being the empiric, and the "trans-cendent" the intrinsic way of perceiving the world.

119. In Thomas Mann's essay "Schopenhauer," he observed "that one can think in the spirit of a philosopher without following his message in the least; that one can make into one's own his thoughts in a fashion in which he absolutely would not have wanted them to be taken" (EHL) (*GW*, 9: 261).

120. Such tranquillity possibly suggests the Schopenhauerian concept of ultimate unity (*ein*) and the peace (*fried*) after the insight, *Einsicht* or *Erkenntnis*, in contrast to the *principium individuationis*.

121. The literal translation emphasizes Thomas Mann's message (*STD*, 133; *GW*, 8: 216).

122. In "Tristan" Thomas Mann does not emphasize the mountain imagery, even though the loftiness of the drama in this setting is obvious. This reference and numer-ous other motifs in this story develop into major themes in *The Magic Mountain*.

123. Thomas Mann later crystallized the many characteristics of Dr. Leander's appearance and personality into two well-rounded figures of *The Magic Mountain*, Dr. Behrens and Dr. Krokowski. Dr. Behrens's leading characteristic is his service to science, while the tendency to dominate the minds of others and the diabolic black pointed beard are Dr. Krokowski's characteristics.

124. Thomas Mann's impressions of Mitterbad, which he visited in July 1901, may have merged with those he received during his visit to his wife Katia, then ill with bronchitis, at Davos in 1911. Certain similarities do exist between the Einfried of "Tristan" and the sanatorium of Mann's *The Magic Mountain*, completed in 1924. No indications whatsoever exist that he was planning a "sanatorium" novel in 1901 or that he consciously used material from "Tristan" when he wrote *The Magic Mountain*.

125. The English version of the standard translation is incomplete (*GW*, 8: 217).

126. *STD*, 135. "Langsam, Gabriele, *take care* [in English], mein Engel, und halte den Mund zu" (*GW*, 8: 218). A reference to Thomas Mann's earlier notes from Florence indicates that the expression "my angel" demonstrates his associations with Mary Smith. Klöterjahn in "Tristan" repeatedly calls his wife his "angel." His English expression is another manifestation of his English snobbery; he is wearing English tweeds and eats an English breakfast with the English family. There are repeated references to Gabriele as an angel (see "Archangel," "Archangel Gabriel," and "Angelus"). In his Schopenhauer essay Thomas Mann wrote: "Man is the potential redeemer of nature. The mystic Angelus Silesius says: 'O man, all living love thee; there is much press about thee, / All run to thee that they may reach their God'" (*ETD*, 392)

127. The connotations and sound of the name "Klöterjahn" all indicate crude clumsiness. The parts of the compound have a long and varied history in German: In

the Middle High German "*kluter*" means the modern German *locken*, to attract or allure; and "*Kluter*" is often compounded with a noun as in "*Kluterspil*" (*Lockspiel*) or "*Kluterwort*" (*verlockendes Wort*) (Oskar Schade, "Kluter," *Altdeutsches Wörterbuch*, 1969 ed., 2 vols., 500). Other meanings include "*Kluter*" (*Fleck*, Schmutz) and "*Kluterwort*" (*wertlos Wort*) used as a noun: *Kluterie* means *Gauklei* or *Täuschung* (Matthias Lexer, "Kluter," *Mittelhochdeutsches Handwörterbuch*, vol. 1 [Leipzig, n.d.], 1872 ed., p. 1641). Jan or Ian is a diminutive of Johann, or John in Scandinavian, or Jahn or Johan in low German dialect. All of the foregoing proves that Thomas Mann intended to pack all the grotesque connotations possible into a name fitting Mr. Klöterjahn but not his wife.

128. The English translation "frosty air" (*STD*, 135), omits the significant reference to "stillness"; "*in der stillen Frostluft*" (*GW*, 8: 218).

129. "Hinzpeter," the ludicrous name of the Klöterjahn's doctor at home, emphasizes his incapability to grasp the patient's real ailment. "Hinz" is the nickname for "Heinrich," and also is seen in combination with "Kunz." "*Hinz und Kunz*" means "everyman," or "as good as another." It sometimes has the connotation of "keeping up with the Joneses." Combining it with "Peter" provides a humorous connotation, pointing up the man's ordinariness. This recalls Thomas Mann's treatment of Dr. Gudehus in "Der Tod."

130. Viewed from this angle, it might be argued that Mrs. Klöterjahn has lost her equilibrium with respect to the *Wille zum Leben*, but that she was not "contaminated" by insight (via music) and therefore was not necessarily taken fatally from the domination of the *Wille zum Leben*. Losing this equilibrium had been the result of her marrying Mr. Klöterjahn and giving birth to his son. At her death following her piano performance, however, there is no doubt that she is suffering from tuberculosis.

131. The little blue vein is a typical feature of some of Thomas Mann's characters. Gerda Buddenbrook and her son Hanno, both musicians, had a "blue shadow" at the corner of an eye.

132. Schopenhauer writes in his *World as Will and Representation*, vol. 2, bk. 4, chap. 44, "Metaphysics of Sexual Love," 652–53: "The man's love diminishes perceptibly from the moment it has obtained satisfaction; almost every other woman charm him more than the one he already possesses; he longs for variety. On the other hand, the woman's love increases from that very moment. . . . The man, therefore, always looks around for other women. . . . The second consideration is *health*; acute diseases disturb us only temporarily, chronic diseases, or even cachexia, repel us, because they are transmitted to the child" (*Die Welt als Wille und Vorstellung*, vol. 2, bk. 4, chap. 44, p. 1118). Indeed, Klöterjahn seems attached to his wife throughout the story, but he is even more attracted to his business and his everyday life. His assignation with the chambermaid is probably of no emotional importance to him, but it clearly illustrates how much he is ruled by instinct. It also represents Schopenhauer's concept of sexual attraction.

133. Robinson "*Names*," 54–55. ". . . Dr. D. W. Schumann illuminates the significance of Dr. Leander's insistence that the name is *Spinell* rather than *Spinell* by pointing out that a person coming from Lemberg and bearing a name of a mineral would quite clearly be a Jew and that the first name, Detlev, a North German name with 'grass roots' quality, is most incongruous and obviously an adopted name. Mann carefully avoids mentioning Spinell's name at first, but refers to a writer, 'ein exzentrischer Mensch, der den Namen irgendeines Minerals oder Edelsteines führt.' When he finally does introduce the name, it is with special emphasis "Spinell hieß der Schriftsteller . . ., Detlev Spinell war sein Name, und sein Äußeres war underlich." Thus once again Mann has given a strangely incongruous name to an artist." The same incongruity will be noted in the names *Tonio Kröger, François Knaak, Raoul Überbein, Adrian Leverkühn*, and other names in Mann's subsequent works. It has already been noted in the case of Paolo Hofmann.

134. Schopenhauer, *The World as Will and Representation*, vol. 1, bk. 2, pp. 112; vol. 1, bk. 3, p. 257. "The *will* as thing-in-itself is quite different from its phenomenon, and is entirely free from all the forms of the phenomenon into which it first passes when it appears, and which therefore concern only its *objectivity*, and are foreign to the will itself." "The [Platonic] Ideas are the adequate objectivation of the will. To stimulate the knowledge of these by depicting individual things (for works of art are themselves always such) is the aim of all the other arts (and is possible with a corresponding change in the knowing subject). Hence all of them objectify the will only indirectly, in other words, by means of the Ideas" (*Die Welt als Wille und Vorstellung*, vol. 1, bk. 2, p. 143; vol. 1, bk. 2, pp. 292–93).

135. Thomas Mann's Schopenhauer essay, *ETD*, 380. (*GW*, 9: 539–40).

136. "For him the veil of Maya had become transparent and the great deception had left him" (EHL). "Ihm ist der Schleier der Maja durchsichtig geworden die große Täuschung hat ihn verlassen" (*GW*, 9: 554). This is a static peaceful existence as close as possible to the concept of happiness.

137. *ETD*, 384. "'Beautiful,' Kant had declared, 'is what happens without *interest.*' Without interest. That, for Schopenhauer, and rightly, meant without reference to the will" (*GW*, 9: 545).

138. *The World as Will and Representation*, vol. 1, bk. 3, chap. 52, pp. 257–58. "As our world is nothing but the phenomenon or appearance of the Ideas in plurality through entrance into the *principium individuationis* (the form of knowledge possible to the individual as such), music, since it passes over the Ideas, is also quite independent of the phenomenal world, positively ignores it, and, to a certain extent, could still exist even if there were no world at all, which cannot be said of the other arts. Thus music is *immediate* and objectivation and copy of the whole *will* as the world itself is, indeed as the Ideas are, the multiplied phenomenon of which constitutes the world of individual things. Therefore music is by no means like the other arts, namely a copy of the Ideas, but *a copy of the will by itself*, the objectivity of which are the Ideas. For this reason the effect of music is so very much more powerful and penetrating than is that of the other arts, for these others speak only of the shadow, but music of the essence. However, as it is the same will that objectifies itself both in the Ideas and in music, though in quite a different way in each, there must be, not indeed an absolutely direct likeness, but yet a parallel, an analogy, between music and the Ideas, the phenomenon of which in plurality and in incompleteness is the visible world. The demonstration of this analogy will make easier, as an illustration, an understanding of this explanation, which is difficult because of the obscurity of the subject."

139. At the time of "Tristan," *Buddenbrooks* was being printed for publication at the end of the next season. Young Thomas Mann then felt satisfied with his work, at one with the "artists"; but he also felt a sense of emptiness after his prolonged efforts, and he repeatedly expressed fears that this might be the "one and only" novel that he would write.

140. (*ETD*, 386) (*GW*, 9: 547).

141. ". . . That he does nothing of all that he would like to do, and does all that he does not like to do" (*ETD*, 392) (*GW*, 9: 555). This victory is defined as the achievement of the act, free from the *Wille zum Leben*, overcoming its blind power. It is also conceivable as the highest insight of truth against the falsity of the *principium individuationis*, or as the simile of the falling of the veil of Maya.

142. Friedrich Nietzsche, *Thus Spoke Zarathustra*, trans. Walter Kaufmann (New York: Viking, 1954), part 2, chap. 12, pp. 113ff. "'Will to truth,' you who are wisest call that which impels you and fills you with lust? A will to the thinkability of all beings: this *I* call your will. You want to *make* all being thinkable, for you doubt with well-founded suspicion that it is already thinkable" (*Thus Spoke Zarathustra*, 113). The theme of this chapter is: "And life itself confided this secret to me: 'Behold,' it said, 'I am that which must always overcome self'" (115).

143. An attempt to separate Nietzschean concepts from Schopenhauerian is not germane here. Neither Friedemann nor "Bajazzo" could achieve even clownish heroism since neither considered fighting his weaknesses, but glided into self-pitying disgust and despair. The treatment in "Tristan" represents Thomas Mann's deepest personal and intellectual bond with Nietzsche, the unconscious urge he had to overcome himself. This inclination gradually formed a positive rather than a negative conception of the Schopenhauerian *Weltbild* for him.

144. Mann's lines in "Tristan" interestingly compare with his personal writings: "A kind of decorum, a hygienic regimen, for instance, becomes a necessity for some of us. To get up early, to get up ghastly early, take a cold bath, and go out walking in a snowstorm" (*STD*, 142). (The German text refers to snow, not snowstorm.) (*GW*, 8: 229). In a letter to Grautoff, 20 Jan. 1895, he wrote, "I have lately developed almost into an ascetic. In my beautiful hours I rave about aesthetic sensuality, the sensuality of the *Geist*, the *Geist*, the soul and the mood in general" (EHL).

145. Her "insight" or *Erkenntnis* might also be called "genius," meaning a metaphysical perception of an intuitive and a priori nature, reaching beyond the imitation of the *principium individuationis* toward a vision of peaceful unity.

146. Such prohibition of musical self-expression comes directly from the tradition of the German *Märchen*, acquiring a special significance since the publication of E. T. A. Hoffmann's fantastic short story "Rat Krespel," revived in Offenbach's opera *The Tales of Hoffmann*. The similarities between the plot and imagery of "Tristan" and those of "Rat Krespel" are the more suggestive because Thomas Mann was deeply attracted to Hoffmann's works. Hoffmann presented his themes with a combination of the realistic and the fantastic, a combination that helped Thomas Mann greatly to achieve his "dual vision" (*doppelte Optik*) in "Tristan." Gabriele Klöterjahn especially parallels Hoffmann's Antonia because both young women are barred from performing music at the risk of their lives. The connection of music with death is not new, nor is the suggestion that the violinist in particular has an affinity with the demonic. How far the Mephistophelean element should be speculated upon in the Hoffmann-derived material or in the interpretation of Mann's "Tristan" is debatable, but certainly the motifs of death and the prohibition of music are related to concepts in "Rat Krespel." The notion of "seduction by music" may also involve an Old Testament allusion to the forbidden "Tree of Knowledge," or, as here, "Insight." Other similar motifs in the two works are the father-daughter relationships; the glowing red spot on Antonia's cheek when she sings, which recalls the blue vein on Gabriele's forehead; and the emphasis on the "ugly" names "Krespel" and "Klöterjahn."

147. This represents the creation of a "world representation" ("*Vorstellung*") of his own, the reality of which cannot be proved with ordinary pragmatic or logical arguments.

148. *Wollen* is the infinitive form of "to *want*" or "to *wish for*." *Der Wille* is the German equal of *the Will*. In the German text, *wollte* is italicized, although italics do not appears in the English translation (*STD*). The repetition of "will," so highly significant, does not appear in the English translation (*STD*).

149. Schopenhauer, *The World as Will and Representation*. "Diese letztere bestätigt meinen Satz, daß der Intellekt so gut wie Klauen und Zähne nichts anderes als ein Werkzeug zum Dienst des Willens ist" (*Die Welt als Wille und Vorstellung*, vol. 2, supplement to bk. 3, chap. 31, p. 241).

150. Ibid., vol. 2, supp. to bk. 4, chap. 48, pp. 604–5. "It represents the guilt not as being established simply by existence itself, but as arising through the act of the first human couple. This was possible only under the fiction of a *liberum arbitrium indifferentiae*, and was necessary only on account of the Jewish fundamental dogma, into which that doctrine was here to be implanted. . . . Therefore Augustine taught in his books *De Libero Arbitrio* that only Adam before the Fall was man guiltless and had a

free will, whereas for ever after he is involved in the necessity of sin. . . . But of course Jewish theism, on to which the myth was grafted, must have received marvelous additions in order to attach itself to that myth. Here the fable of the Fall presented the only place for the graft of the old Indian stem. It is to be ascribed just to this forcibly surmounted difficulty that the Christian mysteries have obtained an appearance so strange and opposed to common sense. Such an appearance makes proselytizing more difficult; on this account and from an inability to grasp their profound meaning, Pelagianism, or present-day rationalism, rises up against them, and tries to explain them away by exegesis, but in this way it reduces Christianity to Judaism (pp. 1180–81).

151. "Und nun heißen Sie nicht mehr Eckhof, sondern anders, und haben den kleinen gesunden Anton und leiden ein wenig an der Luftröhre" (*GW*, 8: 236). In choosing Klöterjahn and bearing his child, Gabriele's vital balance was disrupted. She had given all her physical strength to the service of the *Wille zum Leben*, leaving herself debilitated, and the diagnosis of her ailment cleverly indicates her progress toward insight. At the moment she begins to play the piano, her life reaches its turning point, after which she will be able to overcome the *Wille zum Leben*; at this point in the story, Spinell's comment is a little enigmatic, but it proves that he has had his own clear insight of his *"Vorstellung"* all along.

152. Käte Hamburger has commented, "Before, all the romantic form of the process of death in Thomas Mann emerges very clearly through the phenomenon of illness, which is an important element of his art and is in close relation to the phenomenon of death in his works. But illness had been made a subject of philosophical inquiry at first by the Romantics, especially Novalis" (EHL). Käte Hamburger, *Thomas Mann und die Romantik, eine problemgeschichtliche Studie* (Berlin: Junker und Sunnhaupte Verlag, 1932), 63. Fiction does not present a more shocking opposition than the robustness of Klöterjahn and the stillness of Gabriele.

153. German Romanticism has been considered a Neoplatonic intellectual and spiritual movement demanding complete dedication and becoming a way of life (*Lebensweise*). Numerous followers of the German Romantic school did convert to Roman Catholicism, attracted to the mystic medieval charm of Gothic cathedrals, cloisters, and religious chants, as opposed to the established church of that time. The Platonism and the fervent insight of St. Augustine's *"unio mystica"* had far more appeal for the German Romantics than did the Aristotelianism of Thomas Aquinas.

154. Schopenhauer designates the everlasting human substance left after the body has been integrated into nature as its biological survival in the species in vol. 2, supplement to book 4 of *Die Welt als Wille und Vorstellung*, chap. 44, "Metaphysik der Geschlechtsliebe" (The Metaphysics of Sexual Love).

155. Richard Wagner, "Zukunftsmusik," in *Richard Wagner: Sämtliche Schriften und Dichtungen* (Leipzig: n.p., n.d.), 123.

156. Thomas Mann's knowledge of and feeling for music is well illustrated in the choice of selections Gabriele plays. She plays a Chopin nocturne first, presumably to warm up—the lyric nocturne op. 9, no. 2, with one solo voice. It breaks down the tension of indecision, twilight, and the presence of *Rätin* Spatz. Gabriele then plays two more nocturnes of more complicated structure, the latter possibly with two voices. Only then does Spinell discover the Wagnerian transcription. Technically such transcriptions are extemely demanding, and a performance would have exhausted Gabriele both intellectually and physically, since she had not been practicing regularly and she was playing an unfamiliar instrument. Gabriele not only breaks her doctor's rules in yielding to Spinell's wishes, but by increasing both her physical and *geistig* effort, she comes to exemplify Schopenhauer's concept of *Erkenntnis* and the overcoming of the *principium individuationis* (see Schopenhauer, *The World as Will and Representation*, vol. 1, bk. 4, chap. 68).

157. (*STD*, 153; *GW*, 8: 244). Also compare the reference to music to Antonia's

song in E. T. A. Hoffmann's "Rat Krespel." The motif of stillness as a foreshadowing of the ultimate quietude of death recurs significantly here. Schopenhauer says: "On the other hand, all true and pure affection, and even all free justice, result from seeing through the *principium individuationis*; when this penetration occurs in all its force, it produces perfect sanctification and salvation, the phenomenon of which is the state of resignation previously described, the unshakable peace accompanying this, and the highest joy and delight in death" (vol. 1, bk. 4, chap. 68, p. 398).

158. In Schopenhauerian terms, this is the separation caused by the *principium individuationis* counteracted by the magic potion. Tristan and Isolde cannot overcome the separation because of the veil of Maya that blinds their *Erkenntnis*.

159. In "Tristan," Thomas Mann handles the insensitivity of *Rätin* Spatz to Gabriele's Wagner performance with biting satire, similar to his "burlesque" treatment of the male Klöterjahns. This satire is thus intended for the representatives of the *Wille zum Leben*. The two music lovers are left alone together in the drawing room, just barely illuminated by the flickering candles at the piano.

160. *STD*, 154 (*GW*, 8: 245). The English passage reads: "Ah, boundless, unquenchable exultation of union in the eternal beyond! Freed from torturing error, escaped from fettering space and time, the Thou and the I, the Thine and the Mine at one forever in a sublimity of bliss!"

A literal rendering, however inaesthetic, of the climax is helpful: "Ah, overabundant and insatiable rejoicing of the union in the eternal beyond (hereafter) of things! Freed of torturing error, having escaped from fettering Time and Space, the Thou and the I, the Thine and the Mine are fused into sublime ecstasy" (EHL).

161. The potion actually undoes the *principium individuationis* without freeing them from the veil of Maya and giving them Insight; the potion (the music) does not free them from the restrictions of their bodies, and so their longing here is the greatest torment, entirely without remedy.

162. The *Erkenntnis* (insight or knowledge) attained in Schopenhauer's philosophical system through art, especially music, is contrary to Wagner's, which leads to a state in which the highest bliss is the freedom from the powerful active pressure of the *Wille zum Leben*, permitting a state of quietude not existing in the world of will and representation.

163. *STD*, 154 (*GW*, 8: 246). See also Wagner, *Tristan und Isolde*, act 2, scene 1, 11. 215–16. The "world" means not only the physical globe, but the existential universe, and only in this sense does the statement of Tristan, "I am the world," signify that union "with me" opens up the knowledge of the entire sphere of life.

164. Letter to Hilde Distel, Munich, 14 March 1902.

165. "That in some sense music must be related to the world as the depiction of the thing depicted, as the copy to the original, we can infer from the analogy with the remaining arts, to all of which this character is peculiar; from their effect on us, it can be inferred that that of music is on the whole of the same nature, only stronger, more rapid, more necessary and infallible. Further, its imitative reference to the world must be very profound, infinitely true, and really striking, since it is instantly understood by everyone, and presents a certain infallibility by the fact that its form can be reduced to quite definite rules expressible in numbers, from which it cannot possibly depart without entirely ceasing to be music. Yet the point of comparison between music and the world, the regard in which it stands to the world in the relation of a copy or a repetition, is very obscure. Men have practiced music at all times without being able to give an account of this; content to understand it immediately, they renounce any abstract conception of this direct understanding itself" (Schopenhauer, *The World as Will and Representation*, vol. 1, bk. 2, chap. 52, p. 256).

166. *Richard Wagners sämtliche Schriften und Dichtungen*, 12 vols., Breitkopf and Härtel, ed. E. F. W. Siegel (Leipzig: Linnemann, n.d.), 7: 123. ". . . in the musical

execution of 'Tristan' there is no repetition of words, but in the structural web of the words and verses the entire width of the melody is preconceived, that is, the melody is readily constructed.

"If I had succeeded overall with this procedure, you would consequently have given me credit for [demonstrating] that it would necessarily be able to produce a far more intimate union of the poetry with the music than would the earlier [procedure]; and if I at the same time could hope that you would grant more value to the poetic execution of my 'Tristan' than to my earlier works, then you would have to conclude from this circumstance that the totally preconceived musical form is above everything else advantageous to poetic work" (EHL).

Richard Wagner's art is best conceived through the correspondence and inter-dependence of the genres of poetry, music, and dance, known as *Gesamtkunstwerk*, which function together to convey the metaphysical, unsubstantialized concept which is his message. His highest mystical achievement is his concept of *Liebestod* ("Love-Death"), which incorporates the emotional and intellectual essences of Wagner's *Weltanschauung* at the time *Tristan und Isolde* was written. The lover's expression of longing (*Sehnsucht*) is the expression of the power to overcome the *principium individuationis*. When they do overcome it, they overcome the "representation" of the material world and gain insight into the "truth," real existence for the bliss of union. In this sense, the theme is universally relevant, for in joining the means of expression of the various genres of art, Wagner achieved a maximum fusion (unity) between the components of his theme and thus a maximum power of expression in his artistic communication of experience.

167. The central issue is Schopenhauer's *Die Welt als Wille und Vorstellung*, where "*Welt*" stands for the imaginative rationalization by the Intellect, which builds a state of conscious objectivation. "*Welt*" is more a mental image than a tangible set of objects or people and it may be seen in countless forms, depending on the angle of the "*Weltanschauung*" from which one views the world. When Schopenhauer uses the phrase "World as Will," he refers to the blindly powerful aspect of the world that is activated by the *Wille zum Leben*. When the Will and the Representation or mental image (*Vorstellung*) are considered, with the Representation indicating a concept or mental image, the World (sphere of existence) is raised to an intellectual and imaginative force on the level of ephemeral existence: a Representation (*Vorstellung*). The power of the blind will, whether the bare reproductive instinct or its objectivated rationalized form, is projected into the vision of the "*Vorstellung*," which is built on the "*principium individuationis*." The blind will can be overcome by the will of a "genius" in order to attain insight into "reality," the calm unity of existence. Such *Erkenntnis* is hidden usually by the veil of Maya. "World" therefore can signify these things: first, blind will rationalized (on the false concept of *Welthunger* [world-hunger]); second, the *principium individuationis*; or third, the *Erkenntnis* into ultimate unity.

168. See "Gerächt," Dunja's comment: "Entfleischte Brunst," in reference to *Tristan und Isolde*. The comment can at best be inadequately rendered as "disembodied lust."

169. *STD*, 155 (*GW*, 8: 246). Thomas Mann's musical devices are far more elaborate than those used in "Little Lizzy," since he now has strengthened his link to the work of E. T. A. Hoffmann with Wagnerian musical theory, the full appreciation of which is limited to readers familiar with music.

170. Gabriele now takes the place of Isolde dying for the love of Tristan, personifying it much as does the actress who represents Donna Anna in E. T. A. Hoffmann's "Don Juan."

171. Rat Krespel's Antonia had a strange red spot on her cheeks when she sang, a physical manifestation of her being chosen for an extraordinary gift to Art—and of her consequent death.

172. This is the last meeting between Gabriele and Spinell in "Tristan."

173. *Tristan und Isolde* is not mentioned again, and there are only short references to the "longing motif" (*Sechnsuchtsmotiv*).

174. Thomas Mann describes the colors of Spinell's room as typical of the mineral spinel.

175. Thomas Mann would later shift to another tone and define his own position as artist and *Bürger* in "Tonio Kröger."

176. Spinell's idealization seems utterly ridiculous to Klöterjahn, but the question whether the girls around the wishing well were singing or knitting, or whether Gabriele wore a little golden crown on her hair, merely shows the two differing viewpoints, Spinell's and Klöterjahn's. Spinell's imagination had certainly provided extra details to the visions from Gabriele's life, but though such insight cannot be taken literally, since they are the artist's means of communication; Spinell is, after all, a writer. His eyes are "formed to see" and objectify dimensions out of reach of the rationalization governed by Klöterjahn's *Wille zum Leben*.

177. The motif of decadence and refinement familiar from *Buddenbrooks* is insistently repeated: "An ancient stock, too exhausted and refined for life and action, stood there at the end of it days; its latest manifestations were those of art: violin notes, full of that melancholy understanding which is ripeness for death . . ." (*STD*, 159; *GW*, 8: 252).

178. *STD*, 164; *GW*, 8: 260. Thomas Mann stresses the contrast between Gabriele's stillness and the foolish commotion of the quarrel between Spinell and Klöterjahn. Klöterjahn's excited babbling does contain important information. He reveals Gabriele's letter to him, the fact that she did not kiss her little son, and finally the doctors' diagnosis; all of these illustrate her breaking away from the domination of the *Wille zum Leben* in her path toward death.

179. It does not suit Spinell to fortify himself with brandy, and no occult experience like van der Qualen's can be expected, not even as act of self-rejection, like Lobgott Piepsam's. Spinell, in facing the dominance of the *Wille zum Leben* in this world of representation, the shouting Klöterjahn and the sparkling spring day, knows that he must come to terms with this dimension he so hates. The cognac is merely his attempt to find ease in a difficult situation.

180. Spring called the desperate little Herr Friedemann and Tobias; Spinell also must face its archetypes of reborn life. Like Thomas Mann's earlier heroes, Spinell must face his defeat alone.

181. These are the exact words *Rätin* Spatz used about the dying Gabriele.

182. Spinell does not hum the *Liebestod*, the portion Gabriele probably hummed on her deathbed, but Spinell is no Tristan; Spinell's eternal fate is the *Sehnsuchtsmotiv*.

183. These were also shown in certain of Wagner's theoretical writings, especially the "*Zukunftsmusik*," and in Thomas Mann's own essays on Wagner. However, he referred very seldom to Wagner's theoretical writings.

184. The important inherent comic factor in the intellect refers to Schopenhauer.

185. S. Fischer had originally wanted "Tristan" for the *Neue deutsche Rundschau* but found the completed work "unsuitable."

Chapter 4. *Bürger* and *Künstler*: The Contour of a New Beginning

1. Thomas Mann's 1901 notebooks, especially Notebook no. 7, contain material pertinent to his new novel project, "Die Geliebten," and his notes for *Fiorenza*.

2. See Nietzsche's "Richard Wagner in Bayreuth," 1874, and "Schopenhauer als Erzieher," also 1874.

3. Armin Martens was the son of a Lübeck mill owner. He was born in 1878 and was Thomas Mann's casual schoolmate for several years. Never paying the author any real attention, Martens left Lübeck at age sixteen to become a strolling actor and died an alcoholic in a German settlement in Africa. On 9 March 1955, Thomas Mann wrote about Martens to Hermann Lange: ". . . completely without inflection (probably intentionally), the name Armin Martens passes in your catalogue among other names, even though it deserves to have been underlined in red. Because I have loved him—he was in fact my first love, and a more delicate love, one filled with more spiritual suffering, would never be my lot. One does not forget such a thing, even if 70 eventful years pass over it. It may seem ridiculous, but I preserve a memory of this passion of innocence like a treasure. It is only too understandable that he did not know what to do with my raving when I confessed this to him on a 'great' day. It was because of [both] me and him. It [the love] then died away, much before he [did] himself, whose charm had already suffered damaged from puberty. . . . But I have built a monument to him" (EHL). Thomas Mann's "monument" to Armin Martens was the figure of Hans Hansen in "Tonio Kröger."

4. Thomas Mann recorded emotional and intellectual expressions at this time in his unpublished notebooks under the heading of a new novel project, "Die Geliebten." This material is held by the Thomas Mann Archives in Zurich. Even though Mendelssohn paraphrases some details of this project, the only scholarly presentation of this material in print is "Zu Thomas Manns 'Maja'-Project" by Hans Wysling, in Paul Scherer and Hans Wysling, *Quellenkritische Studien zum Werk Thomas Manns* (Bern/Munich: Francke Verlag, 1967). Future references to this highly valuable source of material on Thomas Mann's unpublished writings are abbreviated as "Wysling: 'Maja.' "The passage quoted in text is found on pp. 27–28.

5. *Summary* of "The Hungry Ones": Detlef, a writer, depressed that his beloved Lilli prefers a young painter, leaves a party in a bitter mood; he meets a starving man and speculates on physical and intellectual starvation. He finally realizes that any "hunger" is painful and needs reciprocal understanding.

6. In his *Birth of Tragedy*, Nietzsche used the term "hungry" in a manner germane to the topic of Thomas Mann's "The Hungry Ones":

> Our art reveals this universal distress: in vain does one depend imitatively on all the great productive periods and natures; in vain does one accumulate the entire "world-literature" around modern man for his comfort; in vain does one place oneself in the midst of the art styles and artists of all ages, so that one may give names to them as Adam did to the beasts: one still remains eternally *hungry*, the "critic" without joy and energy, the Alexandrian man, who is at bottom a librarian and corrector of proofs, and wretchedly goes blind from the dust of books and from printers' errors. (Nietzsche/Schlechta, 1: 102)

Friedrich Nietzsche, *The Birth of Tragedy*, trans. Walter Kaufmann (New York: Random House, 1967), 113.

7. In the light of the Schopenhauer material cited with "Tristan," "hunger" is considered here as the longing for the principle of unity that contrasts with the *principium individuationis*. The strongly developing *Bürger* motif in Thomas Mann's writing at this time and the growing theme of personal sensitivity weaken the Schopenhauerian "hunger" theme to the limit of recognition, but a close reading of the last two paragraphs of "The Hungry Ones" reveals it clearly.

8. The actual concept is also expressed as the dissolution of the veil of Maya.

9. The English translation of "The Hungry Ones" omits the important mention of blond hair, an essential thematic motif that points toward the theme of "Tonio Kröger." ". . . her head slightly on one side . . ." (*STD*, 168); ". . . den blonden Kopf etwas schief geneigt . . ." (*GW*, 8: 265).

10. The imagery of darkness is apparent in "The Hungry Ones," as for example *STD*, 170: "He was overpowered by the desire to avoid the field, to seek out stillness and darkness. . . ." (*GW*, 8: 267). An obvious example is unfortunately not observed in the English translation. "Why did you not hug your misery in the shadow instead of taking your stand under the lighted windows. . . ." (*STD*, 172). Literally this reads: "Why don't you stay defiantly and proudly in the dark, but rather take your place under lighted windows. . . ." (EHL). "Warum bleibst du nicht trotzig und stolz im Dunkel, sondern nimmst deinen Platz unter erleuchteten Fenstern. . . ." (*GW*, 8: 269–70).

11. The name of this small Danish resort is spelled "Aalsgard" on modern maps, but in "Tonio Kröger" Thomas Mann used the spelling "Aalsgaard," as he did in his letters as well as on the bill he paid there. Hans Wysling's *Bild und Text bei Thomas Mann* (Bern/Munich: Francke Verlag, 1975), 38, contains the facsimile copy of a bill issued to Thomas Mann by the hotel at Aalsgaard. The price was very modest, and the bill reveals that he stayed there only five days. The hotel was reputable but not expensive or fashionable. Mendelssohn reports that the hotel burned down shortly after Thomas Mann's stay.

12. Thomas Mann wrote of his feeling about Italy in "Tonio Kröger." (*STD*, 110–11; *GW*, 8: 305–6).

13. Except for scattered notes, no description of Thomas Mann's vacation at Aalsgaard exists, but he must have written in detail about it to Grautoff, since he wrote to him a year later (9 September 1900): "Just don't let the letter from Aalsgaard get lost. I might very well use it later" (EHL). No trace of the earlier letter has ever been found. It is possible that in 1900, twenty-one days prior to his entering military service, he began either working on or planning "Tonio Kröger."

14. On 4 February 1901, S. Fischer accepted the unabridged version of *Buddenbrooks*. The contract was to follow that March.

15. Thomas Mann wrote to Ehrenberg 6 January 1902 "I, too, am working—that means I am forcing and tormenting myself sometimes almost unbearably with doubts, hesitations, inability, and the hypersensitivity of my artistic conscience . . . At the same time I am in a hurry, a hurry! because the volume of short stories which is to appear by the beginning of the fall, and which my publisher wants to print in the summer, is not yet done" (EHL).

16. Mendelssohn, *Zauberer*, 516, comments that the central section embodies the theme of "Tonio Kröger," while the preceding and concluding sections symmetrically interpret the theme, like two wings of an altar.

17. Walter Kaufmann's spelling ("Apollinian") is used as closer to Nietzsche's term than the more usual "Apollonian."

18. *GW*, 11: 410.

19. Faust, with Mephistopheles and Homunculus, represents the spirit of the North; Helen stands for the spirit of the South.

20. ". . . in a purely artistic sense, it may be that its musical qualities were not what most endeared it ["Tonio Kröger"] to its readers. Here perhaps for the first time I learned to use music to mold my style and form. Here for the first time I grasped the idea of epic prose composition as a tough texture woven of different themes, as a musically related complex. . . ." (*SML*, 32; *GW*, 11: 116). This refers to a theoretical dependence on music rather than to a structural technique.

21. *Summary*: The schoolboy Tonio Kröger, son of a successful North German businessman in an old Hanseatic town and a Latin mother, experiences pain-filled love for his schoolmate Hans Hansen and later for Ingeborg Holm, both healthy, handsome, and happily average people. Once his father dies and he himself is grown, Tonio Kröger leaves the town and moves southward to begin his career as a writer. One spring day Tonio Kröger confesses his frustrations to a friend, Lisabeta Ivanovna, a

painter of Russian origin. They seriously discuss the concept of literature and the definition of the artist (*Künstler*), and Tonio Kröger decides to travel to the North on vacation and seek out his own origins. In his home town again, he is not recognized and is nearly arrested. Later the communion he feels with the North Sea impresses him deeply and long-forgotten feelings overwhelm him. At the goal of his journey, the Danish seaside resort of Aalsgaard, Tonio Kröger thinks he recognizes Hans and Ingeborg again. In a letter to Lisabeta Ivanovna, Tonio Kröger expresses his realization that he can now accept his feelings and his love for the commonplace as part of his artistry (*Künstlertum*).

22. In the second paragraph of the German text, Thomas Mann refers to Wagner's "Wotan's hat" (*Wotanshut*) and Jupiter's beard in a happy school-boy mixture of Germanic and classical elements. Wotan's costume, requiring a high helmet with phantasmagorical Valhalla wings above each ear, reflects Thomas Mann's involvement with Wagnerian music and refers humorously to his school memories. None of this is discernible in the English translation (*STD*, 85).

23. See the final lines of the story: "There is longing in it, and a gentle envy; a touch of contempt and no little innocent bliss" (*STD*, 132).

24. Thomas Mann's comment in his notebook, "Skandinavischer Name" (Scandinavian name), shows his search for such a name for this character. Hans Wysling and Paul Scherer, "Dokumente zur Entstehung des 'Tonio Kröger', archivalisches aus der nach-*Buddenbrooks*-Zeit," in *Quellenkritische Studien zum Werk Thomas Manns* (Bern/Munich: Francke Verlag, 1967), 53. This study contains important contributions on the *Die Geliebten* material in reference to "Tonio Kröger." It will be cited hereafter as "Wysling: 'Tonio Kröger.'"

25. The imagery of the blond versus the dark coloring and the contrast inherent in the ambivalent name "Tonio Kröger" can in no way be taken as an indication of "racism" on Thomas Mann's part, nor should it be associated with Nietzsche's imagery of the "blond beast" (*blonde Bestie*). See Nietzsche/Schlechta, 2: 786, 787, and 980, describing a concept which is irrelevant in this context.

26. In *Betrachtungen eines Unpolitischen*, Thomas Mann wrote, "No one will prevent me from finding in the cause and origin of Wagner's yearning, of his world-eroticism, all that which Nietzsche called his double optics, a capacity sprung from the need to fascinate not only the finest—that is natural—but also the great masses of the dull; I say: sprung from necessity, because I am convinced that each *Künstler* without exception does that, which himself is, which corresponds to his own personal need" (EHL) (*GW*, 11: 108).

27. Novalis believed that everyone at one time or another was privileged to view the *blaue Blume*, and that it then was a matter of existential decision for him to remain with the *Erdgeist* or to renounce it in order to become a poet.

28. Thomas Mann's correspondence with Grautoff and with his brother Heinrich, as well as some comments in his notebooks, reveals that Tonio's hypersensitivity was directly modeled on his own reactions to Martens and Ehrenberg.

29. Tonio wants to walk Hans home, he offers him his volume of Schiller, and he does not even want to see Hans Hansen become more like himself.

30. Freudian scholars might detect homoerotic symptoms in the relationship between Tonio and Hans, but psychoanalytical theories must be separated from Tonio's feelings. "Tonio Kröger" is not a case study but a piece of fiction assembled by the taste and imagination of its author. The term "erotic" in its popular sense appears to suggest a basic sexual or sensual character, but in actuality it may describe a force that is intellectual, spiritual, or metaphysical. "Erotic" expresses an intense experience resulting from the interplay of contrasting elements that inherently contain the capacity for mutual attraction. If this attraction of two diametrically opposed sides is brought into a field of magnetism, which the German Romantics called the *Magnetis-*

mus der Gegenpole, the individual can realize a special delight at its consummation. The term is most commonly applied to the attraction of the opposite sexes, to such an extent that it seems customary to associate "eroticism" with sexual experiences. However, the term "erotic" here is applied to intellectual-erotic, spiritual-erotic, and emotional-erotic experiences, if the prerequisites of contrast and attraction noted above are present.

Thomas Mann himself referred repeatedly to Wagner's *Tristan und Isolde* as expressing a "metaphysical-erotic" theme, the tension between the longing for sexual union between human beings dominated by the *principium individuationis* and the longing of Tristan and Isolde for an unbounded union, an insight which the mystery of their love had given them. The blissful union of their love beyond life without separation and fleshly limits is the manifestation of the latter desire. The two overcoming powers of the *Wille zum Leben* and the "will to love" creates at the climax a bliss achieved through metaphysical experience that might be called "erotic." The masterly ironic humor displayed at the clownish interaction of the completely intellectual capacities of Spinell and Klöterjahn represents the parody of an "intellectual" eroticism. Sensitivity, indeed, can also cause similar experiences through its inherent tension. Nietzsche's concept of the dithyramb may be conceived of as the culmination of the Apollinian and the Dionysian impulses, also belonging to the conceptual sphere of the "erotic."

31. This recalls the *Wonne der Wehmut* (delight of sorrow) of the *Sturm und Drang* period.

32. Thomas Mann wrote in "Das Bild der Mutter," 11 December 1930: "I wish that the general public had not jumped to conclusions in identifying some figures of my narrations with real life. More than one critic, convinced that as a writer I am strictly bound to the autobiographical, has thoughtlessly quoted passages from 'Tonio Kröger' in which I characterized the mother of the hero as if they were words that I have written about my own mother . . ." (EHL).

In "Theodor Storm," written in July 1930, Thomas Mann referred to his description of Tonio Kröger's father, saying that he had "strayed away considerably from the biographical with this description . . . the figures of these *geistig* fathers of his story are of Storm and Turgenev, . . . melted into the father figure of the tall, melancholically meditative white-bearded man with the field flower in his buttonhole . . ." (EHL) (*GW*, 9: 247).

33. *STD*, 88. "Wir sind doch keine Zigeuner im grünen Wagen, sondern anständige Leute, Konsul Krögers, die Familie der Kröger . . ." (*GW*, 8: 275). This "pattern-phrase," i.e.—appears in *STD*, 88, 91, 99, 118; *GW*, 8: 275, 279, 291, 317, and becomes an important formal tool to express the theme.

34. See *STD*, 88, in which the translator makes this passage into question, a misleading change from the original. "Wer so blaue Augen hätte, dachte er, und so in Ordnung und glücklicher Gemeinschaft mit aller Welt lebte wie du!" (*GW*, 8: 276).

35. Robinson, "Names," 63. "The name *Jimmerthal* suggests *Jammerthal*, the vale of tears. The connotation is appropriate, for Jimmerthal brings Tonio close to tears." Thomas Mann wrote to Stanley Godman 14 May 1945 (in English): "I have to admit that I cannot furnish you with any further information about the Lubeck organist Jimmerthal than you already possess. I doubt that when I chose the name for Tonio Kröger's schoolmate I was thinking of the organist. It was simply that the name was familiar to me from my early childhood days. I learned from you for the first time that Jimmerthal wrote a book about Buxtehude" [H. Jimmerthal, *Dietrich Buxtehude. Historische Skizze* (Lübeck: Kaibel, 1877)].

36. The Italian sound of "Tonio" (which in German would be Anton) is usually acknowledged as the motif which emphasizes the origin of the boy's mother. However, the name can be traced further back, to ideas introduced into Thomas Mann's work

from Leoncavallo's *Pagliacci* at the time Thomas Mann was writing "Der Bajazzo."

37. The English translation (*STD*, 92), "His heart beat richly," does not carry the German connotations of "Damals lebte sein Herz," literally translated "Then his heart was alive." This motif recurs in the German at significant spots in the story, but this is not shown in the standard English translation, which uses different vocabulary each time the phrase recurs. *STD*, 92, 97, 121, 131 (only the last is literally translated); *GW*, 8: 281, 287, 322, 336).

38. "There was longing in it, and a heavy-hearted envy, and a little bit of contempt and an utterly chaste bliss" (EHL) (see also *STD*, 92). The emphasis on *"keusche"* stresses the nonsexual, nonpragmatic, nonegotistical love that brings about Tonio's bliss, which is the joy he takes in sharing the experience of Schiller's *Don Carlos* with Hans Hansen: the desire of bringing the treasure of his mind and heart to his beloved (*STD*, 88, 92, 132: *GW*, 8: 276, 281, 256).

39. The love for Hans/Armin occurred before the age of natural puberty.

40. Robinson, "Names," 63. "The name François Knaak bears a similarity to the name Tonio Kröger. Both names are incongruous mixtures of rather exotic first names and commonplace family names."

41. Ibid., 62–63. "The name Magdalena, that of the reformed prostitute, combined with a family name which means to propagate, suggests promiscuity not exactly in keeping with the character of the affectionate little girl who is perpetually down in the dance. It may be a sort of perverse *Namenwitz* (joke of name). But the name, like that of the hero, is certainly not one of the '*allgemein anerkannte Namen, die niemand befremdeten*'" ('common names which did not alienate anyone'—EHL).

42. Thomas Mann's mother never remarried. Therefore, some of the references in this story to Tonio's mother ought not to be considered part of the autobiographical detail.

43. The role of the Intellect as Thomas Mann had presented it in Schopenhauerian terms in "Tristan" is perceptible. Tonio's snobbery has enmeshed him in the *principium individuationis*, completely isolated him and made him hostile to everyone else. He thus loses the chance to gain any rapport with the happy blond "others."

44. The English translation of the pertinent passage is: "But as his health suffered from these excesses . . ." (*STD*, 99). The German text does not provide any reason for the decline in Tonio's health: ". . . wie seine Gesundheit geschwächt ward, verschärfte sich seine Künstlerschaft . . ." (*GW*, 8: 291). (". . . as his health became weaker his artistry was sharpened . . ." [EHL].)

45. Käte Hamburger's comment on the polarity of life and *Geist* is germane here: ". . . So it is no wonder that in the early phase of German Romanticism one problem, which previously could not have been considered significant, now becomes important: the problem of *illness*, which must be considered as a product of the union of the polarity of life and death, life as such [a product] gaining a *Geistes*-historical significance. . . . And out of the union of these polarities into this basic spiritual mood, which Thomas Mann happened to call Romantic, the problem of disease was engendered, which infiltrates his work in many aspects and which, in *The Magic Mountain*, becomes the hero of the action itself. The problem of the *Geist* and the problem of Death become in the idiosyncratic union of a Romantic experience the metaphysical basis upon which Thomas Mann's work of art is built" (EHL) (Käte Hamburger, *Thomas Mann und die Romantik* [Berlin: Junker und Dünnhaupt, 1932], 12–13). Käte Hamburger's sensitivity in capturing the secret of Thomas Mann's concept of the dynamism of the contrasting polarities even before he had written *Joseph und seine Brüder* is impressive, especially since it would seem that at the time he wrote "Tonio Kröger" Thomas Mann himself would have been incapable of this definition.

46. Thomas Mann first spelled the name with a *v* and later changed it to *w*. This name is ". . . probably a reference to Pushkin, in whose *Queen of Spades* the coun-

tess's stepdaughter is called 'Lisaweta Iwanowna'" (EHL) (Paul Scherer and Hans Wysling, *Quellenkritische Studien zum Werk Thomas Manns* [Bern/Munich: Francke Verlag, 1967], 330). The English spelling is Lisabeta Ivanovna.

47. The connotations of the word "confused" used in the English translation do not correctly reflect those of the original German "*verworren*."

48. The word *Pointieren*, meaning to point, to bring to a point, or to express (an idea) pointedly has intriguing connotations; it also is used in German gambling jargon, meaning "to punt" or "to prick." *Point* in French means the same thing as it does in American English: a point and an emphasis: "to make a point." Each notion pertains to Thomas Mann's fiction, but the word is also used repeatedly and emphatically in the German translation of Pushkin's *Queen of Spades*. In "Tonio Kröger" Lisabeta Ivanovna chooses the rules of the game, because neither Adalbert nor Tonio can, being intoxicated with spring. Lisabeta, the accomplished artist, chooses and arranges her challenging words, and she wins when Tonio chooses to travel north because of their enlightening conversation. In German "nun mache ich . . . diese kleine Pointe [emphasis] und Wirkung [effect]," is not a usual phrase, and seems here like shop talk or professional jargon. "*Pointe*" and "*Wirkung*" are represented in the English translation by only the word "effect," only vaguely rendering both words, and the strangeness of the unusual word "*Pointe*" (first used by Adalbert and repeated several times) is lost in the translation.

49. Thomas Mann often combined the mysterious Russian-Slavic qualities with powerful sensuous attraction, as in Dunja Stegemann, Tadzio in "Death in Venice," and Clavdia Chauchat in *The Magic Mountain*.

50. In his *Quellenkritische Studien zum Werk Thomas Manns*, 52, Hans Wysling observes that in Thomas Mann's *Notizbuch* 7, p. 68, he uses the expression "*Litteratenhochmut*" (fierceness of a literary man) as early as 30 January 1902. He continues: "On the next page it says, 'Tonio Kröger had written verses in his youth. In Denmark they occur to him again, and he writes some more'" (EHL). This indicates Tonio's pride in writing poetry, a pride similar to that which he took in knowing *Don Carlos* and "Immensee," like Paolo Hofmann's pride in knowing Heine's works. This "*Litteratenhochmut*" applies to Thomas Mann's downgrading of the *Bürgerlich* in his early years—until, in fact, Tonio Kröger admitted his love for the commonplace.

51. "This glorification of 'Life' at the expense of the *Geist*, this lyricism which had such poor consequences on German thinking—there was only one way to assimilate myself to it: irony" (EHL) (*GW*, 11: 110).

52. "'. . . I confessed to you my love of life, or what I call life. I ask myself if you were aware how very close you came to the truth, how much my love of 'life' is one and the same thing as my being a *bourgeois*'" (*STD*, 131; *GW*, 8: 337).

53. The spring represents the Schopenhauerian *Wille zum Leben*, also conceivable as Nietzsche's Dionysian element.

54. This may represent either the rationalizing power or the notion of the Apollinian art.

55. See also *STD*, 99 (*GW*, 8: 290). The connotation of the word *Erkenntnis* has changed significantly from the highest "insight" namely the overcoming of the Schopenhauerian *Wille zum Leben* to Tonio's rejection of rational power.

56. The "swindler" (*Hochstapler*) was originally a charlatan who makes the world appear to be something it is not, also a crook, fraud, or rogue. This concept later developed into the most powerful of Thomas Mann's last themes, in *Bekenntnisse des Hochstaplers Felix Krull*, where the hero, with all the wit and charm of the picaro actually places himself beyond conventions and even ethics, thus acquiring a detached view of society.

57. "I had at that time a curiously long-suffering technique: after finishing a work I would black out all the deletions with a thick cross-hatching of ink and by this means

produce a clean copy of sorts. The cross-hatching must not be blotted, it had to dry; so in the last stage all the sheets were spread out over the floor and the furniture" (*Sketch of My Life*, 31–32; *GW*, 11: 115).

58. This sequence of ideas builds up a contrast to Tonio Kröger's concluding statement. It is an excellent example of the difficulty in translating Thomas Mann's work. The words *empfinden* and *fühlen* (and *Empfindung* and *Gefühl*) once translated have similar significations: "to perceive through the senses," "to feel," etc. They carry quite different connotations in "Tonio Kröger," however, because *empfinden* is used for concepts related to the sensual and passionate instinctive forces, while *fühlen* is reserved for the sensitivity of the *Geist*. The latter becomes the capacity to "feel" intangible concepts, such as the love for the blond, blue-eyed *Bürger*. With careful examination this tiny detail which seems to be illogical falls into place, but Tonio Kröger himself is unaware of these details at this point in the story. He and the reader achieve understanding together.

59. Now Tonio focuses on the artistic concept "from behind the scene," pitying the naïveté of the impressed people who do not understand ". . . that a 'properly constituted, healthy, decent man never writes, acts or composes. . . . At the time of *Zarathustra*, Nietzsche wrote: 'Everything I had said about Wagner was false. I felt it already in 1876: everything in him is ungenuine; . . .' " Roger Nicholls has observed, "Again, as in 'The Hungry' the values of Wagner's ultimate image are brought up in the light of bitter, passionate doubt, rejection and masochistic distortion reflecting Nietzsche's attitudes especially in *The Case of Wagner*" (Nicholls, *Nietzsche*, 32).

60. Thomas Mann's feelings toward Wagner were becoming more dramatic, that is, more emotional and at the same time more critical, especially after he completed "Tristan." See Mann's important essay on this subject, "Über die Kunst Richard Wagners" (1911); while Nietzsche's influence upon Mann became more philosophical.

61. "*Papyros*" is the German equivalent of the Russian word for cigarette. Russian cigarettes are usually made from very strong tobacco. They also have long holder-like paper attachments, hence the Russian name.

62. For Thomas Mann, *Literat* ("man of letters") does not have the same connotations as *Künstler*, which describes the aesthetically creative individual. He often used *Literat* to refer to Spinell in "Tristan."

63. Thomas Mann wrote in his "Schopenhauer" essay (1938): "What defines the saint? That he does nothing that he wants to do and does everything that he does not want to do" (EHL). (*GW*, 9: 555).

64. Literally, this term indicates a disgust at the "insight"-*Erkenntnis* by rationalization, which is an instinctive self-protective reaction, a rejection of the profanation of life's phenomena.

65. "Alles verstehen hieße alles verziehen" (*GW*, 8: 300), is translated into French in the English translation: "Tout comprendre c'est tout pardonner" (*STD*, 106). It seems improper to translate the German text into French rather than English, because it deemphasizes the effect of this well-known line. Thomas Mann certainly knew it and could have written it in French himself, since he used French in many of his other works both before and after "Tonio Kröger."

66. See *STD*, 107. Thomas Mann did not use the liturgical Latin expression "*credo*." The expression *erledigt* is not accurately translated by "finished."

67. See *STD*, 108. "Admirable" is not an accurate rendition of *liebenswürdig* (*GW*, 8: 302).

68. " 'Sie sind ein Bürger auf Irrwegen, Tonio Kröger—ein verirrter Bürger' " (*GW*, 8: 231). The standard English translation is "You are a bourgeois on the wrong path, a *Bourgeois manqué*" (*STD*, 110). In French *manqué* signifies "failure" in the sense of "having missed." There is a great difference between a *Bürger* who had lost his way and strayed into another category as the text states, and a *Bürger* who has

failed at being a *Bürger*. The German text does not use the French expression.

Lisabeta's statement that Tonio is a *Bürger* gone astray can evoke differing opinions, but Thomas Mann himself wrote in *Betrachtungen eines Unpolitischen* (chapter entitled *"Bürgerlichkeit"* [Summer 1916]): *"Bürger*-like *Künstlertum* is a paradox brought to reality, a paradox after all, a double quality, a dividedness in each case, in spite of the legitimacy which this *geistig* way of life has, especially in Germany. . . . It is the old song from Tonio Kröger: 'I stand between two worlds, but I am not at home in either one and therefore it is a little difficult for me.' But is one, perhaps, German exactly because of this? Is not the German nature the middle, the one in the middle, the one that mediates and so the German [is] the man in the middle in grand style? But now that it is [supposed to be] German to be a *Bürger*, so it is perhaps even more German to be something between *Bürger* and *Künstler* and also something between a patriot and a Pan-European, in between a protester and a Westerner, a conservative and a nihilist . . ." (EHL) (*GW*, 12: 10ff.).

69. "Dilettante" not only carries its usual cultural-historical significance, but it also implies the character of an unqualified impostor, a naïve pretentious uninitiate, like the versifying lieutenant.

70. These are Thomas Mann's italics. The English translation for *"erledigt,"* "in peace," does not encompass the word's meaning. *"Erledigt"* carries an even stronger meaning than "settled"; English has no equivalent expression. The translation "I am expressed" is the translator's version (*STD*, 110; *GW*, 8: 305).

71. The descriptive passages relating to Tonio's Danish vacation, particularly those dealing with the North Sea, were closely modeled on Thomas Mann's own trip to Denmark in the late summer of 1899.

72. Thomas Mann had "devoured" both Scandinavian and Russian literature. He specifically mentioned the works of Ibsen and had even acted in *The Wild Duck*. He also was familiar with the works of Strindberg, Hamsun, and Keilland, and with the poetry of Bang.

73. Tonio's relationship with Hamlet is a self-identification and an admission of his close *geistig* relationship with Shakespeare's Danish prince. Just as Goethe had marked his Wilhelm Meister's awakening by his affinity to Hamlet, at the moment when Tonio Kröger makes his existential step into life, Thomas Mann links Tonio's quest to Hamlet's own.

74. Thomas Mann employs the vocabulary of the German Romantic writers, the vague and meaningful *"Ausgangspunkt."* The *Lebensweise* of the Romantic poet was an unceasing yearning toward his ultimate origin.

75. The mood of this comment is closely related to Tonio's words to Lisabeta in section four: "'On the inside, as an artist, one is always sufficiently an adventurer [as well]. On the outside, one shall dress well, for the devil's sake, and behave like a decent person'" (EHL). See also *STD*, 102.

76. Thomas Mann wrote to Hilde and Lilli Distel from Munich on 8 October 1903: "Please accept my thanks for your two postcards (the one with the sneezing lion) . . . ," which demonstrates that the expression describing the lions was not a casual description coined for "Tonio Kröger."

77. *STD*, 113. The English version uses "ardent," which has misleading connotations.

78. *STD*, 113. The English version uses the expression *de rigueur*, but no French is used in the original. A literal rendition is: "where it was important to make a neat and flawless impression" (EHL) (*GW*, 8: 310).

79. Together with the violin, the walnut tree, and the Gothic fountain, the wind was one of those beloved elements that enabled Tonio to write poetry.

80. When Thomas Mann made his own visit to Lübeck, he looked up no one, not even his friend Ida Boy-Ed, at whose house he was entertained in later days when he went to lecture at Lübeck.

81. The fictional Buddenbrooks house was a combination of Thomas Mann's birthplace, the home of Heinrich Johann Mann, and the house of his grandparents Kröger. Such details, never mentioned in earlier parts of "Tonio Kröger," are familiar from *Buddenbrooks*.

82. This foolish name means "sea-rabbit." Its spelling, "Haase," emphasizes the Nordic element.

83. As he reads over the policeman's shoulder, Tonio Kröger is pleased with the *"Pointe und Wirkung"* he has worked out. The repetition of this motif refers to the technical excellence of the kind that Adalbert the novelist mentioned when he withdrew into a coffeehouse from the disturbances of spring. Whether this *"Pointe und Wirkung"* is a value judgment of art or Tonio's clever technical trick to capture the reader's sympathy is debatable.

84. The English translation cannot convey the low German dialect, which Thomas Mann's text renders phonetically (see also *STD*, 120). It is the primitive melody of this Nordic version of his tongue that attracts Tonio. The young businessman's deeply felt trivia is a witty caricature of Klopstock's *"Frühlingsfeier"* (*GW*, 8: 319).

85. The English text (*STD*, 121) does not mention "heart," a foreshadowing of the later "awakening of the heart," leading to the leitmotif. The English translation (*STD*, 121) misreads the passage: "his heart was full" (*GW*, 8: 321–22).

86. Kaufmann, *The Birth of Tragedy*, 107 (section 17): "In this New Dithyramb, music is outrageously manipulated so as to be the imitative counterfeit of phenomenon, for instance of a battle or a storm at sea; and thus, of course, it has been utterly robbed of its mythopoeic power. For if it seeks to arouse pleasures only by impelling us to seek external analogies between a vital or natural process and certain rhythmical figures and characteristic sounds of music; if our understanding is to content itself with the perception of these analogies; we are reduced to a frame of mind which makes impossible any reception of the mythical; for the myth wants to be experienced vividly as a unique example of a universality and truth that gaze into the infinite. The truly Dionysian music presents itself as such a general mirror of the universal will: the vivid event refracted in this mirror expands at once for our consciousness to the copy of the external truth."

87. The parallelism between the orgiastic theme inherent in both the Faustian *Walpurgisnacht* and the Dionysian feast as viewed in *The Birth of Tragedy* is consciously or unconsciously exploited by Thomas Mann. In "Tonio Kröger" he used more Faustian motifs, while he predominantly emphasizes Dionysian imagery in "Death in Venice." Indeed, Thomas Mann succeeded in powerfully expressing the deep emotional yearnings of both Goethe and Nietzsche in his own works of art.

88. Goethe in the *"Walpurgisnacht"* not only rejects the sensual trupitude of Mephistopheles and his peers, but also the depravity of the Philistines.

89. *GW*, 8: 323. The English translation (*STD*, 122) is inaccurate.

90. *STD*, 130. "Even if I in my own person had written the nine symphonies and *The World as Will and Representation* and painted the 'Last Judgment,' you would still be right to laugh . . ." (EHL) (*GW*, 8: 334). It is significant that Thomas Mann includes Schopenhauer's work here, where he makes Tonio Kröger list the highest artistic creations he can think of.

91. The enigmatic Danish girl represents poetry to Tonio, as Mignon did for Goethe's Wilhelm Meister, dying away when Wilhelm chose the love of life.

92. See *STD*, 131. This is the first time that the English translation uses Thomas Mann's choice of words: ". . . for his heart was alive." The leitmotif has surfaced to a high point that the German text carefully prepared.

93. The key Romantic expression *"Heim"* connotes a longing for the ultimate through the concept of "spiritual homeland." "Nostalgia" used in the English translation is correct, but it loses the original meaning of *"Heim"* (*STD*, 130; *GW*, 8: 336).

94. "Germanic" here refers to the Nordic or "barbaric" stock as opposed to the classical Greco-Roman. Ultimate beauty thus is represented by the South, in particular the most beautiful woman of the classical world, Helen of Troy.

95. At the classical *Walpurgisnacht*, the three visitors from the North are Faust, Mephistopheles, and Homunculus. Faust is God's creation, searching for Helen and longing for ultimate Beauty; Mephistopheles, the fallen angle, is hunting for foul erotic excess; Homunculus, a manmade artifact, seeks a material part of life into which he can unite his sterile *Geist*, and attain a genuine life-giving nature. While Homunculus strives for human existence, Faust strives toward the quintessence of beauty, symbolized in the Greek classical ideal of beauty, Helen. Faust represents the longing of the Northern Germanic man, striving for the vital solution of overcoming the self. After the experience of the classical *Walpurgisnacht*, Faust passes to his next stage, in which he is able to recall Helen into his own sphere of being. Mephistopheles, the third visitor from the North, does not find his goal in the classical *Walpurgisnacht*, and so his trip is a failure.

96. His reference to *Liebe* (love) is taken from 1 Corinthians 13: 1: ". . . if I speak in the tongues of men and of angels, but have not love, I am a noisy gong or as a clanging cymbal."

97. Thomas Mann's letter to Katia at the end of August (n.d.) 1904, shows how deeply autobiographical this passage of "Tonio Kröger" actually is: "T[onio] K[röger] had loved 'Life,' the blue-eyed commonplace, nostalgically mockingly and hopelessly. And now? A being, sweet as the world—and good, and uncommon, and able to meet me with *Geist* and goodness" (EHL).

98. Thomas Mann gives his concept of "disdain" (*Verachtung*) in a letter to Katia at the end of August 1904: "Until now when I loved, I always simultaneously disdained. The mixture of longing and disdain, ironic love, had been the actual quality of my feelings" (EHL).

99. In *Betrachtungen eines Unpolitischen*, 1916, Thomas Mann wrote: "The thing was that, while in *Buddenbrooks* only the Schopenhauerian-Wagnerian influence, [namely] the ethical-pessimistic and the epic-musical, could come to expression, in 'Tonio Kröger' the Nietzschean cultural developmental element [gained] position" (EHL).

100. Walter E. Berendsohn lists the languages into which Thomas Mann's work has been translated, giving approximate numbers of publications up to 1975 (Walter E. Berendsohn, *Thomas Mann: Artist and Partisan in Troubled Years* [Birmingham: Univ. of Alabama Press, 1975], 2).

101. *Summary*: In the cavalry officers' casino of a small German town, the *Schwalben* (swallows), a group of female singers, entertain the officers, mostly aristocrats, and their families. This mixture of social elements is most unusual. Baroness Anna, the young wife of the exuberant cavalry captain Baron Harry, is present, and with increasing anxiety she watches her husband noisily flirting with one of the young singers. When the baroness sees him give the girl his wedding band for a joke, the baroness decides to leave the ballroom. Suddenly the girl approaches her, apologizes, and kisses her hand. Alone in the night, the baroness experiences a moment of true happiness.

102. Thomas Mann wrote to Samuel Fischer on 4 December 1903, "At the moment I am writing a sketch. . . 'The Child Prodigy.' It will be better than 'A Gleam,' which. . . I consider as having been just tossed off. . . " (EHL).

103. Kurt Martens should not be confused with Thomas Mann's other friend, Armin Martens.

104. Under the working title of *Casino-Novelle* there is another note:

Casino-Novelle
"Bakerboy
To ride on the sidewalk
Pistol shooting on the marketplace" (EHL) in reference
to p. 117 of notebook 7. See Wysling: "Maja," 34.

105. As noted above, "The Hungry Ones" was written around the time that Thomas Mann was working on the Tonio/Lisabeta passage of "Tonio Kröger," and evidently he took several passages from "The Hungry Ones" and used them literally in "Tonio Kröger," so that the smaller story clarified his ideas.

106. The word *Huhn* (hen) receives an umlaut (*ü*) in the plural and diminutive. The name thus suggests a comic meaning ("Henman" or "chickenman"), which sounds even more ridiculous when combined with the rank of "*Rittmeister*" (cavalry captain), literally translated "riding master." The lady's intelligence approximates a hen's.

107. Gabriele was a light brunette, without the dark Latin coloration of other artistic and sensitive protagonists.

108. "*Avantageur*" is a now archaic expression derived from French and used in the eighteenth and nineteenth centuries in Germany to designate a "gentleman cadet." The French verb *avantager* means "to prefer," or "to give advantage." Thomas Mann may have emphasized this expression to point out that if the *Schwalbe* had been able to choose, she might have preferred the *Avantageur* to the Baron. The *Avantageur*, being rather similar to the Baroness, contrasts with the Schwalbe. Kurt Martens, who told Thomas Mann this anecdote, recalled it from the time when he himself was an *Avantageur*.

109. "Yellow saddle," a caricature of a German noble-sounding name.

110. Other passages of "Tonio Kröger" indicate Thomas Mann's dependence on the original draft of "The Hungry Ones." The passages in the two stories where the hero leaves the dance hoping that the beloved girl will call him back are very important. These appear in "The Hungry Ones" (*STD*, 170; *GW*, 8: 267), and in "Tonio Kröger" (*STD*, 97; *GW*, 8: 287), where Tonio is sixteen, and later, in Aalsgaard, when he is a man (*STD*, 131; *GW*, 8: 336), demonstrating his postadolescent maturation. Both passages in "Tonio Kröger" clearly derive from the lines in "The Hungry Ones," but again, the rich appeal to happiness and the life that emerges from suffering in "Tonio Kröger" becomes more powerfully evocative of Thomas Mann's growing vision. An interesting comparison may be made between "The Hungry Ones" (*STD*, 170; *GW*, 8: 267) and the fourth section of "Tonio Kröger," where the concepts of the *Künstler* are discussed. Another possible comparison is between the distorted, negative trend of the Wagnerian *Tristan und Isolde* motifs in "The Hungry Ones" (*STD*, 168; *GW*, 8: 265) and the similar passage of "Tonio Kröger" (*STD*, 105; *GW*, 8: 299).

111. The little Pringsheim daughter had been christened Katherina Hedwig and as a little girl was first called Käthe, and later Kati. After 1892, she was remembered as Katja. A governess, Mme. Griselle, employed to teach the Pringsheim children French, had worked a considerable time as governess in Russian aristocratic families, and she called the little girl Katja. Thomas Mann spelled the name in this manner, while Mrs. Mann herself spelled her name Katia.

112. Katia Mann, *Meine ungeschriebenen Memoiren*, ed. Elisabeth Plessen and Michael Mann (Nordlingen: S. Fischer, 1975), 2.

113. Thomas Mann, letter to Katia, end of May 1904: ". . . I . . . have observed you often with my opera glasses, before we knew each other" (EHL).

114. Alfred Pringsheim, 1805–1941, Katia's father, was a passionate Wagnerian who had known the composer personally and once had even become involved in a dual

on Wagner's account. Pringsheim was also an independently wealthy art collector, and he built a house on the Arti Straße, destroyed during World War II. Pringsheim was professor of mathematics at the University of Munich, where he took a late promotion rather than follow the custom of renouncing his Jewish religion. He left Nazi Germany with his wife for Switzerland in 1939. Mrs. Pringsheim, née Dohm, was the daughter of the writers Ernest and Hedwig Dohm. Though her parents were Jewish, she and her four children were raised as Christians. Her eldest son Peter was a professor of physics. Heinz, a cavalry lieutenant in World War I, became an archaeologist and an active music critic; the youngest children were the twins Katia and Klaus.

115. He often mentions a sore throat, constipation, nervous tension, and digestive disorders. Dr. Cabrini (see n. 2 to chap. 1) notes that much of Thomas Mann's idiosyncratic behavior, such as fatigue, shyness, depression, and late sexual maturity is probably traceable to a glandular deficiency.

116. Katia Pringsheim, 1882–1980, was the first woman to graduate from the Munich gymnasium, after which she studied mathematics at the University of Munich. She married Thomas Mann 11 February 1905; they had six children.

117. This was written from the summer of 1906 to February 1909 and first published in *Die neue Rundschau* 20, nos. 1–9 (January–September 1909). This charming novel, the only one Thomas Mann wrote between *Buddenbrooks*, 1901, and *The Magic Mountain*, 1924, is not discussed here in detail.

118. *Summary*: The setting is a festive concert starring Bibi Saccellaphylaccas, the infant prodigy. The thoughts of the child pianist, of his impresario and of his mother, as well as of the various colorful characters of his audience individually, and then collectively the crowd's reactions, express Thomas Mann's ideas on artist-audience relations, the artist's position bridging his obligation to the ever-powerful business machinery and his own artistry. The theme of the sketch is reflected through a series of interior monologues. The action—the concert—is simple, and at its close each character returns to his own path in life.

119. "The Infant Prodigy" is a sketch, not a novella, and so the distinction between "plot" and "theme" is vital. "Plot" is the controlling frame, a simple and distinct succession of episodes. By themselves these episodes, or rather the actions in them, do not make the plot. The plot is actually an abstraction, representing the existing relationship between incidents. An apparently natural interaction that nevertheless must always remain plausible must rule within the unity of the work of art, which Aristotle defines as "the structural union of the parts, such that if any one of them is displaced or removed, the whole will be disjointed and disturbed."

120. The German text uses a sparkling active present tense, but the English translation, by comparison, seems halting. A period in the first line of the English version adds brusqueness, detracting from the melodic German impression reinforcing the sudden quieting of the crowd (*STD*, 172; *GW*, 8: 333).

121. The translation alternates "people" and "audience" in this opening paragraph. The English "audience," a collective noun, demonstrates the unity of those attending the concert. In the original German, "*Leute*" is used seven times and "*Leutehirn*" twice, while the English uses "audience" three times, "people" twice, "average man" once, with one "*Leute*" omitted completely in translation. Also, where Thomas Mann used another word, such as "crowd" or "spectators," the English translation adds one "average man," one "regular man," "audience" twice more, and "people" also twice more. This naturally obliterates the meaning Thomas Mann gave to his leitmotif "*Leute*". Thomas Mann coined the word "*Leutehirn*," a leitmotif, which expresses the workings of the average collective mind. Another interesting detail in this first paragraph is the inclusion in the German text of the Nietzschean expression "*Herrscher*" and "*Herdenführer*" (literally "ruler" and "herd-leader"). "*Herdenführer*" implies that "*Leute*" is synonymous with "*Herde*" (literally "people" and "herd"), a group led

by the *Führer* who begins the applause. Such fine connotation is lost in translation.

122. One of Thomas Mann's sons, born much later, was called "Bibi" when he was small.

123. He would run home after school for a sandwich and then go to his violin lessons, which began in the fall of 1883 under Herr Winkelmann.

124. Mendelssohn, *Zauberer*, 81.

125. The English translation is confusing; but the German words, *"Hoheit," "Scharlatanerie," "heilige Funken," "Verachtung,"* and *"heimlichen Rausch"* convey Thomas Mann's meaning unmistakably.

126. "The Infant Prodigy" is one of Thomas Mann's most often anthologized short stories. Often editorial comments suggest that blond blue-eyed siblings supposedly show Nazi tendencies in Thomas Mann, referring to the expression describing the girl's features as *"reinrassig[en] Gesicht"* and the name of her officer-brother, Adolf. Thomas Mann's perseverant blond, blue-eyed leitmotif on the one hand, and the dates of the story and of Hitler's first appearance in history, on the other, prove such suggestions are unfounded.

127. Letter to Heinrich Mann, 27 February 1904: ". . . *Buddenbrooks* has [sold] 18 thousand, and the [volume of] novellas before the 3rd . . . and now I already have more money than I can use up at the moment" (EHL).

128. Katia Mann, *Meine ungeschriebenen Memoiren*, ed. Elisabeth Plessen and Michael Mann (Frankfurt am Main: S. Fischer, 1975), 25 (hereafter referred to as *Memoiren*).

129. Robinson remarks on "the significance of the choice of a Biblical name, that of one of the most thought-provoking of all of the Old Testament prophets" ("Names," 37).

130. *Summary*: On Good Friday in a rustic suburb, an odd assemblage attends the Prophet Daniel's lecture in his attic flat. The "novelist," who obviously knows only the "rich lady," is, like the lady, an outsider. These two are humorous personifications of Thomas Mann himself and Mrs. Pringsheim. Since the Prophet himself is absent, his disciple, arriving at the exact moment the meeting was to commence, delivers the address. His tense personality is an effective backdrop to the eccentric content of the lecture. Thomas Mann's art focuses the characters and the circumstances with brilliant wit. The novelist, obviously in love with the rich lady's daughter Sonja (Katia), is cheered up when he receives the lady's permission to send flowers to her daughter.

131. See Mendelssohn, *Zauberer*, 605.

132. Ibid., 604.

133. Whether Thomas Mann named the daughter of the rich lady "Sonja" only because of its similarity in sound to "Katia," or because he wanted to emphasize its Slavic sound cannot be determined. Other Slavic names in Thomas Mann's fiction are "Dunja," "Detlef," and "Lisabeta Ivanovna."

134. Fritz Kaufmann's comment is germane: "Reviewing his *Stories of Three Decades*, he [Thomas Mann] finds in nearly all of them 'an allegory of the life of the artist' in his dubious grandeur, even though their mood and meaning undergo considerable change from period to period . . . the ego is objectified and the object animated from within" (Fritz Kaufmann, *Thomas Mann: The World as Will and Representation* [New York: Cooper Square Publishers, 1973], 34).

135. The terminology here refers to *The World as Will and Representation* (*Die Welt als Wille und Vorstellung*).

136. *STD*, 283. "Hier ist das Ende, das Eis, die Reinheit und das Nichts" (*GW*, 8: 362).

137. "The Hungry Ones," *STD*, 170; *GW*, 8: 267; and "Tonio Kröger," *STD*, 131; *GW*, 8: 336.

138. Napoleon's son was known as *l'Aiglon*.

139. Savonarola is mentioned in this story probably because Thomas Mann was still not done with *Fiorenza*, where Savonarola is one of three allegorical representations of his own concept of *Leben*, *Kunst*, and *Geist*. Robespierre and Savonarola were both involved with bloody cultural and social revolutions, but except for their puritanism there is no connection or affinity between them.

140. Thomas Mann, interestingly, uses the word *"Verlesung,"* which indicates either "reciting" or "misreading," for the prophetic utterances, rather than the more usual *"Vorlesung,"* which indicates "lecture" or "reading."

141. K. Mann, *Memoiren*, 26.

142. *Fiorenza*, a dramatic work, is not discussed in detail here. It holds a key position in Mann's intellectual development.

143. Reference to the tragic ending in Ibsen's *Master Builder*, but used as an adjective.

144. *Summary*: "A Weary Hour" is a forceful dramatic sketch offering a static portrait of the "poet," a representation of Schiller, but resembling Thomas Mann himself, in his study one night. There is no plot action; the *monologue intérieur* exclusively discloses the ideas, the problems, and the character of the "poet." This "psychological study" ends with the "poet"'s overcoming his *geistig* crisis and realizing the value of suffering to one who creates.

145. The German *"schwer"* has both physical and abstract meanings, standing for both "heavy" and also "difficult." In idiomatic usage it also connotes "grave," "serious," "severe," and "hard." "Weary" accurately translates the German *"müde," "erschöpft," "überdrüssig," "lästig,"* or *"beschwerlich,"* all of which indicate dejection or extreme fatigue.

146. Schiller's fatal illness began in 1791 and he died in 1805. Schiller had moved to Jena in 1794; he wrote the aesthetic essay *"Über naive und sentimentalische Dichtung"* in 1795; he completed the first version of *Wallenstein* in 1796 and rewrote it in 1797; *Wallenstein* was finally completed and he moved to Weimar in 1799.

147. Goethe is not mentioned by name either.

148. Schiller married Charlotte von Lengefeld on 22 February 1790 in the village church in Wenigenjena. The attractive oil portrait by Ludovike Simanowitz, 1794, now at the Schiller National Museum, shows a tall, slender, dark-haired and dark-eyed girl with open, intelligent features and light complexion, very similar to the photographs of Katia Pringsheim at the time of her marriage to Thomas Mann. Schiller's first child, Karl, was born 14 September 1794 in Ludwigsburg, followed by other children.

149. On 11 January 1797 Schiller wrote, ". . . In these gloomy and oppressive winter days everything matures slowly, and it is difficult to find the proper form" (EHL), and there are references to the poet's poor health in his 7 February 1797 and 5 December 1797 letters.—Thomas Mann's health, especially in 1904–5, had not been good; he often mentions headaches, sore throats, and stomach disorders.

150. The search for a clearer definition of "nature" led the Swiss philologists Bodmer and Breitinger to challenge Aristotle; and Johann Elias Schlegel rose up, for the first time in German literature, to define the intentionally ignored question: What was actually meant by "nature"? Johann Elias Schlegel also attempted to define "nature" itself.

151. Friedrich von Schiller, *Schillers Werke* (Frankfurt am Main: Insel Verlag, 1966), 4: 287.

152. Ibid., 293.

153. Ibid., 362.

154. In the German original there is no mention of a "man." The *"sentimentalische"* indicates not merely Goethe the person, but also the "other" side, as in the explicatory passage above (*GW*, 8: 378).

155. These lines relate to the message of creation expressed by Tonio Kröger (*STD*, 132; *GW*, 8: 338), but they have gained considerably in power and beauty.

156. The protagonist of Lessing's *Nathan der Weise*.

157. *Schillers Werke*, 4: 119.

158. Ibid., 300.

159. When Thomas Mann was temporarily separated from Katia, he wrote to her in May of 1904: "Your black hair, the pearly pallor of your face beneath it. . . ."; and in the middle of August of the same year: ". . . the dark shine of your eyes, the pearl-like paleness of your sweet, wise and expressive face beneath the black hair" (EHL). This description also recalls the appearance of Baroness Ada in "Der Wille zum Glück."

160. Paul Scherer and Hans Wysling, *Quellenkritische Studien zum Werk Thomas Manns* (Bern and Munich: Francke Verlag, 1967), 51–52.

161. Such is precisely the synthesis of "Tonio Kröger."

162. Scherer and Wysling, *Quellenkritische Studien*.

163. His sources were Erdmannsdöroffer's *Deutsche Geschichte vom Westfälischen Frieden bis zu Friedrich dem Großen* and Oncken's *Zeitalter Friedrichs des Großen*.

164. *Summary*: Siegmund and Sieglinde Aarenhold, twin children of a wealthy Jewish railroad speculator, attend the opera *Die Walküre* eight days previous to Sieglinde's planned wedding to the insignificant government functionary von Beckerath. Frenzied by the Wagnerian music, they commit incest in an absurd imitation of the characters in the opera.

165. Thomas Mann, "Sang réservé" (Paris: Grasset, 1931).

166. Thomas Mann, *Wälsungenblut* (Munich: Phantaseus Verlag, Bibliophile, 1921). *Luxusausgabe als Privatdruck*, illustrated by Thomas Theodor Heine.

167. "Bride and sister / you are to your brother— / so may the race of Volsungs flourish!" ("Braut und Schwester / bist du dem Bruder— / so blühe denn Wälsungenblut!")

168. Both Siegmund and Sieglinde express the "avenging" motif: "though I was outlawed / and you were dishonored, / joyful revenge / now greets us in our happiness!"

169. Thomas Mann, "Über die Kunst Richard Wagners" (1911) (*GW*, 10: 840–41).

170. Thomas Mann's conception of these characters was strongly influenced by Paul Bourget's *Cosmopolis*, in which Hafner, a wealthy Jewish businessman, and his angelic daughter Fanny are typical members of dilettante cosmopolitan society.

171. The gift has not been identified, but Thomas Mann praised it in his letter of 18 February 1905, shortly after the wedding. Heinrich might have been absent because he urgently wanted to finish a novel in his usual Italian residence or for a more personal reason.

172. Wayne Andrews, *Siegfried's Curse* (New York: Atheneum, 1972), 291–325.

173. Thomas Mann often used the expression "Jewish issue" or "Jewish problem" (*Judenfrage*) in his famous anti-Nazi speeches from the United States.

174. Mendelssohn, *Zauberer*, 589.

175. Compare similar effects of Wagnerian music on Little Herr Friedemann and Bajazzo.

176. Thomas Mann wrote to his brother Heinrich, 17 January 1906:

. . . in returning from my trip in December, I found the rumor that I had written a strongly "anti-Semitic" (!) short story in which I had frightfully compromised my wife's family. . . . I sent off a few bossy telegrams with orders to Berlin, and I arranged that the January issue of the *Rundschau*, which was already set and ready, would appear *without* "The Blood of the Walsungs." (EHL)

177. "Was wird mit him sein? *Beganeft* haben wir ihn, den *Goy!*" *"Beganeft"* is a rude Yiddish expression. *"Goy"* is a derogatory Yiddish term for a Christian.

178. *STD*, 319; *GW*, 8: 410. Thomas Mann wrote to Heinrich on 5 December 1905: "... *beganeft* breaks through the style, that must be admitted. Before this, all of this sort of thing was avoided and covered up [in the story], the words "Jew" [and] "Jewish" do not appear ... *Beganeft* does not fit such an ironic discretion, even though it is perfectly well-founded psychologically. And the style is to me, in an immoral way, almost as important as the psychology ..." (EHL).

179. Léon Daudet, "Thomas Mann: Sang réservé," *Candide* 8, no. 394 (10 Jan. 1931): 4.

180. In 1903, Lieutenant Fritz Oswald Bilse had published a book exposing the misdeeds of the military, *Aus einer Kleinen Garnison. ein militärisches Zeitbild.* He was tried for slander, but he proved most of his statements to be true. This case had a great deal of publicity and writings of this sort were popularly called *"Bilse Roman."* When a critic suggested that even *Buddenbrooks* was a *"Bilse Roman"* because of its many references to people and life in Lübeck, Thomas Mann was exasperated, and he was impelled in 1906 to write "Bilse und ich." This essay also pertains to the "Blood of the Walsungs" scandal.

181. Wagner closely studied Old Norse manuscripts, especially the *Volsunga Saga*, when he developed the settings and plots of his operas.

182. "Beckerath" is an artificially constructed imitation of a noble name; "Becker" or "baker" is a very common German family name among the lower middle "town burgher" class, recalling the trade in the family's ancestry. "Rath" (the old spelling of "Rat"), meaning "advisor" or "counselor" is a frequently used inconsequential ministerial rank for white collar workers even today. "Becke[r]-rath" is thus a paradoxical combination of a pleasant sound with connotations of philistinism.

183. *STD*, 302, 305, 307, 312, 316; *GW*, 8: 387, 391, 394, 401, 407.

184. *STD*, 302, 307; *GW*, 8: 387, 394.

185. It is a popular belief in Middle and Southern Europe that this physiological feature indicates an intense sexual drive.

186. *Zampa* is an *opéra-comique* by Louis Hérold, with libretto by Mélesville. It had its premiere at the Opéra-Comique, 3 May 1831. Zampa, leader of a pirate gang, invades the island of Castle Lugano and compels Camille to abandon her betrothal and marry him instead. During the pirates' celebration of this event, Zampa derisively places a ring on the finger of a statue of Alice, a girl he has betrayed, and the statue refuses to release the ring. Camille now escapes. As Zampa attempts to pursue her, the statue drags him to his death in the sea. The overture is a well-known concert number. (See David Ewen, *Encyclopedia of the Opera* [New York: Hill and Wang, 1955], 551–52.) The names of the parents' horses, Percy and Leiermann, have no special connotations. The name Percy or Perceval was the name of one of Thomas Mann's own dogs and the name of the high-strung collie in *Royal Highness*. Leiermann suggests the montonous rhythm of trotting.

187. Wagner also depended on fragrances for inspiration. Little Herr Friedemann's savoring his rose, a more refined pleasure, also points up Siegmund's abandonment to his senses.

188. The thematically related essay, "Bilse und ich," was published in the 15 and 16 February 1906 issues of the *Münchner neueste Nachrichten*.

189. This medium-length novel was completed in February of 1909 and published by S. Fischer that year.

190. This fragmentary effort, which Thomas Mann abandoned in 1911, was published as "Felix Krull" in *Stories of Three Decades*. He took up the "Felix Krull" project again in January 1951, and the novel *Bekenntnisse des Hochstaplers Felix Krull* was finished in April 1954. The early fragment of the work was also published as

"Bekenntnisse des Hochstaplers Felix Krull. Bruchstücke aus einem Roman" (*Der Theaterbesuch*, bk. I, chap. 5), "Almanach des S. Fischer Verlags" 25 (1911): 273–83, a work not discussed in detail in this study. Important contributions are: Hans Wysling's "Archivalisches Gewühle zur Entstehungsgeschichte der 'Bekenntnisse des Hochstaplers Felix Krull,'" in Scherer and Wysling, *Quellenkritische Studien*, 234–57, and Hans Wysling's *Narzissmus und illusionäre Existenzform, Zu den Bekenntnissen des Hochstaplers Felix Krull*, (Bern and Munich: Francke Verlag, 1982), in *Thomas Mann Studien*, vol. 5.

191. A pertinent discussion of this essay, "Geist und Kunst, Thomas Manns Notizen zu einem Literatur-Essay," was edited and commented upon by Hans Wysling.

192. On 19 March 1906, S. Fischer renewed Thomas Mann's contract for the next seven years, until 15 June 1913. The conditions offered Thomas Mann were the same as Gerhart Hauptmann's, considered the highest financial contract for a writer in Germany at that time. Thomas Mann was also to receive special pay for anything published in the *Neue deutsche Rundschau*. Fischer and his wife Hedwig even considered Thomas Mann a part of their family (*Verlagsfamilie*), and the two couples frequently met socially.

193. Wysling, "Maja," 329 (n. 27), observes that Thomas Mann had outlined the story in his ninth notebook, p. 14. He had observed: "to 'Maya' (or a short story)" ("zu Maja [oder Novelle])," clearly marking his original intent to make the episode part of the planned Maya fiction.

194. *Summary*: Ernst Becker, a successful bank executive has married the beautiful Angela, who has come to dominate social events and the town's imagination with her beauty and witty appeal. He is envied and admired for his luck in having found such an attractive wife. At one of the splendid dinner parties at the Becker's, the enthusiastic guests toast the admired hostess, praising her extraordinary qualities. Suddenly, pale and disturbed, Becker rises, bursting out with bitter complaint of his wife's repulsive qualities and exposing her vicious private life. The embarrassed company disperses, Becker withdraws into a mental asylum, and soon the Beckers leave town.

195. Wysling, "Maja," 329. Here Thomas Mann referred to his source in the works of Buddha in his notebook no. 9, p. 34 (*GW*, 8: 411).

196. In his Schopenhauer essay Thomas Mann clearly defined the nature of the "veil of Maya," clarifying the reasoning in "Anekdote."

197. "Ernst" is a common German name meaning "serious."

198. "The Metaphysics of Sexual Love," in *The World as Will and Representation*.

199. The similarity of the scene to the final scene of *Doctor Faustus*, written forty years later is significant: "'. . . All this bespoke and beknown, will I now to take leave to play you a little out of the construction which I heard from the lovely instrument of Satan and which in part the knowing children sang to me.' He stood up, pale as death. 'This man,' in the stillness one heard the voice of Dr. Kranich, wheezing yet clearly articulate, 'This man is mad. There has been for a long time no doubt of it. . .'" (*Doctor Faustus*, trans. H. T. Lowe-Porter [New York: Alfred A. Knopf, 1948], 503; *GW*, 6: 666–67). "Still it is not clear, whether out of the Doctor Faustus material should come an independent short story or a partial plot of the 'novel-carpet' [Maya]" (EHL) (Wysling, "Maja," 37).

200. *Summary*: "The Railway Accident" is an autobiographical story about a novelist who travels with his manuscript in his suitcase and becomes the victim of a railway accident. The high point occurs when the novelist believes his manuscript has been destroyed, and feels that he will have to start the work all over again. The story has a happy ending, however.

201. "Die Fragmente zu Thomas Manns Fürsten-Novelle. Eingeführt und ediert von Hans Wysling" *Quellenkritische Studien zum Werk Thomas Manns*, referred to as Wysling: "Fürsten-Novelle."

202. ". . . Thomas Mann went. . . to the Weißen Hirschen in Loschwitz, near Dresden, where Fischer had booked him into the Villa Thalblick and expected him at the sanatorium of Dr. Lahmann. This sanatorium Weißen Hirsch, on the Elbe had a great reputation at that time and into the twenties" (EHL) (Mendelssohn, *Zauberer*, 693).
203. Angelus Gottfried Thomas Mann (Golo) was born 27 March 1909.
204. Thomas Mann wrote it in the summer of 1906 and finished it in February 1909. In November 1908 he worked on the last chapter; at the end of the month he took a trip to the Semering with Arthur Schnitzler and Jakob Wassermann. In the first part of December he was invited to read from *Royal Highness* in Vienna where he met Hugo von Hofmannsthal. *Royal Highness* was first published in *Die neue Rundschau* 20, nos. 1–9 (1909) between January and September.
205. Further details on this crisis in Heinrich Mann's life appear in Nigel Hamilton, *The Brothers Mann* (New Haven: Yale Univ. Press, 1979), chaps. 7–8.
206. Heinrich Mann wrote a play, *Schauspielerin* (1911), inspired by the fate of his sister Carla; Thomas Mann did not approve of the exposure.
207. Thomas Mann, letter to Heinrich, 27 February 1904.
208. On 10 October 1910 the Mann family moved to a new apartment close to the Herzogsplatz, Mauerkirchstraße 13.
209. *Summary*: This modest "Travemünde idyll" describes a fist fight between the titular heroes, who psychically and physically personify the qualities of the "blond" and the "dark." The victory of the "blond" is due less to his qualities than to the ones his opponent lacks. The concepts embodied in Tonio Kröger and Hans Hansen are duplicated in the fighters and the bystanders, the unidentified narrator of the story and Johnny Bishop. Personal experience (as in "The Railway Accident") is expressed when the psychological impact of the situation governs the narrator's mood; at the close, he also feels the urge to fight. The short fight ends when Jappe crushes Do Escobar's nose. The unsatisfied spectators, not finding any other amusement, turn the festive event into a disorganized jumble.
210. Letter of Thomas Mann to Hans von Hülsen, 27 February 1911: "My mother told me the name Do Escobar, and she, if I am not completely mistaken, knew someone with that name" (EHL).
211. *STD*, 331. Literally: "Johnny rejoices wholeheartedly at the battle. . ." (EHL) (*GW*, 8: 430).
212. *STD*, 215. "Was für ein unbegreiflicher Affe. . ." (*GW*, 8: 284). "Tonio Kröger," section 2: it is clear that not only the name but also the personality of François Knaak is identical with the character in "Tonio Kröger".
213. Henry Hatfield, *Thomas Mann* (Norfolk: New Directions, 1951), 29, and Nigel Hamilton, 146.

Chapter 5. An Artist's Call and Fate: The Nature of Beauty

1. K. Mann, *Memoiren*, 70.
2. Ibid., 72.
3. Mendelssohn, *Zauberer*, 872–73, provides another version: "Only in 1964, nearly ten years after Thomas Mann's death, did his Polish translator Andrzej Dolegowski, discover a trace of Wladyslaw Moes, then 68 years old, and looked him up in the Mokotow district of Warsaw. Moes was able to provide him [Dolegowski] with numerous pictures and many details from family chronicles. There were, accurately, two Polish families, both from Warsaw, who spent their vacations together at the Grand Hôtel des Bains at the Lido: the Baroness Moes with her daughters and her picture-pretty son Wladyslaw, and her friend Mrs. Fudakowska with her children, among them Janek, Wladyslaw's friend and companion at the beach" (EHL).

4. *Summary*: The mature, world-famous, and lonely writer, Gustav von Aschenbach, who has attained excellence by hard work, self-discipline, and the suppression of his natural emotions, feels a sudden urge to leave his daily routine and to vacation in the South. Once in Venice he encounters a Polish family with a teenage son who, it seems to Aschenbach, possesses perfect beauty. Aschenbach, the servant of Apollinian harmony of form and clear thought, indulges in contemplation of the aesthetic experience the youngster's features offer. He realizes that beauty is the only quality that is necessarily bound to the material apparition in order to attain its substantiation. The sirocco harms Aschenbach's health, and his sense of self-preservation convinces him to leave Venice, but when he learns that his suitcase is missing, Aschenbach follows his secret wish to stay in Venice after all. The weather clears and Aschenbach, still admiring the young Pole, Tadzio, expresses in a work of art the concept of beauty he has experienced in viewing the boy; in his having brought the concept in his writing to the world of the senses, it becomes corruptible. Thomas Mann presents a delicate duel between the balanced Apollinian beauty of clear thought and the Dionysian intoxication of the instincts in the mind and heart of the aging writer. Asiatic cholera then stalks Venice, a growing motif which parallels Aschenbach's decline. The Venetians try to keep this peril secret in order to retain their tourist business, and as the epidemic ravages the city, Aschenbach gradually succumbs to his addiction with Tadzio's beauty, and he loses his judgment, his sense of proportion, and his poise, a victory for the Dionysian forces. The day he learns of the Polish family's forthcoming departure, Aschenbach goes down to the beach; as his eyes trace Tadzio's features, for him comparable to a Greek god's, Aschenbach, smitten by the cholera, loses consciousness, and soon after, his death is announced to the shocked, respectful world.

5. Letter from Thomas Mann to Elisabeth Zimmer, 9 June 1915.

6. The symbolic significance of the Goethe episode in relation to Thomas Mann's "problem of being an artist" (*Künstlerproblem*) was so vivid that he disregarded exact historical facts and mingled encounters between Goethe and Philippine Lade in Wiesbaden in 1815 with the Marienbad episode with Ulrike von Levetzow in 1821. (See letter to Hans von Hülsen, 3 October 1913, and also Thomas Mann's letter to Julius Bab, 2 March 1913.)

7. Herbert Lehnert, *Thomas Mann, Fiktion, Mythos, Religion* (Stuttgart: Kohlhammer, 1965), 99. Future references are "Lehnert."

8. This essay appeared as "Auseinandersetzungen mit Richard Wagner" in *Der Merkur* (Vienna), July 1911, and its original is available at the Thomas Mann Archives, Zurich, 78. 1911, nos. 31–32, pp. 476–77. The article was later known in reedited form as "Über die Kunst Richard Wagners," 1922 (*GW*, 10: 840). Herbert Lehnert's study on this essay is of great value. See also Wysling, "Geist und Kunst," as well as Manfred Dierks, *Studien zu Mythos und Psychologie bei Thomas Mann* (Bern and Munich: Francke Verlag, 1972), referred to as Dierks, *Studien*.

9. He elaborated on these in "Geist und Kunst" and his Krull project.

10. Thomas Mann's conversation in 1918 with Otto Zarek as described by Otto Zarek in "Neben dem Werk," *Die Neue Rundschau*, June 1936, 621, and *GW*, 10: 842.

11. See Thomas Mann's letter to Ernst Bertram, 16 October 1911, ". . . unmögliche Conception"; also to Wilhelm Herzog, 8 December 1911. Thomas Mann's letter to Hans von Hülsen, 21 July 1912, notes, "My short story has departed just now to Bie. I am curious if the fish will bite [literally: he will bite]; I would rather doubt it" (EHL). Oscar Bie was the editor of *Die Neue deutsche Rundschau*. The hesitation about the reception of the story is noticeable, since Thomas Mann realized that his story would be often and basically misinterpreted.

12. Today international action is being taken to save the city from pollution.

13. *Asche* in German means ashes, an archetype of death. In *Doctor Faustus* the town of Kaisersaschern becomes a leitmotif.

14. On 2 June 1782, his fiftieth birthday, Goethe received his patent of nobility from Emperor Joseph II in recognition of his services. The age of thirty is the traditional hero's age in the Western world: Christ, Dante, Faust, Zarathustra, etc. Aschenbach is thus a man past maturity and on his way to old age, which may represent dignity, but if dignity is lost, age becomes pitiful. Nothing is more repulsive than an old man who clowns, having lost self-respect and discipline and wisdom, a victim of raging. Typical of Thomas Mann's realism is that Gustav von Aschenbach is in the difficult age which today is often called "the male menopause," a time of change and instability. The reference here to Goethe is significant.

15. This was Thomas Mann's own daily routine. After cold water and a walk, the best morning hours were invariably reserved for work, and after a nap he used the afternoon and evening for cultural and personal activities. The routine he had adapted in his bachelor years was observed by Katia who took charge of the household with energetic circumspection; she allowed nothing and no one to disturb her husband during the precious morning hours he reserved for work.

16. The German expression to "swing" or "*schwingen*" versus "schweifen" (to sweep) deserves emphasis.

17. Thomas Mann does not refer to him by either the words *Dichter* or *Künstler*, which express the ideal; nor does he use *Literat*, which tends toward the derogatory. Use of the word "writer" (*Schriftsteller*) provides a sober neutral expression plainly referring to Aschenbach's trade.

18. Thomas Mann developed a pattern of compounds of either *schweifen* or *schwingen* (to swing or balance). In the first paragraph of "Death in Venice," *fortschwingen* is a creative life power, a word that does not recur in the story. *Aufschwingen* connotes "upswing" (to reach a height); and *ausschweifen* develops extremely negative connotations of immorality and dangerous excess or debauchery. Because of the different words used in the translation, the pattern words in the German text are pointed out in the discussion. See note 16.

19. The emphasis on "still" in the German text: "stillere und stillere Wege" (*GW*, 8: 444) is minimized in the translation (*STD*, 378). "Still" introduces here the death motif as it did in "Tristan." Aschenbach is on his way home (*Heimweg*) in the "setting sun" (*sinkende Sonne*, omitted in translation). The sun, being the attribute of Apollo, is a significant symbol in the story.

20. His meeting the mysterious figure near the entrance to the cemetery might be seen as only an insignificant episode seized upon by Aschenbach's overheated imagination, but it might also be an expression of his subconscious desires, the Dionysian element personified as the peculiar wanderer, a mythic element. The wanderer's looks poetically foreshadow death at the entrance to the cemetery. His unexpected influence on Aschenbach indicates he is the vehicle for "death before death," the sinister power that intoxicates the mature, highly disciplined writer, driving him to abandon his *Künstlerwürde*.

21. *STD*, 380. "Vaulting unrest" stands for "*schweifende Unruhe*." The word "*schweifen*" means "to roam," "ramble," "stray." It is the fraction that will form "*ausschweifen*." See notes 16 and 18.

22. See Thomas Mann's letter to Hedwig Fischer, 14 October 1912. "It does not end well, the dignity of the 'hero and poet' is basically shaken. It is a real tragedy."

23. In her translation, H. T. Lowe-Porter reorganized and regrouped the first paragraph. The German text discusses the intellectual references first and then reveals Aschenbach's birthplace and family circumstances, a pattern repeated at the beginning and the end of chapter 2 in the German text.

24. See also *STD*, 382 and *GW*, 8: 450.

25. Thomas Mann planned "Ein Elender" ("A Miserable One"), as a character study built on allegations against two of Thomas Mann's critics: see Theodor Lessing,

"Wider Thomas Mann," in *Die Schaubühne* 6, no. 10 (March 1910): 253–57; "Gegen Thomas Mann," in *Das literarische Echo* 12, no. 13 (April 1910): 975–77; and Alfred Kerr, "Tagebuch," *Pan* 3, no. 27 (April 1913): 635–41. The lamentable story of "Ein Elender," with the sad outline suggested in "Death in Venice," was never written.

26. The title "Geist und Kunst" belonged to an essay that Thomas Mann never finished.

27. Aschenbach's unnamed birthplace begins with *L*, as does Thomas Mann's native Lübeck. Aschenbach's foreign-born mother, to whom he owed his foreign features, also rather resembles Julia Mann. Though not blond like his father or brother Heinrich, Thomas Mann was definitely not the Latin type: he seemed to be pleased, however, to parallel Latin looks with characteristics of his own.

28. *STD*, 383. "*Durchhalten*" (to hold out) is quoted in German in the English text.

29. At this point the German text uses the word "*Zucht*," translated as "discipline." The German word also means "breeding" "rearing," "discipline," and "drill." "*Zuht*" in Old High German and Middle High German also connotes "high breeding," "good manners," "politeness," "noble character"; "*Zuht*" with "*masse*" = "moderation," represented in the Middle High German Golden Age the most esteemed moral value.

30. See *STD*, 384. The translation's emphasis on "spiritual" does not appear in the original.

31. *Anmut* translates as "beauty" but is also conceived of as "grace," and "charm." In Schiller's concept it means the natural visible expression of inner values by bodily gestures, poise, "grace," and "charm." To physical beauty it adds the abstraction of high standards, such as self-esteem, purity, harmony, innocence, etc. Because of this plurality of connotations the word "grace" is used here.

32. See also the letter of Thomas Mann to Josef Ponten, 6 June 1919.

33. *STD*, 285; *GW*, 8: 453.

34. The expression and even the idea are omitted from the translation (*STD*, 385). See notes 16, 18, and 21.

35. *STD*, 385. "*Moralisten der Leistung*" (*GW*, 8: 453) is also referred to above as "*Leistung-Ethiker*." On 18 January 1946, Thomas Mann wrote to Hans Albert Maier: "From Thomas Buddenbrook, the heroic 'Leistung Ethiker,' to Gustav Aschenbach, to the good soldier Joachim Ziemßen in the 'Magic Mountain'—this motif returns in my work."

36. In *Betrachtungen eines Unpolitischen*, February 1918, Thomas Mann scrutinies his own position: "Insofar as there is in me also something of this 'determination,' this yielding to 'the indecent psychologizing of the past era in its lax and formless *tout comprendre*—of a will thus, which one might call unnaturalistic, anti-impressionistic, anti-relativistic, which however in the artistic as well as in the moral [sphere] was a 'will' and not merely morally a 'surrender'" (EHL). (*GW*, 12: 28) In "Mein Verhältnis zur Psychoanalyse" ("My Relationship with Psychoanalysis" [EHL]) (summer of 1925), Thomas Mann wrote, "And one can also find on the other side, that improperly brought among people it [psychoanalysis] could [grow] into an instrument of evil, an enlightenment of an anticultural mania [that would] dismantle and discredit and have second thoughts against it [culture]." This was written after the *Magic Mountain*, in which Hans Castorp rejected Dr. Krokowski's "soul detection" techniques, but prior to "Mario the Magician."

37. *STD*, 386. "Unanständiger Psychologismus der Zeit" (*GW* 8: 455), an often-cited phrase, literally "the indecent psychologizing of the era," conveys a biting irony not present in the translation.

38. *STD*, 388. "ausschweifende Leidenschaften" (*GW*, 8: 457). See notes 16, 18, 21, and 34.

39. *STD*, 338 fails to include this significant detail. This concept of the sea is recognizable in Gustav von Aschenbach's coming experiences of life.

40. This is reminiscent of the Venusberg scene in Wagner's opera *Tannhäuser*.

41. Omitted in translation.

42. Dante was allowed to descend into hell, climb purgatory, and see Heaven in order to relate God's love and truth in his poetry. Dante explicitly refers to Venice in the "Inferno," canto 21.

43. Both here and later Charon is associated with the gondolier. Charon is a mythological boatman paid to ferry dead souls across the Styx and Acheron rivers of Hell.

44. Wine and intoxication are attributes of the god Dionysus.

45. The gondola with its elegant swanlike S-shaped prow, symbolizes Venice's Grand Canal. The six points or teeth to the left are the six Sestrieri, for the sections of the city: San Marco, Rialto, Santa Croce, Dorso Duro, Cannaregio, and Castello. The only tooth toward the right is Giudecca Island. The decor between the first and second tooth and that between the third and fourth tooth represent the islands of Murano and Burano. (Information from Dr. Geraldo Vettorazzo of the University of Padua.)

46. Wealthy travelers in the early years of the twentieth century never carried their own unlimited luggage, which included formal wear for hotel meals. A trunk was usually oblong or square, like a chest with a handle on each end, similar to a coffin.

47. The imagery of the gondola and its mysterious gondolier hints at Charon rowing the soul to the realm of Hades. Charon never delivered without pay, so coins were customarily placed in the mouths of the dead to assure a successful journey. The color black as symbol of mourning, thought to signify death, dates from the first part of the 17th century after the Plague in Venice and was reinforced by 19th-century art such as *The Tales of Hoffmann*, in which the Venice scene focused on Death travelling by gondola. This well-rooted notion, however, is a misconception, since the color of mourning in Venice was red, not black. According to Dr. Geraldo Vettorazzo of the University of Padua, the black color refers to an attempt to limit the gondola's excessive decoration, which came from competition among the Venetian patricians as to whose gondola was richest. The Venetian Republic (*La Serenissima*) was very careful to avoid any kind of rivalry between members of the nobility (*patrizi*) and so ordered everyone to have black gondolas. This order was made into law on 8 October 1562. Whether Thomas Mann was acquainted with these facts is not certain, but in any case these beliefs give additional flavor to the story.

48. This is the real name of the hotel where Thomas Mann had also stayed with Katia and Heinrich. It still exists and the hotel staff exhibits his former living quarters and sells postcards showing his window. This is one of the few hotels on the Lido with a view directly toward the open sea. After the successful film adaptation of "Death in Venice," interest in visiting this hotel has increased and it has been modernized since Mann stayed there in 1911. The rooms are now air-conditioned and have phones and television; the facade and the decor, however, have been preserved. The only important changes outside are a large modern swimming pool on the grounds and beach houses have been built replacing the cabañas and umbrellas Thomas Mann describes.

49. Mann had had a substantial interest in Bourget's *Cosmopolis*, which, with his personal reminiscences of Italy, Riva, and Aalsgaard formed an important motif of *The Magic Mountain* twelve years later.

50. Thomas Mann calls attention to the Nietzschean imagery of the Apollinian and Dionysian forces.

51. In the German text, *Traum* ("dream") appears twice near the end of this paragraph; "dream" is the realm of Apollo, the god of beauty and symbolic form, and a part of the vocabulary of the German Romantic School.

52. *STD*, 398 (*GW*, 8: 472). In the *STD*, "stagnant" should be replaced with "rotting," in contrast to the "carbolic" odor later.

53. Nicholls, *Nietzsche*, 90. "There is one particular connecting link between Nietzsche in Venice and the action of Mann's story that may have been in Mann's mind when he worked out his theme. Nietzsche tells in letters from Venice in May, 1886, how he is forced to leave the city he had loved so much by the oppressiveness of the climate. 'I cannot hold out in Venice,' he complained to his mother, 'my eyes torture me.' Three weeks later he wrote to his sister: 'I came away from Venice just at the right time; meanwhile the cholera has come into the open and the city is encircled by land and sea quarantines.'" (Nicholls quotes *Gesammelte Briefe*, vol. 5, pt. 2, p. 672. Cf. letter to Peter Gast, ibid., vol. 4, p. 249, and the letter to his sister, ibid., vol. 5, pt. 2, p. 637.)

54. The statue of Apollo from the island of Lemons (480 B.C.) is of Parian marble.

55. See also *STD*, 401 (*GW*, 8: 475). The deckchair where the dying Aschenbach has his last vision foreshadows his deathbed. Even though Aschenbach does not even sense his end, his longing and his relationship to the ultimate here represented by the sea do not change. Eros, companion of Aphrodite, was considered the son of Day and Night out of Chaos, and brought harmony to Chaos.

56. She married Thomas Mann's brother-in-law Heinz Pringsheim later; she was a painter who lived in Paris and knew a Polish friend whom she located after some difficulty.

57. The strawberries he ate, associated here with the sudden onset of hot weather, become a key motif in "Death in Venice." Aschenbach first eats healthy luscious fruit, and second, dead-ripe near-rotting merchandise; the heat makes him buy them from a street vendor, ignoring his hotel meal schedule.

58. *STD*, 401. (*GW*, 8: 476). The poised Tadzio's antipathy toward the Russians indicates a clash between basically opposing characters. Tadzio, an Apollo figure, counters Dionysus, whose attribute is instinct. The classical Apollo had a vengeful temper and always won in contests.

59. This detail emerges powerfully in chapter 5, when Aschenbach has a dream of a Dionysian orgiastic feast. The Dionysian magic slowly overcomes his self-discipline and will.

60. The "rationalizing power" which serves the *Wille zum Leben* appears in "Tristan." This and other references to Schopenhauer do not represent an exclusive and structured *Weltanschauung* in "Death in Venice."

61. *STD*, 404 (*GW*, 8: 478). Scholars have noted that Thomas Mann used the motif of poor teeth as a recurrent pattern of decadence and decay. His letter to Rudolf Fleischmann of 16 June 1952 makes it doubtful whether Thomas Mann only visualized decaying teeth and other recurrent physical characteristics or consciously developed them to make his point (letter originally written in English): "The observation of your daughter's literature professor is strange. I had not been conscious of any tendency on my part to describe poor teeth, and so far nobody had noticed it. The professor made a discovery there. I only remember that Hanno Buddenbrook had many toothaches, and that also the teeth of young Tadzio in 'Death in Venice' are not quite perfect. But otherwise? Perhaps the professor could make a little list."

62. *STD*, 404, "revolution"—translation of "*Umschwung*" (*GW*, 8: 480) from the verb "*umschwingen*," literally "swing around." This oscillation is described with a word belonging to the "*schwingen*" versus "*schweifen*" pattern words. See notes 16, 18, 21, 34, and 38.

63. The inner city of Venice is plagued by tourists; souvenir shops and dense crowds make walking difficult. But narrow, picturesque alleys lead to hidden peaceful piazzas where fountains, the stone memorials of long-past ages that once sustained life, are now forgotten by sightseers and abandoned by the Venetians. The fountains' loneliness illustrates the fading of appreciation for the values that built them. Thomas Mann loved fountain imagery, and later in *Joseph and His Brothers* he gave the foun-

tain a major role in expressing the relativity of time as an entrance to an infinite dimension. Aschenbach attains his insight while resting on the rim of such a fountain, and later surrenders his service to Apollo at the same spot.

64. *STD*, 406–7. Some sensitive details are omitted in the translation.

65. *STD*, 406 (omitted): "... *unmöglichen und verbotenen Aufenthalt*" (*GW*, 8: 483).

66. Omitted in translation: "... *eine unglaubliche Heiterkeit*" (*GW*, 8: 484).

67. Apollo, twin brother of Artemis, was god of the sun and bringer of fertility to the earth; his attributes are light, purity, and truth. Helios, also a god of the sun, crossed the heavens daily in his golden chariot drawn by four white horses. His Roman counterpart was Sol (*STD*, 409). "Pontos" (omitted) (*GW*, 8: 486) is an early god of the sea, son of Uranus, the personification of the sky and heavens, and Gaea, who was created after Chaos, personified Mother Earth. Oceanus, son of Uranus and Gaea, is the personification of Ocean. Apollo, who gives prophecy, is also the god of music and lyric poetry. He is a vengeful god envisioned with a lyre and a bow, and the laurel tree is sacred to him.

68. *STD* uses "lost trunk" (409); "*verirrte Last*" (*GW*, 8: 487).

69. See also *STD*, 410 (*GW*, 8: 488). The original German text instead of "sea" mentions *Okeanos* = Oceanus, the personification of the Ocean, entirely surrounding earth, from which all sweet water sources sprang. The reference to Oceanus widens the concept into the infinite, and links it to a ritualistic sacrifice to the Sun.

70. *STD*, 2; *GW*, 8: 489–90). This description recalls the features of the Apollo Belvedere in the Vatican Museum.

71. This topic was widely discussed by the eighteenth-century aesthetic theorists, especially Johann Elias Schlegel, and later Lessing.

72. "*Rausch*" (intoxication) is an attribute of Dionysus.

73. "*Meerrausch*" might also signify the murmur of the sea, the word *Rausch* carrying a double significance. Here *Meerrausch* stands for the Dionysian and *Sonnenglast* for the Apollinian component in the imagined ritual. Thomas Mann's text smoothly allows the multitude of there mythical images to flow in the atmosphere he presents. To stop to identify them is first distracting, but then rewards the reader with enriched vision. See also Nymphs (nature goddesses) of the group of Dryads, Naiads, Oceanids ruling over springs and rivers; the Nymphs presided over streams, mountains, woods, and more. Achelous was a river god who took the shape of a bull and in wrestling with Hercules lost one horn; the nymphs offered it to the Goddess of Plenty and it became the Horn of Plenty.

74. Thomas Mann's thematic development parallels Plato's *Phaedrus*. See the *Phaedrus*, in Irwin Edman, ed., *The Works of Plato* (New York: Modern Library, 1956), referred to here as Pl. *Ph*. "Death in Venice"; distorts the Platonic dialogue, for here only Socrates speaks. Aschenbach's vision includes the Platonic setting near a plane of trees; Plato's Phaedrus challenges the theme of the dialogue on theoretical grounds: "My tale, Socrates, is one of your sort, for love was the theme which occupied us—love after a fashion: Lysias has been writing about a fair youth who was being tempted, but not by a lover; and this was the point: he ingeniously proved that the non-lover should be accepted rather than the lover" (Pl. *Ph*., 213–14). Socrates' explanation exhibits deep insight into the plight of the "lover" and the "non-lover," thoughts closely related to the tragic story of Aschenbach and Tadzio. Plato's Socrates says of himself, "For I was saying, I want to know not about this, but about myself: am I a monster more complicated and swollen with passion than the serpent Python, or a creature of a gentler and simpler sort, to whom Nature has given a diviner and lowlier destiny? But let me ask you, friend: have we not reached the plane-tree to which you were conducting us?" (Pl. *Ph*., 266–67). (Aschenbach's dream vision also refers to a plane tree.) About love Socrates says: "Everyone sees that love is a desire, and we

know also that non-lovers desire the beautiful and good. Now in what way is the lover to be distinguished from the non-lover?" (Pl. *Ph.*, 275).

75. *STD*, 403; (*GW*, 8: 479).

76. Pl. *Ph.*, 272. "Socrates: 'Well, but you and I expected to praise the sentiments of the author, or only the clearness, and roundness, and finish.'"

77. Nietzsche overcame Schopenhauer's "worldview" (*Weltbild*) by uniting rather than destroying the Apollinian and Dionysian forces. According to Nietzsche, the balance of the Apollinian and the Dionysian brings the writer to his highest creativity; the balance creates success out of symbolic and formal expression (Apollinian) and instinctive emotional and sensual (Dionysian) forces. Thomas Mann questions this balance and its attribution to the highest "dignity of the artist" (*Künstlerwürde*) and denies it in the fate of Aschenbach. Aschenbach the artist, not really qualifying for Thomas Mann's own concept of the *Künstler*, attempts to unite the opposites, representing an ironic version of Nietzsche's suggestion of contravening the merciless thesis of the Schopenhauerian world order.

78. Pl. *Ph.*, 276. "Now exist many names, and many members, and many forms, and any of these forms when very marked gives a name, neither honourable nor creditable, to the bearer of the name. . . . And now I think that you will perceive the drift of my discourse; but as every spoken word is in a manner plainer than the unspoken, I had better say further that the irrational desire which overcomes the tendency of opinion toward right, and is led away to the enjoyment of beauty, and especially of personal beauty, by the desire which [is] her own kindred—that supreme desire, I say, which by leading conquers and by the force of passion is reinforced, for this very force, receiving a name, is called love."

79. Pl. *Ph.*, 280–1. "Does not your simplicity observe that I have got out of dithyrambics into heroics, when only uttering a censure on the lover? And if I am to add the praises of the non-lover what will become of me? Do you not perceive that I am already overtaken by the Nymphs to whom you nave mischievously exposed me? And therefore I will only add that the non-lover has all the advantages in which the lover is accused of being deficient."

80. After his death, this pure, noble, and intense piece of literature brought Aschenbach still more renown, since his readers could not realize the circumstances and motivation of its creation.

81. This Apollinian symbolic expression is dissimilar to *Anmut*. See note 31.

82. Nietzsche: Dionysian orgiastic feast; Goethe's *Walpurgisnacht*.

83. Thomas Mann's use of Plato is masterful. While Plato's Socrates, the wise teacher, praises the nonlover to Phaedrus, the Socrates of "Death in Venice" praises the lover. His message, however, represents Nietzsche's position vis-à-vis Socrates, and hence this message is a deceptive rationalization and profanation of the intangible subject in Aschenbach's corruption. Hereafter, by following the words of Plato's Socrates, Aschenbach's fate provides additional insight to the novella.

84. Pl. *Ph.*, 273. "Socrates: '. . . Who, for example, could speak on this thesis of yours without praising the discretion of the non-lover and blaming the indiscretion of the lover?' Phaedrus: '. . . and I will allow you to start with the premise that the lover is more disordered in his wits than the non-lover.'"

85. Jan Fudakowski and Wladyslaw Moes had both noticed "the old man"; also in the story the mother and the governess were aware of Aschenbach following Tadzio. Probably the two boys were innocently curious, and mischievously teased the strangely behaving man.

86. *STD*, 414; *GW*, 8: 494.

87. *Zucht* = breeding; *Zügellosigkeit* = licentious folly.

88. *Instinktverschmelzung* = "the mingling of instincts," an expression coined by Thomas Mann, is perfectly appropriate in this context.

89. Pl. *Ph.*, 280. "'. . . and that in making such a choice he was giving himself up to a faithless, morose, envious, disagreeable being, hurtful to his estate, hurtful to his bodily health, and still more hurtful to the cultivaton of his mind, than which there neither is nor ever will be anything more honoured in the eyes both of gods and men. Consider this, fair youth, and know that in the friendship of the lover there is no real kindness; he has an appetite and wants to feed upon you: "As wolves love lambs so lovers love their lovers."'"

90. Eos's brother is Helios, the driver of the sun's four-horse chariot. Eos's passionate love had seduced many, among them Cephalus, Cleitos, and Orion. This image of passionate promiscuity penetrates the mood of the awakening Aschenbach through the splendor of the morning sky.

91. *STD*, 416. "Grazing herds" *"weidende Herden"* (*GW*, 8: 496). Apollo was the protector of shepherds and herds. Zephyrus, the West Wind, and Boreas, the North Wind, sons of Eos, loved Hyacinthus, son of Amyclas, King of Laconia, who was also loved by Apollo. The Winds caused Hyacinthus's death by directing Apollo's discus at him. Out of Hyacinthus's blood grows the flower called the hyacinth.

92. since Narcissus is associated with self-adoration, Tadzio's smile cannot be interpreted as flirtatious. (Probably young Baron Moes's smile was mischievously curious.)

93. Pl. *Ph.*, 276: "The desire of eating, for example, which gets the better of the higher reason and the other desires, is called gluttony, and he who is possessed by it is called a glutton; the tyrannical desire of drink, which inclines the possessor of the desire to drink, has a name which is only too obvious, and there can be as little doubt by what name any other appetite of the same family would be called;—it will be the name of that what happens to be dominant.

94. The first scene took place in Munich in May, and since it took Aschenbach several weeks to put his affairs in order, his departure for Italy took place in June. He stayed a week and a half at Pola and then four weeks in Venice.

95. *STD*, 418. "World about him." *"Außenwelt"* (*GW*, 8: 499), literally "outer world." The vision concentrated on the self and the considerable emphasis on inner emotions and reactions makes the ordinary seem strange and inferior. Aschenbach's focus on anyone not involved with him and his feelings for Tadzio makes *"Außenwelt"* highly significant. In *The Magic Mountain* the dichotomy between the Magic Mountain and the world below becomes a major theme.

96. *STD*, 418. "Sickness." *"Übel"* (*GW*, 8: 499). The German connotations include "bad," "wicked," "sick," "evil," "misfortune." Beyond the Asiatic cholera and physical death the story treats Aschenbach's loss of *Würde* (dignity) in sliding into the arms of Dionysus, the "death before death." (See note 20.) *"Übel"* here is described as "bad," not limiting the term to "sickness."

97. Pl. *Ph.*, 278. "The lover will be the first to see what, indeed, will be sufficiently evident to all men, that he desires above all things to deprive his beloved of his dearest and best and holiest possession, father, mother, kindred, friends, of all who he thinks may be hinderers or reprovers of their most sweet converse; . . ."

98. *STD*, 419 omits *"Abenteuer"* and *"Außenwelt."*

99. A word for the sensual experience of smelling, mixing the concept with stench and smell, with a derogatory connotation.

100. *STD*, 420. ". . . meet his lover's eyes" is not in the original German text.

101. This passage is omitted in the English translation.

102. The guitar is derived from the ancient stringed cithara (*Kithara*), which appears ca. 1700 B.C. in Asia, one of the most ancient stringed instruments of the Semitic races. The cithara (not to be confused with the lyre) was popular in ancient Greece as the instrument of professional accompanists for voice and dance performances. Contests for solo performance on the cithara were instituted at the Eighth

Pythian Games, and one of the principal events for aulos and cithara was the *nomos pythikos*, describing Apollo's slaying of the mysterious Python. "The degeneration of music, as art, among the Romans and its gradual degradation by association with sensual amusement of corrupt Rome, nearly brought about its [the cithara's] extinction at the end of the 4th century" (*Encyclopaedia Britannica*, 11th ed., s.v. "Guitar"). After this time, the instrument began to evolve into the modern guitar.

103. Tadzio, the incorporation of beauty, Apollo, Narcissus, and Eros, spurns the display.

104. The vocabulary is applicable to an epidemic, and the ecstasy is reminiscent of the Dionysian orgiastic dithyramb.

105. *STD*, 426. "*Traumbann*" (*GW*, 8: 510): in the German "dream-spell," the *Traum* belongs to Apollinian and Romantic terminology—the "spell" overlapping the concept of Dionysian intoxication.

106. This may refer to the *nomos pythikos*, the cithara contest in which the vengeful Apollo won a final victory over Dionysus.

107. ". . . ausschweifende[r] Genugtuung erfüllte sein Herz." The "*ausschweifen*" word pattern (see notes 16, 18, 21, 34, 38, and 62) expresses Aschenbach's exuberance like that of a lover who for the first time believes he has the beloved in reach of his desires. Docility to his mood and the idea of Tadzio's vulnerability to death gave Aschenbach this emotional impulse. "He who is victim of his passions and the slaves of pleasure will of course desire to make his beloved as agreeable to himself as possible. Now to him who has a mind diseased anything is agreeable which is not opposed to him, but that which is equal or superior is hateful to him, and therefore the lover will not brook any superiority or equality on the part of his beloved; he is always employed in reducing him to inferiority. And the ignorant is the inferior of the wise, the coward of the brave, the slow of speech of the speaker, the dull of the clever. These, and not these only, are the mental defects of the beloved;—defects which, when implanted by nature, are necessarily a delight to the lover, and, when not implanted, he must contrive to implant them in him, if he would not be deprived of his fleeting joy" (Pl. *Ph.*, 277).

108. *STD*, 427. "*mephitischen Odem*" (*GW*, 8: 512). The word *Odem* is the archaic form for breath. The emphasis on "ancient" and "breath" personifies the poisonous, bad-smelling vapor significantly related to the development of the concept "bad."

109. *STD*, 380; *GW*, 8: 447.

110. Here the Greek mythological imagery is heavily emphasized, paralleling Nietzsche's approach in the *Birth of Tragedy*. Aschenbach's orgiastic dream differs widely from Goethe's classical *Walpurgisnacht*.

111. The flute is the instrument of Pan. In a contest between Pan playing the flute (pipe) and Apollo playing the lyre, Midas awarded the prize to Pan. Pan is father of the satyr Silenus, who has horns, goat's hooves, a beard, and a snub nose. Pan and the satyrs are part of the Dionysian wine orgies. The *u* sound associates Tadzio with Dionysian orgiastic experiences.

112. The translation cannot convey the exquisite strength of Thomas Mann's imagery or sound patterns. Mounting intoxication gradually overpowers Aschenbach, and his *geistig* dignity, no longer able to resist, succumbs to degradation and falls.

113. Pan's name led to the word "panic," because of the fear of woods at night. This pertains to Aschenbach's jungle vision and his fear before the Dionysian orgy.

114. *STD*, 432. "*unwürdig*" and "*Unzucht*" (*GW*, 8: 517–18). The German uses the negative prefix to words expressing the concepts "dignity" (*Würde*) and "breeding" (*Zucht*).

115. *STD*, 433. The English translation uses "colour of ripe strawberries" in describing the lipstick: "*zartes Karmin*" (*GW*, 8: 519). Thomas Mann's text only mentioned strawberries twice, first when Aschenbach consumed gorgeous healthy ripe

berries at the beach, and later the overripe infected fruits, obviously the source of contagion. "But what pleasure or consolation can the beloved be receiving all this time? Must he not feel the extremity of disgust when he looks at an old shrivelled face and remainder to match, which even in a description is disagreeable, and quite detestable when he is forced into daily contact with his lover?" (Pl. *Ph.*, 279).

116. *STD*, 435. "Knowledge" does not adequately render Schopenhauer's concept nor is it identical with Tonio's idea: this *Erkenntnis* is a boundless experience—an end result of "Tout connaître c'est tout pardonner," a formless loss of self-respect (see *STD*, 414; *GW*, 8: 494), and the fusion of the adventure of the "outer world" and the heart.

117. See notes 16, 18, 21, 34, 38, 62, and 107.

118. The translation cannot express the nuances of this stylized composition, so strongly accompanied by the auditory effects of the language; the cinematographic version of "Death in Venice" partially succeeded in doing so.

119. Mendelssohn, *Zauberer*, 871–73, reports that Jan Fudakowski had indeed been called "Jaschu" or "Jaschiu." The Polish translator of the story Andrzej Dolegowski, reports that Tadzio, Baron Moes, said, "'At the same time my friend Janek was in Venice with his parents. In the novella he is called "Jaschu," as we always called him. I liked to play with him, even though I could not stand his rude ways. The holds which he used at wrestling were not fair. Therefore our friendship ended'" (EHL).

120. Mendelssohn, *Zauberer*, 873: "Andrzej Dolegowski reports a conversation with Baron Moes, 'I was taken for a very pretty child, and women admired me and kissed me in passing when I walked by. I had been painted and sketched. In my memory, however, all this seemed to remain quite insignificant to me; I had exactly the childlike relaxed way which spoiled and early-maturing children sometimes exhibit. In "Death in Venice" this is described better than I could'" (EHL).

121. See also *STD*, 437. In the English translation, part of this passage is unfortunately omitted; the last phrase refers to the last imaginary Socrates-Phaedrus conversation.

122. Thomas Mann's letter to Paul Amann, 9 October 1915. "What I had in mind was the problem of *Künstlerwürde*, something like the tragedy of mastery . . ." (EHL).

123. The best of the letter is originally in English.

Chapter 6. New Humanism: Fading of Formal Genre Limitations

1. *Der Untertan*, a novel, was finished that year. Thomas Mann had not read it yet. Heinrich Mann was unable to publish it until 1918, at the Kurt Wolff Verlag, Leipzig Munich. (*The Man of Straw*, trans. Ernest Boy-Ed) [London: Hutchinson, 1947].)

2. Correspondence of this period shows that Ernst Bertram was regularly invited to the Mann house even during Katia's absence. The children liked him, and his friendship with Thomas Mann from 1914 to 1918 is significant. While Thomas wrote his *Betrachtungen eines Unpolitischen*, Ernst Bertram was working on a study of Nietzsche; they regularly exchanged notes and read to each other from their work (*Nietzsche, Versuch einer Mythologie* [Bonn: H. Bouvier & Co., 1918]).

3. Among others, Thomas Mann corresponded in 1913–14 with Kurt Martens, Schnitzler, Wedekind, Hofmannsthal, Stefan Zweig, and Ida Boy-Ed, his writer friend in Lübeck.

4. Julia Mann, Thomas Mann's sister was also born in Lübeck (1877). She lived most of her life in Munich and married the bank director Dr. Joseph Löhr. The mar-

riage had some difficulties, and her health was delicate. She committed suicide in 1927.

5. Carla Mann, Thomas's favorite sister, was an actress and committed suicide on 30 July 1910. Thomas wrote to Heinrich: "It is the bitterest things that could have happened to me. My sense of fraternal solidarity makes it seem as though Carla's act has put our existence into question, has broken the bond between us . . ." (Hamilton, *Brothers*, 142).

6. "Naturally I am at your disposal [on] August 12" (EHL). Thomas Mann, letter to Heinrich, 30 July 1914.

7. To Magdelena (Nelly) Kilian, from Munich.

8. Thomas Mann had always been painstaking in financial matters, and his debts oppressed him, though his financial situation was not appreciably different from that of other writers. The Mann family was relatively comfortable, even in those difficult times.

9. See a colorfully detailed description of the Poschingerstraße home and daily life, in Mendelssohn, *Zauberer*, 952–55, and also Katia Mann, *Memoiren*, 38–39.

10. Thomas Mann's descriptions of the land surrounding the Poschingerstraße home are best in "A Man and His Dog."

11. The essay (not translated) was published in *Die neue Rundschau* 25, no. 11 (Berlin, 1914): 1471–84, and later in *Friedrich und die große Koalition* (Berlin: Fischer, 1915), 7–31.

12. Thomas Mann, letter to Hans Rademacker, 30 November 1914.

13. The military postcard from 25 November 1914 is filed at the Thomas Mann Archives in Zurich.

14. Thomas Mann, letter to Clarence B. Boutell, 21 January 1944.

15. First published in *Svenska Dagbladet* (Stockholm), 11 May 1915, under the title "Thomas Mann om Tyskland och Världskriget"; also appeared in German in *Die neue deutsche Rundschau* (Berlin) 26, no. 6 (June 1915): 830–36 under the title "Brief an die Zeitung 'Svenska Dagbladet' Stockholm."

16. *Friedrich und die große Koalition. Ein Abriß für den Tag und die Stunde* (Berlin: Fischer, 1915), 119–31.

17. To Paul Amann, 25 March 1915: "The *Geist* of Prussianism, one cannot doubt it any longer, had accomplished its German mission and it is fated today to be overcome. What I heartily wish is that this overcoming should not happen in a catastrophic manner with abuse and shame . . ." (EHL).

18. Mendelssohn, *Zauberer*, 1050, points out that the terminology used by Thomas Mann in this period of intellectual anxiety, especially *Geist, Voluntarismus, Determinismus,* and *Ästhetizismus,* fluctuates between different, sometimes opposing, connotations. His concepts of *Politik, Demokratie,* and *Zivilisation* act in a similar fashion.

19. Katia Mann has commented, " . . . but the brothers had grown widely apart at that time and also politically, because Heinrich had become oriented toward the French-Latin [position], while by contrast my husband, according to his cultural roots, was entirely German, absolutely German."

20. Thomas Mann, letter to Ernst Bertram, 24 January 1916.

21. Thomas Mann wrote a letter to Maximilian Brantl, 31 December 1915, asking him for a copy of the Zola article. Thomas Mann speaks of "issues" in the plural, though the entire essay was published in a single issue of *Weißen Blätter*, which supports the assumption that Thomas Mann had not yet seen Heinrich's work in print and that his brother had not sent him a copy to read as he usually did. "Zola," *Die weißen Blätter* 2, no. 11 (Nov. 1915): 1312–82. Heinrich Mann finished the "Zola" essay on 15 October.

22. K. Mann, *Memoiren*, 36.

23. *Betrachtungen eines Unpolitischen* was written from the fall of 1915 to February 1918. It was first published in Berlin by Fischer, 1918.

24. Thomas Mann's pre-1918 diaries have been destroyed, but the 1918–21 diaries exist.

25. Thomas Mann's diary entry for Sunday, 23 March 1919.

26. "What the devil was he to do in this galley?" (Molière, *Les Fourberies de Scapin*); "Verglieche dich! Erkenne, was du bist!" (Goethe, *Tasso*).

27. On 16 March 1918, the "monster" (*das Untier*) was mailed to the publisher.

28. Thomas Mann's unpublished letter to Kurt Martens, 1 June 1917.

29. The Tölz residence was sold in August 1917, to Dr. Willy Weigand.

30. See Thomas Mann's letter to Paul Amann September 1915.

31. The story of Bauschan's acquisition and his deeds is narrated in "A Man and His Dog" ("Herr und Hund"). Thomas Mann wrote about Bauschan's death to Mrs. John J. Little: "I thank you very much for letting me know of your sympathy with the deceased Bauschan. It is a long time since we had to inter the good creature in Munich. Soon after the publication of his book he succumbed to pneumonia . . ." (20 July 1944; originally in English).

32. "Herr und Hund. Ein Idyll" was written from the middle of March to October 1918. First German edition by Knorr & Hirth, Munich, 1919, followed by *Herr und Hund. Gesang vom Kindchen. Zwei Idyllen* (Berlin: Fischer, 1919). In English, *Bauschan and I*, trans. Herman George Scheffauer (London: Collins, 1923; New York: Holt, 1924). (*STD*: "A Man and His Dog").

33. Thomas Mann, letter to Hans von Hülsen, 15 October 1918: "I have just now finished 'A Man and His Dog'" (EHL).

34. Preserved diaries: *Tagebücher 1918–1921*, ed. Peter de Mendelssohn (Frankfurt am Main: S. Fischer, 1979). "On 21 May 1945, [however], he noted that he had in the execution of a long cherished project destroyed old diaries, by burning them in the outdoor stove known as an 'incinerator' in the yard of his California house. . . . All points toward the reason that he did not destroy the 1918–21 diaries in May 1945 because he still needed them and planned to use them as background material for the novel 'Doktor Faustus' as he had used them for the novel before the date of the burning" (EHL) (Introd., v–vi). The diaries start with 11 September 1918.

35. Written between December 1918 and March 1919. First published in *Der neue Merkur* 3, nos. 1–2 (April/May 1919): 16–32 and 87–97.

36. "The power of love becomes free and trustful / Only when we have learned to know our own fate and knowingly / Have overcome it, clearly to rule it as a man. / Gratefully we learn then also about love which we experience, / While the striving of the youth ungratefully sweeps over it" (EHL) (*GW*, 8: 1073).

37. Thomas Mann's letter to Rupprechtpresse, 25 March 1921: "*Hermann und Dorothea*, the heartiest, most settled, most noble, most naïve and most moral among Goethe's poems . . . was the high ideal that floated before me during the improvisation of my poem . . ."(EHL).

38. "I feel completely the stimulation the material had upon Goethe" (EHL). This was in reference to Goethe's project on "Achilles." "Ich empfinde vollkommen den Reiz, den der Stoff auf Goethe ausgeübt hat" (*Diary*, Wednesday, 26 February 1919).

39. Owing to neglect by his physician, Dr. Lampe, Heinrich Mann's simple case of influenza worsened and was complicated by appendicitis and peritonitis. Thomas Mann sent his brother a bouquet with a note: "Dear Heinrich, accept my hearty greeting and best wishes with these flowers,—I was not permitted to send them sooner. Those were difficult days which lie behind us, but now we are over the hill and will advance more easily together, if you feel as I do" (EHL).

40. Already on 11 September 1921, Thomas Mann had spoken with S. Fischer about shortening the *Betrachtungen*. The version of *Betrachtungen* in the *Gesammelte Werke* was criticized by Arthur Hübscher as a "conscious distortion" of the original. Thomas Mann responded in "Kultur und Sozialismus," March 1928.

41. *Diary*, Tuesday, 8 April 1919.
42. *Diary*, Wednesday, 9 April 1919.
43. See Thomas Mann's letter to Joseph Chapiro, December 21, 1921.
44. January 1922, Thomas Mann went to Budapest, where he met the Hungarian critic Georg Lukács for the first time. It has been suggested that Lukács served as a model of a character in *The Magic Mountain*.
45. Thomas Mann, letters to Desider Kosztolányi, 16 March 1924, and to Félix Bertaux, 23 July 1924.
46. *Summary*: The formerly well-to-do family of a history professor, Doctor Cornelius, is disrupted by the changing times. The postwar inflation and the generation gap are especially troublesome for the older generation. The older children have a party and the youngest, the twins, are permitted to participate. The names "Lorchen" and "Beißer" are used here in their original forms instead of "Ellie" and "Snapper" of the translation. Little Lorchen, whom the professor loves dearly, is overcome by a strong emotion for one of the guests, wishing passionately that Herr Hergesell could somehow be her "brother." When the heartbroken little girl weeps bitterly, the anxious father can only thank Mr. Hergesell for coming up to the nursery to calm the child. The times seem out of joint, with unknown passions shattering people's *geistliche* equilibrium. Amidst all the frustrations of the world, the professor feels one stable point, his deep love for his little daughter.
47. So Thomas Mann wrote to Erich Ebermayer, 2 September 1924. The story ("Unordnung und frühes Leid"), written April and May 1925, was published in *Die neue Rundschau* 36, no. 6 (June 25): 578–611.
48. On 11 March 1923 Thomas Mann's mother, Julia Mann, died in Wassling.
49. "On 11 January 1923 France invaded the Ruhr, and by April the Reichsbank was unable to back the mark with its gold reserves. At the end of May [1923] a dollar cost 70,000 Marks, at the end of June 150,000, by mid-August one-half million Marks, by late September 160 million. The Fascists had triumphed in Italy the previous October, and English to all intents and purposes now withdrew from Europe. The future looked bleak" (Nigel Hamilton, *The Brothers Mann* [New Heaven: Yale Univ. Press, 1979], p. 205).
50. Thomas Mann, letter to Hans Heinrich Borcherdt, 3 March 1926: "'Unordnung und frühes Leid,' eine Inflationsgeschichte. . . .'"
51. In July 1926 Erika Mann was to marry Gustaf Grüngens, chief director of the Hamburger Chamber Theater. This marriage ended in divorce in 1929. She married the British poet W. H. Auden in June 1935.
52. In a letter to Ernst Bertram, 4 February 1925, Thomas Mann identifies this character as being drawn from their own employee: "Our rattlebrained Ludwig is already trained as a chauffeur . . ." (EHL). The fictional name humorously blends the prestigious first name Xaver and the last name Kleinsgutl (small fortune) fitting his position.
53. Hans Wysling in *Dichter über ihre Dichtungen: Thomas Mann*, vol. 2, no. 14, notes: "Professor Cornelius is, according to a comment in a letter from Ernst Bertram, 2 January 1926, to Ernst Glöckner, a 'cross' between Mann and Bertram. Thomas Mann had also planned originally to dedicate the novella to Ernst Bertram. Bertram however declined: the story was in spite of all its qualities 'not dear to him' because of 'the disclosures' about the children" (EHL).
54. Lorchen is modeled after Elisabeth, Thomas Mann's daughter, the little heroine of "Gesang vom Kindchen."
55. These directly refer to Katia, who since the birth of "*Kindchen*" Elisabeth had been ailing. The doctors had recommended terminating her next (sixth) pregnancy, which she refused to do. After the birth of her last child, Michael, on 21 April 1919, Katia Mann had a hard time regaining her strength. Nevertheless she did her best to run the household in spite of soaring inflation.

56. In *Sketch of My Life*, Thomas Mann described ". . . the playful little tale ['Disorder and Early Sorrow'], in which I paid a sort of indulgent homage to disorder, but in truth I love order, love it as nature, as a profoundly legitimate necessity, as the inner fitness and clear correspondence of a productive plan of life" (63) (*Lebensabriß*, *GW*, 11: 135).

57. The childhood picture of Michael Mann also corresponds to this description, but the "father," Thomas Mann, by no means resembles this portrait, so even though family features are introduced into the story, they do not match the Mann family's relations and appear randomly.

58. The name is suitable even though it has ambiguous connotations. *Her* literally means "here" and does not seem germane here. *Herr*, meaning lord or gentleman, contrasts with *Gesell* (chap/fellow/journeyman/apprentice), giving a good idea of the young man's dual nature: he tries to act in a "proper" fashion, but is basically simple and natural, doing his very best to please the professor. *Heer* (army or multitude) harmonizes with *Gesell* as a fellow of the multitude.

59. Referred to as "Germania." Nineteenth-century romantic illustrations represented "Germania" as a large, strong, blond Teutonic figure.

60. The original spelling renders the woman's dialect with untranslatable ironic humor.

61. "Because affirmation must have some psychological truth, the 'historical man' (basically pious man) in times of revolution features the most melancholy and also the most comic figure" (EHL) ("Unordnung und frühes Leid"; see also *STD*, 506; *GW*, 626).

62. Mid-November 1923 saw the establishment of the "*Rentemark*," the consolidation marking the end of inflation. The story is set prior to this date.

63. April 1925.

64. At that time Thomas Mann began work on the essay "Goethe and Tolstoy" and he finished "Mario and the Magician."

65. "Okkulte Erlebnisse" was finished in December 1922 and published in *Die neue Rundschau* in March 1924.

66. Hermann Ebers, the artist, showed Thomas Mann, in the winter of 1923, his paintings illustrating biblical scenes of the Joseph story.

67. 28 September 1929.

68. "Über die Ehe," August 1925 (*GW*, 10: 191–207).

69. "Lübeck als geistige Lebensform" (*GW*, 11: 376–98), written 1–28 May 1926, was presented in Lübeck's Stadttheater, 5 June 1926, on the occasion of the 700th anniversary of the town of Lübeck.

70. "Die Stellung Freuds in der modernen Geistesgeschichte" (*GW*, 10: 256–80). First published as "Psychoanalytische Bewegung" (Vienna, May/June, 1929).

71. "Rede über das Theater" (*GW*, 10: 281–98) was written for the opening of the Heidelberger Festspiele, 8 July 1929.

72. Julia Mann died in Wessling, 11 March 1923, at age seventy-three.

73. She committed suicide 11 May 1927.

74. A Mediterranean cruise on the "*General San Martín*," 2–25 March 1925.

75. *Joseph und seine Brüder*, a tetralogy, was written between 1926 and 1943. Vol. 1, *Die Geschichte Jakobs*, Berlin: Fischer, 1933 (*GW*, 9); vol. 2, *Der junge Joseph*, Berlin: Fischer, 1934 (*GW*, 4); vol. 3, *Joseph in Ägypten*, Vienna: Bermann und Fischer, 1936 (*GW*, 5); vol. 4, *Joseph, der Ernährer*, Stockholm: Bermann-Fischer, 1943 [Stockholmer Gesamtausgabe] (*GW*, 5). *Joseph and His Brothers*, trans. H. T. Lowe-Porter, London: Knopf, 1934 (vol. 1); 1935 (vol. 2); 1938 (vol. 3); 1948 (vol. 4).

76. Written August to September 1929. First published under the title "Tragisches Reiseerlebnis," Velhagen & Klasings *Monatshefte* 44, no. 8 (April 1930): 113–36.

77. *Summary*: The family [narrated in the first person] vacations in Italy, and after

various depressing and disturbing incidents under a gray sirocco sky, they attend the performance of a magician, Cavaliere Cipolla. The magician turns out to be not a master of magic arts, but a charlatan of extraordinary hypnotic power. After numerous demonstrations of his talents the magician abuses the naïve unsophisticated Mario, a young villager and waiter at the hotel, by making him believe that he, the magician, is the girl Mario loves, and so hypnotically forces Mario to kiss him—all this in the presence of the young man Cipolla calls "Giovanotto," Mario's rival, and the entire audience. When Mario regains his senses he kills the magician with the gun the jealous lover had carried. Thomas Mann clearly describes the abuse of the occult power that hypnotism represents.

78. Chapter 7 ("Fragwürdigstes"), *GW*, 3: 907.

79. The holiday was from 31 August to 13 September 1926. Also see *SML*, 71 and *GW*, 11: 138.

80. See discussion with Lisabeta in "Tonio Kröger" (part 4).

81. Thomas Mann wrote to Otto Hoerth (12 June 1930): "I am especially grateful to you because you recognize my will to justice and do not find any antipathy toward Italy and the Italian spirit in the story" (EHL).

82. In Paris, January 1926, Thomas Mann gave an address to the Centre Européen de la Donation Carnégie pour la paix internationale, at the Carnegie Institute. "Die geistigen Tendenzen des heutigen Deutschlands" was written December 1925 and first published in French as "Les tendances spirituelles de l'Allemagne d'aujourdhui." The German text first appeared in *L'esprit international* (Paris) 1, no. 1 (Jan. 1927): 64–76 (*GW*, 8: 593). This seems a striking contrast to the anti-French and anti-Western attitude he held after Heinrich's Zola essay. However, his new attitude represents Thomas Mann's growth, not contradiction; a feeling of unity does not erase dependence on tradition and inheritance or responsibility toward one's own homeland.

83. The real name of the family pension was the Pensione Regina and the hostess's name was Angela Querci. See Thomas Mann's letter to Hopkins, 27 November 1930.

84. See Thomas Mann's essay "Mein Verhältnis zur Psychoanalyse," 1925, which defines his thinking on the subject at that time (*GW*, 11: 748–49).

85. Discussed in "Okkulte Erlebnisse" written December 1922 and January 1923, first published in *Die neue Rundschau* 35, no. 3 (March 1924): 193–224. It was also presented as a lecture in 1923–24 in Vienna, Budapest, Prague, Madrid, Munich, Berlin, Stuttgart, Heidelberg, and Mannheim. It occurs fictionally in *The Magic Mountain*, especially chapter seven ("Fragwürdigstes," *GW*, 3: 907).

86. *STD*, 550. The word "conjuror" correctly connotes "*Zauberkünstler*," Thomas Mann's "artist-magician." Note the evolution of these terms in Thomas Mann's development.

87. The title of this story was changed from "Ein tragisches Reiseerlebnis" to one involving the word "magician."

88. This pertains to the theme of "Felix Krull."

89. Cipolla defines his doctrine to Signor Angiolieri: ". . . let your zeal be quickened by knowing that there are powers stronger than reason or virtue . . ." (*STD*, 559; *GW*, 8: 700).

90. Krokowski's speech in the chapter titled "Analyse," *Zauberberg* (*GW*, 3: 180–81, chap. 4).

91. Thomas Mann's letter to Otto Hoerth, 12 June 1930: "Mario was not really in love, and the aggressive young man at the main floor was not his luckier rival. But not even the shots are my invention: As I told you regarding this evening, my oldest daughter said: 'I would not have been surprised if he had shot him.' It is only from this moment on that the experience became a novella, and to be able to execute it I needed the anecdotal detail which provided the atmosphere . . . I would not have had otherwise the motivation to narrate it, and if you say: [that] without the hotel manager I

would have let Cipolla live, the truth is actually the other way around: in order to be able to kill Cipolla I needed the hotel manager and the [other] preparatory aggravations. Neither Fuggiero nor the furious gentleman at the beach, nor the princess, would have seen the light of literature" (EHL). Thomas Mann also related his motives in letters to Charles Duffy, 14 December 1945, and to Louis M. Grant, 14 October 1949.

92. Letter to Hans Ulrich Staeps, 18 March 1935.

93. Letter to Charles R. Shearn, 8 September 1949: ". . . However these experiences never went so far as to permit me to see with my own eyes a materialization. . ." (letter originally in English). See also "Okkulte Erlebnisse" (*GW*, 10: 161).

94. Thomas Mann's references to the occult appear in *GW*, 10: 162 and 171.

95. See *GW* 10: 280, 281, and 271–72.

96. "For a long time psychoanalysis had played into the poetry of our culture and will possibly influence it in increasing its influence" (EHL). In "Mein Verhältnis zur Psychoanalyse" (1925) (*GW*, 11: 749).

97. See also *STD*, 551; *GW*, 8: 689).

98. "I cannot excuse our staying, scarcely can I even understand it. . . . Were we under the sway of a fascination . . . which paralyzed our resolve?" (*STD*, 556–57; *GW*, 8: 695).

99. *STD*, 560, or "militaristic somnambulism" (EHL) (*GW*, 8: 701).

100. To Henry Hatfield, 20 April 1947, Thomas Mann wrote, "'Mario and the Magician' should not be regarded too much as an allegory. It is simply a story of human affairs which should interest the reader for its own sake and not for some hidden meaning" (Thomas Mann, letter to Louis M. Grant, 14 October 1949; letter originally in English).

101. *Joseph and His Brothers*, part I ("Descent in to Hell"), 3 (*Joseph und seine Brüder.* "Höllenfahrt," *GW*, 4: 9).

102. He had written *Lotte in Weimar* from 11 November 1936 to 26 October 1939. Its first German publication was in Stockholm by Bermann-Fischer, 1939 (*Stockholmer Gesamtausgabe der Werke von Thomas Mann*). Its first English publication, *The Beloved Returns: Lotte in Weimar*, trans. H. T. Lowe-Porter (New York: Knopf, 1940), was followed by *Lotte in Weimar* (London: Secker & Warburg, 1941).

103. Thomas Mann wrote the story from 1 January to 28 July 1940. Its first German publication was in Stockholm by Bermann-Fischer, 1940; its first English edition was "The Transposed Heads. A Legend of India," trans. H. T. Lowe-Porter (New York: Knopf, 1941; London: Secker & Warburg, 1941). Quotations are from the Knopf edition, referred to as *TH*. The subtitle is not included in the *GW* version.

104. On 27 May 1938 Thomas Mann accepted President Harold W. Dodds's offer to serve Princeton University as Lecturer in Humanities for the next academic season, 1938–39. He gave seminars on *Faust* and *The Magic Mountain*, and three public lectures (28–29 November 1938, "On Faust"; 17 January 1939, "On Richard Wagner"; and 13 February 1939, "On Sigmund Freud").

105. Thomas Mann, letter to Agnes E. Meyer, 22 March 1940: "I do not believe that even if we stayed here, I would allow myself such amusements again. I have to be completely free for Joseph IV, which is to be ready for my 70th birthday (or possibly a few years earlier)" (EHL). Thomas Mann's letter to Ida Herz, end of September 1940 (n.d.): "We are returning to Princeton for the winter but we have bought a lot here with 7 palms and a lot of lemon trees and will probably build. . . " (EHL).

106. Pacific Palisades, California, 740 Amalfi Drive, a temporary home until early February 1942, when they moved into their new house at 1550 San Remo Drive.

107. The ten years between Thomas Mann's two last pieces of short fiction are not treated here in detail.

108. At that time the Nobel Prize, 200,000 Marks, was worth a considerable

amount, especially after the Wall Street crash of October 1929. Thomas Mann was advised by friends and fans not to invest the money in Germany. Such investments were not very successful; Mann gained invitations, book sales, and prestige as the real values of his Nobel Prize.

109. Thomas Mann, letter to Maximilian Brantl, 8 April 1930.

110. In "Deutsche Ansprache," 17 October in Berlin, Thomas Mann warned against Social Democratic trends ("Deutsche Ansprache: Ein Appell an die Vernunft" [Berlin: S. Fischer, 1930]).

111. In May 1931, Thomas Mann met to cooperate with Jules Romains and André Gide. Lecture on Freud and "Europa als Kulturgemeinschaft." Shortly after, Thomas Mann attended the "Comité Permanent des Letters et des Arts" in Geneva, and met among others Paul Valéry and Béla Bartók.

112. Among the articles included in the *Festschrift* are: "Goethe als Repräsentant des bürgerlichen Zeitalters" (*Neue Rundschau*, April 1932); "Ansprache bei der Einweihung des erweiterten Goethe-Museums in Frankfurt am Main"; "Goethes Laufbahn als Schriftsteller" (Munich/Berlin/Zurich: Corona, February 1933); "Vortrag auf der Goethe-Gedenkfeier" (Neue Theater, P.E.N Club, Prague, March 1932); "Festvortrag auf der Feier von Goethes 100. Todestag" (Preußische Akademie der Künste, Berlin, 18 March 1932); "Festgabe zum Goethejahre 1932" (Halle, 1932), and more. Some of these studies have been reprinted several times.

113. 230 out of 608 votes. On 8 August 1932 in the *Berliner Tageblatt*, Thomas Mann spoke strongly about the ". . . real nature of this popular disease, this mishmash of hysteria, muffled romanticism, the megaphone Germanism of caricature and turning into a mob everything that is German . . ." (EHL).

114. On 30 January 1933 Adolf Hitler became chancellor of Germany.

115. "Leiden und Größe Richard Wagners," *Die neue Rundschau*, April 1933.

116. 23 February, "Wagner Gedenkfeier," Wagner Vereinigung.

117. 14 February, P.E.N. Club, in the Palais des Beaux Arts.

118. 18 February, twice: in the Théatre des Ambassadeurs, and in the Foyer de l'Europe.

119. For information referring to Heinrich Mann's circumstances, see Hamilton, *Brothers*, chap. 13, "Exile".

120. Near Zurich, Schiedhaldenstraße 33.

121. By Henry Goddard Leach, 30 May 1934.

122. German Department, "Goethe Vortrag," 4 June 1934.

123. Among many others were his honorary doctorate from Harvard University, June 1935; Thomas Mann Archives, planned at Yale, April 1937, and founded in 1938; and his honorary doctorate from Columbia University, 1938. *Stories of Three Decades* appeared with Thomas Mann's introduction in New York, published by Alfred A. Knopf, 1936.

124. *Die Geschichte Jakobs*, 1933, and *Der junge Joseph*, 1934, are the warmest and most personal exemplars of Thomas Mann's fiction.

125. Their silver wedding anniversary was 11 February 1930.

126. *Lotte in Weimar* had been finished at the end of October 1939. Its first German publication was in *Stockholmer Gesamtausgabe der Werke von Thomas Mann* (Stockholm: Bermann-Fischer, 1939); it was translated by H. T. Lowe-Porter as *Lotte in Weimar* (New York: Knopf, 1940; London: Secker and Warburg, 1941).

127. "The Coming Victory of Democracy," written 21 November to 10 December 1937. First publication, "Vom zukünftigen Sieg der Demokratie" (Zurich: Oprecht, 1938), Sonderheft der Zeitschrift *Maß und Wert*.

128. Written 13 January to 18 May 1938; first publication, Stockholm: Bermann-Fischer, 1938 (Schriftreihe "Anblick"). In Thomas Mann's letter to Kuno Fiedler, 21 December 1937, he writes: "(I now read Schopenhauer again systematically, with

greatest joy and admiration: what he taught is put aside, but how he taught is what stands)—so I am lost for letter writing." (Thomas Mann here probably hints jokingly at Nietzsche: "what he had taught is laid aside / what he lived, will stand") (EHL).

129. A translation of the Schopenhauer essay serves as an introduction to *The Living Thoughts of Schopenhauer*, ed. Alfred O. Mendel (New York/Toronto: Longmans, Green and Co., 1939). (*GW*, 9: 528.)

130. Thomas Mann, letter to Agnes Meyer, 5 January 1940.

131. The Italian term *burlesco*, from *burla*, means "a jest," or "mockery"; "a comic or satirical imitation" of something; "a derisive caricature" or "parody." The Italian *grottesco* means "odd," from *grotta*, a grotto, so called from imitation designs found in excavations. Other meanings include "in or of a style in which forms of persons and animals are intermingled with foliage, flowers, fruits, etc. in a fantastic design; characterized by distortions or striving incongruities in appearance, shape, manner, etc., fantastic, bizarre; ludicrously eccentric or strange, ridiculous, absurd" (Webster).

132. Thomas Mann repeats this reference, notably in letters to Ida Heerz, 18 February 1941; Karl Kerényi, 18 February 1941; Harry Slochower, 30 August 1941; Anton W. Heinitz, 9 June 1944; Walter Rilla, 26 August 1944; Hans Eichner, 10 March 1947, and more ("*metaphysischer Spaß*" or "*Scherz*"). In a letter originally written in English to Walter Rilla he used the word "jest."

133. Thomas Mann, letter to William E. Bohn, 19 August 1944: ". . . it ["The Transposed Heads"] was justly considered as a minor work to which one attached little importance" (typewritten letter, originally in English).

134. Käte Hamburger: "De ombytta huvudena," Göteborgs Handels-och Sjöfarts-Tidning, 4 February 1941.

135. See Thomas Mann's letter to Käte Hamburger, 19 April 1941. He had this letter in mind when he wrote to Agnes E. Meyer, 15 May 1941: "In fact it [the story] has become increasingly better in my eyes since I finished it. I have to admit . . . [that I am] sincerely not far from considering it a masterpiece" (EHL). In a later letter to Agnes E. Meyer, 26 May 1941, Mann used the same term, "superior," that he had used to Käte Hamburger. A comment he made later to Erna Zutermann, 26 August 1942, shows how important Käte Hamburger's opinion was to him: "Dr. [Käte] Hamburger herself, had already sent me the [her] wise article on 'The Transposed Heads,' and it was very pleasant to know that this very fine appreciation of my little work had appeared in Sweden (EHL).

136. Thomas Mann, letter to Harry Slochower, 30 August 1941.

137. See also *The Beloved Returns: Lotte in Weimar*, translated from the German by H. T. Lowe-Porter (New York: Alfred A. Knopf, 1957), 451–52. (*GW*, 8: 930).

138. *Summary*: The three protagonists—Sita of the beautiful hips, descended from a line of warriors, her husband Shridaman, a white-skinned Brahman heir, and his friend Nanda, a well-built dark-skinned shepherd from the common people—are accompanied by the omnipotent presence of the World-Mother with the thunderous voice, the goddess Dewi, Durga, or Kali. The two young men see Sita ritually bathing and reciting her prayers. Schridaman, who has fallen in love with her, later marries her, and when Sita becomes pregnant they set out with Nanda to visit Sita's parents in a neighboring village. They lose their way and arrive instead at the temple of the World Mother, where pious Schridaman briefly prays. He is overcome by the urge to sacrifice himself to the goddess, miraculously decapitating himself. Tired of waiting, Nanda follows, and moved by the drama he discovers in the temple, he does the same. Finally Sita enters, and feeling understandably faint, she follows the goddess's instructions to replace the heads and resurrect the men. Accidentally or not, Sita, who loved her husband's refined features but was sensually attracted to Nanda's powerful body, exchanges the heads, creating a problem of identity and marital rights, which they solve by consulting a saintly hermit. He judges that the head bears the individual's

identity. After a few happy years, the intellect of the husband who has ideal facial features and an athletic form slowly begins to modify the body, while the head as well takes on the coarser characteristics of the body. Sita feels a growing urge to see the combination with the Nanda head and she takes her little son with her to find Nanda, who has become a hermit. He has changed, just as Schridaman has. After Sita spends a night of love with Nanda, Schridaman appears in the grove. The three acknowledge the impossibility of a dignified life under these circumstances and agree that only death can unite them properly. After the two men have ritually slain each other, Sita follows them—as their widow—into death on the funeral pyre. Reverent believers tend their little son, who perfectly unites all their qualities, except that he is a little pale and nearsighted.

139. "The Transposed Heads" was written after the first publication of *Stories of Three Decades* in a separate volume (copyright since 1930 by Alfred A. Knopf, 6 June 1936). The story will be referred to as *TH*.

140. Thomas Mann, letters to Lotte Lehmann, 2 August 1941, and to Louise Servicen, 13 February 1948.

141. Thomas Mann, letter to William E. Bohn, 19 August 1944 (letter originally in English).

142. Thomas Mann referred to the source of the setting and plot for "The Transposed Heads" in a letter to Käte Hamburger, 19 April 1941: "I found the anecdote in four lines in Heinrich Zimmer's [book]. . . ." The reference is to Zimmer's *Die indische Weltmutter*, in *Eranos-Jahrbuch 1938* (Zurich: Rhein-Verlag, 1939), 175–220.

143. *TH*, 18. The translation uses the word "hush," but not consistently, so the repetition does not become obvious (*GW*, 8: 719).

144. *TH*, 105. ". . . Schridaman and he [Nanda] could not love without each other because they were so different . . ." (*GW* 8: 761).

145. Suggested also as representing homosexuality.

146. A hilariously paradoxical version of an Augustinian *unio mystica*, here spiced with jesting sensuality.

147. The balance before and after the heads are transposed:

I. Originally: Shridaman = *Geist*   Nanda = Nature

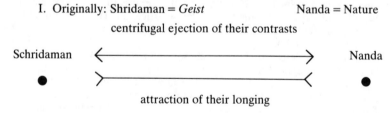

centrifugal ejection of their contrasts

attraction of their longing

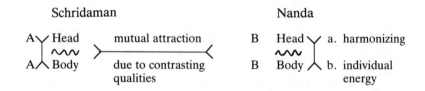

II. After Sita transposed the heads:

$\begin{array}{c}A\uparrow \text{ Head}\\ \hline B\downarrow \text{ Body}\end{array}$ No more attraction $\begin{array}{c}B\uparrow \text{ Head}\\ \hline A\downarrow \text{ Body}\end{array}$ a. contrasting

due to mixed qualities   b. equalling

= Result: mixture = A/B
            B/A

III. Sita = Beauty   first choice: A Head + B Body = temporal happiness
                       second choice: B Head + A Body = 1 night of love =
                                                          need of solution

IV. Samadhi-Andhaka (Sita's child)

$\left.\begin{array}{l}= C/A + C/B\\ C/A = \text{short sighted}\\ C/B = \text{pale skin}\end{array}\right\}$ viable version: genealogical formula of a metaphysical jest.

148. Thomas Mann, letter to Agnes E. Meyer, 18 June 1941: "Yes, Tonio, Hans and Inge are now united in the grave of flames. Peace to their ashes!" (EHL).

149. See Thomas Mann's letter to Louise Servicen, 13 February 1948. The "I" and "My" concepts are also defined and discussed in Heinrich Zimmer's *Maya, der indische Mythos* (Zurich: Räscher Verlag, 1952), 331.

150. *TH*, 5. (*GW*, 8: 713).

151. Whether the fragrance of the jasmine predominates in India is debatable, but Thomas Mann often used jasmine to express similar moods in his early fiction. See "Gefallen" and "Little Herr Friedemann."

152. Exaltation = *Begeisterung*. The same word is used at the moment when Schridaman, overcome by ecstasy in the prescence of the World Mother, is endowed with superhuman faculties and ritually decapitates himself. *Begeisterung* represents the existential moment of conscious transcendence from the finite to the universal and is identified with the Schopenhauerian *geniale Erkenntnis*; Thomas Mann also uses it as the moment of artistic (*künstlerisch*) creative insight.

153. *TH*, 45. "Denn sie ist Alles und nicht nur Eines: Leben und Tod, Wahr und Weisheit, Zauberin und Befreierin, weißt du das nicht? Weißt du nur, daß sie der Geschöpfe Schar betört und bezaubert, und nicht auch, daß sie hinausführt über das Dunkel der Befangenheit zur Erkenntnis der Wahrheit? Dann weißt du wenig und hast ein allerdings schwer umfassendes Geheimnis nicht erfaßt: daß nämlich die Trunkenheit, die sie uns antut, zugleich die Begeisterung ist, die uns zur Wahrheit und Freiheit trägt. Denn dies ist es, daß was fesselt, zugleich befreit, und daß es die Begeisterung ist, welche Sinnenschönheit und Geist verbindet."

154. *TH*, 48. "'Denn wie Schönheit und Geist zusammenfließen in der Begeisterung, so Leben und Tod in der Liebe!'" (*GW*, 8: 734).

155. This deodorizes the breath, humorously characterizing Nanda's earthbound thinking.

156. *TH*, 69. (*GW*, 8: 744). The imagery of the dark, of woods, of going astray, and words such as "*Verwirrung*" and "*irren*" are widely used in Novalis's Romantic vocabulary and are also well known from "Tonio Kröger."

157. She is only partially right about Schridaman, because Nanda commits suicide not to reenter the World Mother but to join Schridaman in death.

158. When Sita wants to commit suicide by hanging herself on the tree, World
Mother bellows, expressing, in her own way, Schopenhauer's ideas: "My ears are full
as it is of these quack philosophers who say that human existence is a disease, com-
municating itself through lust from one generation to the next—Take your neck out of
the noose, or you'll get your ears boxed!" (*TH*, 98) (*GW*, 8: 758).

159. Thomas Mann, letter to Caroline Newton, 28 July 1940: "I nasally dictate this
because after Katia acquired a bronchial complaint here, I have now acquired a sinus
infection. The paradisal climate is dangerous because of the sun and shadow and one
must be very cautious. My head was devastated and empty for a few days, as [chaotic]
as the world before creation, and the end of the Indian novella had turned unusually
sour for me. Now I am in the process of closing this intermezzo off, and then I can
finally pursue the real thing in the prison-fortress of the Nile island" (EHL). (Comment on the conclusion of "The Transposed Heads" and his continuation of the work
on the *Joseph* cycle.)

160. *TH*, 184–85: "For where two of us are, the third will always be lacking; forgive
me then, that I could not hold out longer with you but overcome by pity sought out the
lonely friend-head."

161. See also *TH*, 186–87. ". . . because from [my] father's side, Sumatra, there
still flows some warrior blood in my veins, and against something so base as polyandry
everything in me revolts; in all the fleshly weakness and confusion one still has [one's]
pride and honor as a higher being!" (EHL) ". . . denn von seiten meines Vaters
Sumatra fließt noch einiges Kriegerblut in meinen Adern, und gegen etwas so Tief-
stehendes wie die Vielmännerei empört sich alles in mir: In aller Schwäche und Wirr-
nis des Fleisches hat man doch seinen Stolz und seine Ehre als höheres Wesen!"

162. "The Transposed Heads" has been compared to Voltaire's work. In a letter to
Agnes E. Meyer, 3 July 1941, Thomas Mann points out that he had read *Candide*
while writing this story. Voltaire's theme, though, bitterly rejects Leibniz's ideas, not
at all a parallel of the witty parody of Schopenhauer's system that Mann incorporated
in "The Transposed Heads." Nevertheless, Voltaire's humor and trenchant wit are
comparable to Mann's own humane and ironic talent.

163. Thomas Mann, letter to Christian Gauss, 17 June 1941.

164. Thomas Mann, letter to Agnes E. Meyer, 8 July 1940.

165. Thomas Mann, letter to Caroline Newton, 1 September 1940: " Ich habe jetzt
nur den Schlußband des Joseph im Kopf. . . "

166. "*Die vertauschten Köpfe. Eine indische Legende,*" written 1 January–28 July
1940. First German edition, Stockholm: Bermann-Fischer 1940. English trans. by
H. T. Lowe-Porter, New York: Knopf, 1941; London: Secker and Warburg, 1941.

167. The Manns moved into their new house 5 February 1943: 1550 San Remo
Drive, Pacific Palisades, Calif.

168. In October 1942 a political essay collection, *Order of the Day*, was published.

169. 17 November 1942: lecture in the Library of Congress Auditorium: "On the
Joseph Novels."

170. Written between 18 January and 13 March 1943. First German publication in
Die Tat (Zurich), 27 March–17 April 1945, and Los Angeles: Pacific Press, 1945 (edition of 500 copies, published by Ernst Gottlieb and Felix Guggenheim). First English
publication "Thou Shalt Have No Other Gods Before Me," in *The Ten Commandments*, trans. George R. Marek (New York: Armin Robinson: Hermann Rauschning;
London: Simon and Schuster, 1943). Here the shorter German title, "Gesetz," will be
used, while the English translation will be referred to as *GTZ*. This is the only story of
Thomas Mann's which was suggested by other than his own inspiration. Armin Robinson decided to create a Metro-Goldwyn-Mayer film featuring the Ten Commandments, presented from a political angle: how Hitler had worked against the divine
laws. He received the cooperation of world-famous authors: Hermann Rauschning,

Thomas Mann, Rebecca West, Franz Werfel, John Erskine, Bruno Frank, André Maurois, Sigrid Undset, Hendrik W. van Loon, and Louis Bromfield. When the film was dropped, he was able to get acceptance for the publication of a book on the topic from Simon and Schuster, 1943. In spite of the writers involved, the book had a poor reception and sale. Thomas Mann published his story separately after the essay collection came out.

171. *Summary*: "Das Gesetz" is not a novella but a freely rendered biblical narrative with a widely known plot and fictional elements. Thomas Mann expresses his message in his presentation of the plot and his emphasis on motives. After the introduction, he narrates Moses' origin, not as a Jewish foundling, but the fruit of a romantic liaison of the Pharaoh's daughter with a Jewish slave. Raised by Jewish foster parents, Moses soon leaves his Egyptian school and, after killing an Egyptian guard, flees to Midian. Besides his wife, he is passionately taken by a "Moorish" woman, his concubine. This Moses, plagued by ordinary weaknesses, teaches the Jews (his natural father's people) about the "invisible god" and urges the Pharaoh to release the Jews from slavery. Only after the tenth plague can the Jews leave Egypt, passing miraculously through the Red Sea, winning a victory at Kadesh Oasis in the desert of Paran held by the Amalekites, eating manna from heaven to stay alive. When after forty days on Mount Sinai, Moses returns with his ten commandments carved in stone and outlined with his blood, he finds the people adoring a golden calf. Outraged, he crushes the idol and also ruins the stone tablets. Joshua, his military leader and executive officer, is furious when Moses returns to Mount Sinai to rewrite the commandments. Upon his return, his significant speech to the Jews defines Thomas Mann's theme, ending the story.

172. See Käte Hamburger, *Thomas Mann: Das Gesetz. Dichtung und Wirklichkeit* vollständiger Text der Erzählung, Dokumentation, (Frankfurt am Main and Berlin: Verlag Ullstein GMBTL, 1964), 114 (Chapter: "Dokumentation aus: Die Bibel, altes Testament").

173. Letter to Otto Basler, 11 September 1945, ". . . I have given the features of Michelangelo to my Moses, not the ones of his Moses, but his very own, to show the tremendous effort of the man struggling with rebellious matter . . ." (EHL).

174. This is obviously fictional, not historical. See the classic work of Ignatius Donnelly, *Atlantis: The Antediluvian World* (N.Y.: Harper, 1882; reprint, New York: Gramercy Publishing Co., 1985).

175. Michelangelo's statue of an impressive Moses is in Rome's church of San Pietro in Vincoli. The only details taken from the sculpture of Moses by Michelangelo, rather than the person of Michelangelo himself who had personality similarities with Mann's Moses, are the "rays like horns . . . out from the locks of his forehead." (*GTZ*, 61; *GW*, 8: 867)

176. See Hans Rudolf Vaget, *Thomas Mann, Kommentar zu sämtliche Erzählungen.* (Munich: Winkler Verlag, 1984), 280–83.

177. *Summary*: Rosalie von Tümmler, a widow, lives a comfortable, eventless, middle-class life, with her children Anna, a spinster disabled from birth, an abstract painter, and her mother's sensitive, intelligent confidante, and Edward, the considerably younger high school senior who strongly resembles his late father. Their peaceful existence is suddenly shattered by the appearance of a young American, Kent Keaton, who, after having suffered permanent injuries, has been honorably discharged from the military; now he manages by giving English lessons to members of Düsseldorf society. Edward, too, will take lessons from Kent. The nature-loving, gray-haired Rosalie with her youthful figure, is first attracted to, then passionately in love with, the young American tutor. From the beginning it is clear that Rosalie had recently experienced her menopause and that she suffers at the thought of being "half a woman." Mother and daughter discuss their emotions. One morning Rosalie triumphantly

announces to her daughter that again, miraculously, her menstruation has recurred and she believes she is right in sharing her passion with her son's youthful tutor. On a sunny spring Sunday, the family and the tutor take an excursion to visit the rococo castle of Holterhof and feed the famous black swans (hence the English title) on the estate. The confrontation of Rosalie and the splendid black swans becomes the dramatic turning point of the story. Moments later, escaping into a secret passage of the castle, Rosalie passionately confesses her love to the young American. Later the same night, she is found unconscious in her blood, and after an emergency exploratory operation, her doctors declare that Mrs. von Tümmler has a terminal uterine cancer. The postmenopausal hemorrhage that was mistaken by Rosalie as the reawakening of her youth had been a symptom of the deadly disease, activated by an unknown stimulus. Rosalie takes the "betrayal" (hence the German title) with serenity and dies peacefully sometime after the operation. Will be referred to as *TBS*.

178. Thomas Mann, letter to Anna Jacobson from Kilchberg, 3 May 1954: "I think that 'The Black Swan' is a quite good title as 'Die Betrogene' was impossible to translate into English." Thomas Mann usually defended his ideas about details to be rendered his way in the translations. This comment supports the interpretation given here. Helen T. Lowe-Porter was approaching eighty and declined the translation. Willard R. Trask, her successor, translated the story, which was published by Knopf, New York, and Secker and Warburg, London, 1954.

179. Hamilton, *Brothers*, 365.

180. Leaving his practice in Berlin in 1936, Dr. Rosenthal emigrated to the United States, where he established himself in Beverly Hills, Calif., in 1938. Dr. Rosenthal first diagnosed a malignancy in Thomas Mann's lung tissues in surgery in Billings Hospital, Chicago, 15–25 May 1946. The surgery was successful, but naturally the topic of cancer left a deep impression, reflected in "The Black Swan."

181. 7 Feb. 1953; 9 Feb. 1953.

182. Thomas Mann, letter to Grete Nickish: 1 Feb., 7 Feb., 20 Feb. 1953.

183. Hamilton, *Brothers*, 165.

184. Thomas Mann, letter to Wolfgang Schneditz, 17 Dec. 1953: "The book is often received as one lacking good taste, which seems to me to be a quite primitive reaction . . ." (EHL). Brendan Gill wrote, in a review in the *New Yorker*, 10 July 1954: "Thomas Mann is at his clinical best and literary worst in 'The Black Swan'. . . an outstanding birthday present for gynecologists. . . ."

185. In Thomas Mann's letter to Karl Kerényi, late September 1953. (No reference to exact date available.)

186. Thomas Mann, letter to Hans Reisiger, 21 March 1953.

187. "*Gegen-sich-selbst-leben*" ("Die Betrogene" *GW*, 8: 931). In the translation, "living in contradiction to herself" (*TBS*, 105). The translation carries the same idea, but not the rhythm and music of the German original.

188. The same concept is expressed in the Schopenhauer essay: "dass er nichts tut was er möchte, und alles tut was er nicht möchte" ("that he does nothing he wishes to do and does all that he does not want to do"; EHL) (*GW*, 9: 555).

189. Titus Heydenreich, "Eros in der Unterwelt. Der Holterhof—Ausflug in Thomas Manns Erzählung 'Die Betrogene,'" in *Interpretation und Vergleich. Festschrift für Walter Pabst*, ed. E. Leube and L. Schrader, 79–95 (Berlin, 1972).

190. Letter to Alexander Moritz Frey, 2 October 1953; to Wolfgang Schneditz, 17 December 1953; to Hans Mayer 29 December 1953; to Theodor W. Adorno, 12 March 1955.

191. *Bekenntnisse des Hochstaplers Felix Krull*, written January 1910–1913, continued and finished January 1951–April 1954. First published as *Bekenntnisse des Hochstaplers Felix Krull. Buch der Kindheit* (Vienna, Leipzig, Munich: Rikola-

Verlag, 1922). *Bekenntnisse des Hochstaplers Felix Krull. Der Memoiren erster Teil* (New York and Frankfurt am Main: Fischer, 1954).

192. Hamilton, *Brothers*, 371.

193. "Thomas Mann," by Hans Wysling, with the cooperation of Marianne Fischer, in *Dichter über Dichtungen*, vols. 1–3, published by Rudolf Hirsch and Werner Vordtriede. These volumes have detailed lists of events and references on Thomas Mann's life in the appendix.

194. "Versuch über Schiller. Zum 150. Todestag des Dichters—seinem Andenken in Liebe gewidmet." Written 13 September 1954 to 10 January 1955 (Berlin and Frankfurt am Main: Fischer, 1955)

195. Thomas Mann's birthday, 5 June 1955, was observed by the entire educated world. A reception was offered by the Zurich township, and the same afternoon the Kilchberg community honored him in the Conrad Ferdinand Meyer House. The festivities went on for days in Switzerland and Munich.

BIBLIOGRAPHY

Works by Thomas Mann (in German)

"Auseinandersetzungen mit Richard Wagner." *Merkur: Österreichische Zeitschrift für Musik und Theater* 2 (July 1911): 21–23.

Briefe an Otto Grautoff 1894–1901 und Ida Boy-Ed 1903–1928. Edited by Peter de Mendelssohn. Frankfurt am Main: S. Fischer Verlag GmbH, 1975.

Briefe 1889–1936. Edited by Erika Mann. Frankfurt am Main: Fischer Taschenbuch Verlag, 1979.

Dichter über ihre Dichtungen. Edited by Hans Wysling. "Thomas Mann: Teil I, 1889–1917." Heimeran/S. Fischer, n.d. "Thomas Mann: Teil II, 1918–1943." Munich: Heimeran Verlag, 1979. "Thomas Mann: Teil III, 1944–1955." Passau: Ernst Heimeran Verlag, 1981.

Gesammelte Werke in dreizehn Bänden. Frankfurt am Main: S. Fischer Verlag GmbH, 1974.

Tagebücher 1918–1921. Edited by Peter de Mendelssohn. Frankfurt am Main: S. Fischer Verlag GmbH, 1979.

Tagebücher 1933–1934. Edited by Peter de Mendelssohn. Frankfurt am Main: S. Fischer Verlag GmbH, 1977.

Tagebücher 1935–1936. Edited by Peter de Mendelssohn. Frankfurt am Main: S. Fischer Verlag GmbH, 1978.

Tagebücher 1937–1939. Edited by Peter de Mendelssohn. Frankfurt am Main: S. Fischer Verlag GmbH, 1980.

Tagebücher 1940–1943. Edited by Peter de Mendelssohn. Frankfurt am Main: S. Fischer Verlag GmbH, 1982.

Tagebücher 1944–1946. Edited by Peter de Mendelssohn. Frankfurt am Main: S. Fischer Verlag GmbH, 1986.

Thomas Mann an Ernst Bertram, Briefe aus den Jahren 1910–1955. Edited by Inge Jens. Pfüllingen: Verlag Günther Neske, 1960.

Thomas Mann Briefe an Paul Amann 1915–1952. Edited by Herbert Wegener. Lübeck: Verlag Max Schmidt-Romhild, 1959.

Thomas Mann–Heinrich Mann Briefwechsel 1900 bis 1949. Edited by Hans Wysling. Frankfurt am Main: Fischer Taschenbuch Verlag, 1975.

Works by Thomas Mann (in English)

The Beloved Returns. Lotte in Weimar. Translated by H. T. Lowe-Porter. New York: Knopf, 1957.

"The Black Swan." Translated by Willard R. Trask. New York: Knopf, 1964.

Doctor Faustus. The Life of the German Composer Adrian Leverkühn as Told by a Friend. Translated by H. T. Lowe-Porter. New York: Knopf, 1948.

Essays of Three Decades. Translated by H. T. Lowe-Porter. New York: Knopf, 1976.
"German Letter." *Dial* 73 (19 Nov. 1922): 645–54.
Letters of Thomas Mann 1889–1955. Translated by Richard and Clara Winston. New York: Knopf, 1971.
"The Little Grandma." *Nassau Lit.*, 1942, 3–11.
A Sketch of My Life. Translated by H. T. Lowe-Porter. New York: Knopf, 1960.
Stories of Three Decades. Translated by H. T. Lowe-Porter. New York: Knopf, 1974.
"The Transposed Heads: A Legend of India." Translated by H. T. Lowe-Porter. New York: Knopf, 1941.

Secondary Sources

Abendroth, Walter. *Schopenhauer.* Reinbek bei Hamburg: Rowohlt Taschenbuch Verlag, 1967.
Adorno, Theodor W(iesengrund). "Form und Gehalt des zeitgenössischen Romans." *Akzente* (Munich) 1, no. 5 (1954): 410–23.
———. *Philosophie der neuen Musik.* Edited by J. C. B. Mohr. Tübingen: Paul Siebeck, 1949.
Aiken, Conrad, "Children and Fools." In *The Stature of Thomas Mann*, ed. Charles Neider, 165–67. New York: New Directions, 1947.
Alberts, Wilhelm. *Thomas Mann und sein Beruf.* Leipzig: Xenien Verlag, 1913.
Amann, Paul. "Deux romanciers allemands. Emil Strauss et Thomas Mann." *L'Effort libre* (Poitiers) 1, nos. 15/18 (March 1912): 513–40.
———. "Politik und Moral in Thomas Manns 'Betrachtungen eines Unpolitischen.'" *Münchner Blätter für Dichtung und Graphik* 1, no. 2 (1919): 25–32, 42–48.
Amstein, Max. "Gedanken zum Werk Thomas Manns." *Neue Schweizer Rundschau* (Zurich) 17 (May 1949): 12–28.
Andersch, Alfred. "Mit den Augen des Westens (Thomas Mann als Politiker)." *Texte und Zeichen* 1, no. 1 (1955): 85–100.
———. "Thomas Mann als Politiker." In *Die Blindheit des Kunstwerks und andere Aufsätze*, 41–60. Frankfurt am Main: Suhrkamp Verlag, 1965.
Arens, Hans. "Analyse eines Satzes von Thomas Mann." *Beihefte zur Zeitschrift "Wirkendes Wort,"* no. 10. Düsseldorf: Pädagogischer Verlag Schwann, 1964.
Arnold, Armin. "D. H. Lawrence und Thomas Mann." *Neue Zürcher Zeitung* (Zurich), 29 Nov. 1959, 5.
———. "D. H. Lawrence and Thomas Mann." *Comparative Literature* 13, no. 1 (Winter 1961): 33–38.
Arnold, Heinz Ludwig, ed. *Text und Kritik.* Sonderband. Munich, 1976.
Arntzen, Helmut. *Der moderne deutsche Roman. Voraussetzungen, Strukturen, Gehalte.* Heidelberg: Wolfgang Rothe Verlag, 1962.
Bab, Julius. "Gedanken im Kriege (Herbst 1914)." In *Das Erwachen zur Politik.* Berlin: Oesterheld, 1920.
Baer, Lydia. "Death and Thomas Mann." In *The Stature of Thomas Mann*, ed. Charles Neider, 281–86. New York: New Directions, 1947.
Bahr, Hermann. *Zur Überwindung des Naturalismus. Theoretische Schriften, 1887–1904.* Edited by Gotthart Wunberg. Stuttgart: Kohlhammer, 1968.
———. *Der Antisemitismus. Ein internationales Interview.* Berlin: S. Fischer, 1894.

————. *Fin de siècle*. Berlin: A Zoberbier, 1891.

————. *Zur Kritik der Moderne. Gesammelte Aufsätze.* Zurich: Verlagsmagazin J. Schabelitz, 1890.

Banuls, André. "Schopenhauer und Nietzsche in Thomas Manns Frühwerk." *Études Germaniques* 31, no. 2 (April–June 1976): 129–47.

Basilius, Harold A. "Thomas Mann's Use of Musical Structure and Techniques in 'Tonio Kröger.'" *Germanic Review* 19, no. 4 (Dec. 1944): 284–308.

Bauer, Arnold. *Thomas Mann.* Berlin: Colloquium Verlag, 1960.

Baumgart, Reinhard. "Betrogene Betrüger: Zu Thomas Manns letzter Erzählung und ihrer Vorgeschichte" In *Thomas Mann*, ed. Heinz Ludwig Arnold, 2, erw. Aufl., 123–31. Munich, 1982.

————. "Beim Wiederlesen Thomas Manns." In *Sinn und Form. Beiträge zur Literatur*, ed. Deutsche Akademie der Künste. Sonderheft Thomas Mann, 178–85. Berlin: Rütten und Loening, 1965.

Bauschinger, Sigrid. "'Völlig exceptionelle Kinder.' Vom Bürgerlich-Individuellen zum Mythisch-Typischen bei Thomas Mann." In *Psychologie in der Literaturwissenschaft. Viertes Amherster Kolloquium zur modernen deutschen Literatur*, ed. Wolfgang Paulsen. Heidelberg: Lothar Stiehm Verlag, 1970.

Becagli, Carla. "Invito alla lettura di Thomas Mann." In *Sezione Straniera*, 20. Milano: Mursia, 1978.

Becher, Hubert, S. J. "Thomas Mann unter den Patriarchen." *Stimmen der Zeit* 126, 64, no. 6 (March 1934): 372–83.

Beharriel, Frederick J. "Never without Freud. Freud's influence on Mann." In *Thomas Mann in Context*, ed. Kenneth Hughes, 1–16. Worcester, 1978.

————. "Psychology in the early works of Thomas Mann." *PMLA* 77 (1962): 148–55.

Bellmann, Werner, ed. *Erläuterungen und Dokumente: Thomas Mann: Tonio Kröger.* Stuttgart: Reclam, 1983.

Benét, Stephen Vincent, and Rosemary Benét. "Thomas Mann Honored by the Free World." *New York Herald Tribune*, 29 June 1941.

Berendsohn, Walter A(rthur). *Thomas Mann, Künstler und Kämpfer in bewegter Zeit.* Lübeck: M. Schmidt-Romhild, 1965.

Bertaux, Félix. "Introduction." In *La Mort à Venise*, 3d. ed. Paris: Editions Kra, 1929.

Bertram, Ernst. *Nietzsche. Versuch einer Mythologie.* Bonn: H. Bouvier und Co., 1965.

————. "Das Problem des Verfalls." *Mitteilungen der Literaturhistorischen Gesellschaft Bonn* (Dortmund) 2, no. 2, (9 Feb. 1907): 72–79.

————. "Thomas Manns 'Betrachtungen eines Unpolitischen.'" *Mitteilungen der Literaturhistorischen Gesellschaft Bonn* (Bonn) 11, no. 4 (1917/18): 77–105.

Bihalji-Merin, Oto. "Thomas Mann. Weltsicht und Selbstvollendung." In *Sinn und Form. Sonderheft Thomas Mann*, 85–111. Berlin: Rütten und Loening, 1965.

Björklung, Beth. "Thomas Mann's 'Tobias Mindernickel' in light of Sartre's 'Being for Others.'" *Studies in Twentieth Century Literature* 2 (1978): 103–112.

Blisset, William. "Thomas Mann: The Last Wagnerite." *Germanic Review* 35, no. 1 (Feb. 1960): 50–76.

Blume, Bernhard. *Thomas Mann und Goethe.* Bern: A Francke Verlag, 1949.

————. "Thomas Manns Goethebild." *PMLA* 59, nos. 1,2,3 (March, June, Sept. 1944): 261–90, 556–84, 851–68.

Böckmann, Paul. "Lessings Begründung der klassischen Symbolform." *Zeitschrift für Deutschkunde* 50 (1936): 413–28.

──────. "Die Bedeutung Nietzsches für die Situation der modernen Literatur." *Deutsche Vierteljahrsschrift für Literatur und Geistesgeschichte* (Stuttgart) 27, no. 1 (1953): 77–101.

Böhme, Hartmut. "Thomas Mann: 'Mario und der Zauberer.' Position des Erzählers und Psychologie der Herrschaft." *Orbis Litterarum* 30 (1975): 286–316.

Bohnen Klaus. "Ein literarisches 'Muster' für Thomas Mann: J. P. Jacobsens 'Niels Lyhne' und 'Der kleine Herr Friedemann.'" *Littérature et culture allemandes*, 1985, 197–215.

Bolkosky, Sidney. "Thomas Mann's 'Disorder and Early Sorrow': The Writer as Social Critic." *Contemporary Literature* 22 (1981): 218–33.

Borcherdt, Hans Heinrich. "Das 'Vorspiel' von Thomas Manns *Königliche Hoheit*. Eine Interpretation." *Wirkendes Wort* (Düsseldorf) 4 (Sept. 1954): 359–65.

Braak, Meno ter. "The Beloved Returns." In *The Stature of Thomas Mann*, ed. Charles Neider, 181–87. New York: New Directions, 1947.

Braches, Ernst. "'Der Tod in Venedig': 1. Goethe in Marienbad." *Optima: Cahier voor literatur en boekwezen* (Amsterdam) 2, no. 2 (April 1984): 93–102.

──────. "'Der Tod in Venedig': 2. Venetië bespiegeld." *Optima: Cahier voor literatur en boekwezen* 2, no. 3 (1984): 296–306.

──────. "'Der Tod in Venedig': 3. Commentaar bej hoofdstuk I." *Optima: Cahier voor literatur en boekwezen* 2 no. 4 (December 1984): 273–89.

Braemer, Edith. "Aspekte der Goethe-Rezeption Thomas Manns." In *Vollendung und Grösse Thomas Manns. Beiträge zu Werk und Persönlichkeit*, ed. Georg Wenzel, 162–95. Halle/Saale: Verlag Sprache und Literatur, 1962.

Brann, Henry Walter. "Thomas Mann und Schopenhauer." In *Sonderdruck aus dem XXXXIII. Schopenhauer Jahrbuch für das Jahr 1962*, ed. Arthur Hübscher. Frankfurt am Main (10 June 1980).

Brettschneider, Rudolf. "Die Entdeckung des 'Wälsungenblut.'" *Bücherstube: Blätter für Freunde des Buches und der zeichnenden Künste* 1, nos. 3/4 (Oct. 1920): 110–12.

Brock, Erich. "Ein gern vergessenes Buch Thomas Manns—'Betrachtungen eines Unpolitischen.'" *Orbis Litterarum* (Copenhagen) 13: 3–6.

Brown, Calvin Smith. Music and Literature. A Comparison of the Arts. Athens Univ. of Georgia Press, 1948.

Brück, Max von. "Thomas Mann—das späte Werk." *Die Gegenwart* (Freiburg/Brsg.) 3, no. 19 (1 Oct. 1948): 11–18.

Buchwald, Reinhard. *Führer durch Goethes Faustdichtung*. Stuttgart: Alfred Kroner Verlag, 1964.

Bürgin, Hans, and Hans-Otto Mayer. *Thomas Mann: A Chronicle of His Life*. University: University of Alabama Press, 1969.

Burke, Kenneth. "Thomas Mann and André Gide." In *The Stature of Thomas Mann*, ed. Charles Neider, 253–64. New York: New Directions, 1947.

Carbe, Monika. "Thomas Mann: 'Die vertauschten Köpfe.' Eine Interpretation der Erzählung." Diss., Philipps-Universität Marburg/Lahn, 1970.

Carlsson, Anni. "Das Faustmotiv bei Thomas Mann." *Deutsche Beiträge* (Munich) 3, no. 4 (1949): 343–62.

──────. ed. *Hermann Hesse–Thomas Mann Briefwechsel*. Frankfurt am Main: Suhrkamp S. Fischer, 1968.

Cassirer, Ernst von. "Thomas Manns Goethe-Bild. Eine Studie über 'Lotte in Weimar.'" *Germanic Review* 20, no. 3 (1945): 166–94.

Clar, O. "Thomas Manns 'Betrachtungen eines Unpolitischen.'" *Eiserne Blätter*, no. 26 (1919): 470–74.

Clement, Clara Erskine. *Venice, the Queen of the Adriatic*. Boston: Dana Estes and Co., 1893.

Cohn, Dorrit. "The second author of 'Der Tod in Venedig.'" *Probleme der Moderne: Studien zur deutschen Literatur von Nietzsche bis Brecht. Festschrift für Walter Sokel*, ed. Benjamin Bennett, Anton Kaes, and William J. Lillyman, 223–45. Tübingen, 1983.

———. *Transparends. Narrative Modes for Presenting Consciousness in Fiction*. Princeton, 1978.

Corngold, Stanley, Victor Lange, and Theodore Ziolkowski. "Thomas Mann and the German Philosophical Tradition: Two Essays on Nietzsche." In *Thomas Mann 1875–1955*. Princeton: Princeton Univ. Press, 1975.

———. "The Mann Family." In *Thomas Mann 1875–1955*, 46–53. Princeton: Princeton Univ. Press, 1975.

Curtius, Mechthild. *Erotische Phantasien bei Thomas Mann: "Wälsungenblut," "Bekenntnisse des Hochstaplers Felix Krull," "Der Erwählte", "Die vertauschten Köpfe," "Joseph in Aegypten."* Königstein/TS.: Athenäum, 1984.

Daemmrich, Horst. "Thomas Mann's Concept of Culture: An Introduction to *Betrachtungen eines Unpolitischen*." M. A. thesis, Wayne State University, 1959.

Dehmel, Richard. *Aber die Liebe. Zwei Folgen. Gedichte von Richard Dehmel*. Berlin: Fischer Verlag, 1912.

DelCaro, Adrian. *Dionysian aesthetics: The Role of Destruction in Creation as Reflected in the Life and Works of Friedrich Nietzsche*. Frankfurt am Main: Lang, 1981. Therein: Novel: "Thomas Mann's *Doktor Faustus*. Nietzsche contra Wagner," 119–24.

"Deutsche Schriftsteller über Thomas Mann." In *Thomas Mann*, ed. Heinz Ludwig Arnold, 2. erw. Aufl., 195–237. Munich, 1982.

Dierks, Manfred. Rezension von Hans Wysling: "Narzissmus und illusionäre Existenzform." Ca. 1982.

———. *Studien zu Mythos und Psychologie bei Thomas Mann*. Bern/Munich: Francke Verlag, 1972.

———. "Thomas Manns psychoanalytischer Priester. Die Rolle der Psychoanalyse im 'Zauberberg.'" In *Geistesgeschichtliche Perspektiven. Rückblick—Augenblick—Ausblick*. Bonn: H. Bouvier und Co., 1969.

Dohm, Hedwig. "'Der Tod in Venedig.' Novelle von Thomas Mann." *Der Tag* (Berlin), 23 Feb. 1913.

Ebermayer, Erich. "Thomas Manns Jugendnovelle 'Gefallen.'" *Die Literatur* (Berlin) 27, no. 8 (May 1925): 459–61.

Eichner, Hans. *Thomas Mann. Eine Einführung in sein Werk*, 2d ed. Bern/Munich: Francke Verlag, 1961.

———. "Aspects of Parody in the Work of Thomas Mann." *Modern Language Review* 47, no. 1 (1952): 30–48.

Eifler, Margaret. *Thomas Mann: Das Groteske in den Parodien "Joseph und seine Brüder," "Das Gesetz" und "Der Erwählte."* Bonn, 1970.

Emrich, Wilhelm. "Formen und Gehalte des zeitgenössischen Romans." *Universitas. Zeitschrift für Wissenschaft, Kunst und Literatur* 11, no. 1 (Jan. 1956): 49–58.

————. "Das Problem der Symbolinterpretation in Hinblick auf Goethes 'Wander-jahre.'" *Deutsche Vierteljahrsschrift für Literaturwissenschaft und Geistesgeschichte* 26, no. 3 (1952): 331–52.

Erlich, Gloria Chasson. "Race and Incest in Mann's 'Blood of the Walsungs.'" *Studies in Twentieth Century Literature* 2 (1978): 113–26.

Euripides. *The Bacchae of Euripides*. Translated by Donald Sutherland. Lincoln: Univ. of Nebraska Press, 1968.

Evans, Tamara S. "'Ich werde Besseres machen...' Zu Thomas Manns Goethe-Nachfolge in 'Tonio Kröger.'" *Colloquia germanica: International Zeitschrift für germanische Sprach-und Literaturwissenschaft*, 15, no. 1/2 (1982): 86–97.

Ewen, David. *Encyclopedia of the Opera*. New York: Hill and Wang, 1955.

Exner, Richard. "Zur Essayistik Thomas Manns." *Germanisch-Romanische Monatsschrift* 12, no. 1 (Jan. 1962): 51–78.

Fadiman, Clifton P. "Thomas Mann's Obsession." *Nation* (New York), 11 Feb. 1931.

Faesi, Robert. *Thomas Mann. Ein Meister der Erzählkunst*. Zurich: Atlantis Verlag, 1955.

————. "Grenzen und Gipfel von Thomas Manns Welt." *Neue Rundschau* (Frankfurt am Main) 66, no. 3 (March 1955): 373–91.

Ferenczi, S., and Otto Rank. *Entwicklungsziele der Psychoanalyse*. Leipzig/Wien/Zurich: Internationaler Psychoanalytischer Verlag, 1924.

Feuerlicht, Ignace. *Thomas Mann*. New York: Twayne Publishers, 1968.

————. "Thomas Manns mythische Identification." *German Quarterly* 36, no. 2 (March 1963): 141–51.

Finney, Gail. "Self-Reflexive Siblings. Incest as Narcissism in Tieck, Wagner and Thomas Mann." *German Quarterly* 56 (1983): p. 243–56.

Fleissner, Else M. "Stylistic Confusion in Thomas Mann's Indian Legend, 'The Transposed Heads.'" *Germanic Review* 18, no. 3 (Oct. 1943): 209–12.

Förster-Nietzsche, Elisabeth, ed. *The Nietzsche-Wagner Correspondence*. Translated by Caroline V. Kerr. New York: Liveright, 1949.

Fradkin, Ilja. "'Der Zauberberg' und die Geburt des modernen intellektuellen Romans." In *Sinn und Form. Sonderheft Thomas Mann*, trans. Gerhard Dick, 74–84. Berlin, 1965.

Frank, Bruno. "Death in Venice." Translated by E. B. Ashton. In *The Stature of Thomas Mann*, ed. C. Neider. New York: New Directions, 1947,

————. "Thomas Mann. Eine Betrachtung nach dem 'Tod in Venedig.'" *Neue Rundschau* 24, no. 5 (May 1913): 656–69.

Frank, John G. "Letters by Thomas Mann to Julius Bab." *Germanic Review* 36, no. 3 (Oct. 1961): 195–204.

Freese, Wolfgang. "Thomas Mann und sein Leser: Zum Verhältnis von Antifaschismus und Lesererwartung in 'Mario und der Zauberer.'" *Deutsche Vierteljahrsschrift für Literaturwissenschaft und Geistesgeschichte* 51, 4 (Dec. 1977).

Frizen, Werner. "Von Weibes Wonne und Wert: Über eine Frauengestalt Thomas Manns und den Misogyn Schopenhauer." *Etudes germaniques* 36, no. 1 (1981): 306–17.

————. *Zaubertrank der Metaphysik: Quellenkritische Überlegungen im Umkreis der Schopenhauer-Rezeption Thomas Manns*. Frankfurt am Main, Bern: Lang, 1980.

Frühwald, Wolfgang. "'Der christliche Jüngling im Kunstladen.'" Milieu und Stilparodie in Thomas Manns Erzählung 'Gladius Dei.'" In *Bild und Gedanke, Festschrift für Gerhart Hauptmann*, ed. V. G. Schnitzler, p. 324–42. Munich, 1980.

Furness, Ronald. "Ludwig Derleth und die Proklamationen." *Forum for Modern Language Studies* 15 (1979): 298–304.

Gagnebin, Murielle. "La Bisexualité psychique dans 'Les Têtes inverties' de Thomas Mann." *La Revue d'esthétique* 33 (1980): 303–17.

Ganeshan, V. "'The Transposed Heads' by Thomas Mann: An Indian legend or a metaphysical jest?" *Journal of the School of Languages* (New Dehli) 5 (1977/ 1978): 1–13.

Garrin, Stephen H. "Thomas Mann's 'Mario und der Zauberer': Artistic means and didactic ends." *Journal of English and Germanic Philology* 77, no. 1 (1978): 92–103.

Gide, André. "Europe Beware!" In *The Stature of Thomas Mann*, ed. Charles Neider. New York: New Directions, 1947.

Gisselbrecht, André. "Thomas Manns Hinwendung vom Geist der Musikalität zur Bürgerpflicht." In *Sinn und Form. Beiträge zur Literatur. Sonderheft Thomas Mann*, ed. Deutsche Akademie der Künste, 291–334. Berlin: Rütten and Loening, 1965.

Gregor, Martin. *Wagner und kein Ende. Richard Wagner im Spiegel von Thomas Manns Prosawerk. Eine Studie.* Bayreuth: Edition Musica, 1958.

Gronicka, André von. "Ein 'symbolisches Formelwort' in Thomas Manns 'Zauberberg.'" *Germanic Review* 23, no. 2 (April 1948): 125–30.

———. "'Myth Plus Psychology.' A Stylistic Analysis of 'Death in Venice.'" *Germanic Review* 31, no. 3 (Oct. 1956): 191–205.

———. "Thomas Mann and Russia." *Germanic Review* 20, no. 2 (April 1945): 105–37.

Grützmacher, Richard H. "Die moderne Auffassung des Todes mit besonderer Berücksichtigung von Thomas Mann und Goethe." *Geisteskultur* (Berlin) 36 (1927): 183–96.

Gustafson, Lorraine. "Xenophon and 'Der Tod in Venedig.'" *Germanic Review* 21, no. 3 (Oct. 1946): 209–14.

Guttmann, Bernhard. "Der Unpolitische nach vierzig Jahren." *Die Gegenwart*, no. 273 (1956): 730–32.

Haase, Horst. "Thomas Mann—ein ungarischer Schriftsteller?" *Weimarer Beiträge* 21, no. 9 (1975): 171–77.

Haiduk, Manfred. "Bemerkungen zu Thomas Manns Novelle 'Wälsungenblut.'" In *Vollendung und Grösse Thomas Manns. Beiträge zu Werk und Persönlichkeit des Dichters*, ed. Geory Wenzel, 213–19. Halle: Verlag Sprache und Literatur, 1962.

Hamburger, Käte. "Romantische Politik bei Thomas Mann." *Der Morgen* 8, no. 2 (June 1932): 106–15.

———. *Thomas Mann Humanitetens Diktare.* Stockholm: Bokförlaget Natur och Kultur, 1945.

———. *Thomas Manns Roman "Joseph und seine Brüder." Eine Einführung.* Stockholm: Bermann-Fischer Verlag, 1945.

———. *Der Humor bei Thomas Mann. Zum Joseph-Roman.* Munich Nymphenburger Verlagshandlung, 1965.

———. "Zwei Formen Literatursoziologischer Betrachtung." *Orbis Litterarum* 7, nos. 1–2 (1949): 142–60.

———. "Der Epiker Thomas Mann." *Orbis Litterarum* 13, nos. 1–2 (1958): 7–14.

———. *Thomas Manns biblisches Werk: Der Joseph-Roman, die Moses-Erzählung "Das Gesetz".* Munich Nymphenburger, 1981.

Hamilton, Nigel. *The Brothers Mann: The Lives of Heinrich and Thomas Mann, 1871–1950, 1875–1955*. New Haven: Yale Univ. Press, 1979.

Hardwick, Elizabeth. "Thomas Mann at 100." *New York Times Book Review*, 20 July 1975, 103.

Harlass, Gerald. "Das Kunstmittel des Leitmotivs. Bemerkungen zur motivischen Arbeit bei Thomas Mann und Hermann Broch." *Welt und Wort* (Tübingen) 15 (Sept. 1960): 267–69.

Hatfield, Henry C. "The Achievement of Thomas Mann." *Germanic Review* 31, no. 3 (Oct. 1956): 206–14.

———. *Thomas Mann*. Norfolk, Conn.: New Directions, 1951.

———. "Recent Studies of Thomas Mann." *Modern Language Review* (London) 51, no. 3 (July 1956): 390–403.

———. *From "The Magic Mountain": Mann's Later Masterpieces*. Ithaca: Cornell Univ. Press, 1979.

———. "Mario and the Magician." In *The Stature of Thomas Mann*, ed. C. Neider, 168–73. New York: New Directions, 1947.

Haug, Helmut. "Erkenntnisekel. Zum frühen Werk Thomas Manns." In *Studien zur deutschen Literatur*, ed. Richard Brinkman, Friedrich Sengle, and Klaus Ziegler, vol. 15. Tübingen: Max Niemeyer Verlag, 1969.

Havenstein, Martin. *Thomas Mann. Der Dichter und Schriftsteller*. Berlin: Verlag Wiegandt und Grieben, 1927.

Heim, Karl. "Thomas Mann und die Musik." Diss., Universität Freiburg im Brsg., 1952.

Heimann, Bodo. "Thomas Manns 'Doktor Faustus' und die Musikphilosophie Adornos." *Deutsche Vierteljahrsschrift für Literaturwissenschaft und Geistesgeschichte* (Stuttgart) 38, no. 2 (July 1964): 248–60.

Heller, Erich. "The Conservative Imagination. On Thomas Mann's 'Non-Political Meditations.'" *Encounter* 10, no. 2 (1958): 46–56.

———. "Tonio Kröger und der tödliche Lorbeerbaum." *Hamburger Akademische Rundschau* 2 (May/June 1948): 569–85.

———. *Die Wiederkehr der Unschuld und andere Essays*. Suhrkamp Taschenbuch, 396. Therein: "Thomas Mann in Venedig: zum Thema Autobiographie und Literatur," 169–88; "Improvisation über den Begriff des Klassischen; zu Thomas Manns *Lotte in Weimar*," 191–213; "Die Zurücknahme der Neunten Symphonie; zu Thomas Manns Doktor Faustus," 217–34. Frankfurt am Main: Suhrkamp, 1966.

Heller, Peter. "'Der Tod in Venedig' und Thomas Manns Grund-Motiv." In "Thomas Mann: Ein Kolloquium. . . ." 35–83. Bonn, 1978.

Henel, Heinrich. "Erlebnisdichtung und Symbolismus." *Deutsche Vierteljahrsschrift für Literaturwissenschaft und Geistesgeshichte* 32 (1958): 71–98.

Hermes, Eberhard. "Thomas Mann: "Der Tod in Venedig' (1912). Anregungen zur Interpretation." *Der Deutschunterricht* 29, no. 4 (August 1977): 59–86.

Hettner, Hermann. *Literaturgeschichte der Goethezeit*. Munich: Verlag C. H. Beck, 1970.

Heydenreich, Titus. "Eros in der Unterwelt. Der Holterhof-Ausflug in Thomas Manns Erzählung 'Die Betrogene.'" In *Interpretation und Vergleich. Festschrift für Walter Pabst*, ed. E. Leube and L. Schrader, 79–95. Berlin, 1972.

Hirschbach, Frank Donald. "The Education of Hans Castorp." *Monatshefte für deutschen Unterricht, deutsche Sprache und Literatur* (Madison) 46, no. 1 (Jan. 1954): 25–34.

———. *The Arrow and the Lure. A Study of the Role of Love in the Works of Thomas Mann*. The Hague: M. Nijhoff, 1955.

Hofmiller, Josef. "Thomas Manns neue Erzählung." *Süddeutsche Monatshefte* (Munich), May 1913, 218–32.

———. "Thomas Manns 'Tod in Venedig.'" *Merkur* (Stuttgart) 9, no. 6 (June 1955): 505–20.

Holthusen, Hans Egon. *Die Welt ohne Transzendenz. Eine Studie zu Thomas Manns "Dr. Faustus" und seinen Nebenschriften*. Hamburg: H. Ellermann, 1949.

Hülsen, Hans von. "Das Gesicht hinter der Maske." *Blätter des deutschen Theaters* (Berlin) 2, no. 25 (1912): 394–99.

Jacob, Gerhard. *Thomas Mann und Nietzsche. Zum Problem der Décadence*. (Diss., Universität Leipzig, 1926.) Munich: Michael Hampp, 1926.

Jacobson, Anna. "Das Wagner-Erlebnis Thomas Manns." *Germanic Review* 5, no. 2 (April 1930): 166–79.

———. "Das plastische Element im Joseph Roman." *Monatshefte für deutschen Unterricht, deutsche Sprache und Literatur* 37 (Jan. 1945): 417–27.

Jaloux, Edmond. "Préface." In *Thomas Mann's Tonio Kröger, suivi de Le petit Monsieur Friedemann, Heure difficile, L'enfant prodige, Un petit bonheur*, trans. Geneviève Mauru. Paris: Stock, Delamain, et Boutelleau, 1929.

Jancke, Oscar. "Das analytische-kritische Schaffenselement im Werke Thomas Manns." Diss., Universität München, 1921.

Jens, Walter. "Der Rhetor Thomas Mann." *Wort in der Zeit* (Graz) 12, no. 4 (1966): 57–65.

———. *Statt einer Literaturgeschichte*. Pfüllingen: Neske, 1962.

Jodeit, Klaus. "Das geistige Leben Lübecks von 1871 bis 1890, die Umwelt der jungen Brüder heinrich und Thomas Mann." In *Der Wagen, ein lübeckisches Jahrbuch* (1978), 155–64. Lübeck: Hansisches Verlagskontor, 1978.

Jonas, Klaus W. "Thomas Mann in englischer Übersetzung. Erinnerungen an H. T. Lowe-Porter." *Neue Zürcher Zeitung*, 9 June 1963, 5.

Jung, C. G. "Die psychologischen Aspekte des Mutterarchetypus." Edited by Fröbe-Kapteyn. In *Eranos-Jahrbuch 1938*, vol. 6, 403–43. Zurich: Rhein-Verlag, 1939.

Kahler, Erich. "Säkulisierung des Teufels. Thomas Manns Faust." *Neue Rundschau* (Stockholm) 59, no. 10 (Spring 1948): 185–202. Also in *Die Verantwortung des Geistes. Gesammelte Aufsätze*, 143–62. Frankfurt am Main: S. Fischer Verlag, 1952.

———. "Die Verinnerung des Erzählens." *Neue Rundschau* 68 (1975): 501–46.

———. "Untergang und Übergang der epischen Kunstform. *Neue Rundschau* 64 (1953): 1–44.

Kanno, Ken. "Der Ausgang als Ausgangspunkt: Über 'Mario und der Zauberer.'" *Gengobunka Ronshu* (= *Studies in Languages and Cultures*), no. 12 (1982): 293–300.

Kantorovitcz, Alfred. "Thomas Mann im Spiegel seiner politischen Essays." *Ost und West*, no. 8 (1949): 46–68.

———. *Heinrich und Thomas Mann. Die persönlichen, literarischen und weltanschaulichen Beziehungen der Brüder*. Berlin: Aufbau Verlag, 1956.

Kapp, Max. *Thomas Manns novellistische Kunst. Ideen und Probleme, Atmosphäre und Symbolik seiner Erzählungen*. Munich: Drei Masken Verlag, 1928.

Karst, Roman. *Thomas Mann oder der deutsche Zwiespalt*. Vienna, Munich, Zurich: Molden, 1970.

Karsunke, Yaak. "'. . . von der albernen Sucht, besonders zu sein': Thomas Manns 'Der Tod in Venedig' wiedergelesen." In *Thomas Mann*, ed. Heinz Ludwig Arnold, 2. erw. Aufl., 85–93. Munich, 1982.

Kasdorff, Hans. *Der Todesgedanke im Werke Thomas Manns.* (Diss., Univ. of Greifswald, 1932.) Leipzig: Eichblatt, 1932.

Kaufmann, Fritz. "Thomas Manns Weg durch die Ewigkeit in die Zeit." *Neue Rundschau* 67, no. 4 (1956).

———. *Thomas Mann. The World as Will and Representation.* New York: Cooper Square Publishers, 1973.

———. "Thomas Mann und Nietzsche." *Monatshefte für deutschen Unterricht* 36, (Nov. 1944): 345–50.

Kaufmann, Walter A. *Nietzsche: Philosopher, Psychologist, Antichrist.* Princeton: Princeton Univ. Press, 1950.

———. *Basic Writings of Nietzsche.* New York: Modern Library, 1968.

Kerényi, Karl. *Labyrinth-Studien. Labyrinthos als Linienreflex einer mythologischen Idee.* Zurich: Rhein-Verlag, 1950.

———. "Die goldene Parodie. Randbemerkungen zu den "Vertauschten Köpfen.'" *Neue Rundschau* 67, no. 4 (1956): 549–56.

———. "Der Erzschelm und der Himmelstürmer. Ein Kapitel aus der Heroenmythologie der Griechen." *Neue Rundschau* 66, no. 3 (June 1955): 312–23.

———. "Die Entstehung der olympischen Götterfamilie." *Mitteilungen zur Kulturkunde* 4 (1950): 127–38.

———. *Die griechisch-orientalische Romanliteratur in religionsgeschichtlicher Beleuchtung.* Tübingen: J. C. B. Mohr Verlag, 1927.

———. "Kroll, Gott und Hölle." Spec. ed., *Gnomon. Kritische Zeitschrift für die gesamte klassische Altertumswissenschaft* 9, no. 7 (July 1933).

———. Introduction to *Platon. Über die Liebe und Unsterblichkeit.* Zurich: Rascher Verlag, 1946.

———. "Thomas Mann und ein neuer Humanismus." *Merkur* 1, no. 4 (1947): 613–15.

———. *Das göttliche Kind in mythologischer und psychologischer Betrachtung.* Amsterdam: Pantheon, 1940.

Kerényi, Magda. A Bibliography of C. Kerényi. Princeton: Princeton Univ. Press, 1976.

Kessel, Martin. "Studien zur Novellentechnik Thomas Manns." *Edda* (Oslo) 25, 15, no. 2 (1926): 250–356.

Kirsch, Edgar. "Die Verungleichung des Gleichen. Ein Beitrag zur Analyse des Identitätsproblems in 'Doktor Faustus.'" In *Vollendung und Grösse Thomas Manns. Beiträge zu Werk und Persönlichkeit*, 204–12. Halle/S.: Verlag Sprache und Literatur, 1962.

Kluge, Gerhard. "Das Leitmotiv als Sinnträger in 'Der kleine Herr Friedemann.' Ein Versuch zur frühen Prosadichtung Thomas Manns." *Jahrbuch der deutschen Schillergesellschaft* 11 (1967): 484–526.

———. Hans Wysling: "Thomas Mann. Narziss [*sic*] und illusionäre Existenzform." *Deutsche Bücher*, Amsterdam, no. 1, 1984.

Koelp, Clayton. "Mannn, Hoffmann and 'Callot's Manner.'" *Germanic Review* 52 (1977): 260–73.

Koopmann, Helmut. "Thomas Manns Bürgerlichkeit." In *Thomas Mann 1875–1975: Vorträge in München . . .*, ed. Beatrix Bludau, 39–60. Frankfurt am Main, 1977.

————. "Thomas Mann und Schopenhauer." In *Thomas Mann und die Tradition*, edited by Peter Pütz, 180–200. Frankfurt am Main: Atheneum Verlag, 1971.

————. "Thomas Mann. Theorie und Praxis der epischen Ironie." In *Thomas Mann. Wege der Forschung*, vol. 135, pp. 351–85. Darmstadt: Wissenschaftliche Buchgesellschaft, 1975.

————. "Hanno Buddenbrook, Tonio Kröger und Tadzio: Anfang und Begründung des Mythos im Werk Thomas Manns." In *Gedenkschrift für Thomas Mann 1875–1975*, vol. 2, Sonderreihe, ed. Rolf Wiecker. Copennagen: Text und Kontext, 1975.

Koopmann, Helmut, and Peter-Paul Schneider, eds. *Heinrich Mann: Sein Werk in der Weimarer Republik*. Zweites internationales Symposium, Lübeck, 1981. Frankfurt am Main. Klostermann, 1983.

Krey, Johannes. "Die gesellschaftliche Bedeutung der Musik im Werk von Thomas Mann." *Wissenschaftliche Zeitschrift der Friedrich-Schiller-Universität Jena. Gesellschafts- und Sprachwissenschaftliche Reihe* 3, nos. 2/3 (1953/54): 301–32.

Krishnalal, Shridharani. "Thomas Mann Spins a Fable of Brahmin India." *New York Herald Tribune*, 8 June 1941.

Kurz, Paul Konrad. "Thomas Mann und die Ironie." *Stimmen der Zeit* (Freiburg im Brsg.) 179, 92, no. 6 (1967): 446–60.

Landmann, Michael, and Judith Marcus-Tar. "Thomas Mann und Georg Lukács." *Neue Deutsche Hefte*, no. 175 (September 1982): 627–30.

Lange, Victor. "Thomas Mann in Exile." In *Thomas Mann 1875–1955*, ed. Stanley Corngold, Victor Lange, and Theodore Ziolkowski, 39–45. Princeton: Princeton Univ. Press, 1975.

————. "Thomas Mann the Novelist." In *Thomas Mann 1875–1955*, ed. Stanley Corngold, Victor Lange, and Theodore Ziolkowski, 1–8. Princeton: Princeton Univ. Press, 1975.

Lawson, Marjorie. "The Transposed Heads of Goethe and Thomas Mann." *Monatshefte für deutschen Unterricht, deutsche Sprache und Literatur* (Madison) 34 (Feb. 1942): 87–92.

Lehnert, Herbert. "'Tristan,' 'Tonio Kröger' und der 'Tod in Venedig.' Ein Strukturvergleich." *Orbis Litterarum* (Copenhagen: Munksgaard) 24 (4 November 1969): 271–304.

————. "Thomas Manns 'Unordnung und frühes Leid.' Entstellte Bürgerwelt und ästhetisches Reservat." In *Text und Kontext. Festschrift für Steppen Steffenson*, ed. R. Wiecker, 239–56, Munich, 1978.

————. "Tonio Kröger and Georg Bendemann: Artistic alienation from bourgeois society in Kafka's writings. Perspectives and personalities; studies in modern German literature honoring Claude Hill," 222–37.

————. *Thomas Mann. Fiktion, Mythos, Religion.* In *Sprache und Literatur*. Stuttgart: Kohlhammer, 1965.

Leibrich, Louis. "L' engagement politique de Thomas Mann en 1914." *Les Langues Modernes* 46, no. 1A (1952): 63–71.

————. "Experience et philosophie de la vie chez Thomas Mann." *Etudes Germaniques* 9, no. 4 (Oct./Dec. 1954): 291–307.

————. Review of *Dichterüber Dichtungen*, by Thomas Mann, edited by Hans Wysling. *Etudes germaniques* 36, no. 4 (1981): 484–85.

———— and Hermann Kurzke. "Auf der Suche nach der verlorenen Irrationalität: Thomas Mann und der Konservatismus." Würzburg, 1980. *Etudes germaniques* 35, no. 2 (1980): 220–21.

—— and Hans Wysling. "Narzissmus und illusionäre Existenzform." *Etudes germaniques* 38 no. 3 (1983): 384.

Lem, Stanislaw. "Über das Modellieren der Wirklichkeit im Werk von Thomas Mann." In *Sinn und Form. Beiträge zur Literatur*, ed. Deutsche Akademie der Künste, Sonderheft Thomas Mann, 157–77. Berlin: Rütten und Loening, 1965.

Leppmann, Wolfgang. "Der Amerikaner im Werke Thomas Manns." In *Deutschlands Amerikabild*, ed. Alexander Ritter, 390–400. Hildesheim, 1977.

Lerch, Eugen. "Ursprung und Bedeutung der sogenannten 'Erlebten Rede.'" *Germanisch-Romanisches Monatsheft* 16 (1928): 459–78.

Lesser, Jonas. "Of Thomas Mann's Renunciation. A Chapter of German Metaphysics." *Germanic Review* 25, no. 4 (Dec. 1950): 245–56; 26, no. 1 (Feb. 1951): 22–33.

Lewisohn, Ludwig. "Death in Venice." In *The Stature of Thomas Mann*, ed. Charles Neider, 124–28. New York: New Directions, 1947.

Lindsay, J. M. "Thomas Mann's First Story, 'Gefallen.'" *German Life and Letters* 28 (April 1975): 297–307.

Lindtke, Gustav. *Die Stadt der Buddenbrooks. Lübecker Bürgerkultur im 19. Jahrhundert*. Lübeck: Verlag Max Schmidt-Römlich, 1965.

Lion, Ferdinand. *Thomas Mann. Leben und Werk*. Zurich: Verlag Oprecht, 1947.

Lotze, Dieter P. "Balduin Bählamm und Tonio Kröger." *Wilhelm-Busch Jahrbuch, 1978: Mitteilungen der Wilhelm-Busch–Gesellschaft*, no. 44, p. 36–42.

Lublinski, S. *Die Bilanz der Moderne*. Berlin: Verlag Siegfried Cronbach, 1904.

Lüdecke, Heinz. "Thomas Manns dialektisches Goethe-Bild." *Aufbau*, no. 10 (Oct. 1952): 941–46.

Lukács, Georg von. *Die Seele und die Formen. Essays*. Berlin: Egon Fleischel and Co., 1911.

——. "In Search of the Bourgeois." In *The Stature of Thomas Mann*, ed. Charles Neider, 469–73. New York: New Directions, 1947.

——. "Thomas Manns Gegensatz zur Dekadenz der Gegenwart." *Heute und Morgen* (Düsseldorf), no. 6 (1955): 331–39.

——. *Thomas Mann*. Berlin: Aufbau Verlag, 1949.

——. *Essays on Thomas Mann*. Translated by Stanley Mitchell. New York: Howard Fertig, 1978.

Maas, Joachim, "Thomas Mann. Geschichte einer Liebe im Geiste." *Neue Rundschau. Thomas-Mann-Sonderheft* (1945): 91ff.

Mádl, Antal. "Thomas Mann als Schriftsteller und Politiker." *Német filologiai Tanulmányok IX* (*Arbeiten zur deutschen Philologie*), 5–16. Debrecen: Kossuth Lajos Tudományegyetem, 1975.

Maier, Hans Albert. *Stefan George und Thomas Mann. Zwei Formen des dritten Humanismus in kritischem Vergleich*. Zurich: Speer Verlag, 1947.

Maitre, Hans Joachim. "Thomas Mann Aspekte der Kulturkritik und seiner Essayistik." In *Studien zur Germanistik, Anglistik und Komparatistik*, ed. Armin Arnold, vol. 3. Bonn: H. Bouvier und Co., 1970.

Mann, Golo. "Ein Stück Erinnerung." *Kulturelle Monatshefte*, 20 (Dec. 1960): 72–76.

Mann, Julia. *Aus Dodos Kindheit. Erinnerungen*. Constance: Rosgarten Verlag, 1958.

Mann, Katia. *Meine ungeschriebenen Memoiren*. Edited by Elisabeth Plessen and Michael Mann. Frankfurt am Main: S. Fischer, 1975.

Mann, Klaus. *Der Wendepunkt. Ein Lebensbericht*. Frankfurt am Main: Fischer Verlag, 1952.

Mann, Michael. *Das Thomas-Mann Buch. Eine innere Biographie in Selbstzeugnissen.* Frankfurt am Main: Fischer Bücherei, 1965.

———. "Thomas Mann: Wahrheit und Dichtung." *Deutsche Vierteljahrsschrift für Literaturwissenschaft und Geistesgeschichte* 50, nos. 1/2 (April 1976): 203–12.

Mann, Monika. *Vergangenes und Gegenwärtiges.* Munich: Kindler Verlag, n.d.

Marcel, Gabriel. "Thomas Mann et Nietzsche." In *Hommage de la France à Thomas Mann à l'occasion de son quatre-vingtième anniversaire,* 41–47. ed. Martin Flinker. Paris: Editions Flinker, 1955.

Martens, Kurt. *Roman aus der Décadence.* Berlin: F. Fontane und Co., 1898.

———. "Über erotische Dichtung." *Berliner Tageblatt und Handels-Zeitung,* Abendausgabe, 9 Dec. 1907.

———. "Der Tod in Venedig." *Zwiebelfisch* (Munich) 5, no. 2 (1913): 62–63.

Martini, Fritz. *Das Wagnis der Sprache: Interpretationen deutscher Prosa von Nietzsche bis Benn.* Stuttgart: Klett Verlag, 1954.

———. "Thomas Mann." In *Denker und Deuter im heutigen Europa,* 1: 113–18. oldenburg, Hamburg: Stalling, 1954.

Mason, Eudo C. "Thomas Mann und Rilke." *Orbis Litterarum* 13, ncs. 1/2 (1958): 15–26.

Mater, Erich. "Zur Wortbildung und Wortbedeutung bei Thomas Mann." In *Vollendung und Grösse Thomas Manns. Beiträge zu Werk und Persönlichkeit des Dichters.* 141–48. Halle/S., 1962.

Maury, Geneviève. "L'Allemagne et la démocratie d'après les idées de Thomas Mann." *Revue de Genève* (Feb. 1921): 183–94.

Mautner, Franz. "Die griechischen Anklänge in Thomas Manns 'Tod in Venedig.'" *Monatshefte* (Madison) 44 (Jan. 1952): 20–26.

Mayer, Hans. "Thomas Manns 'Doktor Faustus': Roman einer Endzeit und Endzeit des Romans." In *Von Lessing bis Thomas Mann.* Pfüllingen: Neske, 1959.

———. *Thomas Mann. Werk und Entwicklung.* Berlin: Volk und Welt, 1950.

———. *Von Lessing bis Thomas Mann. Wandlungen der bürgerlichen Literatur in Deutschland.* Pfüllingen: Neske, 1959.

———. "'Der Tod in Venedig': Ein Thema mit Variationen." In *Literaturwissenschaft und Geistesgeschichte: Festschrift für Richard Brinkmann,* 711–24. Tübingen, 1981.

———. "Tod in Venedig: Ein Thema mit Variationen." *Die Tageszeitung,* Sonderausgabe 2 (10 Oct. 1980): 11–14.

Meier, Bernhard. "Gustav von Aschenbachs Verfall: Studien zur Symbolik in Thomas Manns Erzählung 'Der Tod in Venedig'" *Blätter für den Deutschlehrer,* March 1980, vol. 1.

Menchen, Henry Louis. Introduction to *The Nietzsche-Wagner Correspondence,* ed. Elisabeth Förster-Nietzsche, trans. Caroline V. Kerr. New York: Liveright, 1949.

Mendelssohn, Peter de. *Der Zauberer: Das Leben des deutschen Schriftstellers Thomas Mann,* vol. (1875–1918). Frankfurt am Main: S. Fischer, 1975.

———. *Nachbemerkungen zu Thomas Mann.* 2 vols. Frankfurt am Main: Fischer Verlag, 1982.

Mercanton, Jacques. "Thomas Mann in seinen Briefen." In *Sinn und Form. Beiträge zur Literatur,* ed. Deutsche Akademie der Künste. Sonderheft Thomas Mann, 379–87. Berlin: Rütten und Loening, 1965.

Michael, Wolfgang. "Stoff und Idee im 'Tod in Venedig.'" *DVjs* 33 (1959): 13–19.

————. "Thomas Mann auf dem Wege zu Freud. "*MLN* 65 (1905): 165–71.

————. "Über die Jugenddichtung Thomas Manns." *Monatshefte für deutschen Unterricht* 31 (1945): 413, 415.

Moeller, Hans. "Thomas Manns venezianische Götterkunde, Plastik und Zeitlosigkeit." *DVjs* 40 (1966): 184–205.

Motylowa, Tamara. "Thomas Mann und die Erneuerung des Realismus." In *Sinn und Form*, ed. Deutsche Akademie der Künste. Sonderheft Thomas Mann. Berlin: Rütten and Loening, 1965.

Mühler, Robert. "Thomas Mann und Karl Kerényi." In *Phaidros: Zeitschrift für die Freunde des Buches und der schönen Künste, Folge 2*. Vienna: H. Bauer Verlag, 1947.

Müller, Fred. *Thomas Manns Erzählungen, Interpretationen*. Munich: Oldenbourg, 1972.

Müller-Salget, Klaus. "Der Tod in Torre di Venere: Spiegelung und Deutung des italienischen Faschismus in Thomas Manns 'Mario und der Zauberer.'". *Arcadia: Zeitschrift für vergleichende Literaturwissenschaft* 18, no. 1 (1983): 50–65.

Mumford, Lewis. "The Magic Mountain." In *The Stature of Thomas Mann*, ed. Charles Neider, 150–155. New York: New Directions, 1947.

Neider, Charles. "The Artist as Bourgeois." In *The Stature of Thomas Mann. A Critical Anthology*. New York: New Directions, 1947.

————, ed. *The Stature of Thomas Mann. A Critical Anthology*. New York: New Directions, 1947.

Nicholls, R. A. "Nietzsche in the Early Work of Thomas Mann." *Modern Philology* 45 (1955).

Nitsche, Roland. "Ein humanistischer Briefwechsel. Thomas Mann, Karl Kerényi und der Geist des Mythos." *Forum* 7, no. 84. (Dec. 1960).

Noble, C. A. M. "Erkenntnisekel und Erkenntnisfreude: Über Thomas Manns Verhältnis zu Sigmund Freud." *Revue des langues vivantes* 37, 38, no. 2 (1972).

Northcote-Bade, James. "The background to the 'Liebestod' plot pattern in the works of Thomas Mann." *Germanic Review* 59 (1984): 11–18. "Die Wagner-Mythen im Frühwerk Thomas Manns." In *Abhandlungen zur Kunst, Musik- und Literaturwissenschaft*, vol. 167. Bonn: Bouvier Verlag, 1975.

Pache, Alexander. "Thomas Manns epische Technik." *Mitteilungen der literaturhistorischen Gesellschaft Bonn* 2 (1907): 43–71.

Pätzold, Kurt. "Zur politischen Biographie Thomas Manns (1933)." *Weimarer Beiträge* 21, no. 9 (1975): 178–81.

Peacock, Ronald. "Das Leitmotiv bei Thomas Mann." *Sprache und Dichtung* 54 (1934): 1–68.

Pestalozzi, Karl. "Geistesgeschichte" (betr. Thomas Manns Novelle "Gladius Dei"), 70–80. *Seminar Literaturwissenschaft—heute . . .* Zurich: Ropress, 1977.

Peter, Hans Armin. *Thomas Mann und seine epische Charakterisierungskunst*. In *Sprache und Dichtung*, vol. 43. Bern: Paul Haupt, 1929.

Peters, Arno. "Freunde des Sozialismus: Thomas Mann." *Periodikum für wissenschaftlichen Sozialismus*, no. 5 (1959): 51–60.

Pietsch, Ulrich, ed. Kunst und Kultur Lübecks im 19. Jahrhundert. Contributions by Beiträgen von Wult Schadendorf et al. Lübeck: Museum für Kunst und Kulturgeschichte, 1981. Vol. 4 of *Hefte zur Kunst und Kulturgeschichte der Hansestadt Lübeck*. Therein: "Die Brüder Heinrich und Thomas Mann," by Hans Wysling, 69–110.

————. Museum Drägerhaus: Kurzführer: Kunst und Kultur Lübecks im 19. Jahrhundert. Contributions by Beiträgen von Wult Schadendorf et al. Lübeck: Museum für Kunst und Kulturgeschichte, 1981. Therein: "Die Brüder Mann: Heinrich Mann—Thomas Mann—Buddenbrooks—Ida Boy-Ed, Thomas Mann und Lübeck," 25–31.

Politzer, Heinz. "Thomas Mann und die Forderung des Tages." *Monatshefte* 46 (Feb. 1954): 65–79.

Priestley, J. B. "An Exchange of Letters." In *The Stature of Thomas Mann*, ed. Charles Neider, 1275–76. New York: New Directions, 1947.

Pringsheim, Klaus. "Thomas Mann in Exile: Roosevelt, McCarthy, Goethe, and Democracy," 20–34. In *Thomas Mann, ein Kolloquium* (Bonn, 1978).

Pütz, Heinz-Peter. *Kunst und Künstlerexistenz bei Nietzsche und Thomas Mann.* Bonn: H. Bouvier und Co., 1963.

————. "Thomas Mann und Nietzsche." In *Thomas Mann und die Tradition.* Frankfurt am Main: Athenäum Verlag, 1971.

Pütz, Peter. "Thomas Manns Wirkung auf die deutsche Literatur der Gegenwart." In *Thomas Mann*, ed. Heinz Ludwig Arnold, 2d erw. Aufl, 169–79. Munich, 1982.

Rasch, Wolfdietrich. "Das Problem des Anfangs erzählender Dichtung." In *Stil-und Formprobleme in der Literatur*. Heidelberg: 1959, pp. 448–53.

————. "Eine Beobachtung zur Form der Erzählung um 1900. Das Problem des Anfangs erzählender Dichtung." In *Stil- und Formprobleme in der Literatur*. International Federation for Modern Languages and Literatures, 7th Congress, Heidelberg, 1957. Heidelberg: Carl Winter Universitätsverlag, 1959.

————. "Thomas Mann und die Décadence." In *Thomas Mann 1875–1975: Vorträge in München*, ed. Beatrix Bludau, 271–84. Frankfurt/Main, 1977.

Reed. T. J. "Mann and Turgenev—A First Love." *German Life and Letters* 17 (1964): 313–18.

————. *Thomas Mann: "Der Tod in Venedig." Text, Materialien, Kommentar mit den bisher unveröffentlichten Arbeitsnotizen Thomas Manns.* Munich: Hanser, 1983.

Rehbock, Theda. "Thomas Mann–Friedrich Nietzsche." In *Die menschliche Individualität: Festschrift zum 85. Geburtstag von Prof. Dr. Herbert Cysarz*, 29–76. Munich, 1981.

Rehfeld-Kiefer, Margarete. *Groteske Züge in der Personengestaltung des mittleren und späten Werkes Thomas Mann.* (Diss., Philipps Universität Marburg/Lahn, 1965.) Munich: Dissertationsdruck Schön, 1965.

Reiss, Günter. "Herrenrecht. Bemerkungen zum Syndrom des Autoritären in Thomas Manns frühen Erzählungen." In *Gedenkschrift für Thomas Mann 1875–1975*, Sonderreihe, vol. 2, ed. Rolf Wiecker. Copenhagen: Verlag Text und Kontext, 1975.

————. *Allegorisierung und moderne Erzählkunst. Eine Studie zum Werk Thomas Manns.* Munich: Wilhelm Fink Verlag, 1970.

Requadt, Paul von. "Jugendstil im Frühwerk Thomas Manns." *Deutsche Vierteljahrsschrift für Literaturwissenschaft und Geistesgeschichte* 40 (1966): 206–16.

Rice, Philip Blair. "Thomas Mann and the Religious Revival." In *The Stature of Thomas Mann*, ed. Charles Neider, 358–71. New York: New Directions, 1947.

Richter, Bernt. "Psychologische Betrachtungen zu Thomas Manns Novelle 'Mario und der Zauberer.'" In *Vollendung und Grösse Thomas Manns. Beiträge zu Werk und Persönlichkeit*, 106–17. Halle/Saale: Verlag Sprache und Literatur, 1962.

Riess, Curt. "Interview with Thomas Mann." *Direction* 2, no. 3 (Dec. 1939): 4–5.

Riley, Antony W., Klaus W. Jonas, et al. "Die Thomas-Mann-Literatur: Bibliographie der Kritik." *Seminar: A Journal of Germanic Studies* 16, no. 2 (1980): 119–20.

Robinson, Walter L. "Name-Characterization in the Works of Thomas Mann." Diss., Univ. of Texas, 1959.

Rohner, Ludwig. *Der deutsche Essay. Materialien zur Geschichte und Ästhetik einer literarischen Gattung.* Neuwied/Berlin: Luchterhand, 1966.

Rolland, Romain. "Les Idoles." *Journal de Genève*, 4 Dec. 1914.

———. *Au-dessus de la Mêlée.* Paris: Société d'Editions Littéraires et Artistiques, 1915.

Rümmele, Doris. "Mikrokosmos im Wort. Zur Ästhetik der Namengebung bei Thomas Mann." Diss., Albert-Ludwigs Universität Freiburg im Brsg., 1969.

Sagave, Pierre Paul. "Art et bourgeoisie dans l'oeuvre de Thomas Mann." *Revue germanique*, no. 2 (1937): 125–33.

———. *Réalité sociale et idéologie religieuse dans les romans de Thomas Mann.* Paris: Société d'Edition Les Belles Lettres, 1954.

Sauer, Paul Ludwig. "Der hinkende Staat: Über einen Schmarren Thomas Manns, genannt 'Das Eisenbahnunglück.'" *Wirkendes Wort* 30, no. 5 (1980): 311–22

Sautermeister, Gert. "Sozialpsychologie, Marxismus." (Betr. Thomas Manns Novellen "Der Tod in Venedig" und "Mario und der Zauberer"), 53–69. *Seminar Literaturwissenschaft—heute. . . .* Zurich: Ropress, 1977.

Sautermeister, Gert. *Thomas Mann: "Mario und der Zauberer."* Munich, Fink, 1981. *Text und Geschichte: Modellanalysen zur deutschen Literatur*, vol. 5.

Schädlich, Michael. "Der Mythos bei Thomas Mann." In *Die Zeichen der Zeit: Evangelische Monatsschrift*, 7: 177–82. Berlin/DDR, 1984.

Schaper, Eva. "Zwischen den Welten. Bemerkungen zu Thomas Manns Ironie." In *Literatur und Gesellschaft. Festausgabe für Benno von Wiese*, 330–64. Bonn: Bouvier/VVA, 1963.

Schärer, Hans-Ruedi. *Thomas Manns Verhältnis zu seinem Bruder Heinrich 1914–1922.* Zurich: Deutsches Seminar der Universität, 1980/81.

Scher, Steven Paul. "Kreativität als Selbstüberwindung: Thomas Manns permanente 'Wagner-Krise.'" In *Rezeptions der deutschen Gegenwartsliteratur. . . ,* 263–74. Stuttgart: Kohlhammer, 1976.

Scherer, Paul, and Hans Wysling. *Quellenkritische Studien zum Werk Thomas Manns.* In *Thomas-Mann-Studien*, vol. 1. Bern/Munich: Francke Verlag, 1967.

Schickel, René. "Glossen." *Die weissen Blätter* 2, no. 7 (July 1915): 924–26.

Schiller, Friedrich. *Schillers Werke.* Edited by Benno von Wiese. Nationalausgabe. Vol. 20. Weimar: Hermann Bohlaus Nachfolger, 1962.

Schilling, Otto Erich. "Noch—Moderne Musik? oder, Der Kultus der Konsequenz." *Wort und Wahrheit* 9 (1954).

Schirnding, Albert von. "Die Tochter des Zauberers: Zum ersten Band der Briefausgabe von Erika Mann." *Süddeutsche Zeitung* (Munich), 6 Feb. 1985.

Schlappner, Martin. *Thomas Mann und die französische Literatur. Das Problem der Décadence.* Diss., Universität Bern, 1950. Saarlouis: Hansen Verlag, 1950.

Schmeisser, Marleen. "Friedrich der Grosse und die Brüder Mann." *Neue Deutsche Hefte*, Nov. 1962, 97–106.

Schmidt, Ernst A. "Künstler und Knabenliebe. Eine vergleichende Skizze zu Thomas Manns 'Tod in Venedig' und Vergils zweiten Ekloge." *Euphorion* 68 (1974): 437–46.

Schneck, Erna H. "Women in the Works of Thomas Mann." *Monatshefte für den deutschen Unterricht* 32, no. 4 (1940): 145–64.

Schochow, Maximilian. "Der musikalische Aufbau in Thomas Manns Novelle 'Tonio Kröger.'" *Zeitschrift für deutsche Bildung* 4 (1928): 244–53.

Schöffler, Heinz. "Grundmotive und Grundproblematik der Jahrhundertwende in der Dichtung von Friedrich Huch und Thomas Mann. Versuch einer geistesgeschichtlichen Synthese." Diss., Universität Münster, 1948.

Schömann, Milian. "Thomas Mann und die deutsche Sozialdemokratie." *Das freie Wort*, no. 27 (1931): 18–22.

Schopenhauer, Arthur. *The World as Will and Representation.* Translated by E. F. Payne. New York: Dover Publications, 1958.

———. *Die Welt als Wille und Vorstellung.* Cologne: Atlas Verlag. n.d.

Schrenck Notzing, Baron von. *Phenomena of Materialization.* Translated by E. E. Fournier d'Albe. London: Kegan, Paul, Trench, Trübner and Co.; New York: Dutton and Co., 1920.

Schröter, Klaus, ed. *Thomas Mann im Urteil seiner Zeit. Dokumente 1891–1955.* Hamburg: Christian Wegener Verlag, 1969.

———. *Thomas Mann in Selbstzeugnissen und Bilddokumenten.* Reinbeck Bei Hamburg: Rowohlt, 1964.

Schultz, Stefan H. "Das Menschenbild Thomas Manns." *Monatshefte* 39 (1947): 173–86.

Schuster, Peter-Klaus. "Als München leuchtete: Kunsthistorische Anmerkung zu einer Erzählung von Thomas Mann." *Süddeutsche Zeitung*, 9–11 June 1984.

Schwarz, Egon. "Faschismus und Gesellschaft: Bemerkungen zu Thomas Manns 'Mario und der Zauberer.'" In *Dichtung, Kritik, Geschichte: Essays zur Literatur 1900–1930*, 212–30. Göttingen, 1983.

Schwarz, Egon. "Fascism and society: Remarks on Thomas Mann's novelle 'Mario and the magician'". *Michigan Germanic studies* 2, no. 1 (Spring 1976): 47–67.

Seidlin, Oskar. "Picaresque Elements in Thomas Mann's Works." *Modern Language Quarterly* 12 (1951): 183–200.

———. "Stiluntersuchung an einem Thomas Mann-Satz." *Monatshefte* 39 (1947): 432, 448.

———. "Thomas Manns 'Versuch über Schiller': Die Zurücknahme einer Zurücknahme." In *Literaturwissenschaft und Geistesgeschichte: Festschrift für Richard Brinkman*, 692–710. Tübringen: Niemeyer, 1981.

Seitz, Gabriele. *Film als Rezeptionsform von Literatur: Zum Problem der Verfilmung von Thomas Manns Erzählungen "Tonio Kröger," "Wälsungenblut," und "Der Tod in Venedig."* Munich: Tuduv-Verlagsgesellschaft, 1979.

Sell, Friedrich Carl. "The Problem of Anti-Intellectualism." In *The Stature of Thomas Mann*, ed. Charles Neider, 484–94. New York: New Directions, 1947.

Seypel, Joachim. "Adel des Geistes: Thomas Mann und August von Platen." *Deutsche Vierteljahrsschrift für Literatur und Geistesgeschichte* 33 (1959): 565–73.

Sichtermann, Hellmut. "Karl Kerényi. Mit einem Anhang: Ein Gästebuch aus Palestrina." *Arcadia. Zeitschrift für vergleichende Literaturwissenschaft*, ed. Horst Rüdiger, 2, no. 2 (1976): 150–77.

Sjörgen, Christine Oertel. "The variant ending as a clue to the interpretation of Thomas Mann's 'Wälsungenblut.'" *Seminar: A Journal of Germanic Studies* 14, no. 2 (1978): 97–104.

————. "Wendelin and the theme of transformation in Thomas Mann's 'Wälsungenblut.'" *Comparative Literature Studies* 14, no. 4 (1977): 346–59.

Slochower, Harry. "Thomas Mann and Universal Culture." *Southern Review* 4 (1938–39): 726–44.

————. "Mann's Latest Novels." *Accent* 4, no. 1 (Fall 1943): 3–8.

Smikalla, Karl. "Die Stellung Thomas Manns zur Romantik." Diss., Bayrische Julius-Maximilian-Universität Würzburg, 1953.

Somerhage, Claus. *Eros und Poesie. Über das Erotische im Werk Thomas Manns.* Bonn: Bouvier/VVA, 1982.

Sonner, Franz Maria. *Ethik und Körperbeherrschung: Die Verflechtung von Thomas Manns Novelle "Der Tod in Venedig" mit dem zeitgenössischen intellektuellen Kräftefeld.* Opladen: Westdeutschen Verlag, 1984.

Sørensen, Bengt Algot. "Die symbolische Gestaltung in den Jugenderzählungen Thomas Manns." *Orbis Litterarum* 20, no. 2 (1965): 85–97.

————. "Der 'Dilettantismus' des Fin de siècle und der junge Heinrich Mann." *Orbis Litterarum* (n.d.): 251–304.

Sorg, Bernhard. *Zur literarischen Schopenhauer-Rezeption im 19. Jahrhundert.* Heidelberg: Carl Winter Universitätsverlag, 1975.

Speirs, R. C. "Some psychological observations on domination, acquiescence and revolt in Thomas Mann's 'Mario und der Zauberer.'" *Forum for Modern Language Studies* 16, no. 4 (1980): 319–30.

Spelsberg, Helmut. "Thomas Manns Durchbruch zum Politischen in seinem kleinepischen Werk." Diss., Philipps-Universität Marburg/Lahn, 1971.

Staiger, Emil. *Goethe.* Zurich: Atlantis Verlag AG, 1963.

Steinbach, Ernst. "Gottes arme Mensch. Die religiöse Frage im dichterischen Werk von Thomas Mann." *Zeitschrift für Theologie und Kirche* (Tübingen) 50, no. 2 (1953): 207–42.

Stöcklein, Paul. "Konträre Goethedeutungen." *Hochland,* August 1949, 587–93.

Strich, Fritz. "Thomas Mann, oder Der Dichter und die Gesellschaft." *Der kleine Bund* 106, no. 254 (3 June 1955).

————. *Dichtung und Zivilisation.* Munich: Meyer and Jessen, 1928.

Struc, Troman S., and E. L. Marson. "The ascetic artist: Prefigurations in Thomas Mann's 'Tod in Venedig.'" *Seminar: A Journal of Germanic studies* 16, no. 2 (1980): 120–22.

Szemere, Samuel. *Kunst und Humanität. Eine Studie über Thomas Manns ästhetische Ansichten.* Berlin: Akademie-Verlag; Budapest: Akademiai Kiadó, 1966.

Szenessy, Mario. "Über Thomas Manns 'Die Betrogene.'" *Deutsche Vierteljahrsschrift für Literaturwissenschaft und Geistesgeschichte* 40 (1960): 217–47.

Szondi, Peter. "Versuch über Thomas Mann." *Die neue Rundschau* 67, no. 4 (1956): 557–63.

Thalmann, Marianne. "Thomas Mann. 'Tod in Venedig.' Eine Aufbaustudie." *Germanisch-Romanische Monatsschrift* 15 (1927): 374–78.

Thomas, R. Hinton. "Death in Venice." In *Thomas Mann. The Mediation of Art,* 59–83. Oxford: Clarendon Press, 1956.

Vaget, Hans Rudolf. *Intertextualität im Frühwerk Thomas Manns: "Der Wille zum Glück."* Northampton, Mass., 1985.

————. "Georg Lukács, Thomas Mann and the Modern Novel." In *Thomas Mann in Context,* ed. K. Hughes, 38–65. Worcester, Mass., 1978.

————. "The most sensational self-portrait and self-critique of German character? A review of some recent Wagner literature in English." *German Quarterly* 54 (1981): 202–14.

———. "Sang réservé in Deutschland: Zur Rezeption von Thomas Manns 'Wälsungenblut.'" *German Quarterly* 57 (Summer, 1984): 367–76.

———. *Thomas Mann: Kommentar zu sämtliche Erzählungen.* Munich: Winkler, 1984.

———. "Thomas Mann und Wagner" In *Literatur und Musik*, ed. Steven Paul Scher. Bern: Erich Schmidt Verlag, 1984.

———. "Auf dem Weg zur Repräsentanz: Thomas Mann in Briefen an Otto Grautoff, 1894–1901." *Neue Rundschau*, (Frankfurt am Main) 2–3 (1980): 58–82.

Venable, Vernon. "Death in Venice." In *The Stature of Thomas Mann*, ed. Charles Neider, 120–41. New York: New Directions, 1947.

Venohr, Lili. *Thomas Manns Verhältnis zur russischen Literatur. Osteuropastudien der Hochschule des Landes Hessen, Reihe III. Frankfurter Abhandlungen zur Slawistik*, vol. 1. Meisenheim/Glan: Verlag Anton Hain, 1959.

Villari, Pasquale. *Life and Times of Girolamo Savonarola.* Translated by Linda Villari. New York: Charles Scribner's Sons, 1896.

Völker, Klaus. "Thomas Mann beim 'Simplicissimus.'" In *Sinn und Form. Beiträge zur Literatur*, ed. Deutsche Akademie der Künste, Sonderheft Thomas Mann, 396–99. Berlin: Rütten und Loening, 1965.

von Rieckmann, Jens. "Brüderliche Möglichkeiten: Thomas Manns 'Tonio Kröger' and Heinrich Manns 'Abdankung.' N.d., n.p.

Walser, Martin. "Ironie als höchstes Lebensmittel, oder: Lebensmittel der Höchsten." In *Thomas Mann*, ed. Heinz Ludwig Arnold, 2d enl. ed., 5–26. Munich, 1982.

Wandrey, Conrad. "Thomas Mann und sein 'Zauberberg.'" *Der neue Merkur* (Stuttgart/Berlin) 8 (Feb. 1925): 421–36.

Wanner, Hans. *Individualität, Identität und Rolle: Das frühe Werk Heinrich Manns und Thomas Manns Erzählungen "Gladius Dei" und "Der Tod in Venedig."* Munich: Tuduv-Verlagsgesellschaft, 1976.

Wapnewski, Peter. "Tristan, keine Burleske: Zu Thomas Manns Novelle." In *Tristan, der Held Richard Wagners*, 150–70. Berlin, 1981.

Warning, Rainer. "Rezeptionsästhetik" (betr. Thomas Manns Novelle "Der Tod in Venedig"). *Seminar Literaturwissenschaft—heute*," 30–40.

Weigand, Hermann. "The Magic Mountain." In *The Stature of Thomas Mann*, ed. Charles Neider, 156–64. New York: New Directions, 1947.

———. "Der symbolisch-autobiographische Gehalt von Thomas Manns Romandichtung 'Königliche Hoheit.'" *PMLA* 46, no. 3 (Sept 1931): 867–79.

———. "Thoughts on the Passing of Thomas Mann." *Germanic Review* 31 (1956): 115ff.

Weiss, Walter. "Konkurrierende Ansätze sprachlicher Beschreibung und Deutung: Angewendet auf die Erzählung 'Beim Propheten' vom Thomas Mann." In *Thomas Mann 1875–1955: Vorträge in München*, ed. Beatrix Bludau, 484–99. Frankfurt am Main: S. Fischer, 1977.

———. "Thomas Manns Kunst der sprachlichen Integration." *Wirkendes Wort. Beihefte zur Zeitschrift. Special Edition.* Vol. 13 (1964), 5–100.

Wenzel, Georg, ed. *Vollendung und Grösse Thomas Manns. Beiträge zu Werk und Persönlichkeit des Dichters.* Halle/Saale: Verlag Sprache und Literatur, 1962.

Wessling, Berndt W., ed. *Bayreuth im Dritten Reich: Richard Wagners politische*

Erben: Eine Dokumentation. Basel: Weinheim, 1983. Therein: "Der Fall Thomas Mann. Protest der Richard Wagner—Stadt München"; "Thomas Mann, Richard Wagner und die Müncher Gralshüte"; Willie Schuh. Tagebucheintrag Oskar Loerkes"; "Erwiderung auf den Protest der Richard Wagner—Stadt München"; "Thomas Mann," 202–17.

West, Paul. "Thomas Manns Verlegenheit." *Sinn und Form*, ed. Deutsche Akademine der Künste. Sonderheft Thomas Mann, 224–37. 1965.

Wetzel, Heinz. "Erkenntnisekel: Motivkorrespondenzen zwischen Heines 'Götterdämmerung' und Thomas Manns 'Tonio Kröger.'" *Heine Jahrbuch*, 1981, 163–69.

Wich, Joachim. "Groteske Bekehrung des 'Vergnügens am tragischen Gegenstand.' Thomas Mann Novelle 'Luischen' als Beispiel." *Deutsche Vierteljahrsschrift für Literaturwissenschaft und Geistesgeschichte* 50, nos. 1–2 (April 1976): 213–37.

Wilhelm, Friedrich. "Thomas Mann über seine indische Legende." *Euphorion. Zeitschrift für Literaturgeschichte* (Heidelberg) 64, nos. 3–4 (1970): 399–403.

Wilkinson, Elisabeth M. *The Place of "Tonio Kröger" in Thomas Mann's Work*. Blackwell's German Texts. Oxford: Basil Blackwell, 1971.

———. "Aesthetic Excursus on Thomas Mann's Akribie." *Germanic Review* 37 (Oct. 1956): 225–35.

———. "Über den Begriff der künstlerischen Distanz." *Deutsche Beiträge zur geistigen Überlieferung* (Bern) 3 (1975): 69ff.

Winau, R. "Krankheit und Künstlertum in frühen Erzählungen Thomas Manns." *Sonderdruck aus Verhandlungen XX. Internationalen Kongress für Geschichte der Medizin Berlin, 22–27 August 1966*. Hildesheim: Georg Olms Verlagsbuchhandlung, 1968.

Winkler, Franz. "Re: Thomas Manns 'Wälsungenblut'." (Contains a letter of Thomas Mann to F. W. of 14 Nov. 1951.) *Aufbau*, 29 Oct. 1976.

Winkler, Michael. "Tadzio-Anastasios: A note on 'Der Tod in Venedig.'" *MLN* (German issue) 92, no. 3 (1977): 607–9.

Winston, Richard. *Thomas Mann. The Making of an Artist 1875–1911*. New York, 1981.

Wirtz, Erika A. "Zitat und Leitmotiv bei Thomas Mann (1953–54)." In *Thomas Mann*, ed. Helmut Koopmann. *Wege der Forschung*, vol. 335, pp. 64–78. Darmstadt: Wissenschaftliche Buchgesellschaft, 1975.

Wolff, Hans M. *Thomas Mann*. Bern: Francke Verlag, 1957.

Wolff, Uwe, and Hinrich Siefkan, "Thomas Mann: Goethe—Ideal der Deutschheit: Wiederholte Spiegelungen 1893–1949." *Zeitschrift für deutsche Philologie* 100, no. 4 (December 1981): 613–18.

Wolffheim, Hans. "Das 'Interesse' als Geist der Erzählung." *Euphorion* 47 (1953): 351–89.

Wolfradt, Willi. "Thomas Manns Bekenntnis." *Der neue Merkur* 3, no. 1 (1919): 69–70.

Wright, John. "'La commedia è finita': An Examination of Leoncavallo's *Pagliacci*." *Italica* 55, no. 2 (Summer 1978): 167–79.

Wysling, Hans. "Die Brüder Heinrich und Thomas Mann." In *Kunst und Kultur Lübecks im 19. Jahrhundert*, ed. Museum für Kunst und Kulturgeschichte der Hansestadt Lübeck, 69–110. Lübeck, 1981.

———. "Kolloquium über das Werk Thomas Manns, vor allem über 'Tonio Kröger.'" Leitung: Hans Wysling. *Jahresberichte des germanistischen Institut der Swanseigakuin-Universität* 23 (1981): 47–72.

——. "Schopenhauer-Leser Thomas Mann." Sonderdruck aus dem 64. *Schopenhauer-Jahrbuch für das Jahr 1983*, 61–79.

——. "Thomas Manns Rezeption der Psychoanalyse" In *Probleme der modernen Studien zur deutschen Literatur. Festschrift für Walter Sokel.* Tübingen: Max Niemeyer Verlag, 1983.

——. ". . . eine sehr ernste und tiefgehende Korrespondenz mit meinem Bruder. . ." Zwei neuaufgefundene Briefe Thomas Manns an seinen Bruder Heinrich. Sonderdruck aus *Deutsche Vierteljahrschrift für Literaturwissenschaft und Geistesgeschichte* 55, no. 4 (1981): 654–64.

——. ". . . eine fast tödliche Bereitschaft." Sonderabdruck aus *Schweizer Monatshefte* 63, nos. 7/8 (July/August 1983).

——. "Thomas Manns Verschlußsache. Die Tagebücher sind jetzt zugänglich." *Rheinischer Merkur* (Koblenz), 22 Aug. 1975, 15.

——. "Bogen und Leier." *Bulletin* 81 (March 1975): 33–35.

——. "Thomas Mann. Irritation und Widerstand." *Schweizer Monatshefte* 55, no. 7 (Oct. 1975): 553–66.

Zimmer, Heinrich. "Die indische Weltmutter." In *Eranos-Jahrbuch 1938*, 175–220. Zurich: Rhein-Verlag 1939.

Ziolkowski, Theodore. "Thomas Mann and the Emigré Intellectuals." In *Thomas Mann 1875–1955*, ed. Stanley Corngold, Victor Lange, and Theodore Ziolkowski, 24–38. Princeton: Princeton Univ. Press, 1975.

——. "Thomas Mann as a Critic of Germany." In *Thomas Mann 1875–1955*. Princeton: Princeton Univ. Press, 1975.

Zmegac, Viktor. "Die Musik im Schaffen Thomas Manns." *Zagreber Germanistische Studien*, 1. (Philosophische Fakultät der Universität Zagreb. Seminar für deutsche Philologie, Zagreb, 1959.)

——. "Zur Form und Funktion des Erzähleinsatzes bei Thomas Mann." In *Sinn und Form. Beiträge zur Literatur*, Sonderheft Thomas Mann, 255–67. Berlin: Rütten und Loening, 1965.

Zweig, Arnold. "Das Wunderkind." (Teildruck der Rezension von Thomas Manns Novelle, erstmals erschienen in "Die Schaubühne," Berlin, Jg. 10, no. 52, 31.12.1914.) In *Arnold Zweig, 1887–1968. Werk und Leben in Dokumenten und Bildern . . .*, 64.

Zweig, Stefan. "The Beloved Returns." In *The Stature of Thomas Mann*, ed. Charles Neider, 188–90. New York: New Directions, 1947.

INDEX

Character names appear in full capital letters.